Global Issues

2009 EDITION

CQ PRESS

A Division of SAGE
Washington, D.C.

SELECTIONS FROM **CQ RESEARCHER**

CQ Press
2300 N Street, NW, Suite 800
Washington, DC 20037

Phone: 202-729-1900; toll-free, 1-866-4CQ-PRESS (1-866-427-7737)

Web: www.cqpress.com

Cover design: Kimberly Glyder
Cover photo: AP Photo/Jerome Delay

♾ The paper used in this publication exceeds the requirements of the American National Standard for Information Sciences—Permanence of Paper for Printed Library Materials, ANSI Z39.48-1992.

Printed and bound in the United States of America

12 11 10 09 08   1 2 3 4 5

A CQ Press College Publishing Group Publication

Executive director	Brenda Carter
Acquisitions editor	Charisse Kiino
Development editor	Dwain Smith
Marketing manager	Christopher O'Brien
Production editor	Allyson Rudolph
Compositor	Olu Davis
Managing editor	Stephen Pazdan
Electronic production manager	Paul Pressau
Print and design manager	Cynthia Richardson
Sales manager	Linda Trygar

ISSN: 1559-8047
ISBN: 978-0-87289-615-4

Contents

Annotated Contents

The 16 *CQ Researcher* reports reprinted in this book have been reproduced essentially as they appeared when first published. In the few cases in which important developments have since occurred, updates are provided in the overviews highlighting the principal issues examined.

CONFLICT, SECURITY AND TERRORISM

Rise in Counterinsurgency

U.S. troops are using new tactics in Iraq and Afghanistan. Instead of trying to defeat the enemy by brute force, they are focusing on counterinsurgency — protecting civilians and relying on them to provide information on enemy activity. But some military experts argue that too much emphasis on "winning hearts and minds" is weakening the skills needed in conventional combat — from rapid infantry advances to accurate artillery marksmanship to tank tactics. Counterinsurgency advocates concede that some of these capabilities may decline, partly because U.S. foes on today's Third World battlefields do not have air power or armor. Still, they say no rational enemy would challenge the powerful U.S. military in a traditional, World War II–style conflict. But even battle-hardened veterans of today's conflicts acknowledge that military forecasting is an inexact science and that the biggest danger can be planning ahead — for last year's war.

Separatist Movements

When Kosovo declared its independence on Feb. 17, 2008, thousands of angry Serbs demonstrated to protest the breakaway region's secession from Serbia. Less than a month later, Chinese authorities battled Buddhist monks in Lhasa, the legendary capital of Tibet, where separatist resentments have been simmering since China occupied the Himalayan region more than 50 years ago. These protests were the latest flashpoints in some two dozen separatist "hot spots" — the most active of roughly 70 such movements around the globe. They are part of a post–World War II independence trend that has produced a nearly fourfold jump in the number of countries worldwide, with 26 of those new countries emerging since 1990. Some nations, like the far-flung Kurds and the Sri Lankan Tamils, are fighting fiercely to establish a homeland, while others — like Canada's Québécois — seem content with local autonomy. A handful of national movements have become de facto states that are as yet unrecognized by the United Nations, including Somaliland, Taiwan, South Ossetia and Nagorno-Karabakh.

U.S. Policy on Iran

In October 2007 President George W. Bush said Iran's nuclear program raised the specter of World War III. Then Vice President Dick Cheney warned of "serious consequences" if Iran stayed on course as a "terror-supporting state." The heated rhetoric was widely seen as calculated to raise the specter of military action against Iran. Indeed, President Mahmoud Ahmadinejad calls the United States an international bully that is keeping Iraq violent to justify continued occupation. He also vows to maintain Iran's nuclear development program, which he says is not for creating weapons. But many observers — Israelis particularly — see Iran's effort as a grave threat, prompting some U.S. hawks to advocate a preemptive strike on Iranian nuclear facilities. Other Iran-watchers say military action could further endanger U.S. forces fighting next door in Iraq. They urge the administration to aid dissidents rather than counter Iran by military force.

Radical Islam in Europe

The recent spate of foiled terrorist plots by Muslim extremists in Great Britain, Germany and Denmark is a grim reminder that radical Islam continues to pose a serious threat in Europe. Some experts warn that Europe could export its brand of terrorism to the United States, since many of Europe's 15 million Muslims carry European passports that give them easy access to this country. European capitals like London have provided a haven for terrorists to organize, some critics say, because countries like Britain have failed to integrate Muslims into mainstream society. But other experts blame international terrorist networks, which recruit from a small minority of estranged European Muslims. Others argue that in fighting terrorism at home, countries like France have gone too far in curbing Muslims' civil liberties. Concerned that their secular Western values are under threat from conservative Muslims, some European countries are considering limiting immigration and requiring new citizens to adopt the national language and beliefs.

HUMAN RIGHTS

Torture Debate

Countries around the globe — including the United States — are using coercive interrogation techniques in the fight against terrorism that critics say amount to torture. Despite international laws banning the practice, authoritarian nations have long abused prisoners and dissidents, and a handful of democracies have used torture in recent decades against what they considered imminent threats. U.S. soldiers in Iraq say they would torture suspects to save the lives of their comrades. Human rights advocates worry that the use of torture by the United States is legitimizing its use globally and destroying America's moral authority to speak out against regimes that abuse prisoners in far worse ways. U.S. officials credit "enhanced interrogation" methods with averting terrorist attacks. But many experts say information gained by torture is unreliable.

Crisis in Darfur

More than two years after government and rebel fighters signed a peace agreement in Sudan, violence is still rampant in the Darfur region. At least 2.4 million people have been displaced and up to 400,000 have died since 2003, and observers say the situation is getting worse. Rebel groups have splintered into more than a dozen warring factions, bandits are attacking relief workers and drought threatens to make 2009 among the deadliest years in Darfur's history. Despite pressure from religious and human-rights groups, the international community seems unable — or unwilling — to find a lasting solution. A year after the United Nations authorized the world's largest peacekeeping force in Darfur, only 37 percent of the authorized personnel have been deployed, and no military helicopters have been provided. The International Criminal Court is considering genocide charges against Sudanese president Omar Hassan al-Bashir, but some fear an indictment would trigger more violence than justice. Some say China, Sudan's largest trading partner and arms supplier, should pressure Sudan to end the violence.

Women's Rights

Women around the world have made significant gains in the past decade, but tens of millions still face significant and often appalling hardship. Most governments now have gender-equality commissions, electoral gender quotas and laws to protect women against violence. But progress has been mixed. A record number of women now serve in parliaments, but only 14 of the world's 193 countries currently have elected female leaders. Globalization has produced more jobs for women, but they still constitute 70 percent of the world's poorest inhabitants and 64 percent of its illiterate. Spousal abuse, female infanticide, genital mutilation, forced abortions, bride-burnings, acid attacks and sexual slavery remain pervasive in some countries, and rape and sexual mutilation have reached epic proportions in the war-torn Democratic Republic of the Congo. Experts say without greater economic, political and educational equality, the plight of women will not improve, and society will continue to suffer the consequences.

Human Rights in China

When the curtain rose on the 2008 Summer Olympics in Beijing, China eagerly showcased its hypersonic economic growth and its embrace of what it calls the "rule of law." But 19 years after its bloody suppression of protesters in Tiananmen Square, China also displayed its human-rights record for all to judge. Human-rights advocates say the sheen of Chinese progress and prosperity hides repression and brutality by the Chinese Communist Party, including the violent repression of pro-independence protesters in Tibet, forced abortions stemming from China's one-child policy and the trampling of basic freedoms of speech, religion and assembly. Chinese government officials say their nation of 1.3 billion people has made huge strides on the legal and human-rights fronts and that the West has no business interfering in China's internal affairs.

ENERGY AND THE ENVIRONMENT

Global Food Crisis

Food prices spiked around the world in 2007 and 2008, bringing hunger and unrest to many developing countries, along with pain at the checkout counter for lower-income American families. In North Korea, for example, where 35 percent of the population is undernourished, the price of the major food staple, rice, soared 186 percent, and overall food prices rose 70 percent. With 2.1 billion people around the world living on less than $2 a day, such price increases may plunge hundreds of millions into malnutrition and starvation. Drought, high oil prices that make food transport pricey and diversion of corn for use as a biofuel all contributed to the price spike. Globalization — which has led poor countries to abandon domestic food crops in favor of commodity crops for export — also has been blamed. The crisis also has sparked international tension over the impact of wealthy nations' farm subsidies and meat-heavy diets, which take many more resources to produce than grain- or legume-based diets.

Energy Nationalism

A world thirsting for imported oil and gas is seeking new supplies in Central Asia and Africa, where many nations have nationalized their energy resources. In a dramatic reversal from 30 years ago, government-owned or -controlled petroleum companies today control 77 percent of the world's 1.1 trillion barrels of oil reserves. While the emergence of these rising petrostates has helped diversify the world's energy sources, many are considered oil "hot spots" — vulnerable to disruption from international terrorists or domestic dissidents. In addition, many of the petrostates are blending politics and energy into a new "energy nationalism," rewriting the rules of the world's energy markets and restricting international oil corporations' operations. Russia's confrontational energy policies alarm its neighbors, and critics say a booming China is combing the world for access to oil and gas resources without concern for suppliers' corruption or human rights violations. Many also worry that growing competition for dwindling oil supplies will lead to greater risks of international conflict.

Oil Jitters

Vastly increased demand for oil in rapidly modernizing China and India, warfare and instability in the Middle East and the weakening U.S. dollar have revived fears of a new energy crisis. Gasoline shortages — and the accompanying lines at gas stations — were thought to have ended with President Jimmy Carter's administration. But as 2008 began, American drivers were paying more than $3 a gallon, and crude oil hit a milestone — $100 a barrel. Some oil experts predict even bigger price shocks as oil-producing nations use more and more of their own oil, and energy demand jumps 50 percent by 2030. Some experts predict an oil "production crunch" within four to five years that will have severe geopolitical and economic impacts, and one expert says the energy supply-demand gap could create "social chaos and war" by 2020. In any event, the days of cheap, plentiful oil appear to be over, and motorists may have to learn how to conserve energy.

DEMOCRATIZATION

Dealing with the 'New' Russia

Winston Churchill once famously called Russia "a riddle wrapped in a mystery inside an enigma." Viewed from Washington, or any Western capital, Churchill's observation still rings true in today's post-Soviet era. On May 7, 2008, Dmitry Medvedev became Russia's third president. But no one knows how much clout he will exercise, given that he appointed his powerful predecessor, Vladimir Putin, as prime minister, a post that until now has been only marginal. Medvedev vows to fight corruption, strengthen the judicial system and reduce the vast country's bloated, entrenched bureaucracy, but so far his power base remains a mystery, as does his future relationship with Putin. Also a mystery: who the next U.S. president will be and how he will deal with the Kremlin's new power-sharing arrangement.

The New Latin America

Latin America is struggling to redefine its soul. The region's once ubiquitous military dictators in dark glasses have been replaced by a new generation of democratically elected leaders. Under their tutelage Latin America is enjoying steady growth and trying to bridge the notoriously deep chasm between rich and poor citizens.

Wealth and global trade have brought a new sense of cohesion and an unprecedented regional identity, while newly empowered women and indigenous and mixed-race populations are transforming the political landscape. Amid these positive signs, experts ask whether the future belongs to the more moderate, market-oriented democracies — such as those in Brazil, Chile, Mexico and Argentina — or to the more radical, left-wing populism inspired by Venezuela's bombastic socialist leader Hugo Chávez. Meanwhile, with the United States preoccupied in Iraq and elsewhere, the European Union, the Gulf States and China are increasing their economic presence in the region as U.S. influence declines.

Afghanistan on the Brink

In 2004, the Bush administration could still claim democracy was taking hold in Afghanistan and that the country was on the road to economic recovery. Four years later, Afghanistan is dangerously close to sliding back into lawlessness and chaos as more than 50,000 NATO and U.S.-led coalition troops battle a resurgent Taliban movement and a still-robust al Qaeda. A recent spike in civilian deaths — caused by terrorist suicide bombers and stepped-up air attacks by NATO and allied forces — also threatens to turn a war-weary population against the Western troops and the shaky, new Afghan government. President Hamid Karzai's authority barely extends beyond Kabul, and the country's only successful economic sector is its burgeoning drug trade. Afghan women have seen their newfound rights shrink as Islamic fundamentalism elbows its way back into the courts and social system. Meanwhile, neighboring Pakistan has been unable or unwilling to prevent the Taliban and al Qaeda from using its mountainous border areas as a safe haven. Some Afghans and international experts believe recovery is still possible — but they say time is of the essence.

INTERNATIONAL POLITICAL ECONOMY

The Troubled Dollar

Since World War II, the powerful U.S. dollar has symbolized American economic might and fueled an expanding global economy. Foreign central banks stash dollars in their vaults as secure reserves, and most international financial transactions occur in dollars. But since 2002, America's record-high trade and federal budget deficits have severely weakened the dollar, which has lost 21 percent of its value against other leading currencies. That has helped to push oil and food prices higher around the globe, causing suffering among the poor and painful economic adjustments for others. Foreign investors — who in 2007 held more than half of the U.S. Treasury's $3.5 trillion worth of debt — had begun to lose confidence in the dollar even before the current Wall Street financial crisis and Washington's struggles to craft a rescue plan. Experts now debate whether in the coming decade the dollar could collapse in value against other currencies or even be replaced as the world's currency of choice by the euro — or, eventually, by China's yuan.

China in Africa

China is expanding its presence and influence across Africa. Sino-African trade has jumped nearly six-fold in recent years, and some 800 Chinese businesses operate across the continent. After centuries of enslavement, colonization and failed economic policies imposed by the West, Africans are attracted by China's no-strings-attached model of aid and investment. But while China is helping to build new ports and roads, it also is inundating Africa with low-cost goods and labor, resulting in the loss of many African businesses and jobs. Moreover, China's ever-growing demand for oil and other natural resources has led it to invest in oil-rich countries like Sudan, which has been condemned by the West for genocidal practices or human-rights abuses. In response, the United States and other Western nations are playing catch-up in the race for African oil, while scrambling to hold onto their once-historic dominance over Africa's other resources and markets.

Preface

I n this pivotal era of international policymaking, scholars, students, practitioners and journalists seek answers to such critical questions as: Has globalization been good for women? Will the euro surpass the dollar as the world's anchor currency? Would a nuclear-armed Iran endanger the United States? Students must first understand the facts and contexts of these and other global issues if they are to analyze and articulate well-reasoned positions.

The 2009 edition of *Global Issues* provides comprehensive and unbiased coverage of today's most pressing global problems. This edition is a compilation of 16 recent reports from *CQ Researcher*, a weekly policy brief that explains difficult concepts and provides balanced coverage of competing perspectives. Each article analyzes past, present and possible political maneuvering, is designed to promote in-depth discussion and further research and helps readers formulate their own positions on crucial international issues.

This collection is organized into five subject areas that span a range of important international policy concerns: conflict, security and terrorism; human rights; energy and the environment; democratization; and international political economy. Twelve of these reports are new to this edition.

Global Issues is a valuable supplement for courses on world affairs in political science, geography, economics and sociology. Citizens, journalists and business and government leaders also turn to it to become better informed on key issues, actors and policy positions.

CQ RESEARCHER

CQ Researcher was founded in 1923 as *Editorial Research Reports* and was sold primarily to newspapers as a research tool. The magazine was renamed and redesigned in 1991 as *CQ Researcher*. Today, students are its primary audience. While still used by hundreds of journalists and newspapers, many of which reprint portions of the reports, *Researcher*'s main subscribers are now high school, college and public libraries. In 2002, *Researcher* won the American Bar Association's coveted Silver Gavel Award for magazine excellence for a series of nine reports on civil liberties and other legal issues.

Researcher staff writers — all highly experienced journalists — sometimes compare the experience of writing a *Researcher* report to drafting a college term paper. Indeed, there are many similarities. Each report is as long as many term papers — about 11,000 words — and is written by one person without any significant outside help. One of the key differences is that the writers interview leading experts, scholars and government officials for each issue.

Like students, staff writers begin the creative process by choosing a topic. Working with *Researcher*'s editors, the writer identifies a controversial subject that has important public policy implications. After a topic is selected, the writer embarks on one to two weeks of intense research. Newspaper and magazine articles are clipped or downloaded, books are ordered and information is gathered from a wide variety of sources, including interest groups, universities and the government. Once the writers are well informed, they develop a detailed outline and begin the interview process. Each report requires a minimum of 10 to 15 interviews with academics, officials, lobbyists and people working in the field. Only after all interviews are completed does the writing begin.

CHAPTER FORMAT

Each issue of *CQ Researcher*, and therefore each selection in this book, is structured in the same way. A selection begins with an introductory overview, which is briefly explored in greater detail in the rest of the report.

The second section chronicles the most important and current debates in the field. It is structured around a number of key issues questions, such as "Are globalization and regional integration fueling separatism?" and

"Will China's exploding growth lead to Western-style democracy?" This section is the core of each selection. The questions raised are often highly controversial and usually the object of much argument among scholars and practitioners. Hence, the answers provided are never conclusive but rather detail the range of opinion within the field.

Following those issue questions is the "Background" section, which provides a history of the issue being examined. This retrospective includes important legislative and executive actions and court decisions to inform readers on how current policy evolved.

Next, the "Current Situation" section examines important contemporary policy issues, legislation under consideration and action being taken. Each selection ends with an "Outlook" section that gives a sense of what new regulations, court rulings and possible policy initiatives might be put into place in the next five to ten years.

Each report contains features that augment the main text: sidebars that examine issues related to the topic, a pro/con debate by two outside experts, a chronology of key dates and events and an annotated bibliography that details the major sources used by the writer.

ACKNOWLEDGMENTS

We wish to thank many people for helping to make this collection a reality. Thomas J. Colin, managing editor of *CQ Researcher*, gave us his enthusiastic support and cooperation as we developed this edition. He and his talented staff of editors and writers have amassed a first-class collection of *Researcher* articles, and we are fortunate to have access to this rich cache. We also thankfully acknowledge the advice and feedback from current readers and are gratified by their satisfaction with the book.

Some readers may be learning about *CQ Researcher* for the first time. We expect that many readers will want regular access to this excellent weekly research tool. For subscription information or a no-obligation free trial of *Researcher*, please contact CQ Press at www.cqpress.com or toll-free at 1-866-4CQ-PRESS (1-866-427-7737).

We hope that you will be pleased by the 2009 edition of *Global Issues*. We welcome your feedback and suggestions for future editions. Please direct comments to

Charisse Kiino, Chief Acquisitions Editor, College Publishing Group, CQ Press, 2300 N Street, NW, Suite 800, Washington, DC 20037; or send e-mail to ckiino @cqpress.com.

—The Editors of CQ Press

Contributors

Thomas J. Colin, managing editor of *CQ Researcher*, has been a magazine and newspaper journalist for more than 30 years. Before joining Congressional Quarterly in 1991, he was a reporter and editor at the *Miami Herald* and *National Geographic* and editor in chief of *Historic Preservation*. He holds a bachelor's degree in English from the College of William and Mary and in journalism from the University of Missouri.

Brian Beary, a freelance journalist based in Washington, D.C., specializes in EU-U.S. affairs and is the U.S. correspondent for *Europolitics*, the EU affairs daily newspaper. Originally from Dublin, Ireland, he worked in the European Parliament for Irish member Pat "The Cope" Gallagher in 2000 and at the EU Commission's "Eurobarometer" unit on public opinion analysis. A fluent French speaker, he appears regularly as a guest international relations expert on various television and radio program. Apart from his work for *CQ Researcher*, Beary also writes for the *European Parliament Magazine* and the *Irish Examiner* daily newspaper.

Peter Behr recently retired from *The Washington Post*, where he was the principal reporter on energy issues and served as business editor from 1987 to 1992. A former Nieman Fellow at Harvard College, Behr worked at the Woodrow Wilson Center for Scholars and is working on a book about the history of the U.S. electric power grid.

Thomas J. Billitteri, a freelance journalist in Fairfield, Pa., has had more than 30 years' experience covering business, nonprofit institutions and related topics for newspapers and other publications. He has written previously for *CQ Researcher* on teacher education, parental rights and mental-health policy. He holds a bachelor's degree in English and a master's degree in journalism from Indiana University.

Marcia Clemmitt is a veteran social-policy reporter who joined *CQ Researcher* after serving as editor in chief of *Medicine and Health*, a Washington-based industry newsletter, and as staff writer for *The Scientist*. She has also been a high school math and physics teacher. She holds a bachelor's degree in arts and sciences from St. John's College, Annapolis, and a master's degree in English from Georgetown University.

Roland Flamini is a Washington-based correspondent who writes a foreign-affairs column for *CQ Weekly*. Fluent in six languages, he served as *Time* magazine's bureau chief in Rome, Bonn, Beirut, Jerusalem and the European Common Market and later served as international editor at United Press International.

Karen Foerstel is a freelance writer who has worked for the *Congressional Quarterly Weekly Report* and *Daily Monitor*, *The New York Post* and *Roll Call*, a Capitol Hill newspaper. She has published two books on women in Congress: *Climbing the Hill: Gender Conflict in Congress* and *The Biographical Dictionary of Women in Congress*. She currently lives and works in London. She has worked in Africa with ChildsLife International, a nonprofit that helps needy children around the world, and with Blue Ventures, a marine conservation organization that protects coral reefs in Madagascar.

Sarah Glazer specializes in health, education and social-policy issues. Her articles have appeared in *The New York Times*, *The Washington Post*, and *The Public Interest* and *Gender and Work*, a book of essays. Glazer has covered energy legislation for the Environmental and Energy Study Conference and reported for United Press International. She holds a bachelor's degree in American history from the University of Chicago.

Peter Katel is a veteran journalist who previously served as Latin America bureau chief for *Time* magazine in Mexico City, and as a Miami-based correspondent for *Newsweek* and the *Miami Herald*'s Spanish language edition *El Nuevo Herald*. He also worked as a reporter in New Mexico for 11 years and wrote for several nongovernmental organizations, including International Social Service and the World Bank. He has won several awards, including the Interamerican Press Association's Bartolome Mitre Award. He is a graduate of the University of New Mexico with a degree in university studies.

Seth Stern is a legal affairs reporter at *CQ Weekly*. He has worked as a journalist since graduating from Harvard Law School in 2001, including as a reporter for the *Christian Science Monitor* in Boston. He received his bachelor's degree at Cornell University's School of Industrial and Labor Relations and a master's degree in public administration from Harvard's Kennedy School of Government. He is coauthoring a biography of Supreme Court Justice William J. Brennan Jr.

1

Rise in Counterinsurgency

Peter Katel

American soldiers shell Taliban positions in eastern Afghanistan after coming under rocket fire in October 2006. The United States is sending more troops to Afghanistan and planning to emphasize counterinsurgency tactics. But some military experts argue that too much emphasis on "winning hearts and minds" of the local population could weaken the military skills needed in conventional combat.

E arly this summer, after savage fighting, elements of the 24th Marine Expeditionary Unit forced Taliban fighters out of Afghanistan's Helmand Valley, an area they had dominated for two years. Now it was time to talk.

The commander of Alpha Company, from the 6th Marine Regiment's First Battalion, Capt. Sean Dynan, a soft-spoken Annapolis graduate and fourth-generation fighter, addressed wary members of the village council in Amir Agha.

"I know that all of you want to just live your lives and that you don't want us to interfere with what you're doing on a daily basis," Dynan told two dozen men gathered in the marketplace. "It is our intention to help and to protect you." [1]

But making friends was proving difficult in a country at war since the failed Soviet occupation of the 1980s. "America came here telling us they're going to help us, but these are all tricks, the same tricks that Russia played — then they started killing us," Sayid Gul, an opium-poppy grower and merchant, told Bill Gentile, a PBS journalist embedded with the Marines. "We don't trust them any more, the foreigners." Gul was trying to get the Marines to pay him for damaging his house during a battle with the Taliban. [2]

Despite the villagers' wariness, Dynan's efforts at on-the-ground diplomacy reflect the Pentagon view that similar counterinsurgency tactics have led to a notable lessening of violence in Iraq this year.

Support for counterinsurgency is a key tenet of Defense Secretary Robert M. Gates' new National Defense Strategy, which lays out a hearts-and-minds approach for the last phase of what the Bush administration once labeled the "global war on terror" and now dubs "the long war."

From *CQ Researcher*, September 5, 2008.

Military and Civilian Casualties Decline in Iraq

The number of deaths among civilians and U.S. troops in Iraq has markedly decreased since 2006. There were 822 military deaths in 2006, and less than one-third as many so far this year (left). Iraqi civilian deaths dropped during the same period from nearly 17,000 two years ago to less than 4,000 this year. Much of the decline has been credited to new American counterinsurgency tactics, which were accompanied by a temporary troop buildup. In Afghanistan, however, troop deaths have already surpassed 100 for 2008, more than the tally in 2006. In response, the U.S. is planning to shift more troops to Afghanistan to facilitate counterinsurgency strategy.

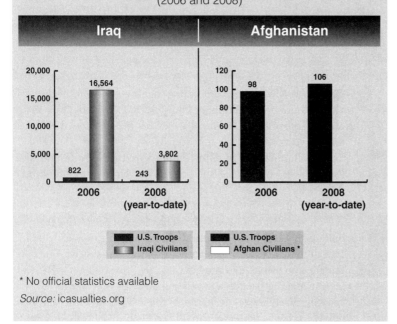

Deaths in Iraq and Afghanistan
(2006 and 2008)

* No official statistics available

Source: icasualties.org

"Military efforts to capture or kill terrorists are likely to be subordinate to measures to promote local participation in government and economic programs to spur development," the document says, "as well as efforts to understand and address the grievances that often lie at the heart of insurgencies." [3]

That strategy may sound more Peace Corps than Army and Marines. But counterinsurgency advocates argue they're guided by practicality, not bleeding-heart humanitarianism. Even after major fighting ends in Iraq and Afghanistan, the United States and its allies will be facing so-called asymmetric conflicts against foes who

know every nook and cranny of their home terrains, says John A. Nagl, a newly retired Army lieutenant colonel and leading counterinsurgency expert, now a senior fellow of the nonpartisan Center for a New American Security. He has proposed the formation of a 20,000-strong corps of Army advisers to work with U.S.-friendly governments facing insurgencies or potential insurgencies.

"Our conventional superiority is going to drive our enemies to fight us asymmetrically," says Nagl, who served as operations officer of an armored battalion early in the Iraq War and later helped write the *U.S. Army-Marine Corps Counterinsurgency Field Manual.* But that doesn't mean U.S. troops will be sitting ducks for traditional military operations, he says. "Even understanding that we've been focusing on counterinsurgency, you're still not going to want to mass tanks against the United States," he says, because American pilots would make short work of enemy armor.

Beware of such certainties, some military experts warn. One of the most vocal skeptics, Iraq combat veteran Lt. Col. Gian P. Gentile, argues that counterinsurgency advocates have drawn a false distinction between full-on, World War II-style combat and asymmetrical warfare. Recent events, he says, show that these varieties of combat can be used simultaneously.

As an example, Gentile points to Israel's painful experience in Lebanon during the 34-day war in the summer of 2006. Israeli troops who had been using counterinsurgency tactics in the Palestinian territories unexpectedly found themselves facing Hezbollah fighters in Lebanon employing conventional military tactics instead of guerrilla warfare to defend their territory. Hezbollah killed 119 Israeli soldiers, a shockingly high death toll for Israel. [4]

"I use that as a way to think about conflicts the United States might face in the future," says Gentile, who commanded an armored reconnaissance squadron in Baghdad in 2006, often confronting unseen enemies. Now a history professor at the United States Military Academy at West Point, he notes that the United States must continue to be ready in the future to deal with potential foes, such as Iran and North Korea, with big conventional armed forces.

After Gentile spoke, the Aug. 8 Russian invasion of the Republic of Georgia, a strong U.S. ally, prompted a wave of speculation about a rebirth of the Cold War — a period during which U.S. and Soviet forces trained incessantly for full-scale conflict in Europe. But, for now, at least, Secretary Gates said, "I don't see any prospect for the use of military force by the United States in this situation." [5]

In fact, the counterinsurgency-versus-conventional-warfare debate first began during the Cold War years, long before Gentile and Nagl — who both hold doctoral degrees — won their combat decorations in Iraq.

President John F. Kennedy came into office in 1961 determined to challenge Soviet-sponsored guerrilla insurgencies in societies scarred by colonialism or social injustice. Kennedy expanded the limited U.S. advisory effort in Vietnam, pushing for greater use of the military's "unconventional warfare" unit, Army Special Forces. But after Kennedy's assassination, the conflict turned into a full-scale war that emphasized the conventional-war strategy known as "attrition" — trying to force surrender by killing large numbers of enemy troops (see p. 11).

Military experts and historians still argue over whether attrition would have succeeded if the U.S. public hadn't forced an end to the war, or whether an early and total commitment to counterinsurgency warfare would have turned the tide. In any case, from the end of the Vietnam War until 2001, U.S. counterinsurgency operations were mounted as advisory missions — not major troop commitments — as in El Salvador during the 1980s. Indeed, the biggest post-Vietnam military operation, the Persian Gulf War of 1991, followed conventional lines — massive forces of aviation, artillery and armored infantry deployed against another nation-state's military.

Conventional warfare also dominated the early phase of the Iraq War, though Defense Secretary Donald H. Rumsfeld modified it by demanding use of a relatively small, highly mobile ground force, reinforced by massive airpower.

The planning focused solely on toppling Saddam Hussein and defeating his forces, not on what would follow the invasion. "We are not in Iraq to engage in nation-building," Rumsfeld wrote in *The Washington Post* six months after the U.S. invasion in March 2003. "The sooner Iraqis can take responsibility for their own affairs, the sooner U.S. forces can come home." [6]

But nation-building found favor in the Bush administration after U.S. forces came under attack both from Sunnis and Shiites in the years following the invasion.

Nation-building and counterinsurgency are closely related. "Counterinsurgency is nation-building in the face of armed opposition," in Nagl's definition. The Bush administration signaled its new strategy with the 2007 appointment of a new top commander for Iraq, Gen. David H. Petraeus, who co-directed preparation of the 2006 *U.S. Army-Marine Corps Counterinsurgency Field Manual*, the first publication of its kind for more than 20 years.[*]

Petraeus made his first priority the protection of Iraqi civilians, a shift in emphasis from pouring all resources into hunting and killing enemies. (*See graphs, p. 2.*)

For American military personnel, deaths have fallen to 221 in the first seven months of 2008 — from 740 during the same period last year. [7] Meanwhile, deaths among Iraqi security forces and civilians have fallen from more than 14,000 during the first seven months of 2007 to about 4,300 during the same period in 2008. [8]

One of Petraeus' key tactics was forging ties with Sunni tribes who were rebelling against the group Al Qaeda in Iraq and eroding the power of militias on whom Shiite civilians had depended for protection. As a result, says military-affairs specialist Stephen Biddle, who served on Petraeus' staff in 2007, "By late 2007 you had a situation in which all major internal combatants, for perfectly rational, perfectly self-interested reasons, had declared cease-fires — observing ceasefires of necessity." Biddle is a senior fellow at the Council on Foreign Relations think tank.

Skeptics argue, however, that counterinsurgency strategy had little to do with the increasing stability — because the United States never faced a true insurgency in Iraq or

---

[*] Petraeus will take over this month as head of U.S. Central Command, which covers the Middle East, North Africa and Central Asia; he will be replaced in Iraq by Gen. Raymond Odierno.

in Afghanistan. "We're not defending legitimate governments against foreign-inspired insurgencies," says Douglas A. Macgregor, a former Army colonel who served in the Persian Gulf War. "We've established puppet regimes designed to implement our will, and provoked rebellions against those regimes." Macgregor now consults for the defense industry and writes on military affairs.

Still, says Carter Malkasian, a military expert who has advised Marines in Iraq and Afghanistan, precisely labeling U.S. strategy and the nature of the war in Iraq matters less than the ultimate result. "What wins wars?" he asks. "There's very powerful argument to be made that tactics are much less important than economics and politics." In Iraq, Sunni tribes' turning against Al Qaeda in Iraq proved more decisive than U.S. strategy, he says.

Moreover, argues Air Force Maj. Gen. Charles J. Dunlap Jr., treating counterinsurgency largely as a low-tech exercise of winning the trust of poor villagers downplays what modern air power can accomplish.

"In the early part of the Afghanistan war, the Taliban assumed we would fight like the Russians, and they could simply hold out," Dunlap says. "What the Taliban didn't know about was the advent of laser-guided and precision munitions. Suddenly they're in positions they've held for years, and their foxholes are being vaporized by B-52s they didn't see or hear. What unhinges an adversary is knowing that he's helpless against his opponent's weapons."

Nevertheless, air power without solid intelligence on the ground can be catastrophic. In late August, U.N. investigators and an Afghan government commission said a U.S. air strike in western Afghanistan had killed 90 civilians, including 60 children. The U.S. military said 30-35 insurgents, including a Taliban commander, had been killed, along with five to seven civilians. But two members of the Afghan parliament said tribal enemies of the targeted community had fed false information to the U.S. military about a Taliban presence. [9]

Gen. David D. McKiernan, U.S. commander of the NATO force in Iraq, countered later that the civilian casualty number had been deliberately inflated. "We regret the loss of civilian life, but the numbers that we find on this target area are nowhere near the number reported in the media. We believe there was a very deliberate information operation orchestrated by the insurgency, by the Taliban," he told *The New York Times*. [10]

Taliban adaptability to U.S. tactical and strategic shifts helps explain the insurgents' comeback of the past several years.

That's one reason why Alpha Company's Marines made sure that farmer-merchant Gul finally got reimbursed for his damaged house.

Even so, Gul and his fellow villagers could be forgiven for still keeping the Americans at arms' length. Soon after the Marines entered the village of Amir Agha, they were led to the body of a man lying on a path, his throat slit. The message, villagers said, was clear: Don't cooperate with the Americans.

As the wars in Iraq and Afghanistan continue, here are some of the key issues being debated:

Is counterinsurgency the next wave of warfare?

The two world wars and the Korean War featured massive, mechanized armies in conventional, head-to-head confrontations. In Vietnam, however, the enemy used both guerrilla and "conventional" tactics. They inflicted such heavy casualties — more than 58,000 U.S. personnel killed — that it broke America's political will — even as massive U.S. bombing failed to demoralize the North Vietnamese.

Some military experts now say the United States demonstrated such technological superiority and raw military power in Iraq and Afghanistan that future enemies will utilize guerrilla warfare and counterinsurgency rather than head-on confrontations.

Indeed, says counterinsurgency advocate Nagl, the recently retired Army lieutenant colonel, Iraq and Afghanistan also have shown that innovative, guerrilla-style tactics can be highly effective against the U.S. military, especially in countries that are culturally and linguistically remote for most Americans.

Most foes of the United States "cannot compete tank to tank, fighter plane to fighter plane; that's a recipe for suicide, and they all know it," he says. "However, they've watched insurgencies in Iraq and Afghanistan tie us in knots. We're improving, but if you want any chance against the United States you're going to fight us asymmetrically."

Other military thinkers say conventional warfare is still very much a possibility. West Point history professor Gentile, a leading skeptic of the counterinsurgency thesis, warns against "narrowly conceiving the possibilities of future conflict." Hypothetically, he says, the possible collapse of North Korea could force an intervention by South Korea and the United States and a confrontation with North Korean troops who've decided to make a stand.

Moreover, North Korea and other potential enemies could build up their conventional-war capabilities to give them an edge over U.S. forces whose priority has become counterinsurgency, Gentile says. "If you're building an army to deal with irregular war and counterinsurgencies, and then you put that army into a [conventional warfare] scenario in Iran or North Korea, then things start to get worrisome and complicated."

Retired Army Col. Peter Mansoor, who served as executive officer to Gen. Petraeus, argues that North Korea and Iran are highly unlikely to emerge as U.S. opponents in conventional wars. A conflict on the Korean peninsula probably would turn into a counterinsurgency as U.S.-backed South Korean forces crossed into North Korea, he says. And U.S.-Iran combat almost certainly would see Iranians taking a counterinsurgency page from the Shiite Mahdi Army or even Sunni insurgents in Iraq, he adds.

"If you look around the world today, you have to stretch the imagination to find an area where we're going to be fighting a high-intensity land war in the near future," Mansoor says. "The people saying we have to scale back our efforts in Iraq in order to train for high-intensity combat that may come somewhere down the line are off-target."

But some military challenges defy predictions and rate higher on the threat scale than developing-world insurgencies, some experts caution. "The first priority of the military has to be to defend against existential threats, threats to the survival of the nation," says Air Force Maj. Gen. Dunlap. "I am still a believer that only a nation-state can destroy the United States. Therefore, we need to be absolutely sure that we can defend against any out there that might want to try to destroy or coerce us."

In practice, Dunlap says, defending against that level of menace means maintaining, refining and constantly inventing the high-tech weaponry that gives the United States a major advantage. "There are adversaries out there who are building against our capability," he says. "We want to push them away from even thinking about using force against us, by staying ahead."

Should the Army form an advisers corps?

Training and advising local security forces is a major strategic role for U.S. forces in Iraq and NATO in Afghanistan. As each country's troops and police gradually assume complete responsibility, goes the theory, the foreign presence can diminish. In July, Lt. Gen. James

Marine Maj. Gen. John Kelly and Gov. Maamoun Sami Rashid al-Alwani transfer security control of Anbar Province — once the center of Iraq's Sunni insurgency — from U.S. to Iraqi security forces on Sept. 1, in Ramadi, the provincial capital. The turnover reflected the success of the recent U.S. troop "surge" and the increased use of counterinsurgency tactics.

M. Dubik, former head of the U.S. training program in Iraq, told Congress that Iraqi ground forces would be fully capable by mid-2009. [11]

The proposal by former Lt. Col. Nagl would create a 20,000-strong corps of Army advisers who could be deployed whenever or wherever needed in the future. Creating a corps would not only make more advisory work possible but also formally recognize the activity as a military specialty — making it attractive to ambitious career officers for whom advisory work can now sidetrack them from the promotion ladder.

Sending in U.S. advisers, of course, isn't a 21st-century innovation. During the "small wars" period before World War II, U.S. troops created and trained national police forces in Haiti and Nicaragua. [12]

Similarly, in 1980-92 American military advisers played a crucial role during El Salvador's civil war against left-wing guerrillas. And advisers are now working with the Colombian military in its fight against nominally left-wing insurgents. (See "Current Situation," p. 16.)

But advisory missions can expand in scope. The U.S. role in Vietnam began in 1955, when President Dwight D. Eisenhower ordered the Military Assistance and Advisory Group to Vietnam. In 1960, there were only 685 advisers and trainers. In 1964, the United States began a massive troop buildup that eventually reached more than half a million. In 1972, American forces returned to an advisory role after President Richard M. Nixon instituted his "Vietnamization" program and withdrew U.S. combat troops. Ultimately, however, the U.S.-advised Vietnamese forces broke under unrelenting pressure from North Vietnamese forces. (*See "Background," p. 8.*)

As the Vietnam experience demonstrates, limiting the U.S. role to training doesn't necessarily prevent escalation. Nor is victory guaranteed to U.S.-trained forces.

Still, even some military experts who criticize the growing emphasis on counterinsurgency are warming to the idea of an advisory corps. "Insurgencies prosper when they can cast themselves as the protectors of the indigenous people from foreign forces," says Air Force Maj. Gen. Dunlap. "You overlay that with the negative views that many people have of America and Americans, and we ought to look for opportunities to have a small footprint. John Nagl's adviser corps is perfect. The 'face' of the counterinsurgents largely will be other indigenous people, not U.S. troops, and that's a good thing."

In what might seem like an unexpected twist, Dunlap sees the adviser corps proposal as strengthening his own case for maintaining a strong high-tech program. Assigning relatively small groups of advisers to other countries will allow the Air Force and other branches to keep their advanced weaponry projects under way, something that might not be possible if major U.S. contingents were assigned to every insurgency of interest to the United States. "At the same time we can also help them with air power, logistics and intelligence — things that are hard for some of these countries to do."

But it's not certain that advising and training are jobs that the vast majority of U.S. military personnel are equipped to carry out. Retired Army Col. Macgregor, who writes on military affairs, ridicules the idea that "we are going to turn conventional soldiers into Renaissance men who speak multiple languages and become friends with people all over the Arab world."

The reality behind the counterinsurgency drive, Macgregor argues, is a revival of 19th-century imperialist notions that Western powers have complete freedom of military maneuver in poor and developing countries. "I can do more by pulling in a hospital ship and some Navy ships into a river port in Zaire and inoculating thousands of children, offloading food and medicine and building some electrical infrastructure than I can with an adviser corps," he says.

But Nagl, who came up with the adviser corps idea, says the proposal isn't designed simply to generate good will. Advisers would be dispatched to countries in which shooting wars are under way now — to Iraq and Afghanistan, for starters. "I believe that we will continue to have an advisory role in both countries for a number of years," he says, "and professional, dedicated advisers will be essential to our success in both. I believe we should continue to adapt to meet the needs of wars we're actually fighting."

The creation of a corps would make advisory work part of the military career track. Hence, Nagl and others say, officers who spend years working with foreign military units wouldn't lose out to contemporaries who took the conventional steps up the promotion ladder by rotating through a variety of combat positions. Now advisory work has taken on considerable urgency. "We're building these teams now," Nagl says. "Are we building them as well as we possibly can — giving them every possible advantage given the importance of their role in two wars?"

But even some experts who view military advising favorably dispute the notion that it's the foundation stone on which U.S. strategy in Iraq and Afghanistan rests. "I'm not sure I see as powerful an upside as [Nagl] does," says Biddle, at the Council on Foreign Relations. "There's a gain, but it's not as decisive and overwhelming as a lot of advocates would argue."

Above all, Biddle argues, technical improvements in soldiering don't necessarily make the difference between winning and losing. "Military performance is partly a function of the politics of the war in which a soldier is fighting," he says. In Iraq, "I don't care how much training Shiites get, they're not going to be reliable defenders of Sunnis."

Is the emphasis on counterinsurgency weakening the military?

For military professionals, few issues are more critical than ensuring that their forces are prepared for the kinds of conflicts that lie ahead. History is filled with sorry tales of generals and politicians who looked to the past instead of the future.

The most recent example comes from the Republic of Georgia. Its military has been getting intensive U.S. training for service in Iraq, where 2,000 Georgian troops had been bolstering the U.S.-led presence. But their counterinsurgency training did them little good against

Russian invaders who pushed into Georgia with tanks and armored personnel carriers supported by warplanes. "Against the Russians, Georgian command and control withered quickly, and army and police units were operating on their own, often at cross-purposes or overlapping missions," *The New York Times* reported. [13]

In a reverse case, Gen. William Westmoreland, commander of U.S. forces in Vietnam from 1964-1968, insisted on using World War II-style tactics, focusing on wiping out major enemy formations, and claimed that the strategy was working. Subordinates who presented data to the contrary were silenced. Meanwhile, "The general's staff officers manipulated body counts and kill ratios and reports of desertion and falling morale among the enemy to gradually compile these proofs of imminent victory he now displayed to the newsmen," wrote Neil Sheehan, a journalist in Vietnam who later authored a Pulitzer Prize-winning history of the war. [14]

Vietnam figures prominently in today's counterinsurgency debate. Gen. Petraeus, who graduated from West Point in 1974, two years after U.S. combat forces withdrew from Vietnam, wrote his doctoral thesis at Princeton University on the war's lessons.

Vietnam, he wrote, reinforced military skepticism about counterinsurgency. Even those who supported counterinsurgency in principle expressed doubt about its suitability for U.S. forces. "As one U.S. officer put it, 'I submit that the U.S. Army does not have the mind-set for combat operations where the key terrain is the mind, not the high ground. We do not take the time to understand the nature of the society in which we are fighting, the government we are supporting or the enemy we are fighting.' " [15]

If Petraeus himself had any reservations about counterinsurgency, Iraq changed his mind. He has become a leading advocate of stepping up the U.S. counterinsurgency capability and may have influenced Defense Secretary Gates to adopt that view as well. "We cannot kill our way out of this endeavor," Petraeus said in June in a three-page "Commander's Counterinsurgency Guidance" to U.S. forces. "We and our Iraqi partners must identify and separate the 'reconcilables' from the 'irreconcilables.' . . . We must strive to make the reconcilables a part of the solution, even as we identify, pursue and kill, capture or drive out the irreconcilables." [16]

But, despite the apparent success, so far, of the strategy, some military men warn that it's damaging the military.

An American soldier rescues an elderly woman near Danang during combat in Vietnam in February 1970. At the beginning of the Vietnam War, President John F. Kennedy pushed for greater use of the military's "unconventional warfare" unit, Army Special Forces, but after his assassination the conflict turned into a full-scale war.

"The U.S. Army commitment in Afghanistan and Iraq for the past six-plus years has turned the Army, at least in terms of operational capabilities, into pretty much a counterinsurgency-only force," says Gentile of West Point. "People will say that the Army can quickly turn around from a counterinsurgency focus to fighting at the higher end of conflict. That is not at all clear to me."

Gentile argues in *Armed Forces Journal* that the rhythms of counterinsurgency warfare differ substantially from those of high-intensity combat. For instance, if a roadside bomb kills or wounds a soldier, the enemy who planted the bomb may be unknown, preventing U.S. troops from doing what they would do in battle — strike back immediately. "The longer the soldier stays in Iraq and the more casualties [are] taken by a combat unit, the more the discernible links between these actions, reactions and counteractions that demonstrate progress get fuzzy," he wrote. [17]

Mansoor, Petraeus' former executive officer, counters that the war in Iraq has given troops plenty of opportunity to sharpen their battle skills. "Talk to a soldier who fought in Baquba, or Karbala or Fallujah," he says, naming cities where U.S. troops fought pitched battles against Sunni insurgents or Shiite militias, "and ask, 'Were you in high-intensity combat?' Damn right, they were."

Mansoor does concede that some conventional-war skills, such as air defense, may have eroded in wars in which the enemies have no aircraft. "That, to me, given the lack of immediate threat around the world, argues for putting more of these capabilities in the reserve component."

Air Force Maj. Gen. Dunlap is among those who oppose that idea, given that conventional threats could appear suddenly. And he questions the underlying view that overall combat capability has remained up to snuff. "In a full-up war, the other guy has airplanes," he says. "Our troops have gone a very long time without suffering air attack or serious armored attack; they haven't even been under an extended artillery barrage. They're not thinking very much about what it takes to fight a country that might put hundreds of thousands of well-equipped troops in the field to oppose them in a combined arms battle."

Dunlap points to the intense but limited nature of the current wars as the reason for lack of experience fighting conventional armies. Sunni insurgents, Shiite militias and the Taliban fight without air power, without artillery and sometimes without any vehicles, maneuvering in small groups through difficult terrain. Many military thinkers who have been through these campaigns, Dunlap says, "seem to conceive of all future war as being some replay of what they saw in Iraq or Afghanistan; in a way, these great minds are almost prisoners of their own experience."

For some experts, the question is whether that lack of experience in conventional war is harmful. "Certainly, the Army doesn't have as much time to train on large-unit conventional warfare as 10 years ago," says Steven Metz, chairman of the Regional Strategy and Planning Department and a professor of national security affairs at the U.S. Army War College's Strategic Studies Institute. "The Army may be less proficient at tank gunnery. But I don't see where that creates unacceptable risk. Show me somebody else we are likely to fight that is moving ahead of us in tank gunnery."

BACKGROUND

'Small Wars'

Before the era of global warfare, U.S. military forces fought, or conducted advisory operations in, a number of limited foreign conflicts, all in former European colonial possessions. In some cases — but not all — U.S. troops, mainly Marines, used what are now called counterinsurgency strategies. [18]

At the dawn of the 20th century, American troops helped the Philippines win freedom from Spain in 1898. But the United States' annexation of the country in 1899 provoked a rebellion by Filipinos who had fought against Spain. They surrendered after four years of combat.

Muslim inhabitants of the southern Philippines, the Moros, whom Spain had never completely subjugated, waged a longer struggle against the Americans. The insurgency lasted about 12 years. For much of that time, U.S. forces followed a strategy of harsh repression. After Gen. John J. Pershing took command, he tried a more humane approach, but too late to repair relations with the population. The Moros were finally defeated by U.S. military.*

During the same period, U.S. Army troops and Marines joined a multinational effort to suppress a Chinese nationalist insurgency known as the Boxer Rebellion. The insurgents (who had formed a secret society, The Righteous Harmony of Fists) were rebelling against Western powers' granting themselves extensive trade privileges in China — without consulting China. The "Boxers," supported by the Imperial Chinese government, began in 1900 to attack railroads and other facilities and people associated with the West. The Boxer uprising was a classic anti-colonialist insurgency. The American and allied forces' response came straight from conventional-war doctrine. American and allied forces marched on Peking (now Beijing), seizing the capital in August, 1900. The empress was forced to sue for peace and to endorse all foreign, commercial interests in her country.

Asian conflicts aside, most U.S. military action in the United States' pre-superpower days took place close to home. From 1903 to 1933, U.S. forces intervened 32 times in Latin American and Caribbean countries.

---

* A rekindled separatist movement remains active in the southern Philippines today.

Most of those actions involved little or no fighting. But in Haiti, during an occupation that lasted from 1915 to 1934, the Marine Corps broke a 1915-1920 rebellion against the Haitian government by northern farmers known as *cacos*. The key was U.S. cultivation of allies and informants in farming communities.

American troops played a similar role in Nicaragua in the early-20th century. President William Howard Taft sent Marines to Nicaragua in 1909 to support an insurrection against anti-U.S. dictator José Santos Zelaya. The U.S.-backed rebels won. But in 1925, anti-U.S. nationalist insurgents took up arms against another president, who had just taken power in a coup. Augusto César Sandino, who headed the uprising, scored an initial victory, prompting a call by the government of Adolfo Díaz for U.S. help.

A U.S. Marine contingent couldn't beat the rebels. In a country whose governments had done little to win popular support, Sandino enjoyed a freedom of mobility that the Marines — despite the innovative use of airplanes for surveillance and bombing — couldn't match. Finally, in 1933, the Nicaraguan government persuaded Sandino to call off the insurgency if U.S. forces withdrew. They did so, and Sandino was granted amnesty. But in 1934, troops of the U.S.-equipped National Guard assassinated Sandino, who would become the namesake of the left-wing Sandinista revolution 45 years later.

Global Conflict

The two world wars vaulted the United States into the role of global superpower. America approached that commanding position hesitantly, entering World War I in 1917, after the European nations had been fighting for the better part of three years. [19]

By that time, the conflict in Western Europe, where the war was centered, amounted to a facedown between vast, scarcely mobile armies fighting from trenches. Major tactics included massive artillery barrages, infantry charges and defensive operations based on machine-gun fire. Other newly developed weapons also made their mark: poison gas, the tank, the airplane and the submarine. In this strategic environment counterinsurgency played no part.

President Woodrow Wilson's decision to join in the conflict on the side of England, France, Belgium and Russia pushed the American military establishment into the age of mass mobilization and complicated logistics.

When the war began in Europe in 1914, the U.S. Army stood at fewer than 100,000 men. The United States also lagged in weaponry. From 1898-1915, Congress had appropriated an average of only about $150,000 a year to buy machine guns — a small expenditure even then. In 1916, the appropriation for machine guns jumped to $12 million.

The following year, Congress instituted the draft. As a result, Gen. Pershing was able to have 1.2 million troops quickly shipped to Europe.

Nearly all of them participated in the Meuse-Argonne offensive, an enormous allied attack on German forces that was decisive in ending the war in late 1918.

The Treaty of Versailles, which left Germany with a loss of territory and a punishing debt of $33 billion in reparations, caused intense bitterness in Germany and helped pave the way for World War II. In Japan, an ultranationalist doctrine took hold in the political class, which adopted the belief that Japan was destined to rule East Asia by conquering the region's other nations, as well as Western competitors. The Dec. 7, 1941, Japanese attack on Pearl Harbor plunged America into war. By that time, virtually all of Europe was under Nazi domination, while Japan controlled much of China, the South Pacific and Southeast Asia.

To fight in so many far-flung theaters, the United States built a vast war machine. In 1943, the nation's armament orders included 125,000 aircraft and 500,000 machine guns. By war's end in 1945, the Army alone had 8.3 million men in uniform, 5.4 million deployed overseas.

All that manpower and materiel fed massive military operations, such as D-Day — the June 6, 1944, invasion of Western Europe, in which 156,000 U.S. and allied troops landed on the beaches of Normandy, France. Elsewhere in Europe, massive Soviet forces advanced from the east, and the Allies moved from the west, retaking territory from the enemy before marching into Germany itself, killing or capturing German troops every step of the way. Overall, the Allies' strategy was simply to pound the enemy into unconditional surrender.

In the east, Japan unconditionally surrendered soon after atomic bombs were dropped on Hiroshima and Nagasaki in August 1945, dramatically demonstrating the United States' overwhelming military superiority.

CHRONOLOGY

1900-1933 *U.S. quells insurgencies in former European colonies in Asia, Central America and the Caribbean.*

1941-1961 *U.S. plays decisive role in World War II, then as U.S. Soviet Cold War intensifies, sends military advisers to Vietnam.*

1941-1945 United States enters World War II, helps Allies defeat Germany with relentless and massive offensives on all fronts, then drops atomic bombs on two Japanese cities to force Japan's surrender.

1950-1953 Korean War pits U.S. and South Korea against North Korea and China.

1954 President Dwight D. Eisenhower sends military advisers to South Vietnam, threatened by communist North Vietnam.

1961 President John F. Kennedy authorizes the distinctive green beret for the military's main counterinsurgency fighters, the Army Special Forces.

1965-1990 *Counterinsurgency and conventional strategies both fail in Vietnam, eventually leading to creation and acceptance of "Powell Doctrine" — never to enter into war without massive force and an exit strategy.*

1966 U.S. troop level in Vietnam nears a half-million; Pentagon remains committed to "attrition" strategy.

1968 "Tet Offensive" by North Vietnam weakens Americans' support for war.

1975 North Vietnam conquers the south, two years after the last U.S. combat troops withdraw.

1983 President Ronald Reagan invades Grenada to topple Cuban-supported government. . . . Administration warns Salvadoran government of loss of counterinsurgency aid if human-rights abuse continues during war against left-wing guerrillas.

1989 President George H. W. Bush invades Panama to arrest strongman Manuel Noriega on drug charges.

1990 Iraq invades Kuwait under orders from dictator Saddam Hussein.

1991-2003 *U.S. launches military operations, mostly conventional, from Middle East to the Balkans.*

1991 "Operation Desert Storm," a massive, multinational military offensive led by United States, pushes Iraq out of Kuwait.

1995 President Bill Clinton helps organize NATO bombing of Serbia to counter ethnic cleansing in Bosnia.

1998 NATO air campaign seeks to halt expulsion of ethnic Albanians from Kosovo. . . . Clinton orders missile strike to kill Osama bin Laden after al Qaeda bombing of two U.S. embassies in Africa.

2001 U.S. Special Forces and CIA help anti-Taliban Afghan forces overthrow Taliban in wake of Sept. 11 attacks.

2003 U.S.-led invasion of Iraq uses conventional-war strategy to topple Saddam.

2006-2008 *Mounting U.S. casualties in Iraq spur call for new approach.*

2006 New Army-Marine counterinsurgency manual directs military to become familiar with societies in which insurgents emerge.

2007 Following escalating attacks on U.S. forces, President George W. Bush appoints counterinsurgency strategist Gen. David H. Petraeus as Iraq commander. . . . As troop "surge" brings new U.S. forces into Iraq, Americans build ties with former Sunni insurgents and force main Shiite militia into a cease-fire.

2008 Pentagon embraces counterinsurgency for "long war" against terrorists. . . . Taliban insurgents step up attacks on Western troops and aid workers in Afghanistan. . . . Plans announced for major U.S. military reinforcement in Afghanistan. . . . Russian invasion of Georgia prompts fears of new Cold War.

Korea to Vietnam

America's first post-World War II conflict began in 1950. Like the world wars, the Korean War pitted massive, heavily armed militaries against each other, fighting for territory. Newly created North Korea, a Soviet-bloc country, invaded the also newly created South Korea, a U.S. ally. North Korea was reinforced by its neighbor, the Peoples Republic of China — yet another new government. The hard-fought war never formally ended, but an armistice in 1953 stopped the conflict and left the Korean peninsula divided at the 38th parallel. [20]

The first phase of America's war in Vietnam began the very next year, when communist Vietnamese forces decisively defeated France, which was trying to reestablish control of its long-time colony. An ensuing treaty left the communists established in the north and anti-communists, backed by the United States, in the south.

The early days of U.S. involvement in Vietnam attracted little attention from the general public. As involvement escalated into war, the Vietnam conflict grew into a sociopolitical conflict in the United States — and the stage on which counterinsurgency advocates in the military battled for strategic control with adherents of conventional warfare.

The buildup of forces took place over a span of more than 10 years. President Kennedy, Eisenhower's successor, authorized the military to expand its mission from advice and training to direct combat. Kennedy also signed off on a CIA-backed military coup against South Vietnamese President Ngo Dinh Diem, who was losing political support among his own people and was deemed ineffective at countering the communist guerrillas known as the Vietcong.

Kennedy put much stock in the fledgling U.S. Army Special Forces, viewing the highly trained and culturally adaptable soldiers as the ideal counterinsurgency force. Kennedy personally authorized their distinctive headgear — green berets. [21]

Following Kennedy's 1963 assassination, the military challenge to the south intensified. And in 1964, after two alleged North Vietnamese attacks on U.S. destroyers in the nearby Gulf of Tonkin, off the coast of North Vietnam* President Lyndon B. Johnson pushed a reso-

lution through Congress authorizing the president to "take all necessary measures to repel any armed attack against the forces of the United States and to prevent further aggression." Language that followed specified Southeast Asia as the region involved.

With the Gulf of Tonkin Resolution, the United States began rapidly escalating its forces. Troop strength climbed from 685 advisers in 1960, to 21,000 combat troops in 1964, to 429,000 in 1966 and to a peak of 536,000 in 1968 — with draftees supplying most of the manpower. For their part, the communists put more North Vietnamese Army (NVA) troops into the field, to reinforce the Vietcong.

Gen. Westmoreland, the U.S. commander until July 1968, pursued a "search and destroy" strategy aimed at grinding down the enemy. In the air, meanwhile, American bombers in 1966-1967 carried out major raids against North Vietnamese targets. (Republican presidential candidate Sen. John McCain, R-Ariz., was shot down on one such mission in 1967 and spent more than five years as a North Vietnamese prisoner of war.)

U.S. officials reported inflicting heavy daily losses on the communists, but their resistance never broke. On Jan. 30, 1968, New Year's Day ("Tet") on Vietnam's lunar calendar, the communists launched a massive offensive throughout South Vietnam.

Militarily, the offensive failed, but its scale shattered U.S. public confidence, after years of upbeat bulletins from the White House and the Pentagon. With support for the war eroding, President Johnson limited bombing of North Vietnam, enabling peace talks to start with North Vietnam. Because of the war's unpopularity, Johnson decided not to run for a second term.

On the ground, Gen. Westmoreland was replaced by Gen. Creighton Abrams, who showed more willingness to embrace counterinsurgency strategy focused on winning civilian support.

But with U.S. domestic support still diminishing, President Nixon unveiled a "Vietnamization" strategy of turning military responsibility over to South Vietnam. At the same time, Nixon and North Vietnamese negotiators kept peace talks going, though these were interrupted by the resumption of U.S bombing of North Vietnam. The renewed bombing was aimed at forcing Vietnam into conceding more at the bargaining table. Nonetheless, the North Vietnamese were confident they were nearing victory, even as

---

* The National Security Agency released a study in 2005 concluding that the report of the crucial second attack was based on a mistranslation — a mistake that the agency covered up to avoid admitting the error.

Anthropologists Assist Troops in Iraq

New Pentagon program raises academics' concerns.

The new *Army/Marine Corps Counterinsurgency Field Manual* directs military commanders to study the social codes, rituals and power relationships of the societies in which they're fighting insurgents.

But a Pentagon program that embeds anthropologists and other social scientists with American troops in Iraq and Afghanistan has many academics up in arms.

The goal is to ensure that troops' "activities are better harmonized with the interests of the local population, thereby reducing the need to use lethal force," says anthropologist Montgomery McFate, the program's senior adviser, and a member of the team that wrote the manual. [1]

While the program is calculated to help U.S. troops understand the societies they operate in, its official name — Human Terrain Systems (HTS) — seems more designed to inspire "maximum paranoia," as Defense Secretary Robert M. Gates wryly acknowledged. [2]

Indeed, Gates told the Association of American Universities in April, the name echoes the militaristic sound of other Pentagon programs, including the infamous TALON Reporting System, a database on terrorists that was found to be collecting information on peaceful antiwar protesters. After a burst of unfavorable publicity, the Pentagon shut TALON down in 2007. [3]

But its name aside, Gates said the program is vital in combating a major weakness that affects Americans in general and the military in particular. "Understanding the traditions, motivations and languages of other parts of the world has not always been a strong suit of the United States," he said.

Winning over the academic community is proving equally tough for the Pentagon. Since last year, the Network of Concerned Anthropologists has been gathering signatures of social scientists who oppose HTS as a misuse of their discipline in the service of wars they oppose. [4]

The American Anthropological Association's Executive Board echoed the sentiment last October: "In the context of a war that is widely recognized as a denial of human rights and based on faulty intelligence and undemocratic princi-ples, the Executive Board sees the HTS project as a problematic application of anthropological expertise, most specifically on ethical grounds." [5]

The American Psychological Association, meanwhile, has been debating whether to make a psychologist's participation in military interrogations a violation of the association's code of ethics. That potential professional conflict has taken on a sharper edge than the debate among anthropologists, given the harsh interrogations — many call them torture — of terrorism suspects at Guantánamo Bay by U.S. personnel. [6]

While opposition to the Iraq War is a key reason for the negative response to HTS, a past war also is influencing the debate. David Price, an anthropology professor at St. Martin's University in Lacey, Wash., and a founder of the anti-HTS network, points to a report citing a Pentagon official who linked the program to the Vietnam War-era Civil Operations and Revolutionary Development Support (CORDS) program. The rural-pacification effort led to a program known as Phoenix, which was designed to capture — often, in practice, to kill — Vietcong leaders. [7]

"I am not saying that is what's going on with Human Terrain Teams," Price added during a 2007 radio discussion, but he called the remark of the anonymous Pentagon official citing CORDS "very troubling." [8]

However, neither CORDS nor Phoenix involved recruiting social scientists to unravel the mysteries of Vietnamese rural society. And Col. John Agoglia, director of the U.S. Army Peacekeeping and Stability Operations Institute, responded to Price that Human Terrain doesn't target enemies. "We are trying to get people to resort to using peaceful means, not violent means, to resolve conflict, not having to be beholden to a brutal regime like that of the [Afghan] Taliban." [9]

The anti-HTS academics raise a practical objection as well. Anthropological ethics require that people who speak to social scientists give "voluntary informed consent" to sharing knowledge. "In an environment with so many weapons . . . people are being interviewed and asked things, and the notion they

Nixon sent U.S. forces into Cambodia, a move he said was aimed at destroying North Vietnamese supply facilities, and was also designed to keep pressure on North Vietnamese peace negotiators. On March 29, 1973, the last U.S. combat troops pulled out of Vietnam, and remaining U.S. forces resumed their original advisory mission. South Vietnam finally fell to communist forces on April 30, 1975.

can just say no and not talk to somebody — that's not a concern in a military context, but it's a fundamental concern for social scientists," Price said during the radio exchange. [10]

McFate, who has a doctorate in social anthropology from Yale, responded that rural Afghans "can draw a distinction between a lethal unit of the U.S. military and a non-lethal unit," such as a human terrain team. "If they choose to talk to a human terrain team, they are told exactly what the human terrain team is doing — that they're trying to learn about the society, that they're trying to help the military make better decisions." [11]

Nevertheless, *New York Times* correspondent David Rohde said during the radio discussion that an HTS team member he'd observed in action in Afghanistan carried a weapon by choice. "And she wore a military uniform, which would make her appear to be a soldier to Afghans she wasn't speaking with." [12]

One aspect of HTS efforts is not in dispute: the danger. In the program's first year, two social scientists were killed. Michael Bhatia, an Afghanistan specialist and a doctoral candidate in political science at Oxford University, was killed in May by a roadside bomb in Afghanistan, where he was deployed with the 82nd Airborne Division. In June, Nicole Suveges, a doctoral candidate in political science at Johns Hopkins University, died in the bombing of a District Advisory Council meeting in Sadr City, a sprawling Shiite district of Baghdad. A former U.S. Army reservist, she was embedded in Iraq with the Army's 4th Infantry Division. [13]

Clearly, though the military classifies the social scientists as civilians, enemies don't distinguish them from U.S. troops. And the program's critics suggest that drawing a line between the social scientists' work and the military goal of killing enemies may be impossible. The critics repeatedly cite John Wilcox, assistant deputy undersecretary of Defense for advanced systems and concepts, who gave a presentation in 2007 that cited a "Need to 'Map the Human Terrain' Across the Kill Chain." Accomplishing that task "[prepares] the entire kill chain for the GWOT [global war on terror]," he said. Wilcox was speaking about the development and refinement of air-launched rocket and missile platforms, whose output includes the bombs known as "penetrating weapons." [14]

The terminology may have been identical to the military's social sciences project, McFate says, but the context was entirely different. "He wasn't talking about HTS at all," she says. "It seems apparent to me that he was talking about the benefits of understanding a population for kinetic targeting," military jargon for deadly, direct force. "A lot of people use the words 'human terrain' these days."

---

[1] *U.S. Army-Marine Corps Counterinsurgency Field Manual* (2007), p. 97.

[2] Robert M. Gates, Secretary of Defense, April 14, 2008, www.defenselink.mil/speeches/speech.aspx?speechid=1228.

[3] *Ibid.*; also see Mark Mazzetti, "Pentagon Expected to Close Unit That Tracked Protesters," *The New York Times*, April 2, 2008, p. A24.

[4] See Network of Concerned Anthropologists, http://concerned.anthropologists.googlepages.com.

[5] See "Statement on HTS," American Anthropological Association Executive Board Statement on the Human Terrain System," Oct. 31, 2007, http://dev.aaanet.org/issues/policy-advocacy/Statement-on-HTS.cfm.

[6] See Benedict Carey, "Psychologists Clash on Aiding Interrogations," *The New York Times*, Aug. 16, 2008, www.nytimes.com/2008/08/16/washington/16psych.html?sq=psychologists%20interrogation&st=cse&adxnnl=1&scp=1&adxnnlx=1219068689-IaEQZpGtkMsQbf3nfyL9OQ&pagewanted=print.

[7] See Neil Sheehan, *A Bright Shining Lie: John Paul Vann and America in Vietnam* (1988), pp. 731-732.

[8] "Anthropologists and War," "The Diane Rehm Show," National Public Radio, Oct. 10, 2007, WAMU, http://wamu.org/programs/dr/07/10/10.php. For the report citing the unnamed Pentagon official, see Bryan Bender, "Efforts to aid US roil anthropology," *The Boston Globe*, Oct. 8, 2007, ww.boston.com/news/nation/washington/articles/2007/10/08/efforts_to_aid_us_roil_anthropology/.

[9] *Ibid.*

[10] *Ibid.*

[11] *Ibid.*

[12] *Ibid.*

[13] See "In Memoriam: Nicole Suveges," Human Terrain System, undated, http://humanterrainsystem.army.mil/Suveges.htm; "In Memoriam: Michael Bhatia," Human Terrain System, undated, http://humanterrainsystem.army.mil/Bhatia.htm; James Vaznis, "Afghan bomb kills scholar from Mass.," *The Boston Globe*, May 10, 2008, p. B1; Ovetta Wiggins, "Johns Hopkins Grad Student Dies in Iraq," *The Washington Post*, June 27, 2008, p. B3.

[14] See John Wilcox, assistant deputy under secretary of Defense; director, Joint Capability Technology Demonstration, "Precision Engagement — Strategic Context for the Long War," Department of Defense, unclassified, Feb. 1, 2007, www.dtic.mil/ndia/2007psa_winter/wilcox.pdf.

'Small Wars' II

American military engagements in the 1980s marked a return to the U.S. backyard in Central America and the Caribbean.

The nearby conflicts were marked by deployment of small numbers of U.S. troops, either as advisers, or as rapid-intervention forces ordered to topple unfriendly governments and withdraw.

Officers Cross Swords in Online Debate

"The finest military leaders want differing ideas ruthlessly explored."

A lively public debate on the merits of counterinsurgency strategy in Iraq and Afghanistan is playing out across the ranks in several online publications, including the U.S. Army's "Military Review" and "abu muqawama," a blog on counterinsurgency.

Consider the firefight that resulted when Air Force Maj. Gen. Charles J. Dunlap Jr. criticized aspects of the new Army-Marine Corps counterinsurgency manual and questioned the Pentagon's emphasis on counterinsurgency — at a time when China is building up its high-tech warfare capabilities.

"Are more ground forces to fight lengthy irregular wars the most critical capability for 'the Armed Forces we need for the 21st century?'" Dunlap wrote, quoting President George W. Bush. "Technology can obviate the need for massive numbers of boots-on-the-ground. Soldiers seem to be predisposed . . . to be uncomfortable with any technology that might diminish or even displace the large ground formations so vital to their tradition-driven self-conceptualization." [1]

In response, wrote Air Force Lt. Col. Buck Elton, "Gen. Dunlap's critique of operations in Iraq is unusual and alarming, coming from an active-duty general officer *while* the conflict is ongoing. Advocating the types of wars the Air Force should fight (no ground troops) by only preparing for the wars they want to fight (airpower-centric conflicts with peer competitors), while ignoring the type of fight our enemy wants to fight (al Qaeda's global insurgency) and the wars our president orders us to fight (Afghanistan and Iraq), is a terrible mistake." [2]

Counterinsurgency is an especially important topic for discussion across ranks, says John A. Nagl, an Iraq War veteran who contributed to the counterinsurgency manual, because many senior officers today never got counterinsurgency experience as junior officers. "The Army didn't practice counterinsurgency for a generation, so generals don't necessarily know more about counterinsurgency than captains do," Nagl says. "For the organization to adapt and learn, it has to admit it doesn't have all the answers."

The search for answers isn't for the timid. In a recent article in the *International Herald Tribune*, Lt. Col. Gian P. Gentile, a former battalion commander in Iraq, attacked the conventional view that the "surge" of additional U.S. troops in Iraq brought a fundamental change in U.S. strategy. In fact, Gentile wrote, he and his Baghdad-based troops in pre-surge 2006 were already practicing counterinsurgency. He cited daily small-unit patrols aimed at pro-

President Ronald W. Reagan in 1983 ordered an invasion of the island of Grenada to topple a left-wing government that was deepening its relationship with Cuba. [22]

By the time of the Grenada intervention, Reagan had directed U.S. military and civilian advisers to help run a war in El Salvador against a left-wing insurgency, the *Frente Farabundo Martí de Liberación Nacional* (FMLN). As some U.S. officials acknowledged at the time, maintaining an alliance with the Salvadoran government put the United States on the side of a military and civilian establishment whose preferred strategy was to massacre suspected insurgents and civilian supporters.

In 1983, Vice President George H. W. Bush warned the Salvadoran government that it would lose U.S. aid if human-rights abuses continued. One result was an election deemed fair enough to justify continued military aid. A major offensive by the FMLN in 1989 failed to topple the government but persuaded both sides that a military solution wasn't in the offing. The war came to a negotiated end in 1992. [23]

While that war still raged, Bush, who had become president, ordered a direct military intervention elsewhere in Central America. U.S. troops invaded Panama in 1989 in order to arrest strongman Manuel Noriega, a onetime U.S. ally who had been indicted for drug trafficking. Noriega was captured and sent to the United States, where he was convicted in federal court in Miami.

Continuing the tradition of military action close to home, President Bill Clinton in 1994 sent troops to Haiti to back up President Jean-Bertrand Aristide in reclaiming the presidential seat he had lost in a coup. Aristide was restored, but Haiti remained unstable.

By then, U.S. and world attention had already shifted to the Balkans. After the disintegration of the former

tecting Iraqi civilians — a tactic commonly reported to have begun only when Gen. David H. Petraeus took command of U.S. forces and ordered troops out of big bases and into Baghdad neighborhoods.

With Petraeus in charge, Gentile wrote, "The only significant change is that, as part of the surge strategy, nearly 100,000 Sunnis, many of them former insurgents, were induced to stop attacking Americans and were put on the U.S. government payroll as allies against al Qaeda." [3] Peter Mansoor, who served as Petraeus' executive officer, fired back that Gentile and his troops were, in fact, "commuting" to neighborhoods from forward operating bases, not living in them. "This is the reason why the local Iraqis did not side with his battalion, or others in the city," he wrote. [4]

Another Iraq veteran — "Cavguy" — jumped into the debate on Mansoor's side. "I wish you would stop with the downright, untrue lie that we simply bought off the Sunni tribes," he told Gentile. "We didn't. Yes, money was used as an incentive in several ways. But the Sunnis wanted to get rid of al Qaeda on their own. We simply had the fortitude to help them." [5]

Gentile later responded that he had deliberately used the provocative wording about buying off enemies "because so many have convinced themselves that American military power has been the primary agent for the lowering of violence in Iraq in summer 2007." [6]

Such exchanges are what the military needs, Nagl and Dunlap — who disagree themselves on some major issues — wrote in a joint post on smallwarsjournal.com. "Military professionals know that being challenged intellectually forces them to re-examine their thinking," they wrote. "The finest military leaders want, indeed, demand, that differing ideas be ruthlessly explored. They expect and encourage vigorous debates." [7]

[1] Maj. Gen. Charles J. Dunlap Jr., "Shortchanging the Joint Fight? An Airman's Assessment of FM 3-24 and the Case for Developing Truly Joint COIN Doctrine," Air Force Doctrine Development and Education Center, December 2007, http://aupress.maxwell.af.mil/12 1007dunlap.pdf. For Bush quote see "President's Address to the Nation," The White House, Jan. 10, 2007, www.whitehouse.gov/news /releases/2007/01/20070110-7.html.

[2] Lt. Col. Buck Elton, "Shortchanging the Joint Doctrine Fight: One Airman's Assessment of the Airman's Assessment," Small Wars Journal, July 12, 2008, http://smallwarsjournal.com/mag/2008/07/shortchang ing-the-joint-doctri.php.

[3] See Gian P. Gentile, "Our troops did not fail in 2006," International Herald Tribune, Jan. 24, 2008, www.iht.com/articles/2008/01/24 /opinion/edgentile.php.

[4] Peter Mansoor, "Our troops did not fail; our strategy did," smallwarsjournal.com, Jan. 26, 2008, council.smallwarsjournal.com/show thread.php?t=4782&highlight=Mansoor.

[5] "Cavguy," untitled, Jan. 27, 2008, http://council.smallwarsjournal .com/showthread.php?t=4782&highlight=Mansoor.

[6] Gian P. Gentile, untitled, Jan. 27, 2008, http://council.smallwars journal.com/showthread.php?t=4782&highlight=Mansoor.

[7] Maj. Gen. Charles J. Dunlap, Jr., USAF and Lt. Col. John A. Nagl, USA, "America's Greatest Weapon," Small Wars Journal, May 22, 2008, http://smallwarsjournal.com/blog/2008/05/americas-greatest-weapon-1/.

Yugoslavia, Serbia, the biggest former Yugoslav entity, was pursuing long-held territorial ambitions in Bosnia. [24]

By 1995, Serbian forces were massacring Bosnian Muslims. The Clinton administration, which had shied away from involvement, finally sent U.S. warplanes on NATO bombing missions in Serbia, eventually prompting U.S.-sponsored peace talks. U.S. ground forces went into Bosnia to help enforce the peace deal. In 1999, Serbia forced the expulsion of ethnic Albanians from the Serbian province of Kosovo, prompting a NATO bombing campaign — with U.S. participation — against Serbia, which eventually capitulated to U.N. supervision of Kosovo.

Meanwhile, from Afghanistan, terrorist leader Osama bin Laden had been plotting attacks on U.S. installations. On Aug. 7, 1998, al Qaeda operatives exploded car bombs at American embassies in Dar es Salaam, Tanzania; and Nairobi, Kenya, killing a total of 224 people. On Aug. 20, Clinton ordered retaliatory Tomahawk missile strikes, one on a suspected weapons factory in Sudan and the other on a site in Afghanistan where bin Laden was reportedly holding a meeting. But he had departed before the missiles hit.

Iraq and Afghanistan

In the midst of the new breed of small wars, the Bush administration undertook the biggest U.S. military action since Vietnam. Its trigger was the invasion of tiny Kuwait by Iraq on Aug. 2, 1990. Administration officials feared that Saudi Arabia, a major U.S. oil supplier could be next on the list of Saddam Hussein, the Iraqi dictator. [25]

In the months that followed, Bush ordered a massive influx of U.S. troops and materiel into Saudi Arabia. He also formed an alliance of 48 nations, including some

Arab states, of which 30 contributed personnel to the military campaign being organized in the event that Iraq didn't withdraw from Kuwait. Journalists dubbed the underlying strategic principle, the "Powell Doctrine," after Gen. Colin L. Powell, then chairman of the Joint Chiefs of Staff and a Vietnam veteran. The doctrine — an attempt to repudiate strategies associated with the Vietnam War — called for using military power only to defend vital national interests, to use overwhelming force with clear strategic goals and to have an exit plan. [26]

In effect, the "Powell Doctrine" stands as the alternative to the prolonged campaigns, with restrained use of military force, that characterize present counterinsurgency doctrine.

After Saddam defied attempts through the U.N. to resolve the crisis peacefully, Bush ordered, first, an intense air campaign — "Desert Shield" — and then a full-scale ground offensive to push Iraq out of Kuwait. The ground war — "Desert Storm" — saw the total collapse of Iraqi defenses and lasted just 100 hours. Bush refused to order troops deep into Iraq to topple Saddam. Instead, the so-called Gulf War led to U.N. resolutions designed to bar Saddam from using air power against domestic opponents. "No-fly zones" in northern and southern Iraq were enforced by U.S. and British warplanes. Other U.N. resolutions prohibited Iraq from continuing development of weapons of mass destruction (WMD).

Following the terrorist attacks on the United States on Sept. 11, 2001, the new George W. Bush administration presented intelligence data that seemed to show Iraq was defying the prohibition against WMD, which served as the main justification for the 2003 invasion of Iraq.

By then, U.S. and British troops had aided Afghan guerrilla forces in overthrowing the Taliban regime of Afghanistan, which had welcomed bin Laden as an honored guest. On Oct. 7, 2001, warplanes began bombing and rocketing Taliban targets throughout the country. Special Forces and CIA operatives then linked up with anti-Taliban Afghan guerrillas, who took a series of strategic cities, including Kabul, the capital.

But Afghan fighters and U.S. Special Forces troops failed to capture or kill bin Laden himself. He was believed to have been pinned down in the Tora Bora mountains of southern Afghanistan before apparently escaping into Pakistan. [27]

Meanwhile, the Bush administration was gearing up for "regime change" in Iraq. Saddam's dodging of international inspections, as well as intelligence information

that Powell, by then secretary of State, presented to the U.N. in 2003, made up the bulk of the Bush administration's case for invading Iraq. The invasion was launched on March 19, 2003.

The early years of the U.S. occupation of Iraq were marked by the steady growth of a domestic Sunni insurgency, aided by foreign al Qaeda militants, both anti-American and anti-Shiite (Iraq's majority population), as well as development of an anti-U.S. Shiite militia force. As violence against American forces and among Iraqis escalated, President Bush in 2007 gave military command to Petraeus. His use of counterinsurgency strategy and a "surge" of additional U.S. forces are credited by some with the dramatic reduction in violence that characterized Iraq by the summer of 2008.

But as Iraq grew calmer, the war in Afghanistan — once considered essentially over — was heating up.

CURRENT SITUATION

The Real Test

From the inner rings of the Pentagon to the inner circles of the presidential campaign, a war that had faded from public consciousness is taking on growing importance.

In Afghanistan, the first country to see its government toppled by the United States and its allies in the wake of the Sept. 11 attacks, fighting is intensifying, and the number of U.S. casualties is rising.

The Bush administration is acknowledging the growing danger. In early August, Defense Department officials laid out plans to dispatch up to two more combat brigades — 6,000 to 10,000 troops — to Afghanistan next year, adding to the 36,000 already there. Of the present force, about 18,000 operate under direct U.S. command in counterinsurgency and training, with the remaining 17,500 serving in NATO-led operations. [28]

In addition, the Pentagon is planning to spend $20 billion to expand the Afghan army from 80,000 to 120,000 troops. Counterinsurgency expert Nagl estimates that will require a near-doubling of U.S. trainers and advisers assigned to the Afghan forces.

The Pentagon plans became public amid a steady uptick in bad news from Afghanistan, where 569 U.S. military personnel have been killed since 2001. [29]

Is the new U.S. emphasis on counterinsurgency reducing capabilities for other kinds of warfare?

YES
Col. Douglas A. Macgregor (ret.)
Written for *CQ Researcher*, August 2008

Urging Americans to see operations in Iraq as the warfare of the future implies that the most dangerous adversary American soldiers and Marines will fight is a weakly armed Muslim Arab rebel whose only hope of inflicting damage on U.S. forces is to engage in an insurgency directed against an unwanted U.S. military occupation.

But why would the United States ever willingly seize control of another Muslim country, garrison it and then fight a rebellion (insurgency) against the U.S. military's unwanted presence in that country? The occupation of Iraq is rightly viewed by the occupied Arabs and the rest of the world not as counterinsurgency to defend a legitimate, allied government but as colonial warfare to prop up a puppet regime established by the U.S. occupier.

Thus, exporting democracy at gunpoint with masses of U.S. ground troops is worse than delusional. It's dangerous. And increasing the size of Army and Marine ground forces to perform this mission makes no sense in the 21st century. The history of 20th-century warfare teaches that mass armies are rarely well-trained or effectively commanded. And although capable of great carnage, it's often the ground forces themselves — in the form of half-trained and ill-led troops — that blunder into war's meat grinder.

The next presidential administration will find it must move the Army and Marines away from long-term occupations of foreign territory and toward expeditionary warfare with defined, attainable military objectives, as well as homeland defense.

In the 21st century, what the nation needs are ground-maneuver forces organized and equipped to expand the nation's range of strategic options — forces capable of conducting joint, mobile, dispersed warfare operations against a mix of opponents employing both conventional and unconventional capabilities. Mobile dispersed warfare has replaced warfare with defined, continuous fronts as the dominant form of combat.

But to fight effectively in the environment of mobile, dispersed warfare that will also include weapons of mass destruction, the maneuver forces will need a new organization for combat within a new joint command-and-control structure along with a new approach to acquisition and modernization very different from today's structures with their roots in World War II and the Cold War.

Of course, none of these insights make it easier to predict when and where U.S. forces will fight, but colonial warfare executed from fixed installations is the past, not the future.

NO
Steven Metz
Chairman, Regional Strategy and Planning Department, U.S. Army War College Strategic Studies Institute

Written for *CQ Researcher*, August 2008

Because the U.S. Army has such a wide range of responsibilities it must often adjust its focus, assuring that its training, doctrine, organizations and equipment match the missions it is given. This has happened many times in American history as the global security environment and U.S. strategy changed. Today, this process is again under way as the Army seeks the most effective balance between its ability to fight large-scale, conventional war and to undertake irregular conflict such as counterinsurgency, stabilization operations and reconstruction support.

Like any major change — particularly one involving national security — this is difficult and contentious. Within the Army and the broader community of policymakers and defense experts, some feel that shifting too far toward irregular conflict will diminish the Army's dominance of conventional war. Time that a soldier spends learning how to perform reconstruction projects or understand diverse cultures is time not spent training for war. And, this argument goes, America's dominance at large-scale conventional war fighting is precisely what has made this type of conflict rare in the modern world. Aggressors know they will be crushed, and hence resist their nefarious temptations.

Irregular conflict and conventional war fighting, however, are not diametric opposites. Many skills, capabilities, and technologies apply to both. But an increasing focus on irregular conflict will require time, effort and money. Assuming there is no significant increase in the defense budget or size of the military, this will come at the expense of other things, including preparing for conventional war fighting. This, in turn, will increase the strategic risk if the United States finds itself involved in large-scale conventional war.

The big question is whether this is acceptable. I believe so. The United States will be involved in irregular conflict somewhere in the next decade. The chances of a large-scale conventional war that requires a major commitment of American ground forces — a war that cannot be won by allied armies bolstered by U.S. air and naval forces — are small. I am hard-pressed to think of such a scenario. Even an Army more focused on irregular conflict will remain better at conventional war fighting than any possible enemy. It might be less dominant, but dominant nonetheless. Deterrence will survive.

Ultimately, shifting the Army toward a greater (although not exclusive) focus on irregular conflict entails risk. But given the changes that have taken place in the world during the past decade, it is a risk we must accept.

AFP/Getty Images/Inaldo Perez

After being held in the jungle by leftist guerrillas for more than six years, former Colombian presidential candidate Ingrid Betancourt arrives in Bogota on July 2, 2008, the day she was dramatically rescued with 14 other hostages. U.S. military advisers helped Colombian armed forces, who mounted the bloodless operation. Colombia is widely seen as exemplifying the value of providing U.S. funds and technology — rather than massive troop commitments — to friendly governments.

Even as U.S. combat deaths in Iraq were declining, they began increasing in Afghanistan in 2007, when 232 NATO troops were killed, compared with 191 in 2006. Of those killed, 117 of the 2007 casualties and 98 of those in 2006 were Americans. [30]

Rising death tolls reflect the deep roots that the anti-Western guerrillas — the Taliban — have sunk both at home and in neighboring Pakistan. Those ties are decades old. During the 1980s, when the Reagan administration was funneling aid to Afghan guerrillas — including the future Islamist militants who were fighting Soviet occupiers — Pakistan served as operational headquarters, and Pakistan's Inter-Services Intelligence (ISI) played a key role as intermediary between the Americans and the Afghans.

Now, Afghan President Hamid Karzai is stepping up pressure on Pakistan. "If these people in Pakistan give themselves the right to come and fight in Afghanistan, as was continuing for the last 30 years," he said in June, "so Afghanistan has the right to cross the border and destroy terrorist nests, spying, extremism and killing in order to defend itself, its schools, its peoples and its life." [31]

Whether Karzai is in a position to intervene in far-stronger Pakistan is questionable. Taking another route, Karzai's American allies have been turning up the heat on Pakistan as well. In July, *The New York Times* ran a detailed account of the CIA pressing Pakistan by showing some of its officials detailed evidence of close ties between the ISI and Taliban-linked militants who operate in both Pakistan and Afghanistan. [32]

Pakistani Prime Minister Yousaf Raza Gilani denied ISI-militant links. He called such reports "not believable" and added, "We would not allow that." [33]

As if the Pakistan connection to the Afghan insurgency weren't complication enough, a stratospheric rise in Afghan opium production is making Afghanistan the world's main source of raw material for heroin. The International Monetary Fund reported early this year that opium is, by far, the country's biggest cash crop: 8,200 metric tons in 2007 — 93 percent of the global supply. [34]

Afghanistan's most fertile opium-producing regions are the south and southwest, also the center of Taliban activity. But, wrote Thomas Schweich, former U.S. coordinator for counternarcotics in Afghanistan, "While it is true that Karzai's Taliban enemies finance themselves from the drug trade, so do many of his supporters." [35]

Counterinsurgency doctrine calls for helping an embattled friendly government fight the forces trying to topple it. Schweich posed a challenge that has bedeviled past counterinsurgency campaigns — how to defend a government that seems to be weakening itself from within?

Rory Stewart, an ex-British officer and diplomat who now runs a humanitarian foundation in Kabul, argues that counterinsurgency won't solve the problem. "The preoccupations of the West — fighting terrorism and narcotics — are not the priorities of Afghans," he wrote in *Time* in July. "A smarter strategy would focus on two elements: more effective aid and a more limited military objective. . . . But our troops should not try to hold territory or chase the Taliban around rural areas." [36]

The Colombian Model

The wars in Afghanistan and Iraq are only one aspect of U.S. counterinsurgency strategy. In Colombia, the dramatic July 2 rescue of 15 hostages held by the Revolutionary Armed Forces of Colombia (FARC) illustrated the close relationship between U.S. military advisers and the Colombian armed forces, who mounted the rescue operation.

Afterwards, officials of both governments acknowledged that U.S. military and intelligence personnel had been deeply involved. "This mission was a Colombian concept, a Colombian plan, a Colombian training operation, then a Colombian operation," said William R. Brownfield, U.S. ambassador to Colombia. "We, however, had been working with them more than five years on every single element that came to pass that pulled off this operation, as well as the small bits that we did on this operation." [37]

Those "bits" included interception of FARC radio communications as well as U.S. Special Forces' surveillance of the jungle camp where the hostages were held. Hailed because no shots were fired, the rescue mission fooled guerrillas into turning the hostages over to a humanitarian organization — in fact, the Colombian armed forces. Recently, however, the operation has been tarnished by the revelation that some rescuers bore the Red Cross emblem, a disguise prohibited by the Geneva Conventions because it can open genuine Red Cross workers anywhere in the world to the suspicion that they're really counterinsurgency troops. Colombian President Alvaro Uribe said the Colombian military had lied to him about the matter, calling that a matter that "cannot be excused." [38]

Monitoring the shifting locations of Colombia's crop of opium poppies and coca leaves, and the clandestine laboratories that process the drugs, is central to U.S.-Colombian efforts to defeat the FARC.

Dubbed "Plan Colombia," the eight-year-old partnership targets FARC both militarily and financially. Since the plan went into effect in 2000, the United States has spent approximately $5 billion on military and police aid, as well as economic and human-rights initiatives designed to win the hearts and minds of rural Colombians who once saw the FARC as a force that could protect them from a predatory government. [39]

But as the FARC put "taxing" the drug industry and holding hostages for ransom ahead of its social goals, rural Colombians gradually came to adopt the same loathing of the FARC that became common among urban Colombians of all classes.

"Colombia has progressed — with the strong support of the United States — from a nation under siege by narcoterrorists and paramilitary vigilantes to one poised to become a linchpin of security and prosperity in South America," wrote Defense Secretary Gates and Colombian Defense Minister Juan Manuel Santos. Colombian security forces, "have pushed terrorists and drug traffickers into the farthest reaches of Colombia's mountains and jungles." [40]

To be sure, other illegal organizations profit from the Colombian drug industry. Right-wing anti-FARC forces known generically as "paramilitaries" have made millions from drugs as well. The Colombian strategy toward these groups has focused on negotiated demobilization.

"That process is largely hype," Kenneth Roth, executive director of Human Rights Watch, told Sen. McCain before he visited Colombia in July. "While more than 30,000 individuals supposedly demobilized, Colombian prosecutors have turned up evidence that many of them were not paramilitaries at all, but civilians recruited to pose as paramilitaries. Law enforcement authorities never investigated most of them." [41]

On the whole, however, even counterinsurgency skeptics say Colombia exemplifies the value of investing U.S. funds, expertise and technology — rather than massive troop commitments — in helping friendly governments. "Was it a lot of money?" asks Air Force Maj. Gen. Dunlap. "Well, yes, until you start looking at something like Iraq. We've spent about $5 billion over several years in Colombia. However, the U.S. government is now spending approximately $10 billion a month on the Iraq war." [42]

OUTLOOK

New Threat

Russia's August incursion into the Republic of Georgia exemplifies the speed with which events can alter military forecasts.

As recently as June, the Pentagon's National Defense Strategy had mentioned Russia's conflictive relationship with its neighbors only briefly. "Russia's retreat from democracy and its increasing economic and political intimidation of its neighbors give cause for concern," the strategy document said. "We do not expect Russia to revert to outright global military confrontation, but the risk of miscalculation or conflict arising out of economic coercion has increased." [43]

In the days following Russia's move — which involved ground, air and naval forces — there were no indications that it would start a world conflict. But the conflictive history of Russia and its neighbors, combined with Moscow's new energy wealth and assertiveness, leads some commentators to forecast more trouble to come.

Three days after Russia's strike, Robert Kagan, a conservative international-affairs specialist, treated it as a turning point as important as the fall of the Berlin Wall in 1989. The attack signals a return of "great-power competition, complete with virulent nationalisms, battles for resources, struggles over spheres of influence and territory, and even . . . the use of military power to obtain geopolitical objectives," wrote Kagan, a senior associate at the Carnegie Endowment for International Peace. He had been among the earliest advocates of a U.S. invasion of Iraq. [44]

Whether the United States would have to resort to military force on a vast scale remains a question — one that Kagan doesn't answer. Military experts who've been focusing on that issue tend to think that major deployments of U.S. forces won't occur.

"I don't think that Iraq is a model for the future, just as I don't think Desert Storm is a model for the future," says Metz of the U.S. Army War College's Strategic Studies Institute. His vision of that future differs from Kagan's.

In a new book, Metz argues that the Bush administration's failure to grasp the consequences of invading Iraq reflected a deeper misunderstanding about how global politics has changed. For one thing, the coming military challenges are likely to be "hybrid threats" in which governments mix with non-governmental insurgents over causes including politics, economics and crime and "new extremist ideologies." The great causes for which Americans have gone to war may not be operative.

In this environment, Metz writes, "Iraq may have shown that the world no longer wants a leader. . . . It is not clear that the United States can be an effective leader against hybrid threats in an environment of moral ambiguity." [45]

On the less lofty plane of military hardware, Air Force Maj. Gen. Dunlap argues that air power can flex-

ibly be used across the full spectrum of conflicts. "Today you need equipment that you can use in all kinds of wars," he says.

"The generation coming up now, of our adversaries, is addicted to technology — the Web, cell phones and more — which is a vulnerability that we can use our technology to exploit," he says. "We should not be trying to fight our wars by putting more uniforms on people than our adversaries have. If it's just human beings with guns, they have a lot of people they can work with. We need to work with our asymmetrical advantage, which is our technological prowess."

He adds that high-tech airpower can work well with ground-based counterinsurgency. An enemy who adjusts his movements to avoid being spotted by an unmanned air-surveillance plane can still be caught by troops who've cultivated informants, he says. Joint warfare confounds foes, he says. "They never quite know who or what might kill them. They don't know whether to look up, down or across the street."

Still, the question remains whether a major buildup in counterinsurgency capability will meet the next wave of threats to the United States. Lt. Col. Gentile of West Point warns that the counterinsurgency trend may contain the seeds of future military misadventures. He quotes from a recent book review by counterinsurgency theorist Nagl that argues victory in the "long war" will require soldiers "not just to dominate land operations but to change entire societies." Gentile calls that assertion "breathtaking" in its ambition — an ambition that could go astray as easily as U.S. ambitions did in Vietnam. [46]

Nagl fires back that he's "disappointed" in Gentile for leaving out the remainder of the book review's sentence: ". . . not all of these soldiers will wear uniforms or work for the Department of the Army." The underlying point is that the war of ideas matters more than the war of weapons.

"We have devoted far more attention to killing and capturing our current enemies than countering the pernicious effects of ideology and hatred," Nagl says. "We need a comprehensive U.S. government, nongovernmental-organization and international effort to minimize the factors that cause hatred and fear of the United States. That is a very tall order, but we are not doing it as well as we could."

NOTES

1. A PBS video documentary recorded Alpha Company's experiences. See Bill Gentile, "Afghanistan: The Forgotten War," NOW, July 18, 2008, www.pbs.org /now/shows/428/index.html.

2. *Ibid.*

3. See "National Defense Strategy," June 2008, p. 8, available from InsideDefense.com, http://insidede fense.com/. The document was quoted in Josh White, "Gates Sees Terrorism Remaining Enemy No. 1," *The Washington Post*, July 31, 2008, p. A1.

4. See Peter Katel, "Middle East Tensions," *CQ Researcher*, Oct. 27, 2006, pp. 889-912.

5. See "Secretary of Defense Robert Gates and Vice Chairman, Joint Chiefs of Staff Gen. James Cartwright, DOD News Briefing," Department of Defense, Aug. 14, 2008, www.defenselink.mil/tran scripts/transcript.aspx?transcriptid=4275.

6. See Donald H. Rumsfeld, "Beyond 'Nation-Building," *The Washington Post* (op-ed), Sept. 25, 2003, p. A33; and Thomas E. Ricks, *Fiasco: The American Military Adventure in Iraq* (2006), p. 24.

7. See "U.S. Military Deaths by Year/Month," Iraq Coalition Casualty Count, constantly updated, http://icasualties.org/oif.

8. See "Iraqi Security Forces and Civilian Deaths Details," http://icasualties.org/oif.

9. See Carlotta Gall, "U.S. Killed 90, Including 60 Children, in Afghan Village, U.N. Finds," *The New York Times*, Aug. 26, 2008, www.nytimes.com /2008/08/27/world/asia/27herat.html?scp=1&sq=U .N.Afghanistanairstrike&st=cse. Also see Carlotta Gall, "U.S. Airstrike at Odds with Reports of More Afghan Deaths," *The New York Times*, Sept. 3, 2008, p. A10.

10. See Carlotta Gall, "Joint Inquiry on Deaths of Afghans is Proposed," *The New York Times*, Aug. 29, 2008, www.nytimes.com/2008/08/30/world/asia/30afghan .html?scp=5&sq=afghanistan%20bombing%2090% 20&st=cse.

11. See Steven Lee Myers, "A More Confident Iraq Becomes a Tougher Negotiating Partner for the U.S.," *The New York Times*, July 10, 2008, p. A6.

12. See "Greek Civil War," GlobalSecurity.org, undated, www.globalsecurity.org/military/world/war/greek.htm.

13. See Thom Shanker, "Russians melded Old-School Blitz With Modern Military Tactics," *The New York Times*, Aug. 17, 2008, p. 8.

14. See Neil Sheehan, *A Bright Shining Lie: John Paul Vann and America in Vietnam* (1988), p. 696.

15. Quoted in "Petraeus on Vietnam's Legacy," *The Washington Post*, Jan. 14, 2007, p. B4.

16. See "Multi-National Force-Iraq Commander's Counterinsurgency Guidance," June 21, 2008, www.mnf-iraq.com/images/CGs_Messages/080621 _coin_%20guidance.pdf.

17. See Lt. Col. Gian P. Gentile, "Eating Soup With a Spoon," *Armed Forces Journal*, Sept. 27, 2007, www .armedforcesjournal.com/2007/09/2786780.

18. Unless otherwise indicated, this subsection draws from "American Military History," Chapter 15, updated April 27, 2001, Army Historical Series, Office of the Chief of Military History, United States Army, www.history.army.mil/books/AMH /amh-toc.htm; Alan Axelrod, *Political History of America's Wars* (2007), CQ Press.

19. *Ibid.*

20. Unless otherwise indicated, material in this section is drawn from Axelrod, *op. cit.*

21. See "U.S. Army Special Forces 1961-1971," Department of the Army, 1973, www.history.army .mil/books/Vietnam/90-23/90-23C.htm.

22. Unless otherwise indicated, material in this is drawn from Axelrod, *op. cit.*, Max Boot, "The Savage Wars of Peace: Small Wars and the Rise of American Power," 2002; and "Final Report of the National Commission on Terrorist Attacks Upon the United States," 2004.

23. See Steven Metz, "Counterinsurgency: Strategy and the Phoenix of American Capability," Strategic Studies Institute, U.S. Army War College, Feb. 28, 1995, p. 16, www.strategicstudiesinstitute.army.mil /pubs/display.cfm?pubID=333.

24. For background see Brian Beary, "Separatist Movements," *CQ Global Researcher*, April 2008, pp. 85-114.

25. Unless otherwise indicated, this section is drawn from Axelrod, *op. cit.*; and Steven Metz, "Iraq & the Evolution of American Strategy," 2008.

26. See Paul Richter, "Vietnam Still an 'Invisible Scar' for Army," *Los Angeles Times*, April 10, 2000, p. A1; Rick Atkinson and Bob Woodward, "Prolonged Buildup Reflects Doctrine of Invincible Force," *The Washington Post*, Dec. 2, 1990, p. A1.

27. See Barry Bearak with James Risen, "Al Qaeda Fleeing Toward Pakistan, U.S. Officials Say," *The New York Times*, Dec. 17, 2001, p. A1; James Risen and David Rhode, "A Hostile Land Foils the Quest for Bin Laden," *The New York Times*, Dec. 13, 2004, p. A1.

28. See Thom Shanker, "Gates Pushing Plan to Double Afghan Army," *The New York Times*, Aug. 8, 2008, p. A1.

29. See "Operation Enduring Freedom," Iraq Coalition Casualty Count, constantly updated, http://icasualties.org/OEF/Default.aspx.

30. *Ibid.*

31. Quoted in Carlotta Gall, "Karzai Threatens To Send Soldiers into Pakistan," *The New York Times*, June 16, 2008, www.nytimes.com/2008/06/16/world /asia/16afghan.html?scp=5&sq=Karzai%20Afghanistan %20Pakistan&st=cse.

32. See Mark Mazetti and Eric Schmitt, "C.I.A. Outlines Pakistan Links With Militants," *The New York Times*, July 30, 2008, www.nytimes.com /2008/07/30/world/asia/30pstan.html?scp=2&sq= Pakistan%20Bush%20administration%20CIA%20 Afghanistan&st=cse.

33. Quoted in *ibid.*

34. See "Islamic Republic of Afghanistan: 2007 Article IV Review," International Monetary Fund, February 2008, p. 7, www.csdp.org/research/cr0876.pdf.

35. See Thomas Schweich, "Is Afghanistan a Narco-State," *The New York Times Magazine*, July 27, 2008, www.nytimes.com/2008/07/27/magazine/27 AFGHAN-t.html?sq=Afghanistan%20opium%20 Karzai%20&st=cse&scp=3&pagewanted=all.

36. See Rory Stewart, "How to Save Afghanistan," *Time*, July 17, 2008, www.time.com/time/world/arti- cle/0,8599,1823753,00.html.

37. Quoted in Juan Forero, "In Colombia Jungle Ruse, U.S. Played A Quiet Role," *The Washington Post*, July 9, 2008, p. A1.

38. Quoted in Frank Jordans, "Red Cross: Colombia broke Geneva Conventions," The Associated Press, Aug. 7, 2008, http://ap.google.com/article/ALeq M5gvsvlzZeaZtVTXDZZZQ842X3cT_QD92D20 G00.

39. See Peter Katel, "Change in Latin America," *CQ Researcher*, July 21, 2006, pp. 601-624.

40. See Robert M. Gates and Juan Manuel Santos, "Colombia's Gains Are America's Too," *The New York Times* (op-ed), July 23, 2008, www.nytimes .com/2008/07/23/opinion/23gates.html.

41. See "Letter to Senator John McCain," Human Rights Watch, June 27, 2008, http://hrw.org/eng lish/docs/2008/06/27/colomb19219.htm.

42. See Bill Adair, "The Iraq war, for $100 a month," *Politifact*, April 1, 2008, www.politifact.com/truth- o-meter/article/2008/apr/01/iraq-war-100-month/. Also, Peter Katel, "Cost of the Iraq War," *CQ Researcher*, April 25, 2008, pp. 361-384.

43. See National Defense Strategy, *op. cit.*, pp. 9-11.

44. See Robert Kagan, "Putin Makes His Move," *The Washington Post*, Aug. 11, 2008, p. A15; Robert Kagan, "On Iraq, Short Memories," Sept. 12, 2005, p. A19.

45. See Steven Metz, *Iraq and the Evolution of American Strategy* (2008), p. 200.

46. See John A. Nagl, review of Brian Linn McAllister, "The Ethos of Battle: The Army's Way of War," Royal United Services Institute, April, 2008, www.rusi.org/publication/journal/ref:A480E27319 D27F/ (fee required).

BIBLIOGRAPHY

Books

Axelrod, Alan, *Political History of America's Wars*, CQ Press, 2007.
An invaluable guide by a veteran reference-book editor through the United States' eventful and varied military history, including strategic disputes.

Boot, Max, *The Savage Wars of Peace: Small Wars and the Rise of American Power,* **Basic Books, 2002.**
A fellow at the Council on Foreign Relations chronicles the campaigns of U.S. troops, often in small units, fighting rebels and dictators during the 19th and 20th centuries throughout Latin America, Africa, and Asia.

Metz, Steven, *Iraq & the Evolution of American Strategy,* **Potomac Books, 2008.**
A strategy expert at the U.S. Army War College's Strategic Studies Institute dispassionately analyzes the origins and unfolding of the Iraq War and its consequences for the U.S. military.

Nagl, John A., *Learning to Eat Soup With a Knife: Counterinsurgency Lessons from Malaya and Vietnam,* **University of Chicago Press, 2005 (first published, 2002).**
In a book that influenced present U.S. strategy in Iraq, an Army officer contrasts British success with U.S. failure in fighting Asian communist guerrillas.

Wright, Evan, *Generation Kill: Devil Dogs, Iceman, Captain America and the New Face of American War,* **Berkley Books, 2008.**
A *Rolling Stone* journalist embedded with an elite Marine unit during the invasion of Iraq delivers a vivid account of the collision between conventional warfare strategy and Iraqi realities.

Articles

Dreazen, Yochi J., "Officer Questions Petraeus's Strategy," *The Wall Street Journal,* **April 7, 2007, p. A3.**
Lt. Col. Gian P. Gentile is profiled against the backdrop of his criticisms of the counterinsurgency strategy that's finding favor in the Pentagon.

Gall, Carlotta, and Sangar Rahimi, "Taliban Escalate Fighting With Assault on U.S. Base," *The New York Times,* **Aug. 19, 2008, p. A7.**
Journalists report from Afghanistan on the effects of Taliban growth in strength, geographical reach, and tactical sophistication.

Gentile, Gian P., Lt. Col., "The dogmas of war," *Armed Forces Journal,* **November 2007, www.armed-forcesjour-nal.com/2007/11/3155836.**
A tough critic of the counterinsurgency school argues that the Iraq War doesn't fit the counterinsurgency model.

Massing, Michael, "Embedded in Iraq," *The New York Review of Books,* **July 17, 2008, www.nybooks.com/articles/21617.**
A journalist long critical of the war argues that the accomplishments of the counterinsurgency strategy could be outweighed by the hostilities, ravaged infrastructure and deep Iranian influence that characterize today's Iraq.

Mazzetti, Mark, and David Rohde, "Amid U.S. Policy Disputes, Qaeda Grows in Pakistan," *The New York Times,* **June 30, 2008, p. A1.**
Correspondents track the relationship between expansion of the Taliban's insurgency in Afghanistan and its growing strength in Pakistan.

Petraeus, David H., Lt. Gen., "Learning Counterinsurgency: Observations From Soldiering in Iraq," **http://usacac.army.mil/CAC/milreview/English/JanFeb06/Petraeus1.pdf.**
Written before its author became top commander in Iraq, the article previews the strategy he would follow, with precepts including: "Success in a counterinsurgency requires more than just military operations."

Rohde, David, "Army Enlists Anthropology in War Zones," *The New York Times,* **Oct. 5, 2007, www.nytimes.com/2007/10/05/world/asia/05afghan.html?pagewanted=1.**
A journalist accompanies the first Army-embedded anthropologist as she advises paratroopers in the Afghan countryside who are trying to win villagers' trust.

Reports and Studies

Feickert, Andrew, "Does the Army Need a Full-Spectrum Force or Specialized Units? Background and Issues for Congress," **Congressional Research Service, Jan. 18, 2008, www.fas.org/sgp/crs/natsec/RL34333.pdf.**
Congress' research unit analyzes the debate over establishing large units to deal with counterinsurgency, stabilization and training.

Cordesman, Anthony, "The Afghan-Pakistan War: A Status Report, Second Edition," Center for Strategic and International Studies, July 3, 2008, www.csis.org /media/csis/pubs/080703_afghan_status.pdf.
In the most recent version of a regularly updated report, a veteran strategist concludes that Afghanistan represents a 15-year challenge, in which defeating insurgents should be only part of a bigger nation-building strategy.

For More Information

abu muqawama, http://abumuqawama.blogspot.com/. A blog started by a former Army Ranger veteran of Afghanistan and Iraq that specializes in counterinsurgency developments and debates.

Center for a New American Security, 1301 Pennsylvania Ave., N.W., Washington, DC 20004; (202) 457-9400; www.cnas.org/en/cms/?32. A nonpartisan think tank, organized to formulate new defense policies, that includes several counterinsurgency experts.

Council on Foreign Relations, 58 East 68th St., New York, NY 10065; (212) 434-9400; www.cfr.org A nonpartisan, independent membership organization that promotes understanding of the U.S. role in international relations.

Human Terrain System, http://humanterrainsystem.army .mil/. A military program that embeds social scientists with military units in counterinsurgency campaigns, to help troops understand the societies in which they're operating.

Network of Concerned Anthropologists, http://con cerned.anthropologists.googlepages.com. Academic anthropologists opposed to the military use of social scientists to analyze "human terrain" as part of counterinsurgency strategy.

Small Wars Journal, http://smallwarsjournal.com. An Internet forum, run by Marine veterans, for debating counterinsurgency strategy and tactics.

Strategic Studies Institute, United States Army War College, 122 Forbes Ave., Carlisle, PA 17013; (717) 245-4133; www.strategicstudiesinstitute.army.mil. An armed forces research center that studies counterinsurgency and other issues.

2

AFP/Getty Images

The American Embassy in Belgrade is set ablaze on Feb. 21 by Serbian nationalists angered by U.S. support for Kosovo's recent secession from Serbia. About 70 separatist movements are under way around the globe, but most are nonviolent. Kosovo is one of seven countries to emerge from the former Yugoslavia and part of a nearly fourfold jump in the number of countries to declare independence since 1945.

From *CQ Researcher,*
April 1, 2008.

Separatist Movements

Brian Beary

Angry protesters hurling rocks at security forces; hotels, shops and restaurants torched; a city choked by teargas. The violent images that began flashing around the world on March 14 could have been from any number of tense places from Africa to the Balkans. But the scene took place high in the Himalayas, in the ancient Tibetan capital of Lhasa. Known for its red-robed Buddhist monks, the legendary city was the latest flashpoint in Tibetan separatists' ongoing frustration over China's continuing occupation of their homeland. [1]

Weeks earlier, thousands of miles away in Belgrade, Serbia, hundreds of thousands of Serbs took to the streets to vent fury over Kosovo's secession on Feb. 17. Black smoke billowed from the burning U.S. Embassy, set ablaze by Serbs angered by Washington's acceptance of Kosovo's action. [2]

"As long as we live, Kosovo is Serbia," thundered Serbian Prime Minister Vojislav Kostunica at a rally earlier in the day. [3] Kosovo had been in political limbo since a NATO-led military force wrested the region from Serb hands in 1999 and turned it into an international protectorate after Serbia brutally clamped down on ethnic Albanian separatists. Before the split, about 75 percent of Serbia's population was Serbs, who are mostly Orthodox Christian, and 20 percent were ethnic Albanians, who are Muslim. [4]

Meanwhile, war-torn Iraq witnessed its own separatist-related violence on Feb. 22. Turkish forces launched a major military incursion into northern Iraq — the first big ground offensive in nearly a decade — to root out Kurdish separatist rebels known as the PKK, who have waged a bloody independence campaign against Ankara since 1984. [5]

Separatist Movements Span the Globe

Nearly two dozen separatist movements are active worldwide, concentrated in Europe and Asia. At least seven are violent and reflect ethnic or religious differences with the mother country.

Selected Separatist Hot Spots

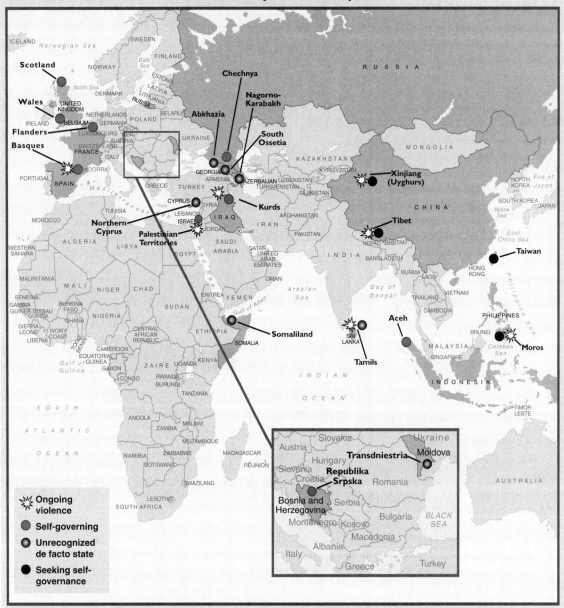

Legend:
- ✺ Ongoing violence
- ● Self-governing
- ◉ Unrecognized de facto state
- ● Seeking self-governance

Sources: Unrepresented Nations and People's Organization, www.unpo.org; *Political Handbook of the World 2007*, CQ Press

Ongoing Separatist Movements

Africa

Somaliland — Militants in this northern Somalia territory established an unrecognized de facto state in the 1990s after the government of Somalia collapsed. The area was ruled by the United Kingdom from 1884 to 1960 and then became unified with the former Italian-ruled Somalia from 1960 to 1989.

Asia/Eurasia

Abkhazia — Independent Soviet republic briefly in 1921. Subsequently united with Georgia. Declared independence in 1992; war with Georgia ensued, which the Abkhaz won with Russian support. Since then, a stalemate has persisted. Up to 300,000 Georgians have fled since the 1990s, leaving an estimated 100,000 Abkhaz as the dominant force.

Aceh — One of the first places where Islam was established in Southeast Asia. Indonesia annexed the territory in 1949 upon becoming independent. Aceh was granted autonomy in 1959 and declared independence in 1976, with thousands dying in violence since then. A further 100,000 were killed in the 2004 Indian Ocean tsunami. A peace agreement was signed in 2005 granting autonomy.

Chechnya — A Muslim region in southern Russia, Chechnya was briefly independent in 1922. It declared independence after the collapse of the Soviet Union, but Russia opposed the secession and went to war with Chechnya from 1994-1996 and again in 1999. It became an autonomous Russian republic after a 2003 referendum.

Kurds — The world's largest ethnic group without its own country resides in Iraq, Iran, Turkey and Syria. The Iraqi Kurds have had autonomy since 1991. In Iran and Turkey they have no autonomy but are relatively free to speak Kurdish. The language is banned in Syria.

Moros — Muslims in the southern Philippines who live primarily on the island of Mindanao. Migration by Christian Filipinos from the north has diluted the Moro population. A militant Islamic fundamentalist group, Abu Sayyaf, is fighting the government to create a Moro Muslim state. Malaysia has committed the most international peacekeeping forces to stem the violence.

Nagorno-Karabakh — Declared independence from Azerbaijan in 1991, followed by a three-year war, during which most of the Azeris fled. A ceasefire has existed since 1994. It is now a de facto independent republic — unrecognized by the international community — populated mostly by ethnic Armenians.

Palestinian Territories — Since the largely Jewish state of Israel came into being in 1948, Arabs from the former Palestine have had no country of their own. The Palestinians live mainly in two non-contiguous areas, the Gaza Strip and West Bank, which Israel occupied in 1967 after a war with Egypt, Jordan and Syria. While the Palestinians have their own civilian administration and neither Israel nor neighboring Arab countries claim sovereignty over them, there is no independent Palestinian state yet because the terms cannot be agreed upon. A violent conflict between Israelis and Palestinians has persisted for decades.

South Ossetia — This region, which became part of Georgia in 1922, tried to become autonomous in 1989, but Georgia refused. After a war from 1990 to 1992 it became a de facto independent republic. Referenda in 1992 and 2006 confirming independence have not been recognized by any other country. Ossetian towns are governed by the separatist government; Georgian towns are overseen by Georgia.

Taiwan — The island off China's southeastern coast was established as a rival Chinese government in 1949 following the defeat of Chiang Kai-shek's Nationalists by Mao Tse-tung's communists. Between 1949 and 1971, it was recognized by most countries as the official government of China, but in 1971 mainland China replaced it as China's representative in the United Nations. In the 1990s, the Taiwanese government started a campaign to become a U.N. member again. Politics is polarized between those favoring unification with China — who won two recent elections — and those seeking official independence.

Tamils — Militant separatists known as the Liberation Tigers of Tamil Eelam (LTTE) have run a de facto state in northern Sri Lanka for many years. The LTTE assassinated Indian Prime Minister Rajiv Gandhi in 1991 for helping Sri Lanka crack down on the Tamils and Sri Lankan Prime Minister Ranasinghe Premadasa in 1993. A ceasefire was declared in 2002, but violence resumed in 2005. The Tamils are predominantly Hindu whereas the majority-Sinhalese community is Buddhist.

The three hotspots reflect the same worldwide phenomenon — the almost inevitable conflict caused when a group of people want to separate themselves from a state that refuses to let them go. Despite today's oft-heard mantra that mankind is living in a global community where borders no longer matter, having a homeland

Asia/Eurasia

Tibet — China took over the Buddhist region in western China by force in the 1950s. Tibet's spiritual leader, the Dalai Lama, fled in 1959 and set up a government-in-exile in India. Recent separatist violence has been fueled by resentment over Chinese immigration into the autonomous region and the government's continued refusal to grant independence. The violence has prompted the Dalai Lama to consider resigning as the head of the exiled government.

Xinjiang — Known as East Turkestan or Chinese Turkistan, this vast region on China's northwest border with Central Asia — which comprises one-sixth of China's land mass — was annexed by China in the 18th century. Its 18 million inhabitants include 47 ethnic groups, including the Turkic-speaking Muslim Uyghurs — who once comprised 90 percent of the population. Today the Uyghurs make up only 40 percent of the inhabitants due to government policies that encourage Han Chinese to migrate there. Although the region has been officially autonomous since 1955, ethnic tensions have escalated in recent years. The U.S. State Department complains of serious human rights abuses against the Uyghurs due to Beijing's efforts to forcibly assimilate them and undermine their culture. China says Uyghur separatists are Islamic terrorists.

Europe

Basque Country — Basques in northeast Spain and southwest France have been pushing for greater autonomy or independence for more than a century. The militant separatist group ETA has killed about 1,000 people since 1968. Spain has granted its Basques extensive political and cultural autonomy but France has not.

Flanders — Flemish nationalism has grown in recent decades in Flanders, the northern part of Belgium where 60 percent of the population lives, most of them Dutch-speaking. Flanders, which has grown wealthier than French-speaking Wallonia to the south, already has extensive autonomy, but most Flemings would like more; many favor full independence.

Northern Cyprus — When Cyprus gained independence from British rule in 1960, relations between the Turks and Greeks on the island quickly deteriorated. Turkey's invasion in 1973 led to the Turkish Cypriots creating their own de facto state in the north that is only recognized by Turkey.

Republika Srpska — This self-governing territory within Bosnia, created in 1992, is populated mainly by ethnic Serbs who opposed Bosnia's secession from Yugoslavia. Moves to integrate it with the rest of Bosnia have failed so far.

Scotland and Wales — Demands by Celtic peoples in the northern and western corners of the United Kingdom for greater control over their affairs resulted in a devolution of power in 1999: A parliament was installed in Scotland and an assembly in Wales.

Transdniestria — First became a part of Moldova in 1812 when Russia captured both territories. From 1917 to 1939 it was part of the Soviet Union, while the rest of Moldova was ruled by Romania. From 1945 to 1991 both parts fell under Soviet rule. In 1992, when Moldova became an independent country Transdniestra seceded amid fear that Moldova would unify with Romania. The Moldovan army was repelled with the support of the Russian army. Its secession has not been recognized internationally. The area is dominated by Russian-speakers, with the Russian military also present.

The Americas (not shown on map)

Bolivia — After Evo Morales, Bolivia's first indigenous president, proposed changing the constitution last year to share more of the country's natural resources with the nation's indigenous highlanders, the mainly European-descended lowlanders have been threatening to secede.

Lakota Nation — This Indian nation of eight tribes living in South Dakota and neighboring states signed a treaty with the United States in 1851 granting them land rights. In 1989 they were awarded $40 million for losses incurred based on an 1868 land-rights treaty. In December 2007 a group of dissident Lakota delivered a declaration of independence to the State Department, which did not respond.

Québec — This majority French-speaking province has been threatening to secede from Canada since the 1960s. In two referenda on independence — in 1980 and 1995 — the Québécois voted to remain part of Canada. Today, they have a large degree of regional autonomy.

Sources: Unrepresented Nations and People's Organization, www.unpo.org; *Political Handbook of the World 2007*, CQ Press

of one's own clearly remains a dream for millions.

Out of more than 70 separatist movements around the globe, about two dozen are active, most in Europe and Asia, and seven of them are violent. And since 1990, more than two dozen new countries have emerged from separatist movements, mostly the result of the disintegration of the Soviet Union and the breaking apart of the former Yugoslavia. [6] Almost half of the 25 successful separatist movements were accompanied by some amount of violence, most of it ethnically based. (*See map and chart, pp. 26-28.*)

In fact, the number of independent countries around the globe has waxed and waned over the past 150 years. During the 19th century, the number declined as the European colonial powers gobbled up territories in Asia and Africa. Then after World War II the number mushroomed as those empires disintegrated. The United Nations has grown from 51 members when it was founded in 1945 to 192 members today (not counting Kosovo). [7] (*See graph, p. 35.*)

Among the groups fighting for independence today, the Kurds are the largest, with approximately 25 million dispersed in Turkey, Iraq, Iran and Syria. [8] Other separatist movements are microscopic by comparison: The South Ossetians — who have seceded from Georgia and formed a de facto but as-yet-unrecognized government — number just 70,000, for example. Some movements, like the Québécois in Canada and the Scottish in the United Kingdom, have been peaceful, while others, like the Tamils in Sri Lanka and Palestinians in Israel, have been violent. Indonesia has had two separatist movements with very different destinies: East Timor (Timor Leste) on Indonesia's eastern tip became independent in 1999 — although it is still struggling to fend for itself, relying on international aid to make up for its severe food shortages — while Aceh in the west has opted for autonomy within Indonesia. [9]

Separatism often triggers serious rifts between the world's major powers. In the case of Kosovo, the United States and its NATO allies — including the United Kingdom, France, Germany, Italy and Turkey — backed the secession. U.S. Assistant Secretary of State Daniel Fried has dubbed it "the last chapter in the dissolution of Yugoslavia," while acknowledging "many things can go wrong and probably will." [10] In stark contrast, Russia steadfastly opposes independence for Kosovo and is standing shoulder-to-shoulder with its historical ally, Serbia.

Outgoing Russian President Vladimir Putin has said, "If someone believes that Kosovo should be granted full independence as a state, then why should we deny it to the Abkhaz and the South Ossetians?" According to Matthew J. Bryza, U.S. deputy assistant secretary of State for European and Eurasian Affairs, Russia is covertly pro-

Protesters at a March rally in Tbilisi, Georgia, want Russia to stop supporting South Ossetia and Abkhazia, two Georgian regions that seceded and formed de facto states. Their placards — which say "Russia! Stop Dealing With the Fates of Small Nations!" — indicate how a separatist movement can become a pawn in a geopolitical tug-of-war. Russia supports the two breakaway states, while most of the international community does not recognize them.

viding material support to South Ossetia and Abkhazia — two de facto states that have emerged from within Russia's political foe, the ex-Soviet Republic of Georgia. [11] The United States and the rest of the international community don't recognize the secession of either state.

Meanwhile, the Chinese government opposes the pro-independence movement among the ethnically Turkic Uyghur people, who live in the western Chinese autonomous region of Xinjiang. China has tried to stifle separatism in its western provinces by promoting mass migration of ethnic Chinese to both Tibet and Xinjiang to dilute the indigenous population. Critics say China used the Sept. 11, 2001, terrorist attacks in the United States as a pretext for clamping down on the Uyghurs, who are Muslim, by claiming they were linked to Islamic terrorist movements like al Qaeda. [12]

China's separatist woes are an embarrassment just four months before the start of the Summer Olympic Games in Beijing — China's chance to shine on the world stage. The Chinese call the Tibetan protests a

World's Newest Country Remains Divided

Kosovo is struggling to be recognized.

Delaware-size Kosovo grabbed the world's attention on Feb. 17 when its ethnic Albanian-dominated government declared its independence from Serbia, triggering street protests among some Serb citizens.

Because of fierce opposition from Serbs both inside Kosovo and in Serbia, a large international presence with armies from six "framework" nations keeps an uneasy peace: The United States controls the east, Ireland the center, Turkey and Germany the south, Italy the west and France the north. [1]

"Do not trust the apparent calm, it's the main difficulty of this mission," says Captain Noê-Noël Ucheida from the Franco-German brigade of the 16,000-strong NATO force in Kosovo. "It can be calm. But it becomes tense in the morning and ignites in the afternoon." [2]

The spotlight fell on Kosovo in 1999 — several years after the break-up of Yugoslavia — when Serbian leader Slobodan Milosevic's brutal campaign to forcibly remove Kosovar Albanians led to NATO having to step in and take the province out of Serb hands. Now Kosovo's 2 million Albanians seem determined to open a new chapter in their history by implementing a U.N. plan granting them internationally supervised independence. Not for the first time, the world's leading powers are divided over a conflict in the Balkans. The United States, Germany, United Kingdom, France and Italy back independence while Serbia, Russia and China oppose it.

Further complicating the issue are the 100,000 Serbs living in Kosovo, including 40,000 concentrated in a zone north of the Ibar River; the remainder are dispersed throughout the south. Just as Kosovo's Albanians fought tooth and nail to free themselves from Serb rule, so the Serbs in north Kosovo are equally resolved to be free of Albanian rule. "They already run their own de facto state," says Nicolas Gros-Verheyde, a French journalist who toured Kosovo just before the declaration of independence. "They are heavily subsidized by the Serbian government in Belgrade, which tops up the salaries of local police officers and supplies the electricity and mobile phone network."

The Ibar River is fast becoming yet another border in the Balkans. "Cars in the north have different registration plates. When Kosovar Serbs drive south, they remove them to avoid being attacked. Our translator, who was Serbian, would not even get out of the car," says Gros-Verheyde. He notes there was much greater contact between the Serb and Albanian communities during his previous visit to Kosovo in 1990, when the Serbian military patrolled the province. "But 15 years of ethnic conflict has bred mistrust and hatred," says Gros-Verheyde.

Daniel Serwer, vice president of the Center for Post-Conflict Peace and Stability Operations at the United States Institute of Peace (USIP), feels Serbia only has itself to blame for losing Kosovo. It drove the Kosovar Albanians to secede by excluding them from the Serbian government, he argues. "If Kosovars had been included — for example by being offered the presidency of Serbia — it might not have seceded. The Serbs want sovereignty over the territory of Kosovo, but they could not care less about the people," he says.

"grave violent crime involving beating, smashing, looting and burning" orchestrated by the Dalai Lama, the Tibetan leader-in-exile. [13] But Western leaders are not buying Beijing's line. Nancy Pelosi, Speaker of the U.S. House of Representatives, traveled to India to meet with the Dalai Lama on March 21 and declared the Tibet situation "a challenge to the conscience of the world." [14]

Despite the international condemnation of China's treatment of the Tibetans, however, the international community and the United Nations (U.N.) — which in 1945 enshrined the right to self-determination in its founding charter — have provided little support to recent separatist movements. Many countries are wary of incurring the wrath of economic giants like China, and international law on separatism is ambiguous, leading to an inconsistent and non-uniform global reaction to separatist movements.

Though several international conventions reaffirm the right to self-determination, they also pledge to uphold the "principle of territorial integrity" — the right of existing states to prevent regions from seceding. "International law grows by practice," says Thomas Grant, a senior fel-

The economy of Kosovo has suffered terribly from two decades of strife throughout the region. With unemployment at 50 percent, thousands have migrated to Western Europe and the United States, sending money back to their families. Much of the country's income is derived from trafficking in drugs, weapons and women, claims Gros-Verheyde. Roads are dilapidated, and electricity is cut off several times a week.

Meanwhile, the international community is ever-present: The mobile phone network for Kosovar Albanians is provided by the principality of Monaco, the euro is the local currency and NATO soldiers' frequent the hotels and restaurants.

"The Albanian part is livelier than the Serbian," says Gros-Verheyde. "The birth rate among the Albanians is very high. They want to increase their population to ensure they are not wiped out."

Kosovo's future remains uncertain. Most of the world's nations have not yet recognized it as an independent country, and many are unlikely to do so, including Spain, Slovakia and Romania, which fear potential secessionist movements of their own. [3] Internally, tensions between the Albanian and Serb communities are unlikely to simply melt away. In fact, relations could further deteriorate over how to divide up the country's mineral resources, most of which lie in the Serb-controlled northern part.

Ethnic Albanians celebrate Kosovo's declaration of independence from Serbia on Feb. 17, 2008. The new state is backed by the United States and key European allies but bitterly contested by Serbia and Russia.

Meanwhile, the world will keep a watchful eye and presence. The European Union (EU) is in the process of deploying a 1,900-strong police and rule-of-law mission to replace a U.N. police force. [4] Indeed, many observers think the EU may hold out the best hope of salvation: Under a plan proposed by the European Commission — and supported virtually across the board in Europe — all Balkan nations would be integrated into the EU, ultimately diminishing the significance of borders and smoothing out ethnic tensions.

In the meantime, NATO holds the fort with a "high-visibility, low-profile" doctrine. "The soldiers have bullet-proof vests but keep them in the vehicles," says Gros-Verheyde. "They carry machine guns on their back but do not walk through villages with a weapon at their hip. A soldier told me the only exception to this was the American soldiers who have been traumatized by Iraq."

---

[1] Nicolas Gros-Verheyde, "One eye on Belgrade, the other on Pristina," *Europolitics*, (EU affairs subscription-based news service), Jan. 22, 2008, www.europolitics.info/xg/europolitique/politiquessectorielles/defense/2 17304?highlight=true&searchlink=true.

[2] Quoted in *ibid.*

[3] Joanna Boguslawska, *Europolitics*, Dec. 14, 2007, www.europolitics .info/xg/europolitique/politiquesexternes/relationsexterieures/215424? highlight=true&searchlink=true.

[4] For details, see Web sites of NATO and U.N. forces, respectively, at www.nato.int/KFOR and www.unmikonline.org.

---

low and legal scholar at the United States Institute of Peace (USIP), an independent institution established and funded by the U.S. Congress that tries to resolve international conflicts. "The legal situation adapts itself to the factual situation." (See box, p. 40.)

Consequently, the international community's response to de facto separatist states varies widely. For example, most of the world refuses to deal with the Turkish Republic of Northern Cyprus, which has been punished with an economic embargo since 1973, when Turkish troops invaded Cyprus and permanently occu-

pied the north, creating a Turkish-dominated de facto state there. Somaliland — which established a de facto state in northwestern Somalia in 1991 after the government in Mogadishu collapsed — has been largely ignored by the world community despite being a relative beacon of stability in the otherwise unstable horn of Africa. [15] The Tamils' campaign to gain independence from Sri Lanka attracts relatively little international diplomatic attention these days, in part, some say, because the area is not considered critical by the major powers.

AP Photo/Al Jacinto

The Moro Islamic Liberation Front — which for decades has fought for an independent state for the Moros, a Muslim group living in the south of the predominantly Catholic Philippines — are negotiating with the government to peacefully settle the dispute.

Meanwhile, the island nation of Taiwan, off the coast of mainland China, is accepted as a global trading partner — the United States alone has 140 trade agreements with the Taiwanese — but not as an independent country. Few countries are willing to challenge Beijing's "one-China" policy, which denies any province the right to secede and sees Taiwan as its 23rd province. [16]

In addition, the world has done nothing — apart from occasionally condemning human rights violations — to prevent Russia from brutally repressing Chechnya's attempt to secede. While separatists there largely succeeded in creating their own state in the 1990s, Moscow has since regained control of it, although an insurgency continues.

The U.N. has no specific unit looking at separatism as a phenomenon. Instead, it usually waits for a conflict to break out and then considers sending a peacekeeping mission to restore law and order.

"U.N. member states are likely to be wary of separatism because of the knock-on effects it can have on themselves," says Jared Kotler, communications officer at the U.N.'s Department of Political Affairs. "Member states are very aware how one movement can encourage another — possibly in their own country."

"Thus far, territorial integrity has always won the debate," says Hurst Hannum, a professor of international law at Tufts University in Medford, Mass., and a specialist in self-determination theory. "This is why Kosovo will be an important precedent despite statements by all concerned that it should not be seen as such."

In Latin America, where most countries won wars of independence in the early 1800s, separatist movements are rare today, although one recently sprang up in Bolivia. Bolivians living in the lowlands, who are mostly of European ancestry, are threatening to secede to prevent the government from redistributing the profits from the nation's oil and gas reserves to the mainly indigenous highlanders. In North America, the United States has not experienced a serious separatist threat since 1861 when 11 Southern states seceded, provoking the Civil War. And while few predict an imminent resurgence of such movements in the United States, diverse secessionist groups are beginning to coordinate their efforts. [17] (*See "At Issue," p. 45.*)

Some separatist movements have been highly successful. For example, since declaring independence from the Soviet Union in 1990, Lithuania has liberalized and grown its economy, consolidated democracy and joined the European Union (EU) and NATO.

Seth D. Kaplan, a foreign policy analyst and author of the forthcoming book *Fixing Fragile States*, has some advice for countries struggling to put out secessionist fires. "Countries that can foster sufficient social cohesion and a common identity while minimizing horizontal inequities are the most likely to stay whole," he says. "Those that don't and have obvious identity cleavages are likely to ignite secessionist movements."

While the world confronts growing separatism, here are some key questions being asked:

Should there be a right of self-determination?

"In principle, yes," says Daniel Serwer, vice president of the Center for Post-Conflict Peace and Stability Operations at the United States Institute of Peace. "But the real question is: What form should self-determination take?"

Self-determination is often interpreted to mean the right to secede and declare independence. But it can take other forms, too, such as local autonomy, similar to what Canada has granted to Québec, or a federal system with a strong central government that protects minority rights.

"In Kosovo, after nine years under U.N. control, young people expected independence," says Serwer. But other minorities have chosen a different path, he adds. For instance, "the Kurds in Iraq were thrown out of their homes" by Saddam Hussein. "They were even gassed. But so far they have not chosen the route of independence."

Gene Martin, executive director of the Philippine Facilitation Project at USIP, notes, "Local autonomy may not be enough for some people, who feel they just do not belong to a country." Plus, he adds, the government's ability or willingness to relinquish its authority also affects whether a minority will push for local autonomy or for full independence. Martin has been involved in brokering peace between the Philippine government and the Moro Islamic Liberation Front, which has for decades fought for an independent state for the Moros, a Muslim people living in southern Philippines.

Marino Busdachin — general secretary of the Hague-based Unrepresented Nations and Peoples Organization (UNPO), which represents 70 nonviolent movements pushing for self-determination — rails against the U.N. for not upholding that right. "Self-determination exists on paper only. It is a trap," he says. "We cannot apply to anyone for it. The U.N. member states block us."

Moreover, he says, seeking self-determination should not be confused with demanding the right to secede. "Ninety percent of our members are not looking for independence," he says.

That's a significant distinction, according to Diane Orentlicher, a professor of international law at American University in Washington, D.C. Although the U.N. has enshrined the right to self-determination, it has never endorsed a right of secession, and no state recognizes such a right. Such a step would be dangerous, she writes, because it would allow minorities to subvert the will of

---

More Than Two Dozen New Nations Since 1990

Since 1990, 26 new countries have declared independence — 15 of them the result of the dissolution of the Soviet Union. Yugoslavia has separated into seven new states, the last one, Kosovo, declaring its independence in February.

Successful Separatist Movements Since 1990

Emerged from Ethiopia (1993)	Emerged from Czechoslovakia in 1993
Eritrea	Czech Republic
	Slovakia
Emerged from Indonesia (2002)	
Timor Leste	**Emerged from Yugoslavia**
	Bosnia and Herzegovina (1992)
Emerged from the Soviet Union (1991)	Croatia (1991)
	Kosovo (2008, from Serbia)
Armenia Kazakhstan Russia	Macedonia (1991)
Azerbaijan Kyrgyzstan Tajikistan	Montenegro (2006)*
Belarus Latvia Turkmenistan	Serbia (2006)*
Estonia Lithuania Ukraine	Slovenia (1991)
Georgia Moldova Uzbekistan	

* For three years, Serbia and Montenegro existed as a confederation called Serbia & Montenegro, and then split into separate countries.

Sources: Unrepresented Nations and Peoples' Organization, www.unpo.org; *Political Handbook of the World 2007*, CQ Press, 2007; Tibet Government-in-exile, www.tibet.com.

---

the majority. "Minorities could distort the outcome of political processes by threatening to secede if their views do not prevail," she writes. [18]

Dmitry Rogozin, Russia's ambassador to NATO, shares that view. "If the majority wants to live in a shared state, why does the minority have the right to break away?" he has asked. [19] "Look at Berlin. You could say it's the third-largest Turkish city [because of the large number of people of Turkish origin living there]. If tomorrow the Turks living in Berlin want to create a national state in the city, who can be against it?"

"The challenge for the West in Kosovo," says self-determination legal expert Hannum at Tufts, is to recognize its independence without implicitly recognizing its right to secede — just as "the West pretended that the former Yugoslavia 'dissolved' as opposed to recognizing the secession of its various parts."

The State Department's Bryza, who deals with conflicts in Abkhazia, South Ossetia and Nagorno-Karabakh, a separatist enclave in Azerbaijan, agrees. "It is

AP Photo/Gemunu Amarasinghe

Female Tamil Tiger fighters undergo training at a hideout deep in Tiger-controlled territory northeast of Colombo, Sri Lanka, in 2007. The Tamils, who comprise 18 percent of Sri Lanka's population, began fighting for independence in 1983 — a struggle that has resulted in the deaths of some 70,000 people. Tamils now control large swathes of the country.

bar is placed very high because you want to preserve the state, as that is the mechanism you use to claim your right of secession."

This is why, argues Serwer, ethnic Albanians in Macedonia, which borders Kosovo, do not have the right to secede. "If they called for independence — and I don't think they want this — I would say 'nonsense,' because they have their rights respected. It is only when other forms of self-determination — like local autonomy — are blocked that secession becomes inevitable."

Meto Koloski — the president of United Macedonian Diaspora, which campaigns for the rights of Macedonian minorities in Greece, Bulgaria, Albania, Serbia and Kosovo — says, "Everyone should have a right to self-determination, their own identity, language and culture but not to their own state."

Secession also is problematic — even if backed by a clear majority of those in the seceding region — because the minority opposed to secession could end up being oppressed. "Secession does not create the homogeneous successor states its proponents often assume," writes Donald Horowitz, a professor of law and political science at Duke University in Durham, N.C. "Guarantees of minority protection in secessionist regions are likely to be illusory; indeed, many secessionist movements have as one of their aims the expulsion or subordination of minorities in the secessionist regions. [20]

"There is an inevitable trade-off between encouraging participation in the undivided state and legitimating exit from it," he continued. "The former will inevitably produce imperfect results, but the latter is downright dangerous." [21]

Some would argue that certain separatist movements have no legal basis because the people concerned already exercised their right of self-determination when their country was first founded. "The whole self-determination theology is very slippery," says a U.S. government official with extensive knowledge of the separatist conflict in Aceh, Indonesia. "We support the territorial integrity of Indonesia. We never concluded that the human rights situation in Aceh was intolerable."

Jerry Hyman, governance advisor at the Center for Strategic and International Studies in Washington, highlights an often-overlooked point: "We have to ask how economically and politically viable are states like Transdniestria? If you apply this [right to secede] to Africa, it could explode. At best, Africa is a stained-glass window." Economic viability tends to be ignored when

unreasonable to have self-determination as the only guiding principle," he says. "If we did, the world would live in utter barbarity."

Fixing Fragile States author Kaplan believes separatism makes sense in a few cases, such as Kosovo and Somaliland. "But, generally, the international community is right to initially oppose separatism," he says.

So when should a group have the right to secede? "When you are deprived of the right to participate in government, and there are serious violations of human rights, such as genocide," says the USIP's Grant. "The

assessing separatist claims, he says, because the "we're special" argument usually prevails.

"If they are not viable, they will end up like East Timor, relying on the international community financially," he says.

Are globalization and regional integration fueling separatism?

Several organizations and treaties have emerged in recent years to encourage more regional integration and cross-border trade. The EU is the oldest and largest, but newer arrivals include the Association of Southeast Asian Nations (ASEAN), the African Union (AU), the Latin American trading blocks ANDEAN and MERCOSUR and the North American Free Trade Agreement (NAFTA). In addition, the World Trade Organization (WTO) is working to abolish trade barriers globally. Experts differ over whether these organizations promote or discourage separatism.

The Peace Institute's Grant believes they can encourage it. "What are the political impediments to independence?" he asks. The new states are not sustainable as a small unit, he says, adding, "If you reduce the significance of national borders and improve the free movement of people, goods and capital, you remove that impediment."

For instance, the possibility of being part of the EU's single market makes an independent Kosovo a more viable option and has seemingly suppressed Albania's desire to merge with the Albanians in Kosovo to create a Greater Albania. Asked if Albania had a plan to establish a Greater Albania, Foreign Minister Lulzim Basha said, "Yes, we do. It has a blue flag and gold stars on it," describing the EU flag. "Today's only goal is integration into NATO and the EU as soon as possible." [22]

Günter Dauwen, a Flemish nationalist who is director of the European Free Alliance political party in the European Parliament, says the EU fuels separatism by

Number of Countries Reaches All-time High

The number of countries in the world has increased sixfold since the 1800s, when European colonization was at its peak. The greatest jump occurred after World War II, when Europe gave up its colonies amid a worldwide movement for independence. The United Nations, which includes nearly all of the world's countries, now has 192 members. The U.N. has not yet recognized Kosovo, which declared its independence in February.

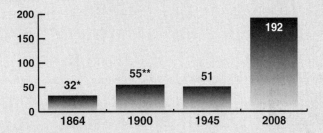

Number of Countries Recognized Worldwide, 1864-2008

* Includes several states in Australia and New Zealand that were part of the British Empire; Finland and Poland were considered part of Russia; Africa is omitted entirely, since its interior was largely unmapped at that time. Since the U.S. Civil War was in progress, the Confederate States were counted as a separate country.

** The British Empire is counted as a single country, as are the French, German and Dutch empires; Austria-Hungary is considered one country and includes both Liechtenstein and Bosnia-Herzegovina; Finland and several Asian dependencies are counted as part of Russia; Turkey includes five states.

Sources: The Statesman's Year Book, 1864 and 1900; United Nations

not adequately ensuring respect for regions. Dauwen is campaigning for more autonomy and possibly independence for Flanders, the mostly Dutch-speaking northern half of Belgium that already has a large degree of self-government. "The national capitals control the EU. They decide where funds for regional development go. This creates terrible tension."

Over-centralization of decision-making is particularly acute in Spain, he says, where it has triggered separatism in the region of Catalonia in the northeast and Galicia in the northwest. In addition, France suppresses regionalist parties in Brittany, Savoy and the French Basque country, he says. "When we complain to the EU, its stock answer is that only nation states can devolve power to the regions."

Dauwen points out that the European Court of Human Rights (ECHR) has condemned countries for

C H R O N O L O G Y

1776-1944 *Nation states gradually eclipse multi-ethnic empires as the dominant form of government.*

1776 Britain's American colonies declare independence, triggering war.

Early 1800s Spanish and Portuguese colonies in Latin America become independent.

1861 Eleven Southern U.S. states secede, sparking Civil War. After four years of bitter fighting, the South loses and is reintegrated into the union.

1918 At the end of World War I new European states are created from the ashes of the Hapsburg and Ottoman empires.

1919 U.S. President Woodrow Wilson champions the "right of self-determination" but fails to get it adopted by the League of Nations.

1939 World War II breaks out. Borders shift as Germany, Japan and Italy occupy neighboring countries before being defeated by the Allies.

1945-1989 *More new states emerge as colonies gain independence, but borders are left largely intact.*

1945 U.N. charter includes the right of self-determination.

1949 China invades and occupies Tibet.

1960 U.N. General Assembly proclaims a Declaration on the Granting of Independence to Colonial Countries and Peoples, heralding the end of the colonial era.

1967 Biafra secedes from Nigeria; is reintegrated after a three-year war.

1975 World's leading powers sign the Helsinki Final Act, guaranteeing peoples the right of self-determination.

1984 A new, violent Kurdish separatist revolt breaks out in Turkey.

1990-2008 *Twenty-six new countries are created after the Soviet Union and Yugoslavia break apart.*

1990 Soviet republics begin resisting Moscow's central control. Lithuania on March 11 becomes the first republic to declare its independence, setting off a chain reaction that leads to the dissolution of the U.S.S.R.

1991 Slovenia and Croatia split from Yugoslavia, accompanied by violence, especially in Croatia. . . . New states emerge from the Soviet Union, as do unrecognized breakaway republics in Nagorno-Karabakh, Chechnya, South Ossetia, Abkhazia and Transdniestra. . . . In Africa, Somaliland separates itself from rapidly disintegrating Somalia.

1992 Bosnia splits from Yugoslavia, provoking a three-year war.

1993 Czechoslovakia splits peacefully into the Czech Republic and Slovakia. . . . Eritrea secedes from Ethiopia after a U.N.-monitored referendum.

1995 A referendum in Québec advocating secession from Canada is rejected by 50.6 percent of Québécois.

1999 North Atlantic Treaty Organization seizes Kosovo from Serbia in response to Serbia's persecution of Kosovar Albanians. . . . East Timor declares independence from Indonesia after 25 years of violence.

2004 The separatist region of Aceh is granted autonomy from Indonesia after a devastating Dec. 26 Indian Ocean tsunami creates a feeling of solidarity between Aceh's separatists and the Indonesian authorities.

2005 Chinese authorize use of force to prevent Taiwan from seceding.

2007 Belgium edges closer to disintegration. . . . In Bolivia, people of European descent threaten to secede in response to fears of losing control over the country's gas reserves.

2008 Taiwanese separatists are defeated in parliamentary elections on Jan. 12. . . . Kosovo declares independence from Serbia on Feb. 17, triggering violent protests among Serbs in Belgrade. Separatist protests in Tibet turn violent on March 14; Chinese send in troops to put down the rebellion.

not respecting the rights of ethnic minorities, but the EU doesn't force its members to comply with those rulings. For instance, he says, the ECHR condemned the Bulgarians for not allowing ethnic Macedonians to form their own political party. But the EU did nothing to force Bulgaria to abide by the ruling, further fueling the desire for separatism.

The State Department's Bryza disagrees. "The opposite works in my experience," he says. "As Hungary and Slovakia have deepened their integration into the EU, the desire of ethnic Hungarians who live in countries neighboring Hungary to become independent is receding. And the possibility for Turkish Cypriots in northern Cyprus [whose de facto state is only recognized by Turkey] to be part of the EU gives them an incentive to rejoin the Greek Cypriot government in the south, which is already in the EU."

Likewise, Ekaterina Pischalnikova — special assistant to the special representative of the secretary-general at the U.N. observer mission in Georgia, which is trying to resolve the Georgia-Abkhaz conflict — says EU regional integration has helped to "mitigate rather than fuel separatist movements."

Busdachin of the Unrepresented Nations and Peoples Organization says the EU "is helping to resolve separatist conflicts in many cases because it has the most advanced regime for protecting minorities." For example, the EU has consistently pressured Turkey, which wants to join the union, to grant the Kurds the right to express their language and culture more freely. Such a move could quell some Kurds' desire for full independence, he says, adding that he would like to see ASEAN, MERCOSUR and other regional organizations follow the EU model.

Author Kaplan — who has lived in Turkey, Nigeria, China and Japan — says regional integration "is only promoting separatism in the EU. Europe is peaceful and prosperous so there is no real need for states. But when you get into the wild jungle, the state is more important." For instance, he explains, "states in Africa and Central America do not want to give up their power, even though they would benefit the most from regionalism."

In Asia, ASEAN has no clearly defined policy on separatism, leaving it up to national governments to decide how to deal with separatist movements. The Shanghai Co-operation Organization (SCO) — set up in 2001 by Russia, China, Kazakhstan, Kyrgyzstan, Uzbekistan and Tajikistan to combat separatism, terrorism and extremism — strongly opposes separatist movements like that of China's Uyghurs. [23]

Ironically, separatism also can fuel regional integration. Many of the countries that have recently joined the EU or intend to do so — Lithuania, Slovakia, Slovenia, Montenegro and Macedonia — were formed from separatist movements. Too small to be economically self-sufficient, they see integration into the EU market as the only way to ensure continued prosperity and stability.

Does separatism lead to more violent conflict?

The recent developments in the Balkans provide strong evidence that separatism can provoke violent conflict — especially when countries divide along ethnic lines, as the former Yugoslavia has done.

Serbia's festering rage over Kosovo's declaration of independence is a prime example. "If this act of secession for ethnic reasons is not a mistake, then nothing is a mistake," said Serbia's Foreign Minister Vuk Jeremić, adding, "Serbia will not go quietly. We will fight, and we will not tolerate this secession." [24]

Serwer at the United States Institute for Peace says, "If you partition a state along ethnic lines, this almost inevitably leads to long-term conflict," especially if the central government resists the separatist movement.

"Secession converts a domestic ethnic dispute into a more dangerous one," according to Duke's Horowitz. "The recurrent temptation to create a multitude of homogeneous mini-states, even if it could be realized, might well increase the sum total of warfare rather than reduce it." [25]

The State Department's Bryza says separatism doesn't have to lead to violence "if leaders of national groups exert wise leadership and temper the ambitions of nationalist groups."

The campaign by Taiwanese separatists to obtain a seat for Taiwan at the U.N. — a March 22 referendum calling for this failed — shows how even nonviolent separatism can trigger conflict. "Bizarre as it may seem, a peaceful referendum in Taiwan may portend war," according to John J. Tkacik, a policy expert at the Heritage Foundation in Washington. He predicted China would invoke a 2005 anti-secession law to justify using "non-peaceful" means to counter Taiwanese separatism. [26] Fear of provoking a war with China is probably the main reason there is so little international support for the Taiwan independence movement.

Bye-Bye Belgium?

More prosperous Flanders wants autonomy.

Belgium experienced a surreal moment in December 2006 when a spoof news program on a French-speaking TV channel announced that Flanders, the country's Dutch-speaking region, had seceded. Footage of the king and queen of Belgium hastily boarding an airplane interspersed with shocked reactions from politicians convinced many viewers that their country was no more. Some even took to the streets to spontaneously rally for the Belgian cause.

But Dutch-speaking Flemings (as those who live in Flanders are called) were offended at how quickly their francophone compatriots (called the Walloons) believed Flanders had seceded. The incident triggered months of national soul-searching about the future of the country.

Fast-forward to the June 2007 general election, when the separatist-leaning Flemish Christian Democrats won the most seats in parliament and demanded that the constitution be amended to devolve more power to the regions, escalating an ongoing dispute between French and Dutch-speaking parties. The controversy became so fierce it took six months to form a government, and even then, it was only provisional, aimed at keeping the country united until the French- and Dutch-speaking communities could agree on a more long-term program. While a coalition pact was finally approved on March 18, bringing an end to the country's nine-month political limbo, the pact says nothing about devolution of powers, so the real battle has still to be fought. [1]

"If the French do not give us more autonomy, it's bye-bye Belgium," says Flemish nationalist Gunter Dauwen, director of the European Free Alliance, a political group that represents 35 nationalist parties in Europe.

Dauwen's party, Spirit, is demanding that unemployment benefits be paid for by the regional governments rather than the federal government. The jobless rate is higher in French-speaking Wallonia. Under Dauwen's plan, the Flemish would not have to subsidize the unemployed Walloons as they do now.

But such a lack of solidarity irks the Francophones. "We are a small country. We should all get the same benefits," says Raphael Hora, an unemployed Walloon. "You can't have a guy in Charleroi (Wallonia) getting less than a guy in Antwerp (Flanders)."

There is also a growing cultural chasm between Flemings and Walloons, he says. "I speak English, Italian, Spanish, Norwegian, German and Polish — but not Dutch. My father never wanted me to learn it."

Roughly 60 percent of Belgians speak Dutch, 39 percent speak French and the remaining 1 percent speak German. The Belgian constitutional system is Byzantine in its complexity, with powers dispersed between governments organized along municipal, linguistic, provincial, regional and national lines.

Hora, who recently moved to Berlin, sees Belgium's breakup as inevitable: "When it happens, I'll come back to Belgium and campaign for Wallonia to rejoin France. We'll be stronger then."

Dauwen insists independence for Flanders is not the goal for now. "My party is not campaigning for independence yet but for a confederation." Contrary to the widespread perception of Flemings as rampant separatists, Dauwen says, "We are all peaceful and not extreme." Flanders' largest pro-independence party, Vlaams Belang, actually lost support in last June's elections, although it remains a major force, garnering about 20 percent of Flemish voters.

According to Jérémie Rossignon, a landscape gardener from Wallonia living in Brussels, "Belgians are not very proud of being Belgian. They do not boast about their achievements and culture." He feels this is a pity, because Belgium has much to be proud of — from its world-renowned beers, chocolates and restaurants to its sports

---

As former U.S. Deputy Secretary of State Robert B. Zoellick said in 2006, "We want to be supportive of Taiwan, while we are not encouraging those that try to move toward independence. Because I am being very clear: Independence means war. And that means American soldiers." [27]

But independence does not always mean war. With a broadly homogeneous population, its own currency, flag, army, government and airline, Somaliland is an example of how a people can effectively secede without causing chaos and violence. Somaliland's isolation from the

stars like tennis champ Justine Henin and the funky fashion designers of Antwerp to the eclectic euro-village that is Brussels.

"There is not much communication between the Francophones and Flemings any more," he continues. "Young Flemings speak English, not French, whereas their parents can speak French."

Meanwhile, he admits, the Francophones "are useless at foreign languages." Foreign-language movies and TV programs are dubbed into French, whereas in Flanders they are subtitled, he notes. The mostly French-speaking monarchy, which is supposed to unify the country, has become another cause of division. Belgium's Italian-born Queen Paola cannot speak Dutch, the language of 60 percent of her subjects, while Crown Prince Philippe has publicly slammed Flemish separatism.

Belgium's predominantly French-speaking capital, Brussels, is located in Flanders, and is seen alternately as a glue holding the country together or an obstacle preventing it from splitting apart. "The Walloons are trying to annex Brussels" by moving to the small strip of land in Flanders that separates Brussels from Wallonia, according to Dauwen. Elected representatives and residents in these municipalities squabble over which language should be used on official documents and street signs. And once a year the Flemings organize a bike ride — known as *Het Gordeel* (the belt) — around Brussels to send a symbolic message that Brussels must not extend itself further into Flanders.

The Francophones feel equally passionately. "The Romans conquered Brussels before the Germans did so we should stay French," says Marie-Paul Clarisse, a lifelong Bruxelloise, who works for an EU-affairs newspaper.

One compromise being floated would turn Brussels into Europe's Washington, D.C., and have it run by the EU, which is based in the city. An even wilder solution calls for tiny Luxembourg to annex Brussels and Wallonia. [2] And as

Belgians Speak Three Languages

The Dutch-speaking portion of Belgium is called Flanders. The southern portion, Wallonia, includes both Francophones and German-speaking citizens. French is the predominant language of Brussels, the capital.

if things were not complicated enough, Belgium also has an autonomous German-speaking community living in Wallonia. No one is quite sure what they want.

Even Rossignon, an ardent defender of Belgium, doubts its future: "The separatists will win out," he predicts, and the new government "will regionalize our country even more than it already is."

---

[1] "New Belgian Coalition Government Reaches Agreement," Agence France-Presse, March 18, 2008, http://afp.google.com/article/ALeq M5jhowUtJkHEsJRfNHhaSlnCb8-Zig.

[2] Laurent Lintermans, "Un Etat federal avec le Luxembourg?" *La Libre Belgique*, Aug. 18, 2007, www.lalibre.be/index.php?view=article&art_ id=364931.

international community has not hindered its development — indeed it has helped, argues author Kaplan.

"The dearth of external involvement has kept foreign interference to a minimum while spurring self-reliance and self-belief," he says.

Martin at the Peace Institute points out that since the end of the Cold War, "most wars have been intra-state. Sometimes borders can be shifted to solve the problem and actually prevent war."

But separatist movements also are frequently manip-

Laws Are Ambiguous on Self-determination

The right to self-determination — which allows people to secede from a mother state if they so choose — appears in various international conventions, including the founding document of the United Nations. But the international documents are ambiguous, because they also espouse the importance of "territorial integrity" — the right of countries not to have their territory dismembered.

International Texts Dealing with Self-determination and Territorial Integrity

U.N. Founding Charter (Article 1) — 1945

- One purpose of the United Nations is "to develop friendly relations among nations based on respect for the principle of equal rights and self-determination of peoples, and to take other appropriate measures to strengthen universal peace."

U.N. Resolution 2625 — 1970

- "Every State has the duty to refrain from any forcible action which deprives peoples referred to in the elaboration of the principle of equal rights and self-determination of their right to self-determination and freedom and independence."
- "Nothing in the foregoing paragraphs shall be construed as authorizing or encouraging any action which would dismember, or impair, totally or in part, the territorial integrity or political unity of sovereign and independent states conducting themselves in compliance with the principle of equal rights and self-determination of peoples and thus possessed of a government representing the whole people belonging to the territory without distinction to race, creed or color."

African Charter on Human and Peoples' Rights (Article 20) — 1981

- "All peoples shall have . . . the unquestionable and inalienable right to self-determination. They shall freely determine their political status and shall pursue their economic development according to the policy they have freely chosen."

Conference on Security and Co-operation in Europe's Charter of Paris for a New Europe — 1990

- "We affirm that the ethnic, cultural, linguistic and religious identity of national minorities will be protected."
- "We reaffirm the equal rights of peoples and their right to self-determination in conformity with the Charter of the United Nations and with the relevant norms of international law, including those related to territorial integrity of states."

Vienna Declaration and Program of Action adopted by World Conference of Human Rights — 1993

- The conference recognizes "the right of peoples to take any legitimate action, in accordance with the Charter of the U.N., to realize their inalienable right of self-determination."

Sources: Organization for Security and Co-operation in Europe, United Nations, University of Hong Kong, University of New Mexico, Unrepresented Nations and Peoples Organization

ulated by external powers as part of a geopolitical chess game that can become violent. "People want independence because of ethnic hatred and because it is in their economic interests to separate. But outside powers help separatists, too," says Koloski, of the United Macedonian Diaspora. For example, the United States, Britain and France support Kosovo's independence because they believe this will help stabilize the region, while Russia and China support Serbia's opposition because they fear it will encourage separatist movements elsewhere, including in their territories.

In some cases — notably Québec, Flanders, Wales and Scotland — separatist movements have not boiled over into violent conflict. In each, the central government granted some self-rule to the separatist region, preventing the situation from turning violent. [28] In addition, the movements were able to argue their case through elected political representatives in a functioning democratic system, which also reduces the likelihood of violence.

"When a country is too centralized and non-democratic, this produces separatist movements that can become violent," says Busdachin at the Unrepresented Nations and Peoples Organization. "The responsibility is 50-50."

But democracy does not always prevent separatism from escalating into conflict. From the 1960s to the '90s, extreme Irish Catholic nationalists in Northern Ireland waged a violent campaign to secure independence from the U.K., all the while maintaining a political party with elected representatives.

How the global community responds to one separatist movement can affect whether a movement elsewhere triggers a war. "Violence is not inevitable," says Flemish nationalist Dauwen. "But ethnic minorities do get frustrated when they get nowhere through peaceful means, and they see those who use violence — for example the Basque separatist movement ETA in Spain — attracting all the headlines."

As a Tamil activist notes, "Whatever we have achieved so far, we have got by force."

BACKGROUND

Emerging Nations

Throughout history separatism has manifested itself in various forms as groups grew dissatisfied with their governments. Even the Roman Empire — which was synonymous with order, peace and civilization in most of its conquered territories — had its Celtic resisters, the Britons and Gauls. [29]

In medieval Europe, the discontented sought to extricate themselves from kingdoms, feudal domains and churches. In the 18th and 19th centuries European colonies in the Americas, Australia and New Zealand began splitting off from the "mother" countries. By the 19th century, with the Hapsburg, Romanov and Ottoman empires on the decline, groups united by ethnicity, language or culture began to cast off their imperial shackles. Then in the late 1800s and early 20th century the major European powers — and the United States — began acquiring and consolidating colonies or territories.

Just three decades after its own war for independence from Great Britain, the United States had to weather its own secessionist storms. In 1814 a handful of New

Yugoslavia Yields Seven New Nations

The former Yugoslavia has broken into seven new countries since 1991, and at least one additional province — the self-governing Republika Srpska in Bosnia and Herzogovina — is threatening to secede. Kosovo, on Serbia's southern border, declared its independence in February. The northern Serbian province of Vojvodina, populated by many Hungarians — is autonomous.

England states opposed to the federal government's anti-foreign-trade policies and the War of 1812 organized a convention in Hartford, Conn., and produced a report spelling out the conditions under which they would remain part of the United States. The U.S. victory against the British in 1815 took the wind out of the initiative's sails, however, and secession negotiations never actually took place.

Then in 1861, largely in response to U.S. government efforts to outlaw slavery, 11 Southern states tried to secede from the union to form their own country. After a bloody, four-year civil war, the South was forcibly reintegrated into the United States in 1865. [30] The U.S. Supreme Court cemented the union with a ruling in 1869 (*Texas v. White*) that effectively barred states from unilaterally seceding. [31]

AP Photo/Yahya Ahmed

In northern Iraq's Qandil Mountains, recruits for a splinter group of the militant Kurdish PKK separatists are training to fight government troops across the border in Iran. Some 16-28 million Kurds are dispersed in Turkey, Iraq, Iran and Syria, making them the world's largest nation without its own country. The PKK wants a single Kurdish state; other Kurds seek either greater autonomy or independence from the countries where they live.

In 1914 nationalist opposition to imperialist expansionism in Europe sparked World War I. Aggrieved at the Austro-Hungarian Empire's annexation of Bosnia, home to many Serbs, 19-year-old Serbian Gavrilo Princip assassinated Archduke Franz Ferdinand, heir to the imperial throne. Many of the new countries created in the post-war territorial division, such as Lithuania and Poland, were constructed along broadly ethnic lines. At the same time the concept of "self-determination" — the right of a nation to determine how it should be governed — emerged, championed by President Woodrow Wilson. [32]

Wilson's effort to enshrine self-determination in the founding statute of the newly created League of Nations was defeated. The idea of holding a referendum to determine who should govern a disputed territory gained support in this period, too. And when the league set up a commission to determine the status of the Åland Islands (it determined Finnish sovereignty), the concept was developed that a people might have the right to secede when the state they belonged to did not respect their fundamental rights. [33]

One group, the Kurds, fared badly in the post-war territorial settlements. Emerging without a state of their own, Kurds repeatedly staged uprisings in Iraq, Iran and Turkey but were suppressed each time. The most recent and bloody of these has occurred in Turkey, where 40,000 people have been killed in an ongoing conflict that began

in 1984. The Kurds in northern Iraq also suffered widespread massacres and expulsions in the late 1980s under Iraqi President Saddam Hussein, but when the United States and its allies defeated Saddam in the 1991 Gulf War, Iraqi Kurds effectively gained self-rule after the U.N. forced Saddam to withdraw from the region. [34]

The Palestinians were also dealt a poor hand in 1948 after their homeland became part of the new state of Israel, populated mainly by Jews fleeing post-war Europe. After winning the Six-Day War in 1967, Israel occupied Palestinian lands on the western bank of the Jordan River and in a narrow strip of land called Gaza. Ever since then, the Palestinians have been fighting to have a country of their own. [35]

Decolonization

The 20th century saw the number of independent countries around the globe more than triple — from the approximately 55 that existed in 1900 to the 192 that make up the United Nations today. [36] Most of the new nations were created in the post-World War II era, as the European powers shed their colonies in Africa and Asia. To ensure that the decolonization process was peaceful and orderly, the United Nations adopted the Declaration on the Granting of Independence to Colonial Countries and Peoples in 1960. [37]

But in practice the emergence of new states was often far from peaceful. Hundreds of thousands of people died in outbreaks of violence during the August 1947 partition of India and Pakistan, which within months went to war with each other over the disputed territory of Kashmir. In 1967 the Igbo people of Biafra tried to secede from Nigeria, triggering a devastating war and famine. Three years later the region was forcefully rejoined to Nigeria. Despite accusations that Nigeria was committing genocide on the Biafrans, the international community did not back Biafra's independence.

The former British colony of Somaliland in the horn of Africa became momentarily independent in 1960 but immediately chose to unite with its fellow Somalis in the newly constituted state of Somalia to the south created from Italy's former colony. When Somalia collapsed into violent anarchy in 1991, Somaliland seceded, and separatist militants installed a civil administration. In northern Ethiopia, Eritrea's 31-year secession struggle finally ended in independence in 1993 after passage of a U.N.-monitored referendum.

In Sri Lanka, which is dominated by Sinhalese people, the minority Tamils — who make up about 18 percent of the population — have been pushing for independence since the 1970s. [38] The Tamils had wielded considerable influence when the island belonged to the British Empire but felt increasingly discriminated against after Sri Lankan independence in 1948. In the late 1970s and early '80s, when Indira Ghandi was India's prime minister, India — which is home to 70 million Tamils — supported the separatist "Tamil Tigers." But in the late 1980s her son and successor, Rajiv Ghandi, dispatched Indian troops to clamp down on the Tigers. He was later assassinated by a female Tamil suicide bomber, Thenmuli Rajaratnam.

Hopes of reconciliation were raised when Sinhalese and Tamil authorities agreed to rebuild areas devastated by the December 2004 Indian Ocean tsunami, which killed some 35,000 Sri Lankans. But the Sri Lankan Supreme Court struck down the agreement.

Dispersed across a vast plateau in the Himalayan mountains, Tibetans are a mostly Buddhist people with a 2,000-year written history and their own language, Tibetan, which is related to Burmese. China claims ownership of the region based on historical links with Tibetan leaders, which were especially strong in the 18th century. The Tibetans refute this claim and insist the region was never an integral part of China and that from 1913 until 1949 Tibet existed as an independent state.

China invaded Tibet in 1949 and 1950, annexed it in 1951 and in 1965 created the Tibet Autonomous Region — a territory less than half the size of the region Tibetans consider their homeland.

Over the past 60 years, according to the Tibetan government in exile, China has brutally repressed the Tibetans, killing 87,000 during the 1959 uprising against Chinese rule and destroying or closing down nearly all of the region's 6,259 monasteries by 1962. China unleashed more death and destruction against the Tibetans in 1966 during the Cultural Revolution, the Tibetans claim. [39]

What Is a Nation?

The words nation, state and country are often used — incorrectly — as if they are interchangeable. But international law and usage today make clear distinctions in the concepts, as set out by U.S. lawyer and diplomat Henry Wheaton in his 1836 text *Elements of International Law*.

A "nation," he wrote, implies "a community of race, which is generally shown by community of language, manners and customs."

A country — or "state" — refers to "the union of a number of individuals in a fixed territory, and under one central authority," Wheaton explained. Thus a state "may be composed of different races of men" while a nation or people "may be subject to several states."

Wheaton noted that in ancient Rome, the philosopher and orator Cicero defined a state as "a body politic, or society of men, united together for the purpose of promoting their mutual safety and advantage by their combined strength."

Source: Henry Wheaton, *Elements of International Law*, 1836.

In other regions, movements to allow ethnic minorities to express their cultures and govern their own affairs have flourished since the 1960s. Such efforts have succeeded among the Welsh in Scotland and the Basques in Spain. In Belgium divisions between Dutch-speakers in Flanders, who make up roughly 60 percent of the population, and the French-speakers of Wallonia widened as more power devolved from the central government to the regions. In Canada separatist aspirations among French-speakers, who make up about 80 percent of the population in the province of Québec, culminated in a 1980 referendum on independence that was rejected by 60 percent of the voters. A subsequent referendum in October 1995 failed by a smaller margin, with 50.6 percent voting No and 49.4 percent Yes. [40]

During the Cold War, the United States, the Soviet Union and others signed the Helsinki Final Act of 1975, which established, among other things, the principle of "equal rights and self-determination of peoples." Latvia, Lithuania and Estonia would later use this to justify seceding from the Soviet Union, according to a U.S. government official involved in overseeing implementation of the act. The 1977 Soviet constitution gave the constituent republics the right to leave the

AP Photo/Martial Trezzini

Wearing symbolic chains, a Uyghur protester in Geneva demands self-rule for the predominantly Muslim, ethnically Turkic Uyghurs in China's autonomous western region of Xinjiang. He also opposes China's one-child policy, which human rights advocates say forces some pregnant mothers to get abortions. China says recent separatist unrest in Tibet has triggered protests in Xinjiang, where some 500 Uyghurs held a demonstration in Khotan on March 23.

Ethno-centrism Surges

The fall of communism in Eastern Europe in the late 1980s and early '90s unleashed a wave of nationalist sentiment that destroyed the two largest multi-ethnic states in the region — Yugoslavia and the Soviet Union. Lithuania got the ball rolling, declaring independence from the Soviets in March 1990. Within two years, 15 new states had emerged from the former Soviet Union and another four in the former Yugoslavia. [43]

Soon several of the new states were experiencing their own secession movements. Russia fought fiercely and successfully to suppress the independence aspirations of the Chechens, a Muslim people with a long history of resisting subjugation by Moscow. Largely Romanian-speaking Moldova saw its Russian-dominated Transdniestria region morph into a de facto yet unrecognized state with the help of the Russian military. Ethnic Armenians in Azerbaijan's Nagorno-Karabakh region set up their own state in 1991, provoking a three-year war during which thousands of Azeris fled. Two regions — South Ossetia and Abkhazia — seceded from Georgia but have yet to be recognized by the international community.

Yugoslavia was torn asunder — eventually into seven new countries — due to the aggressive policies of nationalist leaders like Serbia's president, Slobodan Milosevic (1989-1997) and Croatia's president, Franjo Tudjman (1990-1999). The republics of Slovenia and Croatia in the northwest seceded in 1991, followed by Macedonia in the south and the triangular-shaped Bosnia and Herzegovina in 1992. The tiny republic of Montenegro seceded from Serbia in 2006. The province of Vojvodina in northern Serbia, populated by a substantial number of Hungarians, is autonomous but still part of Serbia.

Montenegro and Macedonia's splits were bloodless and Slovenia's relatively peaceful, but in Croatia and Bosnia hundreds of thousands were either killed, fled persecution or were expelled, leading to the term "ethnic cleansing." NATO helped to take Kosovo, a province in Serbia whose autonomy was withdrawn in 1989, away from the Serbs in 1999 after Milosevic brutally cracked down on Kosova Albanian separatists. Kosovo remained an international protectorate for the next nine years.

The Yugoslav experience highlighted the danger of using referenda to determine the status of territories. The Serbs living in Bosnia, who made up about a third of the population, did not want to secede from Yugoslavia so they boycotted the 1992 plebiscite. When it passed with

U.S.S.R., but the right was not exercised for fear of reprisals from Moscow. [41]

Mikhail Gorbachev — the Soviet leader from 1985 to 1991 whose "glasnost" policy of greater openness to the West proved to be a catalyst for the break-up the U.S.S.R. — had his doubts about self-determination. In his memoirs, he wrote that "the application by a community of its right to self-determination leads regularly to a corresponding attack on the other community. . . . It is obvious that the recognition of the rights of peoples to self-determination should not be absolute." [42]

Could separatism spread to the United States?

YES
Kyle Ellis
Founder, Californians for Independence

Written for *CQ Researcher*, March 2008

Asking whether separatism will spread to the United States is a bit of an odd question to pose in a nation founded through an act of secession from the British Empire.

Secession is at the very foundation of what it means to be American, and over the years since the country was founded many secessionist organizations and movements have kept this American tradition alive.

If you think the Civil War ended the question of secession in the United States, any Internet search you run will show just how wrong you are. Dozens of groups in various states are organizing and agitating for secession.

These groups are getting larger, and more serious ones are being founded all the time. As the leader and founder of one of these new organizations, I would like to offer a little insight as to why I believe the idea of secession will become a lot more popular in the years to come.

Here in California, there is much resentment toward the federal government. People don't like how politicians who live thousands of miles away are able to involve themselves in the creation of California's laws and the allocation of local resources, not to mention the billions of tax dollars sent away each year that are never to be seen again.

Other states have other reasons for wanting independence: Vermonters see the federal government as fundamentally out of touch with their way of life; the Southern states believe their unique culture is being systematically destroyed by the actions of the federal government; and Alaska and Hawaii view the circumstances surrounding their admittance into the Union as being suspect, if not downright undemocratic.

All of these groups view the federal government as broken in such a way that it cannot be fixed from within the system — a valid view considering it is run by two political parties that are fundamentally statist in nature. The two-party system is not even democratic (as we know from the 2000 elections), because it effectively disenfranchises millions of third-party voters due to the winner-take-all nature of political contests.

The federal government also continues to encroach upon individual rights and liberties.

It is natural that marginalized and disenfranchised people will seek to break away from a system they are not a part of, just as the founders of the United States sought to break away from Britain.

NO
Seth D. Kaplan
Foreign Policy Analyst and Business Consultant
Author, Fixing Fragile States: A New Paradigm for Development

Written for *CQ Researcher*, March 2008

Separatism requires a cohesive minority group that dominates a well-defined geographical area and possesses a strong sense of grievance against the central government. All three of these ingredients were present when the United States had its own encounter with separatism: the Confederacy's bid for independence in the 1860s. Southern whites possessed a unique identity, dominated a contiguous territory and were so aggrieved at the federal government that they were prepared to take up arms.

In recent decades, another disaffected and socioculturally distinct group in North America has waged a potent — but in this case nonviolent — campaign for independence: Canada's Québécois. Within the United States, however, no such groups exist today, and none seems likely to emerge in the foreseeable future. Puerto Rico does have a separatist movement, but Puerto Rico is already semi-autonomous and, more to the point, is only an unincorporated organized territory of the United States — not a full-fledged state. Some argue that California is close to reaching a level of economic self-sufficiency that would enable it to survive as an independent state. However, even if California could afford to be independent, neither its sense of difference nor of grievance seems likely to become strong enough to form the basis for a separatist movement.

Some Native American tribes, discontented with their circumscribed sovereignty, might wish to separate but — even if Washington raised no objections — their small populations, weak economies and unfavorable locations (inland, distant from other markets) would not make them viable as independent states.

The cohesiveness of the United States stands in marked contrast to most of the world's large, populous states. China, India, Indonesia and Pakistan all contend with separatist movements today.

Why has the United States escaped this danger? The answer lies in the impartiality of its institutions, the mobility of its people and the brevity of its history. Its robust and impartial institutions do not provide ethnic or religious groups with a strong enough sense of discrimination to ignite separatist passions. Its citizens migrate within the country at an unprecedented rate, ensuring a constant remixing of its population and tempering any geographically focused sense of difference. And its history as a relatively young, immigrant country — where people focus on the future far more than the past — means that few are fiercely loyal to any particular area.

the overwhelming support of the Bosnian Muslims and Croats, the Bosnian Serbs violently resisted integration into Bosnia, and a three-year war ensued. The EU had helped to trigger the referendum by imposing a deadline on the Yugoslav republics to request recognition as independent countries. [44]

In 1993, Czechoslovakia split into the Czech and Slovak republics even though no referendum was held, and opinion polls indicated most citizens wanted to keep the country together. [45] The split came about because the leading politicians decided in 1992 that a peaceful divorce was easier than negotiating a new constitution with the Czechs favoring a more centralized state and the Slovaks wanting more autonomy.

In August 1999 East Timor seceded from Indonesia after a U.N.-supervised referendum. East Timor's annexation by Indonesia in 1975 had never been recognized by the U.N., and the East Timorese were Catholic, unlike the predominantly Muslim Indonesians, since the area had been colonized by Portugal.

The path to independence was a bloody one. The Indonesian military supported anti-independence militias who killed some 1,400 Timorese, causing 300,000 to flee, and destroyed much of the country's infrastructure. Australian-led international peacekeepers helped restore order in September 1999, and Timor Leste became a U.N. member on Sept. 27, 2002. [46]

By contrast, the separatist movement in Aceh has never succeeded in gaining independence, despite a decades-long struggle. Instead, the Free Aceh Movement and the Indonesian government signed a peace treaty in 2005, granting Aceh autonomy. The rapprochement was facilitated by a feeling of solidarity that grew out of the December 2004 Indian Ocean tsunami, which killed more than 130,000 people in Aceh.

CURRENT SITUATION

Balkan Pandora's Box

The shock waves emanating from Kosovo's Feb. 17 declaration of independence show that separatism remains an explosive issue. For Prime Minister Hashim Thaçi, a former separatist guerrilla, "independence is everything for our country and our people. We sacrificed, we deserve independence, and independence of Kosovo is our life, it's our future." [47]

The Kosovars waited until Serbia's presidential elections were over before seceding in order to deny the more nationalistic Serb candidate, Tomislav Nikolic, the chance to make political hay out of the declaration. On Feb. 3, Nikolic narrowly lost to his more moderate opponent, Boris Tadić. Kosovo also deliberately made its declaration before Russia assumed the presidency of the U.N. Security Council on March 1, knowing that Moscow opposes its independence.

At this stage, few expect Serbia to launch a military offensive to take back Kosovo, given the strong NATO presence in the region. The Serbs instead are vowing to diplomatically freeze out any countries that recognize Kosovo. Russia's ambassador to the EU, Vladimir Chizhov, warned in February that such recognition would be "a thorn in our political dialogue." [48] This has not prevented more than 30 countries so far from endorsing Kosovo's independence, including the United States, Canada, Australia and much of Europe.

Some fear that recognizing Kosovo will open a Pandora's box of ethnically motivated separatism. For example, the ethnic Serbs in Bosnia and Herzegovina, who have already largely separated themselves from the rest of Bosnia by creating Republika Srpska, on Feb. 21 pledged to hold a referendum on secession. But the republic's chances of gaining acceptance as an independent country are slimmer than Kosovo's, because both the EU and the United States firmly oppose it.

Romania and Slovakia worry that their large Hungarian minorities could feel emboldened to demand more autonomy or even unification with Hungary. Hungarians in the Romanian region of Transylvania are already demanding that Romanian law recognize their ethnically based autonomy. [49]

Frozen Conflicts

Russia's heavy clampdown on separatists in Chechnya serves as a stark warning to other ethnic groups in the region with separatist leanings not to push for independence. The predominantly Muslim Chechens had managed to gain de facto independence from Moscow in their 1994-1996 war, but Russia recaptured the territory in 1999. Tens of thousands have been killed in these conflicts and hundreds of thousands displaced.

Ethnic violence has also spread to other neighboring republics in the North Caucasus like Dagestan, North Ossetia and Ingushetiya, where disparate rebel groups are fighting for more autonomy or independence. To prevent the Balkanization of Russia, the Putin government cracked down hard on the violence.

Meanwhile, the Central Asian republics of Kazakhstan, Tajikistan, Uzbekistan, Turkmenistan and Kyrgyzstan no longer are as economically integrated as they were during the Soviet era, fueling corruption. Reportedly officials routinely demand bribes from traders and workers seeking to move goods or personnel across the new borders. [50] Some of the new states, like Kyrgyzstan, are weak and at risk of fragmenting or being subsumed by their neighbors. [51]

Transdniestria, Nagorno-Karabakh, South Ossetia and Abkhazia remain unrecognized de facto states, since Moldova, Azerbaijan and Georgia all lack the military or economic strength to recapture the four breakaway territories. The long, narrow valley of Transdniestria — which has a population of Russians, Moldovans and Ukrainians — is "like a Brezhnev museum," according to a U.S. government official involved in reconciliation efforts there, referring to the Soviet leader from 1964 to 1982 whose regime was characterized by stagnation and repression. "It is a nasty place: the rulers repress the Moldovan language, and the economy is largely black market." And Georgia's two secessionist regions — South Ossetia and Abkhazia — are egged on by Russia, according to the State Department's Bryza.

These so-called frozen conflicts have produced "an impasse of volatile stability [where] nobody is happy but nobody is terribly unhappy either, and life goes on, as neither central state nor de facto states have collapsed," writes Dov Lynch, author of a book on the conflicts and director of the U.S. Institute for Peace project. Up to a million people have been displaced, standards of living have dropped as economies barely function, organized crime flourishes and a "profound sense of psychological isolation" prevails. [52]

In one of those ongoing conflicts, the militant Kurdish separatist organization, the PKK, has stepped up its violent campaign against Turkey, which has responded with a military strike into the PKK's base in northern Iraq. [53] The Kurds in northern Iraq already govern themselves. Some pragmatic Kurdish leaders feel their best solution would be to replicate this model in Iran, Syria and Turkey — where they do not have autonomy — instead of pushing for a single Kurdish state.

Meanwhile, the Israeli-Palestinian conflict seems to be edging towards a "two-state solution" under which the Palestinians would be given a state of their own in the West Bank and Gaza in exchange for acknowledgment of Israel's right to exist. However, the region's ongoing violence makes reaching a final agreement problematic.

In Africa, Somaliland looks to be creeping towards acceptance as a state, too. An African Union mission in 2005 concluded that Somaliland's case for statehood was "unique and self-justified" and not likely to "open a Pandora's box." Nevertheless, its neighbors continue to oppose recognizing it formally. [54]

Asian Disputes

The separatist movement in Sri Lanka remains strong. The Tamil Tigers run a de facto state in the northeast and are fiercely fighting the Sri Lankan government, which wants to regain control of the whole country. On Feb. 4 — the 60th anniversary of the country's independence — Sri Lankan President Mahinda Rajapaksa affirmed his commitment to "go forward as a single, unitary state." [55]

According to a Tamil activist who asked not to be identified, Sri Lanka is squeezing the Tamil-controlled area with an economic embargo and preventing international aid organizations from providing humanitarian supplies. Though Pakistan, India and China are helping the Sri Lankan government, the Tamils are holding onto their territory, he says, with the help of Tamils who have fled the country and are dispersed throughout the world. This "diaspora" community is providing funds for weapons that the guerrillas buy covertly from Asian governments, he says.

In Aceh, the 2005 self-rule pact with Indonesia "is working to some extent," according to a U.S. official in Indonesia. With rising crime, high unemployment, little trade with the outside world and little experience in spending public money, "the challenge for the ex-rebels is to become good governors. They need help from the international community," the official says.

Separatism in Taiwan received a blow in the January 2008 parliamentary and March 2008 presidential elections when the Kuomintang Party, which supports reunification with mainland China, trounced the separatist Democratic Progressive Party (DPP), which seeks U.N. membership for Taiwan. [56]

For its part, the United States continues to sit on the fence, reflecting the international community's ambivalence toward Taiwan. According to Susan Bremner, the State Department's deputy Taiwan coordinating adviser, the United States has "not formally recognized Chinese sovereignty over Taiwan and [has] not made any determination as to Taiwan's political status." [57] In the past, however, the United States has said that if China were to bomb or invade Taiwan, it would help defend the island. [58]

In western China, the Uyghurs continue to see their proportion of the population decline as more ethnic Chinese migrate there. Chinese tourists are flooding in, too, as visiting EU official Fearghas O'Beara recently discovered in Kashgar. "The city was as foreign to the Chinese as it was to me," he said. "At times I felt a bit uneasy as well-to-do Chinese people took copious photos of the 'natives' with their quaint habits and clothing." [59]

Eclipsing all these movements are the newest round of protests by Tibetans that began in March, the 49th anniversary of a failed uprising against Chinese rule in Tibet. Protesters in Lhasa on March 14 burned, vandalized and looted businesses of ethnic Chinese immigrants, venting their seething resentment over the wave of immigration that has turned Tibetans into a minority in their capital city. [60] The Tibetans say 99 people were killed, but the Chinese put the figure at 22. [61] Though the Chinese riot police were initially slow to respond, Beijing is now cracking down hard on the protesters. It also is keeping monks elsewhere confined to their monasteries and forcing them to denounce the Dalai Lama. China accuses the exiled leader of orchestrating the violence — calling him "a vicious devil" and a "beast in human form" — even though he has condemned the violence and advocates autonomy rather than outright independence for Tibet. [62]

Before the outbreak of violence, a Chinese Foreign Ministry spokesman had urged the Dalai Lama to drop his "splittist" efforts to attain "Tibetan independence" and do more for average Tibetans. "The Dalai clique repeatedly talks about Tibetan culture and the environment being ruined. But in fact, the Tibetan society, economy and culture have prospered," said spokesman Qin Gang. "The only thing destroyed was the cruel and dark serfdom rule, which the Dalai clique wanted to restore." [63]

The 72-year-old Dalai Lama, Tibet's leader for 68 years, commands enormous respect around the world, as evidenced by U.S. President George W. Bush's decision to telephone China's President Hu Jintao on March 26 to urge the Chinese government "to engage in substantive dialogue" with the Dalai Lama. [64]

Tension over China's suppression of the Tibetans is mounting as some countries consider calling for a boycott of the Beijing Olympics in August to show solidarity with the Tibetans. European foreign ministers, meeting in Brdo, Slovenia, on March 28-29, came out against an outright boycott of the games, although the leaders of France and the Czech Republic are threatening to boycott the opening ceremony. And on April 1, U.S. House Speaker Nancy Pelosi, D-Calif., urged President Bush to reconsider his plans to attend the opening ceremony if China continues to refuse talks with the Dalai Lama.

But Bush at the time was becoming entangled in yet another separatist controversy. Stopping in Ukraine on his way to a NATO summit in Romania, Bush said he supports Georgia's entry into NATO, which Russia opposes. If Georgia were to join the alliance, the NATO allies could be forced to support any future Georgian military efforts to retake South Ossetia and Abkhazia — also strongly opposed by Russia. That would put Georgia in the middle of the same geopolitical chess game that Kosovo found itself in. [65]

Secession in the Americas

Across the Americas, separatist movements are scarcer and weaker than in Europe, Africa and Asia. Perhaps the most significant is the recent flare-up in Bolivia, where the mainly European-descended lowlanders are pushing for greater regional autonomy and are even threatening secession. [66] They are wealthier than the mostly indigenous highlanders and fear that the centralization efforts of indigenous President Evo Morales will loosen the lowlanders' grip on Bolivia's natural resources. Already, Morales has proposed amending the constitution so that oil and gas revenues would be shared evenly across the country. [67]

There are also plans to redistribute a huge portion of Bolivia's land — beginning with its forests — to indigenous communities. Vice Minister of Lands Alejandro Almaraz, who is implementing the project, said recently the tension with the lowlanders was "very painful" and warned that "the east of Bolivia is ready to secede and cause a civil war" to thwart the government's redistribution plans. [68]

In the United States, separatism remains a marginal force, though the movement has never been more visible. "There are 36 secessionist organizations now at work," including in New Hampshire, Vermont, California, Washington state, Oregon and South Carolina, says Kirkpatrick Sale, director of the Middlebury Institute, a think tank on secessionism that he established in 2004.

In Texas, Larry Kilgore — a Christian-orientated secessionist who wants to enact biblical law — won 225,783 votes or 18.5 percent in the March 4 primary for Republican candidate to the U.S. Senate. [69] "If the United States is for Kosovo's independence, there is no reason why we should not be for Vermont's independence," says Sale. "The American Empire is collapsing. It is too big, corrupt and unequal to survive."

Some Native American tribes with limited self-government continue to push for more autonomy. For example, a group of dissident Lakota Indians traveled to Washington in December 2007 to deliver a declaration of independence to the State Department, which did not respond. [70]

OUTLOOK

Ethnocentric Separatism

The growing tendency to construct states along ethnic lines does not necessarily bode well for the future. French philosopher Ernest Renan's warning, delivered in the era of empires and grand alliances, has as much resonance today as it did in 1882: "Be on your guard, for this ethnographic politics is in no way a stable thing and, if today you use it against others, tomorrow you may see it turned against yourselves." [71]

"The Kosovo case is not unique despite the many claims to that effect by European and American diplomats," says Serwer at the United States Institute for Peace. "If people worry about it being a precedent, they should have ensured its future was decided by the U.N. Security Council. That would have created a good precedent for deciding such things." [72]

Though some might support the creation of a U.N. body for assessing separatist claims, U.N. member states would most likely fear it would only serve to give more publicity to separatist causes, writes American University self-determination expert Orentlicher. [73]

The two Western European regions most likely to become independent within the next 10 years are Scotland and Flanders, says Flemish nationalist Dauwen. As for Transdniestria, "the more time that passes, the more likely it will become independent, because the military will resist rejoining Moldova," says a U.S. official working to promote peace in Eastern Europe. The passage of time usually increases the survival odds of unrecognized states, because entrenched elites who profit from their existence fight to preserve them regardless of how politically or economically viable the states are. [74]

The probability of separatist movements morphing into new states also depends on who opposes them. Nagorno-Karabakh, for instance, is more likely to gain independence from Azerbaijan than Chechnya is from Russia because the Azeris are weaker than the Russians.

Political leadership is another factor. When hardliners and extremists rise to power it triggers separatist movements, while the emergence of moderates willing to share power can entice separatist regions to be peacefully and consensually reintegrated into the mother country.

Ethnocentric separatism may also fuel irredentism — annexation of a territory on the basis of common ethnicity. For instance, the Albanians in Macedonia, Kosovo and Albania may push to form a single, unitary state. Ethnic Hungarians living in Romania, Serbia and Slovakia may seek to forge closer links with Hungary; Somalis scattered across Somaliland, Kenya, Ethiopia and Djibouti might decide to form a "Greater Somalia."

"The goal of attaining recognition is the glue holding it together," a State Department official said about Somaliland. "If recognized, I fear that outside powers will interfere more, and it could split."

Likewise, Kurds in Iraq, Turkey, Iran and Syria could rise up and push for a "Greater Kurdistan" encompassing all Kurds. While some countries might support the creation of a Kurdish state in theory, they would be reticent, too, knowing how much it could destabilize the Middle East.

In Southeast Asia, Myanmar (formerly Burma), Thailand and the Philippines are potential separatist hotbeds as tensions persist between the many different ethnic groups, with religious differences further aggravating the situation. [75] "If something moves in the region, it could have a tsunami effect, as happened in Eastern Europe in 1989," says Busdachin at the Unrepresented Nations and Peoples Organization. He adds that most of these groups are seeking autonomy, not independence.

Yet a U.S. official in Indonesia says of Aceh: "I would be very surprised if we would have a new country in 15 years. I don't see that dynamic. Things are moving in the other direction."

And in Taiwan, any push for U.N. membership would worry trading partners like the European Union and the United States, which are keen to maintain good relations with the island but reluctant to anger China.

As for the United States, the strong federal government that emerged during the Great Depression seems to be on the wane as state and local governments increasingly assert their powers. Yet the nation remains well-integrated, and outright secession of a state or group of states seems unlikely. Smaller changes are possible, however, such as the splitting of California into northern and southern states or the evolution of the U.S.-governed Puerto Rico into a new U.S. state or independent country.

In the long term, separatism will fade, author Kaplan believes. "Separatism always appears on the rise when new states are born because such entities do not have the deep loyalties of their people typical of older, successful countries," he says. But as states mature, he notes, the number of separatist movements usually declines.

A starkly different prediction is made by Jerry Z. Muller, history professor at The Catholic University of America in Washington. "Increased urbanization, literacy and political mobilization; differences in the fertility rates and economic performance of various ethnic groups and immigration will challenge the internal structure of states as well as their borders," he wrote. "Whether politically correct or not, ethnonationalism will continue to shape the world in the 21st century." Globalization will lead to greater wealth disparities and deeper social cleavages, he continues, and "wealthier and higher-achieving regions might try to separate themselves from poorer and lower-achieving ones." Rather than fight the separatist trend, Muller argues, "partition may be the most humane lasting solution." [76]

NOTES

1. For detailed accounts of the protests, see *The Economist*, "Trashing the Beijing Road," March 19, 2008, www.economist.com/opinion/displaystory .cfm?story_id=10875823 and Tini Tran, "Tibetan Protests Escalate into Violence," The Associated Press, March 14, 2008, http://news.yahoo.com/s/ap /20080314/ap_on_re_as/china_tibet.

2. Ellie Tzortzi, "US outrage as Serb protesters burn embassy," Reuters, Feb. 21, 2008, www.reuters .com/article/worldNews/idUSL2087155420080221 ?pageNumber=1&virtualBrandChannel=0.

3. See "In quotes: Kosovo reaction," BBC News, Feb. 17, 2008, http://news.bbc.co.uk/1/hi/world/europe /7249586.stm.

4. See European Commission's Web site for political and economic profiles of Serbia and Kosovo, http://ec.europa.eu/enlargement/potential-candidate-countries/index_en.htm.

5. Selcan Hacaoglu and Christopher Torchi, "Turkey launches ground incursion into Iraq," The Associated Press, Feb. 22, 2008, www.washington times.com/apps/pbcs.dll/article?AID=/20080222 /FOREIGN/297026899/1001.

6. For list of current U.N. member states, see the U.N.'s Web site, www.un.org/members/list.shtml.

7. To see growth in U.N. membership, go to www.un .org/members/growth.shtml.

8. See "Kurdistan — Kurdish Conflict," globalsecurity .org, www.globalsecurity.org/military/world/war /kurdistan.htm.

9. Lisa Schlein, "East Timor Facing Food Crisis," June 24, 2007, www.voanews.com/english/archive/2007-06/2007-06-24-voa8.cfm?CFID=213682651&CF TOKEN=33049644.

10. Fried was testifying at a hearing on the Balkans at the U.S. House of Representatives Committee on Foreign Affairs, March 12, 2008. For full testimony go to: http://foreignaffairs.house.gov/testimony .asp?subnav=close.

11. Gary J. Bass, "Independence Daze," *The New York Times*, Jan. 6, 2008, www.nytimes.com/2008/01/06 /magazine/06wwln-idealab-t.html?ref=magazine.

12. Several Uyghurs were detained in the U.S. terrorist prison in Guantánamo Bay, Cuba. According to James Millward, history professor at Georgetown University, Washington, D.C., the Uyghurs' detention in Guantánamo became an embarrassment for the United States when it emerged they were pro-U.S. and anti-China. The U.S. administration decided it could not send them back to China because they would probably be mistreated. Although the United States asked more than 100 other countries to take them, all refused except Albania, where some of the detainees were ultimately expatriated in 2006.

13. Chinese Foreign Ministry spokesperson Qin Gang at press conference, March 18, 2008, www.china-embassy.org/eng/fyrth/t416255.htm.

14. Jay Shankar, "Pelosi Urges Probe of Chinese Claim Dalai Lama Behind Unrest," Bloomberg News,

March 21, 2008, www.bloomberg.com/apps /news?pid=20601101&sid=aDLLITUsmrIg&refer= japan.

15. Seth D. Kaplan, "Democratization in Post-Colonial States: The Triumph of a Societal-Based Approach in Somaliland," in *Fixing Fragile States: A new paradigm for development* (scheduled for publication July 2008).

16. Harvey Feldman, fellow in China policy for the Heritage Foundation, speaking at a discussion on Taiwanese elections in Washington, D.C., Jan. 15, 2008.

17. In November 2004, a group of about 50 secession-ists, gathered for a conference in Middlebury, Vt., signed a declaration pledging to develop cooperation between the various secessionist groups in the United States, including setting up a think tank, The Middlebury Institute, devoted to studying sepa-ratism, secessionism and self-determination. See www.middleburyinstitute.org.

18. Diane Orentlicher, "International Responses to Separatist Claims: Are Democratic Principles Relevant," Chapter 1 of Stephen Macedo and Allen Buchanan, eds., *Secession and Self-Determination* (2003), p. 29.

19. Interview with Nicolas Gros-Verheyde, "Europe should develop its defence policy with Russia," *Europolitics* (EU affairs subscription-based news ser-vice), March 4, 2008, www.europolitics.info.

20. Donald L. Horowitz, "A Right to Secede," Chapter 2 of Macedo and Buchanan, *op. cit.*, p. 50.

21. *Ibid.*, p. 73.

22. Basha was speaking at the Center for Strategic and International Studies in Washington, D.C., on May 5, 2007.

23. Lecture on Shanghai Cooperation Organization by Professor Akihiro Iwashita, visiting fellow at the Brookings Institution, delivered at the Woodrow Wilson International Center for Scholars, Feb. 2, 2008.

24. Jeremic was addressing the European Parliament's Foreign Affairs Committee in Strasbourg, Feb. 20, 2008. See the press release at www.europarl.europa .eu/sides/getDoc.do?pubRef=-//EP//TEXT+IM-PRESS+20080219IPR21605+0+DOC+XML+V0// EN&language=EN.

25. Horowitz, *op. cit.*, p. 56.

26. John J. Tkacik, "Dealing with Taiwan's Referendum on the United Nations," Heritage Foundation, Sept. 10, 2007, www.heritage.org/about/staff/JohnTkacik papers.cfm#2007Research.

27. Zoellick's remark, made at a U.S. congressional hearing on China on May 10, 2006, was quoted in John J. Tkacik, "America's Stake in Taiwan," Heritage Foundation, Jan. 11, 2007, www.heritage .org/Research/AsiaandthePacific/bg1996.cfm.

28. For background, see "Nationalist Movements in Western Europe," *Editorial Research Reports*, April 16, 1969, available at *CQ Researcher Plus Archive*, www.library.cqpress.com.

29. Adapted quote from Ernest Renan, French philoso-pher and theoretician on statehood and nationalism, in his discourse "What is a nation?" widely viewed as the definitive text on civic nationalism (1882).

30. For more details, see Mark E. Brandon, Chapter 10, "Secession, Constitutionalism and American Experience," Macedo and Buchanan, *op. cit.*, pp. 272-305.

31. The case is 74 U.S. 700 (1868), available at http: //caselaw.lp.findlaw.com/scripts/getcase.pl?court=US &vol=74&invol=700.

32. See Patricia Carley, "Self-Determination: Sovereignty, Territorial Integrity, and the Right to Secession," *Peaceworks 7*, March 1996, p. 3, www.usip.org/pubs /peaceworks/pwks7.html.

33. Orentlicher, *op. cit.*, p. 21.

34. For more details, see Washington Kurdish Institute, "The Territorial Status of Kirkuk," position paper, November 2007, http://71.18.173.106/pages/WO-PositionPapers.htm#.

35. For background, see Peter Katel, "Middle East Tensions," *CQ Researcher*, Oct. 27, 2006, pp. 898-903.

36. Figures taken from *The Statesman's Yearbook*, an annual reference book on the states of the world that first appeared in 1864, and from the U.N. Web site, www.un.org/members/list.shtml.

37. For full text of the 1960 U.N. Declaration on the Granting of Independence to Colonial Countries and Peoples, go to www.un.org/Depts/dpi/decolo nization/declaration.htm.

38. For background, see "Sri Lanka," *Political Handbook of the World*, CQ Press (2007).

39. According to the Central Tibetan Administration Web site, www.tibet.net/en/diir/chrono.html.

40. For background, see Mary H. Cooper, "Québec Sovereignty," *CQ Researcher*, Oct. 6, 1995, pp. 873-896.

41. Under Article 72 of the 1977 U.S.S.R. Constitution, "Each Union Republic retains the right freely to secede from the U.S.S.R," www.departments.buck nell.edu/russian/const/1977toc.html.

42. Mikhail Gorbachev and Odile Jacob, ed., *Avant Memoires* (1993), p. 30.

43. The 15 ex-Soviet states could have been 16. Karelia, a region now part of western Russia bordering Finland, used to be a separate Soviet republic until 1956 when its status was downgraded to an autonomous republic within Russia.

44. Orentlicher, *op. cit.*, p. 36.

45. *Ibid.*, p. 33.

46. See CIA, *The World Factbook*, https://www.cia.gov /library/publications/the-world-factbook/geos/tt.html.

47. Reported on CNN.com, Jan. 9, 2008, http://edi tion.cnn.com/2008/WORLD/europe/01/09/kosovo .independence/index.html.

48. Joanna Sopinska, "Russia in last-ditch bid to block Kosovo mission," *Europolitics* (EU affairs subscription-based news service), Feb. 7, 2008, www.europolitics .info.

49. See Medlir Mema, "Kosovo through Central European eyes," Jan. 2, 2008, Center for European Policy Analysis (CEPA), www.cepa.org/digest /kosovo-through-central-european-eyes.php.

50. From lecture by researchers Kathleen Kuehnast and Nora Dudwick at the Woodrow Wilson International Center for Scholars, Nov. 27, 2006.

51. From discussion with Professors Anthony Bowyer, Central Asia and Caucasus Program Manager at IFES, the International Foundation for Election Systems, Eric McGlinchey, associate professor at George Mason University, and Scott Radnitz, assistant professor at the University of Washington, at the School for Advanced International Studies, Dec. 12, 2007.

52. Dov Lynch, *Engaging Eurasia's Separatist States* (2004), pp. 91-93.

53. Al Jazeera, "Toll rises in Turkey-PKK conflict," http://english.aljazeera.net/NR/exeres/3E14DD15-F2D1-4C65-8148-5200DFB3E975.htm.

54. Kaplan, *op. cit.*

55. The president's speech can be viewed in English at www.priu.gov.lk/news_update/Current_Affairs/ca2 00802/20080204defeat_of_terrorism_is_victory_for _all.htm.

56. See "Opposition's Ma wins Taiwan poll," BBC News, March 22, 2008, http://news.bbc.co.uk/2/hi/asia-pacific/7309113.stm.

57. Letter from Susan Bremner, deputy Taiwan coordinating adviser at the U.S. State Department, June 26, 2007, quoted in article by Tkacik, "Dealing with Taiwan's Referendum on the United Nation," *op. cit.*

58. See Peter Brookes, "US-Taiwan Defense Relations in the Bush administration," Nov. 14, 2003, www.heritage .org/Research/AsiaandthePacific/hl808.cfm.

59. Travel diary of Fearghas O'Beara, media adviser to the president of the European Parliament, who toured the region in August 2007.

60. Jim Yardley, "As Tibet Erupted, China Security Forces Wavered," *The New York Times*, March 24, 2008, www.nytimes.com/2008/03/24/world/asia/24tibet .html?ex=1364097600&en=58a6edae8ae26676&ei= 5088&partner=rssnyt&emc=rss.

61. *Ibid.*

62. See "Chinese Crackdown on Tibetan Protests," "The Diane Rehm Show," National Public Radio, March 20, 2008, http://wamu.org/programs/dr/08 /03/20.php#19471; also see Pico Iyer, "A Monk's Struggle," *Time*, March 21, 2007, www.time.com /time/world/article/0,8599,1723922,00.html; also see Louisa Lim, "China's Provinces Feel Crush of Tibet Crackdown," National Public Radio, March 28, 2008, www.npr.org/templates/story/story.php ?storyId=89160575&ft=1&f=1004.

63. "China urges Dalai Lama to drop splittist attempts," Xinhua News Agency, March 11, 2008.

64. See White House press release at www.whitehouse .gov/news/releases/2008/03/20080326-2.html.

65. Joanna Sopinska, "Ministers condemn Tibet crackdown, reject Olympic boycott," *Europolitics*, March 31, 2008, www.europolitics.info. See Peter Baker, "Bush Pushes NATO Membership for Ukraine,

Georgia," *The Washington Post*, April 1, 2008.

66. See Kaplan, *op. cit.*, Chapter 9, "Bolivia: Building Representative Institutions in a Divided Country." Also see Roland Flamini, "The New Latin America," *CQ Global Researcher*, March 2008, pp. 57-84.

67. Flamini, *ibid.*, p. 79.

68. Almaraz was giving a presentation on his land reform proposals at the George Washington University in Washington on March 11, 2008.

69. Primary results posted on *The Austin Chronicle*'s Web site, www.austinchronicle.com/gyrobase/Issue /story?oid=oid%3A599906.

70. Bill Harlan, "Lakota group secedes from U.S." *Rapid City Journal*, Dec. 21, 2007, www.rapidcityjournal.com/articles/2007/12/21/news/local/doc476a99 630633e335271152.txt.

71. Renan, *op. cit.*

72. See Daniel Serwer, "Coming Soon to a Country Near You: Kosovo Sovereignty," *Transatlantic Thinkers*, December 2007, www.usip.org/pubs/usipeace_briefings/2007/1214_kosovo.html.

73. Orentlicher, *op. cit.*, p. 37.

74. Lynch, *op. cit.*, p. 119.

75. See Joseph Chinyong Liow, "Muslim Resistance in Southern Thailand and Southern Philippines: Religion, Ideology and Politics," East-West Center, Washington, 2006, www.eastwestcenter.org/fileadmin/stored/pdfs/PS024.pdf.

76. Jerry Z. Muller, "Us and Them: The Enduring Power of Ethnic Nationalism," *Foreign Affairs*, March/April 2008, www.foreignaffairs.org/20080 301faessay87203/jerry-z-muller/us-and-them.html.

BIBLIOGRAPHY

Books

Kaplan, Seth D., *Fixing Fragile States: A New Paradigm for Development*, Praeger Security International (forthcoming), 2008.
A business consultant who has founded successful corporations in Asia, Africa and the Middle East uses various case studies from around the world to analyze what makes states function and why they become dysfunctional.

Lynch, Dov, *Engaging Eurasia's Separatist States — Unresolved Conflicts and De Facto States*, United States Institute of Peace Press, 2004.
The director of a U. S. Institute of Peace project describes the "frozen conflicts" in the breakaway republics of Transdniestra, Nagorno Karabakh, South Ossetia and Abkhazia.

Macedo, Stephen, and Allen Buchanan, *Secession and Self-Determination: Nomos XLV*, New York University Press, 2003.
In a series of essays, different authors debate whether there should be a right to secede and analyze specific secessionist cases, notably Québec and the pre-Civil War Southern U.S. states.

Articles

"The Territorial Status of Kirkuk," Washington Kurdish Institute, November 2007, http://71.18.173 .106/pages/WO-PositionPapers.htm#.
The institute argues that Kirkuk should be unified with the Kurdish region of northern Iraq.

Mema, Medlir, "Kosovo Through Central European Eyes," Center for European Policy Analysis, Jan. 2, 2008, www.cepa.org/digest/kosovo-through-central-european-eyes.php.
A Balkans scholar explains how many of the countries near Kosovo that have sizeable ethnic minorities are wary of the precedent set by an independent Kosovo.

Muller, Jerry Z., "Us and Them: The Enduring Power of Ethnic Nationalism," *Foreign Affairs*, March/April 2008, pp. 18-35.
A professor of history at Catholic University argues in the magazine's cover story that ethnic nationalism will drive global politics for generations.

Ponnambalam, G. G., "Negotiation with Armed Groups: Sri Lanka and Beyond," Tufts University symposium, April 6, 2006, http://fletcher.tufts.edu /news/2006/04/ponnambalam.shtml.
An academic paper by a member of the Sri Lankan parliament charts the unsuccessful efforts by the Sri Lankan authorities and Tamil separatists to end their conflict.

Renan, Ernst, "What is a Nation?" March 11, 1882, www.tamilnation.org/selfdetermination/nation/renan .htm.
This classic lecture by a French philosopher and theoretician on statehood and nationalism at the Sorbonne University in Paris is viewed as the definitive text on civic nationalism.

Serwer, Daniel, "Coming Soon to a Country Near You: Kosova Sovereignty," *Bertelsmann Stiftung Transatlantic Thinkers series,* **December 2007, www.usip.org/pubs /usipeace_briefings/2007/1214_kosovo.html.**
A conflict resolution expert argues for Kosovo's independence.

Tkacik, John J., "Dealing with Taiwan's Referendum on the United Nations," Heritage Foundation, Sept. 10, 2007, www.heritage.org/about/staff/JohnTkacikpapers .cfm#2007Research.
A China policy scholar assesses how the international community should respond to the ongoing campaign by Taiwanese separatists to obtain a U.N. seat for Taiwan.

Reports and Studies

Carley, Patricia, "Self-Determination: Sovereignty, Territorial Integrity, and the Right to Secession," United States Institute of Peace, Peaceworks 7, March 1996, www.usip.org/pubs/peaceworks/pwks7.html.
A conflict resolution expert outlines the main issues in the self-determination debate, including the uncertainty over what the right entails and who is entitled to claim it.

Gutierrez, Eric, and Saturnino Borras, Jr., "The Moro Conflict: Landlessness and Misdirected State Policies," East-West Center Washington, 2004, www .eastwestcenter.org/fileadmin/stored/pdfs/PS008.pdf.
The authors explain how resentment over not having control of their land has fueled separatism among the Muslim Moros in the southern Philippines.

Millward, James, "Violent Separatism in Xinjiang: A critical assessment," East-West Center Washington, 2004, www.eastwestcenter.org/fileadmin/stored/pdfs /PS006.pdf.
A history professor at Georgetown University in Washington highlights the plight of the Uyghurs, a Turkic people living in western China, where separatist tensions are simmering.

Schulze, Kirsten E., "The Free Aceh Movement: Anatomy of a Separatist Organization," East-West Center Washington, 2004, www.eastwestcenter.org /fileadmin/stored/pdfs/PS002.pdf.
A senior history lecturer at the London School of Economics discusses the history of the separatist movement in the Indonesian province of Aceh since 1976. The paper was published just prior to the brokering of a peace agreement in 2005.

For More Information

Center for Strategic and International Studies, 1800 K St., N.W., Washington, DC 20006; (202) 887-0200; www.csis .org. Think tank focused on regional stability, defense and security.

Centre for the Study of Civil War, P.O. Box 9229 Grønland, NO-0134, Oslo, Norway; +47 22 54 77 00; www.prio.no/cscw. An autonomous center within the International Peace Research Institute, Oslo, that studies why civil wars break out, how they are sustained and what it takes to end them.

Commission on Security and Co-operation in Europe (Helsinki Commission), 234 Ford House Office Building, Washington, DC 20515; (202) 225-1901; www.csce.gov. An independent agency of the U.S. government created to promote democracy, human rights and economic development.

European Free Alliance, Woeringenstraat 19, 1000 Brussels, Belgium; +32 (0)2 513-3476; www.e-f-a.org/home.php. A political alliance consisting of regionalist and nationalist parties in Europe seeking greater autonomy for regions and ethnic minorities through peaceful means.

Middlebury Institute, 127 East Mountain Road, Cold Spring, NY 10516; (845) 265-3158; http://middleburyin-stitute.org. Studies separatism, self-determination and devolution, with a strong focus on the United States.

United Nations Observer Mission in Georgia, 38 Krtsanisi St., 380060 Tbilisi, Georgia; (+995) 32 926-700; www.unomig.org; Established by the U.N. in 1993 to verify that the Georgian and Abkhaz authorities are complying with their ceasefire agreement.

United States Institute of Peace, 1200 17th St., N.W., Washington, DC 20036; (202) 457-1700; www.usip.org. An independent agency funded by Congress to prevent and resolve violent international conflicts and to promote post-conflict stability and development.

Unrepresented Nations and Peoples Organization, P.O. Box 85878, 2508 CN The Hague, the Netherlands; +31 (0)70 364-6504; www.unpo.org. An umbrella organization that promotes self-determination for various indigenous peoples, occupied nations, ethnic minorities and unrecognized states.

Washington Kurdish Institute, 611 4th St., S.W., Washington, DC 20024; (202) 484-0140; http://71.18 .173.106. Promotes the rights of Kurdish people and awareness of Kurdish issues.

VOICES FROM ABROAD

Anatoly Safonov

Deputy foreign minister, Russia

Recognition of Kosovo a potential security threat

"We should not forget that jihadists of terror, who lived a semi-legal life, have settled in Kosovo and in other places since the active phase of the Balkans campaign. However, at the same time, they have kept in touch with al-Qa'idah and other terrorist structures. If Kosovo is recognized, these forces will receive a signal to emerge from the underground. We shall see if our partners adhere to their principles regarding this underground."

Interfax News Agency, February 2008

Vladimir Putin

President, Russia

Putin challenges double standard for Kosovo

"I don't want to say anything that would offend anyone, but for 40 years northern Cyprus has practically had independence. Why aren't you recognizing that? Aren't you ashamed, Europeans, for having these double standards?"

The Guardian (England), February 2008

Zhang Qingli

Communist Party leader, Tibet

Tibetan communists challenge separatist Dalai Lama

"We are currently in an intensely bloody and fiery struggle with the Dalai Lama clique, a life or death struggle with the enemy. . . . As long as we . . . remain of one heart, turn the masses into a walled city and work together to attack the enemy, then we can safeguard social stability and achieve a full victory in this intense battle against separatism."

Canberra Times (Australia), March 2008

Dalha Tsering

Campaign coordinator, Tibetan Community in Britain

Dalai Lama holds back Tibetan violence

"China is one of the most powerful countries in the world, yet it is afraid of one person, and that's the Dalai Lama. He is the only person holding Tibetans from turning violent and confrontational. When his holiness goes, nobody can predict where the situation will go."

Los Angeles Times, March 2008

George Fitzherbert

Tibet scholar, Oxford University

China exacerbates Tibet's frustrations

"Tibetans are rapidly and reluctantly becoming a minority in their own ancestral homelands, in much the same way as Mongolians have already become an almost negligible minority in the equally "autonomous" Chinese province of Inner Mongolia. . . . [By] demonising the Dalai Lama and refusing to compromise an inch on Tibetan aspirations, the Chinese will inevitably exacerbate the already fractious ethnic relations in this vast area of western China."

www.opendemocracy.net/article/ china/democracy_power/tibet_history_china_power, March 2008

Karma Chophel

Speaker, Tibet Parliament-in-Exile

Beware of propaganda

"They [China] use propaganda hoping to fool the world, so we must consider our actions with caution. . . . China is ready to label Tibetans as terrorists in order to win international blessing for their actions. . . . Those who know the true fact of the matter know that this is a genuine outcry and outburst over Chinese misrule."

Agence France-Presse, March 2008

David Miliband

Foreign Secretary, Great Britain

The last piece of the puzzle

"There is a very strong head of steam building among a wide range of countries that do see [Kosovo] as the last piece of the Yugoslav jigsaw and don't see stability in the western Balkans being established without the aspirations of the Kosovar people being respected."

The Associated Press, February 2008

Arcadio Esquivel, *La Prensa*, Panama

3

U.S. Policy on Iran

Peter Katel

Iranian women demonstrate in support of the country's nuclear development program at the uranium conversion facility in Isfahan, about 250 miles south of Tehran. Contrary to U.S. claims, Iran says the program is for peaceful uses of nuclear energy.

From *CQ Researcher*, November 16, 2007.

W hile U.S. troops fight in Iraq, the Bush administration is waging a war of words with neighboring Iran. Bad blood has existed between Washington and Tehran for nearly three decades. But the verbal conflict is getting so intense that even Middle East experts — long accustomed to pugnacious rhetoric — say bullets could start flying.

At issue are Iran's nuclear development efforts and its perceived military support of Iraqi insurgents. Washington says Iran is seeking to develop nuclear weapons, but Iranian President Mahmoud Ahmadinejad says the program is for peaceful uses.

In October, President George W. Bush said he had "told people that if you're interested in avoiding World War III, it seems like you ought to be interested in preventing [Iran] from having the knowledge necessary to make a nuclear weapon." [1]

For his part, Ahmadinejad calls the United States an international bully intent on keeping Iraq violent to justify continued occupation.

"No day passes without people [in Iraq] being killed, wounded or displaced," Ahmadinejad said during an address to the U.N. General Assembly in September. "And the occupiers not only refuse to be accountable and ashamed of their adventure, but speak in a report of a new market for their armaments as a result of their military adventure."

"We're in a serious and dangerous situation," says Bruce Riedel, a senior fellow at the Brookings Institution's Saban Center for Middle East Policy, a centrist think tank. "We'd be better served by lowering the rhetoric."

Meanwhile, hundreds of U.S. troops in Iraq have been killed by sophisticated roadside bombs that Bush and his top military commanders say are coming from Iran, which denies supplying them.

A Major Presence in the Middle East

Heartland of the ancient Persian Empire, Iran is the biggest non-Arab country in the Middle East. It has the biggest Shiite population of any nation and the only officially Shiite constitution in the world. It also maintains the region's biggest military force and is among the world's top petroleum producers.

Iran at a Glance

Population: 65.4 million (July 2007 est.)

Population below poverty line: 40% (2002 est.); Per capita GDP: $8,700

Religion: Muslim 98% (Shiite 89%, Sunni 9%); Other 2% (includes Zoroastrian, Jewish, Christian and Baha'i)

Gross domestic product: $222.9 billion (2006)

Military expenditures: 4.5% of GDP (2005)

Percentage of world's total proven oil reserves: 10%

Ranking among OPEC crude oil producers: No. 2 at 3.8 million barrels per day (Saudi Arabia is No. 1, at 9.2 million)

Natural gas reserves: 974 trillion cubic ft., second-highest in world after Russia (1,680 trillion cubic ft.)

Total military manpower: 545,000 (next highest in the region: Saudi Arabia, 199,500)

Sources: CIA *World Factbook*, updated Nov. 1, 2007; Anthony Cordesman and Martin Kleiber, "Iran's Military Forces and Warfighting Capabilities: The Threat in the Northern Gulf," Center for Strategic and International Studies, 2007; Energy Information Administration, Department of Energy; *Political Handbook of the World, 2007*

Amid the fighting and the fighting words, a glimmer of hope appeared in November. Lt. Gen. Raymond T. Odierno, second in command in Iraq behind Gen. David Petraeus, told reporters on Nov. 1 the number of attacks involving deadly EFPs (explosively formed penetrators) had dropped from 177 in July and August to 105 in September and October.

Defense Secretary Robert M. Gates said Iran had promised to clamp down on shipment of EFPs. "I don't know whether to believe them," Gates said. "I'll wait and see." [2]

Some of the skepticism grows out of Iran's reported role in a 33-day war last year between Israel — America's key Middle East ally — and Lebanon's Hezbollah militia, which was created and armed by Iran. Ahmadinejad has expressed the hope that Israel would be wiped off the map, much as the Soviet Union disappeared. "Was it done through war?" he asked at a September news conference at the United Nations. "No. It was through the voice of the people." [3]

Three weeks later, Bush made his "World War III" remark. And four days after that Vice President Dick Cheney called Iran "the world's most active state sponsor of terror," adding: "The Iranian regime needs to know that if it stays on its present course, the international community is prepared to impose serious consequences. The United States joins other nations in sending a clear message: We will not allow Iran to have a nuclear weapon." [4]

The White House followed the tough talk with new economic sanc-

Iran Ranks Among World Leaders in Energy

Iran ranks third in proven oil reserves, with nearly 140 billion barrels; world leader Saudi Arabia has almost twice as much (left). Iran has nearly a quadrillion cubic feet of natural gas reserves, second only to Russia (right).

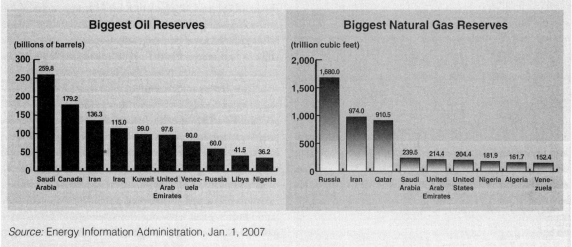

Source: Energy Information Administration, Jan. 1, 2007

tions designed to halt or slow down business transactions for anyone doing business with banks or other companies linked to the Iranian Revolutionary Guard, a military and covert-action agency long accused of supporting and aiding terrorism in the region.

What will the future bring? If past relations between the two countries are a guide, it will be a bumpy ride. In 1953 the United States orchestrated a coup against a nationalist Iranian prime minister, throwing its weight behind the country's pro-Western monarch, Shah Mohammed Reza Pahlavi. The United States, like the then-new state of Israel, saw Iran — successor to the ancient Persian Empire — as a key ally in a dangerous neighborhood. Iran, like other Middle Eastern nations, was Muslim. But Iranians are not Arabs and were seen as distant from the Israeli-Arab confrontation. In 1979 a revolution toppled the shah and installed the anti-American, anti-Israel theocracy that now rules Iran. Since then, U.S.-Iranian relations have been schizophrenic — marked by the 1979-81 hostage crisis involving 52 U.S. Embassy personnel in Tehran but also by quiet cooperation during the U.S.-led invasion of Afghanistan.

Tension has been climbing since Ahmadinejad launched himself globally as a challenger to American power following his election as president in 2005. Yet his real power largely is limited to economic policy. Under Iran's constitu-

tion, a clergyman, elected by a clerical Assembly of Experts, has the last word in all major affairs of state. Only the supreme leader, for instance, can declare war. [5]

Despite the confusing division of power, hawks argue that one thing is clear about the Iranian government: It wants to destroy the United States and Israel. "We're under attack; they're at war with us," says Michael A. Ledeen, who holds the title of "freedom scholar" at the conservative American Enterprise Institute and is the author of a new book on Iran. [6] "They're killing Americans [in Iraq] and intend to kill as many as they can. They want to destroy us." [7]

Other foreign-policy watchers deride such arguments as war-mongering fantasy. "Iran has an economy the size of Finland's and an annual defense budget of around $4.8 billion," wrote Fareed Zakaria, editor of *Newsweek International,* in a widely discussed column. "It has not invaded a country since the late 18th century. The United States has a GDP that is 68 times larger and defense expenditures that are 110 times greater." [8]

Hawks and doves alike place great importance on the survival of Iran's pro-democracy/human rights community, or "civil society." Its members have always risked prison and torture, but increased repression this year is causing renewed alarm. Among other moves, the gov-

A police patrol boat guards the Neka oil terminal on the Caspian Sea on Iran's northern coast. Despite its huge petroleum reserves, Iran has a faltering economy and an 11 percent unemployment rate.

ernment imprisoned several visiting Iranian-American professionals on suspicion of trying to help the Bush administration topple the government. Iran acted after the administration created a $75 million fund to promote civil society in Iran, in part by supporting pro-democracy organizations.

The unintended consequence of that support, some exiled dissidents and their American allies say, is to validate the Iranian government's contention that opposition members are American stooges. "Any Iranian who seeks American dollars will not be recognized as a democrat by his or her fellow citizens," Akbar Ganji, one of Iran's leading democracy activists, wrote in an op-ed in October. "Iran's democratic movement does not need foreign handouts." [9]

U.S. hawks argue that blaming the Bush administration for the latest crackdown ignores history. Iran's government, they point out, was jailing and torturing dissidents long before Bush took office. And, Ledeen says, the dissidents represent Iran's future, so helping them makes more sense than bombing a nuclear site.

In fact, few experts advocate military action. "There's a remarkable consensus across Washington about what the consequences would be," says Michael Rubin, a hawkish American Enterprise Institute scholar who lived in Iran in 1999 and speaks Farsi. "I don't know anyone who thinks a strike is a good idea." Military action, he says, likely would rally Iranians to the government's side. Systematic attacks against U.S. forces in Iraq could also be expected, as could sabotage of oil export facilities in the Persian Gulf, further driving up petroleum prices. [10]

But prominent neoconservative * Norman Podhoretz does advocate air strikes against Iran's nuclear research sites. The United States has "only one terrible choice, which is either to bomb those facilities and retard their program or even cut it off altogether or allow them to go nuclear," said Podhoretz, editor-at-large of *Commentary* magazine." [11]

Podhoretz insisted that Ahmadinejad is today's version of Adolf Hitler. "If we allow Iran to get the bomb," he argued, "people 50 years from now will look back at us the way we look back at the men who made the Munich Pact with Hitler in 1938 and say, 'How could they have let this happen?' "

Most experts scoff at such analogies, despite Iran's hostility to Israel. "The idea that Iran presents to the region and world a threat as big as Hitler's is absurd," says Iranian-born historian Shaul Bakhash of George Mason University, who is Jewish. "Iran is very unlikely to get involved in military adventures abroad."

Israel's reported bombing on Sept. 6 of a possible nuclear site in Syria — an Iranian ally — has fueled fears of U.S. designs on Iran. But even experts concerned about a U.S. attack worry more about the impact of the Iraq War. "I think the president is telling the truth when he says he doesn't intend to bomb," says Riedel, a former Middle East policy director at the National Security Council. "But the war by proxy we're fighting with Iran

---

* "Neoconservative," or neocon, originally referred to a small band of left-wing writers and academics who jumped to the Republican Party in the 1970s and '80s. It now is applied broadly, usually pejoratively, to strongly pro-Israel supporters of the Bush administration.

in Iraq could escalate unpredictably because of events on the ground."

As tension mounts, here are some of the issues being debated:

Would a nuclear-armed Iran endanger the United States?

Concern about Iran's nuclear development program had been simmering for several years. Worries heated up after Ahmadinejad's election in 2005. But the country's nuclear ambitions actually predate the 1979 revolution that led to the Islamic Republic.

Shortly before his overthrow, the shah had been hoping to obtain reactors and other nuclear technology from the United States, his closest ally. Nuclear-generated power would allow Iran to sell more of its oil abroad, bringing in more much-needed revenue. Today, the Islamic Republic — created by the same men who toppled the shah — justifies its nuclear program on the same grounds. [12]

Iranian officials have declared repeatedly their nuclear program excludes plans for any weapons. "We consider the acquiring, development and use of nuclear weapons inhuman, immoral, illegal and against our basic principles," Deputy Foreign Minister G. Ali Khoshroo said in 2003. [13]

To be sure, Khoshroo served in the administration of reformist President Mohammed Khatami. But his successor, Ahmadinejad, sounded the same note. "We are not after an atomic bomb because it is not useful, and our religion does not allow us to have it," he says on his Web site. [14]

In addition, Iran's alternately compliant and defiant dealings with the international nuclear regulatory system — even before Ahmadinejad's rise — have led experts with connections to the Bush administration to be deeply skeptical of Iran's objectives. "Iran has too often dictated the pace of diplomatic progress, giving the impression that it is playing for time," David Albright, president of the Institute for Science and International Security, wrote in 2004. The apparent aim was to stall the regulatory process until its nuclear facilities were up and running, Albright and a colleague wrote. [15]

So widespread are suspicions, in fact, that even critics of the Bush administration's war talk assume Iran's nuclear program is designed to produce weapons. Retired Gen. John Abizaid, former U.S. commander in the Middle East, faced the issue head-on during a talk in Washington last September. "There are ways to live with a nuclear Iran," he said. "Let's face it, we lived with a nuclear Soviet Union; we've lived with a nuclear China; we're living with other nuclear powers as well." [16]

The American Enterprise Institute's Rubin, among the most prominent advocates of a tough policy on Iran, bluntly rejects Abizaid's thesis: "I think he's wrong."

But Rubin isn't worried about nuclear war. Instead, he argued, nuclear weapons will block any attempts to force Iran to play by international rules. He cited a bombing raid by Turkish warplanes on Iranian territory in 1999, apparently aimed at punishing Iran for sheltering a Kurdish guerrilla organization that had been attacking Turkish troops for years. "After that, Iran stopped sheltering them," Rubin says. "But if Iran has a nuclear deterrent, no one is going to risk correcting its behavior." [17]

Brookings' Riedel, the former Middle East policy director at the National Security Council, says the United States has numerous options for pressuring Iran. "I do not see evidence from Iranian behavior over the last 30 years that this is a crazy state," he says. "Iran's behavior shows an understanding of the limits of its capability." He cites fighting between the United States and Iran during the 1980-88 Iran-Iraq War, when U.S. forces were protecting shipping in the Persian Gulf from Iranian attacks. "In the end, they chose to stop the conflict and to de-escalate," he says.

The question of whether Iran is a fundamentally rational power is crucial to the debate over nuclear intentions. True, deterrence worked against America's adversary in the Cold War, says the American Enterprise Institute's Ledeen, a former National Security Council consultant during the Reagan administration. But, he adds, "The Soviet Union was not governed by insane millenarian fanatics. The [Iranian government] wants to rule the world."

"Millenarian" signifies a belief in an approaching end of days, or change on a cataclysmic scale. For many Shiites, including Ahmadinejad, the return of the holy, historic figure known as the Mahdi, or the "Hidden Imam," would herald such a period. "With his 'second coming' there will be a reign of justice until the return of Jesus" — a revered figure to all Muslims — "at which time the world will end," writes Vali Nasr, a political scientist at Tufts University who specializes in the Shiite world. [18]

But Nasr also argues that the key to the future of the Middle East is the evolution of the historic Shiite-Sunni rivalry. And *Newsweek*'s Zakaria, in a television debate with Podhoretz, noted that past communist dictators had their own version of millenarianism that was just as terrifying, on paper — but not in reality — as

Ahmadinejad Takes Aim at the United States

Tough talk is the president's specialty.

Mahmoud Ahmadinejad may be only 5'2" tall, but he looms large as the embodiment of U.S., Israeli and European fears about Iran and its state ideology of religion-laced nationalism.

Seemingly on any given day, if the Iranian president isn't questioning whether the Holocaust occurred, he's accusing the United States of deliberately keeping Iraq unstable to justify the war or defying international nuclear watchdogs.

"Nations and countries don't have to obey the injustice of certain powers," Ahmadinejad told the U.N. General Assembly on Sept. 26, unmistakably referring above all to the United States. "These powers . . . have lost the competence to lead the world because of their hideous acts." And, he went on: "I officially declare that the age of relations arising from the Second World War, as well as materialistic thoughts based on arrogance and domination, is well over now. Humanity has passed a perilous precipice, and the age of monotheism, purity, affinity, respecting others, justice and true peace loving has commenced." [1]

Ahmadinejad's bill of particulars against the United States and its Western allies includes the creation of Israel, their responsibility for poverty and disease in poor countries and the global arms race.

To be sure, any number of developing-nation leaders — including other Iranian presidents — have leveled similar accusations. But Ahmadinejad's talent for provocative oratory, coupled with his position — albeit largely symbolic — as head of a major oil power, has amplified his voice.

Yet, by all accounts, the former mayor of Tehran owes his 2005 election to the presidency less to his international stands than to the political identity he carved out as the voice of the little man hammered by economic problems. Born in 1956, Ahmadinejad is the son of a blacksmith and a veteran of the horrific eight-year war with Iraq. Afterwards, overcoming many hardships, he earned a doctorate in civil engineering. [2]

"Most people voted for Ahmadinejad because he promised they would never have to feel sad again on New Year's Eve in front of their children," Farshid Bakhtieri, a young computer salesman, said in February. [3]

But those promises haven't been fulfilled, Bakhtieri added. Iranians complain they aren't getting the benefits of Iran's status as a major oil power, as the 11.5 percent official jobless rate indicates. And in June, government-imposed gasoline rationing ignited rioting in Tehran and other cities. Although it has the world's third-largest reserves of oil, Iran has built an insufficient number of refineries to produce enough gasoline — which it provides at low, subsidized rates — to meet growing domestic demand. Thus, the country depends heavily on imports,

Ahmadinejad's. Zakaria quoted the late Chinese ruler, Mao Zedong: "If the worst came to worst and half of mankind died, the other half would remain, while imperialism would be razed from the ground." [19]

Trita Parsi, president of the National Iranian American Council, which advocates a diplomatic resolution of U.S.-Iran tensions, argues that Iran's claim of a peaceful purpose for its nuclear development program is accurate — though weapon construction may be on the agenda as well. If the latter succeeded, he says, the existence of the U.S. and Israeli nuclear deterrent will prevent nuclear war. "Coexistence is possible," he says. "The Iranians are deterrable." Parsi is also author of a new book chronicling the post-revolutionary relationship between Iran, the United States and Israel. [20]

Does U.S. support help pro-democracy dissidents influence Iran's policies?

President Ahmadinejad's frequently bellicose speeches may suggest Iran is ruled, and populated, by religious, revolutionary fanatics. But the country's cadre of human-rights campaigners, labor-union organizers, student activists and investigative journalists is bigger than one might think. "Iranian society has refused to be coerced into silence," wrote Shirin Ebadi, a human-rights lawyer who won the Nobel Peace Prize in 2003. "Human-rights discourse is alive and well at the grass-roots level; civil-society activists consider it to be the most potent framework for achieving sustainable democratic reforms and political pluralism." [21]

Ebadi received the Nobel Prize at the moment when expectations of change reached their highest point in

which require cash outlays. Rationing was designed to reduce Iran's gasoline import payments if international sanctions over the country's disputed nuclear-development activities restrict access to cash. [4]

But average Iranians had little sympathy for the government's rationing strategy. "We live on an ocean of oil," said Kambiz Rahmati, 25, an electronics engineer. "Why should we pay a high price for gasoline or suffer rationing?" [5]

Some Iranian pro-democracy activists tie Ahmadinejad's economic failures to his aggressiveness in the international arena. Indeed, says an exiled dissident, the president might see it in his interest to bait the United States into military action over Iran's insistence on building nuclear facilities. "Limited war would give a good excuse to accuse the foreign states — 'it's their fault that the Iranian economy has problems,' " says Ali Afshari, an exiled student leader who spent nearly three years in prison. "Second, he would use this for a complete militarization of the country, and suppress all dissident activities."

But Iran's supreme leader, Ayatollah Ali Khamenei, doubts even a limited U.S. strike against Iran's nuclear facilities would be strategically advantageous, Afshari theorizes. And Khamenei's opinion counts: Only he can declare war or command the military. [6]

But Khamenei makes few public comments these days. Ahmadinejad has come to be seen as the man in charge because he issues a steady stream of commentary on hot-button issues. About the Holocaust, for instance, he shocked listeners when he said last year: "I will only accept something as truth if I am actually convinced of it." In 2001, Khamenei got only sparse attention when he said Zionists had been "fabricating figures related to the Holocaust." [7]

Such statements don't surprise Shaul Bakhash, an Iranian-born historian at George Mason University in Fairfax, Va. "These statements are not as new as people seem to imagine," he says.

In fact, points out Michael Rubin, a resident scholar at the American Enterprise Institute, Iran's nuclear program has been around much longer than Ahmadinejad. "The presidency in Iran is about style, not substance."

---

[1] Address to 62nd U.N. General Assembly, Sept. 26, 2007, www.president.ir/en/.

[2] See Nazila Fathi, "Blacksmith's Son Emphasized His Modest Roots," *The New York Times*, June 26, 2005, p. A11. See also "Iran-Iraq War (1980-1988)," globalsecurity.org, undated, www.globalsecurity.org/military/world/war/iran-iraq.htm.

[3] Quoted in Kim Murphy, "Iran reformists want U.S. to tone it down," *Los Angeles Times*, Feb. 11, 2007, p. A1.

[4] See Ramin Mostaghim and Borzou Daragahi, "Gas rationing in Iran ignites anger, unrest," *Los Angeles Times*, June 28, 2007, p. A5; Najmeh Bozorgmehr, "Iran pushes on with fuel rationing in face of riots," *Financial Times* (London), June 28, 2007, p. A7. Also see Peter Behr, "Energy Nationalism," *CQ Global Researcher*, July 2007, pp. 151-180.

[5] Quoted in *Los Angeles Times*, ibid.

[6] See Ray Takeyh, *Hidden Iran: Paradox and Power in the Islamic Republic* (2006), pp. 24-25.

[7] Quoted in Christopher De Bellaigue, "Hanging of 'CIA Spy' Dents Iran's Overtures to U.S.," *The Independent* (London), May 24, 2001, p. A19. Ahmadinejad quoted in Michael Slackman, "Deep Roots of Denial for Iran's True Believer," *The New York Times*, Dec. 14, 2006, p. A3.

---

recent years, during the term of reformist President Khatami. Under Ahmadinejad, those hopes have dimmed.

A crackdown that intensified this year included enforcement of the religious code against revealing clothing, including scanty head scarves on women and tight shirts on men. "Those who damage the system under any guise will be punished," Intelligence Minister Gholamhossein Mohseni Ejei warned in April. He accused the civil society movement of conspiring to topple the government. [22]

Controversy over direct American aid for Iranian dissidents leapt to the top of the agenda in 2006, when Secretary of State Condoleezza Rice asked Congress for $75 million to fund activities that included expanding Farsi-language news broadcasts into Iran — and support for Iranian civil-society groups. "The United States will actively confront the policies of this Iranian regime, and at the same time we are going to work to support the aspirations of the Iranian people for freedom in their own country," Rice told the Senate Foreign Relations Committee. Congress granted the request. The administration is now asking for the same amount in 2008. [23]

Debate over the usefulness of the money has been raging since the first request, with most supporters of Iranian civil-society groups opposed to the funding. Human Rights Watch is among several groups lobbying against the program as the House and Senate Appropriations committees negotiate the funding. "Iranian activists don't want it and can't get it," Saman Zarifi, Washington advocate for Human Rights Watch,

Haleh Esfandiari, left, appears on Iranian television after her arrest early last year in Tehran. The Middle East Program director of the Woodrow Wilson International Center for Scholars in Washington spent eight months in jail along with several other U.S. pro-democracy activists. She was released in September 2007. Ali Afshari, a former student human-rights activist, spent most of 2000-2003 in prison, where he endured torture and 400 days of solitary confinement.

said in October. "Second, it supports Iranian government efforts to cast activists as foreign agents." [24]

Earlier in the year, Iran added fuel to the conflict by arresting four visiting American human-rights supporters: Haleh Esfandiari, Middle East Program director of the Woodrow Wilson International Center for Scholars in Washington; Kian Tajbakhsh, an urban planner who had been a consultant to the Open Society Institute of the New York-based Soros Foundation; Parnaz Azima, a reporter for Radio Farda, the Persian-language arm of Radio Free Europe/Radio Liberty; and Ali Shakeri, 59, a mortgage broker and a founding board member of the Center for Citizen Peacebuilding at the University of California, Irvine. After solitary confinement and frequent interrogation, the four were freed. [25]

Iranian citizens, however, have spent years in prison. Ali Afshari, a former student human-rights activist, spent most of 2000-2003 in prison, where he told *CQ Researcher*, he endured 400 days of solitary confinement. He now lives in the United States and is a doctoral student in engineering.

Afshari says U.S. support for the Iranian human-rights movement should be limited to programs that remain within U.S. borders. "In Iranian political culture, it's taboo for any organization to get money from any foreign state," he says. "It harms civil society because the government uses it as an excuse to repress."

Some advocates of tough U.S. action against the Iranian government cite the crackdown as evidence of an urgent necessity for financing as many Iranian pro-democracy organizations as possible. The American Enterprise Institute's Rubin says the arrest of Esfandiari and the other Iranian-Americans shows a government feeling weak. "Governments with self-confidence about their peoples' attitudes don't arrest 67-year-old grandmothers," he says, referring to Esfandiari.

The apparent insecurity begs to be exploited, Rubin argues. As for Afshari's view — which is widely echoed — that U.S. funding would provide a rationale for more repression — Rubin notes that repression is a longstanding tradition in the Islamic Republic. "It's safe to say that crackdowns happened long before democracy funding was an issue," he says.

Bakhash, the Iranian-born historian, disputes the notion that American funding would help those for whom it's intended. "Given the way Iran is now, I don't think it's at all helpful for the American government to be involved directly in such activities," he says. "The sensitivity to foreign funding in the Middle East is huge, enormous. The idea that foreign-funded political groups in-country can cooperate freely with political groups out of the country is a rather difficult concept; it can lead to a charge of treason."

Bakhash has a personal stake in the matter. Esfandiari is his wife, and after her release from eight months of imprisonment she coauthored a piece opposing U.S. government aid to Iranian pro-democracy groups. "Governments should talk to governments," she wrote with Robert Litwak, director of international-security studies at the Wilson Center, "while Iranian and American [non-governmental organizations] should be permitted to interact in a transparent fashion without the intrusion of governments." [26]

But some Iranian exiles argue in favor of American funding. "It's very helpful," says Akbar Atri, a former student activist who was also imprisoned. He dismisses as a well-worn accusation, long predating the Bush administration, that all dissidents are tools of American subversion. "The regime said the American government is helping these Iranians, but before these funds they all the time accused the opposition of being the puppet of U.S. intelligence agencies."

Atri, a longtime student democracy activist who fled Iran in late 2004 while under investigation for his political work, is a member of the Washington-based

Committee on the Present Danger, co-chaired by R. James Woolsey, former CIA director in the Clinton administration, and George P. Shultz, who was secretary of State in the Reagan administration. The organization favors "regime change" in Iran. [27]

Is Iran fomenting instability in Iraq?

The U.S. overthrow of Saddam Hussein did an enormous favor for Iran, which had good reason to consider Iraq's dictator an enormous threat. As the instigator of the 1980-1988 Iran-Iraq War, Saddam was responsible for at least 300,000 Iranians killed and an estimated 700,000 wounded. [28]

U.S. destruction of Iran's enemy would seem to make Iran and the United States de facto allies. But the U.S. military accuses Iran of supplying weapons to anti-American Shiite militias in Iraq. "There is absolutely no question," said Gen. Petraeus, the top U.S. commander in Iraq, "that Iranians are funding, arming, training and even in some cases, directing the activities of extremists and militia elements." [29]

Specifically, Petraeus and Lt. Gen. Odierno say the Iranian Revolutionary Guard Corps is supplying "explosively formed penetrators" (EFPs), roadside bombs that can penetrate vehicle armor. [30]

Iranian officials have consistently denied all such accusations. And U.S. military brass have backed away from disclosing what they call definitive evidence. [31]

But even without conclusive proof, some administration critics call the U.S. allegations plausible. "I think the administration is telling the truth when it says Iran is targeting American soldiers in Iraq and Afghanistan," says Riedel, the ex-CIA and National Security Council official. "What that says to me is that the Iranians are demonstrating that we're vulnerable. I have no doubt the U.S. Air Force and U.S. Navy can inflict enormous pain on Iran, but I also know that Iran can inflict enormous pain on the U.S. in Iraq, the Persian Gulf and diplomatic installations. They're prepared to play hardball with us."

Nonetheless, for some Iran-watchers, the question looming over the war in Iraq is whether Iran could be persuaded to help U.S. forces disengage.

Iran hawks say that hope is futile. Rubin of the American Enterprise Institute argues that Iran has settled on a policy of keeping U.S. forces tied down in Iraq. In testimony last July before the House Foreign Affairs Committee, Rubin cited a July 13 sermon by former Iranian President Hashemi Rafsanjani in which he ridiculed American weakness. "What a superpower is the United States when it can be easily trapped in a small country like Iraq?" he said. [32]

Based on the sermon and other evidence, Rubin testified: "The assumption that Iraq's neighbors seek a peaceful, stable Iraq is false. . . . Iranian strategists believe limited instability [in Iraq] and free rein of pro-Iranian militias to be in their best interest." [33]

Parsi of the National Iranian American Council shares Rubin's analysis, up to a point. "If a larger accommodation doesn't take place, my thinking is that the Iranians will not help stabilize Iraq," he says. "The fear in Iran is that the ultimate goal of the United States is to attack Iran and remove its government." Based on that perception, he says, Iran sees a benefit in American forces facing continued threat in Iraq.

But unlike the Iran hawks, Parsi argues that Iran could become a force for peace in Iraq. "They want something in return — better relations with the United States in which the U.S. recognizes Iranian security interests and doesn't attack Iran.

Hardliners ridicule the notion that any deal can be reached with a government that sees itself as an implacable enemy.

"They're just trying to kill us in Iraq," says Ledeen of the American Enterprise Institute. "We have been looking for a modus vivendi with Iran since 1979." The only conclusion to be drawn, he argues, is that there is no Iranian interest in cooperating with the United States.

Riedel argues that view closes off any possibility of peaceful resolution. "If Iranians believe we are only interested in regime change, we're killing any chance of a serious dialogue," he says. "The Iranians need to know when they enter into any kind of dialogue with us that it is not a subterfuge for overthrowing the Islamic Republic."

In any event, he adds, "If an overthrow is anyone's goal, it's a fantasy." The present Iranian government will not disappear "any time in the near future."

BACKGROUND

Mossadegh Overthrown

Modern U.S.-Iranian relations began with the CIA-engineered overthrow of Prime Minister Mohammed Mossadegh in 1953. Mossadegh, an ardent nationalist,

CHRONOLOGY

1950s-1978 *CIA ousts nationalist prime minister, ushering in an era of close ties to Iran's monarch.*

April 28, 1951 Iran's parliament nationalizes country's oil industry.

Aug. 19, 1953 CIA directs coup that ousts Prime Minister Mohammed Mossadegh, who spearheaded oil nationalization.

1963 Shah Mohammed Reza Pahlavi's U.S.-originated "white revolution" on socioeconomic issues receives 99 percent approval in an obviously rigged referendum that prompts a wave of protests.

1964 More protests greet a new law granting immunity to thousands of Americans working in Iran if they are accused of crimes. . . . Ayatollah Ruhollah Khomeini, a cleric leading the protests, is forced into exile.

1977 President Jimmy Carter toasts the shah in Tehran as a beloved promoter of stability.

Jan. 1978 Officially sponsored publication of an article defaming Khomeini sparks demonstrations.

1979-1989 *Incapable of quelling the protests, the shah flees, and Khomeini returns from exile to become the country's dominant leader under a quasi-parliamentary system dominated by religious leaders.*

Jan. 1979 Shah goes into exile.

Nov. 4, 1979 Shah's arrival in United States for cancer treatment prompts students to storm the U.S. Embassy in Tehran and take 52 hostages.

1980 Iraqi dictator Saddam Hussein, a Sunni, launches a war against Iran's Shiite government — which he perceives as a threat to his regime.

1981 Iran frees the hostages the day Carter leaves office. . . . Crash of a plane carrying Israeli arms for Iran signals Israel's tilt in Iran-Iraq war.

1983 Hezbollah terrorists allied with Iran attack U.S. Embassy and Marine barracks in Beirut, Lebanon, killing 304 Americans.

1986 President Ronald Reagan admits his administration illegally sold weapons to Iran and funneled profits to the "contra" guerrillas fighting Nicaragua's left-wing Sandinista government. . . . U.S. confirms providing intelligence to Iraq to help its bombing campaign against Iran.

1989 Ayatollah Khomeini dies.

1990-2007 *Conservative cleric appointed to Iran's most important post. Relations with the U.S. deteriorate.*

1990 Conservative Ayatollah Ali Khamenei named supreme leader.

1997 Reformist cleric Mohammed Khatami elected president in a landslide.

1998 Khatami seems interested in reopening relations with the U.S.

2000 Dissident journalist Akbar Ganji and other democracy activists imprisoned.

2001 Khatami wins second term. . . . Iranian security forces help U.S. military during invasion of Afghanistan.

2002 Bush calls Iran a member of the "axis of evil," along with North Korea and Iraq.

2005 Populist hard-liner Mahmoud Ahmadinejad elected president following failure of Khatami's reforms.

Dec. 23, 2006 U.S. military says Iran is arming Iraqi militias. . . . U.N. Security Council imposes financial sanctions on Iran for failing to halt uranium enrichment. . . . Iran holds conference on Holocaust, with Holocaust deniers invited.

2007 Security Council orders new sanctions against Iran for its refusal to quit uranium enrichment. . . . Senate resolution demands that the U.S. "combat" Iranian activities in Iraq. . . . President Bush says Iran's nuclear program raises specter of "World War III." . . . Israeli bombing in Syria raises fear of Israeli or U.S. strike on Iran. . . . Ahmadinejad vows no retreat from nuclear program. . . . October talks between Iran and nuclear-watchdog agency produce no agreement.

had been at the center of a crisis that had been building since the late 1940s over the future of Britain's long-standing oil concession, which effectively controlled Iran's major natural resource. [34]

Mossadegh had accepted the post of prime minister from the shah on condition that parliament end the concession, which it did on April 28, 1951. "The anniversary of the passing of the oil nationalization bill," writes historian Ali M. Ansari of the University of St. Andrews in Scotland, "is perhaps the closest thing to an Iranian independence day." [35]

But for the CIA — which worked closely with the British — Mossadegh's nationalization of Britain's Anglo-Iranian Oil. Co. showed him to be a threat to Western interests, and politically unreliable, in a region where the Soviet Union was a looming presence. President Dwight D. Eisenhower approved a coup plan. One attempt failed, leading the shah to take a sudden vacation in Rome. Then, on Aug. 19, 1953, a CIA officer directed a move against Mossadegh, who eventually surrendered. "The shah became the centerpiece of American foreign policy in the Islamic world," writes *New York Times* correspondent Tim Weiner in a recent history of the CIA. But, "A generation of Iranians grew up knowing that the CIA had installed the shah." [36]

Although the United States poured money into Iran after the coup, it didn't buy all Iranians' friendship. Abolhasan Ebtehaj, a government official who lost his post after disputes with American officials, faulted the free-spending U.S. approach. "Not so many years ago in Iran, the United States was loved and respected as no other country, and without having given a penny of aid," he said in a 1961 speech in San Francisco. "Now, after more than $1 billion of loans and grants, America is neither loved nor respected; she is distrusted by most people and hated by many." [37]

The John F. Kennedy administration, which came to power in 1961, pushed the shah even harder to shake up his country's social structure. Arguing that Iran's land-tenure system amounted to "feudalism," creating conditions that made Iran ripe for a communist revolution, the Americans demanded private land ownership for peasants.

But when the shah's so-called "white revolution" occurred, it brought repercussions that the Americans hadn't foreseen. Rural, land-owning aristocrats and members of the clergy, who had been instrumental in pushing out Mossadegh, opposed the change, in some cases more

because it was American-imposed than because of its objectives. The shah, with U.S. encouragement, also proposed the political emancipation of women, which angered conservatives, especially religious leaders.

When a national referendum showed 99 percent approval for the "revolution," riots broke out because the election clearly had been rigged. Ruhollah Khomeini, a previously obscure clergyman, became one of the strongest voices against the shah.

For Iranians, what the shah and his American advisers called reform was something quite different. "The shah's modernization program — which created less an authentic development than a consumer society for privileged elites — quickly enriched the members of the royal family and the court, the entrepreneurs (almost all subcontractors for large Western firms), the powerful merchants, the importers of spare parts and consumer goods, the speculators," wrote French journalist Eric Rouleau in 1980. [38]

Then the United States prompted the shah to introduce legislation granting immunity from the Iranian legal system for any American citizen accused of a crime. On the same day the bill was approved — after the shah fixed the parliamentary vote — Iranian lawmakers also approved a $200 million loan from the United States.

"The dignity of Iran has been destroyed," Khomeini declared. "They wanted a loan, and America demanded this in return." In 1964 Khomeini was sent into exile. [39]

Shah Overthrown

The United States and the shah deepened their relationship in the 1970s. Israel, too, enjoyed close ties to the shah, whose quiet acceptance of the Jewish state enraged Arab governments — and many Iranians. By 1977, there were some 30,000 American government personnel and businesspeople in Iran, President Jimmy Carter noted during a toast to the shah on New Year's Eve in Tehran. [40]

"Iran, because of the great leadership of the shah, is an island of stability in one of the more troubled areas of the world," said Carter, in words that would later embarrass him. "This is a great tribute to you, your majesty, and to your leadership and to the respect and the admiration and love which your people give to you." [41]

Only weeks later, however, the monarchy's collapse began. In January, after the shah-approved publication of a defamatory newspaper article about Khomeini, well-organized street protests broke out in several cities, creating a crisis atmosphere.

Presidential Hopefuls Targeting Iran

Democrats and Republicans disagree on military action.

U.S. military action against Iran may or may not occur, but candidates for the 2008 presidential nomination are fighting about whether it would be a good idea.

For now, the big Iran knockdown is taking place among Democratic candidates. Debate centers on a Sept. 26 Senate resolution urging the United States to "combat, contain and roll back the violent activities and destabilizing influence" of Iran's government inside Iraq and declare the Iranian Revolutionary Guard Corps a terrorist organization. The resolution passed, 76-22. [1]

Former Sen. John Edwards, D-N.C.

Antiwar Democrats called the amendment a barely veiled authorization to scramble warplanes over Iran. "It's an enormous mistake to give George Bush the first step in the authority to move militarily on Iran," said former North Carolina **Sen. John Edwards**. "The resolution on the Iranian Revolutionary Guard did that." [2]

Edwards' comment was aimed not only at the Bush administration but at frontrunner **Sen. Hillary Rodham Clinton**, D-N.Y., who drew fire from antiwar Democrats for supporting the resolution.

Sen. Hillary Rodham Clinton, D-N.Y.

Clinton responded that she hadn't been voting for war. "I oppose any rush to war but also believe doing nothing is not acceptable — diplomacy is the right path," she said in a mailing to prospective primary voters in Iowa. [3]

Perhaps in response to criticism of her vote, Clinton on Oct. 1 signed up as a cosponsor of a bill introduced last March by Sen. Jim Webb, D-Va., that would bar military action against Iran without congressional authorization. [4]

Webb, a Marine combat veteran of Vietnam, was among the critics of the resolution, which had been sponsored by Sen. Joseph Lieberman, I-Conn., whose hawkish views on Iraq cost him the Democratic Senate nomination in his state in 2006, and Sen. Jon Kyl of Arizona, a conservative Republican. "Those who regret their vote five years ago to authorize military action in Iraq should think hard before supporting this approach," he said, "because, in my view, it has the same potential to do harm where many are seeking to do good." [5]

While Clinton's support for Webb's bill might have seemed an opportunistic response to recent attacks, last February she had demanded that Bush make no move against Iran without congressional authorization. [6]

In any case, Clinton's opponents didn't drop the Iran issue. By late October, another front-runner nipping at her heels advocated a sharp break with the Iran policy espoused by the administration — notably going further than Clinton in marking a distance from Bush.

Sen. Barack Obama, D-Ill.

"I would meet directly with Iranian leaders," **Sen. Barack Obama**, D-Ill., told *The New York Times.* "We would engage in a level of aggressive, personal diplomacy. . . . Iran and Syria would start changing their behavior if they started seeing that they had some incentives to do so, but right now the only incentive that exists is our president suggesting that if you do what we tell you, we may not blow you up." Obama didn't vote on the resolution that brought Clinton so much heat.

Among Republican presidential hopefuls, Iran has served mostly as a contest over who can advocate the toughest mea-

Sen. John McCain, R-Ariz.

sures. Arizona **Sen. John McCain** seemed momentarily to have won that contest. In April, sitting in his tour bus, he sang a few bars of the chorus of "Bomb Iran," by Vince Vance and the Valiants, an AM radio favorite of the 1979-1981 hostage-crisis period (based on the Beach Boys' "Barbara Ann"). [7] But after cries of indignation, McCain protested that he'd only been kidding. "People got to lighten up, get a life," McCain said. [8]

Nevertheless, in a more serious setting McCain answered affirmatively when asked at an October debate whether he would take action against Iran — without consulting Congress — to stop it from acquiring nuclear weapons. But he added a proviso — "if the situation . . . requires immediate action to ensure the security of the United States of America." [9]

Former Gov. Mitt Romney, R-Mass.

Former Massachusetts **Gov. Mitt Romney** was widely judged to have stumbled when he answered the same question: "We're going to let the lawyers sort out what he needed to do and what he didn't need to do," Romney said, seemingly referring to whichever president might be facing the issue, "but certainly what you want to do is to have the agreement of all the people in leadership of our government, as well as our friends around the world where those circumstances are available." [10]

Former Mayor Rudolph Giuliani, R-N.Y.

Of all the Republican contenders, former New York City Mayor **Rudolph W. Giuliani** has made the most of the Iran issue. His senior foreign policy adviser on Iran is Michael Rubin of the American Enterprise Institute, who advocates stepping up aid to Iranian democracy activists. Also advising is *Commentary* magazine Editor-at-large Norman Podhoretz, a prominent neocon who calls for bombing Iranian nuclear facilities.

During a September visit to London, Giuliani said that if Iran got close to building a nuclear weapon, "We will prevent them or we'll set them back five or 10 years." He added, "That is not said as a threat. That should be said as a promise." [11]

But even if he won the nomination and the election, Giuliani wouldn't be deciding Iran policy until early 2009. For now, the constant stream of events, speculation, declarations and rumors about Iran is fueling the political process to such an extent that liberal *New York Times* columnist Frank Rich theorized that the Bush administration is keeping the tension high mainly to torment Democratic candidates.

"Whatever happens in or to Iran," Rich wrote, "the American public will be carpet-bombed by apocalyptic propaganda for the 12 months to come."

[1] See Senate Amendment 3017 to HR1585: "To express the sense of the Senate regarding Iran," Sept. 20, 2007, www.govtrack.us/congress/amendment.xpd?session=110&amdt=s3017.

[2] Quoted in Dan Balz, "Iran Becomes an Issue in Democratic Contest," *The Washington Post*, Oct. 25, 2007, p. A7.

[3] *Ibid.*

[4] See "Senator Clinton Announces Co-Sponsorship of Webb Legislation Prohibiting the Use of Funds for Military Operations In Iran," press release, Oct. 1, 2007, www.senate.gov/~clinton/news/statements/details.cfm?id=284618.

[5] Quoted in Shailagh Murray, "Webb Seen as a Potential 2008 Running Mate," *The Washington Post*, Oct. 28, 2007, p. A4.

[6] "Clinton: No Military Action on Iran Without Congressional Authority," press release, Feb. 14, 2007, www.senate.gov/~clinton/news/statements/record.cfm?id=269287.

[7] See "Vince Vance and the Valiants," neworleansbands.net, undated, www.neworleansbands.net/music/bands/161/.

[8] Quoted in Mark Leibovich, "Falling From the Top Lands McCain in a Scaled-Back Comfort Zone," *The Washington Post*, Oct. 7, 2007, p. A1.

[9] Quoted in Adam Nagourney and Marc Santora, "Romney and Giuliani Spar as New Guy Looks On," *The New York Times*, Oct. 10, 2007, p. A1.

[10] *Ibid.*

[11] Quoted in Michael Finnegan, "Giuliani warns Iranians against nuclear ambitions," *Los Angeles Times*, Sept. 20, 2007, p. A15.

To the surprise of observers, the shah and his notorious secret police, SAVAK, proved incapable of coping. In the past SAVAK had arrested, tortured or killed hundreds of thousands of genuine or alleged oppositionists. Israel had a close working relationship with SAVAK, growing out of antagonism between the shah and the Arab states. That relationship fueled popular antagonism toward the Jewish state.

A year later, on Jan. 16, 1979, the shah fled Iran. Two weeks later, Khomeini returned home from exile in Paris, turning the revolutionary process definitively toward his brand of socially conservative, politically aggressive and theocratic Shiite politics. Some secular democrats who were involved in an early provisional government were pushed aside. "At every step of the way, [Khomeini] and his supporters proved more ardent in their faith, more manipulative in their conduct and more merciless in their retaliations," writes Ray Takeyh, a historian and senior fellow at the centrist Council on Foreign Relations. [42]

Khomeini's strategy bore fruit on Dec. 3, 1979, when Iranian voters approved a constitution that created today's Islamic Republic of Iran, directed by a religious leader who would not be accountable to the public or to elected officials. A Guardian Council, mainly clerics, would have the final word on all legislation.

The referendum passed amidst a frenzy of enthusiasm generated by a crisis that still reverberates. A month earlier, on Nov. 4, a band of student militants overran the U.S. Embassy in Tehran, taking 52 hostages, to punish the Carter administration for allowing the shah into the United States for cancer treatment.

Khomeini applauded the takeover, and the United States cut relations with Iran — which haven't been restored to this day. Khomeini's forces, meanwhile, used CIA and other U.S. documents the students found to discredit domestic enemies shown to have connections to the United States. The hostage crisis ended 444 days after it began, with the inauguration of Ronald Reagan on Jan. 20, 1981.

Besides broken diplomatic relations, U.S. sanctions against Iran imposed during the hostage crisis also have survived. The United States first imposed financial penalties on Iran during the crisis, when the Carter administration banned Iranian oil imports and froze Iranian assets in the United States. In 1987, Reagan banned imports of all Iranian goods and services, citing Iranian support for international terrorism. In 1995, Clinton banned U.S. participation in petroleum development in Iran, also citing Iranian support for terrorism as well as efforts to acquire weapons of mass destruction. In 1997 Clinton extended the previous order by explicitly barring Americans from virtually all trade and investments involving Iran — a ban that was eased in 2000 to allow imports of Iranian dried fruits, nuts and caviar. [43]

Israel's Tilt

During the hostage crisis, in September 1980, Saddam Hussein launched a war against Iran over its alleged violation of a bilateral treaty. But, pretext aside, Saddam wanted to crush the new republic. As a Sunni ruling a majority-Shiite populace, Saddam viewed Iran's Shiite government as a powerful threat to his predominantly Sunni regime.

Saddam also posed a serious threat to Israel, given his nuclear ambitions. Iran seemed a lesser danger, despite its anti-Israel rhetoric. But for the United States, still reeling from the hostage crisis, Iran was the main enemy. The Iran-Iraq war would see the United States helping Iraq, while Israel secretly shipped arms to Iran. These alignments later shifted — with the United States toppling Saddam and Israel coming to fear Iran. But even during the 1980s, U.S. officials at one point joined in a scheme with Israel to sell arms to Iran.

During the eight-year war, Israeli leaders occasionally acknowledged their tilt toward Iran. "For 28 of 37 years, Iran was a friend of Israel. If it could work for 28 years . . . why couldn't it [again], once this crazy idea of Shiite fundamentalism is gone?" asked Yitzhak Rabin, Israel's defense minister, in 1987. [44]

But in addition to talking, the Jewish state was supplying arms to Iran. Both countries had reasons to keep the supply line secret, but in July 1981 an Argentine airplane carrying Israeli weapons to Iran crashed, leading to reports of a $200 million arms deal between the two countries. [45]

A few years later, Israeli — and American — arms sales to Iran became front-page news during the so-called "Iran-Contra" scandal. In November 1986, a Beirut newspaper revealed a secret visit to Iran by President Reagan's national security adviser, Robert McFarlane. Weeks later, Reagan admitted his administration had sold weapons to Iran — violating a U.S. arms embargo — and funneled the profits to the "contra" guerrillas fighting Nicaragua's left-wing Sandinista government.

Further complicating an already tangled tale, the Reagan administration also acknowledged it had fed secret intelligence to Iraq from U.S. satellite photos, allowing it to assess damage from bombing strikes on Iranian targets. "Because we could see the fact that Iran at various times clearly had the upper hand, and had the manpower to continue much further than Iraq could," the American assistance was necessary, an unnamed White House official said. [46]

By that time, the United States had another reason to help Iran's enemy. Following the 1982 Israeli invasion of Lebanon, Iran — eager for a base in the Arab countries — helped create the terrorist organization and political movement Hezbollah (Party of God). Its base was Lebanon's marginalized Shiite population, which had turned against Israel.

The following year, Hezbollah was implicated in a deadly bombing that destroyed the U.S. Embassy in Lebanon's capital, Beirut, killing 63 people. Six months later, a Hezbollah truck bomb hit the U.S. Marine barracks in Beirut, killing 241 Marines serving as peacekeepers.

Opinions are divided about whether Iran played a role in a terrorist attack that killed 19 airmen in 1996 at Khobar Towers, an apartment building serving as Air Force quarters near Dhahran, Saudi Arabia. In December 2006, U.S. District Judge Royce C. Lamberth of Washington ruled Iran responsible in connection with a lawsuit by victims' families against the Islamic Republic. [47]

Lamberth's decision echoed Attorney General John Ashcroft's conclusion in June 2001 that "elements of the Iranian government inspired, supported and supervised" the attack. Some experts challenge that conclusion. "There was a paucity of credible evidence," writes historian Ansari. [48]

Rise of Repression

After Khomeini's death in 1989, Iran's clerical overseers chose conservative Ayatollah Ali Khameini as the next supreme leader. "He believes that the mission of the Islamic Republic is to uphold religious norms and resist popular attempts to alter the regime along democratic lines," writes a critic, historian Takeyh. [49]

By the late 1990s, however, the popular call for more democracy was picking up strength. In 1997, by a landslide of nearly 70 percent, voters elected Mohammed Khatami as president. Khatami, a mid-ranking cleric who had emerged as a foe of repression, had studied Western philosophy, from which he quoted freely. And he knew Western social and political norms up close, having lived in Germany. That broader outlook and

experience showed. "State authority cannot be attained through coercion and dictatorship," he had written. [50]

In 1998, Khatami indicated a willingness not only to loosen controls on Iranians but also to enter into negotiations aimed at renewing relations with the United States. Using a 1998 interview with CNN to broadcast his views to the West, Khatami condemned terrorism "in all its forms." And speaking of the hostage crisis — still looming over U.S.-Iranian affairs — Khatami said it grew out of Iranian grievances such as the 1953 coup but also reflected the chaos of a revolutionary period — a condition that no longer applied. "Today, our new society has been institutionalized," he said, "and there is no need for unconventional methods of expression." [51]

In his first year in office, more than 200 new newspapers and magazines and 95 political parties and organizations were permitted. The new freedom sparked public debates on topics that had been out of bounds, including Israel and the Palestinians.

In 2001 Khatami swept into office a second time, with a 77 percent victory. But even supporters admitted that political liberalization had advanced, despite continued repression, while the economy had fallen off a cliff. One-quarter of the workforce was unemployed, and 40 percent of the population lived below the poverty line. [52]

Not surprisingly, the high hopes Khatami had inspired turned into disillusion. Economic disaster aside, Iranians who had hoped for reopening relations with the United States had experienced only disappointment. Iranian-U.S. cooperation early in the invasion of Afghanistan hadn't led to closer ties. "Before and during the war in Afghanistan, the Iranians were quite helpful to the United States," writes Kenneth Pollack, director of Persian Gulf Affairs at the National Security Council in the Clinton administration "They shared our hatred of al Qaeda and the Taliban, and they provided us with extensive assistance on intelligence, logistics, diplomacy and Afghan internal politics." [53]

And yet, the year after the Afghanistan campaign began, Bush in his first State of the Union address called Iran a member of the "axis of evil," along with North Korea and Iraq. "Iran aggressively pursues these weapons [of mass destruction] and exports terror," Bush said, "while an unelected few repress the Iranian people's hope for freedom." [54]

In 2005, Ahmadinejad, then Tehran's mayor, won a presidential-election runoff with 62 percent of the vote. A veteran of the bloody Iran-Iraq War and an engineer of working-class origins, he combined Khomeini-era rhetoric against the United States with denunciations of economic injustice.

Where reformists in Iran had hoped for eventual restoration of relations with the West, the new president and his circle looked to China, India and Russia for capital and trade links. "Our nation is continuing the path of progress and on this path has no significant need for the United States," Ahmadinejad said shortly before his election. [55]

CURRENT SITUATION

New Sanctions

The Bush administration is gearing up to start enforcing a new set of financial sanctions against an Iranian military force that the administration charges with terrorism. The sanctions also are designed to stymie what the administration regards as Iran's nuclear-weapons development program.

On Oct. 25, 2007, the State Department barred U.S. citizens and businesses from dealing with banks, businesses and individuals linked to the Revolutionary Guard, Iran's military logistics agency, or the Aerospsace Industries Organization, both of which the administration says are helping in developing ballistic missiles or nuclear weapons. [56]

The State Department also listed a unit of the Revolutionary Guard — the Qods [Jerusalem] Force — as a terrorist agency. The administration says the force, which has been described as a 5,000-man "unconventional warfare" wing of the Guard, provides "material support" to Lebanon's Hezbollah; three Palestinian organizations, including the militant Palestinian Islamic group Hamas; Afghanistan's Taliban and Shiite militias in Iraq "who target and kill coalition and Iraqi forces and innocent Iraqi civilians." [57]

Administration officials suggested that the sanctions represented a commitment to cracking down on Iran short of war. "We do not believe that conflict is inevitable," said Under Secretary of State for Political Affairs R. Nicholas Burns after the measures were announced. "This decision today supports the diplomacy and in no way, shape or form does it anticipate the use of force." [58]

Whether the sanctions will bite into Iran's nuclear development project is another question. "It is unlikely

that these sanctions are going to impede the Iranian pursuit of nuclear capabilities," says Jon Wolfstahl, a senior fellow at the Center for Strategic and International Studies. "It is not going to seriously affect their financial situation because oil prices have risen so high." [59]

But a former National Security Council (NSC) official, Lee Wolosky, sees the sanctions as capable of slowing down Iran's use of the international financial system. European governments may ignore the sanctions, he acknowledges, but European banks could cooperate, if only to avoid complicating their own dealings with the United States. "Already, a great deal of of informal pressure is being applied to European banks to re-analyze relationships with Iran," he says.

"This has had a certain measure of success," he continues. "You're going to see non-U.S. banks cease to do business with [Iranian entities]." [60]

Days after his remarks, according to *The New York Times*, Western diplomats said most major European banks had quit dealing with the Iranian banks named in the sanction orders, or were getting ready to do so. [61]

The new sanctions have reverberated at the World Bank, where officials said in November they were holding up $5.4 million for four projects in Iran — earthquake relief, water and sanitation, environment management and urban housing. The bank acted because the sanctions left it without an Iranian bank through which to funnel funds. [62]

An Iranian official, meanwhile, scoffed at the new measures. "Sanctions have been imposed on us for the past 28 years," said Saeed Jalili, who recently replaced Ali Larijani as Iran's representative before the International Atomic Energy Agency (IAEA). "The new sanctions, like those before, will have no effect on Iran's policies." [63]

Whatever effects the past sanctions may have had, they clearly haven't stopped Iran's nuclear development efforts, according to Paul Pillar, the CIA's former national intelligence officer for the Near East and South Asia. He worries the latest sanctions raise tensions between Iran and the United States. "They strengthen the positions of the relative hard-liners," Pillar says. "I think we played into the Iranian president's hands." [64]

Iran in the U.N.

Amid the new sanctions, and the stepped-up war of words between Washington and Tehran, the U.N. Security Council is jockeying with Iran over its nuclear program.

Are President Bush's recent statements on Iran dangerously provocative?

YES
Sen. Robert C. Byrd, D-W. Va.
Chairman, Senate Appropriations Committee

Written for *CQ Researcher*, November 2007

Yes. Every day now, it seems that the confrontational rhetoric between the United States and Iran continues to escalate. The main point of contention is Iran's pursuit of nuclear weapons. While few doubt Iran's desire to attain a nuclear bomb, there is little evidence that they are close to acquiring such a capability.

Yet, the White House has been busy unleashing almost daily claims of an imminent nuclear threat in Iran, as it did with Iraq. Fear, panic and chest-pounding do not work well in the conduct of foreign policy. This is a time to put diplomacy to work. There is ample opportunity to coordinate with our allies to constrain Iran's ambitions. But instead of working with our partners, the Bush administration has unveiled new unilateral sanctions against Iran. Instead of direct diplomatic negotiations with Iran, the administration continues to issue ultimatums and threats.

We have been down that path already. We know where it leads. Vice President Cheney recently threatened "serious consequences" — the exact phrase that he used in the run-up to the invasion of Iraq — if Tehran does not acquiesce to U.S. demands. The parallels are all-too-chilling. President Bush warned that those who wish to "avoid World War III" should seek to keep Iran from attaining nuclear weapons. Secretary of Defense Robert Gates has admitted in the press that the Pentagon has drafted plans for a military option in Iran. The president's $196 billion request for emergency war funding included a request for "bunker-buster" bombs that have no immediate use in Iraq.

Taking all of it together — the bellicose rhetoric, the needlessly confrontational unilateral sanctions, the provocative stationing of U.S. warships in the region, the operational war planning and the request for munitions that seem designed for use in Iran — there are reasons for deep concern that this administration is once again rushing headlong into another disastrous war in the Middle East.

The Bush administration apparently believes that it has the authority to wage preemptive war — and can do so without prior congressional approval. That is why I am cosponsoring a resolution with Sen. Richard Durbin, D-Ill., which affirms that any military action taken against Iran must be explicitly approved by Congress before any such action is initiated. The White House must be reminded of the constitutional powers entrusted to the people's branch. Let us halt this rush to another war. Let us not make the same disastrous mistake as we did with Iraq.

NO
Michael Rubin
Resident Scholar, American Enterprise Institute

Written for *CQ Researcher*, November 2007

On Oct. 17, President Bush raised the specter of war with Iran. "If you're interested in avoiding World War III," he said, it's necessary to deny the Islamic Republic "the knowledge necessary to make a nuclear weapon." Condemnation of his comments was swift. Sen. Robert Byrd, D-W. Va., accused the president of using "rhetorical ghosts and goblins to scare the American people, with claims of an imminent nuclear threat in Iran."

Navel-gazing is a Capitol Hill pastime, but such criticism is misplaced. Since the disclosure of Iran's covert enrichment program, International Atomic Energy Agency (IAEA) inspectors — not the CIA or Iranian exiles — report a litany of lies. IAEA inspectors discovered traces of uranium metal used to build bombs, not fuel reactors. IAEA inspectors also found that Iran had experimented with chemical separation of polonium, a material used to initiate nuclear detonation. Iran still has not revealed what rogue Pakistani scientist A.Q. Khan sold on his trip to Tehran.

Diplomacy should always be the strategy of first resort, but its track record with Tehran does not encourage. While it is fashionable to blame Iran's nuclear desire upon U.S. presence in Iraq and Afghanistan, Tehran's program predates such interventions by 15 years. In the name of engagement, the European Union nearly tripled trade with Iran between 2000 and 2005. But rather than invest that windfall in schools and hospitals, the Iranian government — then under reformist control — poured money into its military and centrifuge programs. Tehran has yet to provide the West a single, confidence-building measure.

Iranian diplomats say their program is peaceful, but officials close to Supreme Leader Ali Khamenei suggest otherwise. On Feb. 14, 2005, Ayatollah Mohammad Baqer Kharrazi, secretary-general of Iranian Hezbollah, said, "We are able to produce atomic bombs, and we will do that." Three months later, Gholam Reza Hasani, Khamenei's representative to West Azerbaijan province said, "An atomic bomb . . . must be produced." And, on Sept. 3, 2007, Khamenei himself said, "Iran will outwit the West on the nuclear issue."

Iran's centrifuge cascade, Syria's surprise nuclear plant and North Korea's role in its construction suggest time is limited. To avert escalation, the White House must demonstrate diplomacy to be Tehran's best option. Bush's rhetoric dampens Iran's overconfidence and underscores U.S. seriousness, both in Tehran and at the United Nations. Bashing Bush may make good politics, but it is irresponsible and may hasten the result which Bush's domestic critics most fear.

Mohammed ElBaradei, director of the IAEA, has been trying to negotiate a program of tough inspections to ensure Iran's uranium-enrichment program stops short of producing weapons-quality fuel. While he has argued against trying to stop enrichment altogether, he has also warned that Iran may have to "come clean" about possible past work on weapons development. [65]

"We cannot give Iran a pass right now, because there's still a lot of question marks," ElBaradei said on CNN in late October. He added that the agency hasn't seen any definitive evidence Iran is pursuing an "active weaponization program." [66]

ElBaradei's remarks came about six weeks before he is scheduled to tell diplomats from the United States, Britain, France, Germany, Russia and China whether doubts over Iran's nuclear intentions have been resolved. If not, at least some of those countries favor new U.N. sanctions designed to force Iran's compliance with IAEA regulations.

In early November, the British Foreign Office announced that all six countries had agreed to approve such sanctions, but China and Russia hadn't confirmed Britain's statement. Days earlier, President Vladimir V. Putin asked, "Why make the situation worse, bring it to a dead end, threaten sanctions or even military action?" [67]

The climate surrounding Putin's statement — already made tense by the Foreign Office's announcement and the earlier statements by Bush and Cheney — was further supercharged by military action by Israel. On Sept. 6, Israeli warplanes bombed a building in Syria that American officials said housed a nuclear project aided by North Korea. Israel has maintained official silence and imposed military censorship on its aggressive press. And Syria has denied doing any nuclear work — with North Korea or without it. "The rumors have been deliberately fabricated by Israel to justify its recent act of aggression against Syria," Syrian Prime Minister Mohammed Naji al-Otri said. [68]

Whatever effect the bombing may have had on Syria, Iran was also indirectly a target, some Washington strategists said. "If you are Israel and you are looking at this, the value of striking Syria is that it sends a signal, including to the Iranians," said Michael Green, a former director of Asian affairs at the National Security Council and now an associate professor at Georgetown University's School of Foreign Service. "This follows the Chinese proverb that sometimes you have to kill the chicken to scare the monkey." [69]

Iranian officials gave no sign of being scared, nor of willingness to bend to international pressure to suspend their efforts to enrich uranium. "Suspension is the crucial issue if the Iranians want to get off the hook of more sanctions," said a participant in talks in Rome in October between Iranian negotiators and Javier Solana, foreign policy director of the European Union. "They seem to think they are doing enough." [70]

Last March, and also in December 2006, the Security Council approved sanctions aimed at forcing Iran to stop its enrichment efforts. [71]

The first of those two sets of sanctions banned the import and export by Iran of materials and technology used in uranium enrichment and ballistic missiles. In addition, the assets of 12 Iranian individuals and 10 companies allegedly involved in nuclear and missile work were frozen. [72]

Then, in March, after Iran still hadn't satisfied objections to its nuclear program, the Security Council approved tougher sanctions, including a ban on all weapons sales to Iran and on any grants or loans to Iran not involving humanitarian and development aid. [73]

In the weeks leading up to the scheduled November meeting, the outlook for Iran to back away from enrichment seemed dim, judging by President Ahmadinejad's blunt remarks just before the Rome talks were to start. "Iran will not retreat one iota," he said. "We are in favor of talks, but we will not negotiate with anyone about our right to nuclear technology."

Ahmadinejad's declaration represents one face that Iranian officials have presented to international bodies who try to control the proliferation of nuclear technology.

The other face showed in statements made after Iranian officials met in Rome with E.U. representatives. "We are after no adventure, and we are after no trouble-making," Larijani told reporters. [74]

But, in a further complication for those trying to decode Iran's strategy, Larijani — seen by some as a voice of moderation — was replaced as Iran's chief negotiator on the nuclear issue. Larijani denied that his removal signaled a hardening of Iran's position. Some Iranian politicians didn't buy the denial. "It is very disappointing that the government does not tolerate even views of a person like Mr. Larijani and would eliminate him in such a manner," said Mohammed Hashemi, a former vice president and the brother of former President Ali Akbar Hashemi Rafsanjani. [75]

Larijani's replacement, in fact, was among the latest in a long sequence of events that have prompted suspicion of

Iran's intentions. In 2005, for example, the IAEA reported that Iran had acquired engineering drawings on how to cast uranium into the exact shape of a nuclear bomb core. Equally important, the source of the drawings was the infamous A.Q. Khan of Pakistan, who had made a mission and a business out of selling nuclear plans to developing countries, especially Muslim-majority nations. [76]

Hovering over the entire issue of Iran and nuclear development is the question of when Iran could be ready to produce a nuclear weapon. Defense Secretary Gates has reported that intelligence agencies estimate 2010 at the earliest, or 2015 at the latest. But Israel's military intelligence research chief, Brig. Gen. Yossi Baidatz, told the Israeli parliament in early November that the date could come as early as 2009. Some Israeli officials have suggested that Israel would never let Iran get that far. Sallai Meridor, ambassador to the United States, said in late October that Israel should always be prepared "to preempt, to deter, to defeat if we can." [77]

But Israel's political-military elite isn't of one mind on the subject. Efraim Halevy, Israel's retired chief spymaster, disputes the notion that Iran poses a threat to Israel's existence. "I believe that Israel is indestructible," Halevy told *The Washington Post*. And if Iran does produce an atomic weapon, he said, Israel has "a whole arsenal of capabilities" to deter nuclear aggression from Iran, whose leaders would consider it a religious violation to put their country's survival at risk. [78]

OUTLOOK

Popular Uprising?

What will Iran be like 10 years from now? George Mason University historian Bakhash refuses to hazard a prediction. "There are too many variables," he says.

Indeed, from the 1953 coup to the flight of the shah to the embassy hostage crisis to the horrific war with Iraq — and more — Iran has experienced enough volatility for 10 countries.

"Iran is a very emotional and changeable society; it's better to forecast the next six months," says human-rights activist Afshari, sounding a similar note of caution. But he does sketch out a possible near-term future.

"In the next 10 years, Iranian society will be in a much better situation in the field of democracy and human rights and justice," he says. "A basic change will

have happened. The government can't continue like this. They have to give in to the Iranian people's demands."

Afshari sees the present government as incapable of maintaining its current nuclear development efforts. "It cannot continue outside the control of the international community," he says.

Moreover, he predicts, citing the collapse of the Soviet Union, sweeping changes will be brought about, but not by popular elections. "There will be big social changes — civil disobedience like in Poland, and also like the Islamic Revolution," he says.

Such a scenario could come about, says Iran hawk Rubin of the American Enterprise Institute. But a far bleaker one is equally possible, he says: "Either you're going to have a Romania-style change, or else the regime will have crushed all dissent." [79]

Rubin agrees with Afshari that working within legal channels won't produce the kind of deep change that democracy activists and their supporters abroad support. "If you believe that your legitimacy comes from God, you don't care what 90 percent of the people think." Hence, any hopes are futile that the government would respond even to a massive negative vote, he says.

Rubin's American Enterprise Institute colleague Ledeen depicts the government's position even more starkly. "The problem is not the fanaticism of the people, it's the fanaticism of the regime — a thin veneer on top of a civilized and cultured country. They're pro-Western and pro-American, they understand a lot about self-government, they're well-educated, and they've had constitutions. Why aren't we working for their freedom?"

Parsi, the Iranian-American advocate of a negotiated reduction in tension in Tehran, argues that lowering the level of hostility between the governments will make democratic change more possible in Iran. "If we manage to avoid conflict, if there is significant reduction of tension between the two countries and if Iran is included in the regional political and security structure — in return for significant changes — then Iran can be a constructive player in the region," he says. Indeed, he adds, "Then pro-democracy forces will have greater maneuverability to move Iran in a more democratic direction."

Riedel of the Brookings Institution's Saban Center says the failure of reformist President Khatami to produce fundamental changes shows the obstacles the democracy movement faces. "It is a pretty dramatic demonstration that it's not going to move as fast as its own supporters — or outsiders — would like.

"I'm not an optimist about civil-society movements in the Middle East — not on a 10-year cycle. Maybe 50 years."

For the moment, though, Riedel and other Iran-watchers are paying much closer attention to the immediate future, and the prospects for peace.

"The possibilities of avoiding war — if we can get through the end of the Bush administration, they're reasonably good," he says.

NOTES

1. Quoted in Sheryl Gay Stolberg, "Nuclear-Armed Iran Risks 'World War III,' Bush Says," *The New York Times*, Oct. 18, 2007, p. A6.

2. Quoted in Thom Shanker, "Gates Says Iran Gave Assurances on Explosives," *The New York Times*, Nov. 2, 2007, p. A10.

3. Quoted in Warren Hoge, "Iran's President Vows to Ignore U.N. Measures," *The New York Times*, Sept. 26, 2007, p. A1, www.nytimes.com/2007/09/26/world/26nations.html.

4. See "Vice President's Remarks to the Washington Institute for Near East Policy," The White House, Sept. 21, 2007, www.whitehouse.gov/news/releases/2007/10/print/20071021.html.

5. See Ray Takeyh, *Hidden Iran: Paradox and Power in the Islamic Republic* (2006), pp. 24-25.

6. Other institute scholars include John R. Bolton, former U.S. ambassador to the United Nations, who now criticizes the administration for being soft on North Korea. See John R. Bolton, "Bush's North Korea Meltdown," *The Wall Street Journal*, Oct. 31, 2007, p. A21.

7. See Michael A. Ledeen, *The Iranian Time Bomb: The Mullah Zealots' Quest for Destruction* (2007).

8. See Fareed Zakaria, "Stalin, Mao and . . . Ahmadinejad?" *Newsweek.com*, Oct. 29, 2007, www.newsweek.com/id/57346.

9. See Akbar Ganji, "Why Iran's Democrats Shun Aid," *The Washington Post*, Oct. 27, 2007, p. A21.

10. For analysis of oil market effects, see Steven Mufson, "Strike on Iran Would Roil Oil Markets, Experts Say," *The Washington Post*, Oct. 26, 2007, p. A1.

11. See "Debate Stirs Over Possible U.S. Military Action Against Iran," transcript, Online News Hour, Oct. 29, 2007, www.pbs.org/newshour/bb/middle_east/july-dec07/iran_10-29.html.

12. See Sharon Squassoni, "Iran's Nuclear Program: Recent Developments," Congressional Research Service, updated Dec. 26, 2006, pp. 1-2, http://fpc.state.gov/documents/organization/78477.pdf; Jonathan C. Randal, "Shah's Economic Projects Hit Snags, Periling His Regime," *The Washington Post*, April 2, 1978, p. A22; Susanna McBee, "Shah Reportedly Pledges Neutrality on Oil Prices," *The Washington Post*, Nov. 16, 1977, p. A1.

13. Quoted in Squassoni, *ibid.*, p. 2.

14. Quoted in Thom Shanker and William J. Broad, "Iran to Limit Cooperation With Nuclear Inspectors," *The New York Times*, March 26, 2007, p. A6.

15. David Albright and Corey Hinderstein, "Countdown to Showdown," *Bulletin of the Atomic Scientists*, November/December 2004, p. 67, http://thebulletin.metapress.com/content/y718r48304663rg9/fulltext.pdf.

16. "Smart Power Speakers Series, Gen. John Abizaid (Ret.)," Sept. 17, 2007 www.csis.org/media/csis/events/070917_smartpower_abizaid.pdf.

17. For brief background on the 1999 bombing raid, see "Iran wants compensation for Turkish air raids," Deutsche Presse-Agentur, Aug. 1, 1999.

18. See Vali Nasr, *The Shia Revival: How Conflicts within Islam Will Shape the Future* (2006), p. 67.

19. See "Debate Stirs. . . .," *op. cit.*; see also Andrew Higgins, "The bomb-makers of Asia," *The Independent* (London), Nov. 21, 1991, p. A29.

20. Trita Parsi, *Treacherous Alliance: The Secret Dealings of Israel, Iran, and the United States* (2007).

21. See Shirin Ebadi and Hadi Ghaemi, "The Human Rights Case Against Attacking Iran," *The New York Times*, Feb. 8, 2005, p. A25. For background on Ebadi see "Shirin Ebadi, The Nobel Peace Prize 2003, Autobiography," http://nobelprize.org/nobel_prizes/peace/laureates/2003/ebadi-autobio.html.

22. Quoted in Bourzou Daragahi, "Iran tightens the screws on internal dissent," *Los Angeles Times*, June 10, 2007, p. A1.

23. Quoted in Glenn Kessler, "Rice Asks for $75 Million to Increase Pressure on Iran," *The Washington Post*, Feb.

16, 2006, p. A1. See also Adam Graham-Silverman, "Family Planning Programs and Policy Fuel Senate Debate on Spending Bill," *CQ Today*, Sept. 26, 2007.

24. Quoted in Robin Wright, "Cut Iran Democracy Funding, Groups Tell U.S.," *The Washington Post*, Oct. 11, 2007, p. A15.

25. See Neil McFarquhar, "Iran Frees One Detainee as Another Family Waits in Hope," *The New York Times*, Sept. 20, 2007, p. A12; Tony Barboza, "Diplomacy in New York: Divestment; OC man freed from Iran prison," *Los Angeles Times*, Sept. 25, p. A10.

26. See Haleh Esfandiari and Robert S. Litwak, "When Promoting Democracy is Counterproductive," *Chronicle of Higher Education*, Oct. 19, 2007, http://chronicle.com/free/v54/i08/08b00701.htm.

27. See Eli Lake, "An Iranian Student Makes His Escape In face of Charges," *The New York Sun*, Jan. 3, 2005, www.nysun.com/article/7065. See also, "Iran — An Update," Committee on the Present Danger, Jan. 23, 2006, www.committeeonthepresentdanger.org/portals/4/iranpaperjan23.pdf.

28. See "Iran-Iraq War (1980-1988)," undated, globalsecurity.org, www.globalsecurity.org/military/world/war/iran-iraq.htm.

29. Quoted in Cesar G. Soriano, "General discusses Iran's, al-Sadr's influence in Iraq," *USA Today*, June 14, 2007, p. A13.

30. See Michael R. Gordon, "U.S. Says Iran-Supplied Bomb Is Killing More Troops in Iraq," *The New York Times*, Aug. 8, 2007, p. A1.

31. Quoted in Sam Enriquez, "Conflict in Iraq: Guarding the Border; Officer Sentenced," *Los Angeles Times*, Oct. 20, 2007, p. A1.

32. For the full report on Rafsanjani's sermon see "Rafsanjani: World should admire Iran's nuclear achievements," IRNA — Islamic Republic News Agency, July 13, 2007, republished at Globalsecurity.org, www.globalsecurity.org/wmd/library/news/iran/2007/iran-070713-irna02.htm

33. See "Policy Options in Iraq," House Foreign Affairs Committee, Committee Testimony, July 17, 2007.

34. Except where otherwise indicated, this subsection is drawn from Ali M. Ansari, *Hidden Iran* (2006); and (for details of the CIA's role) Tim Weiner, *Legacy of Ashes: The History of the CIA* (2007), pp. 81-92.

35. See Ansari, *op. cit.*, pp 36-37.

36. See Weiner, *op. cit.*, p. 92.

37. Quoted in *ibid.*, p. 46. See also, Frances Bostock and Geoffrey Jones, *Planning and Power in Iran: Ebtehaj and Economic Development Under the Shah* (1989), pp. 160-161.

38. See Eric Rouleau, "Khomeini's Iran," *Foreign Affairs*, fall 1980.

39. Quoted in Ansari, *op. cit.*, p. 53.

40. Unless otherwise indicated, material in this subsection and the one that follows is drawn from Ansari, *op. cit.*; Takeyh, *op. cit.*; Trita Parsi, *Treacherous Alliances: The Secret Dealings of Israel, Iran, and the U.S.* (2007), p. 62; and Rouleau, *op. cit.*

41. See "Tehran, Iran, Toasts of the President and the Shah at a State Dinner," Dec. 31, 1977, The American Presidency Project, www.presidency.ucsb.edu/ws/index.php?pid=7080&st=&st1=.

42. See Takeyh, *op. cit.*, p. 23. Also see Shaul Bakhash, *The Reign of the Ayatollahs: Iran and the Islamic Revolution* (1990).

43. See Bernard Gwertzman, "Iraq Gets Reports From U.S. for Use in War With Iran," *The New York Times*, Dec. 16, 1986, p. A1. U.S. Department of the Treasury, *op. cit.*

44. Quoted in Glenn Frankel, "Israeli Critical of U.S. Policy in Gulf War," *The Washington Post*, Oct. 29, 1987, p. A33.

45. See Benjamin Weiser, "Behind Israel-Iran Sales, 'Amber' Light from U.S.," *The Washington Post*, Aug. 16, 1987, p. A1.

46. Quoted in Gwertzman, *op. cit.*; See also Bob Woodward, "CIA Aiding Iraq in Gulf War," *The Washington Post*, Dec. 15, 1986, p. A1.

47. See Carol D. Leonnig, "Iran Held Liable in Khobar Attack," *The Washington Post*, Dec. 23, 2006, p. A2.

48. See Ansari, *op. cit.*, p. 180; Ashcroft quoted in Barbara Slavin, "14 indicted in barracks bombing," *USA Today*, June 22, 2001, p. A6.

49. See Takeyh, *op. cit.*, pp. 33-34. For background, see Katel, *op. cit.*

50. Quoted in Takeyh, *op. cit.*, p. 44.

51. See "Iranian President Favors People to People Dialogue," CNN "Worldview," Jan. 7, 1998.

52. See John Ward Anderson, "With Stalemate Ended, Khatami Takes Oath in Iran," *The Washington Post*, Aug. 9, 2001, p. A12.

53. See Kenneth M. Pollack, "Don't Count on Iran to Pick Up the Pieces," *The New York Times*, Dec. 8, 2006, p. A35.

54. See "The President's State of the Union Address," The White House, Jan. 29, 2002, www.white-house.gov/news/releases/2002/01/20020129-11.html.

55. Quoted in Takeyh, *op. cit.*, p. 133.

56. See "Fact Sheet: Designation of Iranian Entities and Individuals for Proliferation Activities and Support for Terrorism," Treasury Department, Oct. 25, 2007, www.treasury.gov/press/releases/hp644.htm.

57. See Anthony H. Cordesman and Martin Kleiber, "Iran's Military Forces and Warfighting Capabilities," Center for Strategic and International Studies, 2007, pp. 78-79.

58. Quoted in Helene Cooper, "In Sanctioning Iran, U.S. Plays Its 'Unilateralism' Card," *The New York Times*, Oct. 26, 2007, p. A12.

59. Wolfstahl spoke during a conference call on Oct. 25, 2007, with journalists arranged by the National Security Network, an organization of former Democratic officials. He served as special policy adviser on non-proliferation at the Department of Energy in the Clinton administration.

60. Wolosky, now a Washington attorney, served as transnational threats director at the National Security Council under Clinton and, briefly, President George W. Bush. He spoke during the National Security Council conference call on Oct. 25, 2007.

61. See Steven R. Weisman, "U.S. Sanctions Force World Bank to Halt Some Iran Aid," *The New York Times*, Nov. 3, 2007, p. A14.

62. *Ibid.*

63. Quoted in Nazila Fathi, "Iranians Dismiss Sanctions From U.S.," *The New York Times*, Oct. 27, 2007, p. A7.

64. Pillar spoke during the National Security Council conference call on Oct. 25, 2007.

65. Quoted in Elaine Sciolino and William J. Broad, "To Iran and its Foes, an Indispensable Irritant," *The New York Times*, Sept. 17, 2007, p. A1. Also see Kenneth Katzman, "Iran: U.S. Concerns and Policy Responses," Congressional Research Service, updated Aug. 6, 2007, p. 20, http://fpc.state.gov/documents/organization/91002.pdf.

66. Quoted in Maggie Farley, "U.N. still probing Iran nuclear case," *Los Angeles Times*, Oct. 30, 2007, p. A4.

67. Quoted in "Britain Reports Plan for New Sanctions on Iran," *The New York Times* [Reuters], Nov. 30, 2007, p. A7.

68. Quoted in Joby Warrick and Robin Wright, "Suspected Location of Syria's Reactor Cleared," *The Washington Post*, Oct. 26, 2007, p. A17. See also, Mark Mazzetti and Helene Cooper, "Israeli Nuclear Suspicions Linked to Raid," *The New York Times*, Sept. 18, 2007, p. A11; Glenn Kessler and Robin Wright, "Israel, U.S. Shared Data on Suspected Nuclear Site," *The Washington Post*, Sept. 21, 2007, p. A1.

69. Quoted in David E. Sanger, "Pre-emptive Caution: The Case of Syria," *The New York Times*, Oct. 14, 2007, p. A8.

70. Quoted in Elaine Sciolino and Peter Kiefer, "Iran Has New Nuclear Negotiator, But Similar Stance," *The New York Times*, Oct. 24, 2007, p. A6.

71. See "Uranium Enrichment," U.S. Nuclear Regulatory Commission, Sept. 20, 2007, www.nrc.gov/materials/fuel-cycle-fac/ur-enrichment.html.

72. See Helene Cooper, "Diplomats to Begin Drafting New U.N. Sanctions on Iran," *The New York Times*, Feb. 27, 2007, p. A9.

73. See "Security Council tightens sanctions against Iran over uranium enrichment," UN News Centre, March 24, 2007, www.un.org/apps/news/story.asp?NewsID=21997&Cr=Iran&Cr1#.

74. *Ibid.*

75. *Ibid.*

76. See David E. Sanger and William J. Broad, "Bush and Putin Want Iran to Treat Uranium in Russia," *The New York Times*, Nov. 18, 2005, p. A1. See also Douglas Frantz, "From Patriot to Proliferator," *Los Angeles Times*, Sept. 23, 2005, p. A1, and Roland Flamini, "Nuclear Proliferation," *CQ Global Researcher*, January 2007, pp. 1-26; and Mary H. Cooper, "Nuclear Proliferation and Terrorism," *CQ Researcher*, April 2, 2004, pp. 297-320.

77. Meridor quoted in Hilary Leila Krieger, *Jerusalem Post*, online edition, Oct. 23, 2007, www.jpost .com/servlet/Satellite?pagename=JPost%2FJPArticle %2FShowFull&cid=1192380626865; Baidatz quoted in Mark Weiss and Sheera Claire Frenkel, "Mofaz: 2008 is decisive for stopping Iran's nuclear drive," *Jerusalem Post*, online edition, www.jpost .com/servlet/Satellite?cid=1192380749027&page-name=JPost%2FJPArticle%2FShowFull.

78. Quoted in David Ignatius, "The Spy Who Wants Israel to Talk," *The Washington Post*, Nov. 11, 2007, p. B7.

79. The 1989 Romanian revolution, one of the last nails in the coffin of Eastern and Central European communism, toppled dictator Nicolae Ceausescu, who was shot by firing squad on national television, along with his wife, Elena. See William Horsley, "Romania's bloody revolution," BBC News, Dec. 12, 1999, http://news.bbc.co.uk/2/hi/europe/574200.stm.

BIBLIOGRAPHY

Books

Ansari, Ali M., *Confronting Iran: The Failure of American Foreign Policy and the Next Great Crisis in the Middle East*, **Basic Books, 2006.**
A historian at the University of St. Andrews in Scotland chronicles and analyzes the complexities of the U.S.-Iran relationship.

Ledeen, Michael A., *The Iranian Time Bomb: The Mullah Zealots' Quest for Destruction*, **St. Martin's Press, 2007.**
The Iranian leadership is far more dangerous than most Westerners realize, argues a longtime Iran hawk.

Parsi, Trita, *Treacherous Alliance: The Secret Dealings of Israel, Iran, and the U.S.*, **Yale University Press, 2007.**
An adjunct professor at Johns Hopkins University's School of Advanced International Studies traces the shifting alliances that have marked the crucial three-way relationship.

Takeyh, Ray, *Hidden Iran: Paradox and Power in the Islamic Republic*, **Times Books, 2006.**
A Middle East expert at the Council on Foreign Relations explores the twists and turns of Iranian politics.

Articles

Barboza, Tony, "Iranians in U.S. weigh the price of activism," *Los Angeles Times*, **Sept. 16, 2007, p. B1.**
The imprisonment of liberal Iranian-Americans visiting their homeland sends a chill through the Iranian exile community.

Daragahi, Borzou, "Iran tightens the screws on internal dissent," *Los Angeles Times*, **June 10, 2007, p. A1.**
The Iranian regime is intensifying its repression of pro-democracy Iranians and those who break dress codes.

Daragahi, Borzou, "U.S.-Iran rivalry has a familiar look," *Los Angeles Times*, **July 5, 2007, p. A6.**
The complicated, tense standoff between the United States and Iran has parallels to the Cold War.

Hersh, Seymour M., "Shifting targets: The administration's plan for Iran," *The New Yorker*, **Oct. 8, 2007, www.newyorker.com/reporting/2007/10/08/071008fa_ fact_hersh.**
A leading investigative journalist reports that administration strategy on Iran has met some detours and complications.

Montagne, Renee, (host), "The Evolution of Iran's Revolutionary Guard," National Public Radio, (transcript), www.npr.org/templates/transcript/transcript .php?story Id=9371072.
Iran experts discuss the Iranian force at the center of the U.S.-Iran standoff.

Sciolino, Elaine, "To Iran, Iraq May Be the Greater Satan," *The New York Times*, **Nov. 3, 2002, Sect. 4 (*News of the Week in Review*), p. 14.**
In the run-up to the Iraq War, a veteran correspondent examines the complicated world of Middle Eastern alliances.

Wright, Robin, "Free Thinker; Iranian Dissident Akbar Ganji at Libert to Speak His Mind, at Least Until he Goes Back Home," *The Washington Post*, Aug. 14, 2007, p. C1.
A celebrated dissident assesses the grim state of civil liberties and democracy in Iran, but plans on returning.

Reports

Clawson, Patrick, and Michael Eisenstadt, "Deterring the Ayatollahs: Complications in Applying Cold War Strategy to Iran," Washington Institute for Near East Policy, July 2007, www.washingtoninstitute.org/templateC04.php?CID=280.
Washington think tank scholars compiled essays on how Iran might be persuaded not to develop nuclear weapons.

Cordesman, Anthony H., "Iran's Revolutionary Guards, the Al Quds Force, and Other Intelligence and Paramilitary Forces," Center for Strategic and International Studies, Aug. 16, 2007, (draft), www.csis.org/media/csis/pubs/070816_cordesman_report.pdf.
A veteran military analyst describes what is known about the key Iranian military and unconventional-warfare units.

Katzman, Kenneth, "Iran: U.S. Concerns and Policy Responses," Congressional Research Service, Aug. 6, 2007, http://fpc.state.gov/documents/organization/91002.pdf.
A dispassionate run-down of the issues at stake in the faceoff between the United States and Iran.

Sadjadpour, Karim, "Iran: Reality, Options, and Consequences — Iranian People and Attitudes," testimony to House Committee on Oversight and Government Reform, Subcommittee on National Security and Foreign Affairs, Oct., 30, 2007, www.carnegieendowment.org/files/2007-10-30_ks_testimony.pdf.
An associate at the Carnegie Institute for International Peace with extensive experience in Iran reports that public alienation from the government is unlikely to lead to popular revolt in the near future.

Yaphe, Judith S., and Charles D. Lutes, "Reassessing the Implications of a Nuclear-Armed Iran," Institute for National Strategic Studies, National Defense University, 2005, www.ndu.edu/inss/mcnair/mcnair69/McNairPDF.pdf.
A book-length study examines Iran's nuclear ambitions, including their effects on Israel.

For More Information

American Enterprise Institute, 1150 17th St., N.W., Washington, DC 20036; (202) 862-5800; http://aei.org. Conservative think tank advocates hawkish policies on Iran.

Committee on the Present Danger, P.O. Box 33249, Washington, DC 20033; (202) 207-0190; www.committeeonthepresentdanger.org. Conservative organization favors regime change in Iran.

National Iranian American Council, 1411 K St., N.W., Suite 600, Washington, DC 20005; (202) 386-6325; www.niacouncil.org/index.php. Favors negotiations to establish a new U.S. relationship with Iran.

Saban Center for Middle East Policy, Brookings Institution, 1775 Massachusetts Ave., N.W., Washington, DC 20036; (202) 797-6000; www.brookings.edu/saban.aspx. Studies U.S. policy options in the region.

U.S. Department of State, 2201 C St., N.W., Washington, DC 20520; (202) 647-4000; www.state.gov/p/nea/ci/c2404.htm. Web site provides information on events and policy matters regarding Iran.

Washington Institute for Near East Policy, 1828 L St., N.W., Suite 1050, Washington, DC 20036; (202) 452-0650; www.washingtoninstitute.org. Think tank that devotes much attention to Iran.

4

Radical Islam in Europe

Sarah Glazer

Pakistani Muslims burn the Danish flag in Karachi on Feb. 14, 2006, to protest Danish newspaper cartoons they said blasphemed the Prophet Mohammed. Worldwide protests sparked by the cartoons reflected many young Muslims' feeling that the Muslim world is under attack by the West.

AP Photo/Shakil Adil

From *CQ Researcher,*
November 1, 2007.

A recent spate of attempted terrorist plots by Muslims in Europe has revived questions about how much of the threat is homegrown — the outgrowth of disaffection among European Muslims — and how much is orchestrated abroad.

On Sept. 4 German authorities announced they had foiled a plan to blow up an American military base in Frankfurt. Their arrest of a member of Germany's large Turkish community — long considered one of Europe's most peaceful Muslim immigrant groups — along with two German-born converts to Islam raised new questions about Germany as a locus of radicalization and its success at integrating Muslim residents.

Police said the planned explosion could have been more deadly than the 2004 train bombings in Madrid, which killed 191 people, and the 2005 London transit attack that killed 52 commuters. [1]

On the same day as the announcement of the German arrests, Muslims in Copenhagen were charged with planning a bombing attack in Denmark, suggesting that domestic discontent in the country — where Muslim immigrants complain of job discrimination and a newspaper triggered worldwide protests among Muslims two years ago by publishing cartoons seen as ridiculing Mohammed — may have provided fertile ground for Islamic terrorism. [2]

This past summer, Britons were shocked to learn that Muslims suspected of trying to blow up the Glasgow, Scotland, airport on June 30 included middle-class Indian and Middle Eastern doctors working for the National Health Service — not alienated youths without jobs. The news came the day after the same suspects had allegedly tried to set off a car bomb outside a London nightclub and just before the anniversary of the July 7, 2005, London transit

More European Muslims Favor Suicide Bombings

Muslims in France, Spain and Great Britain are twice as likely as American Muslims to condone suicide bombings of civilians. About one in six Muslims in the three countries say bombing civilians to defend Islam is justifiable.

Can the suicide bombing of civilians to defend Islam be justified?

Muslims who said yes in . . .

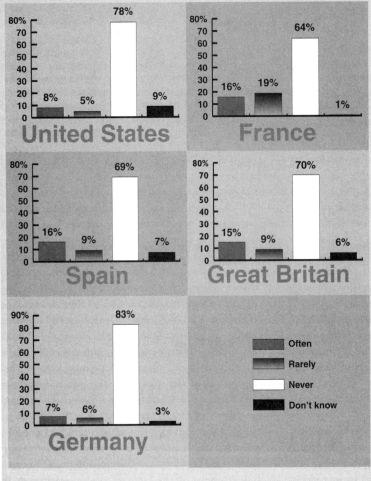

United States
- Often: 8%
- Rarely: 5%
- Never: 78%
- Don't know: 9%

France
- Often: 16%
- Rarely: 19%
- Never: 64%
- Don't know: 1%

Spain
- Often: 16%
- Rarely: 9%
- Never: 69%
- Don't know: 7%

Great Britain
- Often: 15%
- Rarely: 9%
- Never: 70%
- Don't know: 6%

Germany
- Often: 7%
- Rarely: 6%
- Never: 83%
- Don't know: 3%

Legend:
- Often
- Rarely
- Never
- Don't know

* Percentages may not total 100 due to rounding.

Source: "Muslim Americans: Middle Class and Mostly Mainstream," Pew Research Center, May 2007

bombings. One of the suicide bombers from that attack had left a video in a strong Yorkshire accent — a startling reminder that "a British lad" had been radicalized at home even if he also had links to militants abroad. [3]

All three events spurred soul-searching in Britain, Germany, Denmark, Scotland and elsewhere. Experts often blame Western foreign policies, including the war in Iraq, for the young Muslims' outrage and their feeling that the Muslim world is under attack by the West. But the long-held belief by some European leaders that opposing the Iraq War would immunize their countries from Muslim terrorist attacks appeared dashed by the plot in Germany, which opposed the war. Authorities said the bombing scheme was linked to Germany's military presence in Afghanistan. [4]

To what extent does the violence that Europe is experiencing reflect a failure to integrate immigrants and their children into Western society?

"There is a sense in our societies that the radicalism was not created by the United States [foreign policy] but caused by the lack of integration," Christoph Bertram, the former director of the Institute of Security Affairs in Berlin, told *The New York Times* the week after the German and Danish arrests. [5]

Reflecting that concern, British Prime Minister Gordon Brown in July announced that in addition to beefing up border police he was proposing a fourfold increase in "hearts and minds" programs like citizenship classes in Britain's 1,000 *madrasas* (Islamic religious schools, usually attached to a mosque), and

English-language training for imams.

"A tough security response is vital, but to be safe in the longer term we need to reach people before they are drawn into violent extremism," said Hazel Blears, Britain's Secretary of State for Communities and Local Government. [6]

Other analysts argue that radical fundamentalism originates from increasingly well-organized international networks seeking out and finding the few estranged individuals ready to commit violence. The German and Danish plotters were said to have received training and instructions in Pakistan. And in September, European authorities warned that a newly strengthened al Qaeda, operating from the lawless, tribal border region between Pakistan and Afghanistan, was stepping up plans to target Europe and the United States. [7]

Meanwhile, a recent New York City Police Department (NYPD) intelligence report concluded that the terrorists involved in the 2004 Madrid bombings, the London transit attack and the group in Hamburg, Germany, that planned the Sept. 11, 2001, terrorist attacks in the United States were "unremarkable" local residents, some with advanced degrees from European universities. Moreover, the report said, the process of radicalization seems to be accelerating, and terrorists are getting younger. "We now believe it is critical to identify the al Qaeda-inspired threat at the point where radicalization begins," the report said, a conclusion shared by a 2006 British intelligence report. [8]

Jytte Klausen, a professor of comparative politics at Brandeis University who has studied the profiles of 550 alleged terrorists arrested since the 9/11 attacks, disputes the idea that terrorism is primarily the fruit of "homegrown" radicals who have not been integrated into society. "This is not primarily about integration, though better integration might be preventative," she says. "It has a lot to do with transnational networks and ethnic origins: Political developments in Pakistan are getting filtered through Britain's back door; the radical groups piggyback on the migrant stream."

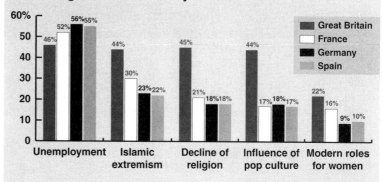

Jobs Are Top Muslim Concern

Most Muslims in Europe worry more about unemployment than about religious and cultural issues, such as the rise of extremism and the decline of religion. They are least concerned about the role of women in modern society.

Percentage of Muslims very worried about . . .

Legend: Great Britain, France, Germany, Spain

	Great Britain	France	Germany	Spain
Unemployment	46%	52%	56%	55%
Islamic extremism	44%	30%	23%	22%
Decline of religion	45%	21%	18%	18%
Influence of pop culture	44%	17%	18%	17%
Modern roles for women	22%	16%	9%	10%

Source: "Muslims in Europe: Economic Worries Top Concerns About Religious and Cultural Identity," Pew Global Attitudes Project, July 2006

British writer Ed Husain describes his recruitment in the 1990s in London by Islamists — Muslims who advocate an Islamic state, in some cases by violent means — in his 2007 memoir *The Islamist.* Husain argues that two factors prompt those drawn to political Islamic ideology to contemplate violence: the scorn heaped on non-Muslims by radical fundamentalists and the growing conviction that the world's Muslims need their own transnational state — or caliphate — governed by strict religious law, called sharia.

But others, like sociologist Tahir Abbas of England's University of Birmingham, say the notion of a Muslim caliphate is still an abstract one — an aspiration that isn't much different from European nations joining together in the European Union. And some of the London organizations where Husain says he was radicalized, such as Hizb ut-Tahrir and the controversial East London Mosque, claim they do not advocate violence to achieve the goal of a global Islamic state. Some groups say they only advocate the return of an Islamic state in Muslim countries. For example, Hizb ut-Tahrir says it works to bring "the Muslim world" under the caliphate but that in the West it does "not work to change the system of government." [9] (*See sidebar, p. 98.*)

European Muslims Emphasize Islamic Identity

A majority of European Muslims consider their Islamic identity more important than their national identity (top). Christians in the same countries, however, say citizenship comes first (bottom).

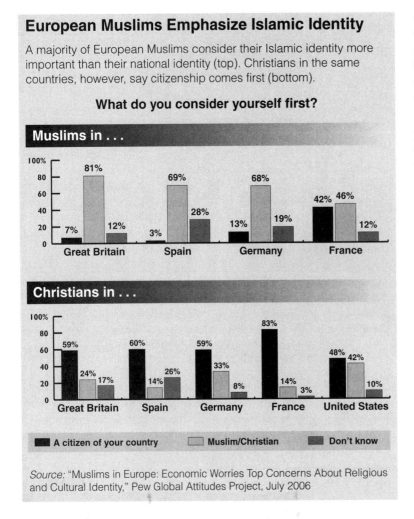

What do you consider yourself first?

Muslims in . . .

Great Britain: 7%, 81%, 12%
Spain: 3%, 69%, 28%
Germany: 13%, 68%, 19%
France: 42%, 46%, 12%

Christians in . . .

Great Britain: 59%, 24%, 17%
Spain: 60%, 14%, 26%
Germany: 59%, 33%, 8%
France: 83%, 14%, 3%
United States: 48%, 42%, 10%

■ A citizen of your country   ☐ Muslim/Christian   ■ Don't know

Source: "Muslims in Europe: Economic Worries Top Concerns About Religious and Cultural Identity," Pew Global Attitudes Project, July 2006

Some Muslim leaders in Britain, including Syed Aziz Pasha, secretary general of the Union of Muslim Organizations of the UK and Ireland, have pushed for sharia law in Britain — but only as it pertains to family matters like marriage, and only for Muslims. One poll shows about a third of British Muslims would rather live under sharia. [10]

Husain, a former member of Hizb ut-Tahrir, remains skeptical of the group's nonviolent stance: "The only difference between Islamists from Hizb ut-Tahrir and jihadists is that the former are waiting for their state and caliph before they commence jihad, while the latter believes the time for jihad is now." [11]

Meanwhile, most experts agree that Muslims in Europe have not been as easily incorporated into society

as they have in the United States, which might explain their openness to radical ideas. Polls show Muslims in France, Spain and Britain are twice as likely as U.S. Muslims to say suicide bombs can be justified. (*See graph, p. 82.*) Notably, support in Europe for suicide bombings is highest among Muslim adults under age 30 — supporters make up 35 percent of young Muslims in Great Britain and 42 percent in France. There were an estimated 15 million Muslims in the European Union in 2006, not counting the 70 million Muslims in Turkey. [12]

One measure of European Muslims' alienation from Western governments and news sources is the surprisingly large majorities who don't accept that recent terrorist acts were carried out by Muslims. An astonishing 56 percent of British Muslims don't believe Arabs carried out the 9/11 attacks, according to a poll by the Pew Research Center, a result commonly explained as acceptance of one of the conspiracy theories blaming Jews, Israel's secret police or the Bush administration. [13] But Abbas, who is Muslim himself, suggests another explanation for the widespread skepticism: Most Muslims are in denial because they are so shocked at the thought that fellow Muslims could carry out such a violent act.

Experts on Islam also hasten to point out that sympathizing with suicide bombers or sharing fundamentalist beliefs doesn't mean one will become a terrorist. Some of the fear about the call for an Islamic state by groups like Hizb ut-Tahrir — a group that calls for the end of Israel and which Britain has considered banning — is misplaced, Abbas believes. "People look at the surface, see dogma and . . . see it as a menacing threat. Yes, lots of people are hotheaded and mad, but they dip in and out of these organizations just as often as they're sprouting up. Young people need to find themselves, need to search for meaning to their lives," he says.

Yet, even if a group doesn't advocate terrorism to achieve an Islamic state, parties advocating Islamic rule through peaceful means should also be resisted because they aim to establish a "totalitarian" theocracy, argues Martin Bright, a journalist who has investigated radical links to Muslim groups in Britain. "We make a mistake if we think that just because people are engaged in the electoral process that's necessarily a good thing; Mussolini and Hitler were also engaged in the electoral process," says Bright, political editor at the *New Statesman*, a left-leaning political weekly published in London. Radical asylum seekers are often careful not to commit violence in Britain and other European countries that accept them for fear of deportation, he says, but still support jihad abroad.

When Muhammad Abdul Bari — secretary general of the British Muslim Council, an umbrella group representing Muslims — suggested last year that British non-Muslims adopt more Islamic ways, including arranged marriages, one critic interpreted it as a call for adopting sharia law. [14] A recent BBC documentary reported that sharia courts in Nigeria, operating strictly according to Koranic prescriptions, have ordered limbs amputated as a punishment for thievery, public flogging and stoning of women accused of adultery. [15] Critics like Bright say that given the potential for such brutal punishments, accompanying repressive attitudes towards women and frequently virulent anti-Semitism, the real struggle facing the West is about ideology, not terrorism.

The recent foiled bombing attempts have prompted calls in England and France to allow police to detain terrorist suspects for longer periods to give police more time to investigate. But groups like Human Rights Watch say Muslims are already bearing the brunt of law enforcement and immigration policies that violate their human rights. [16] In the long run, terrorist crackdowns can be counter-productive if they merely alienate mainstream Muslims, say civil liberties advocates.

By failing to heed moderate Muslims' warnings in the 1990s that clerics were preaching violence, law-enforcement services in Britain alienated the very communities they need to help them, says Hisham A. Hellyer, Senior Research Fellow at the University of Warwick and author of a forthcoming report from the Brookings Institution in Washington on counterterrorism lessons from Britain for the West. An important lesson for the West, he says, is to not cut off contact with

AP Photo/Peter MacDiarmid

A mangled bus is a grim reminder of the four rush-hour suicide bombings by Muslim terrorists that killed 52 London commuters and injured hundreds in July 2005. The attacks added to Europeans' concerns about how well they were integrating Muslim immigrants and their children.

Muslim groups who may be conservatively religious but not violent.

Some experts, including Director of National Intelligence Mike McConnell, fear the United States could be the next target of European terrorists. McConnell told the Senate Judiciary Committee in September that al Qaeda is recruiting Europeans for explosives training in Pakistan because they can more easily enter the United States without a visa. [17]

Peter Skerry, a professor of political science at Boston College who is writing a book about Muslims in America, says homegrown terrorists are less likely in the United States because there is more ethnic diversity among American Muslims, and they are more educated and wealthier than European Muslims. They are also less of a

Foreign Domination Sparked Radical Islamic Thoug

Muslim writers protested British, U.S. interventions.

The radicalization of Islam has historic roots reaching back to the 1930s, '40s and '50s, when Muslim writers were also protesting colonialism and what they saw as imperialistic British and U.S. interventions in the Middle East.

The Muslim Brotherhood, founded in Egypt in 1928, sought to couple resistance to foreign domination with establishment of an Islamic state run by sharia law, which imposes strict interpretations of the *Koran*. The Brotherhood at first worked closely with the secret Free Officers revolutionary movement led by Gamal Abdel Nasser and Anwar al-Sadat, which aimed at overthrowing the British regime and the Egyptian royal family.

But after the group's military coup toppled the Egyptian monarchy in 1952, Nasser's regime sorely disappointed the Brotherhood as insufficiently Islamic. A failed assassination attempt on Nasser by an embittered Brotherhood member in 1954 prompted the secular government to brutally suppress the movement and imprison its leaders.

One of those imprisoned leaders was Sayyid Qutb, known by his followers as "The Martyr," whose anti-Western writings would become extremely influential in the jihadist movement. In 1948, while on a study mission to the United States, he wrote with distaste of the sexual permissiveness and consumerism he saw, comparing the typical American to a primitive "caveman."[1] Alienated by America's hedonism, he argued the only way to protect the Islamic world from such influences would be to return to strict Islamic teachings.

Qutb spent most of the last decade of his life imprisoned in Egypt, where he was tortured. While in prison he wrote *Milestones*, his famous work espousing his vision of Islam as inseparable from the political state, and concluded the regime was a legitimate target of jihad.[2] He was convicted of sedition in 1966 and hanged.

The ideas of writers like Qutb have been adopted by radical Islamic groups (Islamists) today, generating concern in the West. An updated version of *Milestones*, published in Birmingham, England, in 2006 and prominently displayed at the bookstore next to the controversial East London Mosque contains a 1940s-era instruction manual by another member of the Muslim Brotherhood with chapter headings like "The Virtues of Killing a Non-Believer for the Sake of Allah" and "The Virtues of Martyrdom."[3]

The Muslim Brotherhood was "really the first organization to develop the idea that you could have an Islamic state within the modern world," according to *New Statesman* political editor Martin Bright.[4]

Although the Brotherhood is sometimes represented as moderate in comparison to jihadist groups like al Qaeda, Bright notes its motto remains to this day: "Allah is our objective. The Prophet is our Leader. The *Qu'uran* [*Koran*] is our constitution. Jihad is our way. Dying in the way of Allah is our highest hope." In 1981, Sadat, who had become Egypt's president, was assassinated by four members of a Brotherhood splinter group.[5]

Robert S. Leiken, director of the Immigration and National Security Program at the Nixon Center in Washington, D.C., recently interviewed leaders of the Brotherhood in Europe and the Middle East. He concluded the organization "depends on winning hearts through gradual and peaceful Islamization" and is committed to the electoral process. However, the group does authorize jihad in countries it considers occupied by a foreign power.[6]

For instance, Yusuf al-Qaradawi, the Brotherhood's spiritual leader, has supported suicide bombing in the Palestinian occupied territories and called it a duty of every Muslim to resist American and British forces in Iraq.[7]

Jamaat-e-Islami, the radical Asian offshoot of the Muslim Brotherhood, originated in British India first as a religious movement in 1941 and then as a political party committed to an Islamic state in 1947. It is the oldest religious party in Pakistan and also has wings in Bangladesh and Kashmir.

presence. Muslims constitute less than 1 percent of the U.S. population, compared to an estimated 8-9 percent in France, 5.6 percent in the Netherlands, 3.6 percent in Germany and 3 percent in Britain.[18]

But the European experience has American law enforcers casting a worried glance eastward, and some are redoubling efforts to forge links with American Muslims.[19] As they do, here are some of the debates taking place in academic, political and citizen arenas in Europe and the United States:

The party was founded by Abdul A'la Maududi, a Pakistani journalist who promoted a highly politicized, anti-Western brand of Islam. In his writings, Maududi asserts that Islamic democracy is the antithesis of secular Western democracy because the latter is based on the sovereignty of the people, rather than God.

Maududi was the first Muslim to reject Islam as a religion and re-brand it as an ideology — political Islam. His writing strongly influenced Qutb during his years in prison. British former radical Ed Husain writes that the organizations in London where he first heard Islam described as a political ideology in the 1990s — the Young Muslim Organization and the East London Mosque — both venerated Maududi. [8]

But while Maududi urged gradual change through a takeover of political institutions, Qutb argued for "religious war," seizing political authority "wherever an Islamic community exists," and jihad "to make this system of life dominant in the world." [9]

In support, Qutb cited the Prophet Mohammed's declaration of war on the infidels of Mecca. Qutb tarred all Christian, Jewish and Muslim societies of his time as *jahili* — disregarding divine precepts — because their leaders usurped Allah's legislative authority. "When I read *Milestones*, I felt growing animosity toward the *kuffar* (non-Muslims)," Husain writes. [10]

Husain would eventually move on to an even more radical group, Hizb ut-Tahrir (Party of Liberation), founded in Jerusalem in 1953 by Palestinian theologian and political activist Taqiuddin an-Nabhani. While Qutb and Maududi argued that Muslims had a religious duty to establish an Islamic state, Nabhani "provided the details of how to achieve it," writes Husain — through military coups or assassinations of political leaders. [11]

Today, Hizb ut-Tahrir says it seeks to establish a caliphate, or Islamic state governing all Muslims, through an "exclusively political" rather than violent method. [12] However, the group was recently denounced by a former senior member, Maajid Nawaz, who told the BBC that according to the group's own literature, the caliphate is "a state that they are prepared to kill millions of people to expand." [13]

Today, reverence for the writings of Qutb or Maududi should be a litmus test for any Islamist group's level of radicalism, according to Husain. But University of Birmingham sociologist Tahir Abbas cautions that Maududi's writing "is about trying to fight off the yoke of colonialism as much as developing a pan-Islamic identity. When it comes to Maududi, he's writing for his time — and people take it out of context."

Indeed, to the uninitiated, the writings of both Qutb and Maududi come across as rather dry, if fiercely loyal, interpretations of the *Koran* as the supreme word.

Still, Maududi's party, Jamaat-e-Islami, has spawned its share of leaders preaching violent hatred against the West. Hossain Sayeedi, a Jamaat-e-Islami member of the Bangladesh Parliament, has compared Hindus to excrement. In public rallies in Bangladesh, he has urged that unless they convert to Islam, "let all the American soldiers be buried in the soil of Iraq and let them never return to their homes." [14]

---

[1] Sayyid Qutb, *Milestones* (2006), p. 8.

[2] For background, see Peter Katel, "Global Jihad," *CQ Researcher*, Oct. 14, 2005, pp. 857-880.

[3] Qutb, *op. cit.*, p. 266.

[4] Martin Bright, "When Progressives Treat with Reactionaries: The British State's Flirtation with Radical Islamism," *Policy Exchange*, 2006, p. 21.

[5] *Ibid.*, p. 14.

[6] Robert S. Leiken and Steven Brooke, "The Moderate Muslim Brotherhood," *Foreign Affairs*, March/April 2007, pp. 107-119.

[7] Bright, *op. cit.*, p. 20.

[8] Ed Husain, *The Islamist* (2007), p. 24. In this book, Maududi is spelled Mawdudi.

[9] Qutb, *op. cit.*, p. 86.

[10] *Ibid.*

[11] *Ibid.*, pp. 91, 96.

[12] "Radicalisation, Extremism & 'Islamism,'" *Hizb ut-Tahrir Britain*, July 2007, www.hizb.org.uk/hizb/images/PDFs/htb_radicalisation_report.pdf.

[13] Richard Watson, "Why Newsnight's Interview with Former HT Member is Essential Viewing," BBC, Sept. 13, 2007, www.bbc.co.uk/blogs/newsnight/2007/09/why_newsnights_interview_with_former_ht_member_is.html.

[14] Quoted in Bright, *op. cit.*, p. 22.

Has Europe's terrorism been caused by a failure to integrate Muslims into society?

In the early 1990s, the isolation of the Bangladeshi neighborhood in East London where writer Husain grew up made it relatively easy for radical Islamist groups to recruit him to their vision of a transnational Islamic state, he writes in his memoir.

The lack of contact with mainstream British culture and society helps explain why many young Muslims insist that the recent attack on the Glasgow airport and

Europe Has Many Low-income Muslims

Approximately one-fifth of Muslims in Europe are considered low-income, leading some terrorism experts to conclude that economic deprivation triggers extremism. In the United States, where there have been few terrorist attacks, only 2 percent of Muslims are considered low-income.

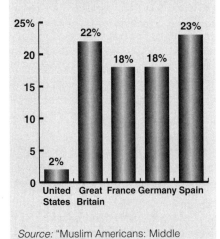

Percentage of Muslims Considered Low-income

Source: "Muslim Americans: Middle Class and Mostly Mainstream," Pew Research Center, May 2007

major terrorist attack was likely in their country in the next 12 months, to consider Muslims a threat to national security and to believe Muslims had too much political power in their country. [20]

French immigration historian Patrick Weil, a senior research fellow at the University of Paris' National Center for Scientific Research, says France accepts Muslims as fellow citizens and friends more easily than the British.

"The English have fought [work and educational] discrimination among the elite, and they've been quite successful, but they've been bad at cultural integration," he says. In France, it's the opposite: "We're very bad at ending discrimination but much better at integration."

Among the Europeans polled, the French are the most likely to have Muslim friends, accept a son or daughter marrying a Muslim and think Muslims are unjustly the subject of prejudice. [21] In the same vein, more French Muslims think of themselves as French first and Muslim second than in the other three countries polled, according to a Pew survey. [22] (See graph, p. 84.)

That may help explain why France has been spared a major Muslim terrorist attack since the mid-1990s. The 2005 riots in Paris' poorer, heavily Muslim suburbs were protests against racial and economic discrimination driven by a desire to be part of France, rather than a separatist Muslim movement, Weil and other experts believe. Even when Muslims were protesting France's 2004 head-scarf ban in public schools, their chant was decidedly Francophile: "First, Second, Third Generation: We don't give a damn: Our home is Here!" [23]

Weil, a member of a commission appointed in 2003 by former French President Jacques Chirac that recommended banning "conspicuous religious symbols" in schools, claims the headscarf ban has helped to integrate Muslims into France's secular system and has given Muslim girls a better chance at educational equality. As evidence, he points out the ban was implemented without the need for police enforcement. The *Koran* became a bestseller during the head-scarf debate, a sign that non-Muslims wanted to learn more about Islam, he says. The head-scarf rule "includes you in the system" of basic French values, he says.

But John R. Bowen, an anthropologist at Washington University in St. Louis and author of *Why the French Don't Like Headscarves*, thinks the ban incurred resentment in the Muslim community. Nevertheless, he argues in a recent article, Muslims and non-Muslims in France

9/11 itself must be the creation of the government and the media, Husain believes. "When you're in that world, what others say [has] no meaning," he says. "You see them as non-believers headed for hell anyway."

But integration is a two-way street, and Husain says the traditional coldness of the English toward outsiders makes it difficult for anyone to easily enter their society.

Supporting that view is a *Financial Times* poll conducted last August that found Britons are more suspicious of Muslims than are other Europeans or Americans. Only 59 percent of Britons thought it possible to be both a Muslim and a citizen of their country, a smaller proportion than in France, Germany, Spain, Italy or the United States. British citizens also were the most likely to think a

"are far more willing to get on with the task of building a multireligious society than are the Dutch, British or Spanish — or even Americans." [24]

French Muslims, for instance, are not calling for sharia law, as do many British Muslims, he notes. Partly that's historical: Many North Africans arrive speaking fluent French and have a sense of affiliation to their former colonial power. Most French Muslims also tend to live in more ethnically mixed areas, while in England entire Bangladeshi villages seem to have been plopped down in single neighborhoods.

Most experts also give credit to the French police and domestic intelligence service. "The French really monitor their Muslims closely, so if someone is preaching a radical sermon they'll know right away and have much less compunction than the British to say, 'You can't do that,' or find a way to get rid of the guy" by deporting him, says Bowen.

Surprisingly, a French government adviser on religious affairs, Bernard Godard, who specialized in Muslim neighborhoods while serving with the French police and domestic intelligence service, ascribes France's lack of Muslim terrorism not to the country's policing efforts but to its policy of non-engagement in Iraq. "France is a little country that is not considered dangerous," he says. And it is harder to recruit North African Muslims for terrorism than Middle Easterners, he suggests. "They have no reason to do something against France."

The French also are much more inclusive toward newcomers than their neighbors. The French government gives newly arrived immigrants hundreds of hours of free French-language lessons to help qualify them for employment. In contrast, observes Bowen, the Netherlands recently required would-be immigrants — even the spouses of Dutch residents — to prove that they already speak good Dutch before they arrive, but provide no help in learning the language. "The Dutch are using language to exclude Muslims, the French to integrate them," he says. [25]

Similarly, Germany recently proposed requiring that immigrants show on their naturalization applications that they agree with German public opinion — a tactic some have called the policing of "un-German" thought. Turks and other Muslims see the plan as discriminatory, according to a study by the International Crisis Group (ICG). Nevertheless, the report concluded that Germany's approach to its mainly Turkish Muslim population was "paying off" — judging from the lack of ter-

rorist incidents or riots in Germany compared to the experiences of Britain and France. [26] (The ICG report was issued before the recent foiled German plot.)

But Boston College political scientist Jonathan Laurence, the author of the ICG report on Germany and a book published last year on integration in France, says the recent German plot involving a Turkish resident doesn't change his "cautious optimism." [27]

Since Germany has traditionally treated Turkish immigrants as "guestworkers" rather than citizens, most of today's Turkish population still holds only Turkish citizenship even though half were born in Germany. A 2000 law opened the door to citizenship but under very restrictive rules. Laurence says German Turks have less "political frustration" than Muslims in other European countries because they have lower expectations as a result of German citizenship laws. "They don't feel as entitled to success or mobility because they have not been included in the German dream," he says.

But he doubts that there are "any direct causal links" between a lack of integration and recent terrorist attempts in Europe. "There are too many other poorly integrated groups that don't turn to terror," he says.

If failure to integrate were the cause, "We'd have masses of people joining the jihad, which is not happening," says Jocelyne Cesari, director of Harvard University's Paris-based Islam in the West study group and author of the 2004 book *When Islam and Democracy Meet: Muslims in Europe and the United States.*

In fact, she continues, "All national ideologies in Europe are in crisis," as indicated by France's failure to ratify the EU constitution. [28] And for some young people, Islamic ideologies fill the vacuum left by national identity, she says.

That's what has happened in Britain, argues British *Daily Mail* journalist Melanie Phillips in her book *Londonistan.* England has become the epicenter of Islamic terrorism, she argues, in part because of shame about British national identity. "British society presented a moral and philosophical vacuum that was ripe for colonization by predatory Islamism," she writes. [29] "Driven by postcolonial guilt . . . Britain's elites have come to believe that the country's identity and values are by definition racist, nationalist and discriminatory." [30]

Ironically, points out Brandeis political scientist Klausen, England has the most terrorism in Europe even though it is one of Europe's most integrated countries by

AP Photo/*Bangalore Mirror*

Kafeel Ahmed died of severe burns a month after his attempted car bombing of Glasgow International Airport on June 30, 2007. Iraqi doctor Bilal Abdullah was also in the car and was charged with attempting a bombing. Ahmed, an engineer from India, was among eight Muslims — including three physicians working for Britain's National Health Service — charged in connection with attempted car bombings in Glasgow and London.

ing study of 550 people arrested for terrorism since 9/11, she was surprised to find a high degree of petty-criminal histories, suggesting these are not mainstream Muslims. And a highly traditional, religious background does not seem to be a predictor either. "The argument that democracy is illegitimate is what turns them on," she says.

Although unemployment is high among young Muslim men in Britain, it isn't among terrorists arrested there, according to Klausen, suggesting only a tenuous link between inequality or discrimination and political anger. [31]

So is terrorism the result of a lack of integration or the influence of external terrorist networks? "It's both," according to Robert S. Leiken, director of the Immigration and National Security Program at the Nixon Center, a think tank in Washington, D.C. Europe, he says, currently has two kinds of jihadists: "outsiders" — typically radical imams, asylum seekers or students fleeing from crackdowns against Islamist agitators in the Middle East — and "insiders" — second- or third-generation children of immigrants. [32]

"That's why Britain is the most dangerous country," according to Leiken. "It has the confluence of these two sources of jihad."

Has Britain's multiculturalism fostered social isolation and extremism?

Various books, columns and think-tank reports recently have blamed Britain's multicultural ethos for creating segregation along religious lines and, in some eyes, providing fertile ground for extremist Islamic ideas. Last year Prime Minister Tony Blair's Communities Secretary Ruth Kelly launched a study commission to examine whether multiculturalism * was causing greater ethnic-minority separateness. [33]

By the time the commission reported back in June, the term "multiculturalism" had disappeared from the report in favor of a new buzzword, "community cohesion," which some columnists took as a reflection of the government's growing anxiety about its earlier approach. [34]

Some critics say multiculturalism encourages Britons to elevate Islamic values over British values. Schools have ceased to transmit "either the values or the story of the nation" because in a multicultural classroom, the

measures like education. The young Islamist radicals described in Husain's memoir are all middle class and well integrated, she points out, including Husain, who worked in a bank. "We have a movement of radical groups recruiting among middle-class, upwardly mobile young Muslims," she says.

Klausen blames England's terrorism on international political networks and a generational counterculture that has found violence-prone individuals. In her study of four Danish-born Muslim teenagers convicted in connection with an October 2005 plot to blow up the U.S. embassy in Sarajevo, she found many similarities to the shooters at Colorado's Columbine High School in 1999. In her ongo-

---

* Multiculturalism is often described as the idea that all races, religions and ethnicities should be equally valued and respected.

"majoritarian culture is viewed as illegitimate and a source of shame," writes Phillips in *Londonistan.* [35]

In that vacuum, it's easy for Islamic radicalism to step in, some argue. For instance, in the state school Husain attended in Britain, Muslim children attended separate assemblies managed by a front organization for the revolutionary Islamic movement Jamaat-e-Islami. It then administered tests promoting Islam as an ideology that sought political power. [36]

The debate over British schools' abdication of responsibility for teaching about Islam is strikingly different from the debate in the United States, where the struggle has usually been over whether officially authorized textbooks or curricula should give more prominence to the nation's traditionally ignored ethnic groups. Compared to Canada, where multiculturalism is a curriculum taught from kindergarten, the term in Britain is "a bit murky," creating a "confused debate," says Canadian-born Abdul-Rehman Malik, a contributing editor at *Q-News*, an edgy magazine aimed at young British Muslim professionals.

To some critics, multiculturalism means the funding of local religious groups, which the critics blame for increasing tensions between Muslims and people of other faiths. A report issued this year by Policy Exchange, a conservative London think tank, concludes that the growth of radical Muslim politics has been "strongly nurtured by multicultural policies at the local and national level since the 1980s." [37]

Muslims' focus on religious identity and their sense that they are victims of discrimination "feeds into the broader narrative of victimhood that radical Islam in Britain is all about," says lead author Munira Mirza. "A lot of radical Islam in Britain is about saying, 'We Muslims are under attack; the West is against us.'"

Yet aside from legislation outlawing discrimination, which has been broadened to include religious discrimination, it's hard to point to any one government policy that's explicitly multicultural, says Sarah Spencer, associate director at the University of Oxford's Centre on Migration, Policy and Society and former deputy chairwoman of the government's Commission for Racial Equality.

Rather than multiculturalism causing the separation, "the factors that promote separation are socioeconomic ones," she maintains, such as housing clustered in poor neighborhoods.

Nevertheless, some critics argue that multiculturalism pervades both the public and private sectors in myriad ways, sometimes by just leaving Muslim communities alone.

The London-based Centre for Social Cohesion recently reported that the Islamic sections in public libraries in Tower Hamlets, London's most heavily Muslim borough, were dominated by fundamentalist literature — preaching terrorism and violence against women and non-Muslims. [38] This is a prime example of taxpayer-funded multicultural policy promoting radical Islam, according to center director Douglas Murray. A Muslim seeking to learn more about his faith from the library "couldn't help but be pushed toward the more extreme interpretation," he says.

The "most horrifying example" of let-them-alone multiculturalism, says Murray, is the estimated dozen Muslim women who are murdered in Britain each year in "honor killings" by fathers and brothers. An independent commission is investigating how police handled the case of a 20-year-old Kurdish woman killed by her father after she repeatedly sought help from authorities.

Police "may be worried that they will be seen as racist if they interfere in another culture," said Diana Sammi, director of the Iranian and Kurdish Women's Rights Organization. [39]

Women's advocates have sought legislation to protect women from forced marriages — already outlawed in Norway and Denmark — which they see as strongly linked to honor killings (*see p. 105*). But University of Chicago anthropologist Richard Schweder cautions it's not clear that honor killings in the Muslim community occur with more frequency than passion killings of adulterous partners by Western husbands. Other experts suggest that police may have failed to follow through on these cases for other reasons, perhaps having more to do with their own racism or their attitudes towards domestic violence.

Leiken of the Nixon Center says Britain's "separatist form of multiculturalism" offered radical Islamists from Algeria and other Muslim countries refuge and the opportunity to preach openly during the 1990s at a time when the French government was denying asylum to radical Muslims. [40] Britain's multicultural ideology "meant the legal system was lenient, and police often found themselves in a situation where they couldn't do anything" when moderate Muslims complained about radical clerics taking over their mosques, Leiken says.

CHRONOLOGY

19th Century *European nations colonize much of Muslim world. British colonization of India sparks mass Muslim immigration to Europe by end of century.*

1900-1960s *European rule in Islamic world ends. Muslims establish their own states. . . . Fundamentalist (Islamist) political groups emerge, some espousing a pan-Muslim caliphate. Muslim workers begin emigrating to Europe.*

1928 Radical Muslim Brotherhood is founded in Egypt.

1941 Islamist Jamaat-e-Islami party is founded in Pakistan.

1947-48 Pakistan becomes world's first avowedly Islamist state. . . . Israel is established, displacing Palestinians and creating lasting conflict with Arabs, Muslims.

1952 Col. Gamal Abdel Nasser topples Egyptian monarchy.

1953 Radical Islamic party Hizb ut-Tahrir is founded in Jerusalem.

1954 Brotherhood member tries to assassinate Nasser, who then imprisons leaders, including Sayyid Qutb. Qutb writes *Milestones* — manifesto of political Islam.

1964 *Milestones* is published.

1970s *Movement for Islamic state advances; Europe limits immigration to families, causing more Muslim emigration.*

1979 Iranian Revolution ousts U.S.-backed Reza Shah Pahlavi, brings Ayatollah Ruholla Khomeini to power.

1980s *Saudi Arabia, India, Pakistan and Iran seek to dominate Muslim world, send missionaries to Europe.*

1981 Scarman Report blames racial discrimination for South London Brixton riots, calls for multicultural approach toward Muslims.

1986 French pass strong terrorist-detention laws after spate of bombings.

1987 Saudi millionaire Osama bin Laden forms al Qaeda terrorist network.

1989 Iran's Khomeini calls for murder of Salmon Rushdie for his allegedly blasphemous depiction of Mohammed in *The Satanic Verses.*

1990s *Al Qaeda, other Islamist groups shift from national liberation to terrorism.*

1995 Algerian terrorists bomb Paris Metro.

1998 Al Qaeda calls on Muslims to kill Americans and their allies.

2000s *Islamist terrorists target Europe.*

Sept. 11, 2001 Terrorists attack World Trade Center and Pentagon.

December 2001 British Muslim Richard Reid tries to ignite "shoe bomb" aboard Paris-Miami flight.

2004 France bans Muslim head scarves in public schools. . . . Muslim terrorists kill 191 people in Madrid subway bombing. . . . Radical Islamist kills Dutch filmmaker Theo Van Gogh.

2005 London transit bombings kill 52. . . . Riots erupt in Muslim suburbs of Paris, other French cities.

2006 Danish cartoonist's depictions of Mohammed provoke protests worldwide. . . . Group of 23 mostly British Muslims are arrested on Aug. 10 on suspicion of planning to blow up transatlantic planes. . . . On Sept. 1 Muslims are arrested for running a terrorist camp in Sussex, Britain. . . . Britain expands detention powers against suspected terrorists.

2007 Europe and U.S. reported to be targets of revived al Qaeda. . . . Eight Muslims charged in failed car bombings in London, Glasgow; Bombing plots foiled in Germany, Denmark. British Prime Minister Gordon Brown proposes longer detention for terror suspects; British government encourages expansion of Muslim schools. . . . Spanish court convicts 21 in connection with 2004 Madrid train bombing; clears 3 alleged leaders.

Outspoken multiculturalism critic Kenan Malik, an Indian-born writer and lecturer living in London, complains government leaders were "subcontracting out" their relationship with Muslim citizens by dealing almost exclusively with clerics or official groups like the British Muslim Council, which has been accused of having radical links. And in a report published last year, journalist Bright criticized government officials for championing a group that promotes "a highly politicised version of Islam." [41]

"Why should British citizens who happen to be Muslim rely on clerics?" Malik asks. "It encourages Muslims to see themselves as semi-detached Britons."

Many French experts tend to agree the British laissez-faire approach to multiculturalism failed because the government "created a higher identification with the [religious] group and left all authority with the religious leaders," in the words of Riva Kastoryano, a senior research fellow at the University of Paris' National Center for Scientific Research, who has written a book on multiculturalism in Europe.

Indeed, when it comes to local government funding, Malik said, "multiculturalism has helped to segregate communities far more effectively than racism." [42]

For example, during the 2005 Birmingham riots in Britain, blacks and Asians turned against one another. But 20 years earlier, black and Asian youths had joined together in riots there to protest police harassment and poverty. What changed, according to Malik, was the local government's "multicultural response" — setting up consultation groups and allocating funding along faith lines. "Different groups started fighting one another for funding, and the friction led to the riots between the two communities" in 2005, he says.

But the University of Birmingham's Abbas claims the 2005 riots were triggered by economic issues, ignited by a bogus radio story about a 14-year-old Caribbean girl who supposedly had been raped repeatedly by several Asian men. Abbas says that urban legend fed existing resentments over Asian takeovers of traditionally Caribbean businesses, like hair salons, in an area already suffering from declining jobs and ethnic rivalry over the drug market.

"It had nothing to do with multiculturalism," says Abbas.

Multiculturalism is more of an ideal about how to approach diversity and rid the country of its historic colonial baggage rather than a specific policy, in Abbas' view. To the extent it's been tried it varies greatly from one city to another, he stresses. "Multiculturalism hasn't been given its full testing period yet," he says. "We cannot easily say that because of multiculturalism we have the problems we have."

Would cracking down on terrorism violate civil liberties?

After the most recent foiled bombing plots in Britain, the Labor government proposed extending from 28 days to up to 56 days the period police can hold terrorist suspects without charge — a proposal opposed by both the Conservative and the Liberal Democratic parties.

The government says plots have become so complicated that police need more time to investigate. According to British police, big terrorism cases against one or two suspects can involve the investigation of 200 phones, 400 computers, 8,000 CDs, 6,000 gigabytes of data and 70 premises across three continents. [43]

In unveiling his anti-terror measures, Prime Minister Gordon Brown anticipated resistance from Parliament, which two years earlier had ratcheted down Blair's 90-day detention proposal to 28 days — a doubling of the then-14-day detention period.

"Liberty is the first and founding value of our country," Brown said. "Security is the first duty of our government." [44]

But Human Rights Watch says the extension would violate human rights law. The proposed 28 days is still more than twice as much as any other European country, and the government now releases more than half those accused in terrorism cases without charge, the group points out. [45]

Longer detentions would "clearly discriminate" against Muslim communities and be "counterproductive in making Muslims willing to cooperate with police" because they arouse such resentment, says Ben Ward, associate director for Europe and Central Asia at Human Rights Watch in London. Polls show that more than half of British Muslims already lack confidence in the police, he says. Muslim groups like the Muslim Council of Britain oppose the extension on similar grounds.

Allowing telephone wiretap evidence in court — another change being considered by the government — would be more effective in pursuing terrorist cases, says Ward. Britain is the only Western country that bans wiretap evidence in criminal prosecutions, he says, because its security services oppose revealing their methods.

What Makes a Person 'British'?

Stereotypical views are challenged.

At a North London pub, young professionals with pints in hand were engaged in a favorite national pastime — the Pub Quiz, a competition usually focused on trivia or sports.

But this quiz was different: It came from the test immigrants must take when applying for citizenship — popularly known as the "Britishness test." The 24-question exam was introduced in 2005 after former Home Secretary David Blunkett insisted that new immigrants should have a command of the English language and understand the nature of British life, customs and culture.

Not one of the 100 (mostly British) volunteers passed, an announcement greeted with applause, hilarity and shouts of "Deported!"

Teams with ad hoc names — like "As British as a pint of Guinness" — competed to answer such questions as, How many members are in Northern Ireland's Assembly? Who is the monarch not allowed to marry? and, curiously, What proportion of the United Kingdom population has used illegal drugs?

The highest score was 17, by Rohan Thanotheran, a Sri Lanka-born accountant who has lived in England since 1962. [1]

"Who would bother to learn those facts?" he asked later, suggesting the quiz was a desperate attempt by the government to reclaim nationalism at a time when symbols like the English flag are being hijacked by the far right.

Pub-goers are not the only British citizens who have failed. Member of Parliament Mike Gapes — who has sup-ported the test, saying, "Nationalism is something that should be earned and not just given away" — flunked when 10 of the questions were posed to him during an interview. [2]

The test has been criticized for lengthening the application process and promoting a "siege mentality" among Britons towards foreigners. [3]

Many young people in the pub clearly found the questions comical, and several questioned the very idea of testing someone's "Britishness."

"The meaning of citizenship is not about knowing what percent of Christians in the U.K. are Catholics. Those are things most British citizens don't know. It doesn't make us any less British," said Munira Mirza, a writer, graduate student and founding member of The Manifesto Club, which organized the event to challenge stereotypical views of identity and Britishness.

A slim 29-year-old with shoulder-length black hair, Mirza was born in England of Pakistani Muslim parents. She describes herself as British-Asian but is quick to add that such ethnic and religious labels are "increasingly irrelevant to people, especially of my age, who grow up here and don't think of ourselves as ethnic categories." For example, she resists requests from TV producers to present the Muslim point of view. "You know what they're thinking: 'Only Muslims can connect with other Muslims.' It's quite a close-minded view," she says.

Two other quiz-takers from Muslim backgrounds in this distinctly secular crowd said they sometimes felt forced

---

Of all the counterterrorism measures being proposed in Europe, Human Rights Watch is "most concerned" about the United Kingdom, says Ward. But when it comes to existing practice, many experts consider France the most draconian.

From September 2001 to September 2006, France deported more than 70 people it considers "Islamic fundamentalists," including 15 Muslim imams, according to a recent Human Rights Watch report. [46]

The advocacy group argues that deportations require a much lower standard of evidence than judicial prosecutions and violate human rights because they often expose deportees to torture in their home countries. "Our point is not that all these guys are completely innocent, but even if someone is guilty of involvement in terrorism, France has a duty to make sure they're not sending them back to a place where they're facing threat of torture" — a serious risk even for an innocent person returned home once he's slapped with a terrorist label, says Judith Sunderland, author of the Human Rights Watch report on France's deportations.

"When we talk to people in Muslim communities, there's a lot of fear; they know they're being watched, and they're concerned about what they can say," says

to identify with their parents' foreign heritage because English peers persisted in seeing them as foreigners.

Lani Homeri, 26, a fashionably dressed law student with striking dark eyes and long raven hair, was born in Britain of Iraqi Kurdish parents who emigrated in the 1970s. She finds it odd how frequently she is asked whether she is Muslim, especially, she says, since she wears Western clothing and is "not a practicing Muslim."

A 28-year-old male pub-goer born in Sweden of Iranian parents who had fled the Islamic revolution said hostile questions about Islam from native-born Britons often made him defensive. "I'm agnostic, but when people attack Islam, I start defending it, even though it messed up my country," he said. "People like me, who want a secular government, start to protect their government because it's attacked on stupid grounds."

Misperceptions about Islam could help explain a recent poll conducted by Harris Interactive for the *Financial Times*, which found the British are more suspicious of Muslims than other Europeans or Americans. Only 59 percent of Britons thought it possible to be both a Muslim and a citizen of their country, a smaller proportion than in France, Germany, Spain, Italy or the United States. [4]

Although the poll was taken before the foiled attacks in London and Glasgow in June, the memory of previous attacks, like the 7/7 transit bombings of July 7, 2005, may have hardened British attitudes. British citizens were also the most likely to predict a major terrorist attack in their country in the next 12 months, to consider Muslims a threat to national security and to believe Muslims had too much political power in their country. [5]

Mirza says those polls didn't reflect her own experience living in Britain. But she blames a "multicultural ethos" for forcing people to increasingly identify themselves with a particular ethnic or religious community, whether it is students taught to identify with people of their own race in history class or community leaders jockeying with ethnic groups for government funding.

A report Mirza coauthored for the London think tank Policy Exchange blames the methods Britain uses to encourage multiculturalism — such as providing local funding that can only be claimed by groups defined by ethnic or religious identity — for nurturing "a culture of victimhood" among Muslims, laying the groundwork for young people to turn to Muslim political groups. [6]

The rise of extremist groups is somewhat understandable "at a time when other political identities like 'left' and 'right' are not very appealing," Mirza observes, noting that young people are also gravitating to other forms of extremism, such as violence in the name of animal rights.

"We should be winning these young people over to other ideas," she says. "Unless you deal with that major problem, you will always find people will turn to something else that's offering a vision."

[1] Justin Gest, "How Many of 100 Britons Passed the Citizenship Exam? Not One," Sept. 29, 2007, *The Times* (London), www.timesonline.co .uk/tol/news/uk/article2554235.ece.

[2] Daniel Adam, "Redbridge Fails Britishness Test," *Rising East*, May 2006, www.uel.ac.uk/risingeast/archive04/journalism/adam.htm.

[3] *Ibid.*

[4] Daniel Dombey and Simon Kuper, "Britons 'More Suspicious' of Muslims," *Financial Times*, Aug. 19, 2007, www.FT.com.

[5] *Ibid.*

[6] Munira Mirza, *et al.*, "Living Apart Together: British Muslims and the Paradox of Multiculturalism," *Policy Exchange*, 2007, p. 18.

Sunderland. "We spoke to imams who said anytime they say anything in defense of someone accused of terrorism, they know they will be on someone's watch list." This fear erodes Muslims' trust in law enforcement and makes them less willing to cooperate in terrorism cases, she says.

But Godard, the adviser to the French Interior Ministry who has served as a specialist on Arab communities in both the national police and security services, dismisses her concerns. "Fifteen imams [removed] in 10 years — it's nothing," he says with a shrug.

Human Rights Watch is also concerned about France's use of its "criminal conspiracy" charge, which it says requires a low standard of evidence. "People are being detained for up to two years on very flimsy evidence," says Ward.

Godard shares this concern, complaining that the prosecutorial judges in France's special terrorism courts have "too much power" and that the source of evidence is not made public.

But many French citizens are happy with the system because they think it has kept them safe from terrorism, concedes Sunderland. France's surveillance system may curtail civil liberties, agrees Kastoryano, at the National Center for Scientific Research, but she adds, "This debate is in America, not here; no one here will talk about civil liberties."

As for the government's contention that its spying, secret files, deportations and special courts have been effective against terrorism, Sunderland says, "We don't have the information the French intelligence services have and have no way of verifying if they dismantled terrorist networks and prevented specific attacks, which is what the French government repeatedly claims."

When someone appeals a deportation in France, the only thing the government provides is an unsigned and undated "white paper" summarizing intelligence information, Sunderland says, "but not the sources or methodology, and the defendant can't go behind the information and figure out where it's coming from."

Proponents of expanded powers for the state argue that an exaggerated concern for human rights in England has inhibited authorities from pursuing terrorist suspects compared to France.

After France's experience with terrorists in the mid-1980s, new legislation extended the detention period for suspects. Using the 1986 law, the French "cleaned out outsiders, and the [radicals] went to Britain if they didn't go to jail," claims the Nixon Center's Leiken. By 1994, "that was a big problem in Britain."

By contrast, Britain's 30 years of experience with the Irish Republican Army (IRA) left British police unprepared for today's brand of Islamic terrorism, with no foreign-intelligence capacity and insufficient time to investigate the computer technology used by Islamic plotters, according to Peter Clarke, head of the Metropolitan Police Counter Terrorism Command. That inexperience was evident in the police shooting in the London underground of Brazilian electrician Jean Charles de Menezes on July 22, 2005, mistaken for one of the terrorists who had tried to detonate bombs on London's transit system the day before. The London Metropolitan police force was found guilty Nov. 1 of putting the public at risk during the bungled operation.

Unlike the IRA, Clarke says, today's terrorism threat is global, with players willing to die who are quickly replaced. Networks re-form quickly, no warnings are given and weaponry (like fertilizer bombs) is unconventional, he says. [47]

He cites the case of Dhiren Barot, an al Qaeda plotter who left plans on his laptop computer for killing thousands of people in Britain (and the United States) by detonating underground bombs.

After Barot's arrest in 2004, British police had to "race against time" to retrieve enough evidence from the seized computers and other equipment to justify charges at the end of the permitted period of detention. [48] After that experience, the Terrorism Act of 2006 criminalized "acts preparatory to terrorism," and police proposed extending the period terrorist suspects can be held without charge. [49]

In addition, since 2001 British anti-terror laws have given the government — with public support — more leeway to mine databases for information about individuals. "There was an assumption that if it was necessary to hand over our privacy to the state to provide protection, that it was a price worth paying," says Gareth Crossman, policy director at Liberty, a London-based civil liberties advocacy group. Now, the country has so many cameras trained on citizens "the government's privacy watchdog describes England as 'the surveillance society.' " [50]

A recent Liberty report warns privacy could be invaded in the future because of the government's ability to mine data and watch people on the street. Surveillance cameras, more prevalent in Britain than any other country, are credited with tracing autos involved in past terrorist attempts. But Liberty wants the government to regulate where they're placed and how they're operated (many are installed by private companies) to protect ordinary citizens' privacy. [51]

Legislation passed in Britain would authorize a national ID card, though it hasn't been implemented and may never be because of the cost. But Crossman warns the government could use it to trawl through databases for personal information by profiling "the sort of person that might be involved in terrorist activity — purely on the basis of demographic information. It's a real minefield. A young, Muslim male is basically where it will end up. That's hugely sensitive."

BACKGROUND

Muslim Migration

Modern Muslim immigration to Europe began in the late 19th century as a result of Europe's colonial and trading activity, which largely explains the different ethnic groups in each country and to some extent their degree of acceptance by those societies.

The French conquest of Algiers in 1830 eventually led to French control of Algeria, Morocco and Tunisia. Together, British colonization of India (which included modern-day Pakistan and Bangladesh) and Dutch domination of trade in Asia gave the three European countries control over most of the world's Muslims.

At the end of the 19th century, immigration began on a large scale, as France imported low-paid workers from Algeria and other African territories and other countries recruited workers from their colonies and territories.

Following World War II, countries like England sought workers, including many Muslims, to help with reconstruction. By the 1960s, entire Muslim families had begun to settle in Europe.

By 1974, however, a global economic recession had led many countries to limit migration, allowing entry only for family reunification or political asylum. Paradoxically, the policy led to further immigration by families, the only means of entry. The recession also increased Europeans' resentment of immigrants and their children, who were viewed as competing for jobs.

During the 1980s, Muslims' religious identity became more pronounced as young Muslims — frustrated by job discrimination — turned to their religion as a source of identity. Islamic political movements in Iran, North Africa and South Asia also influenced this trend.

The rise of political Islam encouraged Muslims in Europe to form associations based on religion, which heightened Europeans' fears of Islam as growing numbers of Muslim refugees were arriving from wars in Iran, Iraq, Lebanon, Palestine and Bosnia. At this time, as rivalry broke out between different groups in Saudi Arabia, India, Pakistan and Iran for domination of

More Muslims Identify With Moderates

More than half of the Muslims in France and Great Britain believe a struggle is going on in their countries between moderate and fundamentalist Islamic ideologies (top). Those who see such a struggle identify overwhelmingly with the moderates (bottom). Britain has the largest percentage of Muslims identifying with the fundamentalists.

Do you see a struggle in your country between moderate Muslims and fundamentalists?

Muslims answering "yes" in ...

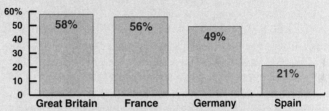

If so, do you identify more with moderates or fundamentalists?

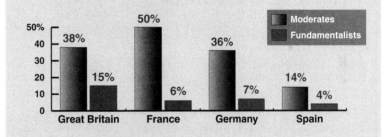

Source: "Muslims in Europe: Economic Worries Top Concerns About Religious and Cultural Identity," Pew Global Attitudes Project, July 2006

Muslim ideology, Europe became a target of missionary and proselytizing efforts, helped along by the distribution of petrodollars — mainly from Saudi Arabia — to create mosques, Islamic schools and even university chairs. [52]

Saudi money supported the spread and teaching of the Wahhabi strand of Islam, the official religion of Saudi Arabia and the guiding spiritual doctrine of al Qaeda. Wahhabism is a fundamentalist form of Islam that preaches strict adherence to Islam's injunctions, including abiding by sharia law.

Radical Mosque Says It Has Changed

But skeptics say its hard-core views are hidden.

The atmosphere at the East London Mosque during a dinner held recently with non-Muslim neighbors could not have been more congenial or ecumenical. Ministers from a local interfaith group and executives in suits from a local hospital philanthropy joined bearded Muslims in skullcaps over plates of Indian food as they broke the Ramadan fast. They had just listened to a mosque lecturer declare, "We're all children of Adam" and "The meaning of Islam isn't terrorism, destruction or violence."

But these reassurances seem at odds with the reputation the mosque developed in the 1990s as a center for radical, young Muslims. And some observers of the London Muslim scene say that beneath its smooth public relations efforts the mosque remains a major center for radical Islam.

"The East London Mosque is at the center of a very sophisticated Jamaat-e-Islami network in Britain," says Martin Bright, political editor for the left-leaning *New Statesman* magazine, referring to the extremist Islamic political party based in Pakistan. "It is essentially the dominant force in the formation of Islamist ideology in Britain — and Europe." Jamaat-e-Islami and other Islamists espouse an Islamic state governed by sharia law.

But on two recent visits to the mosque, including the imam's weekly Friday sermon, talk of radicalism was absent. Instead the imam admonished the congregation for giving too little to charity. ("You give rice, but it's probably not even Basmati.")

Sumaia Begum, 19, a Londoner of Bangladeshi parentage dressed in black from head scarf to figure-concealing skirt, had just listened to the sermon in the secluded second-floor women's section, crowded with Bangladeshis and Somalis in somber black head-coverings. She seemed unaware of the mosque's reputation. "I'd love to live in an Islamic state, but bombing innocent people here — that's not right," she said. "Bearing and raising children — for us, that is our jihad."

Critics of Islamist ideology say mosques like East London often have two faces — a moderate one for the public and a hard-core ideology they might only reveal at summer indoctrination camps for young people.

"At the Friday sermon, which is open to the public, they would not preach hatred," says Irfan Al Alawi, international director of the Center for Islamic Pluralism, a London think tank that promotes religious tolerance. "They would have before 7/7" (the July 7, 2005, London transit bombings). "But when it became obvious they were being investigated because of links with jihadists in Pakistan, they became somewhat cautious."

Throughout the late 1980s, the mosque, located at the heart of London's densest Bangladeshi neighborhood, was home to rival Jamaat-e-Islami factions in Britain, according to British author Ed Husain, a former radical who says he first encountered extremist rhetoric at the mosque in the 1990s, when most of its committee members were affiliated with the movement. [1]

Today, he writes, the Saudi-trained imam of the big mosque continues to lead a faction opposed to modernizing elements and prohibits gatherings of opponents of Islamism and of the strict Saudi version of Islam — Wahhabism. [2]

But Dilowar Khan, the director of the mosque and the gleaming London Muslim Center next door (built with government, private and Saudi funding), says he and his fellow Muslims at the mosque, like Husain, have moved away from the separatist views espoused in the 1990s, with their single-minded focus on replacing secular regimes in the Muslim world with religious states.

Back then, people were interested in Bangladeshi politics, in which Jamaat-e-Islami was very active, he explains.

As Harvard's Cesari explains, since Sept. 11 the apolitical nature of fundamentalist groups has been increasingly questioned as these groups have radicalized their rhetoric against non-Muslims and the West. These movements preach "a theology of intolerance" — referring to all non-Muslims as *kaffir* (or infidel) and aspects of modern life as *haram* (forbidden) — "which can easily become . . . a theology of hate," she writes. Since the 1967 Israeli victory over the Arabs, a feeling of humiliation has combined with a warlike insistence on Islam's superiority over everything Western, democratic and secular. [53]

"Now we're more interested in how to improve our life and image here." For instance, he says, the mosque invites local political candidates as speakers and offers various services, ranging from job counseling to computer education.

While the mosque still may have members who are Wahhabis or followers of Jamaat, it does not define itself by any of those sects, according to Khan. He denies any "formal links" to those groups or to the Tablighi-Jamaat, a hard-line Islamic missionary movement that Al Alawi says has also captured much of the mosque's leadership.

As for Jamaat-e-Islami's central mission — to establish a Muslim state — Khan says, "We believe Islam is a complete code of life. . . . What's wrong with a Muslim country establishing an Islamic state by majority rule?"

What about the party's call for establishing sharia rule? "We're not interested in implementing sharia law in this country," he claims. "If the majority of people in Muslim countries want to implement certain laws in their own country, who am I to tell them, 'Don't do that'?" Later, he emphasized that sharia is the very essence of the religion, adding, "People who are against sharia law are enemies of Islam."

Does he advocate sharia courts like those in Nigeria, which order the amputation of limbs and stoning of women as punishments straight from the *Koran*? "That's only about 1 percent of sharia law," he says, which refers to the vast body of religious observance in Islam, including fasting at Ramadan.

Hisham A. Hellyer, an expert on counterterrorism at the University of Warwick and a former visiting fellow at the Washington-based Brookings Institution think tank, says that while Jamaat-e-Islami did have a presence in Britain's activist groups in the 1980s because of members' involvement in their home countries, "It's a bit of a stretch to say they were the direct wings of these organizations in the U.K." He points out, "It's not unusual for politicians in Britain to have been communists as students, but they mature and grow up. That's what happened to leaders in the Muslim community."

Muslim religious attire is common in the Bangladeshi East London neighborhood of Whitechapel, home to the East London Mosque, one of Britain's largest.

A recent TV documentary dramatized the perception that Muslim mosques are not always what they seem, reporting that Muslim clerics engaged in far more radical language — justifying terrorist bombings, for instance — in private meetings than in public sermons. Since the broadcast, however, some clerics have charged their words were taken out of context. The complaints are being investigated by Britain's broadcasting watchdog. [3]

Such charges and countercharges reflect a problem that Jason Burke, a veteran reporter on the Muslim world for the *British Observer* (of London), says "confronts me daily as a journalist working in the field. Who are our interlocutors? Whose voices best represent the complex, diverse and dynamic societies that are bundled together in that terrible generalization, the 'Muslim world'?" [4]

[1] Ed Husain, *The Islamist* (2007), p. 24.

[2] *Ibid.*, p. 280.

[3] BBC, "C4 Distorted Mosque Programme," Aug. 8, 2007, http://news.bbc.co.uk/1/hi/englan.

[4] Preface by Jason Burke in Martin Bright, "When Progressives Treat with Reactionaries," *Policy Exchange*, 2006, p. 7.

Individual acts of political terrorism in the 1990s and early 2000s fueled fears of radical Islam in Europe. Between 1995 and 1996, a radical Algerian group seeking an Islamic state in Algeria set off bombs on Paris subways and trains. And, prior to the 1998 World Cup soccer tournament in France, the French arrested 100 members of the group in a

preventive action. Radical preachers in Paris and London began to attract young Muslims from the poorer suburbs and cities. Some went to fight in Afghanistan or Iraq, while a few committed terrorist acts at home.

Increased immigration from Muslim countries and high birthrates combined to make Islam the fastest-

Railway workers and police in Madrid examine a train destroyed in a terrorist bombing in March 2004 that killed 191 and injured thousands. In late October, 21 of the 29 people charged were found guilty, including North African men from Algeria, Tunisia and Morocco.

growing religion on the continent, even as ethnic and religious tensions grew. In October 2005 riots erupted in the Muslim suburbs of Paris and other French cities, with the participants complaining of joblessness and discrimination. Muslims also demonstrated against the proposed ban on Muslim girls wearing head scarves at school, which took effect in 2004.

The Madrid train bombings, the 2004 assassination of Dutch filmmaker Theo Van Gogh by a Dutch-Moroccan and the 2005 London subway explosions — all committed by radical Muslims — led European countries to question how well they were integrating Muslim immigrants and their children.

Anthropologist Bowen attributes the differences in how Muslim communities have been absorbed and the types of politics they've adopted in various European countries to the different ways each country treated its colonies and immigrants from those colonies.

In France, Muslim immigrants are clustered in poor, outer suburbs that include a mix of North Africans — such as Algerians, Moroccans and Tunisians — all of whom speak French and grew up under French rule. North Africans often arrived feeling that they were quasi-French citizens, even if they were second-class citizens, says Bowen.

But in Britain many Muslims live in ethnic enclaves in Bangladeshi or Pakistani neighborhoods where Bengali is spoken in stores and banks, and parents of London-born children often speak no English. As

schools in these neighborhoods become 100 percent Asian, some educators are concerned the teaching of English as a first language is being thwarted. [54]

"The French [immigration] story goes back to the beginning of the 20th century," Bowen adds, "whereas in Britain the immigration is much more recent, and the communities are much more closed off."

In addition, he notes, "The French kids from North Africa are more tied into the Muslim Brotherhood, which says, 'Obey the laws of the country you're in, and try to create conditions to live as a Muslim.' There's none of this talk about creating a separate Islamic state that [the radical group] Hizb-ut-Tahrir runs on."

'Londonistan'

The shift to religiously oriented politics in Britain took place in the 1980s and '90s with the increasing embrace of identity politics and the arrival of Islamist political refugees.

After the 1981 rioting in the impoverished Brixton neighborhood of south London, the Scarman Report called for a multiracial, multicultural approach that would recognize the uniquely different needs of ethnic groups. National and local governments awarded funds to groups identifying themselves as ethnic or racial minorities, including ethnic housing associations, arts centers, radio channels and voluntary organizations. Local governments helped set up representative bodies to consult with Muslims over local issues. The funding of conservative religious organizations like the East London Mosque sometimes came at the expense of secular groups, say critics. [55]

The Rushdie affair led to a seminal moment in Muslim identity politics. In 1988 author Salman Rushdie's novel *The Satanic Verses* infuriated Muslims who felt it ridiculed the Prophet Mohammed. British Muslims formed the U.K. Action Committee on Islamic Affairs to protest the perceived blasphemy. Eventually Iran's supreme religious leader, the late Ayatollah Khomeini, issued a religious edict known as a *fatwa* condemning Rushdie to death. But the anti-Rushdie campaign was led primarily from Pakistan by disciples of the deceased Islamist ideologue Abul A'la Maududi, who founded the Jamaat-e-Islami party in India in 1941.

Book burnings in Bradford, England, widely covered by the media, also raised the profile of radical Islamism among young Muslims. The first Gulf War, the Palestinian intifadas of the late 1980s and early '90s and the slaughter of Muslims in Bosnia also discomfited Muslims about their loyalties.

Radical Islam in Britain has evolved under the influence of Islamist groups operating from Pakistan, Bangladesh and the Middle East. According to Policy Exchange, the conservative think tank in London, money poured in from Saudi Arabia and Pakistan for new religious, publishing and education facilities in Britain, shifting the balance "from more traditional and apolitical Muslim organisations toward more internationalist and politically radical groups," especially those leaning toward Wahhabism. [56]

Indeed, as France and other nations forced Islamists to leave in the 1990s, members of the French secret service dubbed the British capital "Londonistan" for its role as a refuge for Islamist groups. [57]

In the weeks following the attacks on the World Trade Center and the Pentagon, many mainstream British news organizations — including the *Guardian* — accepted that the attacks were a response to suffering in the Palestinian territories and to American support of Israel. In interviews, young British Muslims said 9/11 and later the London bombings of 2005 made them identify as Muslims more than they had before. After the Iraq War started in 2003, Islamists joined with left-wing groups and created the Respect Party on an anti-war platform. "Radical Islam's narrative of the victimised *ummah* [Muslim community] has drawn sustenance from broader public anger at U.S. and U.K. foreign policy," says Policy Exchange. [58]

Terrorist Attacks

The current wave of terrorism can be traced to Feb. 23, 1998, when al Qaeda issued a *fatwa* stating that all Muslims had a duty to kill Americans and their allies — civilian or military. Islamic liberation movements began to shift their emphasis to localized, violent jihad. [59]

The Sept. 11, 2001, attacks were directly tied to al Qaeda, as was the attempt three months later by British-born Muslim Richard Reid to blow up an American Airlines flight from Paris to Miami by lighting explosives in his shoes.

Twenty-nine Muslims living in Spain — including first-generation North Africans from Algeria, Tunisia and Morocco — were charged in connection with the March 2004 bombing of four Madrid trains at rush hour, which killed 191 people and injured more than 1,800. [60] The group included petty drug traffickers as

well as university students. Jamal Ahmidan, the plot's Moroccan mastermind, was said to be happily integrated into Spanish society. In October, a Spanish court found 21 people guilty of involvement in the bombing, but three alleged leaders were cleared. [61]

That November, Dutch filmmaker Van Gogh, who had made a film critical of Islam's treatment of women, was stabbed to death on an Amsterdam street by Mohammed Bouyeri, 26, the Amsterdam-born son of Moroccans. Bouyeri, whose radicalism began during a seven-month period in prison, belonged to the Hofsted Group, which had considered bombing the Dutch parliament. [62]

Until the most recent plots, post-2001 terrorist attempts in Europe had been seen as independently planned, even if the organizers took their inspiration from al Qaeda. That appears to have been the case in the 2005 London bus and subway suicide-bomb attacks. The first attack, on July 7, involved four British Muslims — three Pakistanis from West Yorkshire and an Afro-Caribbean Muslim convert. All four had Westernized, unremarkable backgrounds, according to the NYPD. A second attack, intended for three underground trains and a bus on July 21, failed because the bombs did not detonate.

On Aug. 10, 2006, 23 individuals — most British citizens and nearly all Muslim — were arrested on suspicion of plotting to blow up transatlantic airliners using liquid explosives. Three weeks later a group of Muslims was arrested for running a terrorist training camp at a former convent school in Sussex. A total of 68 people were arrested, and al Qaeda is suspected of being centrally involved in the bomb plot. [63]

Several doctors in England were arrested in two incidents — trying to blow up cars near a London nightclub on June 29 and driving a burning jeep into the Glasgow airport the next day.

Although the Sept. 11, 2001, attacks were directed by al Qaeda, they were planned by a group of English-speaking Muslims at a mosque in Hamburg, where they had been radicalized.

"Without a group of radicalized jihadists who had been homegrown in the West to lead this plot, the chances of 9/11 being a success would have been reduced considerably," concluded the NYPD intelligence report. "The Hamburg group underwent a process of homegrown radicalization that matched almost exactly those of Madrid, London, Amsterdam."

Courtesy of Ed Husain

British writer Ed Husain describes his recruitment in the 1990s in London by radical Islamists in his 2007 memoir. Today Husain, a former member of the group Hizb ut-Rahrir, remains skeptical of its nonviolent stance.

But unlike the 7/7 bombers who attacked London, the NYPD observes, when members of the Hamburg group went to Afghanistan to fight, they were re-directed to another target in the West, not to their place of residence. [64]

The North London Central Mosque, better known as the Finsbury Park Mosque, became infamous in the early 2000s for its support of radical Islam under the leadership of its fiery imam, Abu Hamza al-Masri. The mosque's attendees included shoe bomber Reid and 9/11 conspirator Zacarias Moussaoui. After British police raided the mosque on Jan. 20, 2003, it eventually was reclaimed by mainstream Muslims.

However, the London-based think tank Policy Exchange found extremist anti-Western, anti-Semitic literature at the mosque and claims a mosque trustee has said he is prepared to be a suicide bomber against Israel, according to a report released Oct. 30. [65]

Since the 2003 raid, law enforcement and security forces have tried to work with other mosque leaders to prevent the incitement to violence that emanated from Finsbury Park and other Salafi mosques in London in the 1990s. * Among the most notorious clerics were:

---

* Salafi is a term applied broadly to sects that adhere to a supposedly pure form of Islam that they believe was practiced by Islam's ancestors; it often refers to Wahhabis and sometimes to Deobandis, the Muslim Brotherhood and Jamaat-e-Islami.

- Al-Masri, who was sentenced to seven years for incitement to murder in February 2006;
- Abdullah el-Faisal, a Jamaican-born convert sentenced to nine years in 2003 for soliciting the murder of Jews, Americans and Hindus and inciting racial hatred. [66]
- Syrian-born self-styled cleric Omar Bakri Mohammed, who helped establish the radical group Al Muhajiroun and called the 9/11 hijackers the "Magnificent 19," has been banned from Britain and currently lives abroad. [67]

Action against radical clerics was authorized by amendments to Britain's Terrorism Act adopted in 2001, 2005 and 2006, which expanded the definition of terrorist offenses. The most recent changes criminalized "incitement to terrorism," providing assistance to terrorists and providing instruction in the use of firearms and explosives. The British government also has been given greater ability to ban political groups. Last year it considered banning both Hizb ut-Tahrir and Al Muhajiroun, which are both active on college campuses. [68]

CURRENT SITUATION

Worsening Threat

The recent string of disrupted plots in Europe signals a "continuing and worsening" radicalization within Europe's Islamic diaspora and a renewed leadership role for al Qaeda, according to a recent report from the International Institute for Strategic Studies (IISS), a leading security think tank in London. Al Qaeda has regrouped as an organization and now has the capacity to carry out another 9/11-magnitude attack, according to the IISS. [69]

Britain is considered the main target, with up to 30 terrorist plots discovered there — some that would have involved mass-casualty suicide attacks, said British intelligence officials last November. [70] Al Qaeda's Pakistan-based leadership was directing its British followers "on an extensive and growing scale," the officials said, and British authorities said they have their eye on 2,000 individuals involved in such plots. In fact, said Britain's domestic intelligence chief Jonathan Evans on Nov. 5, terrorist recruitment is accelerating so quickly that there could now be twice that many — up to 4,000 — potential terrorists living in Britain. Terrorists are grooming British youths as young as 15 to aid in terrorism and

Should the British government fund Muslim faith schools?

YES Ibrahim Hewitt
Vice Chairman, Association of Muslim Schools, U.K.

Written for *CQ Researcher*, October 2007

The right of any group to establish a school and have it paid for by the state is enshrined in the 1944 Education Act. This is not limited to people of any particular religious or political background. Section 76 of the act goes on to say that "pupils are to be educated in accordance with the wishes of their parents." These provisions grew out of a compromise between church and state concerning the church-run schools then in operation. The state took over control of some of the schools while leaving others more or less in the control of the church. That is the context in which the state funding of Muslim schools exists.

Critics of faith schools — read "Muslim schools" — claim state funding is a historical anomaly that should be abolished. Proponents believe that parental choice has a firm basis in history, as made clear by Section 76. Choice has long been exercised by Anglican, Roman Catholic and Jewish parents, to little or no criticism. Now, many of the criticisms of faith schools are surfacing with the existence of Muslim schools, which were established by parents not unreasonably asking for the same choice in return for paying the same taxes toward education as everyone else.

Faith plays a hugely important part in the life of most Muslims — the notion of a "secular Muslim" is actually a contradiction in terms — and we are enjoined by the *Qu'ran* to "enter into Islam wholeheartedly" and not make any differentiation between religious and secular. It follows, therefore, that the education of our children should be within a framework that recognizes the existence and importance of their faith background.

As parents, we have a legal, moral and religious duty to raise and educate our children to become upright and honest citizens. The fact that the law of the land encourages the existence of faith schools as a core education provision in Britain means that parents from all faiths and none have a choice about their children's schools. Those who would have all schools as religion-free zones offer no such choice while overlooking conveniently that a secular approach is not a neutral approach; it is a conscious desire to remove religion from public life — hardly tolerant in a society where many faiths are represented across different communities.

Human-rights legislation makes clear that people should have freedom of religion; to insist on schools in which faith is the only forbidden f-word is both unreasonable and undemocratic. Muslims' taxes pay for schools of all faiths and none, so why shouldn't some of those taxes be used to fund Muslim schools as well?

NO Terry Sanderson
President, National Secular Society

Written for *CQ Researcher*, October 2007

In a country increasingly divided by religion, the prospect of a hundred or more Muslim schools being brought into the state sector is truly terrifying. The British government, by some upside-down logic, has convinced itself that separating children in schools along religious lines will somehow help create "community cohesion."

The government clings to this opinion in the face of all the evidence. Its own advisers have said Muslim communities are "leading parallel lives," that we as a nation are "sleepwalking into segregation" and that segregated schools are a "ticking time bomb."

At present, there are seven Muslim schools paid for by the state. The rest are operating privately. There is little control over what goes on in the fee-paying schools, and the government argues that by bringing them under state control it would be easier to oversee them and ensure that they teach the national curriculum to an acceptable standard.

But the Muslim parents who took their children out of the state system in the first place did so because they felt that what the state offered was not what they wanted. If the state is not going to provide the strictly Islamic education they desire for their children, then they will simply opt out again and set up more private schools. The state will have to compromise if it wants these people on board.

So, rather than the national curriculum changing Muslim schools, it will be Muslim schools that force the national curriculum to change. Before long we will have schools where girls are forced to wear veils. (This has already been advocated by a leading Muslim educator, even for non-Muslim pupils who might seek a place in the school.) We will have state schools where swimming lessons are not permitted, where male teachers cannot teach girls, where there is no music, no representative art and no sporting activities for females unless they are "modestly dressed" in flowing garments.

Because the Church of England and the Catholic Church have traditionally operated about one-third of Britain's state school system, it is now difficult to argue that other religions should not be permitted to have their own "faith schools." But by permitting Islamic schools into the state system, the government is colluding in the very thing it insists it is against — the further separation of an already-isolated community.

The only way out of this unholy mess is to dismantle the whole system of state-operated religious schools and return them to community control.

have expanded their training bases beyond Pakistan, specifically to Somalia and other areas in East Africa. [71]

Meanwhile, U.S. officials fear Europe's terrorist problems could be exported to the United States because of the ease with which Europeans travel to America. "When you talk to intelligence officials, that's their nightmare," says the Nixon Center's Leiken.

Intelligence officials in Denmark and Washington said at least one suspect in the abortive Copenhagen bombing had direct ties to leading al Qaeda figures. Jakob Scharf, head of Danish intelligence, said Muslim extremists typically are young men, ages 16-25, courted by mentors who identify those predisposed toward a jihadi mindset, radicalize them and put them in touch with others who could help them plan violent action. Denmark became the target of terrorist groups after a conservative Danish newspaper published cartoons two years ago widely seen as mocking Islam. [72]

Fertile Ground

In the past two decades, Europe and the United States have become "crucial battlegrounds" in the rapidly intensifying competition between groups in Saudi Arabia, India, Pakistan and Iran for control of Muslim ideology, according to Harvard's Cesari. [73]

The Saudis spent an estimated $85 billion between 1975 and 2005 to spread fundamentalist Islam by distributing Wahhabi prayer books, dispatching missionaries and imams and building grand mosques in Madrid, Rome, Copenhagen and Great Britain. [74]

The report released last week by *Policy Exchange* found extremist literature — preaching stoning of adulterers, jihad and hatred for non-Muslims — at a quarter of 100 leading mosques and educational institutions visited in England, including the East London Mosque. (*See sidebar, p. 98.*) Much of the material was distributed by Saudi organizations, found in Saudi-funded institutions or written by members of the Wahhabi religious establishment, the report said.

Historically, there have been two paths to violent extremism, notes Brandeis University's Klausen. A political movement seeking Islamic sovereignty includes the Muslim Brotherhood, the Pakistani party Jamaat-e-Islami, Hizb ut-Tahrir, Hamas and Al Muhajiroun.

Competing with them are puritanical groups like the Deobandi sect and the ultra-conservative Tablighi-Jamaat movement, which consider "recent" innovations, such as the mystically oriented practices of the Sufi Muslims and the worship of saints, as impermissible. Like the political groups, these groups glorify suicide but tend to stress theological and moral, rather than political, arguments.

Europe may have proven fertile ground for strict interpretations of Islam, according to Cesari, because some Muslims react to the bewildering range of moral choices in today's globalized Western society with a certain "rigidity of thought and total rejections of cultural pluralism." [75]

But the variety of those arrested for terrorism in recent years suggests there are many reasons young Muslims are drawn to radicalism. For example, about 9 percent are converts, who might have been drawn to other kinds of radical political groups in another era. [76]

For author Husain, one of the few ex-radicals to publicly describe his journey into that world, "it was the serious lack of a sense of belonging here in Britain. We're all left alone like atoms to do our own thing. There's no collective entity. In that vacuum, extremists point to other coherent forms of identity, which are very easy to sign up to."

Questioning Integration

As concern about radical extremism grows, some European governments are rethinking their approach to integrating Muslims and are demanding more from immigrants who want citizenship, including acceptance of their national values.

"It's clear the Dutch and British laissez faire models have outlived their usefulness," says Laurence of Boston College. "No longer will a blank check be given to religious communities to govern themselves. It led to isolation in which a certain extremism thrived."

In the Netherlands the 90-year-old policy of "pillarization," which permits each faith to set up its own faith schools and organizations, is falling out of favor among the Dutch as they see their own socially progressive mores conflicting with Muslim values.

Increasingly, politicians on both the left and right in the Netherlands are saying about Muslims: "We have to be intolerant of the intolerant," says Jan Duyvendak, a professor of sociology at the University of Amsterdam. Applicants for citizenship are shown a film of topless women and two men kissing. The message it's supposed to send: "If you want to come to the Netherlands, you should be tolerant of this," he says.

Scandinavian countries also feel that their culture and values, including gender equality, are increasingly threatened by Muslim communities that "we have quite failed to integrate," Unni Wikan, a professor of social anthropology at the University of Oslo, told a panel recently in London. [77]

Several Scandinavian governments, for example, have outlawed forced marriages of minors, often imported from a Muslim man's native village or clan. In Norway participation in a forced marriage brings up to 60 years in prison. Denmark requires that spouses brought into the country be at least 24 years old. Other European countries are considering similar laws, says Wikan, because "we're afraid we're leading toward a society that's breaking up into ethnic tribes."

Scandinavians and the Dutch also have become concerned about honor killings of young Muslim women thought to have dishonored the clan. "That kind of honor code sacrifices women on the altar of culture," Wikan said. "We don't want such values to become part of Europe."

In France, President Nicolas Sarkozy, who campaigned on a law-and-order immigration platform, proposed DNA testing of immigrants' children seeking to enter the country to prove they're relatives. He has vowed to expel 25,000 illegal immigrants a year. Sarkozy would also set quotas by geographic regions of the world, an approach immigration historian Weil calls "xenophobic" and which he suspects would be focused on disliked minorities. Sarkozy's proposed immigration package will produce a "backlash from Arabs and blacks," Weil warns.

A Belgian proposal to take a tougher stance on immigration, pushed by parties of the right but increasingly adopted by mainstream parties, has been widely interpreted as targeting Muslims. [78]

Changing Course

A British government report earlier this year moved away from the language of multiculturalism, saying friendships with people from other ethnic groups are the best way to prevent prejudice. Prime Minister Brown has also said a sense of Britishness should be the "glue" tying different ethnic groups together. But some teachers are uncomfortable with new requirements that schools teach patriotism, because they are unsure what it is. [79]

After the foiled June plots in Britain and Glasgow, Brown proposed a three-year, $114-million program to win the hearts and minds of Muslims by conducting cit-

izenship classes in Britain's 1,000 *madrasas* and English-language training for imams.

But Faiz Siddiqui, convenor of the Muslim Action Committee representing more than 700 mosques and imams in Britain, pointed out that "excessive sums of money" — by one estimate $14 billion over the last 25 years — were already coming into the country from Saudi Arabia and other countries to support "radical ideology." He also noted that some imams accused of inciting people to murder, like Abu Hamza, already spoke English. [80]

In an investigative report published last year, the New Statesman's Bright found that the British government's main partner in the Muslim community — the Muslim Council of Britain — had links to the religious right both at home and abroad. Leaked memos revealed that the government's decision to make the group its main link to the Muslim community had been heavily influenced by the British Foreign Office, which wanted to maintain connections with opposition movements abroad. [81]

After the report was published, then-Communities Secretary Kelly focused on reaching out to other groups in the community and halted communication altogether with the council, says Bright. One reason for the switch, she said, was the council's boycott of Britain's Holocaust Memorial Day. How Brown will eventually re-connect with the nation's Muslim community remains uncertain.

However, in a speech delivered Oct. 31, Brown's Communities Secretary Blears said the current government "remains absolutely committed" to Blair's shift in priority away from reliance on a few national organizations and toward Muslim groups "actively working to tackle violent extremism." [82]

Muslim Schools

Britain's education department in September recommended that the more than 100 private Muslim schools enter the state-supported system and that faith schools generally should be expanded. The proposal received a deeply divided response. [83] (*See "At Issue," p. 103.*)

The nation's teachers' union expressed concern that the proposal could further divide children ethnically. Moreover, there's no requirement that Muslim schools cover other religions in depth, "which we consider appropriate," said Alison Ryan, policy adviser to the Association of Teachers and Lecturers.

Some moderate Muslims worry the faith schools could become breeding grounds for extremism. Earlier this year, the principal of King Fahd Academy in London confirmed its textbooks described Jews as "apes" and Christians as "pigs" and refused to withdraw them. [84]

Almost half of Britain's mosques are under the control of the conservative Deobandis, who gave rise to the Taliban in Afghanistan, according to a police report cited by the *London Times* in September. [85] And many of them run after-school *madrasas* that could be expanded into state-funded faith schools, some moderate Muslims fear.

But even groups concerned about ethnic separateness acknowledge that a country that supports nearly 7,000 faith schools — mostly Church of England and Catholic — cannot discriminate against Muslims, who currently have only seven state-supported schools. [86] And some hope that with greater government oversight of the curriculum, any tendency toward extremism would be limited.

OUTLOOK

Encouraging Moderation

Concerned that its terrorism problem is largely homegrown, the British government is now trying to curb radicalism. Among other things, the government is trying to encourage moderation by creating a program to educate imams in communicating with young people to reject extremist views and minimum standards for Muslim clerics in prisons and other public institutions to give them the skills to confront and isolate extremists. It is also supporting local governments that are developing their own accreditation programs for imams employed in their city to help them deliver sermons in English, reach out to young people and resist extremist ideology. All these steps are part of a $114 million program announced by Communities Secretary Blears Oct. 31 to build resilience to violent extremism, including citizenship classes in mosque schools. [87]

The government is also using community-policing techniques to get to know Muslims in the neighborhoods where they think terrorists may be living. Dutch, Spanish and Danish authorities are closely watching Britain's approach to see if it stems the tide of radical recruitment.

Next year, a year-old government-backed group aimed at encouraging moderation in mosques, the Mosques and Imams Advisory Board, plans to issue a code of standards to allow its member mosques and imams to be supervised and regulated. The draft code, the Observer reported, would require members to offer programs "that actively combat all forms of violent extremism." Imams would also be expected to make clear to their followers that forced marriages are completely "unIslamic" — as is violence in domestic disputes. [88]

As Oxford University Professor of European Studies Timothy Garton Ash recently observed: "So much now depends on whether the 10 percent" who sympathize with suicide bombers "veer toward the barbaric 1 percent" who thought the London subway bombers were justified or "rejoin the civilized majority." [89]

But Klausen of Brandeis University says that while Britain's new approach has succeeded in establishing links to Muslim leaders, so far it "has failed to build trust among the general Muslim public." [90]

British author Husain says government officials mistakenly think they can deal with radical Islamists' demands rationally. Secular Western leaders have trouble connecting with the annihilation of the West as a religious duty, he says, because they "don't do God."

"Which Islamist demand do you want to do business with?" he asks. "The destruction of Israel? The overthrow of secular government? The establishment of the caliphate? I don't see any of those being up for negotiation," Husain says.

At the same time, it's important not to confuse all conservative religious groups with those committed to terrorism, warns counterterrorism expert Hellyer.

"In a lot of public discourse we have accusations," he says, such as, "This Salafi mosque or this Salafi preacher is 100 percent guilty of all the radical ideologies in the U.K." In fact, he notes, most Salafi Muslims are zealously conservative but not necessarily violent. Those at the Brixton London mosque first attended by shoe bomber Reid tried to dissuade him from radical theologies that preached violence, and as he became increasingly radical he left the mosque. [91]

"I would hate for us to waste resources going after people we don't like rather than people who are a dangerous threat," Hellyer says.

Following the 2005 bombings, the British government launched an Islamic "Scholars' Roadshow" aimed at winning the minds of under-30 Muslims on issues like jihad and extremism. The Muslim magazine *Q-News*, which came out early against suicide bombing, helped organize the event because it agreed with the government that "there needs to be a theological response to violent Islam-inspired radicalism," says contributing editor Malik.

More than 30,000 young Muslims attended — a sign of success. "But we also fought a significant segment of the Muslim community who said: 'Are you promoting Blair's Islam?' " Malik adds.

The British government's tactic of using 'good' Islam to fight 'bad' Islam is likely to be of limited success because it assumes that religious interpretation — not politics — drives radical movements, Brandeis University's Klausen suggests. Terrorists today meet at jihadist video stores, at Internet cafes and in prison — not in mosques, she says. Communities Secretary Blears recently acknowledged this reality, saying the government's new program to counter violent extremism would reach out to young people on the Internet, in cafes, bookshops and gyms. Yet it's hard for outsiders to know which theology to back. The roadshow, for instance, aroused bitter criticism in the press for supporting conservative interpretations of Islam. [92]

The German government, by contrast, has resisted efforts to create a "tame" Islam, saying the state shouldn't influence the theological development of Islam. [93]

Yet the need for Islam-based opposition to extremism is why political moderates like Malik think it was significant when a former senior member of Hizb-ut Tahrir recently denounced the radical group on the BBC. "Here's a guy who in very measured language is saying, 'I reject on theological and philosophical grounds the ideology of an Islamic state,' " while remaining a Muslim, says Malik. He's opening a debate that "needs to happen on Muslim terms."

Winning that debate will be the real challenge, says journalist Bright, and not just because the West is frightened of terrorism. "If people are prepared to blow up individual innocents in atrocities, then we all know what we think about that," he observes. "More difficult is what we do about separatist, totalitarian ideologies and their effects on our young people. That to me is a more serious problem, because far more people are susceptible to that than to becoming terrorists."

NOTES

1. Jane Perlez, "Seeking Terror's Causes, Europe Looks Within," *The New York Times*, Sept. 11, 2007.

2. Nicholas Kulish, "New terrorism case confirms that Denmark is a target," *International Herald Tribune*, Sept. 16, 2007, p. 3, www.iht.com/articles/2007/09/17/europe/17denmark.php.

3. Paul Reynolds, "Bomber Video 'Points to al-Quaeda,' " BBC, Sept. 2, 2005, http://news.bbc.co.uk/1/hi/uk/4208250.stm.

4. See Perlez, *op. cit.*, and Souad Mekhennet and Nicholas Kulish, "Terrorist mastermind, or victim of mistaken identity?" *International Herald Tribune*, Oct. 12, 2007, p. 3.

5. Perlez, *op. cit.*

6. Karen McVeigh, "70 million [pounds] Promised for Citizenship Lessons in Schools and English-speaking Imams," *The Guardian*, July 26, 2007, p. 5.

7. Declan Walsh, "Resurgent Al-Qaida Plotting Attacks on West from Tribal Sanctuary, Officials Fear," *The Guardian*, Sept. 27, 2007. Also see, Jason Burke, "Target Europe," *The Observer*, Sept. 9, 2007, www.guardianunlimited. For background, see Roland Flamini, "Afghanistan on the Brink," *CQ Global Researcher*, June 2007, www.cqpress.com.

8. "Radicalization in the West: The Homegrown Threat," NYPD Intelligence Division, 2007, p. 5. Preventing terrorism by tackling the radicalization of individuals is one part of British intelligence service's four-point strategy: Prevent, Pursue, Protect and Prepare. See also "Countering International Terrorism: The United Kingdom's Strategy," *HM Government*, July 2006, presented to Parliament by the prime minister and secretary of state for the Home Department, www.intelligence.gov.uk.

9. Hizb ut-Tahrir, "Radicalisation, Extremism & 'Islamism,' " July 2007, p. 3, www.hizb.org.uk/hizb/images/PDFs/htb_radicalisation_report.pdf.

10. James Chapman, "Muslims Call for Special Bank Holidays," *Daily Mail*, Aug. 15, 2006.

11. Jane Perlez, "London Gathering Defends Vision of Radical Islam," *The New York Times*, Aug. 7, 2007.

12. Pew Research Center, "Muslim Americans: Middle Class and Mostly Mainstream," May 22, 2007, www.pewresearch.org, pp. 53-54. "Special Report: Islam, America and Europe: Look out, Europe, They Say," *The Economist*, June 22, 2006.

13. *Ibid.*, p. 51. A survey conducted by British Channel 4 in the summer of 2006 found half of Muslims 18-24 believed that 9/11 was a conspiracy by America and

Israel. Cited in Munira Mirza, *et al.*, "Living Apart Together: British Muslims and the Paradox of Multiculturalism," *Policy Exchange*, 2007, p. 58.

14. Cited in Melanie Phillips, *Londonistan: How Britain is Creating a Terror State Within* (2007), p. 302. Also see, "British Should Try Arranged Marriages," *Daily Telegraph*, July 10, 2006, www.telegraph.co.uk/news/main.jhtml?xml=/news/2006/06/10/nterr110.xml.

15. "Inside a Sharia Court," "This World," BBC 2, Oct. 1, 2007, http://news.bbc.co.uk/1/hi/programmes/this_world/7021676.stm.

16. "UK: Extended Pre-charge Detention Violates Rights," Human Rights Watch press release, July 26, 2007, and "In the Name of Prevention: Insufficient Safeguards in National Security Removals," Human Rights Watch, June 2007, http://hrw.org/reports/2007/france0607/1.htm#_Toc167263185.

17. The Associated Press, "Quaeda Using Europeans to Hit U.S., Official Says," *International Herald Tribune*, Sept. 26, 2007, p. 8. McConnell's testimony is at www.dni.gov/testimonies/20070925_testimony.pdf.

18. Peter Skerry, "The Muslim Exception: Why Muslims in the U.S. Aren't as Attracted to Jihad as Those in Europe," *Time*, Aug. 21, 2006.

19. Neil MacFarquhar, "Abandon Stereotype, Muslims in America Say," *The New York Times*, Sept. 4, 2007, p. A12.

20. Daniel Dombey and Simon Kuper, "Britons 'More Suspicious' of Muslims," *Financial Times*, Aug. 19, 2007.

21. *Ibid.*

22. Pew Global Attitudes Project, "Muslims in Europe: Economic Worries Top Concerns about Religious and Cultural Identity," July 6, 2006, http://pew-global.org/reports/display.php?ReportID=254.

23. Presentation by John R. Bowen, University of Chicago International Forum, London, Sept. 29, 2007, as part of "Engaging Cultural Differences in Western Europe" panel.

24. John R. Bowen, "On Building a Multireligious Society," *San Francisco Chronicle*, Feb. 5, 2007.

25. *Ibid.*

26. International Crisis Group, "Islam and Identity in Germany," March 14, 2007, p. 19.

27. Jonathan Laurence and Justin Vaisse, *Integrating Islam: Political and Religious Challenges in Contemporary France* (2006).

28. For background, see Kenneth Jost, "Future of the European Union," *CQ Researcher*, Oct. 28, 2005, pp. 909-932.

29. Phillips, *op. cit.*, p. 22.

30. *Ibid.*, p. 24.

31. Jytte Klausen, "British Counter-Terrorism After 7/7: Adapting Community Policing to the Fight against Domestic Terrorism," *Journal of Ethnic and Migration Studies*, forthcoming, pp. 17-18.

32. See Robert S. Leiken, "Europe's Angry Muslims," *Foreign Affairs*, July/August 2005.

33. Will Woodward, "Kelly vows that new debate on immigration will engage critically with multiculturalism," *The Guardian*, Aug. 25, 2006.

34. Madeleine Bunting, "United Stand," *The Guardian*, June 13, 2007.

35. Phillips, *op. cit.*, p. 25.

36. Ed Husain, *The Islamist* (2007), p. 22.

37. Mirza, *et al.*, *op. cit.*, pp. 6, 18.

38. James Brandon and Douglas Murray, "How British Libraries Encourage Islamic Extremism," Centre for Social Cohesion, August 2007, www.socialcohesion.co.uk/pdf/HateOnTheState.pdf.

39. Emine Saner, "Dishonorable Acts," *The Guardian*, June 13, 2007, p. 18.

40. Leiken, *op. cit.*

41. Martin Bright, "When Progressives Treat with Reactionaries: The British State's Flirtation with Radical Islamism," *Policy Exchange*, 2006, p. 12, www.policyexchange.org.uk/images/libimages/176.pdf.

42. From "Connections," winter 2001, quoted in Tariq Modood, *Multiculturalism: A Civic Idea* (2007), pp. 10-11.

43. Patrick Wintour and Alan Travis, "Brown Sets out Sweeping but Risky 'Terror and Security Reforms,'" *The Guardian*, July 26, 2007, p. 1.

44. *Ibid.*

45. Since 2001, government figures show more than half of those arrested under the 2000 Terrorism Act have been released without charge. Human Rights Watch press release, "UK: Extended Pre-charge Detention Violates Rights," July 26, 2007.

46. Human Rights Watch, "In the Name of Prevention: Insufficient Safeguards in National Security Removals," June 2007, http://hrw.org/reports/2007/france0607/1.htm#_Toc167263185.

47. Peter Clarke, "Learning from Experience: Counter-terrorism in the UK Since 9/11," *Policy Exchange*, 2007, www.policyexchange.org.uk/images/libimages/252.pdf, pp. 19-20.

48. *Ibid.*, p. 27.

49. *Ibid.*

50. See www.liberty-human-rights.org.uk/publications/3-articles-and-speeched/index.shtml.

51. Liberty, "Overlooked: Surveillance and Personal Privacy in Britain," September 2007, www.liberty-human-rights.org.uk.

52. Jocelyne Cesari, *When Islam and Democracy Meet* (2004), pp. 15-16.

53. *Ibid.*, pp. 99-100.

54. Mirza, *op. cit.*, p. 24.

55. *Ibid.*

56. *Ibid.*, pp. 27-28.

57. *Ibid.*

58. *Ibid.*, p. 29.

59. Klausen, *op. cit.*, pp. 14-15. For background, see Peter Katel, "Global Jihad," *CQ Researcher*, Oct. 14, 2005, pp. 857-880.

60. See "Timeline: Madrid investigation," BBC News, April 28, 2004, http://news.bbc.co.uk/2/hi/europe/3597885.stm.

61. NYPD Intelligence Division, *op. cit.*

62. *Ibid.*

63. *Ibid.*, p. 15

64. *Ibid.*

65. Denis MacEoin, "The Hijacking of Islam: How Extremist Literature is Subverting Mosques in the United Kingdom," *Policy Exchange*, 2007, www.policyexchange.org.uk.

66. See "Hate preaching cleric jailed," BBC News, March 7, 2003, http://news.bbc.co.uk/2/hi/uk_news/england/2829059.stm.

67. See "Cleric Bakri barred from Britain," BBC News, Aug. 12, 2005, http://news.bbc.co.uk/2/hi/uk_news/4144792.stm.

68. Klausen, *op. cit.*

69. Richard Norton-Taylor, "Al-Quaida has Revived, Spread and is Capable of a Spectacular," *The Guardian*, Sept. 13, 2007, www.guardian.co.uk/alqaida/story/0,,2167923,00.html. Also see "Strategic Survey 2007," International Institute for Strategic Studies, www.iiss.org/publications/strategic-survey-2007.

70. Peter Bergen, "How Osama Bin Laden Beat George W. Bush," *New Republic*, Oct. 15, 2007.

71. Norton-Taylor, *op. cit.* Jonathan Evans, "Address to the Society of Editors," Nov. 5, 2007, www.mi5.gov.uk.

72. Kulish, Sept. 17, 2007, *op. cit.*

73. Cesari, *op. cit.*, p. 96.

74. Jonathan Laurence, "Managing Transnational Islam: Muslims and the State in Western Europe," March 11, 2006, www.johnathanlaurence.net.

75. *Ibid.*, p. 92.

76. Robert S. Leiken and Steven Brooke, "The Quantitative Analysis of Terrorism and Immigration," *Terrorism and Political Violence* (2006), pp. 503-521.

77. University of Chicago International Forum, London, Sept. 29, 2007.

78. Dan Bilefsky, "Belgians Agree on One Issue: Foreigners," *International Herald Tribune*, Oct. 10, 2007.

79. Jessica Shepherd, "What does Britain Expect?" *The Guardian*, July 17, 2007, p. E1.

80. McVeigh, *op. cit.*

81. Bright, *op. cit.*, p. 28.

82. Hazel Blears, "Preventing Extremism: Strengthening Communities," Oct. 31, 2007, www.communities.gov.uk.

83. "Faith in the System," Department of Children, Schools and Families, Sept. 10, 2007.

84. "We Do Use Books that Call Jews 'Apes' Admits Head of Islamic School," *Evening Standard*, Feb. 7, 2007.

85. Andrew Norfolk, "Hardline Takeover of British Mosques," *The Times* (London), Sept. 7, 2007, www.timesonline.co.uk/tol/comment/faith/article2402973.ece.

86. BBC, "Faith Schools Set for Expansion," Sept. 10, 2007, www.bbc.co.uk.

87. "Major Increase in Work to Tackle Violent Extremism," Department of Communities and Local Government, U.K., Oct. 31, 2007, www.communities.gov.uk/news/corporate/529021.

88. Jo Revill, "Mosques Told to Obey New Code of Conduct," *The Observer*, Nov. 4, 2007, p. 24.

89. Timothy Garton Ash, "Battleground Europe," *Los Angeles Times*, Sept. 13, 2007, www.latimes.com/news/opinion/la-oe-garton13sep13,0,979657.story. Also see Klausen, *op. cit.*: One percent of UK Muslims felt the July 2005 London transit bombers were "right," according to a 2006 poll. Ten percent of Germans sympathized with suicide bombers.

90. Klausen, *op. cit.*

91. See "Who is Richard Reid?" BBC, Dec. 24, 2001, www.bbc.co.uk.

92. Klausen, *op. cit.*

93. International Crisis Group, *op. cit.*, p. 31.

BIBLIOGRAPHY

Books

Bowen, John R., *Why the French Don't Like Headscarves: Islam, the State, and Public Space*, Princeton University Press, 2007.
A Washington University anthropologist looks at the furor that led to the 2004 ban on head scarves in French schools.

Cesari, Jocelyne, *When Islam and Democracy Meet: Muslims in Europe and in the United States*, Palgrave, 2004.
The director of Harvard University's Islam in the West program compares the experiences of European and U.S. Muslims.

Husain, Ed, *The Islamist*, Penguin Books, 2007.
A former Muslim radical in London describes his recruitment by extremist Islamist groups in the 1990s.

Modood, Tariq, *Multiculturalism: A Civic Idea*, Polity, 2007.
A University of Bristol sociologist advocates "multicultural citizenship" to integrate Muslims in Britain.

Phillips, Melanie, *Londonistan: How Britain Is Creating a Terror State Within*, Gibson Square, 2006.
A journalist blames the rise of Muslim radicalism in London on persistent denial by the British government and a craven form of multiculturalism among leftists.

Qutb, Sayyid, *Milestones*, Maktabah Booksellers and Publishers, 2006.
A leader of the Muslim Brotherhood wrote this inspirational text for radical Islamist groups while in an Egyptian prison.

Articles

Bowen, John R., "On Building a Multireligious Society," *San Francisco Chronicle*, Feb. 5, 2007.
France is doing a better job of absorbing Muslims than other European countries.

Leiken, Robert S., and Steven Brook, "The Moderate Muslim Brotherhood," *Foreign Affairs*, March/April 2007.
The Muslim Brotherhood has moved away from violence in favor of using the electoral process to obtain its goal of an Islamic state in Egypt, France, Jordan, Spain, Syria, Tunisia and the United Kingdom, say leaders.

Perlez, Jane, "From Finding Radical Islam to Losing an Ideology," Sept. 12, 2007, *The New York Times*, www.nytimes.com/2007/09/12/world/europe/12britain.html?_r=1&oref=slogin.
A former senior member of the radical group Hizb ut-Tahrir says he left the group because it preached violence.

Ruthven, Malise, "How to Understand Islam," *The New York Review of Books*, Nov. 8, 2007, pp. 62-66.
Influential jihadist thinkers Maududi and Qutb held more rigid views of sharia than many scholars.

Reports and Studies

"In the Name of Prevention: Insufficient Safeguards in National Security Removals," Human Rights Watch, June 6, 2007, http://hrw.org/reports/2007/france0607/.

The group argues that France's policy of deporting imams and others it considers Islamic fundamentalists violates human rights.

"Islam and Identity in Germany," International Crisis Group, March 14, 2007, www.crisisgroup.org.
Issued before the latest foiled plot in Germany, this report downplayed the threat of homegrown terrorism in Germany's Turkish community.

"Radicalisation, Extremism & 'Islamism': Realities and Myths in the 'War on Terror,' " Hizb ut-Tahrir Britain, July 2007, www.hizb.org.uk.
The separatist British group lays out its argument for a caliphate in the Muslim world and denies it espouses violence.

"Radicalization in the West: The Homegrown Threat," New York City Police Department Intelligence Division, 2007, http://sethgodin.typepad.com/seths_blog/files/NYPD_Report-radicalization_in_the_West.pdf.
Muslim terrorists in Europe were generally "well-integrated" into their home countries, according to this study.

Bright, Martin, "When Progressives Treat with Reactionaries: The British State's Flirtation with Radical Islamism," *Policy Exchange*, **2006, www.policyexchange.org.uk.**
The *New Statesman's* political editor says the government was pressured to maintain a relationship with radical Muslim groups.

MacEoin, Denis, "The Hijacking of Islam: How Extremist Literature is Subverting Mosques in the United Kingdom," *Policy Exchange*, **2007, www.policyexchange.org.uk/Publications.aspx?id=430.**
The group visited leading mosques and schools in Britain and found extremist literature preaching hatred against non-Muslims, anti-Semitism and stoning of adulterers.

Mirza, Munira, *et al.,* **"Living Apart Together: British Muslims and the Paradox of Multiculturalism,"** *Policy Exchange*, **2007, www.policyexchange.org.uk.**
A conservative think tank in London blames British multiculturalism policies for dividing people along ethnic lines.

For More Information

Association of Muslim Schools UK, P.O. Box 14109, Birmingham B6 9BN, United Kingdom; +44-844-482-0407; www.ams-uk.org. A Birmingham-based group that "supports and develops excellence in full-time Muslim schools" in the United Kingdom.

Center for Islamic Pluralism, (202) 232-1750; www.islamicpluralism.eu. A Washington-based think tank that is critical of radical Muslim groups.

Centre for Social Cohesion, 77 Great Peter St., Westminster, London SW1P 2EZ, United Kingdom; +44-20-7799-6677; www.socialcohesion.co.uk. A British group critical of Britain's multicultural policy.

Hizb ut-Tahrir, www.hizb.org.uk. Considered one of the more radical Islamic organizations in Britain.

Human Rights Watch, 350 Fifth Ave., 34th Floor, New York, NY 10118-3299; (212) 290-4700; www.hrw.org. An international human rights organization.

Islam in the West Program, Harvard University, 59-61, Rue Pouchet, F-75849 Paris Cedex 17, France; +33-1-40-25-11-22; www.euro-islam.info. A network of scholars who conduct comparative research on Muslims in Europe.

Liberty, 21 Tabard St., London SE1 4LA, United Kingdom; +20-7403-3888; www.liberty-human-rights.org.uk. London-based group, also known as the National Council for Civil Liberties, that advocates for civil liberties.

Muslim Council of Britain, P.O. Box 57330, London E1 2WJ, United Kingdom; +44-845-26-26-786; www.mcb.org.uk. Represents more than 500 Muslim groups, mosques and schools in Britain.

National Secular Society, 25 Red Lion Square, London WC1R 4RL, United Kingdom; +44-20-7404-3126; www.secularism.org.uk. A London-based group that opposes faith schools in Britain.

Policy Exchange, Clutha House, 10 Storey's Gate, London SW1P 3AY, United Kingdom; +20-7340-2650; www.policyexchange.org.uk. A London-based think tank that opposes the British government's multicultural policy and choice of Muslim groups to support.

Saban Center for Middle East Policy, Brookings Institution, 1775 Massachusetts Ave., N.W., Washington, DC 20036; (202) 797-6000; www.brookings.edu/saban.aspx. A Washington-based think tank that studies terrorism.

Stop Islamisation of Europe, +44-122-854-7317; sioe.wordpress.com. A Danish group that has been coordinating street protests in Europe against Islamist stances on issues like sharia.

Mohamed Abdul Bari

Chairman, East London Mosque

Freedom of speech has limits

"Muslims [must] express their feelings peacefully and will call upon the newspapers concerned to apologise for the enormous offence [Mohammed cartoon] and distress caused. The hallmark of any civilized society is not just that it allows freedom of speech, but that it accepts this freedom also has limits."

— The Independent *(England), February 2006*

Ali Selim

Secretary-General Irish Council of Imams

Perpetrators don't speak for all

"In some parts of the world acts of violence against innocent people have created an unhealthy atmosphere which allowed Islamophobia to flourish. To stigmatise every Muslim for a crime perpetrated by a Muslim is just like stigmatising every Christian for a crime perpetrated by a Christian. It is not fair and is absurd."

— The Irish Times, *April 2007*

Salma Yaqoob

Councillor; Sparkbrook, Birmingham, England

Citizenship classes are useless

"Muslims in this country are already British. If Muslims are singled out for citizenship classes, it will only alienate them and make them feel like they are not really British at all. The Muslim community has already condemned extremism. You can't stop extremism through citizenship classes alone."

— Birmingham Evening Mail *(England), May 2006*

Wolfgang Schaeuble

Interior Minister Germany

Our country, our values

"Islam is part of us now. That means Muslims must adapt and not just pay lip service to doing so. They must put up with cartoons, gender equality, possibly insulting criticism — all this is part of our open society."

— Conference on Islam, Berlin, September 2006

Al-Maktoum Institute for Arabic and Islamic Studies

Dundee, Scotland

Education promotes understanding

"There must be better education at university level on Islam and Muslims in today's world, which reflects the needs of our contemporary multicultural society. It is only through multicultural education that we can work to eliminate extremism and fundamentalism."

— Time For Change report, October 2006

Dalil Boubakeur

Chairman, French Council of the Muslim Faith

A religion of peace

"The Prophet founded not a terrorist religion, but on the contrary, a religion of peace. We attach enormous importance to this image and we will not allow it to be distorted. I myself oppose the extremist forms of Islam; we reject this parallel."

— Libération.fr *(France), February 2006*

Tony Blair

Then-Prime Minister United Kingdom

Attacking absurd ideas is crucial

"This terrorism will not be defeated until its ideas, the poison that warps the minds of its adherents, are confronted, head-on, in their essence, at their core. By this I don't mean telling them terrorism is wrong. I mean telling them their attitude to America is absurd; their concept of governance pre-feudal; their positions on women and other faiths, reactionary and regressive."

— Evening Standard *(England), March 2006*

Bassam Tibi

Professor of International Relations, University of Gottingen, Germany

Riots in France pose warning for Europe

"The explosions now are in France, but other countries are sitting on the same time bomb; it's a European time bomb. This is a warning for Europe from the 'no-future' Muslim kids whose lives are wasting all over the continent. Without change, the fighting will come to the streets of Berlin, Amsterdam wherever."

— Boston Globe, *November 2005*

Christo Komarnitski, Bulgaria

5

Torture Debate

Seth Stern

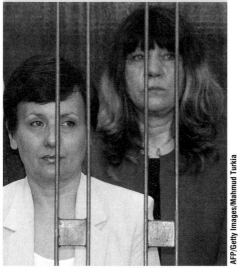

Nurses Valentina Siropoulu, left, and Valia Cherveniashlka are among six Bulgarian medical workers who were tortured while imprisoned for eight years in Libya on charges they infected hundreds of Libyan children with HIV-AIDS. They were released in August. About 160 countries torture prisoners, despite six international treaties banning the practice.

From *CQ Researcher,*
September 1, 2007.

I t is called, simply, waterboarding. A prisoner is strapped to a board with his feet above his head, his mouth and nose covered, usually with cloth or cellophane. Water is then poured over his face, inducing gagging and a terrifying sense of drowning.

The U.S. government — which has been accused of using waterboarding on detainees it suspects are terrorists — denies that it practices torture or cruel, inhuman or degrading treatment. The Central Intelligence Agency (CIA) says it must use what it calls "enhanced interrogation techniques" — to obtain critical information from "enemy combatants" in the war on terrorism. [1] But human rights advocates say waterboarding and other abusive interrogation tactics are prohibited by international law.

To be sure, the United States is far from the worst offender when it comes to mistreating prisoners. Even human rights advocates who complain the most bitterly about the tactics used in America's war on terror say they don't compare to those utilized by the world's worst human rights abusers.

"Nothing the administration has done can compare in its scale to what happens every day to victims of cruel dictatorships around the world," Tom Malinowski, Human Rights Watch's Washington advocacy director, told the U.S. Senate Foreign Relations Committee on July 26. "The United States is not Sudan or Cuba or North Korea." [2]

Indeed, about 160 countries practice torture today, according to human rights groups and the U.S. State Department. [3] In July, for example, six Bulgarian medical workers freed after eight years in a Libyan prison said they had been tortured. "We were treated like animals," said Ashraf al-Hazouz, one of the prisoners, who had been accused of deliberately infecting Libyan children with the HIV-

Torture Still in Use Throughout the World

Some 160 countries practice torture, according to a 2005 survey of incidents reported by the U.S. Department of State and Amnesty International. Besides using torture to solicit information, some countries use it to punish or intimidate dissidents, separatists, insurgents and religious minorities. The Council of Europe accuses the U.S. Central Intelligence Agency (CIA) of using its rendition program to send kidnapped terror suspects to be interrogated in 11 cities — all in countries that practice torture.

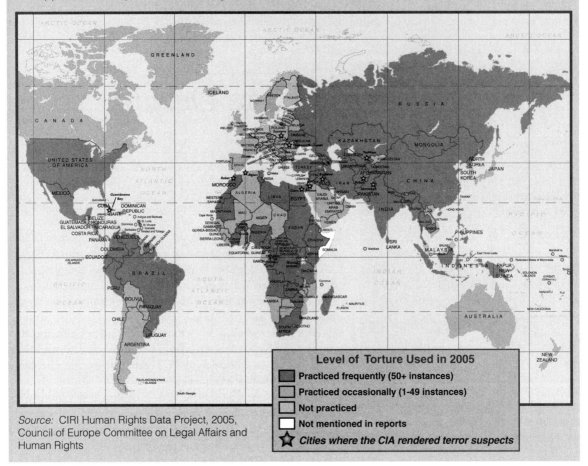

Source: CIRI Human Rights Data Project, 2005, Council of Europe Committee on Legal Affairs and Human Rights

Level of Torture Used in 2005

Practiced frequently (50+ instances)
Practiced occasionally (1-49 instances)
Not practiced
Not mentioned in reports
⭐ *Cities where the CIA rendered terror suspects*

AIDS virus. Hazouz said the Libyans attached electrodes to his genitals and feet, unleashed attack dogs on him and tied his hands and legs to a metal bar, spinning him "like a chicken on a rotisserie." [4]

While other countries' abuse methods may seem more abhorrent, human rights advocates worldwide complain angrily that America's detention and interrogation practices in the post-9/11 war on terror have lowered the bar for torturers worldwide, giving habitual abusers a new justification for their behavior.

America's detention policies since Sept. 11, 2001, "are a gift to dictators everywhere" who "use America's poor example to shield themselves from international criticism and pressure," Malinowski said. Abusive governments now routinely "justify their own, longstanding practices of systematically violating basic human rights norms" by arguing that they — like the United States — must use torture to deal with the threat of international terrorism. [5]

U.S. counterterrorism policies that anger allies and human rights activists include the indefinite detentions

— without a guaranteed trial or right to counsel — of hundreds of alleged terrorists at Guantánamo Bay, Cuba, beginning shortly after 9/11. Then in April 2004 CBS' "60 Minutes II" televised explosive photographs that circulated around the world portraying harsh interrogation methods that reportedly had migrated from Guantánamo to the U.S.-run Abu Ghraib military prison near Baghdad. A year later *The Washington Post* revealed that the CIA was operating so-called "black sites" — secret prisons in Eastern Europe and Southeast Asia where detainees were subjected to extreme interrogation methods, allegedly including waterboarding. [6] Finally, news that the United States was kidnapping terror suspects from foreign locations and transporting them to interrogation sites in third countries with reputations for practicing torture — a tactic known as extraordinary rendition — triggered further global outrage. [7]

By adopting such measures, the United States has lost its moral authority to condemn torture and human rights abuses in other countries, say critics. "It's a very bad precedent for people to be able to say 'the U.S. — the biggest democracy promoter in the world — has to use it, why can't we?' " says physician Bhogendra Sharma, president of the Center for Victims of Torture in Nepal, which treats victims tortured by both the Nepalese government and Maoist guerrillas.

Few American ambassadors today "dare to protest another government's harsh interrogations, detentions without trial, or even 'disappearances,' knowing how easily an interlocutor could turn the

Severe Torture Still Used by Many Nations

According to the U.S. State Department and Human Rights Watch, the following nations are among those condoning widespread and particularly severe forms of torture:

 China: Prison guards are forbidden from using torture, but former detainees report the use of electric shock, beatings and shackles. Among those targeted for abuse are adherents of the outlawed Falun Gong spiritual movement, Tibetans and Muslim Uighur prisoners.

 Egypt: Government interrogators from the State Security Investigations arm of the Ministry of the Interior regularly torture suspected Islamic militants, including prisoners transferred to Egypt by the United States. Victims were kicked, burned with cigarettes, shackled, forcibly stripped, beaten with water hoses and dragged on the floor.

 Indonesia: Security officers in Aceh Province systematically torture suspected supporters of the armed Free Aceh movement, using beatings, cigarette burning and electric shock.

 Iran: Political prisoners are subjected to sensory deprivation known as "white torture" — they are held in all-white cells with no windows, with prison clothes and even meals all in white.

 Morocco: Terrorism suspects detained after a May 2003 attack in Casablanca were subjected to torture and mistreatment, including severe beatings.

 Nepal: Both government security personnel and Maoist rebels employ torture, including beating the soles of victims' feet, submersion in water and sexual humiliation.

Nigeria: Armed robbery and murder suspects are subjected to beatings with batons, horse whips, iron bars and cables.

 North Korea: Captors routinely tortured and mistreated prisoners using electric shock, prolonged periods of exposure, humiliations such as public nakedness, being hung by the wrists and forcing mothers recently repatriated from China to watch the infanticide of their newborn infants.

 Russia: Russian security forces conducting so-called anti-terror operations in Chechnya mutilate victims and dump their bodies on the sides of roads.

 Uganda: Government security forces in unregistered detention facilities torture prisoners with caning and severe beatings and by inflicting pain to the genitals.

 Uzbekistan: Police, prison guards and members of the National Security Service routinely employ suffocation, electric shock, deprivation of food and water and sexual abuse. Prison regulations in 2005 permitted beatings under medical supervision.

Sources: "Human Rights Watch's 2007 World Report;" U.S. State Department "2006 Country Reports on Human Rights Practices"

Views Differ on U.S. Interrogation Tactics

A wide gulf exists between Americans' and Europeans' views of how the United States treats terrorism suspects. Americans are almost evenly split on whether the United States uses torture, but three-quarters of Germans and nearly two-thirds of Britons believe it does. And while just over half of Americans think U.S. detention policies are legal, 85 percent of Germans and 65 percent of Britons think they are illegal.

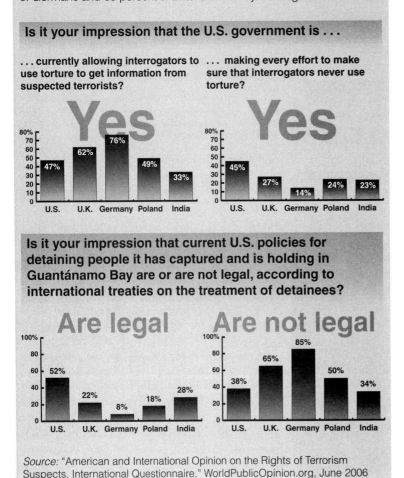

Is it your impression that the U.S. government is . . .

. . . currently allowing interrogators to use torture to get information from suspected terrorists?

. . . making every effort to make sure that interrogators never use torture?

Is it your impression that current U.S. policies for detaining people it has captured and is holding in Guantánamo Bay are or are not legal, according to international treaties on the treatment of detainees?

Source: "American and International Opinion on the Rights of Terrorism Suspects, International Questionnaire," WorldPublicOpinion.org, June 2006

The worldwide anger triggered by America's post-9/11 detention and interrogation policies stems not only from the perception that notorious governments now feel free to continue torturing prisoners. It also stems from widespread perceptions that:

• The United States' overwhelming military and technological superiority have made it arrogant, immune from having to abide by international norms.

• America's pervasive cultural influence has, since 9/11, "normalized" torture by spreading the concept across the globe that torture works and can be legally or morally justified.

• The United States has squandered its historic position as the world's leader in the fight against human rights abuses, opening itself to charges of being a hypocrite.

When the U.S. State Department released its annual report on human rights violators in 2005, both China and Russia said the United States has its own abuses to explain. "Unfortunately, [the report] once again gives us reason to say that double standards are a characteristic of the American approach to such an important theme," said a statement issued by the Russian foreign ministry. "Characteristically off-screen is the ambiguous record of the United States itself." [9]

Disappointment over U.S. tactics has been widespread. *El Tiempo*, a leading newspaper in Bogotá, Colombia, editorialized in 2005: "It seems incredible that these kind of un-civilizing backward steps are coming from a country which declares itself a defender of Western values and which has been so on more than one occasion." [10]

A 2006 survey of 26,000 people in 25 countries found that 67 percent disapproved of U.S. treatment of detainees in Guantánamo and other prisons. Some of the

tables and cite U.S. misconduct as an excuse for his government's own abuses," said a 2007 Human Rights Watch (HRW) report. [8]

Sarah Leah Whitson, HRW's director for the Middle East and North Africa, says when she visits officials in those regions to discuss their use of torture, their first reply now is often, "What about the United States? Go talk to the U.S. government."

highest disapproval rates were among America's closest allies in Europe — which have suffered their own terrorist attacks since 9/11 — and Middle Eastern allies such as Lebanon and Egypt, who fear the growing influence of Islamic extremists. [11]

But the 9/11 attacks did more than raise the profile of the torture debate in the United States. An Australian law professor has become one of the world's most vocal advocates for "life-saving compassionate torture," which he says is justified if it elicits crucial information needed to prevent future terrorist attacks and save innocent lives. (*See "At Issue," p. 131.*)

But critics of that argument point out that torture is not only used to extract life-saving information from terrorists but also to punish political dissidents, suspected criminals — who sometimes are innocent — and religious minorities. China, for instance, tortures members of the Falun Gong spiritual movement, Tibetan dissidents and Muslims from the Uighur region, according to Human Rights Watch.

In Iraq — where former leader Saddam Hussein was notorious for torturing political enemies — the U.S. occupation has not curbed the prevalence of torture by government agents or insurgents. In fact, say human rights advocates, the level of torture perpetrated by the Shiite-dominated Iraqi government and affiliated militias reportedly has escalated as the country has descended into civil strife. (*See sidebar, p. 120.*)

Despite the damage done to America's reputation by its counterterrorism tactics, President Bush in July said he was authorizing the CIA to reopen its overseas black sites. Bush had announced last September that the use of secret prisons had been suspended and that the prisoners were being transferred to Guantánamo. That decision was prompted by the U.S. Supreme Court's ruling that all U.S. detainees, including those held by the CIA, were covered by the Geneva Conventions' guidelines for the treatment of wartime detainees.

The administration said in July 2007 the CIA would comply with the conventions in its treatment of prisoners at the sites. But Bush's new order did not ban waterboarding or any other controversial interrogation techniques and gave interrogators wide latitude if their purpose is to gather intelligence needed to prevent terrorist attacks. [12]

The Bush administration and its supporters argue the United States is operating within the confines of U.S.

Vann Nath, one of only seven people to survive the Khmer Rouge's infamous Tuol Sleng prison, looks at a photo of Kaing Guek Eav, who ran the murderous regime's security service. Eav was recently found living in Cambodia as a born-again Christian. He was indicted by a U.N.-backed tribunal in July for his role in the torture and deaths of 14,000 men, women and children at the facility. His trial is expected to begin in 2008.

and international law and that aggressive interrogation methods are needed to protect against future terrorist attacks. "These are dangerous men with unparalleled knowledge about terrorist networks and their plans for new attacks," President Bush said in 2006. "The security of our nation and the lives of our citizens depend on our ability to learn what these terrorists know." [13]

With America seen as abandoning its role as the world's ethical standard-bearer, human rights groups complain that the European Union (EU) has not stepped up to fill the void. The EU has dragged its feet in questioning U.S. interrogation policies, say critics, and some EU countries have secretly allowed U.S. aircraft to use their airports for rendition flights. Some renditions involved innocent citizens who were tortured in countries long known to abuse prisoners, such as Egypt and

Torture Has Escalated in Iraq

Saddam's brutal legacy survives.

The fall of Saddam Hussein and more than four years of U.S. occupation have done little to curb torture in Iraq. In fact, the level of torture perpetrated by government personnel and militias reportedly has escalated as the country has descended into what many consider a civil war.

The use of torture in Iraq is "totally out of hand," said Manfred Nowak, a U.N. official appointed to study torture around the world, and "many people say it is worse than it had been in the times of Saddam Hussein." [1]

Bodies brought to the Baghdad morgue often bear signs of acid-induced injuries, broken limbs and wounds caused by power drills and nails, said U.N. investigators. [2] The torture is mostly being perpetrated by the largely Shiite ministries of the Interior and Defense as well as by private Shiite militias, according to Sarah Leah Whitson, Human Rights Watch's program director for the Middle East and North Africa.

"The torture committed in the Ministry of Interior facilities we documented is certainly comparable to torture and abuse that's been recorded in the Baath prisons prior to the war," says Whitson.

In 2006 U.S. and Iraqi troops discovered a secret Baghdad prison run by the Interior Ministry, known as Site 4, where some of the more than 1,400 prisoners were found to have been subjected to systematic abuse.

Human rights advocates say the widespread use of torture is being fueled by the breakdown of law and order and the continued employment of officials who previously used torture during Saddam's regime. The weakened Iraqi central government has been unable to rein in the abuse of prisoners in these facilities, despite promises to do so. There has been less documented evidence of torture by Sunni insurgents, Whitson points out. Sunnis usually execute their victims, often by beheading.

A January 2005 report by Human Rights Watch found that police, jailers and intelligence agents — many of whom had similar jobs under Saddam — were "committing systematic torture and other abuses." Despite being "in the throes of a significant insurgency" in which thousands of police officers and civilians are being killed, the report said, "no government — not Saddam Hussein's, not the occupying powers and not

Syria. Besides generating outrage among close U.S. allies such as Canada, the incidents have led to prosecutions in Germany and Italy of Americans allegedly involved in the renditions.

As the Bush administration continues to defend itself against global criticism of its counterterrorism policies, these are some of the questions being asked:

Is torture effective?

Advocates and opponents of torture and other coercive techniques can look at the same evidence about their effectiveness and come to very different conclusions.

Take the case of Khalid Shaikh Mohammed, a senior al Qaeda operative and the alleged principal architect of the 9/11 attacks. He was captured in Pakistan in 2003 and interrogated by U.S. intelligence agents — reportedly using waterboarding — before being transferred to military custody at Guantánamo. [14] In a military hearing in March 2007 the Defense Department released a tran-

script of his confession in which he took credit for 31 different terrorist operations, including planning the 9/11 attacks in the United States and the beheading of *Wall Street Journal* reporter Daniel Pearl.

CIA Director Michael Hayden cited coercive interrogation techniques employed against detainees such as Mohammed (dubbed K.S.M. by intelligence agents) as an "irreplaceable" tool that helped yield information that has helped disrupt several terrorist plots since 9/11. "K.S.M. is the poster boy for using tough but legal tactics," said Michael Sheehan, a former State Department counterterrorism official. "He's the reason these techniques exist." [15]

But opponents of aggressive interrogation techniques, like Col. Dwight Sullivan, head defense lawyer at the Office of Military Commissions, cite Mohammed's serial confessions as "a textbook example of why we shouldn't allow coercive methods." [16]

Some intelligence experts doubt the veracity of portions of Mohammed's information. For one thing they

the Iraqi interim government — can justify ill-treatment of persons in custody in the name of security." [3]

The government of Iraqi Prime Minister Nuri Kamal al-Maliki has been slow to respond to reports of torture by governmental personnel, say human rights advocates. The Iraqi government "made all kinds of promises and commitments to investigate and review" allegations of torture in 2005, Whitson says, but since then the Interior Ministry "has only gone further outside control of the government," as war and sectarian violence have escalated. "There's not a commitment to making this issue a priority."

When British and Iraqi special forces raided the office of an Iraqi government intelligence agency in the southern city of Basra in March 2007, they found prisoners exhibiting signs of torture. Al-Maliki condemned the raid, but not the abuse it uncovered. [4]

Torture has continued since the start of the U.S. military occupation in Iraq. A 2004 report by the International Committee of the Red Cross found that after Saddam's fall Iraqi authorities beat detainees with cables, kicked them in the genitals and hung them by handcuffs from iron bars of cell windows for several hours at a time. [5]

Torture is also being employed in Kurdistan, a semi-autonomous region in northern Iraq that is the most stable part of the country. Human Rights Watch reported in July 2007 that detainees accused of anti-government activities were subjected to torture and other mistreatment. [6]

The torturers are security forces and personnel at detention facilities operated by the two major Kurdish political parties — the Kurdistan Democratic Party and the Patriotic Union of Kurdistan — which operate outside control of the region's government, the report said. Detainees have been beaten, put in stress positions and handcuffed for several days at a time.

Nonetheless, the abuses in Kurdistan do not equal those occurring elsewhere in Iraq. "Certainly the situation in mainland Iraq is much worse," says Whitson.

----

[1] BBC News, "Iraq Torture 'worse than Saddam,' " Sept. 21, 2006.

[2] *Ibid.*

[3] Doug Struck, "Torture in Iraq Still Routine, Report Says," *The Washington Post*, Jan. 25, 2005, p. A10.

[4] Kirk Semple, "Basra Raid Finds Dozens Detained by Iraqi Unit," *The New York Times*, March 5, 2007.

[5] "Report of the International Committee of the Red Cross on the Treatment by the Coalition Forces of Prisoners of War and Other Protected Persons by the Geneva Conventions in Iraq During Arrest, Internment and Interrogation," February 2004, www.globalsecurity.org/military/library/report/2004/icrc_report_iraq_feb2004.pdf.

[6] "Caught in the Whirlwind: Torture and Denial of Due Process by the Kurdistan Security Forces," Human Rights Watch, July 3, 2007, http://hrw.org/reports/2007/kurdistan0707/.

----

don't think a single operative — even one as high ranking as he — could have been involved in 31 separate terrorist plots. And those intimately associated with the Pearl case are highly skeptical that Mohammed himself murdered Pearl, as he claimed.

"My old colleagues say with 100-percent certainty that it was not K.S.M. who killed Pearl," former CIA officer Robert Baer told *New Yorker* writer Jane Mayer. And Special Agent Randall Bennett, who oversaw security at the U.S. consulate in Karachi when Pearl was killed, said "K.S.M.'s name never came up" during his interviews with those convicted in 2002 of the murder. [17]

Skeptics of torture's effectiveness say most people — to end their suffering — will provide false information. For instance, a torture victim deprived of his clothes will feel so "ashamed and humiliated and cold," said retired FBI counterterrorism agent Dan Coleman, "he'll tell you anything you want to hear to get his clothing back. There's no value in it." [18]

Others say torture doesn't work against zealots. "People who are committed to their ideology or religion . . . would rather die than speak up," says Sharma at the Center for Victims of Torture in Nepal.

Both opponents and supporters of coercive interrogation methods, however, agree torture is useful for other purposes. Many countries use torture to punish dissidents, separatists or guerrillas and to intimidate others from joining such groups. "The real purpose of torture is oppression of one or the other kind, to send a signal to anyone who is an opponent that there is a very, very grave risk," says Sune Segal, head of communications for the Copenhagen-based International Rehabilitation Council for Torture Victims, which collaborates with 131 treatment centers around the world. "It's not about soliciting information."

Underlying the debate is the fact that little scientific evidence exists about whether torture works. A recent Intelligence Science Board study concluded that "virtually none" of the limited number of techniques used by

U.S. personnel in recent decades "are based on scientific research or have even been subjected to scientific or systematic inquiry or evaluation." [19]

Darius Rejali, a political science professor at Reed College in Portland, Ore., says regimes that employ torture aren't likely to divulge their findings, and torturers themselves have very little incentive to boast about their work, which is punishable under international law. "Torture travels by back routes," Rejali says. "There's rarely training, so there is no particular mechanism for determining whether it works."

Experienced interrogators who have talked about their work say pain and coercion are often counterproductive. John Rothrock, who as a U.S. Air Force captain in Vietnam headed a combat interrogation team, said he didn't know "any professional intelligence officers of my generation who would think this is a good idea." [20]

Experts say the most effective interrogations require a trained interrogator. Coleman says he learned to build a rapport with even the worst suspects rather than trying to intimidate them. He would patiently work to build a relationship in which the target of his interrogation would begin to trust him and ultimately share information.

You try to "get them to the point, in the intelligence world, where they commit treason," he said. [21]

Is torture ever justified?

Australian law Professor Mirko Bagaric at Deakin University in Melbourne prompted a vigorous public debate in May 2005 when he suggested that torture is sometimes morally justified.

"Given the choice between inflicting a relatively small level of harm on a wrongdoer and saving an innocent person, it is verging on moral indecency to prefer the interests of the wrongdoer," Bagaric wrote in *The Age*, a leading daily paper in Melbourne. Such cases are analogous to a situation in which a wrongdoer threatens to kill a hostage unless his demands are met, he said. "In such a case, it is not only permissible but desirable for police to shoot (and kill) the wrongdoer if they get a 'clear shot.' " [22]

In the United States, Harvard Law Professor Alan Dershowitz has argued that the legal system should adjust to the reality that if it could prevent a catastrophic terrorist attack that could kill millions, interrogators will probably torture a suspect whether or not it's legal. In emergencies, he contends, courts should issue "torture warrants" to interrogators trying to prevent such attacks.

"A formal, visible, accountable and centralized system is somewhat easier to control than an ad hoc, off-the-books and under-the-radar-screen non-system," Dershowitz wrote. [23]

Those who justify torture in certain situations usually invoke a hypothetical "ticking time bomb" scenario in which interrogators torture a suspect to obtain information that can help prevent an imminent attack. Twenty-five years ago, long before the rise of Islamist terrorists, philosophy Professor Michael Levin of the City University of New York hypothesized a similar scenario in *Newsweek*.

"Suppose a terrorist has hidden a bomb on Manhattan Island, which will detonate at noon on 4 July. . . . Suppose, further, that he is caught at 10 a.m. that fateful day, but — preferring death to failure — won't disclose where the bomb is. . . . If the only way to save those lives is to subject the terrorist to the most excruciating possible pain, what grounds can there be for not doing so?" [24]

But opponents of torture say such perfect "ticking time bomb" scenarios occur in the movies, but rarely in real life. Interrogators usually aren't positive they have captured the one person with knowledge of a real plot. And even if they torture such a suspect, it usually won't prevent the attack because his accomplices will proceed without him, critics say.

"I was in the Army for 25 years, and I talked to lots of military people who had been in lots of wars. I talked to lots of people in law enforcement," says James Jay Carafano, a fellow at the conservative Heritage Foundation. "I've never yet ever found anyone that's ever confronted the ticking time bomb scenario. That's not the moral dilemma that people normally face." [25]

"The United States is a nation of laws," says Sen. Patrick J. Leahy, a Vermont Democrat who chairs the Senate Judiciary Committee, "and I categorically reject the view that torture, even in such compelling circumstances, can be justified." Even if harsh interrogation techniques do not rise to the level of torture, he said, they are probably illegal under international laws that prohibit cruel, inhumane or degrading treatment of prisoners.

Law professors and philosophers widely agree that torture is always immoral and should not be legalized. Once torture is allowed in extreme circumstances, they point out, it quickly spreads to less urgent situations. "It has a tendency to just proliferate," says Raimond Gaita, a professor of moral philosophy at King's College in London.

He cites the experience of Israel, which authorized coercive interrogation techniques in 1987 in limited circumstances. But interrogators in the field used more aggressive techniques with more suspects than intended.

Eitan Felner, former director of the Israeli Information Center for Human Rights in the Occupied Territories, writes the lesson of Israel's experience is "the fallacy of believing — as some influential American opinion-makers do today — that it is possible to legitimize the use of torture to thwart terrorist attacks and at the same time restrict its use to exceptional cases." [26]

Instead, torture should remain illegal and interrogators faced with the time-bomb scenario should be in the same legal position as someone who commits civil disobedience, say opponents. "Anyone who thinks an act of torture is justified should have . . . to convince a group of peers in a public trial that all necessary conditions for a morally permissible act were indeed satisfied," writes Henry Shue, a professor of politics and international relations at the University of Oxford. [27]

Human Rights advocates say that — while not explicitly endorsing torture — U.S. policies have changed the dialogue about torture around world. "It used to be these things were automatically bad," says Jumana Musa, advocacy director for Amnesty USA. "Now, there's a cost-benefit analysis and the notion that this isn't really that bad."

Have U.S. attitudes toward torture changed?

Some prominent American politicians and some soldiers, albeit anonymously, have recently endorsed torture as a way to prevent terrorist attacks or save lives.

At a May 2007 GOP presidential debate, Rudolph W. Giuliani, the mayor of New York during the Sept. 11 terror attacks, said if elected president he would advise interrogators "to use every method they could think of" to prevent an imminent catastrophic terror attack. Other candidates were even more explicit, embracing torture with an openness that would have been unheard of before 9/11. California Rep. Duncan Hunter said he would tell the Defense secretary: "Get the information," while Colorado Rep. Tom Tancredo endorsed waterboarding. [28]

Some U.S. military personnel who have served in Iraq express similar attitudes. More than a third of the 1,700 American soldiers and Marines who responded to a 2006 survey said torture would be acceptable if it helped save the life of a fellow soldier or helped get information, and

Getty Images/The Washington Post

An American soldier threatens an Iraqi detainee with an attack dog in one of the graphic Abu Ghraib prison abuse photos that shocked the world in 2004. Human rights advocates worldwide say America's harsh post-9/11 detention and interrogation practices lowered the bar for torturers worldwide. Twelve low-level U.S. military personnel have since been convicted for their roles in the abuse, which an Army investigation described as "sadistic, blatant and wanton criminal" abuse.

10 percent admitted to using force against Iraqi civilians or damaging their property when it wasn't necessary. [29]

But many top U.S. military leaders, interrogators and veterans denounce torture as ineffective and say it will only make it more likely that American captives will be tortured in the future. Sen. John McCain, R-Ariz., who was tortured while a prisoner of war in Vietnam, has spoken out forcefully against torture and led the 2005 effort in Congress to limit the kinds of interrogation methods U.S. military personnel can use.

"We've sent a message to the world that the United States is not like the terrorists. [W]e are a nation that upholds values and standards of behavior and treatment of all people, no matter how evil or bad they are," McCain said. Furthermore, he added, disavowing torture will "help us enormously in winning the war for the hearts and minds of people throughout the world in the war on terror." [30]

A 2006 public opinion survey by the University of Maryland's Program on International Policy Attitudes (PIPA) suggests that most Americans reject the use of torture. The PIPA poll found that 75 percent of Americans agreed that terror detainees had "the right not to be tortured." Fifty-seven percent said the United States should

CHRONOLOGY

1700s *Torture is banned in Europe.*

1754 Prussia becomes first European state to abolish torture; other European countries soon follow suit.

1900-1950 *Torture re-emerges, then is prohibited.*

1917 Russian Revolution gives birth to communism, which will foster totalitarian regimes that will torture perceived enemies of the state.

1933 Nazis take over Germany and soon begin torturing civilian prisoners.

1948 U.N. adopts Universal Declaration of Human Rights banning torture.

1949 Geneva Conventions ban all use of "mutilation, cruel treatment and torture" of prisoners of war.

1950s-1960s *Torture continues, despite international ban.*

1954 France tortures thousands of Algerians during Algeria's war for independence.

1961 Amnesty International is founded after two Portuguese students are jailed for seven years for toasting freedom.

1970s-1990s *Democracies — as well as authoritarian regimes — continue to torture.*

1971 British interrogators use the "five techniques" against Irish Republican Army suspects. European Court of Human Rights calls the methods illegal.

1975 Khmer Rouge takes over Cambodia and soon begins torturing and murdering thousands of detainees.

1978 Human Rights Watch is founded.

1987 Israel authorizes use of aggressive interrogation techniques during widespread Palestinian unrest.

1999 Israel's Supreme Court bans torture and abusive interrogation methods.

2000s-Present *Rise of Islamic terrorist attacks sparks increasing use of torture.*

2001 Muslim terrorists kill 3,000 in Sept. 11 attacks. . . . Hundreds of Muslims are detained in the United States and Afghanistan. . . . Fox Television's "24" begins showing U.S. agents using torture.

2002 First "enemy combatants" captured in Afghanistan arrive at Guantánamo naval base in Cuba. President Bush says they will be treated humanely, but that they are not protected by Geneva Conventions. . . . In September Syrian-born Canadian Maher Arar is detained during a stopover in New York and is sent to Syria for interrogation, where he is tortured.

March 30, 2004 U.S. Supreme Court rules Alien Tort Claims Act can be used to sue human rights abusers.

April 27, 2004 CBS News' "60 Minutes II" airs photographs of U.S. troops abusing prisoners at Abu Ghraib prison in Iraq.

November 2005 *Washington Post* reports the CIA detains terror suspects in secret prisons where detainees allegedly are subjected to coercive interrogation techniques. . . . U.S. government insists it does not torture. Congress passes Detainee Treatment Act, prohibiting torture and mistreatment of prisoners but limiting detainees' rights to challenge their detentions.

2006 On June 29, Supreme Court rules U.S. detainees are subject to the Geneva Conventions. . . . Military Commissions Act authorizes new courtroom procedures for enemy combatants but allows greater flexibility for CIA interrogations.

2007 A German court orders 13 U.S. intelligence agents arrested for their alleged role in rendering a German citizen to Afghanistan. . . . Canada apologizes to Arar for allowing him to be taken to Syria. . . . In July, President Bush authorizes the CIA to reopen secret overseas prisons. . . . International war crimes tribunal in Cambodia indicts former Khmer Rouge leader Kaing Geuk Eav for the torture and murder of thousands of prisoners. . . . Libya admits it tortured Bulgarian medical personnel imprisoned for eight years.

not be permitted to send terror suspects to countries known to torture, and 73 percent said government officials who engage in or order torture should be punished. Fifty-eight percent of Americans said torture was impermissible under any circumstances — about the same percentage as those in countries like Ukraine, Turkey and Kenya — but lower than the percentages in Australia, Canada and France. [31]

Some critics fear that since 9/11 U.S. television shows and movies have changed the way torture is portrayed, making torture more palatable to Americans and the rest of the world.

"It used to be the bad guys who used these techniques," says David Danzig of Human Rights First, a New York-based advocacy group that works to combat genocide, torture and human rights abuses. "You saw it infrequently — an average of four or five times a year — and when you did see it, it was space aliens or Nazis doing it, and it almost never worked. Now it's often the heroes who are using these techniques."

The number of instances of torture portrayed on television jumped from almost none in 1996 to 228 in 2003, according to the Parents Television Council. [32]

Fox Television's "24" has come to symbolize that almost tectonic shift in TV's treatment of torture. The hero of the show — which debuted two months after 9/11 — is Jack Bauer, a member of a unit charged with preventing catastrophic terrorist attacks, including nuclear and poison gas attacks on American cities such as Los Angeles. Bauer and his comrades have been shown using electrical wires, heart defibrillators, physical assaults and chemical injections to obtain information vital to preventing the attacks. [33]

The show's creator has insisted he is not trying to present a realistic — or glamorized — view of torture and that Bauer is portrayed as paying a high psychological price for using torture. [34]

But critics say the show — enormously popular in the United States and throughout the world — is changing how American citizens and soldiers view torture. "The biggest lie that has gained currency through television is that torture is an acceptable weapon for the 'good guys' to use if the stakes are high enough. . . . It is a lie," wrote John McCarthy, a journalist who was held hostage in Lebanon in the late 1980s. He accused the entertainment industry of "minimizing the true horrors of torture by failing to show the very profound impact it has on victims' lives." [35]

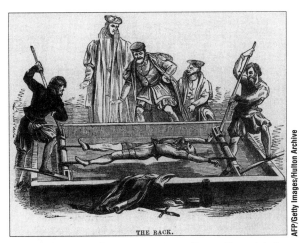

Cuthbert Simpson, a Protestant martyr, suffers on the rack in the Tower of London in 1563. Torture has been used over the centuries to solicit information and to punish political and religious dissenters.

The show "leaves a message with junior soldiers that it's OK to cross the line in order to gather intelligence and save lives," said Danzig.

Senior American military officials were so worried about the show's impact that Brig. Gen. Patrick Finnegan, dean of the United States Military Academy, and top FBI and military interrogators visited the set in 2006. Finnegan told the show's creators it gives U.S. military personnel the wrong idea and has hurt America's image abroad by suggesting the United States condones torture. [36]

The show's impact on world opinion of Americans has been the subject of numerous debates — both in the United States and abroad — including a 2006 panel discussion at the Heritage Foundation. The show reinforces a world view of Americans as people who succeed by "breaking the law, by torturing people, by circumventing the chain of command," said David Heyman, director of Homeland Security at the nonpartisan Center for Strategic and International Studies, which focuses on security issues. [37]

Carafano, the Heritage fellow, said the program "just sort of confirms [the] prejudice" of those "who think ill of us" already. [38]

The show was also debated in June at a conference of North American and European judges in Ottawa, Canada. U.S. Supreme Court Justice Antonin Scalia argued that government agents should have more latitude

Careful Training Creates Soldiers Who Torture

Most defy sadistic stereotype.

Torturers are made, not born. That was the finding of a Greek psychology professor who studied the military regime that came to power in Greece after a 1967 coup.

Until it fell in 1974, the dictatorship carefully trained soldiers to gather information and squelch dissent through torture. That's when Professor Mika Haritos-Fatouros tried to understand how the soldiers had been turned into torturers. In one of the most in-depth studies of torturers ever conducted, she interviewed 16 former soldiers and reviewed the testimony of 21 others and their victims. [1]

Many of her interviewees defy the stereotype of sadistic men who take pleasure in abuse. Haritos-Fatouros found that the torturers were simply plucked from the ranks of ordinary soldiers and trained. One, from a farm family, was a 33-year-old high school teacher married with two children by the time Haritos-Fatouros interviewed him. But for 18 months he had tortured prisoners and ordered others to do so.

The army sought young recruits from rural, conservative families who were physically healthy, of normal intelligence, conformist in nature and compliant. They underwent three months of intensive "training," during which they were broken down physically and mentally — a process that began almost before they arrived at the training facility. The abuse of the torturers-in-training intensified during the subsequent weeks as they were allowed little sleep and ordered to run or hop everywhere they went.

The aim "was to minimize all resistance by instilling in the cadets the habit of obeying without question an order without logic," Haritos-Fatouros wrote. [2] In short, they were programmed to blindly obey authority and dehumanize their victims.

Gradually, they were desensitized to torture. First, they participated in group beatings. One of the torturers said the first time he participated in a group beating he went to his cousin's house and cried. But it got easier each time, he said. Later, they ratcheted up to inflicting electric shocks and other serious abuse.

The underlying goal, Haritos-Fatouros concluded, was making the torturers believe they were "not, in fact, inflicting a savage and horrifying violation upon another human being."

"They brainwashed us," one torturer said. "It was only later we realized that what we did was inhuman. It was only after I finished my military service that it occurred to me that most of us beat up prisoners because we'd been beaten up ourselves." [3]

Another torturer told her, "When I tortured, basically, I felt it was my duty. A lot of the time I found myself repeating the phrases I'd heard in the lessons, like 'bloody communists' and so on. I think I became worse as time went on. I became more a part of the system. I believed in the whole system." [4]

Haritos-Fatouros' chilling conclusion: "We are all, under the right conditions, capable of becoming torturers." [5]

---

[1] Mika Haritos-Fatouros, *The Psychological Origins of Institutionalized Torture* (2003).

[2] *Ibid.*, p. 46.

[3] *Ibid.*, p. 95.

[4] *Ibid.*, p. 82.

[5] *Ibid.*, p. 229.

---

in times of crisis. "Jack Bauer saved Los Angeles," said Scalia. "He saved hundreds of thousands of lives." [39]

Scalia's comments sparked heated retorts from the other judges and a subsequent *Globe and Mail* editorial. "Jack Bauer is a creation of wishful thinking. . . . He personifies the wish to be free of moral and legal constraints. . . . That's why constitutions exist; it's so tempting when fighting perceived evil to call for Jack Bauer." But, left unchecked, the commentary concluded, "Jack Bauer will poison liberty's fount." [40]

The popular TV program, however, doesn't seem to have clouded the vision of a group of American high school students invited to the White House in June to receive the prestigious Presidential Scholar award. They handed President Bush a handwritten letter urging him to halt "violations of the human rights" of terror suspects. "We do not want America to represent torture," said the letter. [41]

BACKGROUND

Ancient Practice

Torture has been embraced by some of the world's most enlightened civilizations. Egyptian wall paintings and friezes depict scenes of horrific treatment of enemies. [42] In ancient Greece, slaves and foreigners could be tortured lawfully but free citizens could not. The same held true in ancient Rome, where free citizens could only be tortured in cases of treason. Slaves could be beaten, whipped, stretched on the rack or burned with hot irons — as long they were not permanently injured or killed. [43]

The use of torture in Europe expanded in the 13th century after Italian city-states began to require stricter proof of guilt in criminal trials. Before that, guilt or innocence was proven by combat or endurance trials in which God was expected to favor the innocent. [44] Under the reforms, defendants could only be found guilty if two witnesses testified against them or the accused confessed to the crime. When there were no witnesses, torture was used to produce confessions, a practice that would persist for the next 500 years in Europe.

Torture was also used to punish prisoners in public spectacles, often attended by cheering crowds. In the technique known as "pressing to plead" weights were piled on the prisoner's body, crushing him until he confessed — or died. Victims were also stretched on a device called the rack — sometimes until their bones were pulled out of their sockets. Britain's King Henry VIII used torture against those who challenged his position as head of the Church of England. Queen Elizabeth I employed torture against those suspected of treason.

Particularly brutal torture methods gained religious sanction during the inquisitions conducted by the Roman Catholic Church to stamp out heresy. In 1252, Pope Innocent IV formally authorized the use of torture against heretics. In Spain for instance, victims were bound to a turning wheel as various body parts — the soles of their feet or the eyes — were brought closer and closer to a fire. In Italy, victims were suspended by their arms — tied behind their backs — from a pulley attached to a beam. The "strappado," as it was called, was then repeatedly jerked to increase the pain. Weights sometimes were attached to the victim's feet to increase the agony, often fracturing bones and tearing limbs from the body. [45]

In the early 17th century, some Europeans tried to regulate torture. Dutch legal scholar Johannes Voet, for instance, argued that torture should only be used when there are "grave presumptions" against the accused. He also suggested that the youngest member of any group of defendants be tortured first, because the youngest was thought most likely to talk. [46]

In 1754 Prussia became the first modern European state to abolish torture. Ten years later, in his seminal book *On Crimes and Punishments*, Italian philosopher and penal reformer Cesare Beccaria denounced torture as "a sure route for the acquittal of robust ruffians and the conviction of weak innocents." The book reflected emerging Enlightenment-era ideals about individual rights and the proper limits on punishment. [47] Within a century, most of Europe had banned torture, in part because convictions without eyewitness testimony or confessions were increasingly allowed, reducing the need for torture. But torture continued to thrive in Africa, Asia and the Middle East. In 1852, for example, leaders of an outlawed religious group in Persia — modern-day Iran — were "made into candlesticks" — with holes dug into their flesh into which lighted candles were inserted. [48]

By 1874, French author Victor Hugo naively declared "torture has ceased to exist." But torture continued to be used against insurgents in Austria and Italy and against opponents of the Tsarist government in Russia.

Changing Norms

By the 20th century, social norms about punishment had changed; the upper classes no longer wanted to watch gruesome public spectacles. Torture sessions became secretive affairs, conducted in prison basements and detention centers. [49]

In the first half of the 20th century, torture was employed by totalitarian governments in countries such as Germany, Russia, Italy and Japan. [50] The Nazis tortured prisoners of war to get information and conducted horrific medical experiments on Jewish and Gypsy civilians in concentration camps. Japanese soldiers severely abused and tortured Allied prisoners.

After the horrors of World War II, torture and lesser forms of abuse known as cruel, inhumane and degrading treatment were outlawed by a series of treaties: the 1948 Universal Declaration of Human Rights, the Geneva Conventions of 1949 and the 1984 Convention Against Torture. (*See box, p. 128.*)

Five International Treaties Ban Torture

Torture has been banned by international treaties since 1948. Key provisions include:

Universal Declaration of Human Rights (1948)

No one shall be subjected to torture or to cruel, inhuman or degrading treatment or punishment.

Adopted by U.N. General Assembly on Dec. 10, 1948, www.un.org/Overview/rights.html.

Third Geneva Convention, Common Article 3 (1949)

Regarding the treatment of civilians and prisoners of war, "the following acts are and shall remain prohibited at any time:

    (a) violence to life and person, in particular murder of all kinds, mutilation, cruel treatment and torture;
    (b) taking of hostages;
    (c) outrages upon personal dignity, in particular humiliating and degrading treatment . . ."

Adopted on Aug. 12, 1949, by the Diplomatic Conference for the Establishment of International Conventions for the Protection of Victims of War, held in Geneva, Switzerland; effective Oct. 21, 1950, www.icrc.org/ihl.nsf/0/e160550475c4b133c12563cd0051aa66?OpenDocument.

International Covenant on Civil and Political Rights (1966)

Article 7
No one shall be subjected to torture or to cruel, inhuman or degrading treatment or punishment. In particular, no one shall be subjected without his free consent to medical or scientific experimentation.

Article 10
All persons deprived of their liberty shall be treated with humanity and with respect for the inherent dignity of the human person.

Adopted the U.N. General Assembly on Dec. 16, 1966, and opened for signature and ratification; became effective on March 23, 1976, www.unhchr.ch/html/menu3/b/a_ccpr.htm.

Torture persisted during the second half of the century, however, particularly in authoritarian countries. For instance, Soviet and Chinese communist regimes tortured political and religious dissidents. Cambodia's murderous Khmer Rouge military regime had a 42-page interrogation manual for use at its Tuol Sleng torture center during the 1970s.

Many repressive regimes were supported by the United States, which was fighting a proxy Cold War with the Soviet Union in developing countries like Vietnam, El Salvador and Guatemala. Because such governments were resisting socialist or communist insurgencies, the United States often provided them with guns, military aid and training, even though they were known to use torture.

In the 1970s, President Jimmy Carter broke with the past by announcing that the nation's foreign policy henceforth would be based on advancing human rights. Congress passed a law requiring the State Department to issue annual reports on the human rights records of any country that received U.S. economic or military aid. [51] Although the law remains on the books and the State Department continues to issue its annual human rights "country reports," the foreign policy focus on human rights faded under Carter's successor, Ronald Reagan, who placed fighting communism above protecting human rights.

Since the 1970s, however, greater scrutiny by Western governments, the U.N., the EU and human rights groups has prompted changes in how countries torture. Increasingly, methods were adopted that don't leave visible scars, such as beating the soles of feet, sleep deprivation, sexual humiliation and electric shock.

Democracies' Experience

It wasn't only communists and dictators who tortured captives after World War II. Democratic countries — including Great Britain, France and Israel — all used torture or other forms of abuse during the last half of the century, usually in response to what they viewed as imminent threats from religious or political dissidents.

But the democracies ended up alienating their own citizens as well as the occupied populations, according to

Protocol Additional to the Geneva Conventions of Aug. 12, 1949, relating to the Protection of Victims of International Armed Conflicts (1977)

Article 75: Fundamental guarantees

1. . . . persons who are in the power of a Party to the conflict . . . shall be treated humanely in all circumstances and shall enjoy, as a minimum, the protection provided by this Article without any adverse distinction based upon race, colour, sex, language, religion or belief, political or other opinion, national or social origin, wealth, birth or other status, or on any other similar criteria. Each Party shall respect the person, honour, convictions and religious practices of all such persons.

2. The following acts are and shall remain prohibited at any time and in any place whatsoever, whether committed by civilian or by military agents:

    (a) Violence to the life, health, or physical or mental well-being of persons, in particular:
        (i) Murder;
        (ii) Torture of all kinds, whether physical or mental;
        (iii) Corporal punishment; and
        (iv) Mutilation;
    (b) Outrages upon personal dignity, in particular humiliating and degrading treatment, enforced prostitution and any form of indecent assault;
    (c) The taking of hostages;
    (d) Collective punishments; and
    (e) Threats to commit any of the foregoing acts.

Adopted by the Diplomatic Conference on the Reaffirmation and Development of International Humanitarian Law applicable in Armed Conflicts on June 8, 1977; became effective on Dec. 7, 1979, www.unhchr.ch/html/menu3/b/93.htm.

Convention Against Torture and Other Cruel, Inhuman or Degrading Treatment or Punishment (1984)

Article 1

. . . the term 'torture' means any act by which severe pain or suffering, whether physical or mental, is intentionally inflicted on a person for such purposes as obtaining from him or a third person information or a confession, punishing him for an act he or a third person has committed or is suspected of having committed, or intimidating or coercing him or a third person, or for any reason based on discrimination of any kind, . . .

Article 2

1. Each State Party shall take effective legislative, administrative, judicial or other measures to prevent acts of torture in any territory under its jurisdiction.
2. No exceptional circumstances whatsoever, whether a state of war or a threat of war, internal political instability or any other public emergency, may be invoked as a justification of torture.
3. An order from a superior officer or a public authority may not be invoked as a justification of torture.

Article 3

1. No State Party shall expel, return ("refouler") or extradite a person to another State where there are substantial grounds for believing that he would be in danger of being subjected to torture.
2. For the purpose of determining whether there are such grounds, the competent authorities shall take into account all relevant considerations including, where applicable, the existence in the State concerned of a consistent pattern of gross, flagrant or mass violations of human rights.

Adopted by the U.N. General Assembly on Dec. 10, 1984, and opened for signature and ratification; became effective on June 26, 1987, www.unhchr.ch/html/menu3/b/h_cat39.htm.

Christopher Einolf, a University of Richmond sociologist who has studied the history of torture. Torture also proved difficult to control once it was authorized.

For instance, France initiated an intensive counterinsurgency strategy — which included torture — in Algeria after the Algerian National Liberation Front began a terrorist bombing campaign in 1956 to force France to cede control of the colony. France's strategy sometimes is cited as evidence that torture works. [52]

But Rejali at Reed College says France succeeded in gathering information because informants voluntarily cooperated — not as a result of torture. And tortured suspects often gave their interrogators the names of rival insurgents, dead militants or old hiding places rather than good information, he says.

Lou DiMarco, a retired U.S. Army lieutenant colonel who teaches at the Command and General Staff College, Fort Leavenworth, Kan., contends the French experience

AP Photo/Jonathan Hayward

Syrian-born Canadian citizen Maher Arar was picked up by the CIA in 2002 at John F. Kennedy International Airport in New York and taken to Syria, where he was imprisoned for a year and tortured with electric cables. He was later cleared of any links to terrorism. Human rights advocates say the CIA's so-called extraordinary rendition program "outsources" torture to countries known to abuse prisoners. The U.S. Justice Department said Syria had assured the United States it would not torture Arar.

in Algeria also proves the difficulty of controlling torture. "In Algeria, officially condoned torture quickly escalated to prolonged abuse, which resulted in permanent physical and psychological damage as well as death," he wrote. [53]

Similarly, the British, facing a spike in Irish Republican Army (IRA) violence in Northern Ireland in 1971, turned to aggressive interrogation techniques, including the "five techniques" — a combination of hooding, noise bombardment, food and sleep deprivation and forced standing. Individually, any one of these techniques could be painful, but taken together, "they induced a state of psychosis, a temporary madness with long-lasting after-effects," wrote John Conroy in his book, *Unspeakable Acts, Ordinary People: The Dynamics of Torture.* [54]

Tom Parker, a former British counterterrorism agent, says extreme interrogation methods had "huge" adverse consequences for Britain: They alienated Ireland — not a natural ally of the IRA — and enabled Ireland to successfully challenge British interrogation methods in the European Court of Human Rights.

Israel approved similar methods in 1987 after its security services were found to be using illegal interrogation techniques on Palestinian detainees in the occupied territories. Officials felt it would be better to allow a few psychological methods and "moderate physical pressure." But coercive methods proved hard to regulate and keep under control. [55]

In 1999, Israel's Supreme Court outlawed such techniques as cruel and inhuman treatment.

Post-9/11 Crackdown

After the 9/11 attacks, aggressive interrogation of suspects became a key — and highly controversial — part of U.S. antiterrorism strategy. On Nov. 13, 2001, President Bush signed an executive order allowing the military to detain and try "enemy combatants" outside the United States.

Defense Secretary Donald H. Rumsfeld announced the next month that enemy combatants detained in Afghanistan would be transferred to Guantánamo. In February 2002 Bush said the United States would treat the detainees humanely but did not consider them legitimate prisoners of war protected by the Geneva Conventions, which ban torture and "cruel, inhuman and degrading treatment."

U.S. interrogators used the same harsh methods designed to train American personnel to resist torture if captured. The so-called "Survival, Evasion, Resistance and Escape" (SERE) techniques included physical and mental pressure ("stress and duress") and sleep deprivation.

Rumsfeld formally approved many of these techniques in December 2002, including prolonged standing, use of dogs and the removal of clothing; he later rescinded approval for some of the methods. [56] Mohammed al-Qhatani — the alleged 20th 9/11 hijacker who had been captured along the Pakistani-Afghan border — says he was interrogated for 20-hour stretches, forced to stand naked while being menaced by dogs and barred from praying during Ramadan unless he drank water, which Islam forbids during Ramadan's fasting periods. The Pentagon said such techniques were designed to "prevent future attacks on America." [57]

Is torture ever justified?

YES

Mirko Bagaric
Professor of Law, Deakin University
Melbourne, Australia

Written for *CQ Researcher*, August 2007

Despite its pejorative overtone, we should never say never to torture. Torture is bad. Killing innocent people is worse. Some people are so depraved they combine these evils and torture innocent people to death. Khalid Shaikh Mohammed, who is still gloating about personally beheading American journalist Daniel Pearl with his "blessed right hand," is but just one exhibit.

Torture opponents must take responsibility for the murder of innocent people if they reject torture if it is the only way to save innocent lives. We are responsible not only for what we do but also for the things we can, but fail, to prevent.

Life-saving torture is not cruel. It is morally justifiable because the right to life of innocent people trumps the physical integrity of wrongdoers. Thus, torture has the same moral justification as other practices in which we sacrifice the interests of one person for the greater good. A close analogy is life-saving organ and tissue transplants. Kidney and bone marrow transplants inflict high levels of pain and discomfort on donors, but their pain is normally outweighed by the benefit to the recipient.

Such is the case with life-saving compassionate torture. The pain inflicted on the wrongdoer is manifestly outweighed by the benefit from the lives saved. The fact that wrongdoers don't consent to their mistreatment is irrelevant. Prisoners and enemy soldiers don't consent to being incarcerated or shot at, yet we're not about to empty our prisons or stop trying to kill enemy soldiers.

Most proponents of banning torture say it does not produce reliable information. Yet there are countless counter-examples. Israeli authorities claim to have foiled 90 terrorist attacks by using coercive interrogation. In more mundane situations, courts across the world routinely throw out confessions that are corroborated by objective evidence because they were only made because the criminals were beaten up.

It is also contended that life-saving torture will lead down the slippery slope of other cruel practices. This is an intellectually defeatist argument. It tries to move the debate from what is on the table (life-saving torture) to situations where torture is used for reasons of domination and punishment — which is never justifiable.

Fanatics who oppose torture in all cases are adopting their own form of extremism. It is well-intentioned, but extremism in all its manifestations can lead to catastrophic consequences. Cruelty that is motivated by misguided kindness hurts no less.

NO

Sune Segal
Head of Communications Unit International Rehabilitation Council for Torture Victims Copenhagen, Denmark

Written for *CQ Researcher*, August 2007

Taking a utilitarian "greater good" approach in the wake of 9/11/2001, some scholars argue that torture is justified if used to prevent large-scale terror attacks. That argument rests on several flawed assumptions.

The claim that torture — or what is now euphemistically referred to as "enhanced interrogation techniques" — extracts reliable information is unfounded. The 2006 *U.S. Army Field Manual* states that "the use of force . . . yields unreliable results [and] may damage subsequent collection efforts." As laid out in a recent *Vanity Fair* article, it was humane treatment — not torture — of a detainee that led to the arrest of alleged 9/11 mastermind Khalid Shaikh Mohammed. In the same article, a U.S. Air Force Reserve colonel and expert in human-intelligence operations, drives home the point: "When [CIA psychologists argue that coercive interrogation] can make people talk, I have one question: 'About what?' "

But even if torture did "work," is it justified when a suspect is in custody and presumed to possess information about an imminent attack likely to kill thousands of people?

No, for several reasons. First, the above scenario assumes the person in custody has the pertinent information — a presumption that is never foolproof. Thus, by allowing torture there would be cases in which innocent detainees would be at risk of prolonged torture because they would not possess the desired information.

Second, it might be argued that mere circumstantial evidence suggesting the detainee is the right suspect is enough to justify torture or that torturing a relative into revealing the suspect's whereabouts is acceptable.

Third, if one form of torture — such as "waterboarding" — is allowed to preserve the "greater good," where do we go if it doesn't work? To breaking bones? Ripping out nails? Torturing the suspect's 5-year-old daughter?

Fourth, torture is not a momentary infliction of pain. In most cases the victim — innocent or guilty — is marked for life, as is the torturer. As a former CIA officer and friend of one of Mohammed's interrogators told *The New Yorker* in an Aug. 13, 2007, article: "[My friend] has horrible nightmares. . . . When you cross over that line, it's hard to come back. You lose your soul."

That's why we refrain from torture: to keep our souls intact. Torture is the hallmark of history's most abhorrent regimes and a violation of civilized values. Taking the "greater good" approach to torture is intellectually and morally bankrupt.

But some within the administration disapproved. In July 2004 Alberto J. Mora, the Navy's general counsel, warned in a 22-page memo that circumventing the Geneva Conventions was an invitation for U.S. interrogators to abuse prisoners. [58]

His prediction was prescient. SERE techniques apparently migrated to U.S. facilities in Afghanistan and Iraq, where they were reportedly employed by inadequately trained and unsupervised personnel. What began as "a set of special treatments" had become routine, wrote Tony Lagouranis, a former Army interrogator in Iraq. [59]

In late 2003 American military personnel at Abu Ghraib prison committed the abuses that generated the most public outrage, thanks to graphic photographs taken by the soldiers involved that eventually were circulated by news media around the world. An Army investigation later detailed "sadistic, blatant and wanton criminal" abuse that included beating detainees with a broom handle, threatening male detainees with rape, sodomizing another with a chemical light stick and frightening them with dogs. [60] Twelve U.S. military personnel have since been convicted for their roles in the abuse.

Mistreatment of Iraqi detainees was not just limited to Abu Ghraib. A military jury convicted Chief Warrant Officer Lewis Welshofer of negligent homicide after an interrogation in a facility in western Iraq in which he put a sleeping bag over the head of Iraqi Gen. Abed Hamed Mowhoush, sat on his chest and covered the general's mouth while asking him questions. American civilian contractors working alongside CIA and military interrogators in Iraq have also been accused of mistreating detainees.

Ever since the 9/11 attacks, a furious legal debate, both inside and outside the Bush administration, has examined the kinds of coercive interrogation methods the military and CIA can employ and the extent to which the United States must abide by international law. In 2005 Congress sought to limit the use by U.S. personnel of cruel, inhumane and degrading treatment in the Detainee Treatment Act. [61]

Then in 2006 the Supreme Court ruled that all prisoners held by the United States — including those in CIA custody — were subject to Common Article 3 of the Geneva Conventions, which outlaws torture or cruel and inhuman treatment of wartime detainees. (*See box, p. 128.*) [62] Later that year Congress passed another bill, the Military Commissions Act, endorsed by the Bush administration. It limited military interrogators to techniques that would be detailed in an updated *Army Field Manual.* The law did not specify, however, which interrogation methods CIA personnel can use — an omission designed to provide flexibility for interrogators at secret CIA facilities where "high value" prisoners are interrogated.

When *The Washington Post* revealed in 2005 that the CIA was operating secret prisons in eight countries in Eastern Europe, Thailand and Afghanistan, the administration had at first refused to confirm the story. [63] In 2006 Bush finally acknowledged the facilities existed, pointing out that, "Questioning the detainees in this program has given us information that has saved innocent lives by helping us stop new attacks — here in the United States and across the world." [64]

In 2007, Human Rights Watch and *The Post* detailed the experience of one former CIA detainee — Marwan Jabour, a Palestinian accused of being an al-Qaeda paymaster — who spent two years in a CIA-operated prison.

Jabour says he was kept naked for the first three months of his detention in Afghanistan. The lights were kept on 24 hours a day, and when loud music wasn't blasted through speakers into his cell, white noise buzzed in the background. And while he was frequently threatened with physical abuse, he says he was never beaten during 45 interrogations. He was also deprived of sleep and left for hours in painful positions. He was ultimately transferred to Jordanian and then Israeli custody, where a judge ordered his release in September 2006. [65]

CIA detainees also reportedly have been subjected to waterboarding and had their food spiked with drugs to loosen their inhibitions about speaking. [66]

The United States did not allow the International Committee of the Red Cross (ICRC) to visit the CIA's detainees until 2006. A subsequent ICRC report based on interviews with 15 former CIA detainees concluded that the detention and interrogation methods used at the "black sites" were tantamount to torture, according to confidential sources quoted in *The New Yorker.* [67]

The United States has strongly denied the ICRC's conclusions and claims the program is closely monitored by agency lawyers. "The CIA's interrogations were nothing like Abu Ghraib or Guantánamo," said Robert Grenier, a former head of the CIA's Counterterrorism Center. "They were very, very regimented. Very meticulous." The program is "completely legal." [68]

Unlike the CIA's secret prisons, the agency's use of so-called "extraordinary renditions" predated the 9/11 attacks. The first terror suspects were rendered to Egypt in the mid-1990s. [69] But the practice expanded greatly after 9/11, with up to 150 people sent to countries such as Morocco, Syria and Egypt between 2001 and 2005. Many, like Abu Omar — an imam with alleged links to terrorist groups — were snatched off the street. Omar, an Egyptian refugee, was kidnapped from Milan in February 2003 and sent to Egypt where he says he was tortured for four years before being released in 2007. [70]

U.S. officials have repeatedly insisted the United States does not send detainees to countries where they believe or know they'll be tortured. [71] But such declarations ring hollow for human rights advocates like Malinowski. "The administration says that it does not render people to torture," he told the Senate Foreign Relations Committee. "But the only safeguard it appears to have obtained in these cases was a promise from the receiving state that it would not mistreat the rendered prisoners. Such promises, coming from countries like Egypt and Syria and Uzbekistan where torture is routine, are unverifiable and utterly untrustworthy. I seriously doubt that anyone in the administration actually believed them." [72]

Renditions usually require the complicity of the countries where the suspects are grabbed. A 2006 report by the Council of Europe's Parliamentary Assembly tried to identify all the member countries that have allowed rendition flights to cross their airspace or land at their airports. [73]

One was the Czech Republic, which reportedly allowed three different jets to land at Prague's Ruzyne Airport during at least 20 different rendition flights, triggering anger from some Czechs. "No 'law enforcement,' 'intelligence,' or 'security' argument in support of torture can ever be anything but inhumane," wrote Gwendolyn Albert, director of the Czech League of Human Rights, in 2006 in *The Prague Post.* [74]

Former CIA operative Melissa Boyle Mahle condemns torture but has defended renditions and the need for absolute secrecy. "Renditions should be conducted in the shadows for optimal impact and should not, I must add, leave elephant-sized footprints so as to not embarrass our allies in Europe," she wrote in a 2005 blog entry. "During my career at the CIA, I was involved in these types of operations and know firsthand that they can save American lives." [75]

CURRENT SITUATION

Rendition Fallout

Kidnapping and shipping off allies' citizens to be harshly interrogated in foreign countries has strained relations with America's friends. Prosecutors in Germany and Italy are attempting to prosecute U.S. personnel for their role in renditions, and the rendition of Canadian citizen Maher Arar to Syria has chilled relations between Canada and the United States.

In Italy, the former chief of Italy's intelligence service is on trial for Omar's 2003 abduction in a case that threatens to ensnare top officials of the current and past Italian governments. A U.S. Air Force colonel and 25 CIA operatives also were indicted but are being tried in absentia because the United States has blocked their extradition. [76]

Similarly, a court in Munich ordered the arrest of 13 American intelligence operatives in January 2007 for their role in the kidnapping of a German citizen interrogated for five months at a secret prison in Afghanistan. But Germany, unlike Italy, does not allow trials in absentia, so an actual trial is unlikely because the United States will not extradite the defendants. [77]

Other European governments may be called to task for their role in U.S. renditions. Investigations have been initiated by Spain, and the Most Rev. John Neill — archbishop of Dublin — said the Irish government compromised itself by allowing rendition flights to land at Shannon Airport.

Meanwhile, on this side of the Atlantic, Canadian-U.S. relations are strained by the case of Syrian-born Canadian citizen Maher Arar. The McGill University graduate was returning to Canada from Tunisia in September 2002 when he landed at John F. Kennedy International Airport in New York during a stopover. U.S. immigration authorities detained him after seeing his name on a terrorist "watch" list.

After two weeks of questioning, he was flown to Jordan and then driven to Syria. During a yearlong detention by Syrian military intelligence, Arar says he was beaten with two-inch-thick electric cables. "Not even animals could withstand it," he said later. [78]

He was released in October 2003. A Canadian inquiry cleared Arar of any links to terrorism and said the Royal Canadian Mounted Police had given U.S. authorities erroneous information about him. Canada's prime minister apologized to Arar in January 2007 and announced an $8.9 million compensation package. Canada has also demanded an apology from the U.S. government and asked that Arar's name be removed from terrorist watch lists. [79]

U.S. federal courts have dismissed a lawsuit by Arar, and Attorney General Alberto R. Gonzales said Syria had assured the United States it would not torture Arar before he was sent there.

But Paul Cavalluzzo, a Toronto lawyer who led the government investigation of Arar's case, calls Gonzales' claim "graphic hypocrisy," pointing out that the U.S. State Department's own Web site lists Syria as one of the "worst offenders of torture."

"At one time, the United States was a beacon for the protection of human rights, whether internationally or domestically. Certainly, the Arar case was one example that lessened [that] view [among] Canadians."

Suing Torturers

Criminal prosecutions and civil lawsuits are pending against alleged torturers in several courts around the world.

In the United States, Iraqis claiming they were mistreated by American military personnel and private contractors are seeking redress under a little-used 18th-century law. The Alien Tort Claims Act, which originally targeted piracy, allows federal courts to hear claims by foreigners injured "in violation of the law of nations or a treaty of the United States."

In May 2007, the American Civil Liberties Union used the law to sue Jeppesen Dataplan Inc., a subsidiary of the Boeing Co., on behalf of three plaintiffs subjected to renditions. The company is accused of providing rendition flight services to the CIA. Two additional plaintiffs joined the suit in August. [80]

The law also was used in a class-action suit against Titan Corp. and CACI International Inc., military contractors that provided translators and interrogation services at Abu Ghraib. The suit asserts the two companies participated in a "scheme to torture, rape and in some instances, summarily execute plaintiffs." CACI called it a "malicious recitation of false statements and intentional distortions." [81]

The law was rarely used until the late 1970s, when human rights groups began suing abusive foreign officials. Since then it has been used to sue a Paraguayan police chief living in Brooklyn accused of torturing and killing a young man in Paraguay, an Ethiopian official, a Guatemalan defense minister and the self-proclaimed president of the Bosnian Serbs.

Advocates of such suits say they are important tools in holding abusers accountable. "It is truly a mechanism that provides for policing international human rights abuses where a criminal prosecution may not necessarily be feasible," says John M. Eubanks, a South Carolina lawyer involved in a suit that relies on the statute. The home countries of human rights abusers often lack legal systems that enable perpetrators to be held accountable.

"America is the only venue where they're going to be able to get their case heard," says Rachel Chambers, a British lawyer who has studied the statute.

Although the U.S. Supreme Court affirmed the use of the statute in 2004, legal experts disagree about just how much leeway the court left for future plaintiffs. [82]

Moreover, the statute can't provide redress in lawsuits against the U.S. government for the mistreatment of prisoners. The United States has successfully challenged such lawsuits by claiming sovereign immunity, a doctrine that protects governments against suits. The same defense has protected individuals sued in their official government capacity, according to Beth Stephens, a professor at Rutgers School of Law, in Camden, N.J. It is unclear how much protection private contractors such as CACI can claim for providing support services for interrogations.

Meanwhile, in Cambodia a U.N.-backed tribunal in July accused former Khmer Rouge leader Kaing Guek Eav of crimes against humanity for his role in the torture and deaths of 14,000 prisoners at Tuol Sleng. Only seven people who entered the prison emerged alive. The trial is expected to begin in 2008. [83]

And in Sierra Leone former Liberian President Charles Taylor is facing a U.N.-backed war-crimes tribunal for his role in financing and encouraging atrocities — including torture — committed during the civil war in neighboring Sierra Leone. The trial has been delayed until January 2008. [84]

The 'Black Sites'

In July, when President Bush authorized the CIA's secret prisons to be reopened, the executive order laid out the administration's position on how the "enhanced interrogation" program will fully comply "with the obligations of the United States under Common Article 3" of the Geneva Conventions, which bans "outrages upon personal dignity, in particular humiliating and degrading treatment."

The president's order said the United States would satisfy the conventions if the CIA's interrogation methods don't violate federal law or constitute "willful and outrageous acts of personal abuse done for the purpose of humiliating the individual in a manner so serious that any reasonable person, considering the circumstances would deem the acts to be beyond the bounds of human decency."

The language appears to allow abusive techniques if the purpose is to gather intelligence or prevent attacks, say critics. "The president has given the CIA carte blanche to engage in 'willful and outrageous acts of personal abuse,' " wrote former Marine Corps Commandant P. X. Kelley and Robert Turner, a former Reagan administration lawyer. [85]

Human rights advocates are troubled by the executive order's lack of an explicit ban on coercive interrogation techniques such as stress positions or extreme sleep deprivation, which military interrogators are explicitly barred from using in the latest *Army Field Manual*, issued in 2006.

Media reports suggested the Bush administration also has sought to maintain other methods, such as inducing hypothermia, forced standing and manipulating sound and light. [86]

"What we're left with is a history of these kinds of techniques having been authorized, no explicit prohibition and we don't know what the CIA is authorized to do," says Devon Chaffee, an attorney with Human Rights First. "This creates a real problematic precedent."

Human rights advocates worry that foreign governments may cite Bush's executive order to justify their own coercive interrogations. "What they did is lower the bar for anybody," says Musa, the advocacy director for Amnesty USA.

In August, the American Bar Association passed a resolution urging Congress to override the executive order. [87] Also that month, Democratic Sen. Ron Wyden of Oregon vowed to block President Bush's nominee to become the CIA's top lawyer. Wyden said he was concerned that the agency's senior deputy general counsel, John Rizzo, had not objected to a 2002 CIA memo authorizing interrogation techniques that stopped just short of inflicting enough pain to cause organ failure or death.

"I'm going to keep the hold [on Rizzo] until the detention and interrogation program is on firm footing, both in terms of effectiveness and legality," Wyden said. [88]

OUTLOOK

No Panaceas

Human rights advocates worry countries that have tortured in the past will feel more emboldened to do so in the future as a result of U.S. government policies.

"This is just empowering the dictators and torturing governments around the world," said Whitson of Human Rights Watch.

They also worry that China, a rising superpower, is an abuser itself and has proven willing to do business with countries with histories of abuse in Central Asia and Africa.

HRW Executive Director Kenneth Roth also complains that — as its membership swells and the difficulty of reaching consensus grows — the European Union appears unable or unwilling to act. "Its efforts to achieve consensus among its diverse membership have become so laborious that it yields a faint shadow of its potential," he says.

The future direction of U.S. interrogation policies could depend heavily on the outcome of the 2008 American presidential election, which will likely determine the fate of what has become the most important symbol of U.S. detention policies: the prison for enemy combatants at Guantánamo. All the Democratic presidential candidates say they would close the facility, according to a study of candidate positions by the Council on Foreign Relations. [89]

On the Republican side, only two candidates — Rep. Ron Paul, R-Texas, and Sen. McCain — have advocated shutting the facility, and neither has been among the leaders in the polls. Mitt Romney, the former Massachusetts governor who has been among the front-runners this summer, suggested doubling the size of Guantánamo if he became president.

But regardless of who wins the election, human rights advocates do not look to a new occupant of the White House as a panacea. Amnesty USA's Musa says new administrations are often skittish about radically changing course from predecessors' foreign policies.

"It's not the absolute cure for all ills," she says.

NOTES

1. See Jonathan S. Landay, "VP confirms use of waterboarding," *Chicago Tribune*, Oct. 27, 2006, p. C5; and "Interview of the Vice President by Scott

Hennen, WDAY at Radio Day at the White House," www.whitehouse.gov/news/releases/2006/10/20061024-7.html. Also see John Crewdson, "Spilling Al Qaeda's secrets; 'Waterboarding' used on 9/11 mastermind, who eventually talked," *Chicago Tribune*, Dec. 28, 2005, p. C15. Also see Brian Ross and Richard Esposito, "CIA's Harsh Interrogation Techniques Described," ABC News, Nov. 18, 2005, www.abcnews.com.

2. Testimony by Tom Malinowski before Senate Committee on Foreign Relations, July 26, 2007.

3. David Cingranelli and David L. Richards, CIRI Human Rights Data Project, 2005, http://ciri.binghamton.edu/about.asp.

4. Quoted in Molly Moore, "Gaddafi's Son: Bulgarians Were Tortured," *The Washington Post*, Aug. 10, 2007, p. A8.

5. "In the Name of Security: Counterterrorism and Human Rights Abuses Under Malaysia's Internal Security Act," Human Rights Watch, http://hrw.org/reports/2004/malaysia0504/.

6. Dana Priest, "CIA Holds Terror Suspects in Secret Prisons," *The Washington Post*, Nov. 2, 2005, p. A1; also see Rosa Brooks, "The GOP's Torture Enthusiasts," *Los Angeles Times*, May 18, 2007, www.latimes.com/news/opinion/commentary/la-oe-brooks18may18,0,732795.column?coll=la-news-comment-opinions.

7. For background see Peter Katel and Kenneth Jost, "Treatment of Detainees," *CQ Researcher*, Aug. 25, 2006, pp. 673-696.

8. Kenneth Roth, "Filling the Leadership Void: Where is the European Union?" *World Report 2007*, Human Rights Watch.

9. Edward Cody, "China, Others Criticize U.S. Report on Rights: Double Standard at State Department Alleged" *The Washington Post*, March 4, 2005, p A14.

10. Lisa Haugaard, "Tarnished Image: Latin America Perceives the United States," Latin American Working Group, March 2006.

11. "World View of U.S. Role Goes from Bad to Worse," Program on International Policy Attitudes, January 2007, www.worldpublicopinion.org/pipa/pdf/jan07/BBC_USRole_Jan07_quaire.pdf.

12. See Karen DeYoung, "Bush Approves New CIA Methods," *The Washington Post*, July 21, 2007, p. A1.

13. See "President Discusses Creation of Military Commissions to Try Suspected Terrorists," Sept. 6, 2006, www.whitehouse.gov/news/releases/2006/09/20060906-3.html.

14. Crewdson, *op. cit.*

15. Jane Mayer, "The Black Sites," *The New Yorker*, Aug. 13, 2007, pp. 46-57.

16. *Ibid.*

17. *Ibid.*

18. Jane Mayer, "Outsourcing Torture," *The New Yorker*, Feb. 14, 2005, p. 106.

19. Intelligence Science Board, "Educing Information, Interrogation: Science and Art," Center for Strategic Intelligence Research, National Defense Intelligence College, December 2006, www.fas.org/irp/dni/educing.pdf.

20. Anne Applebaum, "The Torture Myth," *The Washington Post*, Jan. 12, 2005, p. A21.

21. Henry Schuster, "The Al Qaeda Hunter," CNN, http://edition.cnn.com/2005/US/03/02/schuster.column/index.html.

22. Mirko Bagaric, "A Case for Torture," *The Age*, May 17, 2005, www.theage.com.au/news/ Opinion/A-case-for-torture/2005/05/16/1116095904947.html.

23. Alan Dershowitz, *Why Terrorism Works: Understanding the Threat, Responding to the Challenge*, Yale University Press, 2003, pp. 158-159.

24. Michael Levin, "The Case for Torture," *Newsweek*, June 7, 1982.

25. " '24' and America's Image in Fighting Terrorism," Heritage Foundation Symposium, June 30, 2006.

26. Eitan Felner, "Torture and Terrorism: Painful Lessons from Israel," in Kenneth Roth, *et al.*, eds., *Torture: Does it Make Us Safer? Is It Ever OK? A Human Rights Perspective* (2005).

27. Henry Shue, "Torture," in Sanford Levinson, ed., *Torture: A Collection* (2006), p. 58.

28. See Brooks, *op. cit.*

29. Humphrey Hawksley, "US Iraq Troops 'condone torture,' " BBC News, May 4, 2007, http://news.bbc.co.uk/2/hi/middle_east/6627055.stm.

30. "Bush, McCain Agree on Torture Ban," CNN, Dec. 15, 2005, www.cnn.com/2005/POLITICS/12/15/torture.bill/index.html.

31. "American and International Opinion on the Rights of Terrorism Suspects," Program on International Policy Attitudes, July 17, 2006, www.worldpublicopinion.org/pipa/pdf/jul06/TerrSuspect_Jul06_rpt.pdf.

32. Allison Hanes, "Prime time torture: A U.S. Brigadier-General voices concern about the message the show '24' might be sending to the public and impressionable recruits," *National Post*, March 19, 2007.

33. Evan Thomas, " '24' Versus the Real World," *Newsweek Online*, Sept. 22, 2006, www.msnbc.msn.com/id/14924664/site/newsweek/.

34. Jane Mayer, "Whatever It Takes," *The New Yorker*, Feb. 19, 2007, www.newyorker.com/reporting/2007/02/19/070219fa-fact_mayer?printable=true.

35. John McCarthy, "Television is making torture acceptable," *The Independent*, May 24, 2007, http://comment.independent.co.uk/commentators/article2578453.ece.

36. Mayer, Feb. 19, 2007, *ibid.*

37. Heritage symposium, *op. cit.*

38. *Ibid.*

39. Colin Freeze, "What would Jack Bauer do?," *Globe and Mail*, June 16, 2007, www.theglobeandmail.com/servlet/story/LAC.20070616.BAUER16/TPStory/TPNational/Television/.

40. "Don't Go to Bat for Jack Bauer," *Globe and Mail*, July 9, 2007, www.theglobeandmail.com/servlet/story/RTGAM.20070709.wxetorture09/BNStory/specialComment/home.

41. The Associated Press, "Scholars Urge Bush to Ban Use of Torture," *The Washington Post*, June 25, 2007, www.washingtonpost.com/wp-dyn/content/article/2007/06/25/AR2007062501437.html.

42. See David Masci, "Torture," *CQ Researcher*, April 18, 2003, pp. 345-368.

43. James Ross, "A History of Torture," in Roth, *op. cit.*

44. John Langbein, "The Legal History of Torture," in Levinson, *op. cit.*

45. Brian Innes, *The History of Torture* (1998), pp. 13, 43.

46. Roth, p. 8.

47. Ross, p. 12.

48. Darius M. Rejali, *Torture & Modernity: Self, Society, and State in Modern Iran* (1994), p. 11.

49. *Ibid.*, p. 13.

50. Christopher J. Einolf, "The Fall and Rise of Torture: A Comparative and Historical Analysis," *Sociological Theory 25:2*, June 2007.

51. For background, see R. C. Schroeder, "Human Rights Policy," in *Editorial Research Reports 1979* (Vol. I), available in *CQ Researcher Plus Archive*, http://library.cqpress.com. Also see "Foreign Aid: Human Rights Compromise," in *CQ Almanac*, 1977.

52. Darius Rejali, "Does Torture Work?" *Salon*, June 21, 2004, http://archive.salon.com/opinion/feature/2004/06/21/torture_algiers/index_np.html.

53. Lou DiMarco, "Losing the Moral Compass: Torture & Guerre Revolutionnaire in the Algerian War," *Parameters*, Summer 2006.

54. John Conroy, *Unspeakable Acts, Ordinary People: The Dynamics of Torture* (2001).

55. Miriam Gur-Arye, "Can the War against Terror Justify the Use of Force in Interrogations? Reflections in Light of the Israeli Experience," in Levinson, *op. cit.*, p. 185.

56. Jess Bravin and Greg Jaffe, "Rumsfeld Approved Methods for Guantánamo Interrogation," *The Wall Street Journal*, June 10, 2004.

57. Department of Defense press release, June 12, 2005, www.defenselink.mil/Releases/Release.aspx?ReleaseID=8583.

58. Jane Mayer, "The Memo," *The New Yorker*, Feb. 27, 2006, pp. 32-41.

59. Tony Lagouranis, *Fear Up Harsh: An Army Interrogator's Dark Journey Through Iraq* (2007), p. 93.

60. A summary of the Taguba report can be found at www.fas.org/irp/agency/dod/taguba.pdf.

61. "Bush Signs Defense Authorization Measure With Detainee Provision," *CQ Almanac 2005 Online Edition*, available at http://library.cqpress.com.

62. The case is *Hamdan v. Rumsfeld*, 126 S. Ct. 2749 (2006).

63. Priest, *op. cit.*

64. "President Discusses Creation of Military Commissions to Try Suspected Terrorists," *op. cit.*

65. Dafna Linzer and Julie Tate, "New Light Shed on CIA's 'Black Site' Prisons," *The Washington Post*, Feb. 28, 2007, p. A1.

66. Mark Bowden, "The Dark Art of Interrogation," *The Atlantic*, October 2003.

67. Mayer, Aug. 13, 2007, *op. cit.*

68. *Ibid.*

69. Mayer, Feb. 14, 2005, *op. cit.*

70. Ian Fisher and Elisabetta Povoledo, "Italy Braces for Legal Fight Over Secret CIA Program," *The New York Times*, June 8, 2007.

71. Jeffrey R. Smith, "Gonzales Defends Transfer of Detainees," *The Washington Post*, March 8, 2005, p. A3.

72. Malinowski testimony, *op. cit.*

73. Council of Europe Parliamentary Assembly, "Alleged secret detentions in Council of Europe member states, 2006," http://assembly.coe.int/CommitteeDocs/2006/20060606_Ejdoc162006Part II-FINAL.pdf.

74. Gwendolyn Albert, "With Impunity," *Prague Post*, April 12, 2006, www.praguepost.com/articles/2006/04/12/with-impunity.php.

75. http://melissamahlecommentary.blogspot.com/2005/12/cia-and-torture.html.

76. Elisabetta Povoledo, "Trial of CIA Operatives is delayed in Italy," *The International Herald Tribune*, June 18, 2007.

77. Jeffrey Fleishman, "Germany Orders Arrest of 13 CIA Operatives in Kidnapping of Khaled el-Masri" *Los Angeles Times*, Jan. 31, 2007.

78. Mayer, Feb. 14, 2005, *op. cit.*

79. "Arar Case Timeline," Canadian Broadcasting Company, www.cbc.ca/news/background/arar.

80. Christine Kearney, "Iraqi, Yemeni men join lawsuit over CIA flights," Reuters, Aug. 1, 2007.

81. Marie Beaudette, "Standing at the Floodgates," *Legal Times*, June 28, 2004.

82. The case is *Sosa v. Alvarez-Machain*, 2004, 542 U.S. 692 (2004).

83. Ian MacKinnon, "War crimes panel charges Khmer Rouge chief," *The Guardian*, Aug. 1, 2007.

84. "Taylor Trial Delayed until 2008," BBC News, Aug. 20, 2007, http://news.bbc.co.uk/2/hi/africa/6954627.stm.

85. P. X. Kelley and Robert F. Turner, "War Crimes and the White House," *The Washington Post*, July 26, 2007.

86. Thomas, *op. cit.*

87. Henry Weinstein, "ABA targets CIA methods, secret law," *Los Angeles Times*, Aug. 14, 2007.

88. The Associated Press, "Dem blocking Bush pick for CIA lawyer," MSNBC, Aug. 16, 2007, www.msnbc.msn.com/id/20294826.

89. "The Candidates on Military Tribunals and Guantánamo Bay," Council on Foreign Relations, July 17, 2007, www.cfr.org/publication/13816/.

BIBLIOGRAPHY

Books

Bagaric, Mirko, and Julie Clarke, *Torture: When the Unthinkable Is Morally Permissible*, State University of New York Press, 2007.
Bagaric, an Australian law professor, argues torture is sometimes morally justified and should be legally excusable.

Conroy, John, *Unspeakable Acts, Ordinary People: The Dynamics of Torture*, Random House, 2000.
A reporter examines the history of torture.

Dershowitz, Alan M., *Why Torture Works: Understanding the Threat, Responding to the Challenge*, Yale University Press, 2003.
A Harvard law professor argues that torture will be employed by interrogators, so courts should issue "torture warrants" to bring some legal oversight to the process.

Haritos-Fatouros, Mika, *The Psychological Origins of Institutionalized Torture*, Routledge, 2003.
A sociologist explores the indoctrination of Greek torturers during military rule of the country during the 1970s.

Lagouranis, Tony, *Fear Up Harsh: An Army Interrogator's Dark Journey Through Iraq*, NAL Hardcover, 2007.
A former U.S. Army interrogator describes the use of coercive techniques by American soldiers.

Levinson, Sanford, ed., *Torture: A Collection*, Oxford University Press, 2004.
Essays by academics and human rights advocates examine the historical, moral and political implications of torture.

Rejali, Darius, *Torture and Democracy*, Princeton University Press, 2007.
A Reed College professor and expert on torture traces its history from the 19th century through the U.S. occupation of Iraq.

Articles

"Torture in the Name of Freedom," *Der Spiegel*, Feb. 20, 2006, www.spiegel.de/international/spiegel/0,1518,401899,00.html.
The German news magazine concludes the United States is ceding its moral authority on the issue of torture.

Bowden, Mark, "The Dark Art of Interrogation," *The Atlantic Monthly*, October 2003, www.theatlantic.com/doc/200310/bowden.
An American journalist examines interrogation methods employed by U.S. personnel since the 9/11 terrorist attacks.

Einolf, Christopher J., "The Fall and Rise of Torture: A Comparative and Historical Analysis," *Sociological Theory*, June 2007, www.asanet.org/galleries/default-file/June07STFeature.pdf.
A University of Richmond sociology professor explains the continued prevalence of torture during the 20th century.

Mayer, Jane, "Outsourcing Torture," *The New Yorker*, Feb. 14, 2005, www.newyorker.com/archive/2005/02/14/050214fa_fact6.
The reporter traces the history of the U.S.'s "extraordinary rendition" policy.

Mayer, Jane, "Whatever It Takes," *The New Yorker*, Feb. 19, 2007, www.newyorker.com/reporting/2007/02/19/070219fa_fact_mayer.
The article examines the popular television show "24" and its role in "normalizing" perceptions of torture.

Mayer, Jane, "The Black Sites," *The New Yorker*, Aug. 13, 2007, p. 46, www.newyorker.com/reporting/2007/08/13/070813fa_fact_mayer.
A journalist examines the history of the CIA's secret "black site" prisons for high-value terror suspects.

Ozdemir, Cem, "Beyond the Valley of the Wolves," *Der Spiegel*, Feb. 22, 2006, www.spiegel.de/international/0,1518,401565,00.html.
A Turkish member of parliament discusses a popular Turkish movie that depicts American soldiers mistreating Iraqi civilians.

Reports and Studies

"Alleged secret detentions and unlawful inter-state transfers involving Council of Europe member states," Committee on Legal Affairs and Human Rights Council of Europe Parliamentary Assembly, June 7, 2006, http://assembly.coe.int/CommitteeDocs/2006/20060606_Ejdoc162006PartII-FINAL.pdf.
An organization of European lawmakers examines the role of European governments in U.S. renditions.

"Educing Information, Interrogation: Science and Art," Foundations for the Future Phase 1 Report, Intelligence Science Board, December 2006, www.fas.org/irp/dni/educing.pdf.
Too little is known about which interrogation methods are effective.

"Tarnished Image: Latin America Perceives the United States," Latin American Working Group, www.lawg.org/docs/tarnishedimage.pdf.
A nonprofit group examines Latin American press coverage of U.S. policies, including its interrogation of detainees.

For More Information

Amnesty International USA, 5 Penn Plaza, New York, NY 10001; (212) 807-8400; www.amnestyusa.org. U.S.-affiliate of London-based international human rights organization.

Center for Victims of Torture, 717 East River Rd., Minneapolis, MN 55455; (612) 436-4800; www.cvt.org. Operates healing centers in Minneapolis-St. Paul and Liberia and Sierra Leone. Also trains religious leaders, teachers, caregivers and staff from other NGOs about the effects of torture and trauma.

Human Rights First, 333 Seventh Ave., 13th Floor, New York, NY 10001-5108; (212) 845-5200; www.humanrights-first.org. A New York-based advocacy group that combats genocide, torture and other human rights abuses; founded in 1978 as the Lawyers Committee for Human Rights.

Human Rights Watch, 350 Fifth Ave., 34th floor, New York, NY 10118-3299; (212) 290-4700; www.hrw.org. Advocates for human rights around the world.

International Rehabilitation Council for Torture Victims, Borgergade 13, P.O. Box 9049 DK-1022; Copenhagen K, Denmark; +45 33 76 06 00; www.irct.org. Umbrella organization for worldwide network of centers that treat torture victims.

Medical Foundation for the Care of Victims of Torture, 111 Isledon Rd., Islington, London N7 7JW; (020) 7697 7777; www.torturecare.org.uk. Trains and provides medical personnel to aid victims of torture.

Office of the High Commissioner for Human Rights, 8-14 Ave. de la Paix, 1211 Geneva 10, Switzerland; (41-22) 917-9000; www.unhchr.ch. United Nations agency that opposes human rights violations.

VOICES FROM ABROAD

Tony Blair

Then-Prime Minister, United Kingdom

What's the actual threat?

"People devote the most extraordinary amount of time in trying to say that the Americans, on rendition, are basically deporting people . . . and people spend very little time in actually looking at what the threat is that we face and America faces, from terrorism and how we have to deal with it."

— The Independent *(United Kingdom), February 2006*

Michael Ignatieff

Member of Parliament, Canada

Taking the high ground

"The moral imperative, 'Do not torture, any time, anywhere, in any circumstances,' is mandated by the United Nations convention against torture and other cruel, inhuman or degrading treatment or punishment. The fact that terrorists torture does not change these imperatives. Compliance does not depend on reciprocity."

— Business Day *(South Africa), April 2006*

Basil Fernando

Executive Director, Asian Human Rights Council

A benefit to the elite

"There is still reluctance on the part of Thai elite to eliminate torture. . . . [Those in power fear] police will no longer be an instrument in their hand. They have to accept that police can investigate everyone and that the police will become a friend of the ordinary man."

— Bangkok Post, *July 2006*

Editorial

The Indian Express

We are all capable of torture

"Living in a country where torture has become banal, we know it is just as likely to emanate from disgruntled and disaffected fellow citizens as it is from the institutions mandated to protect us — the army, the police, the paramilitary. When authoritarianism and violence become common currency across classes . . . then nobody has qualms disrespecting the basic tenets of civilised political discourse, behaviour, and transaction."

— November 2005

Manfred Nowak

Anti-Torture Investigator, United Nations

Torturers should pay the costs

"Countries where torture is widespread or even systematic should be held accountable to pay. . . . If individual torturers would have to pay all the long-term rehabilitation costs, this would have a much stronger deterrent effect on torture than some kind of disciplinary or lenient criminal punishment."

— Address before U.N. Human Rights Council, Geneva, April 2007

Narmin Uthman

Minister of Human Rights, Iraq

No torture in Abu Ghraib

"Abu Ghraib prison is currently under the supervision of the Human Rights Ministry, and our [inspection] committees have not found evidence of any use of torture. . . . The change in the treatment of [prisoners by] the jail guards in Abu Ghraib prison has had a great impact on changing the Americans' policy towards Iraqi prisoners in general."

— Al-Arabiya TV (Dubai), February 2006

Larry Cox

Executive Director, Amnesty International

EU needs better policies

"By the EU adopting anemic rules for the commerce of torture instruments, it essentially allows the practice to continue, now with an official wink and nod. These directives fail to provide broad and tough policies to guarantee that businesses do not profit by the sale of these repulsive tools."

— U.S. Newswire, February 2007

Kofi Annan

Then-Secretary-General, United Nations

Torture is torture, by any name

"Fifty-seven years after the Universal Declaration of Human Rights prohibited all forms of torture and cruel, inhuman or degrading treatment or punishment, torture remains an unacceptable vice. . . . Nor is torture permissible when it is called something else. . . . Humanity faces grave challenges today. The threat of terror is real and immediate. Fear of terrorists can never justify adopting their methods."

— Speech during International Human Rights Day, December 2005

HUMAN RIGHTS LESSON 1

ARES.   caglecartoons.com/espanol

Caglecartoons.com/Ares

6

Courtesy of Brian Steidle

Villages continue to be attacked and burned in Darfur by the notorious Arab *janjaweed* militia — aided by aerial bombing by the Sudanese government — despite a two-year-old peace agreement between the government and rebel groups. The prosecutor for the International Criminal Court recently said the government's "scorched earth" tactics amount to genocide, but others say there is insufficient evidence that civilians have been targeted because of their ethnicity.

From *CQ Researcher*, September 1, 2008.

Crisis in Darfur

Karen Foerstel

I t was mid-afternoon when helicopters suddenly appeared and opened fire on the terrified residents of Sirba, in Western Darfur. Then hundreds of armed men riding horses and camels stormed the village, followed by 30 military vehicles mounted with weapons.

"The cars . . . were shooting at everyone, whether a woman, man or child," said Nada, one of the survivors. "They were shooting at us even when we were running away." [1]

Almost simultaneously, another attack was taking place a few miles away in the town of Abu Suruj. Witnesses say Sudanese soldiers and members of the notorious *janjaweed* militia shot people, set homes on fire and stole livestock. Many died in flames inside their huts. Three-quarters of the village was burned to the ground, as government planes bombed the town and surrounding hills where residents had fled for cover.

But that wasn't all. In a third nearby village, Silea, women and girls were raped and two-thirds of the town was destroyed by fire. Among the victims was Mariam, 35, who was shot as she tried to stop looters.

"They told me to leave and not to take anything, and then one of the men on a Toyota shot me, and I fell down," she said. Her father found her and took her by horse-drawn cart to a regional clinic. "I was pregnant with twins, and I lost them while we made the trip," she said. "I lost so much blood." [2]

In all, nearly 100 people were killed and 40,000 civilians driven from their homes in a single day, according to Human Rights Watch (HRW), a global advocacy group. The Sudanese military said the strikes were in retaliation against the Justice and Equality Movement (JEM), an anti-government rebel group that had recently launched a military offensive in the region, attacking a

Conflict Continues Despite Cease-Fire Accords

Darfur is an ethnically diverse area about the size of France in western Sudan — Africa's largest country. It has been wracked by decades of tension — and more recently open warfare — over land and grazing rights between the nomadic Arabs from the arid north and predominantly non-Arab Fur, Masalit and Zaghawa farmers in the more fertile south. A third of the region's 7 million people have been displaced by the conflict, which continues despite numerous cease-fire agreements. The United Nations has set up several camps inside Darfur and in neighboring Chad for those fleeing the violence.

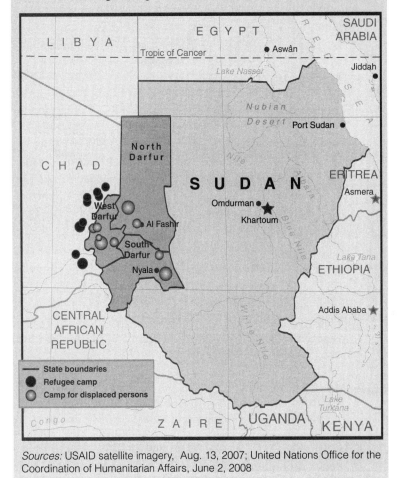

Sources: USAID satellite imagery, Aug. 13, 2007; United Nations Office for the Coordination of Humanitarian Affairs, June 2, 2008

"scorched earth" policy to clear the region and make it easier to go after JEM positions. [3]

Indeed, civilians have been targeted and terrorized throughout the long and bloody fighting in Darfur between non-Arab rebel groups who want to overthrow the Sudanese government and government troops backed by Arabic *janjaweed* militias.* During the peak fighting between 2003 and 2005, from 200,000 to 400,000 people — mostly civilians — died from armed attacks as well as famine and disease. More than 2.4 million Sudanese — about a third of the population — have been forced to flee their homes since 2003; tens of thousands now live in refugee camps across the region. [4]

But the same-day attacks in the three villages did not occur during the period of peak fighting. They occurred on Feb. 8 of this year, nearly two years after rebels and the government signed the Darfur Peace Agreement (DPA) in May 2006.

The continuing conflict has sparked the world's largest humanitarian mission, with more than 17,000 aid workers now stationed in Darfur. [5] And the situation is deteriorating. Observers predict next year will be one of the worst ever.

Growing banditry and lawlessness have made much of Darfur — a region in western Sudan as large as France — inaccessible to aid workers. [6] Rising food prices, drought and a poor cereal harvest also are combining to form what Mike McDonagh, chief of the U.N. Office for Coordination

police station, killing three civilians and detaining local officials.

While HRW criticized the rebels for operating around populated areas, it strongly condemned the Sudanese government for targeting civilians and using a

---

* The word *janjaweed*, which means devil on a horse, is used to describe horsemen from the nomadic Arab tribes in Darfur that have been armed and supported by the Sudanese government.

of Humanitarian Affairs, described as a "perfect storm." [7]

Already, conditions are dire:

- In the first five months of this year, 180,000 Darfuris were driven from their homes. [8]
- More than 4.2 million people in Darfur now rely on humanitarian aid for food, water and medical care. [9]
- Attacks against aid workers have doubled since last year. [10] (*See chart, p. 151.*)
- The U.N. World Food Program was forced to cut its food rations in Darfur by 40 percent this year because of repeated attacks by armed gangs. [11]
- About 650,000 children — half of the region's children — do not receive any education. [12]

While attacks on civilians have decreased since the peace deal was signed, international watchdog groups say the drop has little to do with increased security. "A third of the population has been displaced, so the targets are fewer," says Selena Brewer, a researcher with Human Rights Watch. "But there are far more perpetrators."

The fighting between non-Arab rebels and the Arab-led government's forces — backed by the *janjaweed* — has morphed into all-out lawlessness. The two main rebel groups — the JEM and the Sudanese Liberation Army/Movement (SLA/M) — have splintered into more than a dozen factions that fight among themselves as much as against the government. Moreover, some disaffected *janjaweed* fighters have joined the rebels, and skirmishes between ethnic tribes are increasing. Bandits attack civilians, aid workers and international peacekeepers almost at will. [13]

"We no longer know who is attacking," says Denise Bell, a Darfur specialist with Amnesty International USA.

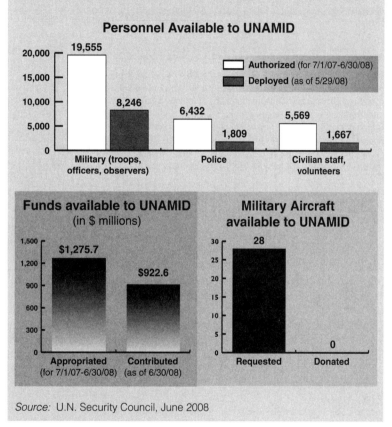

Lack of Resources Hampers Peacekeepers

More than a year after the U.N. authorized the largest peacekeeping force in the world in Darfur, the joint U.N.-African Union (UNAMID) force has received only 37 percent of the nearly 32,000 military, police and civilian personnel that were authorized and 72 percent of the funds. Much of the force's equipment has been delayed by Sudanese customs, hijacked by bandits or simply not provided by international donors. For instance, by the end of May not a single military helicopter had been donated to the force.

Personnel Available to UNAMID

☐ **Authorized** (for 7/1/07-6/30/08)
■ **Deployed** (as of 5/29/08)

Military (troops, officers, observers): 19,555 / 8,246
Police: 6,432 / 1,809
Civilian staff, volunteers: 5,569 / 1,667

Funds available to UNAMID (in $ millions)

Appropriated (for 7/1/07-6/30/08): $1,275.7
Contributed (as of 6/30/08): $922.6

Military Aircraft available to UNAMID

Requested: 28
Donated: 0

Source: U.N. Security Council, June 2008

To make matters even more complicated, Darfur has become the staging ground for a proxy war between Sudan and its western neighbor Chad. The two governments support opposing groups in the region with the goal of launching coup attempts against one another. As arms pour into the area, civilians are the primary victims.

Many describe the conflict as Arabs vs. non-Arabs. "The *janjaweed* . . . would tell us that the black Africans were a lesser race and that they shouldn't be there . . . and that they would drive them out or kill them," said former

During a 2007 visit to Sudan, Chinese President Hu Jintao reviews Sudanese troops with President Omar Hassan al-Bashir. In the run-up to the Beijing Olympics this summer, China came under intense international pressure to use its economic clout as Sudan's biggest oil buyer and weapons supplier to convince Bashir to stop the slaughter in Darfur. Hu convinced Bashir to allow joint U.N.-African Union peacekeeping forces to enter Darfur, but critics say China could do much more.

U.S. Marine Capt. Brian Steidle, whose book about his six months as an unarmed military observer in Darfur was made into an award-winning documentary. [14]

But most observers say the situation is more complicated than that. Nearly all Darfuris speak Arabic, and nearly all are Muslims. Generations of intermarriage have resulted in little physical difference between the groups, and not all Arab tribes have joined the *janjaweed* while some Arab groups have even been targeted themselves — although most of the victims are from the non-Arab Fur, Masalit and Zaghawa ethnic groups.

But poverty, drought and the ongoing conflict have led to increased tensions between Arab groups, who are mainly nomadic, and non-Arabs, who are mainly farmers, as they compete for dwindling land and water resources. [15] The Sudanese government is widely accused of doing all it can to inflame these historical tensions and grow support among its Arab political base in Darfur by arming and recruiting the *janjaweed* to clear the region of non-Arabs.

But most agree race has little to do with government motives. "It's all about divide to rule. It's just the government using one lot of poor people against another lot of poor people," says Gillian Lusk, associate editor of the London-based newsletter *Africa Confidential.*

"It's not about ethnic supremacy. If the so-called Arabs don't help the government, it will kill them, too. It's just renting them."

Although Sudan says its attacks in Darfur comprise a "counterinsurgency" campaign, the prosecutor for the International Criminal Court (ICC) refuted that claim in July when he sought an indictment against Sudanese President Omar Hassan Al-Bashir for genocide and crimes against humanity. [16]

"The most efficient method to commit genocide today in front of our eyes is gang rapes, rapes against girls and rapes against 70-year old women," Chief ICC Prosecutor Luis Moreno-Ocampo said as he described the brutality of the war in Darfur. "Babies born as a result have been called *janjaweed* babies, and this has led to an explosion of infanticide." In addition, he said, "Al-Bashir is executing this genocide without gas chambers, without bullets and without machetes. The desert will do it for them. . . . Hunger is the weapon of this genocide as well as rape." [17]

Many hope the prosecutor's action will pressure Sudan to halt its attacks in Darfur. But others fear an indictment would prompt Bashir to prevent peacekeepers and Western aid organizations from working in Darfur.

"[An indictment] would have very serious consequences for peacekeeping operations, including the political process," U.N. Secretary-General Ban Ki-moon said. "I'm very worried. But nobody can evade justice." [18]

While the ICC is considering charging Bashir with genocide, many aid groups, governments and the United Nations have avoided using the "G-word" to describe the situation in Darfur. Some say the reluctance stems from the fact that international law requires countries to take action to "prevent and punish" genocide. But others, including Amnesty International, say that despite the obvious atrocities, there is insufficient evidence civilians were targeted because of their ethnicity. [19]

The international community also disagrees on how to solve the crisis. While the United States and the United Nations have sanctioned the Bashir government, the move has largely been opposed by China, Russia, Arab nations and the African Union (AU) — a political and economic coalition of African countries.

"China is uniquely positioned to fix this," says Alex Meixner, director of government relations for the Save Darfur Coalition. "They have a fair amount of leverage over Bashir." China buys two-thirds of Sudan's petroleum — much of which comes from the south — and is its largest supplier of weapons. But as a member of the U.N.'s Security Council, China repeatedly has used its veto threat to block action against Sudan. [20]

Over the past year, however, as the Beijing Olympics brought international attention to China's human-rights policies — its government has played a more active role in trying to solve the crisis. It appointed a special envoy to help negotiate a peace settlement and helped convince Sudan to allow a joint U.N.-African Union peacekeeping force — known as UNAMID — to enter Darfur. In July China sent 172 engineers to join the peacekeeping force, bringing China's participation in the mission to more than 300 personnel. [21]

Nearly a year into their mission, however, the force is severely undermanned, underequipped and under constant attack. Although authorized to have 26,000 military and police peacekeepers — the largest deployment in the world — fewer than half that number have been deployed and not a single military helicopter has been donated to the force. (*See graph, p. 145.*) [22]

Darfur is "a test case for international response — or the inability of the international community to respond — to this type of situation," says Imani Countess, senior director for public affairs at TransAfrica Forum, which campaigns for human rights in Africa. "It's a damning indictment against the government of Sudan, because it refuses to end the violence. But it's also a pretty damning indictment of the international community."

AFP/Getty Images/Khaled Desouki

AFP/Getty Images/Ashraf Shazly

Defying the Court

Surrounded by security guards, Sudanese President Omar Hassan al-Bashir (center, top), greets supporters in North Darfur just days after the chief prosecutor at the International Criminal Court accused him of masterminding genocide in the region. Bashir dismissed the accusations as lies and vowed not to cooperate with the court. Soon after the accusation, the Sudanese government convicted and sentenced to death more than three dozen rebels — including these prisoners — in connection with a daring attack last May on Khartoum, the capital, in which more than 200 people were killed.

And while the international community stands by, the situation in Darfur threatens to destabilize the entire region. Millions of refugees from the area are creating

Climate Change Blamed for Darfur Conflict

Nomads and farmers battle for scarce water and arable land.

For generations, Arab nomads in Darfur enjoyed a symbiotic relationship with their farming non-Arab neighbors. As the seasons changed, the nomads would bring their livestock from the arid north to the greener lands to the south during the dry season and then lead them back north during the rainy season. The non-Arabs, who came from several different ethnic groups, would allow the nomads to graze camels, sheep and goats on their farmlands, and in exchange the livestock would provide fertilizer for the farmers' crops. [1]

That relationship, however, began to change about 75 years ago. And today, what had once been a convenient alliance between nomads and farmers has exploded into a bloody war between Darfur's Arabs and ethnic African tribes.

While many blame the bloodshed on political or ethnic divisions, others say climate change lies at the root of the devastation. "It is no accident that the violence in Darfur erupted during the drought," U.N. Secretary-General Ban Ki-moon said. "Until then, Arab nomadic herders had lived amicably with settled farmers." [2]

Most people use "a convenient military and political shorthand" to describe Darfur as an ethnic conflict between Arab militias fighting black rebels and farmers, Ban explained. And, while the conflict involves a complex set of social and political causes, it "began as an ecological crisis, arising at least in part from climate change," he said.

According to the U. N., average precipitation in Sudan has declined 40 percent since the early 1980s. [3] Signs of desertification began emerging as far back as the 1930s. A lake in El-Fashir in northern Darfur reached its lowest water level in 1938, after which wells had to be drilled to tap into underground water supplies. Villages in northern Darfur increasingly were evacuated because of disappearing water supplies. [4]

In the 1980s a severe drought and famine made the northern areas nearly impossible to cultivate, forcing nomadic tribes to migrate even further south and increasingly encroach upon their farming neighbors' more fertile lands. [5] To prevent damage from the nomad's passing herds, the farmers began to fence off their shrinking fertile plots. Violent land disputes grew more and more common.

"Interestingly, most of the Arab tribes who have their own land rights did not join the government's fight," said David Mozersky, the International Crisis Group's project director for the Horn of Africa. [6]

economic and political chaos in Sudan and neighboring countries, and the region's porous borders have turned Darfur into the headquarters for rebels from Chad and the Central African Republic.

The growing crisis also threatens to undo the precarious 2005 Comprehensive Peace Agreement (CPA) that ended the bloody 20-year civil war between North and South Sudan — Africa's longest civil war.

"A lot of attention has been diverted to Darfur," causing backsliding and insufficient funding for implementing the peace agreement, says Bell of Amnesty International. "Darfur threatens to overshadow the CPA. If the CPA falls, the country falls. The international community needs to be much more aware of that."

In June, Jan Eliasson — the U.N.'s special envoy to Darfur — resigned, blaming himself, the U.N. and the international community for not doing enough to bring

peace to the region. He said attention has been too narrowly focused on Darfur alone and that a more comprehensive strategy — addressing the many tensions and conflicts across the region — must now be pursued.

"This simply cannot go on," Eliasson said. "A new generation in Sudan may be doomed to a life in conflict, despair and poverty. The international community should have learned enough lessons from other conflicts where the populations were left to stagnate and radicalize in camps." [23]

As the situation deteriorates in Darfur, these are some of the questions being asked:

Has genocide occurred in Darfur?

In July 2004, the U.S. Congress declared the violence in Darfur "genocide" and urged President George W. Bush to do the same. But for months afterward, Secretary of

A new report by the European Commission predicts that increasing drought and land overuse in North Africa and the Sahel — the semi-arid swath of land stretching from the Atlantic Ocean to the Horn of Africa — could destroy 75 percent of the region's arable land. As land and water resources disappear, the report said, such violent conflicts will increase around the world. [7]

"Already today, climate change is having a major impact on the conflict in and around Darfur," the report said. [8]

Economist Jeffrey Sachs, director of the Earth Institute at Columbia University, said Darfur is an example of the conflicts that increasingly will erupt because of climate change.

"What some regard as the arc of Islamic instability, across the Sahel, the Horn of Africa, Yemen, Iraq, Pakistan and Afghanistan, is more accurately an arc of hunger, population pressures, water stress, growing food insecurity and a pervasive lack of jobs," Sachs wrote earlier this year, using Darfur as an example of a conflict sparked by climate change. [9]

But others say climate change is just an excuse used by the Sudanese government to relieve itself of responsibility. Politics is the real cause of the bloodshed in Darfur, many say, with President Omar Hassan al-Bashir's government bearing full blame for the ongoing violence.

"Jeffrey Sachs and Ban Ki-moon said it's essentially environmental. How dare they?" says Gillian Lusk, associate editor of the London-based newsletter *Africa Confidential*. "The essential issue is the Sudan government went in there and

killed people." And any attempts "to turn it into a primary ethnic or environment issue are dangerous."

Still, many international leaders say Darfur is a warning sign of growing environmental degradation. "Climate change is already having a considerable impact on security," French President Nicolas Sarkozy told an international governmental conference in April. "If we keep going down this path, climate change will encourage the immigration of people with nothing towards areas where the population does have something, and the Darfur crisis will be only one crisis among dozens." [10]

---

[1] Stephan Faris, "The Real Roots of Darfur," *The Atlantic*, April 2007, www.theatlantic.com/doc/200704/darfur-climate.

[2] Ban Ki-moon, "A Climate Culprit in Darfur," *The Washington Post*, June 16, 2007, p. A15.

[3] *Ibid.*

[4] M. W. Daly, *Darfur's Sorrow* (2007), pp. 141-142.

[5] Gerard Prunier, Darfur: The Ambiguous Genocide (2005), pp. 49-50.

[6] Faris, *op. cit.*

[7] "Climate Change and International Security," The High Representative and the European Commission, March 14, 2008, p. 6, http://ec.europa.eu/external_relations/cfsp/doc/climate_change_international_security_2008_en.pdf.

[8] *Ibid.*

[9] Jeffrey Sachs, "Land, Water and Conflict," *Newsweek*, July 14, 2008.

[10] "Climate change driving Darfur crisis: Sarkozy," Agence France-Presse, April 18, 2008, http://afp.google.com/article/ALeqM5h7l_NjlMjZF QWDOwxIbibX5AeuA.

State Colin L. Powell studiously avoided using the word, on the advice of government lawyers.

Under the International Convention on the Prevention and Punishment of Genocide, any signatory country — including the United States — which determines that genocide is occurring must act to "prevent and punish" the genocide. However, while some believe the 1948 treaty requires military intervention to stop the killing, others believe economic sanctions alone are permitted. [24]

The Bush administration used the word to describe what is happening in Darfur only after religious groups launched a lobbying and media campaign condemning the Sudanese government for "genocide." In May 2004, the U.S. Holocaust Memorial Museum issued a "genocide alert" for Darfur, and two months later the American Jewish World Service and the Holocaust

Museum founded the Save Darfur Coalition — an alliance of secular and religious groups calling for international intervention to halt the violence. [25] That August, 35 evangelical Christian leaders said genocide was occurring in Darfur and asked the administration to consider sending troops. [26]

A month later, Powell finally capitulated, telling the Senate Foreign Relations Committee, "We concluded — I concluded — that genocide has been committed in Darfur and that the government of Sudan and the *janjaweed* bear responsibility — and genocide may still be occurring." [27] Powell then called on the U.N. to take action for the "prevention and suppression of acts of genocide." [28] A week later, the United States pushed a resolution through the General Assembly threatening Sudan with economic sanctions if it did not protect civilians in Darfur. [29]

Lynsey Addario

After years of fighting the Sudanese government, rebels in Darfur — like these from the Sudanese Liberation Army/Movement (SLA/M) — have splintered into more than a dozen factions that fight among themselves as much as against the government. Meanwhile, bandits are attacking civilians, aid workers and international peacekeepers almost at will, contributing to rampant lawlessness in the region.

But most other governments and international humanitarian groups — including Amnesty International — say genocidal intent has not been proven.

"There is a legal definition of genocide, and Darfur does not meet that legal standard," former President Jimmy Carter said last year. "The atrocities were horrible, but I don't think it qualifies to be called genocide. If you read the law textbooks . . . you'll see very clearly that it's not genocide, and to call it genocide falsely just to exaggerate a horrible situation — I don't think it helps." [30]

Not surprisingly, Sudan denies targeting ethnic groups in Darfur, instead blaming the massive deaths on tribal conflict, water disputes and collateral military damage. "We do not deny that atrocities have taken place," says Khalid al-Mubarak, a media counselor at the Sudanese Embassy in London. "We do deny that they have been planned or systematic. They happened in an area out of reach of the central government. The government could not have planned or controlled it."

A U.N. commission investigating the conflict also said genocidal intent has not been proven, but it did say Sudanese forces working with *janjaweed* militias had "conducted indiscriminate attacks, including killing of civilians, torture, enforced disappearances, destruction of villages, rape and other forms of sexual violence, pillaging and forced displacement." [31]

"I don't think it matters [whether you call it genocide or not]," says *Africa Confidential's* Lusk. "In terms of legitimizing intervention, it might be important. But no one wants to get involved anyway."

In a joint statement in May, the three leading American presidential candidates at the time — Sens. Barack Obama, D-Ill., Hillary Rodham Clinton, D-N.Y., and John McCain, R-Ariz., — called the situation in Darfur "genocide" and promised, if elected, to intervene. [32]

Some other U.S. politicians — including Democratic vice presidential nominee and Foreign Relations Committee Chairman Sen. Joseph R. Biden, of Delaware — have called for military intervention to halt the mass killings. [33] Susan Rice, a foreign policy adviser to Obama, has called for legislation authorizing the use of force. [34]

But experts say the international backlash against the Iraq War — including the abuse of Muslim prisoners at Abu Ghraib prison by U.S. soldiers — makes intervention in another Muslim country unlikely anytime soon, whether the word genocide is used or not. "Sudan can say all this 'genocide' stuff is a conspiracy to steal [their] oil," says Peter Moszynski, a writer and aid worker with 25 years of experience in Sudan. "With the Iraq backlash, Bashir became bulletproof."

Sudan is Africa's fifth-largest oil producer, with proven reserves of 5 billion barrels. Experts say in the next few years Sudan's daily production could reach 700,000 barrels — enough for nearly 30 million gallons of gasoline a day — about 10 percent of U.S. daily needs. [35]

The United States is also in the awkward position of balancing its national-security interests against calls to end the genocide. Since the Sept. 11, 2001, terrorist attacks in the United States, Sudanese officials have worked closely with the CIA and other intelligence agencies to provide information on suspected terrorists. Although Sudan is on the U.S. list of "state sponsors of terrorism," a 2007 State Department report called Sudan "a strong partner in the War on Terror." [36]

"I am not happy at all about the U.S. working with Sudan," says El-Tahir El-Faki, speaker of the JEM legislative assembly. "Definitely it is genocide in Darfur. They are targeting ethnic people with the aim of eliminating people. . . . It will be contrary to American interest supporting a government that is killing people."

Regardless of what the violence is called, most agree the label is meaningless if nothing is done to stop the killing. "It's like walking down the street and you see someone being beaten up. You don't stop and think whether it's bodily harm or not. You stop and help and let the lawyers figure out the legal side later," says. James Smith, head of the Aegis Trust, a British group that works to halt genocide. "Stopping genocide is more of a political and moral question than a legal one."

"The legal framework exists to prevent or mitigate genocide if the political will is sufficient," he continues. "However, politicians and diplomats create legal ambiguity to mask their disinterest in protecting lives in certain far-away countries."

Would arresting Sudanese President Bashir do more harm than good?

In July, when he asked the International Criminal Court to charge Bashir with genocide and other war crimes, the ICC prosecutor cast aside all the debate over how to label the violence in Darfur. Bashir's motives were "largely political," ICC prosecutor Luis Moreno-Ocampo said. "His pretext was a 'counterinsurgency.' His intent was genocide. . . . He is the mastermind behind the alleged crimes. He has absolute control." [37]

The court is expected to decide this fall whether to accept the charges and issue an arrest warrant. Many heralded the prosecutor's unprecedented request — the first genocide indictment sought for a sitting head of state — as a critical first step to peace in Darfur.

"Darfur has had very little justice of any kind. They've been let down by the African Union, by the U.N. peacekeeping force, by other countries," says *Africa Confidential's* Lusk. "It's about time a small sign of justice appeared on the horizon. Impunity has reigned for 19 years. This action says this is not a respectable government."

But others fear an indictment could spark reprisal attacks against foreign peacekeepers and aid workers by the Sudanese government and could block a peace settlement. Sudan's U.N. ambassador, Abdalmahmood Abdalhaleem Mohamad, said the charges would "destroy" efforts towards a peace agreement in Darfur. "Ocampo is playing

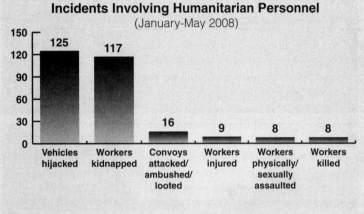

Aid Workers Face Danger

Eight humanitarian workers in Darfur were killed and 117 kidnapped within the first five months of 2008. Rising lawlessness has made parts of Darfur inaccessible to the 17,000 aid workers stationed in Darfur to help the more than 4 million people affected by the ongoing fighting between government and rebel forces, militia attacks and inter-tribal fighting.

Incidents Involving Humanitarian Personnel
(January-May 2008)

Vehicles hijacked	125
Workers kidnapped	117
Convoys attacked/ ambushed/ looted	16
Workers injured	9
Workers physically/ sexually assaulted	8
Workers killed	8

Source: U.N. Office for the Coordination of Humanitarian Affairs

with fire," he said. "If the United Nations is serious about its engagement with Sudan, it should tell this man to suspend what he is doing with this so-called indictment. There will be grave repercussions." [38]

Sudanese officials said that while they would not retaliate with violence, they could not guarantee the safety of any individual. "The U.N. asks us to keep its people safe, but how can we guarantee their safety when they want to seize our head of state?" asked Deputy Parliament Speaker Mohammed al-Hassan al-Ameen. [39]

The Sudanese government, which refused to hand over two other officials indicted for war crimes last year by the ICC, said it would not cooperate with the ICC's latest efforts either.

The United Nations evacuated staff from the region shortly after Ocampo made his announcement. [40] Representatives from the five permanent members of the U.N. Security Council — Britain, China, France, Russia and the United States — met with U.N. officials to discuss the safety of the peacekeeping force in Darfur, which evacuated non-essential staff and cut back on operations that could endanger civilian staff. [41]

Meanwhile, the African Union (AU), the Arab League and others asked the U.N. to delay the ICC legal action, which some say could be used as a bargaining chip to force Bashir to end the killing. "We are asking that the ICC indictment be deferred to give peace a chance," Nigerian Foreign Affairs Minister Ojo Maduekwe said after an emergency meeting on the issue by the African Union's Peace and Security Council in July. China and Russia also support deferring ICC action. [42]

Others fear the request for delay could produce its own backlash — among the rebels. Leaders of JEM and one of the SLA's factions said they will no longer recognize AU efforts to mediate peace because of its request for a deferral. "The African Union is a biased organization and is protecting dictators and neglecting the African people," said Khalil Ibrahim, president of JEM. [43]

Former U.S. Special Envoy for Sudan Andrew Natsios agrees an indictment could derail peace negotiations and make it impossible to hold free and fair elections, scheduled next year. "The regime will now avoid any compromise or anything that would weaken their already weakened position, because if they are forced from office they'll face trials before the ICC," Natsios wrote. "This indictment may well shut off the last remaining hope for a peaceful settlement for the country." [44]

The United States — which, like Sudan, has never ratified the treaty creating the ICC — nevertheless said Sudan must comply with the ICC. But the U.S. envoy to the United Nations has been vague on whether the United States would support a deferral. "We haven't seen anything at this point that could have the support of the United States," said U.S. Ambassador to the United Nations Zalmay Khalilzad. "We certainly do not support impunity for crimes."

But he added, "As you know also, we're not a member of the ICC. So there are various factors in play here. And as I said, I don't see any action on this in the council that would provide impunity anytime in the foreseeable future." [45]

Others point out that efforts to solve the crises diplomatically were faltering long before the ICC prosecutor's recommendations. "The process hasn't gotten anywhere," says veteran aid worker Moszynski. "If we're going to say 'never again,' we've got to do it. Someone must be held accountable."

In any case, he added, the pending ICC charges — and potential indictments — have turned Bashir into an international "pariah," making it nearly impossible for him to play any leadership role on the international stage.

Is China blocking peace in Darfur?

In the year leading up to the Beijing Olympics, U.S. government leaders, human-rights activists and Hollywood's elite used the international sporting event as a platform to criticize China's policy toward Darfur.

China is Sudan's biggest trading partner, weapons supplier and oil-industry investor. It has built a 957-mile-long pipeline in Sudan — one the largest foreign oil projects in China's history. It also has constructed three arms factories in Sudan and provided small arms, anti-personnel mines, howitzers, tanks, helicopters and ammunition. China also has done more than any other country to protect Khartoum from U.N. sanctions. [46]

China "potentially has the most influence with Sudan," says Amnesty International's Bell. "People who are the main [economic] players are able to dictate the rate of progress that is made."

American actress Mia Farrow last year branded the Beijing Olympics the "Genocide Olympics," and Hollywood producer Steven Spielberg stepped down as one of the event's artistic advisers, citing the ongoing violence in Darfur. [47] Last May, a bipartisan group of 108 members of Congress warned the Chinese government that if China did not pressure Sudan to do more to help Darfur, protests and boycotts could destroy the Olympics.

"[We] urge you to protect your country's image from being irredeemably tarnished, through association with a genocidal regime, for the purpose of economic gains," the group wrote. "[U]nless China does its part to ensure that the government of Sudan accepts the best and most reasonable path to peace, history will judge your government as having bank-rolled a genocide." [48]

The day after the letter was sent, China appointed a special envoy for Darfur and since then has made several moves to mitigate the crisis. [49] In addition to sending 315 engineers to join the UNAMID peacekeeping force to build roads, bridges and wells, China last May donated more than $5 million in humanitarian aid and in February handed over a $2.8 million package of financial and development aid. [50] According to China's official news agency, China has given a total of $11 million in humanitarian aid to Darfur, and Chinese companies have spent about $50 million on development projects in the region, including 53 miles of water pipelines. [51]

"We have done as much as we can," said China's assistant foreign minister Zhai Jun. "China remains committed to resolving the Darfur issue and has made unremitting efforts." [52]

But many say China could do much more, and that its millions of dollars in arms sales to Sudan feed the continuing violence. "They've taken some action, but not nearly enough," says Meixner of the Save Darfur Coalition. "They sent engineers to UNAMID, but they're kind of milking that. I look at that as China's having kept these engineers in their back pocket until right before the Olympics."

More meaningful, he says, would be an immediate halt or reduction in China's arms sales to Sudan. According to Amnesty International, China sold Sudan $24 million worth of arms and ammunition in 2005, plus $59 million worth of parts and aircraft equipment. [53]

In March 2005, the U.N. banned the sale of weapons to any combatants for use in Darfur. [54] But earlier this year the BBC reported that China had been providing trucks being used by the Sudanese military in Darfur. China admitted that 212 trucks were exported to Sudan in 2005 but said all were for civilian use and were only later equipped with guns in a defensive move by the government to stave off rebel attacks. [55]

"The Western media and in particular the activities of some nongovernmental organizations have caused China's role to be distorted," said China's Special Envoy to Darfur, Liu Guijin. [56]

China, which repeatedly has opposed or abstained from U.N. votes to sanction or condemn Sudan's actions in Darfur, says diplomacy and humanitarian support are the best path to peace. It has expressed "great concern" over the ICC prosecutor's request for an arrest warrant against Bashir and is considering supporting an effort to delay further action by the court. [57]

Some say such "subtle diplomacy" has persuaded Sudan to reduce military attacks in Darfur and improved conditions for civilians. Former U.S. Envoy Natsios told a Senate hearing last year that Beijing complemented rather than undercut Washington's sanctions-based policy and said China had convinced Sudan to accept UNAMID peacekeepers. "There has been a lot of China-bashing in the West, and I'm not sure, to be very frank with you, that . . . it's very helpful," he told the committee. [58]

Others say that while China is a powerful player in Sudanese affairs, Beijing alone cannot be blamed for the continuing violence. "The finger is pointed first at the Sudan government, and then China . . . and then many other countries," says *Africa Confidential's* Lusk.

John Prendergast, co-chair of the anti-genocide ENOUGH Project, agreed. "Unless China and the U.S. are both exerting much more pressure on Sudan, the crisis will continue to spiral out of control," he said. "China has unique economic leverage, while the U.S. retains leverage based on its ability to confer or withdraw legitimacy." [59]

BACKGROUND

Ostrich Feathers, Ivory and Slaves

The name Darfur comes from the Arabic word "dar," meaning home, and the name of the principal ethnic group of the region, the non-Arab Fur. For centuries, however, Darfur has been home to a wide range of people — both Arab and non-Arab. Darfur is at the crossroads of Africa and the Middle East, and Islamic traders as well as pilgrims traveling to Mecca have long traversed the province — leaving their cultural and religious imprint. [60] Today, around 90 percent of all Darfuris are Muslim. [61] After generations of intermarriage between Arabs and non-Arabs, it is nearly impossible to discern the ethnic ancestry of the people of Darfur, other than through cultural traditions: "Arabs" tend to be nomadic and "non-Arabs" tend to be farmers. Blurring the lines even further, it is not uncommon for people to call themselves Arab one day and non-Arab another. [62]

Around 1650, a Fur sultanate was established, and the region became a prosperous trading center for such goods as ostrich feathers, ivory and black slaves. [63] Over the next two centuries, the sultanate spread across 80 percent of the area known today as Darfur, encompassing 40 to 90 different ethnic groups or tribes. [64] The sultanate was considered one of the region's most powerful kingdoms, wholly separate in culture and heritage from the rest of modern-day Sudan.

In 1899, Egypt and Britain — which had occupied Egypt since 1882 — assumed joint authority over Sudan with the British taking the South and Egyptians taking the North. Even before Sudan came under joint control, Egyptian rulers had for decades occupied northern Sudan, amassing great wealth, largely from kidnapping

CHRONOLOGY

1899-1956 *Colonization sows seeds of poverty and division.*

1899 Britain takes control of mostly Christian southern Sudan; Egypt takes the predominantly Muslim north.

1916 Sudan annexes Darfur.

1956 Britain and Egypt turn control of Sudan over to northern Arab elites.

1957-Early '70s *Multiple coups switch control of Sudan between military and civilian governments; Darfur remains neglected as civil war rages in the east.*

1964 Civilians overthrow Sudan's military government.

1965 Chadian fighters establish bases in Darfur after civil war breaks out in neighboring Chad.

1969 Gen. Jaafar al-Nimeiri takes control of Sudan in military coup.

1972 Sudan's civil war ends when peace agreement is signed in Addis Ababa.

Late '70s-'80s *Darfur serves as staging ground for Chadian rebels; Libya arms Darfuri rebels; rising Islamic extremism sparks renewed civil war in eastern Sudan; famine and drought devastate Darfur.*

1976 Libyan-backed Darfuri rebels attack Khartoum, are defeated. Government tracks down and kills alleged sympathizers in Darfur.

1983 Nimeiri imposes sharia law and nullifies peace agreement, triggering new civil war in eastern Sudan.

1984 Drought devastates Darfur; Arabs and non-Arabs fight over land, water.

1985 Civilian uprising overthrows Nimeiri.

1989-1999 *Civil war intensifies; U.S.-Sudanese tensions increase.*

1989 Gen. Omar Hassan al-Bashir seizes power, embraces militant Islam and hosts al Qaeda's Osama bin Laden.

1993 U.S. lists Sudan as a state sponsor of terrorism.

1996 Sudan expels bin Laden under U.S. pressure.

1997 China agrees to build oil refinery in Khartoum, becomes Sudan's leading weapons supplier.

1998 U.S. bombs Khartoum pharmaceutical factory, claiming it produces chemical weapons, which is never proven.

2000-2005 *War breaks out in Darfur. U.S. says genocide is occurring in Darfur. Civil war in eastern Sudan ends.*

2001 President George W. Bush appoints former Sen. John C. Danforth, R-Mo., as special envoy to Sudan to try to settle the civil war.

2003 Darfur rebels attack North Darfur's capital, marking start of war in Darfur. A cease-fire is reached in the civil war between northern and southern Sudan.

2004 U.S. House of Representatives labels the fighting in Darfur as "genocide." . . . U.N. imposes arms embargo on Darfur and endorses deployment of African Union (AU) peacekeepers.

2005 Sudan's 20-year civil war in the east ends with signing of peace accord.

2006-Present *Darfuri peace deal dissolves; rebel groups splinter; peacekeepers fail to control chaos.*

2006 Darfur Peace Agreement is signed by government and one rebel group.

2007 U.N. creates joint U.N.-AU peacekeeping force.

2008 During run-up to Beijing Olympics, human-rights activists accuse China of abetting genocide in Darfur. . . . International Criminal Court considers indicting Bashir for genocide and war crimes.

black Africans from the South and selling them into slavery. Southern resentment against the North for the brutal slave trade remains today. [65]

Sudan's division between Britain and Egypt set the stage for the clashing cultures and religions that would later lead to the Sudanese civil war that raged for more than 20 years. The Egyptian North — with a higher concentration of Arabic population — was predominantly Islamic, while those in the South were animists or Christians. British missionaries were dispatched to spread the Christian faith in the South.

In 1916, Darfur was annexed by Sudan, merging two states with vastly different cultures and political structures. [66] "There was the problem of differential integration: Darfur is not the Sudan," says Gerard Prunier, author of the book *Darfur: The Ambiguous Genocide.* "Darfur was the easternmost sultanate in Africa, not part of the Nile Valley" as is the rest of Sudan.

And the colonial authorities did nothing to help integrate Darfur into their new state, largely ignoring the former sultanate and giving various tribes semi-autonomous rule over their individual lands. But tribal leaders were often illiterate and corrupt and did little to help Darfur. By 1935, only four government primary schools existed in all of Darfur. [67] Health care and economic development also were non-existent under the colonial rulers, who actually boasted of keeping Darfur poor and powerless.

"We have been able to limit education to the sons of chiefs and native administration personnel," wrote Philip Ingleson, governor of Darfur from 1935 to 1944, "and we can confidently look forward to keeping the ruling classes at the top of the educational tree for many years to come." [68]

Independence and Instability

After World War II, Britain began withdrawing from Sudan and reconnecting the North and South. The British handed power over to northern Arab elites in Khartoum, which became the center of government. [69] Once again, Darfur was ignored.

"Darfur had no say whatsoever over the structure or features of an independent Sudan," Prunier says.

In fact, much of the conflict in Darfur has its roots in the post-independence history of eastern Sudan, which involved a long-running civil war between the Arab- and Muslim-dominated North and the oil-rich, Christian and animist South. Darfur also became a political pawn in strategic maneuverings by Sudan, Chad and Libya,

with each country arming rebel groups in the region to further their parochial interests.

Within months of Sudan's independence in January 1956, the consolidation of power in the Arab North sparked rebellion in the South. Over the next 10 years, a series of political coups alternated the government in Khartoum between military and civilian power, as civil war continued between the North and the South. Yet successive administrations continued to ignore growing poverty and dissent in Darfur. In 1972 the military government of Gen. Jaafar Nimeiri signed a peace agreement in Addis Ababa, Ethiopia, providing substantial power- and wealth-sharing between the North and South but offering nothing to the Darfuris.

However, the North-South tensions remained, and growing conflict in neighboring Chad created even more instability in Sudan. Arab rebels from Chad who opposed their country's Christian government used Darfur as a home base for their own civil war. Libyan leader Muammar Qaddafi — hoping to create a powerful Arab belt stretching into central Africa — supported the Chadian rebels and proposed a unified Arab state between Libya and Sudan, but Nimeiri rejected the offer. Angered by Nimeiri's rejection and Sudan's agreement to end the civil war with the Christians in South Sudan, Qaddafi labeled Nimeiri a traitor to the Arab cause and began arming militant Arab organizations in Darfur who opposed the governments of both Chad and Sudan.

In 1976, Libyan-backed rebels attacked Nimeiri's government in Khartoum but were defeated in three days. The Sudanese military then hunted down and killed Darfuri civilians accused of sympathizing with the insurgents. [70]

Suddenly, after years of neglect, Darfur was getting the attention of Sudan's political leaders — but not the kind it had wanted. The ongoing violence also catapulted Darfur's various local tribes into the broader polarized conflict between "Arabs" and "non-Arabs," depending on which regime they supported. [71]

Making matters worse, a drought and famine in the early 1980s plunged Darfur deeper into poverty and desperation. For the next two decades, the nomadic "Arabs" and the farming "non-Arabs" increasingly fought over disappearing land and water resources. (*See sidebar, p. 148.*) The Arab-led government in Khartoum frequently intervened, providing arms to its nomadic Arab political supporters in Darfur, who in turn killed their farming neighbors. [72]

Arabs Criticized for Silence on Atrocities

Islamic countries also lag in donations, troop support.

The thin, white-haired man living in a U.N. refugee camp in Chad was soft-spoken but fervent as he thanked Americans "and the free world" for the food, medicine and other donations sent to the victims of the conflict in Darfur.

But, he asked a visiting filmmaker intently, tears trickling down his face, "Where are the Arab people? I am Muslim. We receive nothing from Islamic people." [1]

While nations around the world have criticized the Arab-dominated Sudanese government for not halting the rapes and murders of Muslims in the beleaguered region, other Arab governments have been largely silent about the atrocities being committed against Muslims by other Muslims.

"The Islamic world's response to the daily killings and suffering of millions of Muslims in Darfur has been largely silent — from both civil society as well as the institutions and majority of Islamic governments," said the newly formed Arab Coalition for Darfur, representing human-rights groups from 12 Muslim countries. "The Islamic world must decide to end its wall of silence, before it is too late." [2] The coalition made its statement in June before the Organization of the Islamic Conference, an intergovernmental organization of 57 Muslim nations.

Moreover, among the world's Arab governments — many of them awash in petrodollars — only the United Arab Emirates (UAE) earmarked any money ($100,000) specifically for aid to Darfur this year.* The rest of the international community donated more than $100 million, according to ReliefWeb, run by the U.N. Office for the Coordination of Humanitarian Affairs, including $28 million from the European Commission and $12 million from the United States. [3]

Moreover, only 587 of the 12,000 U.N. peacekeepers in Darfur have come from nations belonging to the 22-member Arab League. Of those, 508 were from Egypt, and the rest came from Jordan, Mauritania, Yemen and Libya. [4]

Amjad Atallah, senior director for international policy and advocacy with the Save Darfur Coalition, charges that the Arab League is more worried about protecting Arab leaders than about representing ordinary Arabs. "They seem to have a more compelling need to come to the defense of Arab states than for the people suffering under the regimes," says Atallah.

For its part, the Arab League did help convince Sudan to allow peacekeepers from the joint U.N.-AU peacekeeping mission into Darfur. And in 2004, an Arab League Commission of Inquiry into Darfur publicly condemned military attacks against civilians as "massive violations of human rights." But after Sudan complained, the statement was removed from the Arab League Web site. [5]

And in July, when the International Criminal Court prosecutor sought to indict Sudanese President Omar Hassan al-Bashir for genocide and war crimes, the Arab League expressed "solidarity with the Republic of Sudan in confronting schemes that undermine its sovereignty, unity and stability." The group said the charges would undermine ongoing negotiations to stop the violence in Darfur, and that Sudan's legal system was the appropriate place to investigate abuses in Darfur. [6] The league turned down several

---

* The UAE and Saudi Arabia, however, did contribute a total of $44 million to Sudan as a whole — about 3 percent of the $1.3 billion contributed to Sudan by the international community.

Another Civil War

After the failed coup by Libyan-backed Arab rebels in 1976, Nimeiri tried to appease radical Islamic groups who felt he was disloyal to the dream of a united Arab front. He named leading Islamist opposition leaders to important government posts, including extremist Hassan al-Turabi as attorney general. [73]

The discovery of oil in Southern Sudan in the late 1970s added to the pressure from the increasingly Islamic government to back away from the Addis Ababa peace agreement, because the Arab authorities in the North did not want to share the profits with the Christian South, as the peace deal stipulated. In 1983, Nimeiri ordered the 11-year-old agreement null and void, began imposing strict Islamic law, or sharia, across the country and transformed Sudan into an Islamic state. [74] Southern opposition groups formed the Sudan People's Liberation Army (SPLA) and civil war broke out again.

requests to be interviewed for this article.

While Arab governments have been muted in their criticism of the situation in Darfur, the citizens of Arab countries are more outspoken. According to a poll last year, a vast majority of the public in Morocco, Egypt, Saudi Arabia, the UAE, Turkey and Malaysia think their countries should do more to help Darfur. And more than three-quarters of the Muslim respondents said Arabs and Muslims should be as concerned about the situation in Darfur as they are about the Arab-Israeli conflict.

"The poll shatters the myth that Arabs and Muslims don't care about Darfur," said James Zogby, president of the Arab American Institute, which commissioned the poll. "While they fault news coverage for not being extensive enough, Arabs and Muslims feel compelled by the images and stories they see coming out of Darfur. The poll clearly illustrates a great degree of concern among Muslims, even rivaling that of another longstanding issue to Arabs and Muslims, the Arab-Israel conflict." [7]

Last year, the institute launched an Arabic-language television advertising campaign calling for increased action to help the people of Darfur. The commercial, which featured first-hand accounts in Arabic from victims of the violence in Darfur, concluded by saying, "Palestine, Lebanon, Iraq — Darfur. We must pray for them all." [8]

Getty Images/Marco DiLauro

Darfuri refugees pray at an improvised mosque in a refugee camp in Chad. Arab governments have been largely silent about the Muslim-on-Muslim violence in Darfur and have contributed little aid to the victims.

---

[1] Quoted from "The Devil Came on Horseback" documentary film, Break Thru Films, 2007.

[2] "Arab Panel Scolds Islamic World for Darfur Silence," Agence France-Press, June 20, 2008, http://news.yahoo.com/s/afp/20080620/wl_mideast_afp/sudandarfurunrestrightsislamoic_080620190222. The coalition represents human-rights groups from Egypt, Jordan, Bahrain, Algeria, Iraq, Yemen, Syria, Libya, Mauritania, Kuwait, Saudi Arabia and the Palestinian territories.

[3] "Sudan 2008: List of all commitments/contributions and pledges as of 18 August 2008," U.N. Office for the Coordination of Humanitarian Affairs, http://ocha.unog.ch/fts/reports/daily/ocha_R10_E15391_asof__08081816.pdf.

[4] "UN Mission's Contributions by Country," United Nations, June 2008, www.un.org/Depts/dpko/dpko/contributors/2008/jun08_5.pdf.

[5] Nadim Hasbani, "About The Arab Stance Vis-à-vis Darfur," Al-Hayat, March 21, 2007, International Crisis Group, www.crisisgroup.org/home/index.cfm?id=4722.

[6] "Arab League Backs Sudan on Genocide Charges," The Associated Press, July 19, 2008, http://www.usatoday.com/news/world/2008-07-19-Sudan_N.htm.

[7] "Majorities in six countries surveyed believe Muslims should be equally concerned about Darfur as the Arab-Israeli conflict," Arab American Institute, press release, April 30, 2007, www.aaiusa.org/press-room/2949/aaizogby-poll-muslims-across-globe-concerned-about-crisis-in-darfur.

[8] "AAI Launches Darfur Ads Aimed at Arabic-Speaking International Community," Arab American Institute, press release, Jan. 8, 2007, www.aaiusa.org/press-room/2702/aai-launches-darfur-ads-aimed-at-arabic-speaking-international-community.

In 1985 civilians overthrew Nimeiri, and hopes began to emerge for a new peace settlement. But in yet another coup in 1989, Bashir seized power with the help of the National Islamic Front (NIF) and its leader, former Attorney General Turabi. [75]

Then-Gen. Bashir and the NIF embraced militant Islam and welcomed foreign jihadists, including Osama bin Laden. In 1993, the United States added Sudan to its list of state sponsors of terrorism, and President Bill Clinton imposed economic sanctions against Sudan in 1996 and 1997. In 1998, after U.S. embassies were bombed in Kenya and Tanzania, the United States bombed a Khartoum pharmaceutical factory claiming it was producing chemical weapons. The allegation was never proven. [76]

Meanwhile, Bashir and the NIF launched a bloody counterinsurgency against the South, which became one of the deadliest wars in modern history. An estimated 2 million people died before the fighting ended in 2003.

Human-rights advocates in London call on the international community to stop the violence in Darfur. The conflict erupted in 2003, when ethnic Africans in western Sudan took up arms against the central government in Khartoum, accusing it of marginalizing them and monopolizing resources.

At least one out of every five Southern Sudanese died in the fighting or from disease and famine caused by the war. Four million people — nearly 80 percent of the Southern Sudanese population — were forced to flee their homes. [77]

Throughout the war, China sold arms to Sudan, and in 1997 China — whose domestic oil-production capacity had peaked — agreed to build an oil refinery near Khartoum and a massive pipeline from southern Sudan to Port Sudan on the Red Sea in the north. [78] Bashir declared that the "era of oil production" had begun in Sudan and that the country would soon become economically self-sufficient despite the U.S. sanctions. [79]

Darfur Erupts

Darfur, meanwhile, was suffering from economic neglect, and numerous non-Arab tribes faced repression from government-supported militias. In 2000, the non-Arabs began to fight back, especially after the so-called *Black Book* circulated across the region describing how a small group of ethnic northern tribes had dominated Sudan since independence, at the expense of the rest of the country — especially Darfur.

"When we were writing the book, we were not thinking of rebellion. We wanted to achieve our aims by democratic and peaceful means," said Idris Mahmoud Logma, one of authors and a member of the rebel Justice and Equality Movement. "Later, we realized the regime would only listen to guns." [80]

But international attention remained focused on peace prospects between the North and South, overshadowing the book's impact. The first peace talks began in Nairobi, Kenya, in January 2000. At about the same time, Bashir pushed his former ally, the radical Islamist Turabi, out of power — a move away from religious extremism in the view of the international community. [81]

In 2001, President Bush dispatched former Sen. John C. Danforth, R-Mo., as a special envoy to Sudan to help bring the North and South toward a peace agreement. [82] Just days after the appointment, terrorists attacked the World Trade Center and the Pentagon, prompting Sudan to cooperate with the United States to avoid retaliatory strikes. The two countries soon began sharing intelligence on terrorists, including information about al Qaeda, bin Laden's terrorist organization. [83]

For the next 18 months, as peace negotiators debated splitting wealth and power between the North and South, they never considered sharing any of the pie with Darfur. Moreover, an international community focused on ending the civil war ignored the increasing repression in Darfur and the rebel groups preparing to fight.

In April 2003, just months before a North-South ceasefire was signed in Naivasha, Kenya, Darfuri rebels attacked the airport in El-Fashir, the capital of North Darfur, killing 30 government soldiers and blowing up aircraft. Rebels killed more than 1,000 Sudanese soldiers in the following months. [84]

"The Darfuris saw they had no shot at being part of the process," says Prendergast of the ENOUGH Project. "Leaving these guys out helped reinforce their desire to go to war. Darfur was completely ignored during the first term of the Bush administration, allowing Khartoum to conclude it could do whatever it wanted to in Darfur."

Indeed, Khartoum counterattacked, enlisting the brute force of the desperately poor Arab *janjaweed* militias the government had armed years earlier to settle internal land disputes. Over the next two years, up to 400,000 people died in the conflict by some estimates, and nearly 2.4 million people were displaced. [85] Civilian populations primarily from the Fur, Zaghawa, and Masalit ethnic groups — the same ethnicities as most of the rebel SLA/M and JEM groups — were the main targets.

Through most of the early fighting, global attention remained focused on negotiations to stop the North-South civil war, which officially ended in January 2005 when the government and the SPLA signed the Comprehensive Peace Agreement.

But by then Darfur had already spun out of control. The U.N. human rights coordinator for Sudan the previous April had described the situation in Darfur as "the world's greatest humanitarian crisis," adding "the only difference between Rwanda and Darfur is the numbers involved." [86] Human rights and religious groups had launched a media and lobbying campaign demanding that the international community act. In July 2004, the U.S. House of Representatives called the violence in Darfur "genocide."

A few days later, the U.N. passed its first resolution on Darfur, imposing an arms embargo on militias in the region and threatening sanctions against the government if it did not end the *janjaweed* violence. It also endorsed the deployment of African Union peacekeeping troops. [87] The resolution, the first of a dozen the U.N. would pass regarding Darfur over the next four years, was approved by the Security Council with 13 votes and two abstentions — from China and Pakistan. [88]

"What they've done is produce a lot of pieces of paper," says Brewer, of Human Rights Watch. "But they haven't been reinforced. Khartoum has played a very clever game. They stop aggression just long enough for the international community to look away, and then they start all over again."

Over the past four years rebel groups and Sudanese officials have agreed to a variety of ceasefires and settlements, which one or all sides eventually broke. The most recent — the Darfur Peace Agreement — was reached in May 2006, but only the government and one faction of the SLA/M signed the deal; JEM and another SLA/M faction refused to participate. [89] The SLA/M soon splintered into more than a dozen smaller groups, and fighting grew even worse. [90]

The African Union peacekeepers — under constant attack from rebels and bandits — proved ineffective. So in 2006, the U.N. voted to send international troops to bolster the AU mission. Bashir initially blocked the proposal as a "violation of Sudan's sovereignty and a submission by Sudan to outside custodianship." [91]

But after extended negotiations with China, the AU and the U.N., Bashir finally agreed. In July 2007, the Security Council unanimously voted to send up to 26,000 military and police peacekeepers as part of the joint U.N.-AU force. U.N. Secretary-General Ban heralded the unanimous vote as "historic and unprecedented" and said the mission would "make a clear and positive difference." [92]

But just three months before the peacekeepers began arriving in January 2008, hundreds of rebels in 30 armed trucks attacked a peacekeeping base in the Darfur town of Haskanita, killing at least 10 soldiers, kidnapping dozens more and seizing supplies that included heavy weapons.

"It's indicative of the complete insecurity," said Alun McDonald, a spokesman for the Oxfam aid organization in Sudan. "These groups are attacking anybody and everybody with total impunity." [93]

CURRENT SITUATION

Indicting Bashir

The summer's Olympic Games in Beijing thrust Darfur back into international headlines. Movie stars, activists and athletes have criticized China's continued cozy relationship with the Bashir government and called on the world to stop the violence. Olympic torch-carrying ceremonies in cities around the world were interrupted by protesters complaining about China's support for Sudan and its recent crackdown on dissenters in Tibet. [94]

But even bigger news in the weeks leading up to the Games was the ICC prosecutor's effort to charge Bashir with genocide and war crimes. While, the ICC is not expected to decide until later this year whether to indict and arrest Bashir, the decision could be delayed even further if the Security Council agrees with the AU and others that the indictment should be deferred. The council can defer for 12 months — and indefinitely renew the deferral — any ICC investigation or prosecution. [95]

The ICC's move was not its first against Sudanese officials. On March 31, 2005, the United Nations passed a resolution asking the ICC prosecutor to investigate allegations of crimes against humanity and war crimes in Darfur. After a 20-month investigation, the prosecutor presented his evidence to the court in February 2007 and the court agreed two months later to issue arrest warrants for Sudan's former Interior Minister Ahmad Harun and *janjaweed* leader Ali Kushayb. [96] Bashir has refused to hand over either man, and Harun has since been named head the Ministry of Humanitarian Affairs and oversees the government's activities to aid the victims of the atrocities. [97]

More Than 4.2 Million Affected by Crisis

Continued violence forced nearly 180,000 Darfuris to abandon their homes in the first five months of this year, bringing to 4.2 million the number affected by the ongoing conflict. While from 200,000 to 400,000 have been killed, nearly 2.4 million have been displaced. Many now live in U.N. camps inside Sudan — set up for so-called internally displaced persons (IDPs) — or have fled to refugee camps in neighboring Chad.

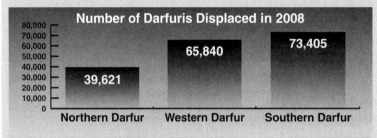

Number of Darfuris Displaced in 2008

Northern Darfur	Western Darfur	Southern Darfur
39,621	65,840	73,405

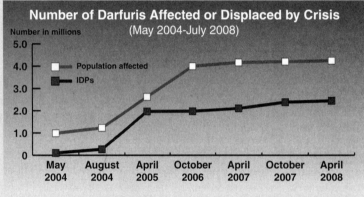

Number of Darfuris Affected or Displaced by Crisis
(May 2004-July 2008)

Number in millions

- Population affected
- IDPs

Sources: Sudan — Darfur: Humanitarian Profile, June 2, 2008, U.N. Office for the Coordination of Humanitarian Affairs; United Nations Sudan Information Gateway

This July, just days after the court's announcement about Bashir, the Sudanese president traveled to Darfur and met with 600 refugees from various tribes, including those he is accused of inflicting war crimes against. He promised to send them farming equipment and to free more than 80 rebels imprisoned last May after an attack on Khartoum's twin city Omdurman. Bashir called the prisoners "boys" and said they would be freed and pardoned — although he did not say when. [98]

Sudan also appointed its own prosecutor to investigate war crimes in Darfur and said it was sending legal teams to the region to monitor the situation. Sudan,

which is not a signatory of the treaty that created the ICC, said its legal system was adequate to look into alleged abuses in Darfur and that it would pass legislation making genocide a punishable crime in Sudan. [99]

International Betrayal

Despite Secretary-General Ban's confidence in the new UNAMID peacekeeping force, deadly assaults against the mission have occurred almost non-stop. The first UNAMID peacekeeper — a civilian police inspector from Uganda — was killed in May, just four months after the new force began arriving.

On July 9, seven peacekeepers were killed and dozens more injured when their convoy was ambushed by hundreds of horsemen and 40 trucks mounted with machine guns and anti-aircraft weapons. The two-hour firefight marked the first time UNAMID had to use force to protect itself, and some observers described it as being near the point of "meltdown." [100]

"The effort being achieved so far is not enough," said, Fadallah Ahmed Abdallah, a Sudanese city official in Darfur working with the peacekeepers. "Sometimes we feel UNAMID itself needs some protection, because UNAMID is not at full strength." [101]

More than a year after the UNAMID force was authorized, only a third of the 26,000 troops are on the ground, and not a single military transport or tactical helicopter among the 28 requested has been deployed to patrol the area — which is the size of France.

On July 31, the day UNAMID's mandate was to expire, the Security Council extended it for a year. [102] Meanwhile, 36 human rights groups — along with Nobel Peace Prize laureate Desmond Tutu and former President Carter — issued a report revealing that countries were not donating helicopters that are desperately needed by UNAMID to restore order. [103] The report said a handful of NATO countries and others that typically contribute aircraft to peacekeeping missions — specifically India, Ukraine, Czech Republic, Italy, Romania and Spain — could easily provide up to 70 helicopters for the mission. (*See graphic, p. 145.*)

"Many of these helicopters are gathering dust in hangars or flying in air shows when they could be saving lives in Darfur," said the report, entitled "Grounded: the International Community's Betrayal of UNAMID." [104]

"It's really shameful," says Brewer of Human Rights Watch. "But it's not just helicopters. They need water, trucks, everything. I don't know whether it's because countries don't have faith in UNAMID, or they don't want to put their troops as risk or if it's fear of being involved in something that will fail."

Brewer also blames the Sudanese government for delaying delivery of peacekeepers' equipment and refusing to accept troops from Western countries. Aside from peacekeepers, aid workers also are being targeted by rebel factions and bandits searching for food and supplies. Eight aid workers were killed in the first five months of 2008, and four times as many aid vehicles were hijacked during the first quarter of this year compared to the same period last year. [105] Armed gangs also attacked 35 humanitarian compounds during the first quarter — more than double the number during the same period last year. [106]

"We are now in the worst situation ever" — even worse than when the government-rebel conflict was at its peak, says Hafiz Mohamed, Sudan program coordinator with Justice Africa, a London-based research and human rights organization.

Life in the Camps

About a third of the Darfuri population has been forced to flee their homes since 2003, with many now living in refugee camps in Darfur or neighboring Chad. Conditions in the camps, like these near Nyala, are harsh. Children (bottom) attend class at a makeshift outdoor school, but about 650,000 don't attend school at all.

"At least in 2004 we only had two rebel movements. Now we have more than 12 SLA factions and more than four JEM factions. Security-wise, Darfur is worse than in 2004."

AP Photo/Nasser Nasser

An African Union (AU) peacekeeper offers bread to two women near the West Darfur town of Murnei. The women said they were raped, beaten and robbed by *janjaweed* militiamen when they left their refugee camp to gather firewood — a common occurrence in Darfur. After being criticized as ineffective, the AU force has been beefed up this year with 10,000 U.N. military and police peacekeepers. Another 16,000 have been authorized.

In May, SLA Unity rebels arrested a dozen Sudanese government employees in Darfur gathering census information for next year's national elections. The rebels, who believe the census will be inaccurate — depriving Darfur of political representation — vowed to try the census takers in military courts as "enemies," which carries the death penalty. [107]

Rebel attacks also are increasing outside Darfur. Last year JEM — which wants to overthrow the Sudanese government — attacked government positions and kidnapped two foreign workers at a Chinese-run oil field in neighboring Kordofan province. "This is a message to China and Chinese oil companies to stop helping the government with their war in Darfur," said JEM commander Abdel Aziz el-Nur Ashr. [108] JEM has said oil revenues are being used to continue the fighting in Darfur.

JEM rebels made their most audacious push against the government in May, when they reached suburban Khartoum before being repelled by Sudanese forces. Sudan immediately cut off diplomatic ties with Chad, which it accused of sponsoring the attack. Chadian officials denied any involvement but accused Sudan of launching a similar attack against their capital three months earlier. [109]

"The entire region is affected by what is happening in Darfur," says Mohamed of Justice Africa. "It's a proxy war. Unless we resolve the relationship between Chad and Sudan, we will not have an agreement for peace in Darfur."

Meanwhile, relations between North and South Sudan are worsening. Both sides remain deadlocked over some of the most contentious issues of the 2005 peace treaty, including how to draw the North-South border and how to split oil profits. The South has a large portion of the country's oil reserves while the North has most of the infrastructure. The South has repeatedly accused the North of not sharing oil revenue fairly, while the North has charged the South with mishandling their portion of the funds. [110]

Under the Comprehensive Peace Agreement (CPA), a referendum is scheduled for 2011 on whether the South will secede from the North. Some wonder if tensions between the two sides will hold until then.

"There are real prospects of another North-South war," says Sudan expert Moszynski. "South Sudan is spending 40 percent of their budget on military. They're preparing for the next war with the North. There are a lot of problems in Sudan. In between all of that, they're not going to sort out Darfur."

Mission Impossible?

While the U.N. has been slow to send in troops and materiel, individual governments and private organizations have provided billions of dollars' worth of food, water, housing, medicine and other humanitarian aid to Darfur and the nearby refugee camps in Chad.

In 2004, when the war between rebels and government forces was at its peak, only 230 relief workers were stationed in the region. [111] Today, there are more than 17,000 national and international aid workers from some 80 NGOs, 14 U.N. agencies and the Red Cross/Red Crescent Movement. [112]

"The humanitarian response has been incredible," providing "a staggering amount of money, a staggering number of people," says Brewer. However, she says she sometimes wonders if people are substituting aid for serious "political engagement to find a solution."

And most agree that only political engagement — coming from a unified global community — can solve the ongoing conflict.

"We need more coordinated diplomacy. We can't have different messages coming from France, China, the U.N., the U.S. and African nations," says Meixner of the Save Darfur Coalition. "Bashir can thwart one or two, but if there's a united front, including China and African nations, it's not so easy."

Would military intervention solve the crisis in Darfur?

YES Hafiz Mohamed
Sudan Program Coordinator
Justice Africa

Written for *CQ Researcher*, August 2008

The current crisis in Darfur has claimed more than 200,000 lives and displaced millions — due primarily to the Sudanese government's counterinsurgency policy, which uses the *janjaweed* as proxy fighters and bombs villages with government aircraft.

Despite more than 16 U.N. Security Council resolutions and authorization of a joint U.N.-African Union peacekeeping mission in Darfur (UNAMID), the mass killing and displacement of civilians continues. The parties to the conflict have signed many cease-fire agreements since 2004, but all of them have been violated, and even the mechanisms for monitoring the cease-fires have failed. Early last month, peacekeepers were attacked in Darfur, primarily because they were outmanned and outgunned. No country has provided them even with helicopters.

Hardliners within Sudan's National Congress Party still believe in a military solution to the crisis and use any means to defeat the Darfuri armed movements. All their rhetoric about being committed to a peaceful solution is just for public opinion and not a genuine endeavor to achieve a peaceful settlement to the conflict. They will only accept peace if they are pressured to do so or feel the war is unwinable.

The regime is in its weakest position since taking power in 1989 and will only cave when it feels threatened. For example, after the International Criminal Court prosecutor initiated proceedings recently to indict the Sudanese president, the government began mobilizing the public to support the president and seek a peaceful resolution.

There is strong evidence that military intervention is needed to stop the killing of civilians and force the Sudanese government to seriously seek a peaceful solution for the crisis. This could start by imposing a no-fly zone on Darfur, which would prevent the government from using its air force to bomb villages and give air support to the *janjaweed*'s attacks; the normal sequences for the attacks on the villages is to start an attack from the air by using the government bombers or helicopter machine guns, followed by attacks by militia riding horses or camels.

A no-fly zone will stop this, and many lives will be saved. The no-fly zone can start by using the European forces based in neighbouring Chad. The UNAMID forces then can be used to monitor movement on the ground and intervene when necessary to stop the ground attacks on villages.

NO Imani Countess
Senior Director for Public Affairs TransAfrica
Forum

Written for *CQ Researcher*, August 2008

For the sake of the 2 million displaced peoples and 200,000 killed, the international community should mount a military force that would protect and restore the dignity and livelihoods to those raped, tortured and maimed by the Sudanese government. But whatever peace comes to Sudan will be the result of those who brought the issue to the world stage: Darfurians supported by millions around the globe who are standing in the breach created by the failures and inaction of the nations of the world.

Truth be told, not one major military or economic power is willing to expend the political capital required to solve the crisis in Darfur.

For the United States, Darfur has become "collateral damage" in the global war on terror. The administration states that genocide is occurring, yet it continues to share intelligence with key Sudanese officials implicated in the tragedy in Darfur — sacrificing thousands of Darfuri lives in exchange for intelligence and extraditions of suspected terrorists.

Other Western nations provide plenty of rhetoric and limited sanctions. But they have failed miserably where it counts: providing adequate support for the joint African Union-U.N. peacekeeping force in Darfur. According to AfricaFocus, UNAMID is "understaffed, underequipped, underfunded and vulnerable to attacks." The U.N. authorized up to 19,555 military personnel for the mission, plus 6,432 police and more than 5,000 civilians. But so far fewer than 8,000 troops and 2,000 police have been deployed, along with just over 1,000 civilians. Critical equipment is lacking, and more than half of the $1.3 billion budget was unpaid as of the end of April.

For the international community as a whole — particularly China and India — continued access to Sudan's oil is the major interest.

If military intervention is not the answer, then what will work? Continued pressure from below. In the United States, the Bush administration was compelled to name the crisis "genocide" because of pressure from faith-based, human-rights and social-justice groups. Across the country, divestment activity — modeled after the anti-apartheid campaigns of the 1970s and '80s — has forced U.S. monies out of Sudan. The transnational human-rights movement will continue to pressure governments, businesses and multilateral institutions to move beyond rhetoric to effective human-centered engagement.

Specifically, he says, multilateral sanctions should be adopted. "Sudan is the test case for multilateralism," he says.

But others say "regime change" is the only viable solution. "I don't think we'll find a political solution for the Darfur crisis if the current government stays in power," says Mohamed of Justice Africa. "Since 1997 we've had six agreements, the CPA, the DPA. This regime will never honor any agreement. . . . If [the international community] managed to overthrow the regime, there is the possibility of a permanent solution."

But Alex de Waal, a program director at the Social Science Research Council in New York and author of *Darfur: A Short History of a Long War*, says global and Arab anger sparked by the Iraq War leaves "zero chance" that the international community will launch any military action against another Muslim country.

However, Obama foreign affairs adviser Rice — a former Clinton-era State Department official — said the U.N. should not let the experience in Iraq deter military action. "Some will reject any future U.S. military action, especially against an Islamic regime, even if purely to halt genocide against Muslim civilians," Rice told a Senate committee in April 2007. "Sudan has also threatened that al Qaeda will attack non-African forces in Darfur — a possibility, since Sudan long hosted bin Laden and his businesses. Yet, to allow another state to deter the U.S. by threatening terrorism would set a terrible precedent. It would also be cowardly and, in the face of genocide, immoral." [113]

Meanwhile, the U.N. has unsuccessfully tried to resurrect peace talks between the Bashir government and rebel groups. Talks in Libya were called off last October after rebel factions refused to participate. [114]

"The last six months have seen some very negative developments," former U.N. Special Envoy Eliasson said upon his resignation in June. If the international community's energy is not mobilized to halt the fighting, he continued, "we risk a major humanitarian disaster again. The margins of survival are so slim for the people of Darfur." [115] The U.N. could start showing its commitment, he said, by stationing his replacement full time in Sudan. Eliasson had been headquartered in Stockholm.

The new U.N. special envoy, Burkino Faso's foreign minister Djibril Bassole, is hopeful. "This will be a difficult mission," he said after his first visit to Sudan in July. "But it's not mission impossible." [116]

OUTLOOK

Bleak Future

As unstable and violent as the past four years have been for Darfur, the next three could be even more tumultuous — for the entire country.

Under Comprehensive Peace Agreement provisions, elections must be held next year — the first in 23 years. In preparation Sudan conducted its first census since 1993 earlier this year, but many doubt that either the census results — or the vote count — will be accurate. [117]

Displaced Darfuris in refugee camps don't trust the government to take an accurate headcount. Indeed, the huge numbers of displaced persons seem to make both an accurate census and democratic elections nearly impossible.

"It's hard to see how elections can take place in a fair and free way in Darfur," says Lusk of *Africa Confidential*. "Half the people are dead, and the other half are in camps."

"The [displaced] people are concerned that if they register to vote while living in the camps, . . . they will lose their land," says Brewer. "There is great lack of clarity in land law."

Some wonder if the Bashir government will back out of the elections altogether, but Sudanese officials insist the polling will be held. "Rebels said the census should not take place, but it did take place," says Mubarak of the Sudanese Embassy in London. "The elections will go ahead."

But elections will at best do little to help the people of Darfur and at worst prompt further violence from those who oppose the results, say some observers. "The elections will have no impact on Darfur — if they happen," says former U.S. Rep. Howard Wolpe, D-Mich., who directs Africa programs at the Woodrow Wilson Center. "At the end of the day, elections have no impact . . . if you haven't built a sense of cohesion or a way of moving forward."

After the elections, the Sudanese people must brace themselves for another potential upheaval — caused by a planned 2011 referendum on Sudanese unity. While the South appears ready to vote for secession, many say Khartoum will never let that happen.

Others say secession could spell dark times for Darfur. "If the South secedes, [Bashir's National

Congress Party] will have greater power in the North, and that is worse for Darfur," says Brewer. "If they vote for power sharing, it could be good for Darfur."

Meanwhile, all eyes are waiting to see whether the ICC will give in to pressure to defer action on Bashir's indictment and how Bashir and the rebel groups will respond to either an indictment or a delay.

The November U.S. presidential election could also bring about some changes. Both McCain and Obama have said they will pursue peace and security for Darfur with "unstinting resolve." And Obama's running mate, Foreign Relations Committee Chairman Biden, was unequivocal last year when he advocated U.S. military intervention. "I would use American force now," Biden said during hearings before his panel in April 2007. "It's time to put force on the table and use it." Biden, who had also pushed for NATO intervention to halt anti-Muslim genocide in Bosnia in the 1990s, said 2,500 U.S. troops could "radically change" the situation on the ground in Darfur. "Let's stop the bleeding. I think it's a moral imperative." [118]

Given the uncertainties of the Sudanese elections, the growing North-South acrimony, the continued fighting between Chad and Sudan and the upcoming ICC decision, most experts say it is nearly impossible to predict what will happen in Darfur in the future.

"Even five years is too far to predict what will happen," says author Prunier. "You have to take it in steps. First look at what happens in 2009, then what happens leading up to the referendum, then what happens after that."

Most agree, however, that whatever future lies ahead for Darfur, it will likely be bleak.

"Sudanese politics is like the British weather: unpredictable from day to day but with a drearily consistent medium-term outlook," de Waal of the Social Science Research Council wrote recently. "There are few happy endings in Sudan. It's a country of constant turbulence, in which I have come to expect only slow and modest improvement. Sometimes I dream of being wrong." [119]

NOTES

1. "They Shot at Us as We Fled: Government Attacks on Civilians in West Darfur," Human Rights Watch, May 2008, p. 18, www.hrw.org/reports/2008/darfur0508/.

2. *Ibid.*, p. 19.

3. *Ibid.*, p. 2.

4. "Darfur Crisis: Death Estimates Demonstrate Severity of Crisis, but Their Accuracy and Credibility Could Be Enhanced," Government Accountability Office, November 2006, pp. 1-2, 7. The U.S. State Department puts the death toll for the period 2003-2005 at between 98,000 and 181,000.

5. "Sudan — Darfur: Humanitarian Profile," United Nations Office for the Coordination of Humanitarian Affairs, June 2, 2008, www.unsudanig.org/library/mapcatalogue/darfur/data/dhnp/Map%201226%20Darfur%20Humanitarian%20Profile%20June%203%202008.pdf.

6. *Ibid.*

7. Sarah El Deeb, "UN warns of bad year in Darfur," The Associated Press, June 22, 2008, www.newsvine.com/_news/2008/06/16/1581306-un-warns-of-bad-year-in-darfur.

8. "Darfur faces potential food crisis unless action taken now, warn UN agencies," UN News Centre, United Nations, June 23, 2008, www.un.org/apps/news/story.asp?NewsID=27114&Cr=darfur&Cr1=.

9. "Darfur 2007: Chaos by Design," Human Rights Watch, September 2007, p. 20.

10. El Deeb, *op. cit.*

11. "Darfur faces potential food crisis," *op. cit.*

12. "Almost Half of All Darfur Children Not in School, Says NGO," BBC Monitoring International Reports, Feb. 29, 2008.

13. Stephanie McCrummen, "A Wide-Open Battle For Power in Darfur," *The Washington Post*, June 20, 2008, p. A1, www.washingtonpost.com/wp-dyn/content/article/2008/06/19/AR2008061903552_pf.html.

14. Quoted from "The Devil Came on Horseback" documentary, Break Thru Films, 2007.

15. Julie Flint and Alex de Waal, *Darfur: A Short History of a Long War* (2005), p. 10.

16. Colum Lynch and Nora Boustany, "Sudan Leader To Be Charged With Genocide," *The Washington Post*, July 11, 2008, p. A1, www.washingtonpost.com/wp-dyn/content/article/2008/07/10/AR2008

071003109.html. Also see Kenneth Jost, "International Law," *CQ Researcher*, Dec. 17, 2004, pp. 1049-1072.

17. Quoted in Hussein Solomon, "ICC pressure shows some result; An arrest warrant for Sudan's President Al-Bashir has resulted in a flurry of activity for change in Darfur," *The Star* (South Africa), Aug. 21, 2008, p. 14.

18. "Court Seeks Arrest of Sudan's Beshir for 'genocide,'" Agence France-Presse, July 14, 2008.

19. For background, see Sarah Glazer, "Stopping Genocide," *CQ Researcher*, Aug. 27, 2004, pp. 685-708.

20. For background, see Karen Foerstel, "China in Africa," *CQ Global Researcher*, January 2008, pp. 1-26.

21. Alexa Olesen, "China Appoints Special Envoy for Darfur," The Associated Press, May 11, 2007; "China paper decries Sudan's Bashir arrest move," Reuters, July 17, 2008; "China boosts peacekeepers in Darfur," Agence France-Presse, July 17, 2008, http://afp.google.com/article/ALeqM5jxVo9_9z2jJ m2wxZW65dyP8CflEw.

22. Neil MacFarquhar, "Why Darfur Still Bleeds," *The New York Times*, July 13, 2008, www.nytimes.com /2008/07/13/weekinreview/13macfarquhar.html.

23. "Darfur's Political Process in 'Troubled State of Affairs,'" U.N. Security Council press release, June 24, 2008, www.un.org/News/Press/docs/2008/sc 9370.doc.htm.

24. Glazer, *op. cit.*, p. 687.

25. Neela Banerjee, "Muslims' Plight in Sudan Resonates with Jews in U.S.," *The New York Times*, April 30, 2006, www.nytimes.com/2006/04/30/ us/30rally.html.

26. Alan Cooperman, "Evangelicals Urge Bush to Do More for Sudan," *The Washington Post*, Aug. 3, 2004, p. A13, www.washingtonpost.com/wp-dyn/articles/A35223-2004Aug2.html.

27. Glenn Kessler and Colum Lynch, "U.S. Calls Killings in Sudan Genocide," *The Washington Post*, Sept. 10, 2004, p. A1, www.washingtonpost.com /wp-dyn/articles/A8364-2004Sep9.html.

28. "The Crisis in Darfur: Secretary Colin L. Powell, Written Remarks Before the Senate Foreign Relations Committee," Secretary of State press release, Sept. 9, 2004.

29. "Security Council Declares Intention to Consider Sanctions to Obtain Sudan's Full Compliance With Security, Disarmament Obligations in Darfur," U.N. Security Council press release, Sept. 18, 2004, www.un.org/News/Press/docs/2004/sc8191.doc.htm.

30. Opheera McDoom, "Statesmen Say Darfur Violent and Divided," Reuters, Oct. 4, 2007, http://africa .reuters.com/wire/news/usnMCD351991.html.

31. "UN Report: Darfur Not Genocide," CNN.com, Feb. 1, 2005, http://edition.cnn.com/2005/WORLD /africa/01/31/sudan.report/. See also Marc Lacey, "In Darfur, Appalling Atrocity, but Is That Genocide?" *The New York Times*, July 23, 2004, p. 3, http://query.nytimes.com/gst/fullpage.html?res=9B0 4E0DC163DF930A15754C0A9629C8B63.

32. Hillary Rodham Clinton, John McCain and Barack Obama, "Presidential Candidates' Statement on Darfur," May 28, 2008, www.cfr.org/publica tion/16359/presidential_candidates_statement_on_dar fur.html?breadcrumb=%2Fregion%2F197%2Fsudan.

33. George Gedda, "Biden Calls for Military Force in Darfur," The Associated Press, April 11, 2007.

34. Susan E. Rice, "The Escalating Crisis in Darfur," testimony before the U.S. House Committee on Foreign Affairs, Feb. 8, 2007, www.brookings.edu/testi mony/2007/0208africa_rice.aspx.

35. Opheera McDoom, "Analysis — Darfur Scares European Investors Off Sudan's Oil," Reuters, Aug. 3, 2007. One barrel of oil produces 42 gallons of gasoline. Also see Energy Information Administration database, at http://tonto.eia.doe.gov/dnav /pet/pet_cons_psup_dc_nus_mbblpd_a.htm.

36. "US Sanctions on Sudan," U.S. Department of State fact sheet, April 23, 2008, www.state.gov/p/af/rls/fs /2008/103970.htm. Also see "Country Reports on Terrorism," U.S. Department of State, April 30, 2007, Chapter 3, www.state.gov/s/ct/rls/crt/2006 /82736.htm.

37. "Situation in Darfur, The Sudan: Summary of the Case," International Criminal Court, July 14, 2008, www.icc-cpi.int/library/organs/otp/ICC-OTP-Summary-20081704-ENG.pdf.

38. Colum Lynch and Nora Boustany, "Sudan Leader To Be Charged With Genocide," *The Washington*

Post, July 10, 2008.

39. *Ibid.*

40. Stephanie McCrummen and Nora Boustany, "Sudan Vows to Fight Charges of Genocide Against Its Leader," *The Washington Post*, July 14, 2008, www.washingtonpost.com/wp-dyn/content/article /2008/07/14/AR2008071400112_pf.html.

41. Mohamed Osman, "Sudan Rejects Genocide Charges Against President," The Associated Press, July 14, 2008.

42. Anita Powell, "AU to Seek Delay in al-Bashir Indictment," The Associated Press, July 21, 2008.

43. Opheera McDoom, "Darfur Rebels Condemn AU on ICC Warrant," Reuters, July 22, www.alertnet .org/thenews/newsdesk/L22832812.htm.

44. Andrew Natsios, "A Disaster in the Making," The Social Science Research Council, Making Sense of Darfur blog, July 12, 2008, www.ssrc.org/blogs/dar fur/2008/07/12/a-disaster-in-the-making/.

45. "Media Stakeout with Ambassador Zalmay Khalilzad," Federal News Service, July 22, 2008.

46. Foerstel, *op. cit.*, pp. 7, 13. Also see "Sudan," *Political Handbook of the World*, CQ Press (2008).

47. Danna Harman, "Activists Press China With 'Genocide Olympics' Label," *The Christian Science Monitor*, June 26, 2007, www.csmonitor.com/2007 /0626/p13s01-woaf.html.

48. "Letter to Chinese President Hu Jintao," Rep. Steven Rothman Web site, May 7, 2007, http://for eignaffairs.house.gov/press_display.asp?id=345.

49. Alexa Olesen, "China Appoints Special Envoy for Darfur," The Associated Press, May 11, 2007.

50. See Jason Qian and Anne Wu, "Playing the Blame Game in Africa," *The Boston Globe*, July 23, 2007, www.iht.com/articles/2007/07/23/opinion/edqian. php; "China boosts peacekeepers in Darfur," *op. cit.*

51. "China envoy: more humanitarian aid to Darfur," Xinhua, Feb. 26, 2008, www.chinadaily.com.cn /china/2008-02/26/content_6483392.htm.

52. Robert J. Saiget, "China says can do no more over Darfur," Agence France-Presse, June 26, 2008, http://afp.google.com/article/ALeqM5gD2S4zFfzj6 CZfnluWi5Kq4eFrgw.

53. Danna Harman, "How China's Support of Sudan

Shields A Regime Called 'Genocidal,' " *The Christian Science Monitor*, June 26, 2007, www.csmonitor .com/2007/0626/p01s08-woaf.html.

54. Security Council Resolution 1591, United Nations, March 29, 2005, www.un.org/Docs/sc/unsc_resolu tions05.htm.

55. "China says BBC's accusation on arms sales to Sudan 'ungrounded,' " Xinhua, July 18, 2008, http://news.xinhuanet.com/english/2008-07/18 /content_8570601.htm.

56. Saiget, *op. cit.*

57. Audra Ang, "China urges court to rethink Sudan arrest warrant," The Associated Press, July 15, 2008.

58. Harman, *op. cit.*

59. Lydia Polgreen, "China, in New Role, Presses Sudan on Darfur," *International Herald Tribune*, Feb. 23, 2008, www.iht.com/articles/2008/02/23/africa/23dar fur.php.

60. M. W. Daly, *Darfur's Sorrows* (2007), p. 1.

61. "Crisis Shaped by Darfur's Tumultuous Past," PBS Newshour, April 7, 2006, www.pbs.org/news hour/indepth_coverage/africa/darfur/political-past .html.

62. Gerard Prunier, *Darfur: The Ambiguous Genocide* (2007), pp. 4-5.

63. Daly, *op. cit.*, p. 19.

64. Prunier, *op. cit.*, p. 10. Also see Flint and de Waal, *op. cit.*, p. 8.

65. Prunier, *op. cit.*, p. 16.

66. *Ibid.*, pp. 18-19.

67. *Ibid.*, p. 30.

68. *Ibid.*

69. Don Cheadle and John Prendergast, *Not On Our Watch* (2007), p. 53.

70. Prunier, *op. cit.*, pp. 45-46.

71. *Ibid.*

72. Cheadle and Prendergast, *op. cit.*, p. 73.

73. *Ibid.*, p. 55.

74. *Ibid.*, p. 56.

75. *Ibid.*, p. 57.

76. Polgreen, *op. cit.*

77. "Sudan: Nearly 2 million dead as a result of the world's longest running civil war," The U.S. Committee for Refugees, April 2001.

78. "Sudan, Oil and Human Rights," Human Rights Watch, September 2003, www.hrw.org/reports /2003/sudan1103/index.htm; "Sudan's President Projects the Export of Oil," *Africa News*, July 13, 1998.

79. "President's Revolution Day Address," BBC Worldwide Monitoring, July 5, 1998.

80. "Crisis Shaped by Darfur's Tumultuous Past," *op. cit.*

81. Prunier, *op. cit.*, p. 88.

82. "President Appoints Danforth as Special Envoy to the Sudan," White House press release, Sept. 6, 2001, www.whitehouse.gov/news/releases/2001/09/200109 06-3.html.

83. Polgreen, *op. cit.*

84. Prunier, *op. cit.*, pp. 95-96.

85. "Darfur Crisis," *op. cit.*, p. 1. Also see Sheryl Gay Stolberg, "Bush Tightens Penalties Against Sudan," *The New York Times*, May 29, 2007, www.nytimes .com/2007/05/29/world/africa/29cnd-darfur.html.

86. Gerard Prunier, "The Politics of Death in Darfur," *Current History*, May 2006, p. 196.

87. Security Council Resolution 1556, United Nations, July 30, 2004, www.un.org/Docs/sc/unsc_resolu tions04.html.

88. "Security Council Demands Sudan Disarm Militias in Darfur," U.N. press release, July 30, 2004, www .un.org/News/Press/docs/2004/sc8160.doc.htm.

89. "Background Notes: Sudan," U.S. State Department press release, April 24, 2008, www.state.gov/r/pa /ei/bgn/5424.htm.

90. Scott Baldauf, "Darfur Talks Stall After Rebels Boycott," *The Christian Science Monitor*, Oct. 29, 2007, www.csmonitor.com/2007/1029/p06s01-woaf.html.

91. Lydia Polgreen, "Rebel Ambush in Darfur Kills 5 African Union Peacekeepers in Deadliest Attack on the Force," *The New York Times*, April 3, 2007.

92. "Secretary-General Urges All Parties to Remain Engaged, As Security Council Authorizes Deployment of United Nations-African Union Mission in Sudan," U.N. Security Council press release, July 31, 2007, www.un.org/News/Press/docs /2007/sgsm11110.doc.htm.

93. Jeffrey Gettleman, "Darfur Rebels Kill 10 in Peace Force," *The New York Times*, Oct. 1, 2005, www .nytimes.com/2007/10/01/world/africa/01darfur.html.

94. For background, see Brian Beary, "Separatism Movements," *CQ Global Researcher*, April 2008.

95. "Arab League Backs Recourse to UN on Sudan War Crimes," Agence France-Presse, July 21, 2008.

96. "The Situation in Darfur, the Sudan," International Criminal Court fact sheet, www.icc-cpi.int/library /organs/otp/ICC-OTP_Fact-Sheet-Darfur-200702 27_en.pdf.

97. "Arrest Now!" Amnesty International fact sheet, July 17, 2007, http://archive.amnesty.org/library/Index /ENGAFR540272007?open&of=ENG-332.

98. Sarah El Deeb, "Sudan's President Pays Visit to Darfur," The Associated Press, July 24, 2008.

99. Abdelmoniem Abu Edries Ali, "Sudan Appoints Darfur Prosecutor," Agence France-Presse, Aug. 6, 2008.

100. Stephanie McCrummen, "7 Troops Killed in Sudan Ambush," *The Washington Post*, July 10, 2008, www.washingtonpost.com/wp-dyn/con-tent/article/2008/07/09/AR2008070900843.html.

101. Jennie Matthew, "Darfur hopes dim six months into UN peacekeeping," Agence France-Presse, June 25, 2008.

102. "Security Council extends mandate of UN-AU force in Darfur," Agence France-Presse, July 31, 2008.

103. "Aid groups urge helicopters for Darfur," Agence France-Presse, July 31, 2008, http://afp.google .com/article/ALeqM5i2aYTRiEePGRmbRqVQb ByF28X_RQ.

104. "Grounded: the International Community's Betrayal of UNAMID — A Joint NGO Report," p. 4, http://darfur.3cdn.net/b5b2056f1398299ffe _x9m6bt7cu.pdf.

105. "Sudan — Darfur: Humanitarian Profile," *op. cit.*

106. "Darfur Humanitarian Profile No. 31," Office of U.N. Deputy Special Representative of the U.N.

Secretary-General for Sudan, April 1, 2008, p. 4, www.unsudanig.org/docs/DHP%2031_1%20Apr il%202008_narrative.pdf.

107. Opheera McDoom, "Darfur rebels say they arrest 13 census staff," Reuters, May 4, 2008, www .reuters.com/article/homepageCrisis/idUSL04471 626._CH_.2400.

108. "Darfur rebels say they kidnap foreign oil workers," Reuters, Oct. 24, 2007, www.alertnet.org/the news/newsdesk/MCD470571.htm.

109. Shashank Bengali, "Darfur conflict stokes Chad-Sudan tensions," McClatchy-Tribune News Service, June 14, 2008, www.mcclatchydc.com /160/story/40518.html.

110. Jeffrey Gettleman, "Cracks in the Peace in Oil-Rich Sudan As Old Tensions Fester," *The New York Times*, Sept. 22, 2007, www.nytimes.com /2007/09/22/world/africa/22sudan.html?fta=y.

111. "Sudan — Darfur: Humanitarian Profile," *op. cit.*

112. "Darfur Humanitarian Profile No. 31," *op. cit.*, p. 6.

113. Susan E. Rice, Testimony before Senate Foreign Relations Committee, April 11, 2007.

114. "Darfur envoys end visit without date for peace talks," Agence France-Presse, April 19, 2008.

115. Steve Bloomfield, "Negotiators quit Darfur, saying neither side is ready for peace," *The Independent* (London), June 27, 2008, www.independent.co .uk/news/world/africa/negotiators-quit-darfur-say-ing-neither-side-is-ready-for-peace-855431.html.

116. "Darfur mediator arrives for a 'difficult mission,'" *The International Herald Tribune*, July 21, 2008.

117. Opheera McDoom, "Counting begins in disputed Sudan census," Reuters, April 22, 2008, www .reuters.com/article/homepageCrisis/idUSMCD2 46493._CH_.2400.

118. Presidential Candidates' Statement on Darfur, *op. cit.*, Gedda, *op. cit.*

119. Alex de Waal, "In which a writer's work — forged in the heat of chaos — could actually save lives," *The Washington Post*, June 22, 2008, p. BW 11, www.washingtonpost.com/wp-dyn/content/article /2008/06/19/AR2008061903304_pf.html.

BIBLIOGRAPHY

Books

Cheadle, Don, and John Prendergast, *Not On Our Watch*, **Hyperion, 2007.**
Cheadle, who starred in the African genocide movie "Hotel Rwanda," and human-rights activist Prendergast explore the Darfur crisis, with tips on how to impact international policy. Forward by Holocaust survivor and Nobel Peace Prize-winner Elie Wiesel, and introduction by Sens. Barack Obama, D-Ill., and Sam Brownback, R-Kan.

Daly, M. W., *Darfur's Sorrow*, **Cambridge University Press, 2007.**
An historian and long-time observer of Sudan traces the complex environmental, cultural and geopolitical factors that have contributed to today's ongoing conflict. Includes a timeline of events in Darfur since 1650.

Flint, Julie, and Alex de Waal, *Darfur: A Short History Of a Long War*, **Zed Books, 2005.**
Two longtime observers of Sudan and Darfur explore the genesis of today's bloodshed and describe the various actors in the conflict, including the region's many ethnic tribes, the *janjaweed* militia, Libyan leader Muammar Qaddafi and the current Sudanese government.

Prunier, Gerard, *Darfur: The Ambiguous Genocide*, **Cornell University Press, 2007.**
A French historian who has authored several books on African genocide provides a comprehensive account of the complex environmental, social and political roots of the ongoing fighting in Darfur.

Articles

"Timeline: Conflict in Darfur," *The Washington Post*, **June 19, 2008, www.washingtonpost.com/wp-dyn/con tent/article/2008/06/19/AR2008061902905.html.**
This brief narrative outlines the fighting in Darfur and various efforts to find peace over the past five years.

Faris, Stephan, "The Real Roots of Darfur," *The Atlantic Monthly*, **April 2007, p. 67.**
Climate change and shrinking water supplies have motivated much of the fighting between Darfur's nomadic Arabs and ethnic African farmers.

Macfarquhar, Neil, "Why Darfur Still Bleeds," *The New York Times*, July 13, 2008, p. 5.
A veteran foreign correspondent discusses the many factors fueling the fighting in Darfur and how international leaders now recommend a comprehensive solution.

McCrummen, Stephanie, "A Wide-Open Battle for Power in Darfur," *The Washington Post*, June 20, 2008, p. A1.
The rebellion in Darfur has devolved into chaos and lawlessness that threatens civilians, aid workers and peacekeepers.

Natsios, Andrew, "Sudan's Slide Toward Civil War," *Foreign Affairs*, May/June 2008, Vol. 87, Issue 3, pp. 77-93.
The former U.S. special envoy to Sudan says that while attention is focused on Darfur another bloody civil war could soon erupt between Sudan's north and south.

Prunier, Gerard, "The Politics of Death in Darfur," *Current History*, May 2006, pp. 195-202.
The French historian discusses why the international community has been unable to solve the crisis in Darfur.

Reports and Studies

"Darfur 2007: Chaos by Design," Human Rights Watch, September 2007, http://hrw.org/reports/2007/sudan0907/.
Through photographs, maps, first-hand accounts and statistics, the human-rights group summarizes the events that led to the conflict and describes Darfuris' daily struggles.

"Darfur Crisis," Government Accountability Office, November 2006, www.gao.gov/new.items/d0724.pdf.
The report analyzes the widely varying estimates on the number of deaths caused by the Darfur conflict and reviews the different methodologies used to track the casualties.

"Displaced in Darfur: A Generation of Anger," Amnesty International, January 2008, www.amnesty.org/en/library/info/AFR54/001/2008.
Using interviews and first-hand accounts, the human-rights group vividly describes the death and destruction in Darfur and recommends ways to end the fighting.

"Sudan — Darfur: Humanitarian Profile," United Nations Office for the Coordination of Humanitarian Affairs, June 2, 2008, www.unsudanig.org/.../darfur/data/dhnp/Map%201226%20Darfur%20Humanitarian%20Profile%20June%203%202008.pdf.
This frequently updated U.N. Web site provides maps and charts illustrating areas hit worst by the crisis, the number of attacks on humanitarian workers and the number of people affected by the fighting.

"They Shot at Us As We Fled," Human Rights Watch, May 2008, www.hrw.org/reports/2008/darfur0508/.
Using first-hand accounts from victims, the report describes how attacks against Darfuri villages in February 2008 violated international humanitarian law.

For More Information

Aegis Trust, The Holocaust Centre, Laxton, Newark, Nottinghamshire NG22 9ZG, UK; +44 (0)1623 836627; www.aegistrust.org. Campaigns against genocide around the world and provides humanitarian aid to genocide victims.

African Union, P.O. Box 3243, Roosevelt St., W21K19, Addis Ababa, Ethiopia; +251 11 551 77 00; www.africa-union.org. Fosters economic and social cooperation among 53 African nations and other governments.

Amnesty International, 1 Easton St., London, WC1X 0DW, United Kingdom, +44-20-74135500; www.amnesty.org. Promotes human rights worldwide, with offices in 80 countries.

Council on Foreign Relations, 1779 Massachusetts Ave., N.W., Washington, DC 20036; (202) 509-8400; www.cfr.org. A nonpartisan think tank that offers extensive resources, data and experts on foreign policy issues.

Human Rights Watch, 350 Fifth Ave., 34th Floor, New York, NY 10118-3299; (212) 290-4700; www.hrw.org. Investigates human-rights violations worldwide.

Justice Africa, 1C Leroy House, 436 Essex Road, London N1 3QP, United Kingdom; +44 (0) 207 354 8400; www.justiceafrica.org. A research and advocacy organization that campaigns for human rights and social justice in Africa.

Save Darfur Coalition, Suite 335, 2120 L St., N.W., Washington, DC 20037; (800) 917-2034; www.savedarfur.org. An alliance of more than 180 faith-based, advocacy and humanitarian organizations working to stop the violence in Darfur.

Social Science Research Council, 810 Seventh Ave., New York, NY 10019; (212) 377-2700; www.ssrc.org. Studies complex social, cultural, economic and political issues.

TransAfrica Forum, 1629 K St., N.W., Suite 1100, Washington, DC 20006; (202) 223-1960; www.transafricaforum.org. Campaigns for human rights and sustainable development in Africa and other countries with residents of African descent.

VOICES FROM ABROAD

Louise Arbour

U.N. High Commissioner for Human Rights

History will judge

"The desperate plight of the people of Darfur has for too long been neglected or addressed with what the victims should rightly regard — and history will judge — as meek offerings, broken promises and disregard."

Voice of America News, December 2006

Liu Jianchao

Foreign Ministry Spokesman, China

Constructive dialogue is necessary

"On this issue, putting up banners and chanting slogans alone can not help resolve the humanitarian issue in Darfur. What is most important is to promote the peace process in Darfur with realistic, constructive and practical action. . . . We also hope relevant people will objectively view China's position on the Darfur issue, and do some concrete things for the people of Darfur in a down-to-earth manner."

Xinhua news agency (China), February 2008

Omar Hassan al-Bashir

President, Sudan

ICC will not hold us back

"Every time we take a step forward, make progress and signs of peace emerge, those people [International Criminal Court] try to mess it up, return us to square one and distract us with marginal issues and false allegations. . . . Ocampo's talk will not bother us or distract us from our work."

The Associated Press, July 2008

Paul Rusesabagina

Celebrated former hotel manager, Rwanda

Too much concern over sovereignty

"When modern genocide has loomed, the United Nations has shown more concern for not offending the sovereignty of one of its member nations, even as monstrosities take place within its borders. Yet 'national sovereignty' is often a euphemism for the pride of dictators. Darfur is just such a case. The world cannot afford this kind of appeasement any longer."

The Wall Street Journal, April 2006

David Mozersky

Horn of Africa Project Director, International Crisis Group

Broader talks needed on Darfur

"The only way to make progress is to give enough time for ongoing rebel unification efforts to succeed and to broaden talks to involve the full range of actors in the conflict. They must seek to identify individuals to represent the interests of these groups at the peace talks, giving specific attention to the representation of women, civil society, the internally displaced and Arabs."

allAfrica.com, December 2007

Kofi Annan

Then Secretary-General, United Nations

'Never again' rings hollow

"To judge by what is happening in Darfur, our performance has not improved much since the disasters of Bosnia and Rwanda. Sixty years after the liberation of the Nazi death camps and 30 years after the Cambodian killing fields, the promise of 'never again' is ringing hollow."

Speech before Human Rights Watch in New York, December 2006

Mustafa Uthman Isma'il

Presidential adviser, Sudan

Death tolls in Darfur are exaggerated

"The United Nations reports indicate that some 200,000 people have been killed in Darfur. However, we, in Sudan, believe that these reports are questionable. They have been prepared by Western organizations that want no good for Darfur. Anyone who follows up on the Western media finds that the situation in Darfur has been clearly exaggerated, as if the developments in Darfur were more serious than what happens in Iraq. More than one million people have been killed in Iraq."

Elaph (England), May 2008

James Smith

Chief Executive Officer, Aegis Trust

More than a civil war

"Painting the crisis in Darfur as merely a civil war encourages further delays — which could cause the loss of thousands of lives. The motives of the perpetrators in Darfur go well beyond territorial conflict. As put by one *janjaweed*: 'We have a dream. We want to kill the Africans.' "

The Guardian (England), September 2006

MOST OF THEM ARE DEAD OR GONE. SO YOU CAN COME IN.

UN

SUDAN DARFUR REGION

HACHFELD

Neues Deutschland/Germany/Rainer Hachfeld

7

Women's Rights

Karen Foerstel

Iraqi teenager Du'a Khalil Aswad lies mortally wounded after her "honor killing" by a mob in the Kurdish region of Iraq. No one has been prosecuted for the April 2007 murder, even though a cell-phone video of the incident was posted on the Internet. Aswad's male relatives are believed to have arranged her ritualistic execution because she had dated a boy from outside her religious sect. The United Nations estimates that 5,000 women and girls are murdered in honor killings around the globe each year.

From *CQ Researcher,*
May 1, 2008.

S he was 17 years old. The blurry video shows her lying in a dusty road, blood streaming down her face, as several men kick and throw rocks at her. At one point she struggles to sit up, but a man kicks her in the face forcing her back to the ground. Another slams a large, concrete block down onto her head. Scores of onlookers cheer as the blood streams from her battered head. [1]

The April 7, 2007, video was taken in the Kurdish area of northern Iraq on a mobile phone. It shows what appear to be several uniformed police officers standing on the edge of the crowd, watching while others film the violent assault on their phones.

The brutal, public murder of Du'a Khalil Aswad reportedly was organized as an "honor killing" by members of her family — and her uncles and a brother allegedly were among those in the mob who beat her to death. Her crime? She offended her community by falling in love with a man outside her religious sect. [2]

According to the United Nations, an estimated 5,000 women and girls are murdered in honor killings each year, but it was only when the video of Aswad's murder was posted on the Internet that the global media took notice. [3]

Such killings don't only happen in remote villages in developing countries. Police in the United Kingdom estimate that up to 17,000 women are subjected to some kind of "honor"-related violence each year, ranging from forced marriages and physical attacks to murder. [4]

But honor killings are only one type of what the international community calls "gender based violence" (GBV). "It is universal," says Taina Bien-Aimé, executive director of the New York-based women's-rights group Equality Now. "There is not one country in the world where violence against women doesn't exist."

Only Four Countries Offer Total Equality for Women

Costa Rica, Cuba, Sweden and Norway receive the highest score (9 points) in an annual survey of women's economic, political and social rights. Out of the world's 193 countries, only 26 score 7 points or better, while 28 — predominantly Islamic or Pacific Island countries — score 3 or less. The United States rates 7 points: a perfect 3 on economic rights but only 2 each for political and social rights. To receive 3 points for political rights, women must hold at least 30 percent of the seats in the national legislature. Women hold only 16.6 percent of the seats in the U.S. Congress. The U.S. score of 2 on social rights reflects what the report's authors call "high societal discrimination against women's reproductive rights."

Status of Women's Rights Around the Globe

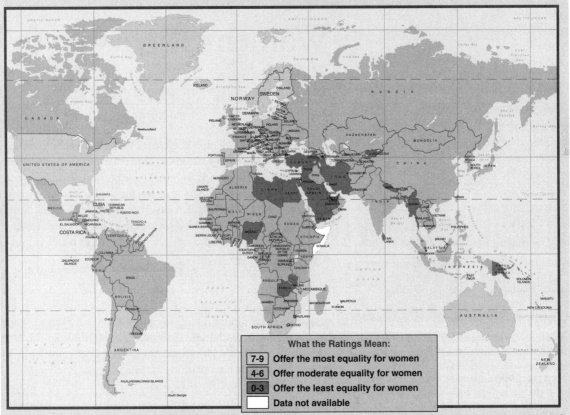

What the Ratings Mean:

7-9	Offer the most equality for women
4-6	Offer moderate equality for women
0-3	Offer the least equality for women
	Data not available

Source: Cingranelli-Richards Human Rights Dataset, http://ciri.binghamton.edu/, based on Amnesty International's annual reports and U.S. State Department annual Country Reports on Human Rights. The database is co-directed by David Louis Cingranelli, a political science professor at Binghamton University, SUNY, and David L. Richards, an assistant political science professor at the University of Memphis.

Thousands of women are murdered or attacked around the world each day, frequently with impunity. In Guatemala, where an estimated 3,000 women have been killed over the past seven years, most involving some kind of misogynistic violence, only 1 percent of the perpetrators were convicted. [5] In India, the United Nations estimates that five women are burned to death each day by husbands upset that they did not receive sufficient dowries from their brides. [6] In Asia, nearly 163 million females are "missing" from the population — the result of sex-selective abortions, infanticide or neglect.

And since the 1990s some African countries have seen dramatic upsurges in rapes of very young girls by men who believe having sex with a virgin will protect or cure them from HIV-AIDS. After a 70-year-old man allegedly raped a 3-year-old girl in northern Nigeria's commercial hub city of Kano, Deputy Police Chief Suleiman Abba told reporters in January, "Child rape is becoming rampant in Kano." In the last six months of 2007, he said, 54 cases of child rape had been reported. "In some cases the victims are gang-raped." [7]

Epidemics of sexual violence commonly break out in countries torn apart by war, when perpetrators appear to have no fear of prosecution. Today, in Africa, for instance, UNICEF says there is now a "license to rape" in eastern regions of the Democratic Republic of the Congo, where some human-rights experts estimate that up to a quarter of a million women have been raped and often sexually mutilated with knives, branches or machetes. [8] Several of the Congolese rapists remorselessly bragged to an American filmmaker recently about how many women they had gang-raped. [9]

"The sexual violence in Congo is the worst in the world," said John Holmes, the United Nations under secretary general for humanitarian affairs. "The sheer numbers, the wholesale brutality, the culture of impunity — it's appalling." [10]

In some cultures, the female victims themselves are punished. A report by the Human Rights Commission of Pakistan found that a woman is gang-raped every eight hours in that country. Yet, until recently, rape cases could not be prosecuted in Pakistan unless four Muslim men "all of a pious and trustworthy nature" were willing to testify that they witnessed the attack. Without their testimony the victim could be prosecuted for fornication

Women's Suffering Is Widespread

More than two decades after the U.N. Decade for Women and 29 years after the U.N. adopted the Convention on the Elimination of All Forms of Discrimination against Women (CEDAW), gender discrimination remains pervasive throughout the world, with widespread negative consequences for society.

According to recent studies on the status of women today:

- Violence against women is pervasive. It impoverishes women, their families, communities and nations by lowering economic productivity and draining resources. It also harms families across generations and reinforces other violence in societies.
- Domestic violence is the most common form of violence against women, with rates ranging from 8 percent in Albania to 49 percent in Ethiopia and Zambia. Domestic violence and rape account for 5 percent of the disease burden for women ages 15 to 44 in developing countries and 19 percent in developed countries.
- Femicide — the murder of women — often involves sexual violence. From 40 to 70 percent of women murdered in Australia, Canada, Israel, South Africa and the United States are killed by husbands or boyfriends. Hundreds of women were abducted, raped and murdered in and around Juárez, Mexico, over the past 15 years, but the crimes have never been solved.
- At least 160 million females, mostly in India and China, are "missing" from the population — the result of sex-selective abortions.
- Rape is being used as a genocidal tool. Hundreds of thousands of women have been raped and sexually mutilated in the ongoing conflict in Eastern Congo. An estimated 250,000 to 500,000 women were raped during the 1994 genocide in Rwanda; up to 50,000 women were raped during the Bosnian conflict in the 1990s. Victims are often left unable to have children and are deserted by their husbands and shunned by their families, plunging the women and their children into poverty.
- Some 130 million girls have been genitally mutilated, mostly in Africa and Yemen, but also in immigrant communities in the West.
- Child rape has been on the increase in the past decade in some African countries, where some men believe having sex with a virgin will protect or cure them from HIV-AIDS. A study at the Red Cross children's hospital in Cape Town, South Africa, found that 3-year-old girls were more likely to be raped than any other age group.
- Two million girls between the ages of 5 and 15 are forced into the commercial sex market each year, many of them trafficked across international borders.
- Sexual harassment is pervasive. From 40 to 50 percent of women in the European Union reported some form of sexual harassment at work; 50 percent of schoolgirls surveyed in Malawi reported sexual harassment at school.
- Women and girls constitute 70 percent of those living on less than a dollar a day and 64 percent of the world's illiterate.
- Women work two-thirds of the total hours worked by men and women but earn only 10 percent of the income.
- Half of the world's food is produced by women, but women own only 1 percent of the world's land.
- More than 1,300 women die each day during pregnancy and childbirth — 99 percent of them in developing countries.

Sources: "Ending violence against women: From words to action," United Nations, October, 2006, www.un.org/womenwatch/daw/public/VAW_Study/VAW studyE.pdf; www.womankind.org.uk; www.unfp.org; www.oxfam.org.uk; www.ipu.org; www.unicef.org; www.infant-trust.org.uk; "State of the World Population 2000;" http://npr.org; http://asiapacific.amnesty.org; http://news.bbc.co.uk

Negative Attitudes Toward Women Are Pervasive

Negative attitudes about women are widespread around the globe, among women as well as men. Rural women are more likely than city women to condone domestic abuse if they think it was provoked by a wife's behavior.

Location	Percentage of women in selected countries who agree that a man has good reason to beat his wife if:						Women who agree with:	
	Wife does not complete housework	Wife disobeys her husband	Wife refuses sex	Wife asks about other women	Husband suspects infidelity	Wife is unfaithful	One or more of the reasons mentioned	None of the reasons mentioned
Bangladesh city	13.8	23.3	9.0	6.6	10.6	51.5	53.3	46.7
Bangladesh province	25.1	38.7	23.3	14.9	24.6	77.6	79.3	20.7
Brazil city	0.8	1.4	0.3	0.3	2.0	8.8	9.4	90.6
Brazil province	4.5	10.9	4.7	2.9	14.1	29.1	33.7	66.3
Ethiopia province	65.8	77.7	45.6	32.2	43.8	79.5	91.1	8.9
Japan city	1.3	1.5	0.4	0.9	2.8	18.5	19.0	81.0
Namibia city	9.7	12.5	3.5	4.3	6.1	9.2	20.5	79.5
Peru city	4.9	7.5	1.7	2.3	13.5	29.7	33.7	66.3
Peru province	43.6	46.2	25.8	26.7	37.9	71.3	78.4	21.6
Samoa	12.1	19.6	7.4	10.1	26.0	69.8	73.3	26.7
Serbia and Montenegro city	0.6	0.97	0.6	0.3	0.9	5.7	6.2	93.8
Thailand city	2.0	0.8	2.8	1.8	5.6	42.9	44.7	55.3
Thailand province	11.9	25.3	7.3	4.4	12.5	64.5	69.5	30.5
Tanzania city	24.1	45.6	31.1	13.8	22.9	51.5	62.5	37.5
Tanzania province	29.1	49.7	41.7	19.8	27.2	55.5	68.2	31.8

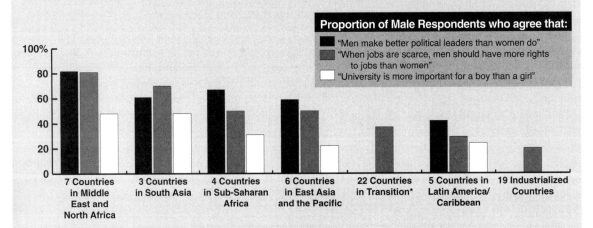

Proportion of Male Respondents who agree that:
- ■ "Men make better political leaders than women do"
- ■ "When jobs are scarce, men should have more rights to jobs than women"
- □ "University is more important for a boy than a girl"

* Countries in transition are generally those that were once part of the Soviet Union.

Sources: World Heath Organization, www.who.int/gender/violence/who_multicountry_study/Chapter3-Chapter4.pdf; "World Values Survey," www.worldvaluessurvey.org

and alleging a false crime, punishable by stoning, lashings or prison. [11] When the law was softened in 2006 to allow judges to decide whether to try rape cases in Islamic courts or criminal courts, where such witnesses are not required, thousands took to the streets to protest the change. [12]

Honor killings are up 400 percent in Pakistan over the last two years, and Pakistani women also live in fear of being blinded or disfigured by "acid attacks" — a common practice in Pakistan and a handful of other countries — in which attackers, usually spurned suitors, throw acid on a woman's face and body.

But statistics on murder and violence are only a part of the disturbing figures on the status of women around the globe. Others include:

- Some 130 million women have undergone female genital mutilation, and another 2 million are at risk every year, primarily in Africa and Yemen.
- Women and girls make up 70 percent of the world's poor and two-thirds of its illiterate.
- Women work two-thirds of the total hours worked by men but earn only 10 percent of the income.
- Women produce more than half of the world's food but own less than 1 percent of the world's property.
- More than 500,000 women die during pregnancy and childbirth every year — 99 percent of them in developing countries.
- Two million girls between the ages of 5 and 15 are forced into the commercial sex market each year. [13]
- Globally, 10 million more girls than boys do not attend school. [14]

Despite these alarming numbers, women have made historic progress in some areas. The number of girls receiving an education has increased in the past decade. Today 57 percent of children not attending school are girls, compared to two-thirds in the 1990s. [15]

And women have made significant gains in the political arena. As of March, 2008, 14 women are serving as elected heads of state or government, and women now hold 17.8 percent of the world's parliamentary seats — more than ever before. [16] And just three months after the brutal killing of Aswad in Iraq, India swore in its first female president, Pratibha Patil, who vows to eliminate that country's practice of aborting female fetuses because girls are not as valued as boys in India. (*See "At Issue," p. 195.*) [17]

Last October, Argentina elected its first female president, Cristina Fernández de Kirchner,* the second

Spain's visibly pregnant new Defense minister, Carme Chacón, reviews troops in Madrid on April 14, 2008. She is the first woman ever to head Spain's armed forces. Women hold nine out of 17 cabinet posts in Spain's socialist government, a reflection of women's entrance into the halls of power around the world.

AP Photo/Bernat Armangue

woman in two years to be elected president in South America. Michelle Bachelet, a single mother, won the presidency in Chile in 2006. [18] During her inaugural speech Kirchner admitted, "Perhaps it'll be harder for me, because I'm a woman. It will always be harder for us." [19]

Indeed, while more women than ever now lead national governments, they hold only 4.4 percent of the world's 342 presidential and prime ministerial positions. And in no country do they hold 50 percent or more of the national legislative seats. [20]

"Women make up half the world's population, but they are not represented" at that level, says Swanee Hunt, former U.S. ambassador to Austria and founding director of the Women and Public Policy Program at Harvard's Kennedy School of Government.

While this is "obviously a fairness issue," she says it also affects the kinds of public policies governments pursue. When women comprise higher percentages of officeholders, studies show "distinct differences in legislative outputs," Hunt explains. "There's less funding of bombs and bullets and more on human security — not just how to defend territory but also on hospitals and general well-being."

---

* Isabel Martínez Perón assumed the presidency of Argentina on the death of her husband, Juan Perón, in 1974 and served until she was deposed in a coup d'etat in 1976; but she was never elected.

Female Peacekeepers Fill Vital Roles

Women bring a different approach to conflict resolution.

The first all-female United Nations peacekeeping force left Liberia in January after a year's mission in the West African country, which is rebuilding itself after 14 years of civil war. Comprised of more than 100 women from India, the force was immediately replaced by a second female team.

"If anyone questioned the ability of women to do tough jobs, then those doubters have been [proven] wrong," said U.N. Special Representative for Liberia Ellen Margrethe Løj, adding that the female peacekeepers inspired many Liberian women to join the national police force. [1]

Women make up half of the world's refugees and have systematically been targeted for rape and sexual abuse during times of war, from the 200,000 "comfort women" who were kept as sex slaves for Japanese soldiers during World War II [2] to the estimated quarter-million women reportedly raped and sexually assaulted during the current conflict in the Democratic Republic of the Congo. [3] But women account for only 5 percent of the world's security-sector jobs, and in many countries they are excluded altogether. [4]

In 2000, the U.N. Security Council unanimously adopted Resolution 1325 calling on governments — and the U.N. itself — to include women in peace building by adopting a variety of measures, including appointing more women as special envoys, involving women in peace negotiations, integrating gender-based policies in peacekeeping missions and increasing the number of women at all decision-making levels. [5]

But while Resolution 1325 was a critical step in bringing women into the peace process, women's groups say more women should be sent on field missions and more data collected on how conflict affects women around the world. [6]

"Women are often viewed as victims, but another way to view them is as the maintainers of society," says Carla Koppell, director of the Cambridge, Mass.-based Initiative for Inclusive Security, which promotes greater numbers of women in peacekeeping and conflict resolution. "There must be a conscious decision to include women. It's a detriment to promote peace without including women."

Women often comprise the majority of post-conflict survivor populations, especially when large numbers of men have either fled or been killed. In the wake of the 1994 Rwandan genocide, for example, women made up 70 percent of the remaining population.

And female peacekeepers and security forces can fill vital roles men often cannot, such as searching Islamic women wearing burkas or working with rape victims who may be reluctant to report the crimes to male soldiers.

Today's historic numbers of women parliamentarians have resulted partly from gender quotas imposed in nearly 100 countries, which require a certain percentage of women candidates or officeholders. [21]

During the U.N.'s historic Fourth World Conference on Women — held in Beijing in 1995 — 189 governments adopted, among other things, a goal of 30 percent female representation in national legislatures around the world. [22] But today, only 20 countries have reached that goal, and quotas are often attacked as limiting voters' choices and giving women unfair advantages. [23]

Along with increasing female political participation, the 5,000 government representatives at the Beijing conference — one of the largest gatherings in U.N. history — called for improved health care for women, an end to violence against women, equal access to education for girls, promotion of economic independence and other steps to improve the condition of women around the world. [24]

"Let Beijing be the platform from which our global crusade will be carried forward," Gertrude Mongella, U.N. secretary general for the conference, said during closing ceremonies. "The world will hold us accountable for the implementation of the good intentions and decisions arrived at in Beijing." [25]

But more than 10 years later, much of the Beijing Platform still has not been achieved. And many question whether women are any better off today than they were in 1995.

"The picture's mixed," says June Zeitlin, executive director of the Women's Environment & Development

"Women bring different experiences and issues to the table," says Koppell. "I've seen it personally in the Darfur and Uganda peace negotiations. Their priorities were quite different. Men were concerned about power- and wealth-sharing. Those are valid, but you get an entirely different dimension from women. Women talked about security on the ground, security of families, security of communities."

In war-torn countries, women have been found to draw on their experiences as mothers to find nonviolent and flexible ways to solve conflict.[7] During peace negotiations in Northern Ireland, for example, male negotiators repeatedly walked out of sessions, leaving a small number of women at the table. The women, left to their own, found areas of common ground and were able to keep discussions moving forward.[8]

"The most important thing is introducing the definition of security from a woman's perspective," said Orzala Ashraf, founder of Kabul-based Humanitarian Assistance for the Women and Children of Afghanistan. "It is not a man in a uniform standing next to a tank armed with a gun. Women have a broader term — human security — the ability to go to school, receive health care, work and have access to justice. Only by

The first all-female United Nations peacekeeping force practices martial arts in New Delhi as it prepares to be deployed to Liberia in 2006.

AP Photo/Mustafa Quraishi

improving these areas can threats from insurgents, Taliban, drug lords and warlords be countered."[9]

[1] "Liberia: UN envoy welcomes new batch of female Indian police officers," U.N. News Centre, Feb. 8, 2008, www.un.org/apps/news/story.asp?News ID=25557&Cr=liberia&Cr1=.

[2] "Japan: Comfort Women," European Speaking Tour press release, Amnesty International, Oct. 31, 2007.

[3] "Film Documents Rape of Women in Congo," "All Things Considered," National Public Radio, April 8, 2008, www.npr.org/templates/story/story.php? storyId=89476111.

[4] "Ninth Annual Colloquium and Policy Forum," Hunt Alternatives Fund, Jan. 22, 2008, www.huntalternatives.org/pages/7650_ninth _annual_colloquium_and_policy_forum.cfm. Also see Elizabeth Eldridge, "Women cite utility in peace efforts," *The Washington Times*, Jan. 25, 2008, p. A1.

[5] "Inclusive Security, Sustainable Peace: A Toolkit for Advocacy and Action," International Alert and Women Waging Peace, 2004, p. 15, www.huntalternatives.org/download/35_introduction.pdf.

[6] *Ibid.*, p. 17.

[7] Jolynn Shoemaker and Camille Pampell Conaway, "Conflict Prevention and Transformation: Women's Vital Contributions," Inclusive Security: Women Waging Peace and the United Nations Foundation, Feb. 23, 2005, p. 7.

[8] The Initiative for Inclusive Security, www.huntalternatives.org /pages/460_the_vital_role_of_women_in_peace_building.cfm.

[9] Eldridge, *op. cit.*

Organization (WEDO). "In terms of violence against women, there is far more recognition of what is going on today. There has been some progress with education and girls. But the impact of globalization has exacerbated differences between men and women. The poor have gotten poorer — and they are mostly women."

Liberalized international trade has been a two-edged sword in other ways as well. Corporations have been able to expand their global reach, opening new businesses and factories in developing countries and offering women unprecedented employment and economic opportunities. But the jobs often pay low wages and involve work in dangerous conditions because poor countries anxious to attract foreign investors often are willing to ignore safety and labor protections.[26] And increasingly porous

international borders have led to growing numbers of women and girls being forced or sold into prostitution or sexual slavery abroad, often under the pretense that they will be given legitimate jobs overseas.[27]

Numerous international agreements in recent years have pledged to provide women with the same opportunities and protections as men, including the U.N.'s Millennium Development Goals (MDGs) and the Convention on the Elimination of All Forms of Discrimination Against Women (CEDAW). But the MDGs' deadlines for improving the conditions for women have either been missed already or are on track to fail in the coming years.[28] And more than 70 of the 185 countries that ratified CEDAW have filed "reservations," meaning they exempt themselves from certain parts.[29] In

Few Women Head World Governments

Fourteen women currently serve as elected heads of state or government including five who serve as both. Mary McAleese, elected president of Ireland in 1997, is the world's longest-serving head of state. Helen Clark of New Zealand has served as prime minister since 1999, making her the longest-serving female head of government. The world's first elected female head of state was Sirimavo Bandaranaike of Sri Lanka, in 1960.

Current Female Elected Heads of State and Government

Heads of both state and government:

 Gloria Macapagal-Arroyo — President, the Philippines, since 2001; former secretary of Defense (2002) and secretary of Foreign Affairs (2003 and 2006-2007).

 Ellen Johnson-Sirleaf — President, Liberia, since 2006; held finance positions with the government and World Bank.

 Michelle Bachelet Jeria — President, Chile, since 2006; former minister of Health (2000-2002) and minister of Defense (2002-2004).

 Cristina E. Fernández — President, Argentina, since 2007; succeeded her husband, Nestor de Kirchner, as president; former president, Senate Committee on Constitutional Affairs.

 Rosa Zafferani — Captain Regent, San Marino, since April 2008; secretary of State of Public Education, University and Cultural Institutions (2004 to 2008); served as captain regent in 1999; San Marino elects two captains regent every six months, who serve as co-heads of both state and government.

Heads of Government:

 Helen Clark — Prime Minister, New Zealand, since 1999; held government posts in foreign affairs, defense, housing and labor.

Luísa Días Diogo — Prime Minister, Mozambique, since 2004; held several finance posts in Mozambique and the World Bank.

 Angela Merkel — Chancellor, Germany, since 2005; parliamentary leader of Christian Democratic Union Party (2002-2005).

 Yuliya Tymoshenko — Prime Minister, Ukraine, since 2007; chief of government (2005) and designate prime minister (2006).

Zinaida Grecianîi — Prime Minister, Moldova, since March 2008; vice prime minister (2005-2008).

Heads of State:

 Mary McAleese — President, Ireland, since 1997; former director of a television station and Northern Ireland Electricity.

Tarja Halonen — President, Finland, since 2000; former minister of foreign affairs (1995-2000).

 Pratibha Patil — President, India, since 2007; former governor of Rajasthan state (2004-2007).

Borjana Kristo — President, Bosnia and Herzegovina, since 2007; minister of Justice of Bosniak-Croat Federation, an entity in Bosnia and Herzegovina (2003-2007).

Source: www.guide2womenleaders.com

---

fact, there are more reservations against CEDAW than against any other international human-rights treaty in history. [30] The United States remains the only developed country in the world not to have ratified it. [31]

"There has certainly been progress in terms of the rhetoric. But there are still challenges in the disparities in education, disparities in income, disparities in health," says Carla Koppell, director of the Cambridge, Mass.-based Initiative for Inclusive Security, which advocates for greater numbers of women in peace negotiations.

"But women are not just victims," she continues. "They have a very unique and important role to play in solving the problems of the developing world. We need to charge policy makers to match the rhetoric and make it a reality. There is a really wonderful opportunity to use the momentum that does exist. I really think we can."

Amidst the successes and failures surrounding women's issues, here are some of the questions analysts are beginning to ask:

Has globalization been good for women?

Over the last 20 years, trade liberalization has led to a massive increase of goods being produced and exported from developing countries, creating millions of manufacturing jobs and bringing many women into the paid workforce for the first time.

"Women employed in export-oriented manufacturing typically earn more than they would have in traditional sectors," according to a World Bank report. "Further, cash income earned by women may improve their status and bargaining power in the family." [32] The report cited a study of 50 families in Mexico that found "a significant proportion of the women reported an improvement in their 'quality of life,' due mainly to their income from working outside their homes, including in (export-oriented) factory jobs."

But because women in developing nations are generally less educated than men and have little bargaining power, most of these jobs are temporary or part-time, offering no health-care benefits, overtime or sick leave.

Women comprise 85 percent of the factory jobs in the garment industry in Bangladesh and 90 percent in Cambodia. In the cut flower industry, women hold 65 percent of the jobs in Colombia and 87 percent in Zimbabwe. In the fruit industry, women constitute 69 percent of temporary and seasonal workers in South Africa and 52 percent in Chile. [33]

Frequently, women in these jobs have no formal contract with their employers, making them even more vulnerable to poor safety conditions and abuse. One study found that only 46 percent of women garment workers in Bangladesh had an official letter of employment. [34]

"Women are a workforce vital to the global economy, but the jobs women are in often aren't covered by labor protections," says Thalia Kidder, a policy adviser on gender and sustainable livelihoods with U.K.-based Oxfam, a confederation of 12 international aid organizations. Women lack protection because they mostly work as domestics, in home-based businesses and as part-time workers. "In the global economy, many companies look to hire the most powerless people because they cannot demand high wages. There are not a lot of trade treaties that address labor rights."

Women Still Far from Reaching Political Parity

Although they have made strides in the past decade, women hold only a small minority of the world's leadership and legislative posts (right). Nordic parliaments have the highest rates of female representation — 41.4 percent — compared with only 9 percent in Arab countries (below). However, Arab legislatures have nearly tripled their female representation since 1997, and some countries in Africa have dramatically increased theirs as well: Rwanda, at 48.8 percent, now has the world's highest percentage of women in parliament of any country. The U.S. Congress ranks 70th in the world, with 89 women serving in the 535-member body — or 16.6 percent.

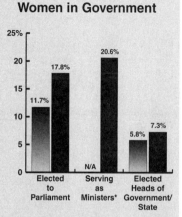

Women in Government

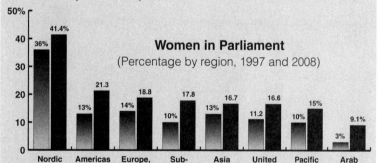

Women in Parliament
(Percentage by region, 1997 and 2008)

* Includes deputy prime ministers, ministers and prime ministers who hold ministerial portfolios.

Sources: Interparliamentarian Union, www.ipu.org/wmn-e/world.htm; State of the World's Children 2007, UNICEF, www.unicef.org/sowc07/; "Worldwide Guide to Women in Leadership" database, www.un.org/womenwatch/daw/csw/41sess.htm.

In addition to recommending that countries embrace free trade, Western institutions like the International Monetary Fund and the World Bank during the 1990s recommended that developing countries adopt so-called structural adjustment economic reforms in order to qualify for certain loans and financial support. Besides opening borders to free trade, the neo-liberal economic

AP Photo/Rajesh Kumar Singh

National Geographic/Getty Images/Melvyn Goldstein

Women's Work: From Hauling and Churning . . .

Women's work is often back-breaking and monotonous, such as hauling firewood in the western Indian state of Maharashtra (top) and churning yogurt into butter beside Lake Motsobunnyi in Tibet (bottom). Women labor two-thirds of the total hours worked around the globe each year but earn only 10 percent of the income.

ble" by replacing long-term contracts with temporary, seasonal and hourly positions — while restricting collective bargaining rights. [35] And countries streamlined and privatized government programs such as health care and education, services women depend on most.

Globalization also has led to a shift toward cash crops grown for export, which hurts women farmers, who produce 60 to 80 percent of the food for household consumption in developing countries. [36] Small women farmers are being pushed off their land so crops for exports can be grown, limiting their abilities to produce food for themselves and their families.

While economic globalization has yet to create the economic support needed to help women out of poverty, women's advocates say females have benefited from the broadening of communications between countries prompted by globalization. "It has certainly improved access to communications and helped human-rights campaigns," says Zeitlin of WEDO. "Less can be done in secret. If there is a woman who is condemned to be stoned to death somewhere, you can almost immediately mobilize a global campaign against it."

Homa Hoodfar, a professor of social anthropology at Concordia University in Montreal, Canada, and a founder of the group Women Living Under Muslim Laws, says women in some of the world's most remote towns and villages regularly e-mail her organization. "Globalization has made the world much smaller," she says. "Women are getting information on TV and the Internet. The fact that domestic violence has become a global issue [shows globalization] provides resources for those objecting locally."

regime known as the Washington Consensus advocated privatizing state-owned businesses, balancing budgets and attracting foreign investment.

But according to some studies, those reforms ended up adversely affecting women. For instance, companies in Ecuador were encouraged to make jobs more "flexi-

But open borders also have enabled the trafficking of millions of women around the world. An estimated 800,000 people are trafficked across international borders each year — 80 percent of them women and girls — and most are forced into the commercial sex trade. Millions more are trafficked within their own countries. [37] Globalization has sparked a massive migration of women in search of better jobs and lives. About 90 million women — half of the world's migrants and more than ever in history — reside outside their home countries. These migrant women — often unable to speak the local language and without any family connections — are especially susceptible to traffickers who lure them with promises of jobs abroad. [38]

And those who do not get trapped in the sex trade often end up in low-paying or abusive jobs in foreign factories or as domestic maids working under slave-like conditions.

But some experts say the real problem is not migration and globalization but the lack of labor protection. "Nothing is black and white," says Marianne Mollmann, advocacy director for the Women's Rights Division of Human Rights Watch. "Globalization has created different employment opportunities for women. Migration flows have made women vulnerable. But it's a knee-jerk reaction to say that women shouldn't migrate. You can't prevent migration. So where do we need to go?" She suggests including these workers in general labor-law protections that cover all workers.

Mollmann said countries can and should hammer out agreements providing labor and wage protections for

AP Photo/Sergei Grits

AFP/Getty Images/Ali Burafi

. . . to Gathering and Herding

While many women have gotten factory jobs thanks to globalization of trade, women still comprise 70 percent of the planet's inhabitants living on less than a dollar a day. Women perform a variety of tasks around the world, ranging from gathering flax in Belarus (top) to shepherding goats in central Argentina (bottom).

domestic workers migrating across borders. With such protections, she said, women could benefit from the jobs and incomes promised by increased migration and globalization.

Should governments impose electoral quotas for women?

In 2003, as Rwanda struggled to rebuild itself after the genocide that killed at least 800,000 Hutus and Tutsis, the country adopted an historic new constitution that, among other things, required that women hold at least 30 percent of posts "in all decision-making organs." [39]

Today — ironically, just across Lake Kivu from the horrors occurring in Eastern Congo — Rwanda's lower house of parliament now leads the world in female representation, with 48.8 percent of the seats held by women. [40]

Before the civil war, Rwandan women never held more than 18 percent of parliament. But after the genocide, the country's population was 70 percent female. Women immediately stepped in to fill the vacuum, becoming the heads of households, community leaders and business owners. Their increased presence in leadership positions eventually led to the new constitutional quotas. [41]

"We see so many post-conflict countries going from military regimes to democracy that are starting from scratch with new constitutions," says Drude Dahlerup, a professor of political science at Sweden's Stockholm University who studies the use of gender quotas. "Today, starting from scratch means including women. It's seen as a sign of modernization and democratization."

Both Iraq and Afghanistan included electoral quotas for women in their new constitutions, and the number of women in political office in sub-Saharan Africa has increased faster than in any other region of the world, primarily through the use of quotas. [42]

But many point out that simply increasing the numbers of women in elected office will not necessarily expand women's rights. "It depends on which women and which positions they represent," says Wendy Harcourt, chair of Women in Development Europe (WIDE), a feminist network in Europe, and editor of *Development,* the journal of the Society for International Development, a global network of individuals and institutions working on development issues. "It's positive, but I don't see yet what it means [in terms of addressing] broader gender issues."

While Afghanistan has mandated that women hold at least 27 percent of the government's lower house seats and at least 17 percent of the upper house, their increased representation appears to have done little to improve women's rights. [43] Earlier this year, a student journalist was condemned to die under Afghanistan's strict Islamic sharia law after he distributed articles from the Internet on women's rights. [44] And nongovernmental groups in Afghanistan report that Afghan women and girls have begun killing themselves in record numbers, burning themselves alive in order to escape widespread domestic abuse or forced marriages. [45]

Having gender quotas alone doesn't necessarily ensure that women's rights will be broadened, says Hoodfar of Concordia University. It depends on the type of quota a government implements, she argues, pointing out that in Jordan, for example, the government has set aside parliamentary seats for the six women who garner the most votes of any other female candidates in their districts — even if they do not win more votes than male candidates. [46] Many small, conservative tribes that cannot garner enough votes for a male in a countrywide victory are now nominating their sisters and wives in the hope that the lower number of votes needed to elect a woman will get them one of the reserved seats. As a result, many of the women moving into the reserved seats are extremely conservative and actively oppose providing women greater rights and freedoms.

And another kind of quota has been used against women in her home country of Iran, Hoodfar points out. Currently, 64 percent of university students in Iran are women. But the government recently mandated that at least 40 percent of university enrollees be male, forcing many female students out of school, Hoodfar said.

"Before, women didn't want to use quotas for politics because of concern the government may try to use it against women," she says. "But women are beginning to look into it and talk about maybe developing a good system."

Quotas can be enacted by constitutional requirements, such as those enacted in Rwanda, by statute or voluntarily by political parties. Quotas also can vary in their requirements: They can mandate the number of women each party must nominate, how many women must appear on the ballot (and the order in which they appear, so women are not relegated to the bottom of the list), or the number of women who must hold government office. About 40 countries now use gender quotas in national parliamentary elections, while another 50 have major political parties that voluntarily use quotas to determine candidates.

Aside from questions about the effectiveness of quotas, others worry about the fairness of establishing quotas based on gender. "That's something feminists have traditionally opposed," says Harcourt.

"It's true, but it's also not fair the way it is now," says former Ambassador Hunt. "We are where we are today through all kinds of social structures that are not fair. Quotas are the lesser of two evils."

Stockholm University's Dahlerup says quotas are not "discrimination against men but compensation for discrimination against women." Yet quotas are not a panacea for women in politics, she contends. "It's a mistake to think this is a kind of tool that will solve all problems. It doesn't solve problems about financing campaigns, caring for families while being in politics or removing patriarchal attitudes. It would be nice if it wasn't necessary, and hopefully sometime in the future it won't be."

Until that time, however, quotas are a "necessary evil," she says.

Do international treaties improve women's rights?

In recent decades, a variety of international agreements have been signed by countries pledging to improve women's lives, from the 1979 Convention for the Elimination of All Forms of Discrimination Against Women to the Beijing Platform of 1995 to the Millennium Development Goals (MDGs) adopted in 2000. The agreements aimed to provide women with greater access to health, political representation, economic stability and social status. They also focused attention on some of the biggest obstacles facing women.

But despite the fanfare surrounding the launch of those agreements, many experts on women's issues say on-the-ground action has yet to match the rhetoric. "The report is mixed," says Haleh Afshar, a professor of politics and women's studies at the University of York in the United Kingdom and a nonpartisan, appointed member of the House of Lords, known as a crossbench peer. "The biggest problem with Beijing is all these things were stated, but none were funded. Unfortunately, I don't see any money. You don't get the pay, you don't get the job done."

The Beijing Platform for Action, among other things, called on governments to "adjust budgets to ensure equality of access to public sector expenditures" and even to "reduce, as appropriate, excessive military expenditure" in order to achieve the Platform goals.

But adequate funding has yet to be provided, say women's groups. [47] In a report entitled "Beijing Betrayed," the Women's Environment & Development Organization says female HIV cases outnumber male cases in many parts of the world, gender-related violence remains a pandemic

Indian women harvest wheat near Bhopal. Women produce half of the food used domestically worldwide and 60 to 80 percent of the household food grown in developing countries.

and women still make up the majority of the world's poor — despite pledges in Beijing to reverse these trends. [48]

And funding is not the only obstacle. A 2004 U.N. survey revealed that while many countries have enacted laws in recent years to help protect women from violence and discrimination, long-standing social and cultural traditions block progress. "While constitutions provided for equality between women and men on the one hand, [several countries] recognized and gave precedent to customary law and practice in a number of areas . . . resulting in discrimination against women," the report said. "Several countries noted that statutory, customary and religious law coexist, especially in regard to family, personal status and inheritance and land rights. This perpetuated discrimination against women." [49]

While she worries about the lack of progress on the Beijing Platform, WEDO Executive Director Zeitlin says international agreements are nevertheless critical in raising global awareness on women's issues. "They have a major impact on setting norms and standards," she says. "In many countries, norms and standards are very important in setting goals for women to advocate for. We complain about lack of implementation, but if we didn't have the norms and standards we couldn't complain about a lack of implementation."

Like the Beijing Platform, the MDGs have been criticized for not achieving more. While the U.N. says promoting women's rights is essential to achieving the millenium goals — which aim to improve the lives of all

CHRONOLOGY

1700s-1800s *Age of Enlightenment and Industrial Revolution lead to greater freedoms for women.*

1792 Mary Wollstonecraft publishes *A Vindication of the Rights of Women*, later hailed as "the feminist declaration of independence."

1893 New Zealand becomes first nation to grant women full suffrage.

1920 Tennessee is the 36th state to ratify the 19th Amendment, giving American women the right to vote.

1940s-1980s *International conventions endorse equal rights for women. Global conferences highlight need to improve women's rights.*

1946 U.N. creates Commission on the Status of Women.

1951 U.N. International Labor Organization adopts convention promoting equal pay for equal work, which has been ratified by 164 countries; the United States is not among them.

1952 U.N. adopts convention calling for full women's suffrage.

1960 Sri Lanka elects the world's first female prime minister.

1974 Maria Estela Martínez de Perón of Argentina becomes the world's first woman president, replacing her ailing husband.

1975 U.N. holds first World Conference on Women, in Mexico City, followed by similar conferences every five years. U.N. launches the Decade for Women.

1979 U.N. adopts Convention on the Elimination of All Forms of Discrimination against Women (CEDAW), dubbed the "international bill of rights for women."

1981 CEDAW is ratified — faster than any other human-rights convention.

1990s *Women's rights win historic legal recognition.*

1993 U.N. World Conference on Human Rights in Vienna, Austria, calls for ending all violence, sexual harassment and trafficking of women.

1995 Fourth World Conference on Women in Beijing draws 30,000 people, making it the largest in U.N. history. Beijing Platform outlining steps to grant women equal rights is signed by 189 governments.

1996 International Criminal Tribunal convicts eight Bosnian Serb police and military officers for rape during the Bosnian conflict — the first time sexual assault is prosecuted as a war crime.

1998 International Criminal Tribunal for Rwanda recognizes rape and other forms of sexual violence as genocide.

2000s *Women make political gains, but sexual violence against women increases.*

2000 U.N. calls on governments to include women in peace negotiations.

2006 Ellen Johnson Sirleaf of Liberia, Michelle Bachelet of Chile and Portia Simpson Miller of Jamaica become their countries' first elected female heads of state. . . . Women in Kuwait are allowed to run for parliament, winning two seats.

2007 A woman in Saudi Arabia who was sentenced to 200 lashes after being gang-raped by seven men is pardoned by King Abdullah. Her rapists received sentences ranging from 10 months to five years in prison, and 80 to 1,000 lashes. . . . After failing to recognize any gender-based crimes in its first case involving the Democratic Republic of the Congo, the International Criminal Court hands down charges of "sexual slavery" in its second case involving war crimes in Congo. More than 250,000 women are estimated to have been raped and sexually abused during the country's war.

2008 Turkey lifts 80-year-old ban on women's headscarves in public universities, signaling a drift toward religious fundamentalism. . . . Former housing minister Carme Chacón — 37 and pregnant — is named defense minister of Spain, bringing to nine the number of female cabinet ministers in the Socialist government. . . . Sen. Hillary Rodham Clinton becomes the first U.S. woman to be in a tight race for a major party's presidential nomination.

the world's populations by 2015 — only two of the eight specifically address women's issues. [50]

One of the goals calls for countries to "Promote gender equality and empower women." But it sets only one measurable target: "Eliminate gender disparity in primary and secondary education, preferably by 2005, and in all levels of education" by 2015. [51] Some 62 countries failed to reach the 2005 deadline, and many are likely to miss the 2015 deadline as well. [52]

Another MDG calls for a 75 percent reduction in maternal mortality compared to 1990 levels. But according to the human-rights group ActionAid, this goal is the "most off track of all the MDGs." Rates are declining at less than 1 percent a year, and in some countries — such as Sierra Leone, Pakistan and Guatemala — maternal mortality has increased since 1990. If that trend continues, no region in the developing world is expected to reach the goal by 2015. [53]

Activist Peggy Antrobus of Development Alternatives with Women for a New Era (DAWN) — a network of feminists from the Southern Hemisphere, based currently in Calabar, Cross River State, Nigeria — has lambasted the MDGs, quipping that the acronym stands for the "Most Distracting Gimmick." [54] Many feminists argue that the goals are too broad to have any real impact and that the MDGs should have given more attention to women's issues.

But other women say international agreements — and the public debate surrounding them — are vital in promoting gender equality. "It's easy to get disheartened, but Beijing is still the blueprint of where we need to be," says Mollmann of Human Rights Watch. "They are part of a political process, the creation of an international culture. If systematically everyone says [discrimination against women] is a bad thing, states don't want to be hauled out as systematic violators."

In particular, Mollmann said, CEDAW has made real progress in overcoming discrimination against women. Unlike the Beijing Platform and the MDGs, CEDAW legally obliges countries to comply. Each of the 185 ratifying countries must submit regular reports to the U.N. outlining their progress under the convention. Several countries — including Brazil, Uganda, South Africa and Australia — also have incorporated CEDAW provisions into their constitutions and legal systems. [55]

Still, dozens of ratifying countries have filed official "reservations" against the convention, including Bahrain,

Egypt, Kuwait, Morocco and the United Arab Emirates, all of whom say they will comply only within the bounds of Islamic sharia law. [56] And the United States has refused to ratify CEDAW, with or without reservations, largely because of conservatives who say it would, among other things, promote abortion and require the government to pay for such things as child care and maternity leave.

BACKGROUND

'Structural Defects'

Numerous prehistoric relics suggest that at one time matriarchal societies existed on Earth in which women were in the upper echelons of power. Because early societies did not understand the connection between sexual relations and conception, they believed women were solely responsible for reproduction — which led to the worship of female goddesses. [57]

In more modern times, however, women have generally faced prejudice and discrimination at the hands of a patriarchal society. In about the eighth century B.C. creation stories emerged describing the fall of man due to the weakness of women. The Greeks recounted the story of Pandora who, through her opening of a sealed jar, unleashed death and pain on all of mankind. Meanwhile, similar tales in Judea eventually were recounted in Genesis, with Eve as the culprit. [58]

In ancient Greece, women were treated as children and denied basic rights. They could not leave their houses un-chaperoned, were prohibited from being educated or buying or selling land. A father could sell his unmarried daughter into slavery if she lost her virginity before marriage. If a woman was raped, she was outcast and forbidden from participating in public ceremonies or wearing jewelry. [59]

The status of women in early Rome was not much better, although over time women began to assert their voices and slowly gained greater freedoms. Eventually, they were able to own property and divorce their husbands. But early Christian leaders later denounced the legal and social freedom enjoyed by Roman women as a sign of moral decay. In the view of the early church, women were dependent on and subordinate to men.

In the 13th century, the Catholic priest and theologian St. Thomas Aquinas helped set the tone for the subjugation of women in Western society. He said women

Women Suffer Most in Natural Disasters

Climate change will make matters worse.

In natural disasters, women suffer death, disease and hunger at higher rates then men. During the devastating 2004 tsunami in Asia, 70 to 80 percent of the dead were women. [1] During cyclone-triggered flooding in Bangladesh that killed 140,000 people in 1991, nearly five times more women between the ages of 20 and 44 died than men. [2]

Gender discrimination, cultural biases and lack of awareness of women's needs are part of the problem. For instance, during the 1991 cyclone, Bangladeshi women and their children died in higher numbers because they waited at home for their husbands to return and make evacuation decisions. [3] In addition, flood warnings were conveyed by men to men in public spaces but were rarely communicated to women and children at home. [4]

And during the tsunami, many Indonesian women died because they stayed behind to look for children and other family members. Women clinging to children in floodwaters also tired more quickly and drowned, since most women in the region were never taught to swim or climb trees. [5] In Sri Lanka, many women died because the tsunami hit early on a Sunday morning when they were inside preparing breakfast for their families. Men were generally outside where they had earlier warning of the oncoming floods so they were better able to escape. [6]

Experts now predict global climate change — which is expected to increase the number of natural disasters around the world — will put women in far greater danger than men because natural disasters generally have a disproportionate impact on the world's poor. Since women comprise 70 per-cent of those living on less than $1 a day, they will be hardest hit by climate changes, according to the Intergovernmental Panel on Climate Change. [7]

"Climate change is not gender-neutral," said Gro Harlem Brundtland, former prime minister of Norway and now special envoy to the U.N. secretary-general on climate change. "[Women are] more dependent for their livelihood on natural resources that are threatened by climate change. . . . With changes in climate, traditional food sources become more unpredictable and scarce. This exposes women to loss of harvests, often their sole sources of food and income." [8]

Women produce 60 to 80 percent of the food for house-hold consumption in developing countries. [9] As drought, flooding and desertification increase, experts say women and their families will be pushed further into poverty and famine.

Women also suffer more hardship in the aftermath of natural disasters, and their needs are often ignored during relief efforts.

In many Third World countries, for instance, women have no property rights, so when a husband dies during a natural disaster his family frequently confiscates the land from his widow, leaving her homeless and destitute. [10] And because men usually dominate emergency relief and response agencies, women's specific needs, such as contra-ceptives and sanitary napkins, are often overlooked. After floods in Bangladesh in 1998, adolescent girls reported high rates of rashes and urinary tract infections because they had no clean water, could not wash their menstrual rags prop-erly in private and had no place to hang them to dry. [11]

were created solely to be "man's helpmate" and advo-cated that men should make use of "a necessary object, woman, who is needed to preserve the species or to pro-vide food and drink." [60]

From the 14th to 17th centuries, misogyny and oppression of women took a step further. As European societies struggled against the Black Plague, the 100 Years War and turmoil between Catholics and Reformers, reli-gious leaders began to blame tragedies, illnesses and other problems on witches. As witch hysteria spread across Europe — instituted by both the religious and non-reli-gious — an estimated 30,000 to 60,000 people were exe-cuted for allegedly practicing witchcraft. About 80 percent were females, some as young as 8 years old. [61]

"All wickedness is but little to the wickedness of a woman," Catholic inquisitors wrote in the 1480s. "What else is woman but a foe to friendship, an unescapable pun-ishment, a necessary evil, a natural temptation, a desirable calamity. . . . Women are . . . instruments of Satan, . . . a structural defect rooted in the original creation." [62]

"In terms of reconstruction, people are not talking about women's needs versus men's needs," says June Zeitlin, executive director of the Women's Environment and Development Organization, a New York City-based international organization that works for women's equality in global policy. "There is a lack of attention to health care after disasters, issues about bearing children, contraception, rape and vulnerability, menstrual needs — things a male programmer is not thinking about. There is broad recognition that disasters have a disproportionate impact on women. But it stops there. They see women as victims, but they don't see women as agents of change."

Women must be brought into discussions on climate change and emergency relief, say Zeitlin and others. Interestingly, she points out, while women are disproportionately affected by environmental changes, they do more than men to protect the environment. Studies show women emit less climate-changing carbon dioxide than men because they recycle more, use resources more efficiently and drive less than men. [12]

"Women's involvement in climate-change decision-making is a human right," said Gerd Johnson-Latham, deputy director of the Swedish Ministry for Foreign Affairs. "If we get more women in decision-making positions, we will have different priorities, and less risk of climate change." [13]

The smell of death hangs over Banda Aceh, Indonesia, which was virtually destroyed by a tsunami on Dec. 28, 2004. 70 to 80 percent of the victims were women.

AP Photo

[1] "Tsunami death toll," CNN, Feb. 22, 2005. Also see "Report of High-level Roundtable: How a Changing Climate Impacts Women," Council of Women World Leaders, Women's Environment and Development Organization and Heinrich Boll Foundation, Sept. 21, 2007, p. 21, www.wedo.org/files/Round table%20Final%20Report%206%20Nov .pdf.

[2] *Ibid.*

[3] "Cyclone Jelawat bears down on Japan's Okinawa island," CNN.com, Aug. 7, 2000, http://archives.cnn.com/ 2000/ASIANOW/east/08/07/asia .weather/index.html.

[4] "Gender and Health in Disasters," World Health Organization, July 2002, www.who.int/gender/other_health/en /genderdisasters.pdf.

[5] "The tsunami's impact on women," Oxfam briefing note, March 5, 2005, p. 2, www.oxfam.org/en/files /bn050326_tsunami_women/download.

[6] "Report of High-level Roundtable," *op. cit.*, p. 5.

[7] "Gender Equality" fact sheet, Oxfam, www.oxfam.org.uk/resources /issues/gender/introduction.html. Also see *ibid.*

[8] *Ibid.*, p. 4.

[9] "Five years down the road from Beijing: Assessing progress," *News and Highlights*, Food and Agriculture Organization, June 2, 2000, www.fao.org/News/2000/000602-e.htm.

[10] "Gender and Health in Disasters," *op. cit.*

[11] *Ibid.*

[12] "Women and the Environment," U.N. Environment Program, 2004, p. 17, www.unep.org/Documents.Multilingual/Default.asp?Document ID=468&ArticleID=4488&l=en. Also see "Report of High-level Roundtable," *op. cit.*, p. 7.

[13] *Ibid.*

Push for Protections

The Age of Enlightenment and the Industrial Revolution in the 18th and 19th centuries opened up job opportunities for women, released them from domestic confines and provided them with new social freedoms.

In 1792 Mary Wollstonecraft published *A Vindication of the Rights of Women*, which has been hailed as "the feminist declaration of independence." Although the book had been heavily influenced by the French Revolution's notions of equality and universal brotherhood, French revolutionary leaders, ironically, were not sympathetic to feminist causes. [63] In 1789 they had refused to accept a Declaration of the Rights of Women when it was presented at the National Assembly. And Jean Jacques Rousseau, one of the philosophical founders of the revolution, had written in 1762:

"The whole education of women ought to be relative to men. To please them, to be useful to them, to make themselves loved and honored by them, to educate them when young, to care for them when grown, to counsel them, to

AP Photo/Khalid Tanveer

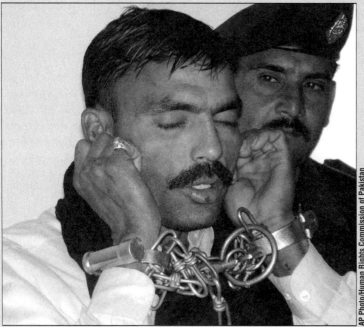

AP Photo/Human Rights Commission of Pakistan

Honor Killings on the Rise

Women in Multan, Pakistan, demonstrate against "honor killings" in 2003 (top). Although Pakistan outlawed such killings years ago, its Human Rights Commission says 1,205 women were killed in the name of family honor in 2007 — a fourfold jump in two years. Nazir Ahmed Sheikh, a Punjabi laborer (bottom), unrepentantly told police in December 2005 how he slit the throats of his four daughters one night as they slept in order to salvage the family's honor. The eldest had married a man of her choice, and Ahmed feared the younger daughters would follow her example.

make life sweet and agreeable to them — these are the duties of women at all times, and what should be taught them from their infancy." [64]

As more and more women began taking jobs outside the home during the 19th century, governments began to pass laws to "protect" them in the workforce and expand their legal rights. The British Mines Act of 1842, for instance, prohibited women from working underground. [65] In 1867, John Stuart Mill, a supporter of women's rights and author of the book *Subjection of Women*, introduced language in the British House of Commons calling for women to be granted the right to vote. It failed. [66]

But by that time governments around the globe had begun enacting laws giving women rights they had been denied for centuries. As a result of the Married Women's Property Act of 1870 and a series of other measures, wives in Britain were finally allowed to own property. In 1893, New Zealand became the first nation to grant full suffrage rights to women, followed over the next two decades by Finland, Norway, Denmark and Iceland. The United States granted women suffrage in 1920. [67]

One of the first international labor conventions, formulated at Berne, Switzerland, in 1906, applied exclusively to women — prohibiting night work for women in industrial occupations. Twelve nations signed on to it. During the second Berne conference in 1913, language was proposed limiting the number of hours women and children could work in industrial jobs, but the outbreak of World War I prevented it from being enacted. [68]

In 1924 the U.S. Supreme Court upheld a night-work law for women. [69]

In 1946, public attention to women's issues received a major boost when the United Nations created the Commission on the Status of Women to address urgent problems facing women around the world. [70] During the 1950s, the U.N. adopted several conventions aimed at improving women's lives, including the Convention on the Political Rights of Women, adopted in 1952 to ensure women the right to vote, which has been ratified by 120 countries, and the Convention on the Nationality of Married Women, approved in 1957 to ensure that marriage to an alien does not automatically affect the nationality of the woman. [71] That convention has been ratified by only 73 countries; the United States is not among them. [72]

In 1951 The International Labor Organization (ILO), an agency of the United Nations, adopted the Convention on Equal Remuneration for Men and Women Workers for Work of Equal Value, to promote equal pay for equal work. It has since been ratified by 164 countries, but again, not by the United States. [73] Seven years later, the ILO adopted the Convention on Discrimination in Employment and Occupation to ensure equal opportunity and treatment in employment. It is currently ratified by 166 countries, but not the United States. [74] U.S. opponents to the conventions claim there is no real pay gap between men and women performing the same jobs and that the conventions would impose "comparable worth" requirements, forcing companies to pay equal wages to men and women even if the jobs they performed were different. [75]

In 1965, the Commission on the Status of Women began drafting international standards articulating equal rights for men and women. Two years later, the panel completed the Declaration on the Elimination of Discrimination Against Women, which was adopted by the General Assembly but carried no enforcement power.

The commission later began to discuss language that would hold countries responsible for enforcing the declaration. At the U.N.'s first World Conference on Women in Mexico City in 1975, women from around the world called for creation of such a treaty, and the commission soon began drafting the text. [76]

Women's 'Bill of Rights'

Finally in 1979, after many years of often rancorous debate, the Convention on the Elimination of All Forms of Discrimination Against Women (CEDAW) was adopted by the General Assembly — 130 to none, with 10 abstentions. After the vote, however, several countries said their "yes" votes did not commit the support of their governments. Brazil's U.N. representative told the assembly, "The signatures and ratifications necessary to make this effective will not come easily." [77]

Despite the prediction, it took less than two years for CEDAW to receive the required number of ratifications to enter it into force — faster than any human-rights convention had ever done before. [78]

Often described as an international bill of rights for women, CEDAW defines discrimination against women as "any distinction, exclusion or restriction made on the basis of sex which has the effect or purpose of impairing or nullifying the recognition, enjoyment or exercise by women, irrespective of their marital status, on a basis of equality of men and women, of human rights and fundamental freedoms in the political, economic, social, cultural, civil or any other field."

Ratifying countries are legally bound to end discrimination against women by incorporating sexual equality into their legal systems, abolishing discriminatory laws against women, taking steps to end trafficking of women and ensuring women equal access to political and public life. Countries must also submit reports at least every four years outlining the steps they have taken to comply with the convention. [79]

CEDAW also grants women reproductive choice — one of the main reasons the United States has not ratified it. The convention requires signatories to guarantee women's rights "to decide freely and responsibly on the number and spacing of their children and to have access to the information, education and means to enable them to exercise these rights." [80]

While CEDAW is seen as a significant tool to stop violence against women, it actually does not directly mention violence. To rectify this, the CEDAW committee charged with monitoring countries' compliance in 1992 specified gender-based violence as a form of discrimination prohibited under the convention. [81]

In 1993 the U.N. took further steps to combat violence against women during the World Conference on Human Rights in Vienna, Austria. The conference called on countries to stop all forms of violence, sexual harassment, exploitation and trafficking of women. It also declared that "violations of the human rights of women

Getty Images/Paula Bronstein

Pakistani acid attack survivors Saira Liaqat, right, and Sabra Sultana are among hundreds, and perhaps thousands, of women who are blinded and disfigured after being attacked with acid each year in Pakistan, Bangladesh, India, Cambodia, Malaysia, Uganda and other areas of Africa. Liaqat was attacked at age 18 during an argument over an arranged marriage. Sabra was 15 when she was burned after being married off to an older man who became unsatisfied with the relationship. Only a small percentage of the attacks — often perpetrated by spurned suitors while the women are asleep in their own beds — are prosecuted.

in situations of armed conflicts are violations of the fundamental principles of international human rights and humanitarian law." [82]

Shortly afterwards, as fighting broke out in the former Yugoslavia and Rwanda, new legal precedents were set to protect women against violence — and particularly rape — during war. In 1996, the International Criminal Tribunal in the Hague, Netherlands, indicted eight Bosnian Serb police officers in connection with the mass rape of Muslim women during the Bosnian war, marking the first time sexual assault had ever been prosecuted as a war crime. [83]

Two years later, the U.N.'s International Criminal Tribunal for Rwanda convicted a former Rwandan mayor for genocide, crimes against humanity, rape and sexual violence — the first time rape and sexual violence were recognized as acts of genocide. [84]

"Rape is a serious war crime like any other," said Regan Ralph, then executive director of Human Rights Watch's Women's Rights Division, shortly after the conviction. "That's always been true on paper, but now international courts are finally acting on it." [85]

Today, the International Criminal Court has filed charges against several Sudanese officials for rape and other crimes committed in the Darfur region. [86] But others are demanding that the court also prosecute those responsible for the rapes in the Eastern Congo, where women are being targeted as a means of destroying communities in the war-torn country. [87]

Beijing and Beyond

The U.N. World Conference on Women in Mexico City in 1975 produced a 44-page plan of action calling for a decade of special measures to give women equal status and opportunities in law, education, employment, politics and society. [88] The conference also kicked off the U.N.'s Decade for Women and led to creation of the U.N. Development Fund for Women (UNIFEM). [89]

Five years later, the U.N. held its second World Conference on Women in Copenhagen and then celebrated the end of the Decade for Women with the third World Conference in Nairobi in 1985. More than 10,000 representatives from government agencies and NGOs attended the Nairobi event, believed to be the largest gathering on women's issues at the time. [90]

Upon reviewing the progress made on women's issues during the previous 10 years, the U.N. representatives in Nairobi concluded that advances had been extremely limited due to failing economies in developing countries, particularly those in Africa struggling against drought, famine and crippling debt. The conference developed a set of steps needed to improve the status of women during the final 15 years of the 20th century. [91]

Ten years later, women gathered in Beijing in 1995 for the Fourth World Conference, vowing to turn the rhetoric of the earlier women's conferences into action. Delegates from 189 governments and 2,600 NGOs attended. More than 30,000 women and men gathered at a parallel forum organized by NGOs, also in Beijing. [92]

The so-called Beijing Platform that emerged from the conference addressed 12 critical areas facing women, from poverty to inequality in education to inadequate health care to violence. It brought unprecedented attention to women's issues and is still considered by many as the blueprint for true gender equality.

The Beijing Conference also came at the center of a decade that produced historic political gains for women around the world — gains that have continued, albeit at a slow pace, into the new century. The 1990s saw more women entering top political positions than ever before. A record 10 countries elected or appointed women as presidents between 1990 and 2000, including Haiti, Nicaragua, Switzerland and Latvia. Another 17 countries chose women prime ministers. [93]

In 2006 Ellen Johnson Sirleaf of Liberia became Africa's first elected woman president. [94] That same year, Chile elected its first female president, Michelle Bachelet, and Jamaica elected Portia Simpson Miller as its first female prime minister. [95] Also that year, women ran for election in Kuwait for the first time. In Bahrain, a woman was elected to the lower house of parliament for the first time. [96] And in 2007, Fernández de Kirchner became the first woman to be elected president of Argentina.

Earlier, a World Bank report had found that government corruption declines as more women are elected into office. The report also cited numerous studies that found women are more likely to exhibit "helping" behavior, vote based on social issues, score higher on "integrity tests," take stronger stances on ethical behavior and behave more generously when faced with economic decisions. [97]

"Increasing the presence of women in government may be valued for its own sake, for reasons of gender equality," the report concluded. "However, our results suggest that there may be extremely important spinoffs stemming from increasing female representation: If women are less likely than men to behave opportunistically, then bringing more women into government may have significant benefits for society in general." [98]

CURRENT SITUATION

Rise of Fundamentalism

Despite landmark political gains by women since the late 1990s, violence and repression of women continue to be daily occurrences — often linked to the global growth of religious fundamentalism.

In 2007, a 21-year-old woman in Saudi Arabia was sentenced to 200 lashes and ordered jailed for six months after being raped 14 times by a gang of seven men. The Saudi court sentenced the woman — who was 19 at the time of the attack — because she was alone in a car with her former boyfriend when the attack occurred. Under Saudi Arabia's strict Islamic law, it is a crime for a woman to meet in private with a man who is not her husband or relative. [99]

After public outcry from around the world, King Abdullah pardoned the woman in December. A government spokesperson, however, said the king fully supported the verdict but issued the pardon in the "interests of the people." [100]

Another Saudi woman still faces beheading after she was condemned to death for "witchcraft." Among her accusers is a man who claimed she rendered him impotent with her sorcery. Despite international protest, the king has yet to say if he will pardon her. [101]

In Iraq, the rise of religious fundamentalism since the U.S. invasion has led to a jump in the number of women being killed or beaten in so-called honor crimes. Honor killings typically occur when a woman is suspected of unsanctioned sexual behavior — which can range from flirting to "allowing" herself to be raped. Her relatives believe they must murder her to end the family's shame. In the Kurdish region of Iraq, the stoning death of 17-year-old Aswad is not an anomaly. A U.N. mission in October 2007 found that 255 women had been killed in Iraqi Kurdistan in the first six months of 2007 alone — most thought to have been murdered by their communities or families for allegedly committing adultery or entering into a relationship not sanctioned by their families. [102]

The rise of fundamentalism is also sparking a growing debate on the issue of women wearing head scarves, both in Iraq and across the Muslim world. Last August Turkey elected a conservative Muslim president whose wife wears a head scarf, signaling the emergence of a new ruling elite that is more willing to publicly display religious beliefs. [103] Then in February, Turkey's parliament voted to ease an 80-year ban on women wearing head scarves in universities, although a ban on head scarves in other public buildings remains in effect.

"This decision will bring further pressure on women," Nesrin Baytok, a member of parliament, said during debate over the ban. "It will ultimately bring us Hezbollah terror, al Qaeda terror and fundamentalism." [104]

But others said lifting the ban was actually a victory for women. Fatma Benli, a Turkish women's-rights activist and lawyer, said the ban on head scarves in public buildings has forced her to send law partners to argue her cases because she is prohibited from entering court wearing her head scarf. It also discourages religiously conservative women from becoming doctors, lawyers or teachers, she says. [105]

Many women activists are quick to say that it is unfair to condemn Islam for the growing abuse against women.

Female farmworkers in Nova Lima, Brazil, protest against the impact of big corporations on the poor in March 2006, reflecting the increasing political activism of women around the globe.

"The problem women have with religion is not the religion but the ways men have interpreted it," says Afshar of the University of York. "What is highly negative is sharia law, which is made by men. Because it's human-made, women can unmake it. The battle now is fighting against unjust laws such as stoning."

She says abuses such as forced marriages and honor killings — usually linked in the Western media to Islamic law — actually go directly against the teachings of the *Koran.* And while the United Nations estimates that some 5,000 women and girls are victims of honor killings each year, millions more are abused and killed in violence unrelated to Islam. Between 10 and 50 percent of all women around the world have been physically abused by an intimate partner in their lifetime, studies show. [106]

"What about the rate of spousal or partner killings in the U.K. or the U.S. that are not called 'honor killings'?" asks Concordia University's Hoodfar. "Then it's only occasional 'crazy people' [committing violence]. But when it's present in Pakistan, Iran or Senegal, these are uncivilized people doing 'honor killings.'"

And Islamic fundamentalism is not the only brand of fundamentalism on the rise. Christian fundamentalism is also growing rapidly. A 2006 Pew Forum on Religion and Public Life poll found that nearly one-third of all Americans feel the Bible should be the basis of law across the United States. [107] Many women's-rights activists say Christian fundamentalism threatens women's rights, particularly with regard to reproductive issues. They also condemn the Vatican's opposition to the use of con-

doms, pointing out that it prevents women from protecting themselves against HIV.

"If you look at all your religions, none will say it's a good thing to beat up or kill someone. They are all based on human dignity," says Mollmann of Human Rights Watch. "[Bad things] are carried out in the name of religion, but the actual belief system is not killing and maiming women."

In response to the growing number of honor-based killings, attacks and forced marriages in the U.K., Britain's Association of Chief Police Officers has created an honor-based violence unit, and the U.K.'s Home Office is drafting an action plan to improve the response of police and other agencies to such violence. Legislation going into effect later this year will also give U.K. courts greater guidance on dealing with forced marriages. [108]

Evolving Gender Policies

This past February, the U.N. Convention on the Elimination of All Forms of Discrimination Against Women issued a report criticizing Saudi Arabia for its repression of women. Among other things, the report attacked Saudi Arabia's ban on women drivers and its system of male guardianship that denies women equal inheritance, child custody and divorce rights. [109] The criticism came during the panel's regular review of countries that have ratified CEDAW. Each government must submit reports every four years outlining steps taken to comply with the convention.

The United States is one of only eight countries — among them Iran, Sudan and Somalia — that have refused to ratify CEDAW. [110] Last year, 108 members of the U.S. House of Representatives signed on to a resolution calling for the Senate to ratify CEDAW, but it still has not voted on the measure. [111] During a U.N. vote last November on a resolution encouraging governments to meet their obligations under CEDAW, the United States was the lone nay vote against 173 yea votes. [112]

American opponents of CEDAW — largely pro-life Christians and Republicans — say it would enshrine the right to abortion in *Roe v. Wade* and be prohibitively expensive, potentially requiring the U.S. government to provide paid maternity leave and other child-care services to all women. [113] They also oppose requirements that the government modify "social and cultural patterns" to eliminate sexual prejudice and to delete any traces of gender stereotypes in textbooks — such as references to women's lives being primarily in the domestic sector. [114] Many

AT ISSUE

Should sex-selective abortions be outlawed?

YES
Nicholas Eberstadt
Henry Wendt Chair in Political Economy, American Enterprise Institute; Member, President's Council on Bioethics

Written for *CQ Researcher*, April 2008

The practice of sex-selective abortion to permit parents to destroy unwanted female fetuses has become so widespread in the modern world that it is disfiguring the profile of entire countries — transforming (and indeed deforming) the whole human species.

This abomination is now rampant in China, where the latest census reports six boys for every five girls. But it is also prevalent in the Far East, South Korea, Hong Kong, Taiwan and Vietnam, all of which report biologically impossible "sex ratios at birth" (well above the 103-106 baby boys for every 100 girls ordinarily observed in human populations). In the Caucasus, gruesome imbalances exist now in Armenia, Georgia and Azerbaijan; and in India, the state of Punjab tallies 126 little boys for every 100 girls. Even in the United States, the boy-girl sex ratio at birth for Asian-Americans is now several unnatural percentage points above the national average. So sex-selective abortion is taking place under America's nose.

How can we rid the world of this barbaric form of sexism? Simply outlawing sex-selective abortions will be little more than a symbolic gesture, as South Korea's experience has shown: Its sex ratio at birth continued a steady climb for a full decade after just such a national law was passed. As long as abortion is basically available on demand, any legislation to abolish sex-selective abortion will have no impact.

What about more general restrictions on abortion, then? Poll data consistently demonstrate that most Americans do not favor the post-*Roe* regimen of unconditional abortion. But a return to the pre-*Roe* status quo, where each state made its own abortion laws, would probably have very little effect on sex-selective abortion in our country. After all, the ethnic communities most tempted by it are concentrated in states where abortion rights would likely be strongest, such as California and New York.

In the final analysis, the extirpation of this scourge will require nothing less than a struggle for the conscience of nations. Here again, South Korea may be illustrative: Its gender imbalances began to decline when the public was shocked into facing this stain on their society by a spontaneous, homegrown civil rights movement.

To eradicate sex-selective abortion, we must convince the world that destrtroying female fetuses is horribly wrong. We need something akin to the abolitionist movement: a moral campaign waged globally, with victories declared one conscience at a time.

NO
Marianne Mollmann
Advocacy Director, Women's Rights Division, Human Rights Watch

Written for *CQ Researcher*, April 2008

Medical technology today allows parents to test early in pregnancy for fetal abnormalities, hereditary illnesses and even the sex of the fetus, raising horrifying questions about eugenics and population control. In some countries, a growing number of women apparently are terminating pregnancies when they learn the fetus is female. The resulting sex imbalance in countries like China and India is not only disturbing but also leads to further injustices, such as the abduction of girls for forced marriages.

One response has been to criminalize sex-selective abortions. While it is tempting to hope that this could safeguard the gender balance of future generations, criminalization of abortion for whatever reason has led in the past only to underground and unsafe practices. Thus, the criminalization of sex-selective abortion would put the full burden of righting a fundamental wrong — the devaluing of women's lives — on women.

Many women who choose to abort a female fetus face violence and exclusion if they don't produce a boy. Some see the financial burden of raising a girl as detrimental to the survival of the rest of their family. These considerations will not be lessened by banning sex-selective abortion. Unless one addresses the motivation for the practice, it will continue — underground.

So what is the motivation for aborting female fetuses? At the most basic level, it is a financial decision. In no country in the world does women's earning power equal men's. In marginalized communities in developing countries, this is directly linked to survival: Boys may provide more income than girls.

Severe gaps between women's and men's earning power are generally accompanied by severe forms of gender-based discrimination and rigid gender roles. For example, in China, boys are expected to stay in their parental home as they grow up, adding their manpower (and that of a later wife) to the family home. Girls, on the other hand, are expected to join the husbands' parental home. Thus, raising a girl is a net loss, especially if you are only allowed one child.

The solution is to remove the motivation behind sex-selective abortion by advancing women's rights and their economic and social equality. Choosing the blunt instrument of criminal law over promoting the value of women's lives and rights will only serve to place further burdens on marginalized and often vulnerable women.

Republicans in Congress also have argued that CEDAW would give too much control over U.S. laws to the United Nations and that it could even require the legalization of prostitution and the abolition of Mother's Day. [115]

The last time the Senate took action on CEDAW was in 2002, when the Senate Foreign Relations Committee, chaired by Democratic Sen. Joseph Biden of Delaware, voted to send the convention to the Senate floor for ratification. The full Senate, however, never took action. A Biden spokesperson says the senator "remains committed" to the treaty and is "looking for an opportune time" to bring it forward again. But Senate ratification requires 67 votes, and there do not appear to be that many votes for approval.

CEDAW proponents say the failure to ratify not only hurts women but also harms the U.S. image abroad. On this issue, "the United States is in the company of Sudan and the Vatican," says Bien-Aimé of Equality Now.

Meanwhile, several countries are enacting laws to comply with CEDAW and improve the status of women. In December, Turkmenistan passed its first national law guaranteeing women equal rights, even though its constitution had addressed women's equality. [116] A royal decree in Saudi Arabia in January ordered an end to a long-time ban on women checking into hotels or renting apartments without male guardians. Hotels can now book rooms to women who show identification, but the hotels must register the women's details with the police. [117] The Saudi government has also said it will lift the ban on women driving by the end of the year. [118]

And in an effort to improve relations with women in Afghanistan, the Canadian military, which has troops stationed in the region, has begun studying the role women play in Afghan society, how they are affected by military operations and how they can assist peacekeeping efforts. "Behind all of these men are women who can help eradicate the problems of the population," said Capt. Michel Larocque, who is working with the study. "Illiteracy, poverty, these things can be improved through women." [119]

In February, during the 52nd session of the Commission on the Status of Women, the United Nations kicked off a new seven-year campaign aimed at ending violence against women. The campaign will work with international agencies, governments and individuals to increase funding for anti-violence campaigns and pressure policy makers around the world to enact legislation to eliminate violence against women. [120]

But women's groups want increased U.N. spending on women's programs and the creation of a single unified agency addressing women's issues, led by an under-secretary general. [121] Currently, four different U.N. agencies address women's issues: the United Nations Development Fund for Women, the International Research and Training Institute for the Advancement of Women (INSTRAW), the Secretary-General's Special Advisor on Gender Issues (OSAGI) and the Division for the Advancement of Women. In 2006, the four agencies received only $65 million — a fraction of the more than $2 billion budget that the U.N.'s children's fund (UNICEF) received that year. [122]

"The four entities that focus on women's rights at the U.N. are greatly under-resourced," says Zeitlin of the Women's Environment & Development Organization. "If the rhetoric everyone is using is true — that investing in women is investing in development — it's a matter of putting your money where your mouth is."

Political Prospects

While the number of women leading world governments is still miniscule compared to their male counterparts, women are achieving political gains that just a few years ago would have been unthinkable.

While for the first time in U.S. history a woman is in a tight race for a major party's nomination as its candidate for president, South America — with two sitting female heads of state — leads the world in woman-led governments. In Brazil, Dilma Rousseff, the female chief of staff to President Luiz Inacio Lula da Silva, is the top contender to take over the presidency when da Silva's term ends in 2010. [123] In Paraguay, Blanca Ovelar was this year's presidential nominee for the country's ruling conservative Colorado Party, but she was defeated on April 20. [124]

And in Europe, Carme Chacón was named defense minister of Spain this past April. She was not only the first woman ever to head the country's armed forces but also was pregnant at the time of her appointment. In all, nine of Spain's 17 cabinet ministers are women.

In March, Pakistan's National Assembly overwhelmingly elected its first female speaker, Fahmida Mirza. [125] And in India, where Patil has become the first woman president, the two major political parties this year pledged to set aside one-third of their parliamentary nominations for women. But many fear the parties will either not keep their pledges or will run women only in contests they are unlikely to win. [126]

There was also disappointment in Iran, where nearly 600 of the 7,000 candidates running for parliament in March were women. [127] Only three won seats in the 290-member house, and they were conservatives who are not expected to promote women's rights. Several of the tallies are being contested. Twelve other women won enough votes to face run-off elections on April 25; five won. [128]

But in some countries, women running for office face more than just tough campaigns. They are specifically targeted for violence. In Kenya, the greatest campaign expense for female candidates is the round-the-clock security required to protect them against rape, according to Phoebe Asiyo, who served in the Kenyan parliament for more than two decades. [129] During the three months before Kenya's elections last December, an emergency helpdesk established by the Education Centre for Women in Democracy, a non-governmental organization (NGO) in Nairobi, received 258 reports of attacks against female candidates. [130]

The helpdesk reported the attacks to police, worked with the press to ensure the cases were documented and helped victims obtain medical and emotional support. Attacks included rape, stabbings, threats and physical assaults. [131]

"Women are being attacked because they are women and because it is seen as though they are not fit to bear flags of the popular parties," according to the center's Web site. "Women are also viewed as guilty for invading 'the male territory' and without a license to do so!" [132]

"All women candidates feel threatened," said Nazlin Umar, the sole female presidential candidate last year. "When a case of violence against a woman is reported, we women on the ground think we are next. I think if the government assigned all women candidates with guns . . . we will at least have an item to protect ourselves when we face danger." [133]

Impunity for Violence

Some African feminists blame women themselves, as well as men, for not doing enough to end traditional attitudes that perpetuate violence against women.

"Women are also to blame for the violence because they are the gatekeepers of patriarchy, because whether educated or not they have different standards for their sons and husbands [than for] their daughters," said Njoki Wainaina, founder of the African Women Development Communication Network (FEMNET). "How do you start telling a boy whose mother trained him only disrespect for girls to honor women in adulthood?" [134]

Seaweed farmer Asia Mohammed Makungu in Zanzibar, Tanzania, grows the sea plants for export to European companies that produce food and cosmetics. Globalized trade has helped women entrepreneurs in many developing countries improve their lives, but critics say it also has created many low-wage, dangerous jobs for women in poor countries that ignore safety and labor protections in order to attract foreign investors.

Indeed, violence against women is widely accepted in many regions of the world and often goes unpunished. A study by the World Health Organization found that 80 percent of women surveyed in rural Egypt believe that a man is justified in beating a woman if she refuses to have sex with him. In Ghana, more women than men — 50 percent compared to 43 percent — felt that a man was justified in beating his wife if she used contraception without his consent. [135] (*See survey results, p. 176.*)

Such attitudes have led to many crimes against women going unpunished, and not just violence committed during wartime. In Guatemala, no one knows why an estimated 3,000 women have been killed over the past seven years — many of them beheaded, sexually mutilated or raped — but theories range from domestic violence to gang activity. [136] Meanwhile, the government in 2006 overturned a law allowing rapists to escape charges if they offered to marry their victims. But Guatemalan law still does not prescribe prison sentences for domestic abuse and prohibits abusers from being charged with assault unless the bruises are still visible after 10 days. [137]

In the Mexican cities of Chihuahua and Juárez, more than 400 women have been murdered over the past 14 years, with many of the bodies mutilated and dumped in the desert. But the crimes are still unsolved, and many human-rights groups, including Amnesty International, blame indifference by Mexican authorities. Now the country's 14-year statute of limitations on murder is forcing prosecutors to close many of the unsolved cases. [138]

Feminists around the world have been working to end dismissive cultural attitudes about domestic violence and other forms of violence against women, such as forced marriage, dowry-related violence, marital rape, sexual harassment and forced abortion, sterilization and prostitution. But it's often an uphill battle.

After a Kenyan police officer beat his wife so badly she was paralyzed and brain damaged — and eventually died — media coverage of the murder spurred a nationwide debate on domestic violence. But it took five years of protests, demonstrations and lobbying by both women's advocates and outraged men to get a family protection bill enacted criminalizing domestic violence. And the bill passed only after legislators removed a provision outlawing marital rape. Similar laws have languished for decades in other African legislatures. [139]

But in Rwanda, where nearly 49 percent of the elected representatives in the lower house are female, gender desks have been established at local police stations, staffed mostly by women trained to help victims of sexual and other violence. In 2006, as a result of improved reporting, investigation and response to rape cases, police referred 1,777 cases for prosecution and convicted 803 men. "What we need now is to expand this approach to more countries," said UNIFEM's director for Central Africa Josephine Odera. [140]

Besides criticizing governments for failing to prosecute gender-based violence, many women's groups also criticize the International Criminal Court (ICC) for not doing enough to bring abusers to justice.

"We have yet to see the investigative approach needed to ensure the prosecution of gender-based crimes," said Brigid Inder, executive director of Women's Initiatives for Gender Justice, a Hague-based group that promotes and monitors women's rights in the international court. [141] Inder's group released a study last November showing that of the 500 victims seeking to participate in ICC proceedings, only 38 percent were women. When the court handed down its first indictments for war crimes in the Democratic Republic of the Congo last year, no charges involving gender-based crimes were brought despite estimates that more than 250,000 women have been raped and sexually abused in the country. After an outcry from

women's groups around the world, the ICC included "sexual slavery" among the charges handed down in its second case involving war crimes in Congo. [142]

The Gender Justice report also criticized the court for failing to reach out to female victims. It said the ICC has held only one consultation with women in the last four years (focusing on the Darfur conflict in Sudan) and has failed to develop any strategies to reach out to women victims in Congo. [143]

OUTLOOK

Economic Integration

Women's organizations do not expect — or want — another international conference on the scale of Beijing. Instead, they say, the resources needed to launch such a conference would be better used to improve U.N. oversight of women's issues and to implement the promises made at Beijing.

They also fear that the growth of religious fundamentalism and neo-liberal economic policies around the globe have created a political atmosphere that could actually set back women's progress.

"If a Beijing conference happened now, we would not get the type of language or the scope we got 10 years ago," says Bien-Aimé of Equity Now. "There is a conservative movement, a growth in fundamentalists governments — and not just in Muslim countries. We would be very concerned about opening up debate on the principles that have already been established."

Dahlerup of Stockholm University agrees. "It was easier in the 1990s. Many people are afraid of having big conferences now, because there may be a backlash because fundamentalism is so strong," she says. "Neo-liberal trends are also moving the discourse about women toward economics — women have to benefit for the sake of the economic good. That could be very good, but it's a more narrow discourse when every issue needs to be adapted into the economic discourse of a cost-benefit analysis."

For women to continue making gains, most groups say, gender can no longer be treated separately from broader economic, environmental, health or other political issues. While efforts to improve the status of women have historically been addressed in gender-specific legislation or international treaties, women's groups now say women's well-being must now be considered an integral part of all policies.

Women's groups are working to ensure that gender is incorporated into two major international conferences coming up this fall. In September, the Third High-Level Forum on Aid Effectiveness will be hosted in Accra, Ghana, bringing together governments, financial institutions, civil society organizations and others to assess whether assistance provided to poor nations is being put to good use. World leaders will also gather in November in Doha, Qatar, for the International Conference on Financing for Development to discuss how trade, debt relief and financial aid can promote global development.

"Women's groups are pushing for gender to be on the agenda for both conferences," says Zeitlin of WEDO. "It's important because . . . world leaders need to realize that it really does make a difference to invest in women. When it comes to women's rights it's all micro, but the big decisions are made on the macro level."

Despite decades of economic-development strategies promoted by Western nations and global financial institutions such as the World Bank, women in many regions are getting poorer. In Malawi, for example, the percentage of women living in poverty increased by 5 percent between 1995 and 2003. [144] Women and girls make up 70 percent of the world's poorest people, and their wages rise more slowly than men's. They also have fewer property rights around the world. [145] With the growing global food shortage, women — who are the primary family caregivers and produce the majority of crops for home consumption in developing countries — will be especially hard hit.

To help women escape poverty, gain legal rights and improve their social status, developed nations must rethink their broader strategies of engagement with developing countries. And, conversely, female activists say, any efforts aimed at eradicating poverty around the world must specifically address women's issues.

In Africa, for instance, activists have successfully demanded that women's economic and security concerns be addressed as part of the continent-wide development plan known as the New Partnership for Africa's Development (NEPAD). As a result, countries participating in NEPAD's peer review process must now show they are taking measures to promote and protect women's rights. But, according to Augustin Wambo, an agricultural specialist at the NEPAD secretariat, lawmakers now need to back up their pledges with "resources from national budgets" and the "necessary policies and means to support women." [146]

"We have made a lot of progress and will continue making progress," says Zeitlin. "But women's progress doesn't happen in isolation to what's happening in the rest of the world. The environment, the global economy, war, peace — they will all have a major impact on women. Women all over world will not stop making demands and fighting for their rights."

NOTES

1. http://ballyblog.wordpress.com/2007/05/04/warning-uncensored-video-iraqis-stone-girl-to-death-over-loving-wrong-boy/.

2. Abdulhamid Zebari, "Video of Iraqi girl's stoning shown on Internet," Agence France Presse, May 5, 2007.

3. *State of the World Population 2000*, United Nations Population Fund, Sept. 20, 2000, Chapter 3, "Ending Violence against Women and Girls," www.unfpa.org/swp/2000/english/ch03.html.

4. Brian Brady, "A Question of Honour," *The Independent on Sunday*, Feb. 10, 2008, p. 8, www.independent.co.uk/news/uk/home-news/a-question-of-honour-police-say-17000-women-are-victims-every-year-780522.html.

5. Correspondance with Karen Musalo, Clinical Professor of Law and Director of the Center for Gender & Refugee Studies at the University of California Hastings School of Law, April 11, 2008.

6. "Broken Bodies, Broken Dreams: Violence Against Women Exposed," United Nations, July 2006, http://brokendreams.wordpress.com/2006/12/17/dowry-crimes-and-bride-price-abuse/.

7. Various sources: www.womankind.org.uk, www.unfpa.org/gender/docs/studies/summaries/reg_exe_summary.pdf, www.oxfam.org.uk. Also see "Child rape in Kano on the increase," IRIN Humanitarian News and Analysis, United Nations, www.irinnews.org/report.aspx?ReportId=76087.

8. "UNICEF slams 'licence to rape' in African crisis," Agence France-Press, Feb. 12, 2008.

9. "Film Documents Rape of Women in Congo," "All Things Considered," National Public Radio, April 8, 2008, www.npr.org/templates/story/story.php?storyId=89476111.

10. Jeffrey Gettleman, "Rape Epidemic Raises Trauma Of Congo War," *The New York Times*, Oct. 7, 2007, p. A1.

11. Dan McDougall, "Fareeda's fate: rape, prison and 25 lashes," *The Observer*, Sept. 17, 2006, www.guardian.co.uk/world/2006/sep/17/pakistan.theobserver.

12. Zarar Khan, "Thousands rally in Pakistan to demand government withdraw rape law changes," The Associated Press, Dec. 10, 2006.

13. *State of the World Population 2000, op. cit.*

14. Laura Turquet, Patrick Watt, Tom Sharman, "Hit or Miss?" ActionAid, March 7, 2008, p. 10.

15. *Ibid.*, p. 12.

16. "Women in Politics: 2008" map, International Parliamentary Union and United Nations Division for the Advancement of Women, February 2008, www.ipu.org/pdf/publications/wmnmap08_en.pdf.

17. Gavin Rabinowitz, "India's first female president sworn in, promises to empower women," The Associated Press, July 25, 2007. Note: India's first female prime minister was Indira Ghandi in 1966.

18. Monte Reel, "South America Ushers In The Era of La Presidenta; Women Could Soon Lead a Majority of Continent's Population," *The Washington Post*, Oct. 31, 2007, p. A12. For background, see Roland Flamini, "The New Latin America," *CQ Global Researcher*, March 2008, pp. 57-84.

19. Marcela Valente, "Cristina Fernandes Dons Presidential Sash," Inter Press Service, Dec. 10, 2007.

20. "Women in Politics: 2008" map, *op. cit.*

21. *Ibid.*; Global Database of Quotas for Women, International Institute for Democracy and Electoral Assistance and Stockholm University, www.quotaproject.org/country.cfm?SortOrder=Country.

22. "Beijing Betrayed," Women's Environment and Development Organization, March 2005, p. 10, www.wedo.org/files/gmr_pdfs/gmr2005.pdf.

23. "Women in Politics: 2008" map, *op. cit.*

24. Gertrude Mongella, address by the Secretary-General of the 4th World Conference on Women, Sept. 4, 1995, www.un.org/esa/gopher-data/conf/fwcw/conf/una/950904201423.txt. Also see Steven Mufson, "Women's Forum Sets Accord; Dispute on Sexual Freedom Resolved," *The Washington Post*, Sept. 15, 1995, p. A1.

25. "Closing statement," Gertrude Mongella, U.N. Division for the Advancement of Women, Fourth World Conference on Women, www.un.org/esa/gopher-data/conf/fwcw/conf/una/closing.txt.

26. "Trading Away Our Rights," Oxfam International, 2004, p. 9, www.oxfam.org.uk/resources/policy/trade/downloads/trading_rights.pdf.

27. "Trafficking in Persons Report," U.S. Department of State, June 2007, p. 7, www.state.gov/g/tip/rls/tiprpt/2007/.

28. Turquet, *et al., op. cit.*, p. 4.

29. United Nations Division for the Advancement of Women, www.un.org/womenwatch/daw/cedaw/.

30. Geraldine Terry, *Women's Rights* (2007), p. 30.

31. United Nations Division for the Advancement of Women, www.un.org/womenwatch/daw/cedaw/.

32. "The impact of international trade on gender equality," The World Bank PREM notes, May 2004, http://siteresources.worldbank.org/INTGENDER/Resources/premnote86.pdf.

33. Thalia Kidder and Kate Raworth, " 'Good Jobs' and hidden costs: women workers documenting the price of precarious employment," *Gender and Development*, July 2004, p. 13.

34. "Trading Away Our Rights," *op. cit.*

35. Martha Chen, *et al.*, "Progress of the World's Women 2005: Women, Work and Poverty," UNIFEM, p. 17, www.unifem.org/attachments/products/PoWW2005_eng.pdf.

36. Eric Neumayer and Indra de Soys, "Globalization, Women's Economic Rights and Forced Labor," London School of Economics and Norwegian University of Science and Technology, February 2007, p. 8, http://papers.ssrn.com/sol3/papers.cfm?abstract_id=813831. Also see "Five years down the road from Beijing — assessing progress," *News and Highlights*, Food and Agriculture Organization, June 2, 2000, www.fao.org/News/2000/000602-e.htm.

37. "Trafficking in Persons Report," *op. cit.*, p. 13.

38. "World Survey on the Role of Women in Development," United Nations, 2006, p. 1, www.un.org/womenwatch/daw/public/WorldSurvey2004-Women&Migration.pdf.

39. Julie Ballington and Azza Karam, eds., "Women in Parliament: Beyond the Numbers," International Institute for Democracy and Electoral Assistance, 2005, p. 155, www.idea.int/publications/wip2/upload/WiP_inlay.pdf.

40. "Women in Politics: 2008," *op. cit.*

41. Ballington and Karam, *op. cit.*, p. 158.

42. *Ibid.*, p. 161.

43. Global Database of Quotas for Women, *op. cit.*

44. Jerome Starkey, "Afghan government official says that student will not be executed," *The Independent*, Feb. 6, 2008, www.independent.co.uk/news/world/asia/afghan-government-official-says-that-student-will-not-be-executed-778686.html?r=RSS.

45. "Afghan women seek death by fire," BBC, Nov. 15, 2006, http://news.bbc.co.uk/1/hi/world/south_asia/6149144.stm.

46. Global Database for Quotas for Women, *op. cit.*

47. "Beijing Declaration," Fourth World Conference on Women, www.un.org/womenwatch/daw/beijing/beijingdeclaration.html.

48. "Beijing Betrayed," *op. cit.*, pp. 28, 15, 18.

49. "Review of the implementation of the Beijing Platform for Action and the outcome documents of the special session of the General Assembly entitled 'Women 2000: gender equality, development and peace for the twenty-first century,'" United Nations, Dec. 6, 2004, p. 74.

50. "Gender Equality and the Millennium Development Goals," fact sheet, www.mdgender.net/upload/tools/MDGender_leaflet.pdf.

51. *Ibid.*

52. Turquet, *et al.*, *op. cit.*, p. 16.

53. *Ibid.*, pp. 22-24.

54. Terry, *op. cit.*, p. 6.

55. "Inclusive Security, Sustainable Peace: A Toolkit for Advocacy and Action," International Alert and Women Waging Peace, 2004, p. 12, www.huntalternatives.org/download/35_introduction.pdf.

56. "Declarations, Reservations and Objections to CEDAW," www.un.org/womenwatch/daw/cedaw/reservations-country.htm.

57. Merlin Stone, *When God Was a Woman* (1976), pp. 18, 11.

58. Jack Holland, *Misogyny* (2006), p. 12.

59. *Ibid.*, pp. 21-23.

60. Holland, *op. cit.*, p. 112.

61. "Dispelling the myths about so-called witches" press release, Johns Hopkins University, Oct. 7, 2002, www.jhu.edu/news_info/news/home02/oct02/witch.html.

62. The quote is from the *Malleus maleficarum* (*The Hammer of Witches*), and was cited in "Case Study: The European Witch Hunts, c. 1450-1750," *Gendercide Watch*, www.gendercide.org/case_witch-hunts.html.

63. Holland, *op. cit.*, p. 179.

64. Cathy J. Cohen, Kathleen B. Jones and Joan C. Tronto, *Women Transforming Politics: An Alternative Reader* (1997), p. 530.

65. *Ibid.*

66. Holland, *op. cit.*, p. 201.

67. "Men and Women in Politics: Democracy Still in the Making," IPU Study No. 28, 1997, http://archive.idea.int/women/parl/ch6_table8.htm.

68. "Sex, Equality and Protective Laws," *CQ Researcher*, July 13, 1926.

69. The case was *Radice v. People of State of New York*, 264 U. S. 292. For background, see F. Brewer, "Equal Rights Amendment," *Editorial Research Reports*, April 4, 1946, available at *CQ Researcher Plus Archive*, www.cqpress.com.

70. "Short History of the CEDAW Convention," U.N. Division for the Advancement of Women, www.un.org/womenwatch/daw/cedaw/history.htm.

71. U.N. Women's Watch, www.un.org/womenwatch/asp/user/list.asp-ParentID=11047.htm.

72. United Nations, http://untreaty.un.org/ENGLISH/bible/englishinternetbible/partI/chapterXVI/treaty2.asp.

73. International Labor Organization, www.ilo.org/public/english/support/lib/resource/subject/gender.htm.

74. *Ibid.*

75. For background, see "Gender Pay Gap," *CQ Researcher*, March 14, 2008, pp. 241-264.

76. "Short History of the CEDAW Convention" *op. cit.*

77. "International News," The Associated Press, Dec. 19, 1979.

78. "Short History of the CEDAW Convention" *op. cit.*

79. "Text of the Convention," U.N. Division for the Advancement of Women, www.un.org/women-watch/daw/cedaw/cedaw.htm.

80. Convention on the Elimination of All Forms of Discrimination against Women, Article 16, www.un.org/womenwatch/daw/cedaw/text/econvention.htm.

81. General Recommendation made by the Committee on the Elimination of Discrimination against Women No. 19, 11th session, 1992, www.un.org/womenwatch/daw/cedaw/recommendations/recomm.htm#recom19.

82. See www.unhchr.ch/huridocda/huridoca.nsf/(Symbol)/A.CONF.157.23.En.

83. Marlise Simons, "For First Time, Court Defines Rape as War Crime," *The New York Times*, June 28, 1996, www.nytimes.com/specials/bosnia/context/0628warcrimes-tribunal.html.

84. Ann Simmons, "U.N. Tribunal Convicts Rwandan Ex-Mayor of Genocide in Slaughter," *Los Angeles Times*, Sept. 3, 1998, p. 20.

85. "Human Rights Watch Applauds Rwanda Rape Verdict," press release, Human Rights Watch, Sept. 2, 1998, http://hrw.org/english/docs/1998/09/02/rwanda1311.htm.

86. Frederic Bichon, "ICC vows to bring Darfur war criminals to justice," Agence France-Presse, Feb. 24, 2008.

87. Rebecca Feeley and Colin Thomas-Jensen, "Getting Serious about Ending Conflict and Sexual Violence in Congo," Enough Project, www.enoughproject.org/reports/congoserious.

88. "Women; Deceived Again?" *The Economist*, July 5, 1975.

89. "International Women's Day — March 8: Points of Interest and Links with UNIFEM," UNIFEM New Zealand Web site, www.unifem.org.nz/IWDPoints ofinterest.htm.

90. Joseph Gambardello, "Reporter's Notebook: Women's Conference in Kenya," United Press International, July 13, 1985.

91. "Report of the World Conference to Review and Appraise the Achievements of the United Nations Decade for Women: Equality Development and Peace," United Nations, 1986, paragraph 8, www.un.org/womenwatch/confer/nfls/Nairobi1985report.txt.

92. U.N. Division for the Advancement of Women, www.un.org/womenwatch/daw/followup/background.htm.

93. "Women in Politics," Inter-Parliamentary Union, 2005, pp. 16-17, www.ipu.org/PDF/publications/wmn45-05_en.pdf.

94. "Liberian becomes Africa's first female president," Associated Press, Jan. 16, 2006, www.msnbc.msn.com/id/10865705/.

95. "Women in the Americas: Paths to Political Power," *op. cit.*, p. 2.

96. "The Millennium Development Goals Report 2007," United Nations, 2007, p. 12, www.un.org/millenniumgoals/pdf/mdg2007.pdf.

97. David Dollar, Raymond Fisman, Roberta Gatti, "Are Women Really the 'Fairer' Sex? Corruption and Women in Government," The World Bank, October 1999, p. 1, http://siteresources.world-bank.org/INTGENDER/Resources/wp4.pdf.

98. *Ibid.*

99. Vicky Baker, "Rape victim sentenced to 200 lashes and six months in jail; Saudi woman punished for being alone with a man," *The Guardian*, Nov. 17, 2007, www.guardian.co.uk/world/2007/nov/17/saudiarabia.international.

100. Katherine Zoepf, "Saudi King Pardons Rape Victim Sentenced to Be Lashed, Saudi Paper Reports," *The New York Times*, Dec. 18, 2007, www.nytimes.com/2007/12/18/world/middleeast/18saudi.html.

101. Sonia Verma, "King Abdullah urged to spare Saudi 'witchcraft' woman's life," *The Times* (Of London), Feb. 16, 2008.

102. Mark Lattimer, "Freedom lost," *The Guardian*, Dec. 13, 2007, p. 6.

103. For background, see Brian Beary, "Future of Turkey," *CQ Global Researcher*, December, 2007, pp. 295-322.

104. Tracy Clark-Flory, "Does freedom to veil hurt women?" *Salon.com*, Feb. 11, 2008.

105. Sabrina Tavernise, "Under a Scarf, a Turkish Lawyer Fighting to Wear It," *The New York Times*, Feb. 9, 2008, www.nytimes.com/2008/02/09/world/europe/09benli.html?pagewanted=1&sq=women&st=nyt&scp=96.

106. Terry, *op. cit.*, p. 122.

107. "Many Americans Uneasy with Mix of Religion and Politics," The Pew Forum on Religion and Public Life, Aug. 24, 2006, http://pewforum.org/docs/index.php?DocID=153.

108. Brady, *op. cit.*

109. "Concluding Observations of the Committee on the Elimination of Discrimination against Women: Saudi Arabia," Committee on the Elimination of Discrimination against Women, 40th Session, Jan. 14-Feb. 1, 2008, p. 3, www2.ohchr.org/english/bodies/cedaw/docs/co/CEDAW.C.SAU.CO.2.pdf.

110. Kambiz Fattahi, "Women's bill 'unites' Iran and US," BBC, July 31, 2007, http://news.bbc.co.uk/2/hi/middle_east/6922749.stm.

111. H. Res. 101, Rep. Lynn Woolsey, http://thomas.loc.gov/cgi-bin/bdquery/z?d110:h.res.00101.

112. "General Assembly Adopts Landmark Text Calling for Moratorium on Death Penalty," States News Service, Dec. 18, 2007, www.un.org/News/Press/docs//2007/ga10678.doc.htm.

113. Mary H. Cooper, "Women and Human Rights," *CQ Researcher*, April 30, 1999, p. 356.

114. Christina Hoff Sommers, "The Case against Ratifying the United Nations Convention on the Elimination of All Forms of Discrimination against Women," testimony before the Senate Foreign Relations Committee, June 13, 2002, www.aei.org/publications/filter.all,pubID.15557/pub_detail.asp.

115. "CEDAW. Pro-United Nations, Not Pro Woman" press release, U.S. Senate Republican Policy Committee, Sept. 16, 2002, http://rpc.senate.gov/_files/FOREIGNje091602.pdf.

116. "Turkmenistan adopts gender equality law," BBC Worldwide Monitoring, Dec. 19, 2007.

117. Faiza Saleh Ambah, "Saudi Women See a Brighter Road on Rights," *The Washington Post*, Jan. 31, 2008, p. A15, www.washingtonpost.com/wp-dyn/content/article/2008/01/30/AR2008013003805.html.

118. Damien McElroy, "Saudi Arabia to lift ban on women drivers," *The Telegraph*, Jan. 1, 2008.

119. Stephanie Levitz, "Lifting the veils of Afghan women," *The Hamilton Spectator* (Ontario, Canada), Feb. 28, 2008, p. A11.

120. "U.N. Secretary-General Ban Ki-moon Launches Campaign to End Violence against Women," U.N. press release, Feb. 25, 2008, http://endviolence.un.org/press.shtml.

121. "Gender Equality Architecture and U.N. Reforms," the Center for Women's Global Leadership and the Women's Environment and Development Organization, July 17, 2006, www.wedo.org/files/Gender%20Equality%20Architecture%20and%20UN%20Reform0606.pdf.

122. Bojana Stoparic, "New-Improved Women's Agency Vies for U.N. Priority," Women's eNews, March 6, 2008, www.womensenews.org/article.cfm?aid=3517.

123. Reel, *op. cit.*

124. Eliana Raszewski and Bill Faries, "Lugo, Ex Bishop, Wins Paraguay Presidential Election," Bloomberg, April 20, 2008.

125. Zahid Hussain, "Pakistan gets its first woman Speaker," *The Times* (of London), March 20, p. 52.

126. Bhaskar Roy, "Finally, women set to get 33% quota," *Times of India*, Jan. 29, 2008.

127. Massoumeh Torfeh, "Iranian women crucial in Majlis election," BBC, Jan. 30, 2008, http://news.bbc.co.uk/1/hi/world/middle_east/7215272.stm.

128. "Iran women win few seats in parliament," Agence-France Presse, March 18, 2008.

129. Swanee Hunt, "Let Women Rule," *Foreign Affairs*, May-June 2007, p. 109.

130. Kwamboka Oyaro, "A Call to Arm Women Candidates With More Than Speeches," Inter Press Service, Dec. 21, 2007, http://ipsnews.net/news.asp?idnews=40569.

131. Education Centre for Women in Democracy, www.ecwd.org.

132. *Ibid.*

133. Oyaro, *op. cit.*

134. *Ibid.*

135. Mary Kimani, "Taking on violence against women in Africa," *AfricaRenewal*, U.N. Dept. of Public Information, July 2007, p. 4, www.un.org /ecosocdev/geninfo/afrec/vol21no2/212-violence-aganist-women.html.

136. Correspondence with Karen Musalo, Clinical Professor of Law and Director of the Center for Gender & Refugee Studies, University of California Hastings School of Law, April 11, 2008.

137. "Mexico and Guatemala: Stop the Killings of Women," Amnesty International USA Issue Brief, January 2007, www.amnestyusa.org/document .php?lang=e&id=engusa20070130001.

138. Manuel Roig-Franzia, "Waning Hopes in Juarez," *The Washington Post*, May 14, 2007, p. A10.

139. Kimani, *op. cit.*

140. *Ibid.*

141. "Justice slow for female war victims," *The Toronto Star*, March 3, 2008, www.thestar.com/News /GlobalVoices/article/308784p.

142. Speech by Brigid Inder on the Launch of the "Gender Report Card on the International Criminal Court," Dec. 12, 2007, www.icc-women.org/news/docs/Launch_GRC_2007.pdf

143. "Gender Report Card on the International Criminal Court," Women's Initiatives for Gender Justic, November 2007, p. 32, www.iccwomen .org/publications/resources/docs/GENDER_04-01-2008_FINAL_TO_PRINT.pdf.

144. Turquet, *et al.*, *op. cit.*, p. 8.

145. Oxfam Gender Equality Fact Sheet, www.oxfam .org.uk/resources/issues/gender/introduction.html.

146. Itai Madamombe, "Women push onto Africa's agenda," *AfricaRenewal*, U.N. Dept. of Public Information, July 2007, pp. 8-9.

BIBLIOGRAPHY

Books

Holland, Jack, *Misogyny: The World's Oldest Prejudice*, Constable & Robinson, 2006.
The late Irish journalist provides vivid details and anecdotes about women's oppression throughout history.

Stone, Merlin, *When God Was a Woman*, Harcourt Brace Jovanovich, 1976.
The book contends that before the rise of Judeo-Christian patriarchies women headed the first societies and religions.

Terry, Geraldine, *Women's Rights*, Pluto Press, 2007.
A feminist who has worked for Oxfam and other non-governmental organizations outlines major issues facing women today — from violence to globalization to AIDS.

Women and the Environment, UNEP, 2004.
The United Nations Environment Programme shows the integral link between women in the developing world and the changing environment.

Articles

Brady, Brian, "A Question of Honour," *The Independent on Sunday*, Feb. 10, 2008, p. 8.
"Honor killings" and related violence against women are on the rise in the United Kingdom.

Kidder, Thalia, and Kate Raworth, " 'Good Jobs' and hidden costs: women workers documenting the price of precarious employment," *Gender and Development*, Vol. 12, No. 2, p. 12, July 2004.
Two trade and gender experts describe the precarious working conditions and job security experienced by food and garment workers.

Reports and Studies

"Beijing Betrayed," Women's Environment and Development Organization, March 2005, www.wedo .org/files/gmr_pdfs/gmr2005.pdf.
A women's-rights organization reviews the progress and shortcomings of governments in implementing the com-

mitments made during the Fifth World Congress on Women in Beijing in 1995.

"The Millennium Development Goals Report 2007," United Nations, 2007, www.un.org/millennium-goals/pdf/mdg2007.pdf.
International organizations demonstrate the progress governments have made — or not — in reaching the Millennium Development Goals.

"Trafficking in Persons Report," U.S. Department of State, June 2007, www.state.gov/documents/organization/82902.pdf.
This seventh annual report discusses the growing problems of human trafficking around the world.

"The tsunami's impact on women," Oxfam briefing note, March 5, 2005, www.oxfam.org/en/files/bn050326_tsunami_women/download.
Looking at how the 2004 tsunami affected women in Indonesia, India and Sri Lanka, Oxfam International suggests how governments can better address women's issues during future natural disasters.

"Women in Politics," Inter-Parliamentary Union, 2005, www.ipu.org/PDF/publications/wmn45-05_en.pdf.
The report provides detailed databases of the history of female political representation in governments around the world.

Ballington, Julie, and Azza Karam, "Women in Parliament: Beyond the Numbers," International Institute for Democracy and Electoral Assistance, 2005, www.idea.int/publications/wip2/upload/WiP_inlay.pdf.
The handbook provides female politicians and candidates information and case studies on how women have overcome obstacles to elected office.

Chen, Martha, Joann Vanek, Francie Lund, James Heintz, Renana Jhabvala and Christine Bonner, "Women, Work and Poverty," UNIFEM, 2005, www.unifem.org/attachments/products/PoWW2005_eng.pdf.
The report argues that greater work protection and security is needed to promote women's rights and reduce global poverty.

Larserud, Stina, and Rita Taphorn, "Designing for Equality," International Institute for Democracy and Electoral Assistance, 2007, www.idea.int/publications/designing_for_equality/upload/Idea_Design_low.pdf.
The report describes the impact that gender quota systems have on women's representation in elected office.

Raworth, Kate, and Claire Harvey, "Trading Away Our Rights," Oxfam International, 2004, www.oxfam.org.uk/resources/policy/trade/downloads/trading_rights.pdf.
Through exhaustive statistics, case studies and interviews, the report paints a grim picture of how trade globalization is affecting women.

Turquet, Laura, Patrick Watt and Tom Sharman, "Hit or Miss?" ActionAid, March 7, 2008.
The report reviews how governments are doing in achieving the U.N.'s Millennium Development Goals.

For More Information

Equality Now, P.O. Box 20646, Columbus Circle Station, New York, NY 10023; www.equalitynow.org. An international organization working to protect women against violence and promote women's human rights.

Global Database of Quotas for Women; www.quotaproject.org. A joint project of the International Institute for Democracy and Electoral Assistance and Stockholm University providing country-by-country data on electoral quotas for women.

Human Rights Watch, 350 Fifth Ave., 34th floor, New York, NY 10118-3299; (212) 290-4700; www.hrw.org. Investigates and exposes human-rights abuses around the world.

Hunt Alternatives Fund, 625 Mount Auburn St., Cambridge, MA 02138; (617) 995-1900; www.huntalternatives.org. A private foundation that provides grants and technical assistance to promote positive social change; its Initiative for Inclusive Security promotes women in peacekeeping.

Inter-Parliamentary Union, 5, Chemin du Pommier, Case Postale 330, CH-1218 Le Grand-Saconnex, Geneva, Switzerland; +(4122) 919 41 50; www.ipu.org. An organization of parliaments of sovereign states that maintains an extensive database on women serving in parliaments.

Oxfam International, 226 Causeway St., 5th Floor, Boston, MA 02114; (617) 482-1211; www.oxfam.org. Confederation of 13 independent nongovernmental organizations working to fight poverty and related social injustice.

U.N. Development Fund for Women (UNIFEM), 304 East 45th St., 15th Floor, New York, NY 10017; (212) 906-6400; www.unifem.org. Provides financial aid and technical support for empowering women and promoting gender equality.

U.N. Division for the Advancement of Women (DAW), 2 UN Plaza, DC2-12th Floor, New York, NY 10017; www.un.org/womenwatch/daw. Formulates policy on gender equality, implements international agreements on women's issues and promotes gender mainstreaming in government activities.

Women's Environment & Development Organization (WEDO), 355 Lexington Ave., 3rd Floor, New York, NY 10017; (212) 973-0325; www.wedo.org. An international organization that works to promote women's equality in global policy.

VOICES FROM ABROAD

Jasvinder Sanghera

Director of Karma Nirvana, A women's project and refuge in Derby, England

Police don't understand honor killing

"The women who ring us for support have said, 'We've been to the police and they don't understand and they're sending us back.' Honor-based violence is far more complex than 'typical' domestic violence and the police are not being trained in how complex it is."

The Guardian (London), June 2007

Kalpana Sharma

The Hindu Newspaper

Young Indian women reject sex-selective abortions

"I know women who have been persuaded to have multiple abortions and who feel absolutely rotten, but they have no choice — either abortion or divorce. But I sense things are changing with a younger generation of very well educated women who are not prepared to put up with this."

Daily Mail (London), July 2006

Hilda Morales

Network of Non-Violence Against Women

Abuse goes unpunished in Guatemala

"Unfortunately, in Guatemala, killing a woman is like killing a fly; no importance is assigned to it . . . . the perpetrators are encouraged to continue beating, abusing and killing because they know that nothing will happen, that they won't be punished."

IPS (Latin America), November 2007

Datuk Seri Abdullah Ahmad Badawi

Prime Minister of Malaysia

Women are an asset

"We have a woman who is the governor of Bank Negara, and she is one of the finest in the world. We have two women vice-chancellors in our universities, and we are in the midst of appointing a third. . . . This is a natural progression . . . as more men realize their female counterparts are playing an equally important role."

New Straits Times (Malaysia), September 2007

Punit Bedi

New Delhi gynecologist

Medical professionals partly responsible for sex-selective abortion

"Just as throughout history euphemisms have been used to mask mass killings, terms like 'female foeticide,'* 'son preference' and 'sex selection' are now being used to cover up what amount to illegal contract killings on a massive scale, with the contracts being between parents and doctors somehow justified as a form of consumer choice."

Sunday Times (London), August 2007

* Feticide, or foeticide, is the killing of a fetus.

Jolly Kamuntu

Lawyer, based in Bukavu, Dem. Republic of Congo

Congolese activists urge the prosecution of war criminals

"The ICC [International Criminal Court] defines rape as a crime of war and a crime against humanity. . . . It has the jurisdiction to arrest the big fish . . . who are in power today. If they are punished, this would intimidate the militias on the ground and give relief to the whole community living through this trauma.

Agence France-Presse, December 2007

Michelle Bachelet

President of Chile

Chilean leader criticizes sexism in Latin America

"In my whole political life I have never seen a male candidate whose clothes and hair are discussed. There is a machismo, and a sexism, and it is not just in Latin America. . . . If a woman talks hard then she is [described as] authoritarian, or else she's soft. [Female politicians] are often asked how they manage the children. They would never ask that of a man."

The Independent (London), April 2008

Dario La Crisis/Dario Castillejos

8

Human Rights in China

Thomas J. Billitteri

Policemen train outside the Olympic Stadium in Beijing on July 21. Concern about terrorism during the Games has led China to take the kinds of actions that have outraged the West and sparked internal unrest, such as the recent public execution of three young men reportedly with terrorist ties. China is hoping the Olympics will showcase its economic and social gains, but critics say the Communist Party still stifles dissent and tramples basic freedoms.

From *CQ Researcher*,
July 25, 2008.

At a ceremony in March in flower-bedecked Tiananmen Square, Vice President Xi Jinping suggested the Beijing Olympics would lead China and people the world over to join hands in creating "a more harmonious and better future." [1]

The event underscored China's hope that 19 years after its violent suppression of protesters in Tiananmen Square, it could present a new face to the world. China's nationalistic pride in its rise as a global power is palpable, and the country is clearly anxious to showcase its hypersonic economic growth and its embrace of what communist officials call the "rule of law."

But human-rights advocates say that while some facets of Chinese society have indeed improved in recent years, repression and inequity still affect millions of people. The critics say that behind the sheen of progress and prosperity — the ubiquitous construction cranes and thousands of new factories — the Chinese Communist Party (CCP) still stifles dissent and tramples basic freedoms of speech, religion and assembly at home and abets human-rights abuses in places like Sudan's Darfur region.

"When you come to the Olympic Games in Beijing, you will see skyscrapers, spacious streets, modern stadiums and enthusiastic people," Teng Biao and Hu Jia, two of China's most prominent human-rights activists, wrote last year. "You will see the truth, but not the whole truth. . . . You may not know that the flowers, smiles, harmony and prosperity are built on a base of grievances, tears, imprisonment, torture and blood." [2]

In April Hu was sentenced to three-and-a-half years in prison. A month before his arrest, he had deplored the "human-rights disaster" in China during testimony via the Internet to the European Parliament's Subcommittee on Human Rights. [3]

China Gets Low Human-Rights Rating

In a survey of citizens in 24 nations, China received lower marks for respecting its citizens' rights than the United States and France but higher marks than Russia, Saudi Arabia and Iran. China's approval ratings were highest among Pakistanis, Nigerians and Tanzanians and lowest in Europe, Japan and the Americas.

Percentage in Selected Countries Who Say Governments Respect the Personal Freedoms of Their People

	United States	France	China	Russia	Saudi Arabia	Iran
United States	75%	66%	14%	23%	13%	8%
Germany	70	86	13	16	24	6
Great Britain	69	78	12	18	14	12
France	65	77	7	14	20	5
Russia	66	67	39	45	23	22
Lebanon	55	87	48	38	64	29
Egypt	44	50	34	29	60	28
Japan	80	78	6	22	24	10
China	50	58	n/a	52	34	38
Pakistan	45	34	66	33	67	56
Brazil	51	53	22	26	11	5
Mexico	50	45	33	28	10	8
Nigeria	72	60	72	40	54	39
Tanzania	67	68	65	50	35	31
Median*	**65%**	**63%**	**30%**	**28%**	**24%**	**10%**

* Median percentages are shown for all 24 countries in the survey, but not all countries surveyed are shown above.

Source: "Some Positive Signs for U.S. Image," Pew Global Attitudes Project, June 2008

In many ways, China's rigid societal control is at odds with its economic revolution and the accompanying rapidly expanding middle class, dynamic new urban architecture and thousands of new laws and regulations. By 2006 the nation boasted 11 million private entrepreneurs and 4.3 million private firms, banned until the early 1980s. China's middle class, barely evident in the early 1990s, had exploded to 80 million people by 2002, and by 2025 is expected to number an astonishing 520 million. [4]

Yet a litany of serious abuses by the Chinese government persists, according to the U.S. advocacy group Freedom House and others, including:

- Imprisoning more journalists than any other country;
- Maintaining one of the world's most sophisticated systems of blocking Web-site access and monitoring e-mail;
- Prescribing the death penalty for scores of non-violent crimes, including tax fraud and "the vague offense of 'undermining national unity.' " Amnesty International estimated 470 people were executed [to] death last year, based on public reports, but said the true figure is thought to be far higher;
- Maintaining a one-child policy that sometimes leads to forced abortions and human trafficking; and
- Repressing religious freedom of Falun Gong adherents, Tibetan Buddhists, Christians, Muslims and others. [5]

Security threats related to the Olympics have led China to take the kind of actions that have outraged the West and sparked internal unrest. In July, an execution squad publicly shot three young men in the public square of the city of Yengishahar. They had been convicted of having ties to terrorist plots, which authorities said were part of an effort to disrupt the Games by a separatist group seeking independence on behalf of Muslim Uyghurs. [6] The executions did not quell fears of terrorism as the Olympics drew nearer, however. At least two died and 14 were injured in a pair of bus bombings in the city of Kunming as authorities tightened security for the Games. [7]

Meanwhile, a scramble this summer to clear Beijing's air and regatta waters in preparation for the Olympics highlighted China's colossal environmental woes, which have sparked thousands of mass protests throughout the country over health and safety issues.

Reconciling the two faces of China — repressive yet forward-looking — is not easy. Many experts note that Beijing's overriding goal is to develop the country as a world power and push its economy into the 21st century while keeping a lid on internal dissent that could weaken the Communist Party — a difficult balancing act given the country's unprecedented speed of change.

Chinese embassy officials in Washington declined to discuss the status of human rights in their country. But in April, Luo Haocai, director of the China Society for Human Rights Studies, said that after three decades of rapid economic development, China is on a path to developing human rights with Chinese characteristics.

"China believes human rights like other rights are not 'absolute' and the rights enjoyed should conform to obligations fulfilled," he said. "The country deems human rights not only refer to civil rights and political rights but also include the economic, social and cultural rights. These rights are inter-related." [8]

The upcoming Olympics — and President George W. Bush's decision to attend the opening ceremonies despite China's human-rights record — has focused attention on the question of how far the West should go in pressing China to improve its human rights. Asked whether Bush's attendance would induce China to concede on its human-rights issues, Foreign Ministry spokesman Qin Gang suggested that any changes would not be influenced by Western pressure.

"We have been committed to improving human rights not on the premise of the will of any nation, group, organization or individual, nor because of a certain activity to be held that makes us concede to the human-rights issue," he said. Still, Qin said, a human-rights dialogue between China and the United States held in May — the first since 2002 — was "positive" and "constructive." [9]

Wu Jianmin, a professor at China Foreign Affairs University and former ambassador to France, said that in trying to modernize, China is "striking a delicate balance" among stability, development and reform. Stability is a "known condition for development," and development is "the aim," he said. "We are facing many prob-

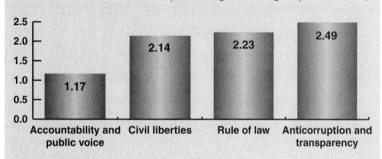

China's Human-Rights Record Is Lackluster

China performs poorly in all four human-rights categories studied by the pro-democracy group Freedom House. On a scale of 0 to 7 — with 7 representing the best performance — China scored less than 3 in all four categories and lowest (1.17) in "accountability and public voice" (free elections, media independence and freedom of expression).

China's Human Rights Report Card, 2007
(on a scale of 0 to 7, with 7 representing the strongest performance)

Accountability and public voice	Civil liberties	Rule of law	Anticorruption and transparency
1.17	2.14	2.23	2.49

Source: "Country Report — China," Freedom House, 2007

lems. I believe that only development can provide solutions. Reform is a driving force. We can't afford to go too fast. Too fast will disturb stability." [10]

Experts caution that China's human-rights picture is highly complex and difficult to characterize without nuance and historical perspective. "Things are moving forward and backward at the same time at different paces at different places," says John Kamm, executive director of the Dui Hua Foundation, a human-rights group in San Francisco and Hong Kong.

China's human rights present a "moving target," adds Margaret Woo, a professor at Northeastern University School of Law and co-editor of the forthcoming book, *Chinese Justice: Civil Dispute Resolution in China.* "It really depends on what time you're talking about, what particular topic, whether you're looking at it in terms of its progress vs. where it is today. It's not an easy, simple yes-or-no answer."

The tension in China between progress and repression emerged in full force after the massive earthquake in Sichuan Province in May, killing nearly 70,000 Chinese. Prime Minister Wen Jiabao and President Hu Jintao both toured the disaster zone, with Wen visiting an aid station and exhorting rescue workers not to give up on

Prominent human-rights activist Hu Jia, right, with his wife Zeng Jinyan in 2007, was sentenced to three-and-a-half years in prison. A month before his arrest, he had deplored the "human-rights disaster" in China.

saving lives, and Hu clasping hands with survivors. [11] But behind the scenes, local Chinese officials have tried to stifle complaints of parents whose children died in collapsed schools, reminding them that disturbing the social order is against the law. [12]

Despite concern over China's human-rights behavior, its rising prominence as an economic powerhouse and national-security ally has led U.S. policy makers to act in ways that satisfy neither Chinese officials nor Western human-rights advocates. In March, just as a massive pro-independence protest erupted in Tibet, leading to violent clashes with Chinese security forces, the State Department removed China from its list of the world's 10 worst human-rights violators. Activists denounced the move, and *The New York Times* opined that removing China from the list "looked like a political payoff to a government whose help America desperately needs on difficult problems." [13] Yet the State Department's annual report on global human rights called China an "authoritarian state" whose record remained "poor." [14] It cited:

- Extrajudicial killings, torture and coerced confessions of prisoners;
- Coercive birth-limitation policies sometimes resulting in forced abortions;
- Severe repression of minorities;
- Use of forced labor, and other violations;

- Judicial decision-making often influenced by bribery, abuse of power and other corruption and a criminal-justice system biased toward a presumption of guilt, especially in high-profile or politically sensitive cases.

In another report in May, the State Department charged that China "continued to deny its citizens basic democratic rights" and called for the government to bring its practices in line with international norms. [15]

Foreign Ministry spokesman Qin called the May report "unreasonable." "We remind the U.S. side to pay more attention to its own human-rights problems, stop interfering in the internal affairs of other countries with such issues as democracy and human rights, and do more things that are conducive to the advancement of Sino-U.S. mutual trust and bilateral relations." [16]

As thousands of foreigners descend upon Beijing for the Olympic Games, here are some of the main questions surrounding human rights in China:

Is China's human-rights record improving?

China is making strides toward protecting personal rights, though experts say the gains are uneven, incomplete and driven by political pragmatism.

"It really depends on how you break it down," says Minxin Pei, a senior associate in the China Program at the Carnegie Endowment for International Peace. The government has, for example, loosened up in recent years on personal freedoms, such as the freedom to travel, while civil or political rights remain "very limited," he says.

It is now "fair game" to discuss public-policy issues such as health care, housing, the environment and education, Pei says, and even to "take government to task for not doing a good job." But, "you cannot challenge the Communist Party in a frontal way and call for democratic elections."

"On balance, human rights are improving because the pressure from society is so enormous," Pei said. "Also, the legitimacy of repression is declining. Even the government understands there are certain things you cannot use force to deal with, and international pressure is also rising."

Cheng Li, a senior fellow at the Brookings Institution think tank in Washington who moved from Shanghai to the United States in 1985, says compared to decades past, human rights in China "are improving, there's no question about that."

Cheng, also a professor of government at Hamilton College, points out that during the Cultural Revolution in the 1960s and '70s, China was "like a prison," and human suffering was widespread. Even 20 years ago, around the time of the Tiananmen Square crackdown, Cheng says, Chinese authorities viewed discussions about human rights as "propaganda or Western hypocrisy."

But in recent years, China gradually has loosened up on some fronts, according to Cheng. He notes that dissidents have been able to give interviews to foreign media, some intellectuals have been critical of the Chinese government and significant progress has occurred toward instituting legal and economic reforms. Although "no fundamental breakthrough" has occurred on such issues as ethnic freedom, Tibet and treatment of the outlawed Falun Gong spiritual movement, "in general terms, China is more open and freer than at anytime in recent history," Cheng says.

Wang Chen, director of the Information Office of China's State Council, said human rights do not advance overnight but rather through "a gradual process."

"China is a developing country with a population of 1.3 billion, and China's human-rights development still faces many problems and difficulties," Wang said. "To respect and protect human rights and promote all-round development of human rights is a long-term arduous task for the Chinese government and Chinese people." [17]

But many China experts are doubtful significant progress will occur in the immediate future. James Mann, a former diplomatic correspondent for the *Los Angeles Times* and now author in residence at Johns Hopkins University's Paul H. Nitze School of Advanced International Studies, says that despite some gains in recent years, China still lacks the freedoms that form the bedrock of civil society in the West.

"If you define human rights to include personal freedoms such as what people can wear and what music they can listen to, then human rights have definitely expanded," says Mann, author of *The China Fantasy: How Our Leaders Explain Away Chinese Repression*. But, "if you define human rights in the truest political sense — the right to oppose the government, the right to dissent — then they've made remarkably little progress over the last 30 years. Each time you think there's been a step forward, you see retrogression."

Kirk Donahoe, assistant director of the Washington-based Laogai Research Foundation, which monitors Chinese human-rights violations, including in the prison system, is similarly downbeat. "The political progress has just not kept pace with the economic progress," he says. "Sure, people's living standards have improved, and a lot of times when you talk to the Chinese people they'll mention living standards and health and medication as being indicative of a better human-rights situation."

But, Donahoe says, "the basic situation has not improved" when measured in traditional Western terms: freedom of speech and religion, the right to criticize the government and dissent from official policy, free elections, and so on.

While China's constitution guarantees certain rights, such as freedom of speech and religion, Donahue says, "as long as there's a one-party system in place, these reforms don't carry much weight."

Human-rights advocates have voiced particular concern over violations in the months leading up to the Olympics. "Over the past year, we have continued to document not only chronic human-rights abuses inside China, such as restrictions on basic freedoms of speech, assembly and political participation, but also abuses that are taking place specifically as a result of China's hosting the 2008 Summer Games," said Sophie Richardson, advocacy director of Human Rights Watch's Asia Division.

"Those include an increasing use of house arrest and charges of 'inciting subversion' as [a] means of silencing dissent, ongoing harassment of foreign journalists despite new regulations protecting them and abuses of migrant construction workers without whose labors Beijing's gleaming new skyline would not exist." [18]

"People do have more choice in their daily lives" than in decades past, says Minky Worden, media director of Human Rights Watch and editor of *China's Great Leap: The Beijing Games and Olympian Human Rights Challenges*. "But if they try to cross one of the invisible red lines by posting something on the Internet, criticizing the government, if they fall afoul of a corrupt party official in their village, the political situation can still be very harsh."

During the one-year run-up to the Olympics, Worden says, Human Rights Watch has seen "a fairly systematic deterioration of human rights across most of the measurable areas. After a couple of decades of progress, we're seeing a retrenchment."

China Holds More Than 700 Political Prisoners

China is detaining or imprisoning 734 political prisoners, according to the Congressional-Executive Commission on China.* Many were convicted of overstepping government speech or media regulations or inciting separatism — as occurred recently in Tibet and Xinjiang Province. Prisoners representing a range of offenses are profiled below.

Selected Political Prisoners in China

Name Reason for detention	Ethnic group	Date of detention	Length of sentence
Adrug Lupoe	Tibetan	Aug. 21, 2007	10 years
Lupoe and other protesters climbed onto a stage where Chinese officials were speaking and called for the Dalai Lama's return to Tibet, freedom of religion and the return of exiled figure Gedun Choekyi Nyima. The Ganzi Intermediate People's Court convicted him of espionage and inciting "splittism."			
Abdulghani Memetemin	Uiyghur	July 26, 2002	9 years
Memetemin provided information to the East Turkistan Information Center, a Munich-based organization advocating independence for Xinjiang Province. The group is designated by China as a terrorist organization. He was sentenced by the Kashgar Intermediate People's Court for "supplying state secrets to an organization outside the country." On top of his prison sentence, he received three years' deprivation of political rights.			
Chi Jianwei	Han	Oct. 18, 2006	3 years
Chi was detained for participating in a sit-in and distributing materials from the Falun Gong spiritual group, which were found in his home. Shangcheng District People's Court charged him with "using a cult to undermine implementation of the law."			
Shi Tao	Han	Nov. 24, 2004	10 years
Shi was convicted of disclosing state secrets to foreigners after disobeying a government order limiting journalists' reports during the 15th anniversary of the Tiananmen democracy protests. Shi e-mailed his notes to the Democracy Forum, a U.S.-based online newspaper. His conviction was based in part on evidence provided by the China office of Yahoo!, which agreed to pay his legal expenses.			
Tenzin Deleg	Tibetan	April 7, 2002	20 years
Deleg was convicted of exploding bombs and scattering separatist leaflets. Deleg and an accomplice were sentenced to death, but Deleg's sentence was commuted to life imprisonment. He is reportedly being treated for heart disease in Chuandong Prison in Sichuan Province.			

* Congress created the commission in 2000 to monitor human rights and the development of the rule of law in China. It consists of nine senators, nine House members and five senior administration officials.

Source: "Political Prisoner Database," Congressional-Executive Commission on China, June 26, 2008

Will China's exploding growth lead to Western-style democracy?

Some China experts say the middle class is the key to China's future.

"If the middle class believes that its interests are being adequately tended to by the state, then there will be less pressure for democracy," says Harry Harding, university professor of international affairs at The George Washington University (GWU). "If they think the state is violating or ignoring their interest, then the desire for democracy can become extremely powerful."

For now, many analysts argue, China's expanding middle class tends to be highly nationalistic, supportive of the central government and concerned that if Western-style rights are given to the country's massive poor population, the interests of wealthier Chinese could suffer.

Johns Hopkins University's Mann says "people tend to assume that as a country becomes more prosperous it will develop an independent civil society. . . . But China seems to be developing a new political model in which the emerging middle class, which as a percentage of the overall population is still small, has much closer ties to the existing regime than we've seen elsewhere. It's not just that they may not be independent enough to push for democracy. They may be threatened by democracy because in China, where you have 500-800 million poor peasants or migrant workers either in the countryside or the edges of cities, there is fear among the emerging middle class that with democracy they will be outvoted, and that their interests will not emerge on top."

Nevertheless, democracy — at least focused on the local level and in a form shaped to Chinese political culture — has been a hot topic within the administration of President Hu. Writing before the 17th Congress of China's Communist Party last fall, Brookings scholar David Shambaugh alerted readers to "expect lots of 'democracy' initiatives."

"While these initiatives do not constitute democratic institutions and procedures as recognized in real democracies, they nonetheless represent serious efforts to broaden what the Chinese describe as 'inner-party democracy,' 'electoral democracy' and extra-party 'consultative democracy,'" he wrote. "All of these forms go under the broad rubric of 'socialist democracy' or 'democracy with Chinese characteristics.' " [19]

Scholars say that while China allows — and sometimes even encourages — criticism of corrupt local party officials, it keeps a tight lid on dissent aimed at the central government out of fear that it could lead to chaos and threaten the party's control.

"At this point in China's political development, there isn't a lively multiparty system, and there isn't an established political institution for political transition," says Northeastern University's Woo. "So imagine if your sole source of legitimacy goes out the window. What's going to happen to the country? They've never been able to figure that one out yet."

Some China scholars argue that China inevitably will move toward some kind of democracy that includes a multiparty political system. "The question for China is not whether, but when and how," says Pei, of the Carnegie Endowment for International Peace. "You can definitely say 20 years from now, China probably will be democratic and will have a multiparty system."

But others are doubtful. In *The China Fantasy*, Mann critiques scenarios often held by policy elites in the West — that capitalism will lead to democracy in China or that social or economic upheavals will undermine the current regime. He poses a third scenario: that China will continue to grow stronger economically but retain its authoritarian ways. The West should not continue to overlook China's human-rights violations at home and its support for repressive regimes elsewhere, he argues.

"[W]e should not assume China is headed for democracy or far-reaching political liberalization," Mann writes. "China will probably, instead, retain a repressive one-party political system for a long time. In fact, such an outcome may not bother the American or European business and government leaders who deal regularly with China; it may indeed be just the China they want.

"But they rarely acknowledge that they would be content with a permanently repressive and undemocratic China. . . . Instead, they foster an elaborate set of illusions about China, centered on the belief that commerce will lead inevitably to political change and democracy." [20]

Should U.S. companies in China push for human-rights reforms?

In April, actress Mia Farrow, chairwoman of the humanitarian group Dream for Darfur, criticized most of the major corporate sponsors of the Beijing Olympics, including Visa and Coca-Cola, for their alleged failure to take meaningful steps to pressure China to help end human-rights abuses in war-ravaged Darfur.

"Because sponsors are desperate to win the hearts and minds of 1.3 billion potential consumers in China, they have been frozen into silence on Darfur," Farrow said. "If the Summer Games go down in history as the Genocide Olympics, it will be because of the Chinese government's support of the regime in Sudan, abetted by the moral cowardice of the sponsors who would not speak out publicly about the genocide in Darfur." [21]

China's growing thirst for oil has led it to deal with resource-rich nations that have been ostracized by the West for human-rights abuses. Sudan, for instance, where more than 200,000 people have died in fighting in the Darfur region since 2003, is one of China's biggest oil suppliers. China repeatedly has blocked efforts by the West to impose sanctions against Sudan and until recently was reluctant even to pressure the Sudanese government to curb the fighting. [22]

But some companies returned fire on Dream for Darfur. Coca-Cola's chief executive called its approach "flawed." "It judges concern by one narrow measure — the degree to which one pushes a sovereign government in public — while ignoring what we and others are doing every day to help ease the suffering in Darfur," wrote Coke CEO Neville Isdell. He added: "Our approach encompasses: immediate relief to those on the ground; investments to address water, one of the conflict's underlying causes; and efforts to bring local and international stakeholders together to develop long-term solutions." [23]

While many scholars and human-rights activists say corporations have an important role to play in pushing China toward human-rights and political reforms, some recommend a more low-key dialogue with Chinese officials while ensuring that their own corporate operations within China are clean of any taint of abuse.

"Private discussion and dialogue instead of finger pointing" is the best approach says the Brookings Institution's Cheng.

In a commentary in *Condé Nast Portfolio*, New York University business Professor Tunku Varadarajan explored the question of whether companies receiving global exposure from sponsoring the Olympics should press for human-rights improvement in China. [24] "At the very least," he wrote, the corporations "owe it to us to show that they are not wholly blind to human-rights issues." While they "cannot be asked to entirely subordinate the interest of their stockholders to those of a more amorphous group of stakeholders," he wrote, "the global practice of capitalism is not a morality-free exercise."

As a first step, advises Georges Enderle, a professor of international business ethics at the University of Notre Dame, companies "should keep their own house in order in China [and] treat their employees decently and according to American standards."

U.S. and foreign companies can help bolster the rule of law in China, he says, by following a major, new labor law in China and help explain to Chinese companies why the law is important. The law requires employers to provide workers with written contracts, restricts the use of temporary workers and makes it more difficult to lay off employees. It also strengthens the role of the Communist Party's monopoly union and allows collective bargaining for pay and benefits. [25]

The law was developed despite stiff objections from many multinational companies, who said it would sig-

nificantly increase labor costs and reduce flexibility. As passed, the measure softened some controversial provisions but kept others. [26]

While it has drawn wide international attention, the law nonetheless "may fall short of improving working conditions for the tens of millions of low-wage workers who need the most help," said *The New York Times* — "unless it is enforced more rigorously than existing laws, which already offer protections that on paper are similar to those in developed economies." [27]

The *Times* pointed out that "abuses of migrant laborers have been endemic in boom-time China" and noted the labor law was passed shortly after Chinese officials and state media exposed the widespread use of slave labor in brick kilns and coal mines. [28]

Michael A. Santoro, a professor of ethics at the Rutgers University business school and author of *Profits and Principles: Global Capitalism and Human Rights in China*, says preaching to the Chinese about human rights simply engenders hostility toward Westerners. But foreign companies, he argues, should be far more aggressive in holding the Chinese government to trade and business standards that China itself committed to when it became a member of the World Trade Organization (WTO) in 2002.

By aggressively enforcing those standards and exercising the rights granted to them under the WTO, he argues, foreign companies could help promote the rule of law in China and provide moral support to citizens who are challenging China's government on political and human-rights issues.

"How many cases do you think foreign companies have brought" against China so far under the WTO rules? Santoro asks. "Try zero." Even if China retaliated, WTO provisions entitle companies to resolve their disputes with the Chinese government through a fair and independent court system in China, Santoro says. And if that fails, he adds, a dispute becomes an international trade case.

"We have this whole legal mechanism in place, and nobody's using it." Instead, business leaders continue "to work within the old paradigm of power in China," using personal connections rather than international law to resolve business disputes.

While not suggesting that multinational businesses always deal with China in the most confrontational way, Santoro says "they need to start thinking about the fact that they have economic rights — and not economic privileges that the [Chinese] government is granting to them."

As flawed as China's judicial system is, Santoro says, "we see very brave Chinese citizens pushing the envelope" on labor, environmental and economic-rights issues in the Chinese judiciary. But he says, "the foreign business community and the foreign legal community are not doing nearly enough to promote the rule of law in China."

BACKGROUND

Mao's Legacy

China's human-rights practices have been under scrutiny for generations. Some scholars have painted Chairman Mao Zedong, who founded the People's Republic of China, as one of history's worst monsters. A controversial 2005 biography claims he was responsible for more than 70 million deaths in peacetime, with nearly 38 million dying of starvation and overwork during the Great Leap Forward and an accompanying famine. [29]

Whatever the true death figure, and notwithstanding that some Chinese continue to revere him, Mao's legacy is widely viewed as shameful. During his disastrous 10-year Cultural Revolution in the 1960s and '70s, even top political and military leaders were subject to arbitrary arrest, torture and extrajudicial execution. [30] Young intellectuals were forced into "re-education" camps to work alongside peasants, Red Guards beat citizens for perceived slights to the authorities and Western music and other cultural expressions were suppressed.

In February 1972 Mao and President Richard M. Nixon met in Beijing in a spectacle that gave American television viewers a window on a China they had not seen for more than two decades. The visit, the first by a U.S. president to China, marked the first steps toward normalizing relations between the two countries and helped lay the groundwork for China's opening to the West.

Following Mao's death in 1976, hopes for democracy grew in China. In 1978 — 30 years ago this year — China adopted a "Reform and Opening" policy, which, while fostering dramatic economic and cultural changes also led to a vast chasm between rich and poor and what critics say has been a legacy of human-rights violations, including relocations of Chinese citizens to make way for new development, government corruption and other abuses.

The push for greater freedom suffered its most notorious setback in 1989, when Chinese tanks crushed a pro-democracy movement in Tiananmen Square and the nearby Avenue of Eternal Peace.

Ma Jian, a well-known Chinese writer, described what happened: "The protests had been set off by the death of the reform-minded party leader Hu Yaobang. College students had camped out in the square — the symbolic heart of the nation — to demand freedom, democracy and an end to government corruption. There they fell in love, danced to Bob Dylan tapes and discussed Thomas Paine's "Rights of Man."

"The city had come out to support the protesters: workers, entrepreneurs, writers, petty thieves. After the tanks drove the students from the square in the early hours of June 4, 1989, nearby shop owners turned up with baskets of sneakers to hand out to protesters who'd lost their shoes in the confrontation. As soldiers opened fire in the streets, civilians rushed to the wounded to carry them to the hospital." [31]

According to the PBS TV program "Frontline," the Chinese Red Cross initially reported 2,600 were killed, then quickly retracted that figure under intense pressure from the government. The official Chinese government figure is 241 dead, including soldiers, and 7,000 wounded. [32]

Ma went on to say that the Communist Party in China rewrote history and "branded the peaceful democracy movement a 'counterrevolutionary riot' and maintained that the brutal crackdown was the only way of restoring order. . . .

"Realizing that their much vaunted mandate to rule had been nullified by the massacre, the party focused on economic growth to quell demands for political change. Thanks to its cheap, industrious and non-unionized labor force, China has since become a world economic power, while the Communist Party has become the world's best friend."

About 130 prisoners are still being held for their role in the Tiananmen protests, according to Human Rights Watch. [33]

The Tiananmen massacre isolated China on the global stage for years afterwards and helped defeat its bid to host the 2000 Olympics. "[W]hen the application was made in 1993, the sounds of the gunshots in Beijing were still ringing in people's ears," according to Chinese journalist Li Datong. [34]

In the nearly two decades since Tiananmen, experts say, China has changed in some significant ways, including the attitude of its youth toward the government. "In

CHRONOLOGY

1890s-1970s *Mao Zedong founds People's Republic of China.*

1893 Mao is born in Hunan province.

1949 Mao leads Communists to power.

1958 Mao launches Great Leap Forward to increase industrial and agricultural production, causes deadly famine.

1959 Great Leap Forward opponent Liu Shaoqi replaces Mao as chairman of the People's Republic.

1966 To reassert his power, Mao launches Cultural Revolution; repression of human rights and religion causes political and social chaos.

1972 President Nixon visits China.

1976 Mao dies; power fight ensues.

1978 China adopts "reform and opening up" policy spurring economic growth and progress on human rights.

1980s-1990s *Economic reforms stimulate development, but pro-democracy efforts meet resistance.*

1982 New Chinese constitution promises to protect freedom of speech, press, assembly, association and other rights, but crackdowns persist.

1987 China sets up China Academic Network, its first computer network.

1989 Military brutally clears pro-democracy demonstration in and around Beijing's Tiananmen Square, resulting in hundreds of deaths.

1991 China's State Council issues white paper on human-rights record.

1993 European Parliament denounces repression in Tibet and opposes China's bid to host 2000 Olympics.

1994 Advocacy groups complain about President Bill Clinton's decision to delink human rights and trade in dealing with China.

1999 Beijing bans Falun Gong spiritual movement as part of continuing repression of Christian house churches, Muslim Uyghurs and others.

2000s *Human-rights abuses continue to mar China's international image.*

2001 Beijing wins bid to host 2008 Summer Olympics. . . . China receives formal approval to join World Trade Organization.

2002 Hu Jintao elected general secretary of Chinese Communist Party.

2002-2004 China suppresses media coverage of SARS outbreak.

2003 Hu Jintao becomes China's president; Wen Jiabao becomes premier.

2004 Zhao Yan, a Chinese researcher working for *The New York Times* in China, is charged with disclosing state secrets to the newspaper; charges are later dismissed.

2007 President Bush meets with President Hu in Australia and emphasizes U.S. concern about human rights. . . . Yahoo! officials defend company's role in jailing of Chinese journalist Shi Tao, sentenced in 2005 to 10 years. . . . Human-rights activist Hu Jia arrested. . . . Dozens of women in southwest China reportedly forced to have abortions.

March 2008 Foreign journalists restricted from traveling to Tibet as monks and other pro-independence demonstrators engage in deadly clashes with Chinese police. . . . State Department removes China from list of top 10 human-rights violators but says its record remains "poor."

April 2008 Olympic Torch Relay hit by anti-China protesters around the world.

May 2008 Earthquake kills nearly 70,000 in central China, opening country to scrutiny by Western reporters and leading to charges of poor building standards and government corruption.

July 2008 China scrambles to deal with environmental woes and prepare the country for start of Olympic Games.

Aug. 8-24 Olympics to be held in Beijing.

1989," says Kamm of the Dui Hua Foundation, "young people were very critical of the government, and that was in line with international outrage over Tiananmen. Today the situation is radically different. You still have international concern over the bad human-rights record, but in China you have extreme nationalism, which basically says 'my country right or wrong' and 'how dare you criticize my government because in doing so you criticize China and by doing that you criticize me.' "

A University of Hong Kong survey this spring found that most Hong Kong residents continue to believe that Chinese students were right to protest at Tiananmen and that the government's reaction was wrong, but 85 percent said human rights in China had improved since 1989. [35]

Catalog of Abuses

China's selection to host the 2008 Games was predicated in part on promises to improve its human rights. Beijing Mayor Liu Qi told the International Olympic Committee the Games "will help promote our economic and social progress and will also benefit the further development of our human-rights cause." [36] Yet, critics charge that China has not lived up to its word.

Some of the criticism stems from its crackdown this spring in Tibet and widely perceived failure to do more to stem abuses in places like Darfur. But rights advocates also express a more general concern over practices within China, despite the economic gains of some citizens in recent years.

"In some limited aspects, there has been some progress" on human rights, says Sharon Hom, executive director of Human Rights in China, an international organization founded in 1989 by Chinese students and scholars. For example, she cites "the 400 million lifted out of absolute poverty."

"However, for the vast majority — the migrants, the rural inhabitants, the urban poor, ethnic-minority groups, Tibetans, Uyghurs, Mongols — which together comprise the vast majority of the 1.3-billion population — the human-rights situation has not only not improved, it has absolutely deteriorated in the last 20 years with respect to the right of individuals to have . . . religious [freedom], cultural freedom [and] the freedom of expression and association."

What's more, Hom says most Chinese continue to lack decent housing, jobs, education and health care and that the problems are so severe the Communist Party has recognized the need for improvement because of the social unrest they have generated.

Hom cautions that it is impossible to know the full extent of human-rights abuses in China because of the centralized control exerted under the one-party system, the state-of-the-art technology to monitor and filter information and the pervasive state-secrets system.

A detailed report last year by Human Rights in China said the state-secrets system "perpetuates a culture of secrecy that is not only harmful but deadly to Chinese society." [37] The system controls the flow of data on everything from the effects of environmental damage in urban industrial areas to forced abortions and deaths among political prisoners, Hom explains. "Anything and everything could be deemed a state secret, even retroactively," she says.

Despite the lack of reliable data, journalists and Western governments have nonetheless compiled thousands of pages of documentation in recent years on human-rights abuses in China. Amnesty International, for example, says it believes a "significant drop in executions" is likely to have occurred since the Supreme People's Court review of death sentences was restored in 2007, but that China remains the world leader in the use of the death penalty, with roughly 68 offenses punishable by death, including non-violent ones such as embezzling and certain drug-related crimes. [38]

In its 2008 report on global human rights, Amnesty estimates that at least 470 people were executed and 1,860 sentenced to death in 2007, based on public reports, "although the true figures were believed to be much higher." [39] Kamm of the Dui Hua Foundation estimates there were 5,000 executions last year, compared with perhaps 15,000 in the late 1990s.

"[D]eath penalty trials continued to be held behind closed doors, police often resorted to torture to obtain 'confessions,' and detainees were denied prompt and regular access to lawyers," the Amnesty report said.

Amnesty's catalog of abuses is far broader than the death penalty. For example, it said "torture in detention remained widespread." Also, "while space for civil society activities continued to grow, the targeting of human-rights defenders who raised issues deemed to be politically sensitive intensified." China continued to tightly control the flow of news and information, Amnesty said, noting that around 30 journalists were known to be in prison along with at least 50 individuals for posting their views on the Internet. (*See sidebar, p. 220.*)

Intimidation of Press Said to Be Widespread

But private media continue to push boundaries.

With the Olympic Games approaching, media representatives and human-rights advocates have stepped up their perennial calls for greater press freedom for both Chinese reporters and foreign correspondents working in China.

Press advocates say China has violated temporary regulations it established 18 months ago that allow foreign correspondents more latitude in covering the country before and during the Games. The rules, which took effect in January 2007, expire in October. In early July China repeated its pledge to abide by the rules, with Li Changchun, a high-ranking Chinese official, encouraging foreign journalists to report "extensively" on the games. [1]

But free-press advocates say reporting efforts by foreign and domestic journalists, Chinese cyber-dissidents, bloggers and others have been anything but unfettered. Shortly before Li's statement, Human Rights Watch released a report concluding that China continued to thwart and threaten foreign journalists.

Drawing on more than 60 interviews with correspondents in China between December 2007 and this past June, the report said correspondents and their sources continued to experience intimidation and obstruction when pursuing articles that could embarrass authorities, uncover official wrongdoing or chronicle social unrest. [2]

Chris Buckley, a senior correspondent for Reuters, was beaten and detained by "plainclothes thugs" last September after interviewing rural citizens seeking redress for abuses by local authorities, Human Rights Watch said. In October, it said, a European TV correspondent experienced similar treatment when trying to report on provincial unrest.

Other groups also have voiced strong complaints about China's disregard for free expression. In a report reissued this year, the New York-based Committee to Protect Journalists cited a "yawning gap between China's poor press-freedom record and promises made in 2001 when Beijing was awarded the Olympic Games." [3] As of early July, more than two dozen Chinese journalists remained in prison, the group said. [4]

Reporters Without Borders, a Paris-based press-advocacy group, said China jails more journalists, cyber-dissidents, Internet users and freedom of expression campaigners than any other country. [5]

But China's journalistic scene is not uniformly bleak. As the nation's economy has boomed, a climate of spirited competitiveness has developed among private Chinese newspapers and magazines, some with a zest for investigative reporting and the willingness and ability to push censorship boundaries. Also, the temporary rules established for the Olympics have helped open a window on China. The rules coincided with this year's massive earthquake in Sichuan Province, which was heavily covered by both Western and Chinese media.

In addition, millions of Chinese were impeded in their quest for religious freedom, with Falun Gong practitioners, Uyghur Muslims, Tibetan Buddhists and underground Christian groups "among those most harshly persecuted."

One-Child Policy

Advocates also point to threats to women's rights in China, including forced abortions, a problem long associated with the government's "one-child" family-planning policy, which restricts the rights of parents to choose the number of children they will have and the interval between births. [40]

The law gives married couples the right to have one birth but allows eligible couples to apply for permission to have a second child if they meet conditions in local and provincial regulations, according to the U.S. State Department's annual review of human rights in China for 2007. Enforcement varied from place to place, and was more strictly applied in cities than rural areas, the report says. [41]

Couples who have an unapproved child must pay a "social compensation fee" up to 10 times a person's annual disposable income. "The law requires family-planning officials to obtain court approval before taking 'forcible' action, such as detaining family members or confiscating and destroying property of families who refuse to pay

Still, journalists have experienced harassment. They were banished from strife-torn Tibet, where riots last March generated some of the biggest international news of the year. [6] And after the earthquake, the *Wall Street Journal* reported, officials in Xianger, a coal-mining town, "prevented foreign reporters from entering areas where schools collapsed, stopped parents from speaking with reporters elsewhere and in some case have threatened parents trying to voice their anger." [7]

Chinese journalists face particular challenges in reporting on issues that government authorities deem threatening to state security or the Communist Party. The Committee to Protect Journalists noted in its report that censorship of domestic reporters in China "remains in force across all regions and types of media," with "all news outlets . . . subject to orders from the Central Propaganda Department" and provincial authorities blocking coverage of sensitive local issues.

Journalists must avoid reporting on the military, ethnic conflict, religion issues (especially the outlawed Falun Gong movement) and the internal workings of the government and Communist Party, the committee said. "Coverage directives are issued regularly on matters large and small. Authorities close publications and reassign personnel as penalties for violating censorship orders." [8]

The committee also noted that even Western Internet service providers have yielded to government pressure, pointing out that Yahoo turned over e-mail account information that led to the imprisonment of a journalist and several dissidents, Microsoft deleted a reporter's blog, and Google "launched a self-censoring Chinese search engine." [9]

In a new book on China, Philip P. Pan, former Beijing bureau chief for *The Washington Post*, describes how Cheng Yizhong, editor in chief of *The Southern Metropolis Daily*, ran an exposé on the *shourong* system, a detention-center network used to enforce a passport policy designed to keep "undesirables" out of cities. After *The Daily* reported on a detainee's death, it was announced that Premier Wen had done away with the *shourong* regulations and was going to shut the detention centers. But *The Daily* paid a high price for its success: Advertisers were directed away from the paper, its general manager was sentenced to prison and Cheng himself was arrested and held for five months. [10]

---

[1] "China pledges media freedom at Olympic Games," The Associated Press, July 11, 2008.

[2] See "China's Forbidden Zones: Shutting the Media out of Tibet and other 'Sensitive' Stories," Human Rights Watch, July 2008, http://hrw.org/reports/2008/china0708/.

[3] "Falling Short," Committee to Protect Journalists, updated and reissued June 2008, p. 8, http://cpj.org/Briefings/2007/Falling_Short/China/china_updated.pdf.

[4] "One month before the Olympics, media face huge hurdles," Committee to Protect Journalists, July 8, 2008.

[5] "2008 Annual report — Asia-Pacific: China," Reporters Without Borders, p. 79, www.rsf.org/IMG/pdf/rapport_en_asie.pdf.

[6] For background, see Brian Beary, "Separatist Movements," *CQ Global Researcher*, April 2008, pp. 85-114.

[7] James T. Areddy, "China Stifles Parents' Complaints About Collapsed Schools," *The Wall Street Journal*, June 18, 2008, p. 10A.

[8] "Falling Short," *op. cit.*, p. 8.

[9] *Ibid.*, p. 9.

[10] Michiko Kakutani, "Dispatches From Capitalist China," *The New York Times*, July 15, 2008. See Philip P. Pan, *Out of Mao's Shadow* (2008).

---

social compensation fees," the report said. "However, in practice this requirement was not always followed."

Hom says that while fines for having an unapproved child are legal under Chinese law, forced abortions are not, and property destruction is not a legal enforcement mechanism set forth in the one-child population policy. "It is the coercive and often illegal implementation of the policy that produces these abuses," she says."

The State Department review drew attention to the role that incentives play in enforcement of the one-child policy. "Officials at all levels remained subject to rewards or penalties based on meeting the population goals set by their administrative region," it said. "Promotions for

local officials depended in part on meeting population targets."

Hom says that "of all the policies introduced by the Communist Party, the one-child population policy is the most hated and the most resisted. The vast majority of the people, meaning the rural-area people — really hate it."

She says she has visited villages where parents have more than one child and even as many as four or five. Those unable to pay the penalty may give birth outside the village and bring the child back later, she says.

While enforcement of China's family-planning policy can vary by place and circumstance, the State Department said that "there continued to be sporadic reports of viola-

Environmental Problems Spark Unrest, Health Woes

Protests reflect rise of citizen activism, hope for future.

In 2005, thousands rioted in a village in southeastern China, breaking windows and overturning police cars to protest factory pollution.

"The air stinks from the factories," said villager Wang Yuehe. "We can't grow our crops. The factories had promised to do a good environmental job, but they have done almost nothing." [1]

The episode marked one of numerous pollution-related protests — many peaceful but some violent — that have occurred in China in recent years as the nation's exploding economic growth has led to some of the world's worst environmental damage in history.

Experts say the problem has had massive human-rights consequences, including an alarming rate of cancer deaths, shrinking access to clean water and forced relocations of citizens to make way for new buildings and infrastructure.

Pollution has haunted the Olympics, too. In the city of Qingdao, for example, thousands of people were mobilized this summer to clean algae from the Yellow Sea, where the Olympic sailing regatta was planned. Concerns arose that the foul-smelling algae would impede sailing competitions. And marathoners have worried that they would have trouble breathing in Beijing's smog-saturated air. To counter the pollution, Beijing officials removed 300,000 high-polluting vehicles from local roads and then temporarily removed half of all vehicles as the Games drew nearer. They also were preparing contingency plans to temporarily close factories in northern China if necessary. [2]

But the problems surrounding the Olympics are only a small drop in a much bigger ocean of ecological blight in China.

Elizabeth Economy, author of *The River Runs Black: The Environmental Challenges to China's Future*, wrote recently in *Foreign Affairs* that "fully 190 million Chinese are sick from drinking contaminated water. All along China's major rivers, villages report skyrocketing rates of diarrheal diseases, cancer, tumors, leukemia and stunted growth." [3]

Economy, who is director for Asia Studies at the Council on Foreign Relations, also noted that in a survey of 30 cities and 78 counties released in 2007, China's Ministry of Public Health blamed worsening air and water pollution for drastic increases in cancer — a 19 percent rise in urban areas and 23 percent rise in rural areas since 2005.

Moreover, Economy wrote, a research institute affiliated with China's State Environmental Protection Administration estimated that 400,000 premature deaths occur each year due to air-pollution-related respiratory diseases — a number she said could be conservative. Indeed, she noted, a joint research project of the World Bank and Chinese government put the figure at 750,000, but Beijing reportedly did not want to release the figure, fearing it would incite social unrest.

China's environmental woes have led to so many stability-threatening mass protests that officials have backed away from some controversial industrial projects.

tions of citizens' rights by local officials attempting to reduce the number of births in their region."

In southwest China, dozens of women were forced to have abortions in 2007 even as late as their ninth month of pregnancy, according to evidence uncovered and reported by National Public Radio. [42]

"I was scared," Wei Linrong told NPR, after 10 family-planning officials came to her home in Guangxi Province in April 2007 and told her and her husband, who already have one child, that they would have to abort their 7-month-old fetus. "If you don't go [to the hospital], we'll

carry you," they told her. Wei said the hospital was "full of women who'd been brought in forcibly." After the baby was aborted, she said, the nurses "wrapped it up in a black plastic bag and threw it in the trash."

In the U.S. Congress, one of the most vocal critics of China's human-rights record has been Rep. Chris Smith, R-N.J. "The one-child policy makes brothers and sisters illegal in China," he said in Beijing this summer. It "relies on forced abortion, ruinous fines and other forms of coercion to achieve its goals. . . . The one-child-per-couple policy has not only killed tens of millions of children and

"China's greatest environmental achievement over the past decade has been the growth of environmental activism among the Chinese people," said Economy. "They have pushed the boundaries of environmental protection well beyond anything imaginable a decade ago."[4]

In her *Foreign Affairs* article, Economy wrote that China's explosive development "has become an environmental disaster."

"Clearly, something has got to give," she wrote. "The costs of inaction to China's economy, public health and international reputation are growing. And perhaps more important, social discontent is rising. The Chinese people have clearly run out of patience with the government's inability or unwillingness to turn the environmental situation around. And the government is well aware of the increasing potential for environmental protest to ignite broader social unrest."[5]

Yet, some observers — even within the ecological arena itself — see reason for hope. In a response to Economy's article entitled "China's Coming Environmental Renaissance," Yingling Liu, China program manager at the Worldwatch Institute, an environmental advocacy group, said Economy "underestimates the level of efforts now under way to address these problems, both in the Chinese government and in the growing private sector, as well as the degree to which the

Heavy pollution envelops Beijing during morning rush hour in June. Officials are temporarily removing half the vehicles from the city before Olympic Games begin in August.

United States and other industrial countries are complicit in China's environmental woes.

"As a Chinese citizen and researcher who has followed these developments for many years, I am more optimistic that China is beginning to turn the corner on its monumental environmental challenges," she wrote.[6]

Also cautiously hopeful is James Fallows, a national correspondent for *The Atlantic Monthly* who lives in China. After visiting a cement plant in Shandong Province that recycles its heat to help generate electricity and researching other "green" projects, Fallows wrote, "China's environmental situation is disastrous. And it is improving. Everyone knows about the first part. The second part is important, too."[7]

---

[1] Jim Yardley, "Thousands of Chinese Villagers Protest Factory Pollution," *The New York Times*, April 13, 2005.

[2] Jim Yardley, "Chinese Algae threatens Olympic Sailing," *The New York Times*, July 1, 2008, p. A6.

[3] Elizabeth C. Economy, "The Great Leap Backward?" *Foreign Affairs*, September/October 2007.

[4] Quoted in James Fallows, "China's Silver Lining," *The Atlantic Monthly*, June 2008.

[5] Economy, *op. cit.*

[6] Yingling Liu, "China's Coming Environmental Renaissance," Worldwatch Institute, Nov. 29, 2007, www.worldwatch.org/node /5510.

[7] Fallows, *op. cit.*

---

wounded their mothers but has led to a serious disparity between the number of boys and girls. The missing girls [phenomenon] is not only a heartbreaking consequence of the one-child policy but is catastrophic for China."[43]

Laws and regulations in China forbid terminating pregnancies based on a fetus's gender, the State Department report said, "but because of the intersection of birth limitations with the traditional preference for male children, particularly in rural areas, many families used ultrasound technology to identify female fetuses and terminate these pregnancies."

China's male-to-female birth ratio for first births in rural areas was about 123 to 100, the report said. The national average in China was about 120 to 100. For second births, the national ratio was 152 to 100.

China's National Population and Family Planning Commission denied a direct connection between family planning and skewed gender ratios at birth, but it promoted expanded programs to raise awareness of the imbalance and improve protection of the rights of girls, the State Department reported.

Great 'Walk' Forward

Despite what often appears as a depressing litany of abuses against China's vast population, especially its poor, many Western observers are guardedly optimistic. George J. Gilboy, a senior fellow at the MIT Center for International Studies, and Benjamin L. Read, an assistant professor in the politics department of the University of California-Santa Cruz, wrote recently that "in contrast to those who see a stagnant China, political and social dynamism is at work."

They point out that to preserve its power, the Chinese Communist Party "has chosen to revitalize itself and to adjust to new social realities, efforts that have intensified since the leadership team of President Hu Jintao and Premier Wen Jiabao came to power in 2002-2003." Still, the authors note that changes are "uneven and fragile" and that "political and social reform in China continues to 'walk,' not march, forward." [44]

Wu, at China Foreign Affairs University, when asked this year what the West doesn't understand about China, replied, "First, they don't like our system. They say, look, your system's not democratic, you don't respect human rights." But, Wu added, "You know why Chinese started the revolution? For human rights. Before 1949 [the] Chinese population [was] 500 million people. Four hundred million people were hungry. And they couldn't go on like that."

The former ambassador to France went on to say that China's massive modernization effort is occurring "for human rights" — "to make Chinese, every Chinese, better." People in the West see China "with Western eyes," he said. "They believe — some of them — we have to behave like them. It's impossible. You are American and I'm Chinese." The Chinese people, he said, are "used to strong central authorities. More than 2,000 years."

Noting America's own long road to women's suffrage and civil rights for blacks, he added, "You are where you are after more than two centuries of revolution. How can you expect others to do the same thing as you? It's impossible." [45]

Wu rejected the notion that people in China are afraid to speak about issues in ways that appear to challenge the country's leadership. "People are expressing themselves," he said — maybe not in the way people in the United States do, he added, "but . . . you are where you are after more than centuries of evolution."

CURRENT SITUATION

Olympic Heat

As the Aug. 8 start of the Olympic Games approaches, emotions over China's human-rights record are rising with the temperature.

"Tragically, the Olympics has triggered a massive crackdown designed to silence and put beyond reach all those whose views differ from the official 'harmonious' government line," said Rep. Smith in Beijing in early July. [46]

He and Rep. Frank R. Wolf, R-Va., said they had come to meet with Chinese citizens pressing for greater political and religious freedoms, but the Chinese authorities pressured or prevented nine activists from meeting with them, according to documents the lawmakers handed out. Wolf and Smith presented officials with a list of 734 Chinese prisoners whom they said were jailed for dissent and urged President Bush not to attend the Games unless major progress on human rights occurred quickly. [47]

But China reacted sharply, saying Smith and Wolf's attempted meetings violated the purported reason for their visit. "The two U.S. congressmen came to China as guests of the United States Embassy to engage in internal communications and consultations" and "should not engage in activities incompatible with the objective of their visit and with their status," said Foreign Ministry spokesman Liu Jianchao. Wolf later called his point "simply ridiculous." [48]

The harsh exchange underscored the degree to which the Olympics have become a major rallying point for Western critics of China's human-rights practices. Some of the sharpest barbs have been reserved for the government's handling of journalists. (*See sidebar, p. 220.*)

Human Rights Watch charges that despite promises to lift media restrictions leading up to the games, China continues to thwart foreign journalists. "[S]ystematic surveillance, obstruction, intimidation of sources and pressure on local assistants are hobbling foreign correspondents' efforts to pursue investigative stories," the group said in early July. [49]

Human Rights Watch added that temporary government regulations in effect until Oct. 17 allow foreign journalists to conduct interviews with consenting Chinese organizations or citizens but do not grant similar freedoms to Chinese reporters. While some correspondents say the regulations have spurred improvements, most say they

Should the U.S. use trade sanctions against China to promote human rights?

YES
Tienchi Martin-Liao
Director, Laogai Research Foundation

Written for *CQ Researcher*, July 2008

It is widely believed that U.S. trade sanctions against Cuba, Iraq, Iran and North Korea have been ineffective. Using economic means to achieve political ends usually fails. Nevertheless, sanctions have been applied repeatedly because they send a clear, disapproving message to the targeted country.

But with China, trade sanctions could be more fruitful. Unlike North Korea or Iran, China is not an isolated country harboring strong anti-American sentiment. It is an emerging superpower intent upon gaining international respect and has gone to great lengths to promote a positive image. If the United States could convince some of its European and Asian allies to support sanctions, the pressure on China would be substantial.

Moreover, communist ideology is bankrupt, and China's leadership now derives its legitimacy almost solely from the booming economy. While a disruption to the enormous U.S.-China trade would affect both countries, the U.S. economy is more flexible than the Chinese economy and probably could more quickly adapt to a sudden fluctuation in trade. Conceivably, just the threat of trade sanctions could convince the Chinese leadership to grant some concessions.

Now, with the Olympics rapidly approaching, China's human-rights situation is worsening. Because President Hu Jintao wants China to be seen as a "harmonious society," peasant workers, environmentalists, human-rights defenders, vagabonds and those with criticisms or grievances are being silenced. The 80,000 protests that occur annually are being crushed at the first sign of trouble. Earlier this year the world saw China crack down on mass demonstrations in Tibet and grieving parents protesting shoddy school construction in Sichuan after the earthquake. The Chinese Communist Party controls the army, police, courts, media, banks and all manufacturing, as well as China's only pseudo-union. It also decides who leaves the country or goes to jail and what can be said, read and heard.

If the United States had made permanent, normalized trade relations with China conditional upon China making reasonable progress on human rights, we might be witnessing the rise of a very different China today. But the Bush administration has adopted a friendly — sometimes almost embracing — China policy. Meanwhile, the suppression of so-called troublemakers and religious and ethnic groups has intensified.

Thus, China is denying freedom to a fifth of the world's population — a problem the United States will have to address at some point. When it does so, economic sanctions should not be out of the question.

NO
James A. Dorn
China specialist and Vice President for Academic Affairs, Cato Institute

Written for *CQ Researcher*, July 2008

Using trade sanctions against China to promote human rights would do the opposite. Unlike trade, protectionism denies individuals the freedom to expand their effective alternatives, thus limiting their choices. Sanctions would fuel the flames of economic nationalism, harm U.S. consumers and embolden hardliners in Beijing.

Before China opened to the outside world in 1978, the state dominated the economic landscape, private property was outlawed and capitalists were considered criminals. Today millions of people engage in trade, private ownership is widespread and civil society is advancing, as was evident in the spontaneous response to the Sichuan earthquake.

In 1995, Jianying Zha wrote in her book *China Pop*, "The economic reforms have created new opportunities, new dreams and to some extent a new atmosphere and new mindsets. . . . There is a growing sense of increased space for personal freedom." That is even truer today as a growing proportion of urban residents own their own homes, and more than 200 million people use the Internet — increasingly to challenge government power.

A 2005 GlobeScan poll of 20 countries found that China had the highest percentage of respondents (74 percent) who agreed that the "free-market economy is the best system on which to base the future of the world." And a 2006 Chicago Council on Global Affairs poll found that 87 percent of those surveyed in China had a favorable view of globalization. That positive attitude toward economic liberalism is good for China and good for the world.

Increasing commercial ties has helped spread the flow of information about alternative forms of government as well as improve living standards in China. Isolating China would do little to advance human rights — as we have learned from North Korea and Cuba. Instead, sanctions would be an act of economic suicide, endanger U.S.-China relations and threaten world peace.

It makes no sense to use such a blunt instrument in an attempt to "advance" human rights in China when trade itself is an important human right. Instead, the United States should continue its policy of engagement and avoid destructive protectionism.

It would be more constructive to welcome China as a normal rising power, admit it to the G-8 and continue the Strategic Economic Dialogue initiated by Presidents Bush and Hu. At the same time, we should not ignore the human rights violations that do occur and use diplomatic pressure to help move China toward a legitimate rule of law.

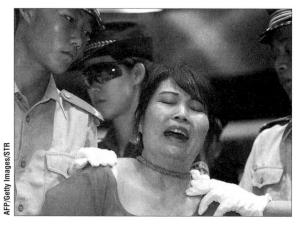

AFP/Getty Images/STR

Drug peddler Wang Xiongyin cries after being sentenced to death in Guangzhou. China imposes the death penalty for many non-violent crimes, including "undermining national unity." Amnesty International estimates 470 people were sentenced to death last year but said the true figure may be far higher.

"have done little to enable them to report on issues government officials are determined to conceal," Human Rights Watch said. "Those include high-level corruption, ethnic conflicts, social unrest, public health crises and the workings of China's large detention system, including prisons, labor camps, mental hospitals and police stations." [50]

Wang Baodong, the Chinese Embassy's spokesman in Washington, wrote in June that the regulations had "given foreign journalists full freedom to report from China in the run-up to and during the Beijing Olympics," noting that more than 25,000 foreign correspondents were expected to cover the event. "Of course," he added, "they are expected to follow China's law, and to present to the world a real China with their pens and lenses." [51]

Johns Hopkins University's Mann doubts the Olympics — or media coverage of the Games — will move China toward greater freedom and human rights.

"I actually thought — wrongly — that in the year or so moving up to the Olympics, there might be some political opening in China," he says. "My frame of reference was a period of about four to six months before [President] Bill Clinton visited China in 1998, when there was a great relaxation in China."

But, Mann continues, the current period "isn't the same. Last fall and this spring, China really got threatened by a series of different events and decided to tighten up the climate. It became more afraid of upheaval. So the reality is, we're going to have an Olympics where the Chinese government now sees it as something to get through," rather than an opportunity for greater opening.

The upheaval in Tibet, the controversy over China's alleged lack of action on Darfur and protests during the Olympic-torch relay are among the events over which the regime felt threatened, Mann says.

Others point to last fall's 17th National Congress of the Communist Party, held every five years in China to praise past leaders, welcome new ones and help shape the country's future direction. In the meeting, President Hu vowed to address social, environmental and corruption problems in China and called for "intra-party democracy" that allows more party officials to participate in decision making. But Hu said the Communist Party must remain "the core that directs the overall situation and coordinates the efforts of all quarters." [52]

In the months leading up to the meeting, says Worden of Human Rights Watch, a "chill . . . went into place" as government officials sought to forestall disruption and protests. For example, she said, the government emptied the "Petitioner's Village" in Beijing, where citizens living outside the capital gathered to seek help from the central government in grievances against local officials.

"At one point [the village] had as many as 10,000 petitioners in Beijing. The last several thousand were cleared out in September before the Party Congress. These are people who have the legal right to petition the government dating back centuries, and they travel from the provinces to do so, often because of egregious cases of corruption, and then the local officials with whom they have the grievances will often send thugs to beat them up and haul them back to their home provinces. That's what's happened to most of them before the Olympics."

Authorities also reportedly cracked down on the Internet, closing tens of thousands of Web sites on which visitors could post opinions. [53]

Despite what many see as China's tightening political atmosphere, many China-watchers say the Olympics inevitably will have some effect on China's internal policies.

In a piece comparing the Beijing Olympics and the 1988 Games in Seoul, South Korea, Richard Pound, a longtime member of the International Olympic Committee, wrote that "no host country of the Olympic Games has ever been the same after the Games . . . especially countries that had been closed or particularly authoritarian. China will not be unaffected. . . . Its size and present governance may mean that the change does not occur as quickly as it might in other countries. Its lack of transparency may also mean that the elements of change are not easily apparent, which will not mean that they are not occurring. Patience and firmness on the part of the international community can be effective catalysts — as can the Olympic Games." [54]

Internet's Impact

China has some 223 million Internet users, almost as many as in the United States. [55] And many think the Internet will continue discomforting Communist authorities and may ultimately bring about human-rights reforms. Despite the government's efforts to control its use, the Internet remains a powerful and pervasive force for change.

For instance, in southwest China's Guizhou Province some 30,000 rioters torched government buildings this summer to protest officials' handling of a teenage girl's death, a case chronicled by Chinese journalists and Internet bloggers. News reports said police called the death a suicide, angering people who believed she was raped and murdered, possibly by someone close to local authorities. [56]

In the ensuing days, however, authorities announced that four officials had been fired for "severe malfeasance" over an alleged cover-up in the case, *The Wall Street Journal* reported. The shift appeared to have resulted from pressure exerted by Chinese journalists and bloggers. When mainstream Web sites began to delete posts on the case, some bloggers got creative, the *Journal* noted, including by writing their postings backward to avert censorship. [57]

While tech-savvy dissidents may be fighting creatively against local corruption and other ills, it is not at all clear how much educated young Chinese will stir things up on the human-rights front, including on tinderbox issues such as Tibetan independence and China's role in the Darfur crisis.

"Educated young Chinese, far from being embarrassed or upset by their government's human-rights record, rank among the most patriotic, establishment-supporting people you'll meet," wrote Matthew Forney, a former Beijing bureau chief for *Time*. [58] He went on to say "most young, ethnic Chinese strongly support their government's suppression of the recent Tibetan uprising."

Forney said the most obvious explanation for young people's unquestioning support of the government is China's education system, "which can accurately be described as indoctrination." He also suggested that few young people experience political repression, most are too young to remember the Tiananmen Square massacre and many lack life experiences that would help them gain perspectives other than the government's viewpoint.

"Educated young Chinese are . . . the biggest beneficiaries of policies that have brought China more peace and prosperity than at any time in the past thousands years," Forney wrote. "They can't imagine why Tibetans would turn up their noses at rising incomes and the promise of a more prosperous future. The loss of a homeland just doesn't compute as a valid concern."

Unless big changes occur in China's education system or economy, Forney concluded, Westerners won't find allies among most Chinese on issues like Tibet and Darfur for some time to come. "If the debate over Tibet turns this summer's contests in Beijing into the Human Rights Games . . . ," he wrote, "Western ticket-holders expecting to find Chinese angry at their government will instead find Chinese angry at them."

OUTLOOK

Chinese-style Change

The West's immediate focus on China may fade once the Olympic Games end, but concern about human-rights reform is likely to persist long into the future.

While China has made "great progress in human-rights construction," said Luo of the China Society for Human Rights Studies, "China's political and economic systems are not perfect." [59]

"The democracy and the legal system are not complete," he continued, "and urban and rural development are imbalanced. There are still problems in employment, education, medical care, housing, social welfare, income distribution, production safety and environmental protection."

But China had never ignored those problems, Luo insisted. "Some Western countries have always adopted a double standard on the human-rights issue and condemned China and other developing countries, but turned a blind eye to their own human-rights problems."

Western experts are variously optimistic and pessimistic about China's human-rights picture, but many agree the Communist Party is likely to pay more attention to citizens' grievances in coming years out of a pragmatic desire to maintain supremacy and keep the country from spinning out of control.

"Over time the government will become more responsive to the demands of its people, and the judicial system will afford more protections for people who are arrested," says the Dui Hua Foundation's Kamm. "We should first be looking at those things, rather than jumping in and saying, will China fully respect human rights by a certain date or be a democracy."

Pointing to the recent Guizhou uprising over the girl's death, Kamm notes that "if that had happened in 1989, it would have been suppressed incredibly hard [and] called a counterrevolutionary riot and the perpetrators put in prison for 20 years or life. Now it's called a mass incident, and the [state-controlled press] has given it extraordinary coverage by Chinese standards."

Still, Kamm says government officials are not acting out of altruism in such cases. They are "being forced to respond more and more to the people . . . in order to stay in power," he says

Northeastern University law Professor Woo says China is trying to move not toward Western-style democracy but toward a model of "soft authoritarianism," in which officials relax some controls to build support for the governing regime.

She notes, for example, the passage in 2007 of a landmark property-rights law designed to provide citizens with a grievance process and adequate compensation when the government takes property for economic development — a huge issue in recent years given the countless Chinese who have been forced out of their homes.

Nonetheless, Woo says, economic reforms have also led China to pull back from health, welfare and labor protections, widening the gap between the rural poor and rising urban middle class and increasing social unrest.

Ultimately, she says, the outlook for human rights in China is mixed. "I don't ever think China will be the same kind of democracy you see in this country," she says. "But I think it has changed a lot."

NOTES

1. "Chinese president announces official start of Olympic torch relay," GOV.cn (Chinese government's official Web portal), March 31, 2008, http://english.gov.cn/2008-03/31/content_933196.htm.

2. Teng Biao and Hu Jia, "The Real China and the Olympics," open letter, Sept. 10, 2007, accessed at Web site of Human Rights Watch, http://china.hrw.org/press/news_release/the_real_china_and_the_olympics.

3. Minky Worden, ed., *China's Great Leap: The Beijing Games and Olympian Human Rights Challenges* (2008), pp. 36-37.

4. All data were cited in corresponding footnotes in Cheng Li, ed., *China's Changing Political Landscape* (2008), p. 2.

5. "Ten Things You Should Know About China," Freedom House, www.freedomhouse.org/template.cfm?page=379.

6. Edward Cody, "Across China, Security Instead of Celebration," *The Washington Post*, July 19, 2008, p. A1.

7. Jim Yardley, "2 Die in Blasts on Chinese Buses," *The New York Times*, July 22, 2008, p. A6.

8. Xinhua News Agency, "China's protection of human rights differs from Western countries," April 21, 2008, http://news.xinhuanet.com/english/2008-04/21/content_8021857.htm.

9. Xinhua News Agency, "Spokesman: China's human rights improvement self-directed," June 3, 2008, www.china-embassy.org/eng/zt/zgrq/t443623.htm.

10. Margaret Warner, interview with former Ambassador Wu Jianmin, PBS' "The NewsHour with Jim Lehrer," May 30, 2008, www.pbs.org/newshour/bb/asia/jan-june08/jianmin_05-30.html.

11. Mary Hennock and Melinda Liu, "China's Tears: The Sichuan earthquake could change the way Chinese see their leaders," *Newsweek*, May 17, 2008, www.newsweek.com/id/137519.

12. James T. Areddy, "China Stifles Parents' Complaints About Collapsed Schools," *The Wall Street Journal*, June 18, 2008, p. 10A.

13. "China Terrorizes Tibet," editorial, *The New York Times*, March 18, 2008.

14. "Country Reports on Human Rights Practices — 2007," U.S. Department of State, March 11, 2008.

15. "2008 Country Reports on Advancing Freedom and Democracy," U.S. Department of State, May 23, 2008, www.state.gov/g/drl/rls/afdr/2008/104760.htm.

16. Xinhua News Agency, "FM: U.S. report on China democracy, human rights 'unreasonable,' http://news.xinhuanet.com/english/2008-06/02/content_8301760.htm.

17. Xinhua News Agency, *op. cit.*, April 21, 2008.

18. Sophie Richardson, "The Impact of the 2008 Olympic Games on Human Rights and the Rule of Law in China," statement to the Congressional-Executive Commission on China, Feb. 27, 2008, http://cecc.gov/pages/hearings/2008/20080227/richardson.php.

19. David Shambaugh, "China: Let a Thousand Democracies Bloom," *International Herald Tribune*, July 6, 2007, accessed at www.brookings.edu/opinions/2007/0706china_shambaugh.aspx.

20. James Mann, *The China Fantasy: How Our Leaders Explain Away Chinese Repression* (2007), p. xiii.

21. "Olympic Corporate Sponsors Still Silent on Darfur," Dream for Darfur, press release, April 24, 2008, www.dreamfordarfur.org/index.php?option=com_content&task=view&id=183&Itemid=51. The report is "The Big Chill: Too Scared to Speak, Olympic Sponsors Still Silent on Darfur," Dream for Darfur, www.dreamfordarfur.org/storage/dreamdarfur/documents/executive_summary_jj_revised.pdf. See also Stephanie Clifford, "Companies Return Criticism From Darfur Group," *The New York Times*, April 25, 2008.

22. For background see Karen Foerstel, "China in Africa," *CQ Global Researcher*, January 2008, pp. 1-26.

23. Neville Isdell, "We help Darfur but do not harm the Olympics," *Financial Times*, April 17, 2008, www.ft.com/cms/s/0/bba2d544-0c88-11dd-86df-0000779fd2ac.html.

24. Tunku Varadarajan, "No Word From Our Sponsors," *Condé Nast Portfolio*, July 2008, p. 21.

25. Joseph Kahn and David Barboza, "China Passes a Sweeping Labor Law," *The New York Times*, June 30, 2007.

26. *Ibid.*

27. *Ibid.*

28. *Ibid.*

29. See Jung Chang and Jon Halliday, *Mao: The Unknown Story* (2005). For a review of the book see Michiko Kakutani, "China's Monster, Second to None," *The New York Times*, Oct. 21, 2005, www.nytimes.com/2005/10/21/books/21book.html?scp=6&sq=mao+and+deaths&st=nyt.

30. Yu Keping, "Ideological Change and Incremental Democracy in Reform-Era China," in Li, *op. cit.*, p. 46. Yu, deputy director of the Bureau of Translation of the Chinese Communist Party Central Committee, also is director of the China Center for Comparative Politics and Economics and director of the Center for Chinese Government Innovations, at Beijing University.

31. Ma Jian, "China's Grief, Unearthed," op-ed, *The New York Times*, June 4, 2008, p. A23.

32. "China in the Red," "Frontline," Public Broadcasting Service, Feb. 13, 2003.

33. Christopher Bodeen, The Associated Press, "Olympic debate focuses on Tiananmen prisoners," *Columbus Dispatch*, June 4, 2008, www.dispatch.com/live/content/national_world/stories/2008/06/04/ap_tianamen_0604.ART_ART_06-04-08_A5_S5AD44G.html?sid=101.

34. Quoted in Worden, *op. cit.*, p. 26.

35. Keith Bradsher, "Vigil for Tiananmen Dead Draws Fewer in Hong Kong," *The New York Times*, June 5, 2008, p. A10, www.nytimes.com/2008/06/05/world/asia/05hong.html?scp=1&sq=%22vigil+for+tiananmen+dead%22&st=nyt.

36. Quoted in Official Web site of the Beijing 2008 Olympic Games, http://en.beijing2008.cn/spirit/beijing2008/candidacy/presentation/n214051410.shtml.

37. "State Secrets: China's Legal Labyrinth," Human Rights in China, http://hrichina.org/public/contents/article?revision%5fid=41506&item%5fid=41421#TOC.

38. "Stop Executions," Amnesty International, www.amnesty.org/en/human-rights-china-beijing-olympics/issues/death-penalty.

39. "Report 2008: The State of the World's Human Rights," Amnesty International, http://thereport.amnesty.org/eng/Homepage.

40. U.S. Department of State, *op. cit.*, March 11.

41. *Ibid.*

42. Louisa Lim, "Cases of Forced Abortions Surface in China," National Public Radio, April 23, 2007,

www.npr.org/templates/story/story.php?storyId=97
66870.

43. Remarks of U.S. Rep. Chris Smith, Beijing, July 1,
2008, accessed at http://chrissmith.house.gov
/UploadedFiles/080701BeijingPresser20001.pdf.

44. George J. Gilboy and Benjamin L. Read, "Political
and Social reform in China: Alive and Walking,"
The Washington Quarterly, summer 2008.

45. Warner, *op. cit.*

46. Chris Buckley, Reuters, "U.S. lawmakers decry
Olympics after dissidents blocked," July 1, 2008,
www.washingtonpost.com/wp-dyn/content/article
/2008/07/01/AR2008070100751.html.

47. *Ibid.* President Bush has said he will attend the
opening ceremony.

48. *Ibid.*

49. "China: Olympics Media Freedom Commitments
Violated," Human Rights Watch, press release, July 7,
2008, www.hrw.org/english/docs/2008/07/03/china
19250.htm.

50. *Ibid.*

51. Wang Baodong, "Opposing view: China welcomes
the world," *USA Today*, June 16, 2008, http://blogs
.usatoday.com/oped/2008/06/opposing-view-2.html.

52. Joseph Kahn, "China's Leader Closes Door to
Reform," *The New York Times*, Oct. 16, 2007, www
.nytimes.com/2007/10/16/world/asia/16china.html
?scp=3&sq=china+and+party+congress&st=nyt.

53. Peter Ford, "Why China shut down 18,401 websites,"
The Christian Science Monitor, Sept. 25, 2007,
www.csmonitor.com/2007/0925/p01s06-woap.html.

54. Richard Pound, "Olympian Changes: Seoul and
Beijing," in Worden, *op. cit.*, pp. 96-97.

55. Geoffrey A. Fowler and Juliet Ye, "Chinese Bloggers
Score a Victory Against the Government," *The Wall
Street Journal*, July 5-6, 2008, p. 7A.

56. *Ibid.* See also, Ye and. Fowler, "Chinese Bloggers
Scale the 'Great Firewall' in Riot's Aftermath," *The
Wall Street Journal*, July 2, 2008, p. 7A.

57. Fowler and Ye, *op. cit.*

58. Matthew Forney, "China's Loyal Youth," *The New
York Times*, April 13, 2008, www.nytimes.com
/2008/04/13/opinion/13forney.html?scp=1&sq=china's
%20loyal%20youth&st=cse.

59. Xinhua News Agency, "Expert: China never shuns
human rights problems," April 21, 2008, http:
//news.xinhuanet.com/english/2008-04/21/content
_8021473.htm.

BIBLIOGRAPHY

Books

**Li, Cheng, ed., *China's Changing Political
Landscape: Prospects for Democracy*, Brookings
Institution Press, 2008.**
A Brookings Institution scholar and professor of government at Hamilton College in Hamilton, N.Y., presents a
collection of scholarly articles on the economic, political
and social challenges facing China.

**Mann, James, *The China Fantasy: How Our Leaders
Explain Away Chinese Repression*, Viking, 2007.**
The author in residence at Johns Hopkins University's
Paul H. Nitze School of Advanced International Studies
and former Beijing bureau chief for the *Los Angeles Times*
argues that "we should not assume China is headed for
democracy or far-reaching political liberalization."

**Santoro, Michael A., *Profits and Principles: Global
Capitalism and Human Rights in China*, Cornell
University Press, 2000.**
A Rutgers University business-ethics professor focuses on
the human-rights responsibilities and contributions of
multinational corporations operating in China.

**Worden, Minky, ed., *China's Great Leap: The Beijing
Games and Olympian Human Rights Challenges*,
Seven Stories Press, 2008.**
The media director of Human Rights Watch presents a
collection of articles by experts on human rights in China.

Articles

**Gilboy, George J., and Benjamin L. Read, "Political
and Social Reform in China: Alive and Walking,"
The Washington Quarterly, summer 2008, www.twq
.com/08summer/docs/08summer_gilboy-read.pdf.**
The head of an international energy firm in China
(Gilboy) who is also a senior fellow at the MIT Center
for International Studies, and an assistant professor at the
University of California-Santa Cruz (Read) argue that

"political and social reforms are alive" in China but that the country "is moving forward at a walking pace . . . on a long, potentially tumultuous path."

Pei, Minxin, "How China Is Ruled," *The American Interest,* **Vol. III, No. 4, March/April 2008, www.the-american-interest.com/ai2/article.cfm?Id=403&MId=18.**
A senior associate in the China Program at the Carnegie Endowment for International Peace argues that "the cost of China's post-1989 strategy resides in its success: The [Communist] Party has been so well protected that its own lassitude has led to internal decay."

Thornton, John L., "Long Time Coming: The Prospects for Democracy in China," *Foreign Affairs,* **January/February 2008, www.foreignaffairs.org/2008 0101faessay87101/john-l-thornton/long-time-coming .html.**
A professor at Tsinghua University's School of Economics and Management in Beijing and chair of the Brookings Institution board says how far China's liberalization will go remains an open question.

Varadarajan, Tunku, "No Word From Our Sponsors," *Condé Nast Portfolio,* **July 2008.**
A business professor at New York University and former assistant managing editor of *The Wall Street Journal* argues that big companies receiving global exposure from the Beijing Olympics should do more to press for human-rights reforms.

Reports and Studies

"China (includes Tibet, Hong Kong, and Macau): Country Reports on Human Rights Practices — **2007," U.S. Department of State, March 11, 2008, www.state.gov/g/drl/rls/hrrpt/2007/100518.htm.**
This annual assessment concludes that human rights "remained poor" last year in China.

"China: Persecution of Protestant Christians in the Approach to the Beijing 2008 Olympic Games," Christian Solidarity Worldwide, produced in association with China Aid Association, June 2008, http: //chinaaid.org/pdf/Pre-Olympic_China_Persecution _Report_in_English_June2008.pdf.
The approach of the Beijing 2008 Olympic Games has been accompanied by a "significant deterioration" in religious freedom for China's Protestant Church, the report says.

"Falling Short: Olympic Promises Go Unfulfilled as China Falters on Press Freedom," Committee to Protect Journalists, June 2008, http://cpj.org/Briefings/2007 /Falling_Short/China/china_updated.pdf.
An update of an August 2007 report, this lengthy document says "China jails journalists, imposes vast censorship and allows harassment, attacks and threats to occur with impunity."

"State Secrets: China's Legal Labyrinth," Human Rights in China, 2007, www.hrichina.org/public /PDFs/State-Secrets-Report/HRIC_StateSecrets-Report .pdf.
The international, nongovernmental organization says that "by guarding too much information . . . the complex and opaque state-secrets system perpetuates a culture of secrecy that is not only harmful but deadly to Chinese society."

For More Information

Amnesty International, 5 Penn Plaza, 16th floor, New York, NY 10001; (212) 807-8400; www.amnesty.org. London-based organization that promotes human rights worldwide.

China Aid Association, P.O. Box 8513, Midland, TX 79708; (888) 889-7757; www.chinaaid.org. Monitors religious persecution in China.

Committee to Protect Journalists, 330 7th Ave., 11th Floor, New York, NY 10001; (212) 465-1004; www.cpj.org. Promotes press freedom around the world.

Dui Hua Foundation, 450 Sutter St., Suite 900, San Francisco, CA 94108; (415) 986-0536; www.duihua.org. Promotes human rights through dialogue with China.

Embassy of the People's Republic of China in the United States, 2300 Conn. Ave., N.W., Washington, DC 20008; (202) 328-2500; www.china-embassy.org/eng. Provides news and other information on China.

Human Rights in China, 350 Fifth Ave., Suite 3311, New York, NY 10118; (212) 239-4495; www.hrichina.org. Founded in 1989 by Chinese students and scholars to promote human rights in China and worldwide.

Human Rights Watch, 350 Fifth Ave., 34th floor, New York, NY 10118-3299; (212) 290-4700; www.hrw.org; Promotes human rights around the world and investigates abuses.

Laogai Research Foundation, 1109 M St., N.W., Washington, DC 20005; (202) 408-8300/8301; www.laogai.org. Documents and reports on human-rights abuses in China.

Reporters Without Borders, 1500 K St., N.W., Suite 600, Washington, DC 20005; (202) 256-5613; www.rsf.org. Paris-based group that promotes press freedom and works to protect safety of journalists.

9

Global Food Crisis

Marcia Clemmitt

Flooded corn crops throughout the Midwest are contributing to rising food prices in the United States and abroad, where higher prices already have plunged millions of poor people into malnutrition and starvation. Drought, high transportation costs stemming from higher oil prices and a growing diversion of corn for use as a biofuel also have contributed to the price hikes.

AFP/Getty Images/David Greedy

From *CQ Researcher*,
June 27, 2008.

S piking food prices have brought pain at supermarket checkout counters for millions of American families this past year, but in many developing countries, the situation is far more severe:

- In Somalia, people who can no longer afford food in markets try to stave off starvation with a watery soup made from the mashed branches of thorn trees. [1]
- In North Korea, where more than a third of the population is undernourished, the price of rice, the major food staple, soared 186 percent between 2007 and 2008, and overall food prices rose 70 percent.
- In Yemen, where 36 percent of the population is undernourished, wheat prices doubled. [2]
- In tiny Burundi, where about half the population is desperately poor, the price tripled for the landlocked nation's food staple, farine noir, a mixture of black flour and ground cassava root. [3]

With 2.1 billion people worldwide living on less than $2 a day and another 880 million living on less than $1 a day, price increases of such magnitude have plunged hundreds of millions into malnutrition and starvation. [4]

The price spikes have several causes, including drought and bad harvests in major food-exporting countries, high oil prices that make food more expensive to chemically fertilize and transport and a growing diversion of corn for use as a biofuel.

Some critics also blame the impact of globalization and the continued use of farm subsidies by industrialized nations, which they say undercut prices in poor countries.

With harvests expected to improve and more land being brought into cultivation, prices are expected to drop somewhat next year, according to

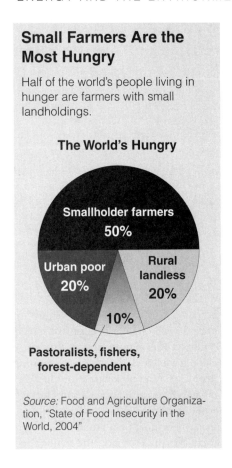

Small Farmers Are the Most Hungry

Half of the world's people living in hunger are farmers with small landholdings.

The World's Hungry

Smallholder farmers
50%

Urban poor
20%

Rural landless
20%

10%

Pastoralists, fishers, forest-dependent

Source: Food and Agriculture Organization, "State of Food Insecurity in the World, 2004"

the United Nations Food and Agriculture Organization (FAO) and the Organization for Economic Cooperation and Development (OECD), representing industrialized nations. [5] Nevertheless, experts warn, serious pressure on the world's food supply poses a long-term threat.

"The era of cheap food may be over," as rising oil prices drive the cost of food production and transport upward, said Haruhiko Kuroda, president of the Asian Development Bank. [6] Over the past several decades, the world's food system has been transformed from local production to a global market, where many countries produce large quantities of just a few crops each, mainly for export, while depending on imports for much of their own food supply.

"A core problem is that 35 countries don't produce enough food to give their residents a 2,000-calorie-per-day diet, even if all their production was being distributed equally" among citizens, says Cornell University Professor of Applied Economics and Management Christopher B. Barrett.

Furthermore, most of the world's population growth now occurs in the very developing nations that are currently unable to produce enough food to feed themselves, Barrett says.

Readjusting the global food system to avoid future crises will require fundamental rethinking of how and where food is produced and how it's allocated, analysts say.

"We're running up against this brick wall called finite resources," mainly the fertile soil and ample water needed to sustain good harvests, says Randall Doyle, an assistant professor of history at Central Michigan University.

"I always tell [food] producers that this whole thing is not rocket science — it's far more complicated," says Jerry L. Hatfield, supervisory plant physiologist at the U.S. Department of Agriculture's (USDA) National Soil Tilth Research Laboratory in Ames, Iowa. To manage water resources successfully, for example, "you have to look at the whole landscape."

"Feeding 6 billion people is really hard," says Curt Ellis, a filmmaker in Portland, Ore., whose documentary on American farming, "King Corn," aired recently on PBS. "I don't think we've figured out the right way to do it."

"We've got to increase the supply," says Mark Alley, a professor of agriculture at Virginia Tech and president-elect of the American Society of Agronomists.

That is especially difficult "in Europe, the United States and Australia, where our ability to exponentially increase food production is quite limited," says Doyle. This means that the most attention must be spent on increasing agriculture yields in developing countries, especially in Africa, where agriculture is least advanced, he says.

However, development experts say, there's no consensus on how future farming should look — what balance should be struck between large-scale industrial farming for export and smaller farms that produce food for local consumption.

"There's no consensus in the global development community about agriculture," says Peter Gubbels, vice president for international programs at World Neighbors, a nonprofit development organization in Oklahoma City that helps poor farmers in developing countries become self-supporting. Nevertheless, "there are growing movements in every country" to return to more local production, he says. "Some call that food sovereignty, and now we're even beginning to see the U.N. and the World Bank" talking about it.

The food crisis has sparked international tension over the rich diets enjoyed by industrialized nations and the fear that, as developing countries add more animal products to their menus, food crises will increase.

"There's still plenty of food for everyone, but only if everyone eats a grain and legume-based diet," said Peter Timmer, a fellow at the Washington-based Center for Global Development. "If the diet includes large . . . amounts of animal protein (not to mention biofuels for our SUVs), food demand is running ahead of global production," he said. [7]

In India, the "middle class is larger than our entire population," said President George W. Bush in May, and "when you start getting wealth, you start demanding better nutrition and better food," including meat, which increases global food demand and "causes prices to go up." [8]

But Indians reacted with outrage to Bush's implication that their diets have fueled food-price spikes. "Bush is shifting the blame to hide the truth," said Devinder Sharma, chair of the New Dehli-based Forum for Biotechnology and Food Security. "We all know that the food crisis is an outcome of the American policy of diverting huge land area from food to fuel production," under a congressional mandate to increase use of biofuels, mainly corn-based ethanol. [9]

While greater consumption of meat in developing countries is a long-term trend, it's not a factor in current price spikes, says Brian Wright, professor of agricultural and resource economics at the University of California at Berkeley. For example, he says, Indians consume only 37 eggs a year per person, and "meat consumption is almost not on the charts."

Other analysts argue that developing countries' farm sectors have been crippled because the United States and other wealthy nations shut out poor nations' farm exports while subsidizing their own farmers to sell abroad below cost.

"The U.S. and the European Union in particular have preached free markets but have been in blatant disregard" of trade rules, which they repeatedly tweak to their own

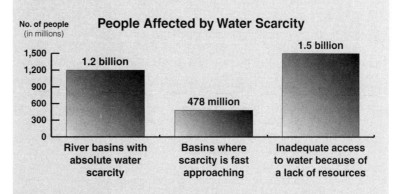

Billions Suffer From Water Scarcity

Three billion people — almost half the world's population — face serious actual or potential water shortages. Most are in the Middle East and North Africa, followed by South Asia and sub-Saharan Africa.

People Affected by Water Scarcity

No. of people (in millions)

- River basins with absolute water scarcity: 1.2 billion
- Basins where scarcity is fast approaching: 478 million
- Inadequate access to water because of a lack of resources: 1.5 billion

Sources: International Water Management Institute, in "World Development Report 2008: Agriculture for Development," The World Bank, 2007

advantage, says Thomas Dobbs, a professor emeritus of economics at South Dakota State University in Brookings. "We produce too much of the wrong kind of thing," then "dump it on Third World markets and remove [those countries'] incentive for local production," he says. [10]

But many U.S. policy makers hotly defend the subsidies. By and large, the United States has not constructed overwhelming trade barriers against agricultural products, said former U.S. Secretary of Agriculture Ann M. Veneman. U.S. farm subsidies "haven't changed market access into this country. At least 91 percent of African produce comes into this country duty free." [11]

Addressing these contentious issues will be difficult because "the poor are voiceless," says Cornell's Barrett. "The loudest and often the shrillest voices are those who aren't paying attention to the billion or so people who are living on a dollar or so a day."

As farmers, scientists and policy makers seek ways to feed a changing planet and expanding population, here are some of the questions that are being asked:

Can enough food be sustainably produced to feed the global population?

Environmentalists warn that water and soil resources soon may be outstripped by growing dietary demands.

Hungry Countries Face Double Whammy

High food prices and climate change trigger unrest.

The recent worldwide price spike for grains and other food staples has left vulnerable populations in many developing countries at risk for malnutrition and starvation. And the growing hunger crisis leaves unstable nations open to "an emerging security problem as well," says Cornell University Professor of Applied Economics and Management Christopher B. Barrett.

But the very instability of many developing nations also leaves them vulnerable to yet another threat — climate change.

Local circumstances largely determine which populations are the most vulnerable, says Johan Selle, director of operations at iJET, an international risk-management consultancy in Annapolis, Md. In rural Kenya, for example, former nomadic peoples "are really struggling," says Selle. "Ten years ago they would have produced their own food," but today many are urban dwellers without enough income to buy imported food at skyrocketing global prices, he says.

The food-price crisis has triggered riots and strikes in more than 30 countries, mostly places where existing political unease has made populations ripe for protest.

Countries like Jordan, which have enough financial stability to subsidize food for their poorest citizens, don't see the unrest, Selle says. But "wherever there's instability, food shortages are the final straw," says Frederic Ngoga Gateretse, iJET regional manager for Africa.

"The capacity of pressure groups to organize" in a country and a population's "history of taking to the streets" largely determine whether the food crisis has triggered unrest, Gateretse says.

Guinea, in West Africa, for example, "is pretty much a failed state, and trade unions there have the capacity to mobilize and get on the streets" after a 10-year struggle of opposition parties trying to remove the current president from office, he says. Guinea has experienced four union-led food strikes, says Gateretse. Trade unions also have been involved in protests in the West African nation of Cameroon, where unrest over food prices lasted for five days in February and left many people dead or injured, he says.

Lack of a stable government or an economic infrastructure also paved the way for food strikes in Haiti, where the unrest was a response to the government's long-term inability to take care of the people, says Selle.

Urban populations have been more likely to riot than rural populations "because the foods they buy to eat are more likely to be affected by price hikes, since they require fuel [to grow, produce and transport], like bread," says Gateretse.

In some countries, riots are unlikely — even with extreme food stress — because citizens fear reprisals. Zimbabwe is suffering from severe shortages, for example, but people know that the military would crush any active rebellion "so they have yet to see protests on the street," says Selle.

In any event, the impact of climate change on harvests worldwide likely means unrest over food supplies will long outlast the current price spike in many developing countries.

Many of the threatened countries lie near the equator and are at high risk for desertification and water shortages, says Gateretse. "Many governments in poor countries do not have the ability to anticipate or handle climate-change-related crises, and no one is training the governments to do so," he says.

"As the economy grows, its demands are outgrowing the Earth," said Lester R. Brown, founder of the Earth Policy Institute, which supports sustainable economic policies. "While the world economy multiplied sevenfold in just 50 years, the Earth's natural life-support systems remained essentially the same. Water use tripled, but the capacity . . . to produce fresh water through evaporation changed little. The demand for seafood increased fivefold, but the sustainable yield of oceanic fisheries was unchanged," he said. [12]

"The bottom line is that it is now more difficult for farmers to keep up with the growing demand for grain," said Brown. "Food insecurity may soon eclipse terrorism as the overriding concern of national governments." [13]

The current American diet, in particular, may not be sustainable, many commentators say.

"Perhaps three Earths would be required to support the current human population if everyone lived the over-consumptive North American lifestyle," noted the environmentalist Web site OilEmpire.us. [14]

Wealthy nations, including the United States, have not offered the help that developing countries need to develop more stable food systems, said Jacques Diouf, director-general of the U.N. Food and Agriculture Organization (FAO). "The developing countries did, in fact, forge policies, strategies and programs that — if they had received appropriate funding — would have given us world food security," but the industrialized nations spent the money on subsidies for their own farmers instead, Diouf said. [1]

But many analysts say that even if aid from wealthy nations had been available, unstable regimes in many nations can't use the aid effectively.

"A lot of developmental solutions are undermined by corruption" in developing countries' governments, says John Walton, a professor of sociology at the University of California at Davis.

"Many of the countries in most trouble are failed states," says Brian Wright, a professor of agricultural and resource economics at the University of California at Berkeley. Without stable and functional governments, countries have "no local research capabilities," without which agricultural science is ineffective, he says. "You can't just take a plant from another country and stick it in the ground." Local researchers must take research findings from elsewhere and figure out how to adapt them to local conditions.

Even the most well-intentioned assistance can easily fail if local government is unstable or corrupt, says Josh N. Ruxin, an assistant professor of public health at New York's Columbia University and director of its Millennium Village Project in Rwanda. "Stability in government is extremely important. It means that interventions can be rolled out large scale, and faster," he says.

"That's one of the reasons I live and work in Rwanda, because now there's a lot of transparency and stability in

government," Ruxin says. "If you look at a place that's extremely corrupt, like Zimbabwe, with bad agriculture policies, you're just hitting your head against the wall."

Farming requires infrastructure, such as roads for farmers to get their crops to market, says Ray Cesca, president of the World Agricultural Forum, which seeks to improve world agriculture. "It's up to the government to build the road, but sometimes the money disappears," he says.

Unfortunately, stable governments are important for moving a population out of poverty and hunger, but poverty and hunger themselves act against development of stable government, says Thomas Dobbs, professor emeritus of economics at South Dakota State University in Brookings. "It's a vicious cycle, and difficult to get out of."

For example, a sustainable system to give a country food security would include "more domestic production, more garden plots" tended over the years right where people live, says Dobbs. "But when there's a civil war and people are moved into camps, that system all falls apart."

There's plenty that industrialized countries like the United States, foundations and other donors can do to help, says Ruxin. For example, "very few governments in sub-Saharan Africa have sufficient agricultural extension [education] to reach all their farmers, and donor funds can have tremendous impact" by helping support such efforts, he says.

And the "failed-state" excuse for not offering assistance doesn't hold water, says Cornell's Barrett. "Of course, nothing productive is going to happen in Zimbabwe, but there are other places with elected governments that don't get support" from wealthy nations. "Donors fiddle" while the future ebbs away, he says.

---

[1] Quoted in Elisabeth Rosenthal and Andrew Martin, "U.N. Issues Warning on Food Crisis," *The New York Times,* June 4, 2008, p. A6.

A factor in recent grain price hikes "is the amount that's being used to increase the meat and milk supply," as more people consume more such foods, says Virginia Tech's Alley. "Can we produce all the food we need? Yes. All we want? Not necessarily."

Furthermore, "there is no way to produce more food without occupying more land and taking down more trees" in the rainforest, said Blairo Maggi, owner of the soybean-producing company Andre Maggi Group and governor of Brazil's Mato Grosso state. [15]

A growing number of analysts argue that today's industrial-style agriculture, which depends heavily on fossil fuels for fertilizer manufacture and long-distance transport, cannot be sustained.

A 2008 report for the intergovernmental group International Assessment of Agricultural Science and Technology for Development, based on input from private- and public-sector participants from developed and developing nations, concluded that "the dominant practice of industrial, large-scale agriculture is unsustainable,

Food Prices Jumped 50 Percent

Prices for several food staples have risen dramatically in recent years. Most have increased by 50 percent, while skim milk powder has more than doubled. Prices are expected to drop in the future, but not back to earlier levels.

Average World Prices for Selected Commodities, 2002-2013

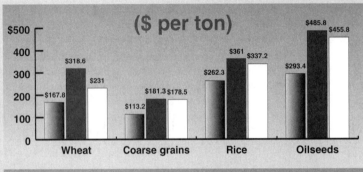

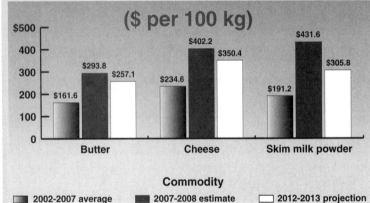

Source: "OECD-FAO Agricultural Outlook 2008-2017," Organisation for Economic Cooperation and Development, 2008

mainly because of the dependence of such farming on cheap oil, its negative effects on ecosystems and growing water scarcity." [16]

As fossil-fuel supplies run out, farm products like corn are increasingly called into service as biofuel, and the heightened demand translates into higher food prices.

"I worry that with biofuels, the food market will end up looking like the worldwide pharmaceutical market. The rich will get theirs, and the poor will die," says Berkeley's Wright. "I would abandon the grain-based biofuels."

Nevertheless, Wright and others say that human effort has vastly increased food production in the past and can continue to do so.

The improvements in agriculture made during the 20th century greatly increased food yields, says Wright. Today there is "some sign that the rate of increase of yields is declining, but there's no evidence that we're going to reach a limit. We still have fairly good yield increases."

"Potentially, can we feed everybody? Of course we can," says Ray Cesca, president of the World Agricultural Forum, which aims to bring together public- and private-sector expertise and resources to improve world agriculture.

Success depends on investing in more agricultural research and then making sure it's implemented, says Wright. "The economic returns on crop research are the highest" returns on any research, he says.

"Earth will have 9 billion people by 2050, and we need a 33 percent jump in food productivity," says Doyle at Central Michigan University 'We need another Green Revolution," he says, referring to the period from the late 1940s through the 1970s, when Western researchers spurred huge crop-yield improvements in developing countries, especially in Asia, using new high-yield grain varieties.

"Do we have the technology to increase the supply? Absolutely," Alley says. "We have better varieties of seeds, methods to control pests," and more. "The issue is implementation of these technologies."

China provides evidence that yields can improve, Alley says. In the early 1990s, some predicted that China's swelling population would soon require it to import virtually all the grain produced on the planet. But within a decade, China had implemented farm improvements that made the country a net grain exporter until as recently as last year, he says.

Developing countries have plenty of unfarmed arable — farmable — land, although barriers exist to its being brought into use, says Cesca. The greatest amounts of potentially arable land that can be used — not counting rainforests — are in Africa, followed by Asia and Latin America, often in the most food-deprived nations, he says. Currently, however, poverty, unstable governments and a lack of business-friendly policies — such as local barriers to setting up banks or getting loans — block development of the land for farming, Cesca says.

Harvests can be improved even in very difficult environments if farmers get help to improve their practices, says Gubbels at World Neighbors.

In many places, such as the Sahel, a dry, semi-tropical belt of shrub- and grasslands that runs across Africa, farmers cannot get into [large-scale] industrial agriculture because "fertilizer costs three to four times as much" as in the United States because of transport costs, Gubbels says. However, small farms can greatly expand their harvests if farmers get help to learn and adopt the best techniques, he says. "A lot of it is building on farmers' own knowledge," but beefing up agricultural-extension programs to teach best practices is vital, he says.

In mountainous areas, for example, few farmers have dug trenches at proper intervals to stem water and soil loss, partly because "it's very labor intensive. But we got people to do this, and now all their neighbors are doing it," with better crops as a result, says Josh N. Ruxin, assistant professor of public health at New York's Columbia University and director of the University's Millennium Village Project in Rwanda.

"A lot of subsistence farmers have just scattered seed and prayed it would produce," but encouraging underutilized practices like sowing seeds in rows to prevent young plants from crowding each other out can greatly increase harvests, even in the most unpromising regions, Ruxin says.

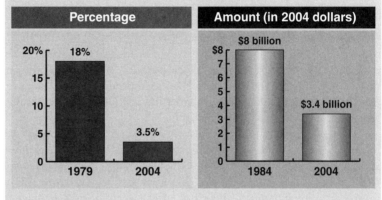

Agricultural Assistance on the Decline

Aid to agriculture amounted to only 3.5 percent of total development assistance in 2004, less than one-fifth the percentage 25 years earlier. Aid to agriculture in 2004 totalled $3.4 billion, less than half of the amount in 1984.

Official Development Assistance for Agriculture

Source: "World Development Report 2008: Agriculture for Development," The World Bank, 2007

Do U.S. farm and trade policies harm poor people in developing countries?

Critics say U.S. policies that give hefty subsidies to American growers encourage developing countries to favor U.S.-produced food at below-market prices. As a result, say critics, farmers in developing countries lose their local markets and grow poorer and developing nations themselves lose their food-production capability, risking famine if imports are unavailable or spike in price.

Other analysts argue, however, that American farmers need financial protection against fluctuating harvests and prices and that, ultimately, global trade is best for everyone.

Trade globalization helps developing countries create modern economies, rather than keeping them mired in a subsistence lifestyle, according to conservative British columnist Janet Daley. "What developing countries need is to develop, not to have their present conditions of life and work preserved like a museum exhibit," she wrote. Replacing globalization with more local food production merely means "sustaining agricultural activity that would not otherwise be sustainable in the global marketplace." [17]

Opening developing-world markets to imports can help those nations in the long run, says Berkeley's

Wright. There can be some value in keeping a modest local ability to produce farm staples like grains, but "globalization is what stops famines," he says. Bad weather or bad farm-sector decision-making can mean severe food shortages, "but if you have another place to get food, you have a safety net."

The argument for importing food rather than striving for agricultural self-sufficiency goes back to Scottish economist Adam Smith, whose 1776 classic *The Wealth of Nations* first described the logic of free-market capitalism. Global free trade in food is the international counterpart of Smith's key "proposition that people within a national economy will all be better off if they all specialize at what they do best instead of trying to be self-sufficient," said Jagdish Bhagwati, a professor of economics and political science at New York's Columbia University. [18]

In fact, the U.S. food market "tends to be fairly open" to developing-country products, said Bob Young, chief economist for the American Farm Bureau, which represents farmers. "The average tariff faced by countries trying to land agricultural products here is around 12 percent. The average tariff faced by our farmers is around 62 percent," making U.S. trade barriers minor compared to those put up by countries in the rest of the world, Young said. [19]

U.S. farmers need subsidies to offset the much stricter food-safety and environmental regulations they face, said Young. U.S. subsidies amount to "compensation to help level the playing field" for the more heavily regulated U.S. farmer, said Young. "We provide protection to other sectors of the economy when they face unfair competition. Why should agriculture be any different?" [20]

The key to determining conditions for the poor is not so much globalization itself but how governments respond to it, say some economists.

"Opening the economy to trade . . . need not make the poor worse off if appropriate domestic policies and institutions are in place," wrote Pranab Bardhan, a professor of economics at the University of California, Berkeley. Cases in point are the developing economies of Mauritius, South Korea and Botswana, whose citizens have prospered in recent years while the lot of the poor stagnated in other countries with similar resources, such as Jamaica, the Philippines and Angola, said Bardhan. [21]

But many commentators criticize U.S. farm and trade policy as harmful and hypocritical.

"The idea that you should import everything that you can buy cheaper from abroad means that you lose your ability to provide your own staples," a dangerous state that threatens nations' food security, says South Dakota State University's Dobbs. "Ironically, this is something the United States would never do" but persists in urging on others, he says.

The United States, Europe and Japan spend about $350 billion a year subsidizing their own farmers, "and at the same time they negotiate trade agreements with other countries requiring them to drop their own farm subsidies," says Gubbels at World Neighbors. "As a result, governments [in developing countries] tell their people, 'Move to the cities,'" thus shrinking their own farm sectors and driving up poverty. He describes a farmer in Ghana who raises chickens but can't sell them profitably in local markets because Europe dumps its excess chicken production in Africa at below-market prices.

A few decades ago, Haiti grew all the rice it needed and was one of the world's largest exporters of sugar and tropical produce, wrote William P. Quigley, a professor of law at Loyola University in New Orleans. But in April, food riots over high prices that threatened to push some families into starvation claimed the lives of six Haitians. [22]

Quigley blames the United States — and the U.S.-backed World Bank and International Monetary Fund — for pushing Haitian leaders to open the way to imports that decimated the country's farms. "In the 1980s, imported rice poured into Haiti, below the cost of what our farmers could produce," said a Haitian priest quoted by Quigley. "Farmers lost their businesses. . . . After a few years of cheap imported rice, local production went way down." [23]

Today Haiti, with an annual per capita income of $400, is the third-largest importer of U.S. rice, writes Quigley. Meanwhile, U.S. rice farmers have been supported by three different government subsidies that averaged more than $1 billion a year since 1998, Quigley said. [24]

In Mexico, U.S.-subsidized corn, imported under the North American Free Trade Agreement (NAFTA), is "swamping small farmers," wrote Conn Hallinan, an analyst for Foreign Policy in Focus, a Washington think tank that seeks diplomatic solutions to international problems. "Some 2 million farmers have left the land, and 18 million subsist on less than $2 a day, accelerating rural poverty and helping to fuel" emigration, he said. [25]

"The extremely high level of U.S. government payments to farmers, while simultaneously encouraging other countries to reduce domestic agricultural supports," is an "egregious example of hypocrisy and double-speak," wrote analysts from the University of Tennessee's Agricultural Policy Analysis Center. [26]

Under World Trade Organization (WTO) agreements, the United States committed to reduce payments to American farmers but found ways around those commitments, which "have risen dramatically since 1996 and stand as a testament to U.S. admonitions to 'do as I say, not as I do,' when it comes to trade liberalization," said the center. "Our farm policy directly affects the livelihoods and sustainability of small farmers around the world." [27]

Do U.S. food aid policies harm people in developing countries?

Historically, the United States has been the largest donor of food to developing nations, tiding numerous countries over crises. [28] But critics of U.S. aid programs argue that much U.S. aid may benefit American producers, including multinational corporations, more than hungry people abroad. Indeed, they say most development aid completely bypasses the poor in rural areas who need help the most.

America's oldest and biggest food aid program, Food for Peace, was signed into law by President Dwight D. Eisenhower in 1954. Since then, it and other programs "have brought together governments, businesses, multilateral institutes such as the U.N. World Food Programme (WFP), and American voluntary organizations in a valuable public-private partnership intended to reduce hunger," wrote Cornell's Barrett and Daniel G. Maxwell, an associate professor of development economics at Tufts University and a former regional director for the charity CARE International.

In its first 50 years, Food for Peace alone "contributed more than 340 million metric tons of food aid to save and improve the lives of many hundreds of millions of poor and hungry people," according to Barrett and Maxwell. [29]

Food aid from the U.S. and other wealthy nations "clearly had a significant role in reducing loss of life during food emergencies in such countries as Ethiopia, Sudan, Somalia, Afghanistan, Rwanda and Haiti," according to analysts at the USDA's Economic Research Service. [30]

During Somalia's 1992-1993 civil war, food aid contributed about 70 percent of Somalians' food consumption and about half of Eritrea's between 2000 and 2004, they wrote. [31]

"The United States has traditionally been the major provider of emergency food aid during international humanitarian disasters," according to the Congressional

Research Service (CRS), Congress' nonpartisan research agency. Historically, the United States "has been the world's largest provider of food aid, both emergency and non-emergency," accounting for just over 55 percent of total food aid in the 1990s. [32]

The resumption this May of U.S. food aid to North Korea is a "very timely" and "hugely significant contribution" that could head off the famine that threatens that country as food prices soar, said Jennifer Parmalee, a spokesperson for the World Food Programme. The U.S. suspended food aid to communist North Korea in 2006 but over the long term has been the country's "biggest historical donor." [33]

A May announcement of a $40 million, three-year food-aid package to Bangladesh will provide "a means and incentive for children to stay in school so Bangladesh can prepare the next generation of leaders," since a large proportion of the aid will feed schoolchildren and pregnant and breastfeeding mothers, said James F. Moriarty, U.S. ambassador to Bangladesh. In 2007, floods and a cyclone destroyed crops in Bangladesh. [34]

But the current structure of aid also causes problems, many analysts say.

"There's an immediate need to reform the way we provide food aid," says Gubbels of World Neighbors. The United States is now "the only developed country that obliges people to buy U.S. grain," thus "tying its food aid to support" for large agribusiness companies like Decatur, Ill.-based Archer Daniels Midland and Minneapolis-based Cargill. Canada and Europe have stopped that practice. The U.S. method is "expensive because you have to ship it all the way over there," says Gubbels.

In addition, "these often are not the foods people are used to," and bringing in tons of food from abroad ends up "degrading local agriculture," Gubbels says. "If you really want to help, give them cash or try to buy the food locally," he says.

The cost to taxpayers of food aid that must be bought from producers in the donor country and then shipped "has been shown to be significantly higher — in many cases 30-50 percent higher" — than aid from alternative sources, said the charity CARE USA. [35]

Moreover, the timing and extent of aid often has more to do with market conditions in wealthy donor countries than with developing-countries' needs, said the international charity Oxfam International. For example, in 1973, many developing countries faced food short-

CHRONOLOGY

1910s-1960s *Famines hit China, Russia and Africa. U.S. farm-support programs are created during the Great Depression.*

1917 War Department's School Garden program urges students to plant vegetable gardens.

1928 Drought-driven famine kills 3 million people in northern China.

1943 Famine in British colony of Bengal — now Bangladesh and western India — kills up to 3 million.

1945 The number of Los Angeles children tending school-yard gardens for the war effort hits 13,000.

1948 In the Green Revolution's first victory, Mexico produces enough grain to feed itself, using high-yield wheat varieties developed by Rockefeller Foundation-backed research.

1968 Four-year drought hits Africa's Sahel.

1970s *Drought and government mismanagement ruin harvests in several countries. World Bank and International Monetary Fund require developing countries to drop farm trade barriers in return for loans.*

1970 American plant-breeding pioneer Norman Borlaug wins the Nobel Peace Prize for improving crop yields in developing countries.

1973 Ethiopian government of Haile Selassie falls after its inaction allows drought to trigger a famine.

1977 India becomes self-sufficient in rice — another victory for the Green Revolution.

1980s-1990s *Large agribusinesses proliferate. Globalization of food-trading systems squeezes out small farms and local food processors. Commodity prices drop worldwide.*

1995 Congress approves Community Food Projects grants to help charities feed hungry people with locally produced food.

1996 President Bill Clinton signs agriculture reform bill to wean farmers off government subsidies over seven years. . . . Floods, drought and the cutoff of food aid from China and the former Soviet Union bring famine to North Korea.

1998 Congress backs off subsidy reform, approving $5.9 billion in emergency farm supports. . . . War and drought cause famine in Ethiopia.

2000s *Congress continues increasing farm subsidies, over objections from the World Trade Organization (WTO). Food shortages hit Zimbabwe after strife over who should control farmlands cripples agriculture in the country, once a major food exporter. Number of U.S. farm households falls to a few hundred thousand from 5 million in the 1930s, while farm output is 10 times larger.*

2001 President George W. Bush calls for cutbacks in farm subsidies to prevent overproduction.

2002 Congress passes farm bill that increases subsidies.

2006 U.S. farm-research budget totals $2.8 billion, down from $6 billion in 1980. . . . U.S. support for developing-country agriculture totals $624 million, down from $2.3 billion in 1980. . . . WTO's Doha Round of international trade talks collapses over disagreement on U.S. and European farm subsidies.

2007 World grain stocks drop to historically low levels. . . . Congress increases requirements for biofuel in the gasoline supply, increasing U.S. demand for corn.

2008 U.N. Food and Agriculture Organization says 850 million people are undernourished. . . . U.N. warns that solving global food problems could cost $30 billion a year. . . . Svalbard Global Seed Vault is opened in Arctic Norway to preserve food-plant biodiversity. . . . International Assessment of Agricultural Knowledge concludes that chemical fertilizer-based industrial farming has depleted soil and water and must be combined with organic and small-farm techniques to keep agriculture sustainable. . . . Congress passes farm bill rejecting Bush administration pleas to end shipment of U.S.-produced food as aid and buy food in developing countries' local markets.

ages, but that same year U.S. Food for Peace shipments dropped to less than a tenth of 1960s levels, according to the charity. The reason? Cereal prices were high around the world so grain producers' revenues from "commercial sales made surplus disposal" of food as aid to developing nations "unnecessary," said the group. [36]

Critics also blast "monetization" — the U.S. practice of shipping American grain to charities in a developing country, which then sell the grain locally and use the proceeds to finance their work. In 2007, CARE announced it would stop accepting monetized food aid by 2009, saying that the process is inefficient and delivers food not to the hungry but only to people who can afford to buy it. [37]

U.S. food aid has focused too much on addressing emergency situations "at the expense of addressing the chronic hunger and poverty that makes these crises so serious," said the charity Catholic Relief Services (CRS). To help countries avoid future food crises, food aid should be accompanied by other assistance, "such as investments in agricultural development aimed at small-scale producers," said CRS. [38]

Only 4 percent of development aid goes to small farmers, even though about 75 percent of those who survive on under a dollar a day live in rural areas, says Gubbels. Instead, most agricultural-development assistance goes to areas near coasts, where climate, land and location make it easier to produce large yields and export harvests efficiently into world trade, he says. A better policy for actually relieving hunger would be to "help the small farmers feed themselves," Gubbels says.

Aid programs should also begin paying for new vitamin- and mineral-fortified ready-to-eat food supplements that developing countries can produce locally, Milton Tectonidis, chief nutritionist for the charity Doctors Without Borders, told CBS News' "60 Minutes." For example, small factories in three African countries now produce Plumpynut — a nutritionist-invented mix of peanut butter, powdered milk, sugar, vitamins and minerals — that can keep otherwise malnourished toddlers healthy for about $1 a day and doesn't require scarce refrigeration or clean water to use.

"In three weeks, we can cure a kid that looked like they're half-dead," Tectonidis said. "There's many countries in Africa now saying, 'We want a factory. We want a factory.' Well let's give it to them," by redirecting some U.S. and European food aid to such projects, he said. [39]

BACKGROUND

Food Riots and Famine

"A hungry man is an angry man," runs a proverb common to nations from Zimbabwe to Scotland. Like hunger itself, protests over food shortages have occurred throughout history.

"America has a history of food riots, though the last were in the Depression," and "I wouldn't be surprised to see them again here," says Rose Hayden-Smith, a fellow in the foundation-funded Food and Society Policy program in Columbia, Mo., and a youth- and community-garden adviser for the University of California's Master Gardener Program. [40] The Civil War saw food riots in the United States, as did the so-called Gilded Age of the 1890s, an era marked by corporate corruption and a rising income gap between rich and poor, she says.

Some food protests are spontaneous revolts by hungry citizens, while others are organized by activists like unions and linked to broader political events.

In Northern France in 1911 rising prices and a meat shortage due to hoof-and-mouth disease spurred women to march "to the markets in protest," demanding "lower prices and dump[ing] carts of eggs and butter if and when their demands were not met," wrote Lynne Taylor, a professor of history at the University of Waterloo in Ontario, Canada. [41]

In Barcelona, Spain, in 1918, women's groups led rioting to protest inflationary food prices during the country's post-World War I economic collapse. Rioting women "attacked bread shops and coal wagons and took over a ship laden with fish," wrote Taylor. When police tried to break up the crowds, "the women turned on them, stripping some officers of their pants" and "thrashing them." [42]

In the 1970s and '80s a "global wave" of food riots in developing countries was sparked by "structural-adjustment" policies imposed by the International Monetary Fund and World Bank as a condition for developing nations to receive loans. These free-market adjustments included "incentives to go from small-farm agriculture to industrial, export-driven agriculture" and requirements to cut government subsidies for items like food staples and bus fare, says John Walton, a professor of sociology at the University of California at Davis.

Often, the result was "prices doubling overnight," triggering protests seen in numerous countries over the decades, he says. "Some countries had 10 or 12 instances

More Than Seeds Needed to Improve Harvests

Poor farmers need access to credit, decent roads.

Worldwide anxiety over food prices could be a good thing if it finally focuses attention on building a sustainable food system for developing countries, agriculture experts say.

"Years ago, if we had the kind of concern we're seeing now, we wouldn't have these problems today," says Ray Cesca, president of the World Agricultural Forum, which seeks to improve world agriculture. For example, the United Nations' Millennium Development Goals include cutting poverty in half by 2015, "but we're going in the opposite direction," Cesca says.

Improving harvests takes investment in more than just seeds and fertilizers. Farmers in developing countries desperately need access to credit to help them through the inevitable ups and downs of farm production, says Peter Gubbels, vice president for international programs at World Neighbors, a nonprofit development group in Oklahoma City.

"When small-scale farmers run out of food, they go to a rich landlord and borrow a sack of grain," says Gubbels. "Then three months later they have to pay it back with interest, which may mean they have to leave their own fields and work as a laborer to pay off the debt." World Neighbors contributes seed money for local farmers' co-ops to create small banks "so that when they fall into need they can borrow from themselves and avoid the cycle of debt and slavery," he says.

Even to sell food in local markets, farmers need basic infrastructure such as roads.

To get a country on the right track, "feeding your own people has got to be the top priority," but many countries "haven't built the infrastructure for it," says Cesca. For example, in U.S. cities there are "central distribution points where everyone can go to buy and sell food, but that takes investment, and somebody needs the foresight to say, 'We'll have to create one of these,' " he says.

Similarly, in many developing countries, "most of the productivity rots in the field because there's no technology in cold storage" to preserve it, says Cesca.

Sub-Saharan Africa exports around $10 billion in food-related products annually, "but the local markets have the potential for around $135 billion" in sales, "so why wouldn't you pay attention to the local markets?" Cesca asks.

In the past, wealthy nations have pushed developing countries to commit most of their agriculture to commodities for export, like coffee or sugar. But in the long run that's a losing strategy, says Josh N. Ruxin, an assistant professor of public health at New York's Columbia University and director of the university's Millennium Village Project in Rwanda. The current price spike aside, since the 19th century prices of basic commodities — like coffee, corn and sugar — "have all gone down," says Ruxin. "Over time, producing only commodities makes people poorer, even if they become more efficient and productive," he says.

A better plan is agricultural diversity, says Ruxin. "We ask, 'What different crops can we produce for both local and national markets?' " says Ruxin. This needs to be thought out carefully, he says. For example, Africa can't export mangoes to Europe because storage and transport are too expensive. "But they can grow mangoes and export dried organic mango strips processed locally."

And mango strips are only the beginning, says Ruxin. On 32 hectares of formerly abandoned land, a farm coop recently planted the first pomegranate trees in Rwandan history in coordination with the federal U.S. African Development Foundation and a Los Angeles-based company, POMWonderful. "Israel and Turkey can only produce so many pomegranates," and there's room for developing nations to get in on the game, says Ruxin. "The answer lies in asking, 'What crops will do well?' "

In the current price crisis, the hungry need immediate aid, Ruxin says. But solving long-term food problems requires patience.

"One reason African farmers don't plant fruit trees is because they take five to eight years to mature, and that doesn't work when you're hungry today," he explains. That's where focused research can help. A new variety of mango tree will produce a 50-fruit crop in two years, increasing to 500 fruits in five years, Ruxin says. "Five hundred mangoes that sell for a dollar apiece" can mean an unheard-of level of wealth for a subsistence farmer, he says.

of strikes and demonstrations." Governments had a variety of reactions, with some working out softer ways of making the prescribed changes, such as making them temporary, says Walton. At the extremes, consequences were harsh for governments and citizens, he says. "Sudan's government fell. Some governments just plowed ahead and repressed the protesters," killing 50 in Morocco and 40 in Cairo, Egypt.

Food crises generally are more political and economic events than natural ones, scholars say.

"Famines themselves, when looked at historically, have turned out not to be about food supply so much as about food distribution," says Walton.

Economic and political inequality lie behind famine, according to Indian economists Jean Dreze, of the Dehli School of Economics, and Amartya Sen, a professor at Harvard University who won the 1998 Nobel Prize in economics. "The developing of modern economic relations and of extensive interdependences even between distant parts of the economy" has created "many new ways in which different sections of the population can see . . . their command over food shift violently and suddenly," they wrote. [43]

For example, the shift to a world economy where virtually every country makes the bulk of its income through trade and where most cheap staple foods are imported has increased the risk of hunger for many, wrote Sen and Dreze. "Pastoralist nomads can be reduced to starvation if the relative price of animal products falls in relation to that of staple food, since their subsistence depends on their ability to sell . . . animal products . . . to buy enough calories from . . . grain. Fishermen may go hungry if the price of fish fails to keep up with that of . . . rice." [44]

The world's growing numbers of wage laborers who own no land that they can farm to tide them over tough times are "particularly vulnerable" to famine in the modern era, Dreze and Sen noted. [45]

Modern-day food crises are most acute in developing nations, many of which were operated for centuries as colonies of European nations, and "the colonial powers invested little in the food production systems" of their colonies, according to the Washington, D.C.-based International Food Policy Research Institute (IFPRI). [46]

As a result of such policies, "by the mid-1960s, hunger and malnutrition were widespread" in the developing world, "which increasingly depended on food aid from rich countries," said IFPRI. [47]

Increasing the Harvest

While the political world has yet to figure out how to ensure that food is distributed fairly, agricultural scientists — boosted by large government investments in research — have been busy, developing farm techniques that increased harvests exponentially.

U.S. and Brazil Produce Most Ethanol

The United States and Brazil made nearly 90 percent of the 40 billion liters of ethanol produced in 2006.* Some critics say the food crisis is partly the outgrowth of diverting land from food to fuel production.

Worldwide Ethanol Production, 2006

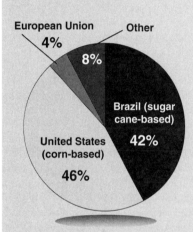

European Union 4%

Other 8%

Brazil (sugar cane-based) 42%

United States (corn-based) 46%

* A U.S. gallon contains 3.78 liters.

Source: "World Development Report 2008: Agriculture for Development," The World Bank, 2007

Beginning in the 1890s, Germany, the United Kingdom and the United States launched major agricultural-research enterprises, says the University of California's Wright. At the time, rising demand from growing populations was forcing farms to expand into less fertile land, but research on higher-yield plants and better growing methods kept yields increasing, says Wright.

"The story of English wheat is typical," according to the IFPRI. "It took nearly 1,000 years for wheat yields to increase from 0.5 to two metric tons per hectare, but only 40 years to climb from two to six metric tons per hectare." [48]

Agricultural disasters themselves often spurred improvements.

Is America's Food System Ripe for Change?

Return to locally grown food is advocated.

Americans spend an average of only 10 percent of their disposable income on food, compared with 50 percent in Indonesia and 30 percent in China. U.S. spending today is also low by historical standards: In 1933, Americans spent about a quarter of their income on food. [1]

Nevertheless, with food prices spiking, more Americans are feeling pain at the supermarket checkout. "Our [monthly] food bills are $600, $700," up from around $400 a year or two ago, said Jomarie Ortiz, the mother of four teenage sons in Bloomfield, N.J. "The cereal [price] was astronomical." [2]

Food experts say the rising prices are but one indication of serious, long-term problems in the American food system, which relies too much on fuel-guzzling long-distance shipping and single-crop, commodity-based agriculture that damages the environment and stints human nutrition needs.

"In the last half-century we made a profound choice to have the bulk of our food system in commodity crops, like corn, soybeans and rice," says Curt Ellis, the Portland, Ore.-based filmmaker of "King Corn," a documentary on American farming that aired recently on PBS television. "These dominate our diets in unrecognizable forms," from the fast-food hamburger made from corn-fed beef to soda sweetened with corn syrup rather than with sugar or honey, he says.

"All across our food shelves are products that are seemingly diverse but actually are not" when you read labels carefully, Ellis says. The result is a meat- and simple-carbohydrate-heavy diet that sees "one-in-three first-graders on the road to developing Type 2 diabetes" and "young people in America today — my generation — potentially having shorter lifespans than their parents," says the 28-year-old Ellis.

In addition, environmentally sustainable farming methods aren't yet the order of the day in American agriculture, despite the real possibility that depleted soils and fluctuating rainfall — partly brought on by climate change — may threaten future harvests.

"Even with our productive crop yields, we've got spots in the heartland with really poor yields because" of soil erosion, depletion of soil nutrients and water problems, says Jerry L. Hatfield, supervisory plant physiologist at the U.S. Department of Agriculture's National Soil Tilth Research Laboratory in Ames, Iowa.

"We need to focus on how reliant we are on a good natural-resource base" of rich soil and sufficient water, Hatfield says. "We can work on this genetic stuff" — breeding or bioengineering higher-yield or hardier plant varieties — "but at a certain point environment" is the determining factor for harvests, he says. "I don't want to be an alarmist, but

In the 1930s, for example, the Great Plains of the United States and Canada — especially Kansas, Oklahoma and the Texas panhandle — turned into a veritable "Dust Bowl." Drought combined with decades of intense, single-crop farming allowed wind to blow the once-rich topsoil away in huge dust clouds, darkening skies all the way to the East Coast and rendering millions of acres of farmland useless.

Out of the disaster came better soil conservation, says the USDA's Hatfield. In fact, "one of the places where we've done the best at conserving soil is the Great Plains," he says, by means such as reduced plowing, which helps keep soil from drying out.

But while the industrialized world increased its farm yields through science in the first half of the 20th cen-

tury, developing countries made little progress, even as their populations soared. By the 1960s, hunger in the developing world, especially Asia, could no longer be ignored. A 1967 report of the President's Science Advisory Committee noted that "the scale, severity and duration of the world food problem are so great that a massive, long-range, innovative effort unprecedented in human history will be required to master it." [49]

At the time, American entomologist and population scientist Paul Ehrlich predicted that hundreds of millions of people would starve to death during the next few decades because Earth was incapable of sustaining the population explosion, says Wright.

"These were very confident predictions in those days," Wright says. "Why didn't it happen? Because of the

I still believe that we're on a path where our soils are continuing to degrade, and when I look at our practices, we could do a lot more" to conserve soil, Hatfield says.

"When you choose to plant 90 million acres with just one crop — corn — it's a thirsty crop, a nitrogen-thirsty crop," so it depletes soil resources and "doesn't make efficient use of the limited water and nitrogen that we have," says Ellis.

Environmentally sustainable farming generally requires more crop diversity, says Thomas Dobbs, professor emeritus of economics at South Dakota State University in Brookings. "You can't just do corn/soybean cropping," as farms from Ohio to North Dakota mostly do today, he says. "You also have to have small grains like wheat or oats and some plants like clover or alfalfa," which take nitrogen from the air and return it to the soil where it acts as a fertilizer, he says.

Some farmers argue that they can't diversify their fields because under current law they can only get government subsidies by keeping many acres in corn and soybeans, says Hatfield. "But if we focused on food security, we'd think about changing to a more diverse system of crops."

The American food system has been nationalized, with little food grown close to where it's eaten, and changing that is job No. 1 in the eyes of many food analysts, as fossil-fuel prices rise.

"In a petroleum-limited world, the best solutions are the ones you can find close to home," says Ellis. "It's unfathomable to me that Iowa can feed the whole country with corn but grows so few fruits and vegetables," even though "fruits and vegetables used to grow just fine there."

"In Virginia 10 or 12 years ago, we developed a good system with a nice niche for growing fall broccoli, but we couldn't compete with California's competitive advantage because of their climate and [higher] yield," says Mark Alley, a professor of agriculture at Virginia Tech. But with fuel prices rising "that's changing" back in favor of more local growing, he says.

But switching to locally grown produce will require rebuilding a lost food infrastructure.

"We've created a national food system, stripping rural areas of food-processing capabilities," says Rose Hayden-Smith, a youth- and community-garden adviser for the University of California's Master Gardener Program. Processing and distribution infrastructure will need to be rebuilt from the ground up, she says.

Furthermore, urban farming and home and city-lot community gardening should be brought back in a big way, says Hayden-Smith. "We need the government to introduce 'victory gardens' again," she says. "They were phenomenally successful, especially in World War II, when America was able to export much more food to our starving European allies" because the "citizen gardener" — including schoolchildren — produced so much of the food eaten in U.S. homes, says Hayden-Smith.

"I'd like to see the White House put in a garden," just like first lady Eleanor Roosevelt did, she says.

_____

[1] "Americans Spend Less than 10 Percent of Disposable Income on Food," *Salem-News* [Salem, Ore.], July 19, 2006, www.salem-news.com.

[2] Andrew Martin and Michael M. Grynbaum, "Costs Surge for Stocking the Pantry," *The New York Times*, March 15, 2008, p. A1.

increase in crop yields, and that didn't happen by accident" but through investments in research, he says. "Indians have a life expectancy in the 60s today, up from the 40s to 50s several decades ago," and much of that comes from better nutrition. "There is about a third more food available per person in the world today than when Ehrlich was writing."

Beginning in the mid 1940s and accelerating in the '60s, the Rockefeller and Ford foundations began promulgating new farming products and techniques in developing countries, including improved irrigation, better crop-management techniques and, first and foremost, new varieties of wheat, rice and other grains that were more responsive to modern chemical fertilizers. [50]

This so-called Green Revolution provided "the highest return on a public investment in recorded history," says Cornell's Barrett. For an amount variously estimated at between several hundred million and 1 billion dollars, "we kept a billion people from falling into poverty and moved a billion out of poverty. That's a remarkable accomplishment."

By the 1990s, nearly 75 percent of Asian rice came from Green Revolution seeds, along with about half the wheat planted in Africa, Latin America and Asia and about 70 percent of the world's corn, according to Food First, an Oakland, Calif.-based anti-hunger think tank. [51]

More recently, however, the limits of the Green Revolution's achievements have become clear.

For one thing, "we basically became complacent" about agriculture's achievements, and "investments in research have slowed radically," says Barrett. Furthermore, "we took

Grain and rice vendors wait for customers at a market in Beijing, China, in July 2007. Farm improvements made China a net exporter of grain until last year, when high prices began putting food staples out of the reach of many Chinese.

for granted that agricultural yields were going to continue to improve," partly because of continued heavy use of fertilizers. "But now — with worries about the environment growing — fertilizer use has dropped off," meaning that continual yield increases are no longer assured, he says.

Finally, the focus on agricultural yield does nothing to change economic and political problems that are root causes of most famines, said Food First. "If the poor don't have the money to buy food, increased production is not going to help them." [52]

Subsidies and Trade

Congress enacted its first farm-subsidy legislation in 1933, during the Great Depression, to ensure farmers had a stable enough income to keep farming, even in tough times. [53]

"Since then, in various ways and to varying degrees, Congress has sought to raise farm income through a combination of commodity-specific price supports and supply controls, mainly import restrictions," according to trade analysts at the Cato Institute, a libertarian, Washington-based think tank. [54]

Subsidies "originally were intended to raise farm prices and incomes from Depression levels and to provide greater income stability," wrote South Dakota State University's Dobbs. "The goal was to maintain a nation of moderate-sized family farms." [55]

In the second half of the 20th century, however, the food-supply web changed dramatically. International

trade in food commodities swelled, huge food-processing companies gained control of international food markets and giant agribusinesses squeezed out small and medium-sized family farms. These developments led critics to argue that wealthy nations' farm subsidies should be scrapped.

"Only 8 percent of producers receive 78 percent of subsidies," with 80 percent of farmers getting an average subsidy of under $1,000, wrote Keith Ashdown, vice president for policy at the Washington advocacy group Taxpayers for Common Sense. "Farm payments are based on production levels, so the bigger the farm, the bigger the government check," and the family farmers whom subsidies originally were designed for see virtually no assistance today. [56]

Intense constituent pressure on farm-state politicians has kept subsidies in place, however.

For example, U.S. guarantees of a minimum price to sugar producers and trade barriers to keep foreign sugar out have long raised concerns, and the U.S. House in 1996 came within five votes of abolishing the sugar supports, wrote Mark A. Groombridge, a research fellow at the Cato Institute and now a special assistant in the State Department's Office of Arms Control. Since 1996, however, Congress has actually increased sugar supports, despite widespread criticism. [57]

Beginning in 1995, the WTO has worked toward international consensus on rules to lower trade barriers worldwide. Since 2001, the trade organization has focused on reducing agricultural trade barriers in the so-called Doha Development Round of negotiations.

The Doha Round has stalled, however, mainly because wealthy nations refuse to alter their subsidy programs while insisting that developing nations abandon their own trade barriers and farm supports. For example, both U.S. cotton subsidies and the European Union's sugar programs have been found in violation of WTO rules, but the programs have not been revised, said the Cato Institute analysts. [58]

In 2003, at a street protest against WTO talks being held in Cancun, Mexico, Lee Kyung Hai, a South Korean farmer and former director of the Korean Advanced Farmers Union, committed suicide by stabbing himself in the heart; he was carrying a banner that read "WTO Kills Farmers." [59]

Earlier, Lee had spoken of another farmer who committed suicide by swallowing poison, after falling into serious debt. "I was powerless to do anything but hear the howling of my friend's wife," he said. [60]

Is the U.S. ethanol fuel program worsening the world food crisis?

YES
Gawain Kripke
Senior Policy Adviser, Oxfam America

From testimony before the House Energy and Commerce Subcommittee on Energy and Air Quality, May 6, 2008

Diversion of corn to ethanol is playing a significant role in reducing corn supplies for food and feed. In 2008 the U.S. Department of Agriculture estimates that 3.1 million bushels of U.S. corn will be used to produce biofuels. That's an increase of nearly 50 percent over the 2.1 million bushels last year and close to twice the 1.6 million bushels of 2006.

In 2008 the U.S. will convert approximately one-quarter (23.7 percent) of our corn production into biofuels. We're rapidly diverting larger portions of our corn supply to fuel, leaving less for food.

For about 1.2 billion people around the world, corn is the preferred staple cereal. Consider that the U.S. produces more than 40 percent of the world's corn supply. Dedicating 3.1 million bushels of corn for ethanol this year will take more than one-tenth of the global corn supply off the market for food and feed. Furthermore, the U.S. exports nearly twice as much corn as all the other exporters combined. So, reduced supply and/or higher prices in the U.S. corn market have significant implications for the rest of the world.

Although ethanol mandates and subsidies directly impact corn prices, they also have cascading impacts on other agricultural commodities. Higher corn prices are encouraging farmers to commit more acreage and agricultural inputs to corn. This leaves less for other crops, especially soybeans, which are often planted in alternate years with corn. As a result, production for other commodities is lower and prices are higher.

Higher corn prices also lead consumers to choose other, cheaper cereals to substitute for food or feed. Over time, this increased demand increases the prices for other commodities.

"Biofuel demand has propelled the prices not only for corn but also for other grains, meat, poultry and dairy through cost push and crop and demand substitution effects," according to the [International Monetary Fund's] World Economic Outlook.

The International Food Policy Research Institute (IFPRI), one of the premier organizations tracking food and hunger issues, estimates that biofuels will drive up corn prices by between 27 percent and 72 percent by 2020, depending on the scenario. Other commodities such as oil seeds used for biodiesel fuel would rise by 18 percent to 44 percent. "In general, subsidies for biofuels that use agricultural-production resources are extremely anti-poor, because they implicitly act as a tax on basic food, which represents a large share of poor people's expenditures," the IFPRI said.

NO
Rick Tolman
CEO, National Corn Growers Association

From testimony before the House Energy and Commerce Subcommittee on Energy and Air Quality, May 6, 2008

Recently, the media and ethanol critics have demonized corn ethanol and attempted to solely blame rising food costs on higher commodity costs and government policies promoting renewable fuel.

In attempting to justify their opposition to ethanol expansion and the Renewable Fuels Standard (RFS) enacted by Congress in 2007, opponents continue to claim that higher corn prices are causing higher retail food prices. A look at the facts surrounding food prices simply doesn't support that logic.

More so, the effects of $120-per-barrel oil have far-reaching effects on the consumer price for food. A recent study by the Oregon Department of Agriculture details the factors affecting food price: a growing middle class in Latin America and Asia; drought in Australia; low worldwide wheat stocks; increases in labor costs; a declining U.S. dollar; regional pests, diseases, droughts and frost; and marginal impacts from ethanol demand for corn and sugarcane.

One recent study found that a $1-per-gallon increase in the price of gas has three times the impact on food prices as does a $1-per-bushel increase in the price of corn.

In fact, just 19 cents of every consumer dollar can be attributed to the actual cost of farm products like grains, oilseeds and meat. Retail food products like cereals, snack foods and beverage corn sweeteners contain very little corn. Consider that even when corn is priced at $5 per bushel, a standard box of corn flakes contains less than eight cents' worth of corn.

Corn is a more significant ingredient for meat, dairy and egg production. Still, corn represents a relatively small share of these products from a retail price perspective. As an example, according to the National Cattlemen's Beef Association, it takes about three pounds of corn to produce one pound of beef. This equates to 27 cents' worth of corn in a pound of beef when corn is $5 per bushel.

Because corn and other grains constitute such a small portion of retail food products, higher grain prices are unlikely to have any significant impact on overall food inflation, according to a number of experts. According to [U.S. Department of Agriculture] economist Ephraim Liebtag, a 50 percent increase in corn prices translates to an overall increase of retail food prices of less than 1 percent. Similarly, a recent analysis by Informa Economics found that higher corn prices "explain" only 4 percent of the increase in retail food prices.

CURRENT SITUATION

Price Spike

Skyrocketing prices for food staples are fueling protests around the world this year.

"In 2006, no one was predicting this current price boom," says David Orden, a senior research fellow at the International Food Policy Research Institute and a professor of economics at Virginia Tech. A constellation of supply-and-demand factors came together to drive prices skyward, and though "good crops are forecasted this year, they are not harvested yet, so people are still nervous" enough about future food availability to keep demand high, he says.

High demand and a historically low supply of commodities like grain are the main drivers of the price spike. For example, "we're at historic lows of grain inventories," says Cornell's Barrett. "In the U.S. we have less than one month's supply when there are usually three or four."

A long-term drought that has slashed Australia's grain exports has also contributed to a scare that caused some other rice-producing countries to ban their exports, out of fear they would not have enough to feed their own people, says Berkeley's Wright.

Most recently, a disastrous May 2 cyclone devastated crops in Myanmar, which had been among the few countries expected to export rice in 2008. [61]

Demand pressures also are driving up prices.

Notably, in its 2005 energy bill, Congress mandated adding 4 billion gallons of renewable fuel — mostly corn-based ethanol — to the U.S. gasoline supply in 2006, with increased amounts added in succeeding years. [62]

The mandate drives up demand and prices for corn, says Barrett. And in our processed-food world, corn demand is already much higher than many realize, he says. "Corn feeds chickens and sweetens soft drinks" to name just a few uses, Barrett says. Rising corn prices also drive up prices for meat and other sweeteners like sugar cane, he says.

Investors are also driving the price spike. Many have been dabbling in the grain markets as other investment sectors, such as housing, have become unstable in the past year. [63] The new investors also have encouraged "some speculators to withhold grain from the market in hopes of selling it for a higher price later," says Central Michigan University's Doyle.

But while speculation has been a factor in recent price spikes, it "will not in the long term keep prices high, because there's only so much wheat or corn . . . that someone can hold off the market . . . because it is a perishable product," said Dean Baker, co-director of the Center for Economic and Policy Research in Washington.

To some extent, the demand-supply equation will come into balance naturally and food prices will drop again, says Barrett. To meet high demand, "farmers will put more land into cultivation and use more fertilizers," he says. But the poorest countries will have the most trouble making adequate adjustments, he says. "Poor farmers can't get credit" to put in irrigation systems, for example, he says.

Columbia University's Ruxin says the price surge could actually lead to a new era of smarter agricultural development in developing countries.

"The overall direction over the decades" has been to steer African nations toward large-scale industrial farming of products for export to Europe and the United States, but "overnight that policy has been stood on its head," Ruxin says. Today, "if you're a poor, subsistence-level farmer and eat what you produce and maybe trade a little, and prices go up 60 percent, your food is suddenly extremely valuable, and your ability to get into the market is greater," which could help build local agriculture, he says.

"We're asking how can we help smaller farms cooperate" to produce for local and regional markets, where buyers have been hit exceptionally hard by the price of imported grain. Thanks in part to the price spike, "the jury is clearly coming down on the side of producing more locally, and that was not the picture five years ago," says Ruxin.

Farm Bill

A flurry of attention followed April statements by U.N. food officials branding recent food-price spikes as signs of a long-term disaster in the making.

High food prices are "creating the biggest challenge that the [World Food Programme] has faced in its 45-year history, a silent tsunami threatening to plunge more than 100 million people on every continent into hunger," said WFP Executive Director Josette Sheeran. [64]

"We must take immediate action in a concerted way," said U.N. Secretary-General Ban Ki-moon. [65]

But food and farm politics are intensely national and too easily override international concerns. A case in point, say critics, is the new U.S. farm bill, which Congress overwhelmingly approved in May, 318-106 in the House and 85-15 in the Senate, overcoming an earlier presidential veto. [66]

The bill trims some farm subsidies and increases the percentage of funding for U.S. nutrition programs, such as food stamps and the Fresh Fruit and Vegetable Snack Program for schools, said House Agriculture Committee Chairman Collin Peterson, D-Minn., a supporter of the bill. [67]

"Today's overwhelming vote was an indication that we produced a strong, bipartisan farm bill that is good for our farmers and ranchers and essential to our state," said Sen. Amy Klobuchar, D-Minn., a member of the Senate Agriculture Committee. [68]

But the legislation comes in for harsh criticism from others.

The farm bill "is a travesty, it's disgusting" says Berkeley's Wright. "When farmers are richer than ever and the poor can't eat, they gave $10 billion more to farmers."

Singled out for special censure are the legislation's protections for U.S.-produced sugar, particularly championed by Peterson, whose home state of Minnesota is a major sugar-beet producer.

The bill raises subsidies for U.S. sugar producers and requires imported sugar to be used for ethanol production, not food, "virtually locking in an 85 percent share of the U.S. market for domestic . . . growers, even though a number of foreign countries can grow sugar more cheaply," wrote trade analyst Daniel Griswold of the Cato Institute. The sugar provisions interfere with free trade and drive up prices for American consumers, he insisted. [69]

"This farm bill just heads in the wrong direction in terms of our international obligations," which is why President Bush vetoed it, said Deputy Secretary of Agriculture Chuck Conner. "We would expect [nations that trade with the United States] to protest in every way they can." [70]

During the more than year-long battle over the new bill, the legislation's architects also remained at odds with President Bush and many anti-poverty groups over changes the White House wanted in food-aid programs. U.S. food aid currently comes in the form of U.S.-produced food that U.S. transport companies ferry to developing countries, where it is either handed out or sold in local markets by charities that use the proceeds to provide various kinds of assistance.

The White House pushed to turn a quarter of the American aid — about $400 million annually — into cash to buy food in developing countries' own regional markets, a move that Bush and several charities, including CARE

and Oxfam, say would provide more food more quickly and cost less by cutting transport times and costs. [71]

Congress' nonpartisan auditing agency, the Government Accountability Office (GAO), agreed. The amount of food actually delivered as U.S. aid actually dropped by 52 percent between 2002 and 2007 because transport and other associated costs rose, said the GAO. [72]

But the Bush plan runs afoul of U.S. food producers and shippers. Accordingly, Congress approved only a small pilot program — totaling $60 million over four years — to test overseas purchasing. [73]

Gloria Tosi, a lobbyist for companies that transport American food aid, called even the tiny pilot program "a bad idea." [74]

OUTLOOK

Environmental Concerns

The science of farming traditionally has focused on increasing harvests, but today concerns have shifted to making farming environmentally sustainable. The change was prompted by soaring prices for fossil fuels that power farm machinery and are used in fertilizer manufacturing, plus dawning awareness that soil and water resources are rapidly being depleted.

In the United States, "One thing we need to focus on is how reliant we are on a good natural-resource base" — mainly soil and water — says the USDA's Hatfield. "Even with our productive yields we've still got spots in the heartland with really poor yields" due to erosion and depletion of soil nutrients, he says.

In India and Pakistan, farmers "are mining the groundwater deeper and deeper," depleting future stores, says South Dakota State University's Dobbs.

Climate change is adding to the troubles. In China, Australia and Africa, deserts are encroaching on once-fertile lands, says Doyle at Central Michigan University. "Where the hell is all the food going to be grown?"

Transport of food in a globalized marketplace is "a huge issue with the price of diesel fuel as it is today" and oil supplies dwindling, says Virginia Tech's Alley, president-elect of the American Society of Agronomists.

Farmers must soon reevaluate many practices in light of environmental needs.

"About two years ago, I was in northwestern Iowa to talk about reducing tillage" — plowing fields less to reduce soil erosion and depletion, recalls Hatfield. "I asked, 'What are you going to do when diesel fuel goes above $3 a gallon?' And they looked at me as if I were from Mars," he says. But today, "Farmers are asking different questions, like 'How do I reduce my tilling? How do I use manure' " to replace fossil-fuel-based fertilizer?

The debate is heating up right now about the best means to maximize harvests in sub-Saharan Africa and other challenging environments, and industrial, fossil-fuel-based farming is not necessarily winning, says Dobbs. A large study by Great Britain's University of Essex found that "sustainable practices . . . led to a 96 percent increase in per-hectare food production," showing that "there's potential for a lot of increased productivity without abandoning small-farm agriculture," he says.

But others say that tough times may lead to increased acceptance of high-tech methods, including so-called genetically modified foods — crop varieties created by gene manipulation in the biotechnology lab — of which many consumers are wary. [75]

In Australia and New Zealand, for example, there was a great deal of resistance" to transgenic crops — which may someday be cheaper and drought-resistant — but as food prices go up, the opposition is starting to be muffled, says Doyle.

Food shortages and the resulting unrest "are not going to go away tomorrow by any stretch of the imagination," says Johan Selle, an international risk-management expert, in Annapolis, Md.

"When a businessman is getting $5 for a loaf of bread, he will not bring it down to $2. We are going to see this for another five, six, seven years," he says. "Unless someone — the U.S., the U.N., the World Trade Organization — takes the lead" to create a more stable system, "we're going to struggle for a long time."

NOTES

1. Jeffrey Gettleman, 'Famine Looms as Wars Rend Horn of Africa," *The New York Times*, May 17, 2008, p. A1.

2. "The List: The World's Most Dangerous Food Crises," *Foreign Policy*, April 2008, www.foreignpolicy.com.

3. Maria Bartiromo, "Food Emergency: On the Front Line With the U.N.'s Josette Sheeran," Facetime, *Business Week*, May 1, 2008, www.businessweek.com.

4. For background, see "Agriculture for Development, World Development Report 2008," World Bank, Oct. 19, 2007, http://econ.worldbank.org/WB SITE/EXTERNAL/EXTDEC/EXT-RESEARCH /EXTWDRS/EXTWDR2008/0,,contentMDK:214 10054~menuPK:3149676~pagePK:64167689~piPK :64167673~theSitePK:2795143,00.html.

5. "Agricultural Outlook 2008-2017," United Nations Food and Agriculture Organization (FAO) and the Organization for Economic Cooperation and Development (OECD).

6. Quoted in Laurie Garrett, "Food Failures and Futures," Council on Foreign Relations working paper, May 15, 2008, www.cfr.org/content/publica tions/attachments/CGS_WorkingPaper_2.pdf.

7. "Asian Rice Crisis puts 10 Million or More at Risk: Q&A With Peter Timmer," Center for Global Development, April 21, 2008, www.cgdev.org.

8. Quoted in Rama Lakshimi, "Bush Comment on Food Crisis Brings Anger, Ridicule in India," *The Washington Post*, May 8, 2008, p. A18.

9. Quoted in *ibid*.

10. For background on globalization and world trade, see Samuel Loewenberg, "Anti-Americanism," *CQ Global Researcher*, March 2007, pp. 51-74; Brian Hansen, "Globalization Backlash," *CQ Researcher*, Sept. 28, 2001, pp. 761-784, and Mary H. Cooper, "World Trade," *CQ Researcher*, June 9, 2000, pp. 497-520.

11. Quoted in Elizabeth Becker, "U.S. Defends Its Farm Subsidies Against Rising Foreign Criticism," *The New York Times*, June 27, 2002.

12. Lester R. Brown, *Outgrowing the Earth: The Food Security Challenge in an Age of Falling Water Tables and Rising Temperatures* (2005), p. 3.

13. *Ibid.*, p. 8.

14. "Peak Grain: Feeding Nine Billion After Peak Oil and Climate Change," OilEmpire.us Web site, www.oilempire.us/peak-grain.html.

15. Quoted in Tom Philpott, "Food Crisis Resolved!" "Gristmill blog," *Grist*, http://grist.org, April 28, 2008.

16. Stephen Leahy, "Africa: Reinventing Agriculture," Inter Press Service, April 15, 2008, http://all africa.com. For background see Peter Behr, "Looming Water Crisis," *CQ Global Researcher*, February 2008, pp. 27-56.

17. Janet Daley, "Forget Fairtrade — Only Free Trade Can Help Poor," *Daily Telegraph* (United Kingdom), Feb. 25, 2008, www.telegraph.co.uk.

18. Jagdish Bhagwati, "Protectionism," *The Concise Encyclopedia of Economics*, Library of Economics and Liberty Web site, www.econlib.org.

19. Daniel T. Griswold and Bob Young, "Online Debate: Should the United States Cut Its Farm Subsidies?" Council on Foreign Relations, April 27, 2007, www.cfr.org.

20. *Ibid.*

21. Pranab Bardhan, "Does Globalization Help or Hurt the World's Poor?" *Scientific American*, March 26, 2006, www.sciam.com.

22. Bill Quigley, "30 Years Ago Haiti Grew All the Rice It Needed. What Happened?" *Counterpunch*, April 21, 2008, www.counterpunch.org/quigley04212008.html.

23. *Ibid.*

24. *Ibid.* For background see Peter Katel, "Haiti's Dilemma," *CQ Researcher*, Feb. 18, 2005, pp. 149-172.

25. Conn Hallinan, "The Devil's Brew of Poverty Relief," *Foreign Policy in Focus*, July 19, 2006, www.fpif.org.

26. Daryll E. Ray, Daniel G. De La Torre Ugarte and Kelly J. Tiller, "Rethinking U.S. Agricultural Policy: Changing Course to Secure Farmer Livelihoods Worldwide," Agricultural Policy Analysis Center, University of Tennessee, September 2003, p. 2.

27. *Ibid.*

28. For background, see Mary H. Cooper, "Foreign Aid After Sept. 11," *CQ Researcher*, April 26, 2002, pp. 361-392.

29. Christopher B. Barrett and Daniel G. Maxwell, "Recasting Food Aid's Role," *Policy Brief*, Cornell University Department of Applied Economics and Management, August 2004, www.aem.cornell.edu/faculty_sites/cbb2/papers/BM_policybrief.pdf.

30. Shahla Shapouri and Stacey Rosen, "Fifty Years of U.S. Food Aid and Its Role in Reducing World Hunger," *Amber Waves*, U.S. Department of Agriculture Economic Research Service, September 2004, www.ers.usda.gov.

31. *Ibid.*

32. Charles E. Hanrahan, "Indian Ocean Earthquake and Tsunami: Food Aid Needs and the U.S Response," Congressional Research Service, April 8, 2005.

33. Quoted in "North Korea Welcomes Resumption of U.S. Food Aid," Agence France-Presse, May 17, 2008, http://news.yahoo.com. For background, see Kenneth Jost, "Future of Korea," *CQ Researcher*, May 19, 2000, pp. 425-448.

34. Quoted in "U.S. Giving Bangladesh $40 million in Food Aid," The Associated Press, May 4, 2008, www.msnbc.msn.com.

35. Quoted in Matthew Bolton and Michael Manske, "Non-Emergency Food Aid: A Resource in the Fight Against Hunger and a Tool for Development," policy statement, Counterpart International, www.hungercenter.org/international/documents/Michael%20Manske%20Non%20Emergency%20Food%20Aid.pdf.

36. "Food Aid or Hidden Dumping: Separating Wheat from Chaff," *Oxfam Briefing Paper 71*, March 2005, www.oxfam.org/en/files/bp71_food_aid_240305.pdf.

37. For background, see Eben Harrell, "CARE Turns Down U.S. Food Aid," *Time*, Aug. 15, 2007, www.time.com/time/nation/article/0,8599,1653360,00.html.

38. "Food Aid for Food Security," Catholic Relief Services, http://crs.org/public-policy/food_aid.cfm.

39. Quoted in "A Life Saver Called 'Plumpnut,' " "60 Minutes," June 22, 2008, www.cbsnews.com/stories/2007/10/19/60minutes/main3386661.shtml.

40. For background on food riots, see B.P. Garnett, "Mob Disturbances in the United States," *Editorial Research Reports*, Oct. 20, 1931. Available at *CQ Researcher Plus Archive*.

41. Lynne Taylor, "Food Riots Revisited," *Journal of Social History*, winter 1996, p. 483.

42. *Ibid.*

43. Jean Dreze and Amartya Sen, *Hunger and Public Action* (1989), p. 4.

44. *Ibid.*, p. 5.

45. *Ibid.*, p. 6.

46. "Green Revolution: Curse or Blessing?" International Food Policy Research Institute, 2002, www.ifpri.org.

47. *Ibid.*

48. *Ibid.*

49. Quoted in *ibid.*

50. For background, see "The Green Revolution & Dr. Norman Borlaug," The Norman Borlaug Institute for Crop Improvement, www.nbipsr.org.

51. "Lessons from the Green Revolution," Food First Web site, April 8, 2000, www.foodfirst.org.

52. *Ibid.*

53. For recent background, see David Hosansky, "Farm Subsidies," *CQ Researcher*, May 17, 2002, pp. 433-456, and Brian Hansen, "Crisis on the Plains," *CQ Researcher*, May 9, 2003. For historical background, several articles appear in *Editorial Research Reports*, including B. W. Patch, "Government Subsidies to Private Industry," April 26, 1933, and Charles E. Noyes, "Government Payments to Farmers," Sept. 3, 1941.

54. Daniel Griswold, Stephen Slivinski and Christopher Preble, "Ripe for Reform: Six Good Reasons to Reduce U.S. Farm Subsidies and Trade Barriers," Center for Trade Policy Studies, Cato Institute, Sept. 14, 2005.

55. Thomas Dobbs, "Is It Too Late for Progressive Farm and Food Policy Reforms? Critical Decisions Facing Congress," *Dailykos.com* Web site, Jan. 26, 2008, www.dailykos.com.

56. Keith Ashdown, "Congress Continues with Corruption and Failure: Handouts to Large Agribusiness Corporations," *The Progress Report* Web site, www.progress.org/2005/tcs176.htm.

57. Mark A. Groombridge, "America's Bittersweet Sugar Policy," Center for Trade Policy Studies, Cato Institute, Dec. 4, 2001.

58. Griswold, *et al.*, *op. cit.*

59. John Ross, "Bridging the Distance," *San Francisco Bay Guardian*, Sept. 17, 2003.

60. Quoted in *ibid.*

61. For background, see "Myanmar Cyclone Aftermath: Rice Shortage," *The Daily Green* Web site, May 7, 2008, www.thedailygreen.com.

62. For background, see Ben Lieberman, "The Ethanol Mandate Should Not Be Expanded," *Heritage Foundation Backgrounder* #2020, March 28, 2007, www.heritage.org/Research/energyandenvironment/bg2020.cfm.

63. For background, see Marcia Clemmitt, "Mortgage Crisis," *CQ Researcher*, Nov. 2, 2007, pp. 913-936, and Kenneth Jost. "Financial Crisis," *CQ Researcher*, May 9, 2008, pp. 409-432.

64. Quoted in Thalif Deen, "A Silent Tsunami Threatening the Global Population," *Daily News* [Sri Lanka], April 30, 2008, www.dailynews.lk.

65. Quoted in *ibid.*

66. For background see "The 2008 Farm Bill Enacted Into Law," American Farmland Trust Web site, www.farmland.org.

67. Quoted in Peter Shinn, "Farm Bill Heads for Congressional Passage Next Week," Brownfield Network Web site, May 8, 2008, www.brownfieldnetwork.com.

68. Quoted in Pamela Brogan, "Coleman, Klobuchar Vote to Override Bush Veto," *Saint Cloud* (Minnesota) *Times*, May 23, 2008, www.sctimes.com/apps/pbcs.dll/article?AID=/20080523/NEWS01/105220105/0/archives.

69. Daniel Griswold, "Ag Committee Chair Demands Higher Food Prices," Cato-at-liberty blog, Cato Institute, May 5, 2008, www.cato-at-liberty.org.

70. Quoted in Greg Hitt, "Farm Bill May Hinder Trade Talks," *The Wall Street Journal*, May 14, 2008, p. A2.

71. For background, see Missy Ryan, "Congress Spurns Bush's Call for Food Aid Switch," Reuters, from Yahoo! News Canada Web site, May 8, 2008, http://ca.news.yahoo.com; Michael Janofsky and Christopher Swann, "Congress Resists Speeding U.S. Food Aid, Benefiting Archer, APL," Bloomberg News, May 19, 2008, www.bloomberg.com.

72. "Foreign Assistance: Various Challenges Impede the Efficiency and Effectiveness of U.S. Food Aid," Government Accountability Office, April 2007, www.gao.gov/new.items/d07560.pdf.

73. *Ibid.*

74. Quoted in Janofsky and Swann, *op. cit.*

75. For background, see David Hosansky, "Food Safety," *CQ Researcher*, Nov. 1, 2002, pp. 897-920, and David Hosansky, "Biotech Foods," *CQ Researcher*, March 30, 2001, pp. 249-272.

BIBLIOGRAPHY

Books

Brown, Lester B., ***Outgrowing the Earth: The Food Security Challenge in an Age of Falling Water Tables and Rising Temperatures,*** **W. W. Norton, 2005.**
An environmentalist argues that climate change and resource depletion demand major changes in the global food system.

Federico, Giovanni, *An Economic History of World Agriculture*, 1800-2000, Princeton University Press, 2005.
A professor of economic history at the European University Institute in Florence, Italy, describes how farming remade itself over two centuries to feed a growing world.

Pollan, Michael, *The Omnivore's Dilemma: A Natural History of Four Meals*, Penguin, 2007.
A journalist chronicles the path of common foods through America's food-production systems.

Sen, Amartya, *Poverty and Famines: An Essay on Entitlement and Deprivation*, Oxford University Press, 1983.
A Nobel Prize-winning economist argues that there is enough food to feed the world, but many poor people can't get enough money to buy the food.

Vernon, James, *Hunger: A Modern History*, Harvard University Press, 2007.
A history professor at the University of California, Berkeley, argues that views about hunger shifted in the 20th century.

Articles

"The New Face of Hunger," *The Economist*, April 19, 2008, pp. 32-34.
Soaring food prices may be a sign of a world food system that needs large-scale overhaul to be sustainable.

Akl, Aida F., "Market Speculation Drives Food Prices," *Voice of America News*, May 16, 2008, www.voanews.com.
A surge of commercial and private investment in grain markets is a small but significant contributing cause of rising food prices.

Bello, Walden, "Manufacturing a Food Crisis," *The Nation*, May 15, 2008, www.thenation.com.
A professor of sociology at the University of the Philippines and a critic of globalization argues that contemporary trade policies have crippled developing-country food markets.

Hedges, Stephen J., "Grain Prices Grow, But So Do Risks," *Chicago Tribune*, May 26, 2008, www.chicago

tribune.com/news/nationworld/chi-grain_hedgesmay27,0,1989503.story.
Many grain farmers aren't benefiting from skyrocketing commodity prices.

Janofsky, Michael, and Christopher Swann, "Congress Resists Speeding U.S. Food Aid, Benefiting Archer, APL," Bloomberg.com, May 29, 2008, www.bloomberg.com.
American food-aid policies benefit industrial food producers and shipping companies and limit the amount of aid taxpayers' dollars can buy.

Philpott, Tom, "Sticker Shock" Gristmill blog, *Grist*, April 25, 2008, http://gristmill.grist.org.
A writer for an environmental magazine explains the causes of the food-price spike.

Reports and Studies

"Foreign Assistance: Various Challenges Impede the Efficiency and Effectiveness of U.S. Food Aid," Government Accountability Office, April 2007.
Congress' nonpartisan auditing arm finds that U.S. food-aid practices reduce the amount, timeliness and quality of the food assistance the U.S. provides to hungry populations.

"Signing Away the Future," Oxfam International, March 2007, www.oxfam.org/en/files/bp101_regional_trade_agreements_0703/download.
An international charity argues that trade agreements are cutting developing countries out of the global economy.

Constantin, Anne Laure, "A Time of High Prices: An Opportunity for the Rural Poor," Institute for Agriculture and Trade Policy, April 2008, www.iatp.org.
A nonprofit group that promotes family farming argues that current food-price spikes may provide a window for countries to beef up their local farm production.

Griswold, Daniel, "Grain Drain: The Hidden Cost of U.S. Rice Subsidies," Cato Institute, November 2006, www.freetrade.org/node/539.
An analyst for a libertarian think tank argues that U.S. supports to rice producers distort markets and hurt farmers and consumers in the United States and abroad.

Riedl, Brian M., "Seven Reasons to Veto the Farm Bill," Backgrounder #2134, Heritage Foundation, May 12, 2008, www.heritage.org/Research/Agriculture/bg2134.cfm.

A conservative think tank argues that U.S. farm subsidies benefit wealthy large-scale farmers but not struggling family farms.

Schnepf, Randy, "High Agricultural Commodity Prices: What Are the Issues?" Congressional Research Service, May 6, 2008, www.iatp.org/tradeobservatory/library.cfm?refid=102843.

Congress' nonpartisan research office provides a primer on the food-price spike.

For More Information

Agribusiness Accountability Initiative, www.agribusinessaccountability.org. Think tank and advocacy group that supports alternatives to large agribusinesses; sponsored by the Des Moines, Iowa-based National Catholic Rural Life Conference.

American Farm Bureau, 600 Maryland Ave., S.W., Suite 1000W, Washington, DC 20024; (202) 406-3600; www.fb.org. Independent organization representing the interests of U.S. farmers.

Center for Trade Policy Studies, Cato Institute, 1000 Massachusetts Ave., N.W., Washington, DC 20001-5403; (202) 842-0200; www.freetrade.org. Libertarian think tank analyzes farm policies as an advocate of global free markets.

Food First — Institute for Food and Development Policy, 398 60th St., Oakland, CA 94618; (510) 654-4400; www.foodfirst.org. Think tank and advocacy group that works to eliminate hunger.

Grist, 710 Second Ave., Suite 860, Seattle, WA 98104; (206) 876-2020; www.grist.org. Environmental journalism group provides information on sustainable farming and other green issues.

International Assessment of Agricultural Knowledge, Science and Technology for Development, www.agassessment.org. International intergovernmental group that has produced expert assessments of future global food and agriculture needs.

International Food Policy Research Institute, 2033 K St., N.W., Washington, DC 20006-1002; (202) 862-5600; www.ifpri.org. Part an international network of food-policy groups seeking sustainable solutions to hunger.

King Corn, www.pbs.org/independentlens/kingcorn. Web site for a public-television documentary on the dominant role of corn in U.S. farming and food supply.

La Via Campesina, Jl. Mampang Prapatan XIV No. 5, Jakarta Selatan, DKI Jakarta, Indonesia 12790; +62-21-7991890; www.viacampesina.org. International organization that represents the interests of peasant farmers, small landholders, farmworkers and rural, landless people.

Organization for Competitive Markets, P.O. Box 6486, Lincoln, NE 68506; www.competitivemarkets.com. Think tank and advocacy group that promotes government-regulated free markets in agriculture.

World Agricultural Forum, One Metropolitan Square Plaza, Suite 1300, Saint Louis, MO, 63102; (314) 206-3218; www.worldagforum.org. International group that brings together government, business, academic and non-governmental groups to seek solutions for global food problems.

World Neighbors, 4127 N.W. 122nd St., Oklahoma City, OK 73120; (405) 752-9700; www.wn.org. Provides training and support for rural communities in developing countries to improve their farm yields and make other community improvements.

10

Energy Nationalism

Peter Behr

The Caspian Sea oil town of Neft Dashlari ("Oil Rocks") produces more than half of Azerbaijan's crude oil. Built in 1947 on a chain of artificial islands, the facility contains 124 miles of streets, schools, libraries and eight-story apartments housing some 5,000 oil workers. Energy companies are targeting the Caspian Sea and other areas in the search for non-Persian Gulf oil sources.

Getty Images/Reza

From *CQ Researcher*,
July 1, 2007.

Westerners saw the Soviet Union's 1991 collapse as a defining triumph of democracy, but Russian President Vladimir Putin has called it "the greatest geopolitical catastrophe of the century." [1] Today, to the growing unease of leaders in Washington and Europe, Putin is bent on erasing the wounds of what some Russian leaders call the "16 lost years" since the break-up and reclaiming Russia's position as a superpower. His weapon: the country's considerable energy resources.

With $500 million pouring into its coffers daily from oil and gas exports, Moscow is raising its voice — and using its elbows — in international business negotiations. During the winter of 2005-06, Russia temporarily cut off natural gas deliveries to Ukraine and Western Europe over a pricing dispute. [2] Putin also jailed Russian oil tycoon Mikhail Khodorkovsky after he challenged government energy plans and political control. And to the dismay of Washington, Moscow is considering energy investments in increasingly bellicose Iran and enticing former Soviet states Turkmenistan and Kazakhstan to channel new Caspian Sea natural gas production through Russia's existing and planned pipelines — supplies that will be vital to Europe.

"The truth is that Russia, having first scared its neighbors into [joining] NATO by its bullying behavior, is currently outmaneuvering a divided and indecisive West on almost every front, and especially on energy," said *The Economist*, the respected British newsweekly. [3]

Oil and politics have always made a volatile blend — particularly in the Middle East. But Russia's recent in-your-face actions represent a new strain of energy nationalism being practiced by Russia and a handful of emerging petrostates in Africa, Central Asia and Latin America that are nationalizing or taking greater control over

"Hot Spots" to Supply Most of World's Energy

To reduce dependence on the unstable Persian Gulf, an oil-hungry world is turning to sources in Central Asia, Africa and Russia. But most of these "emerging" producers have either nationalized their oil industries or are considered vulnerable to terrorists or dissidents. By 2010, according to the U.S. Energy Information Agency, 58 percent of global daily oil production will be at risk because it originates or passes through one of the world's oil "hot spots," including Saudi Arabia, Russia, Iraq, Nigeria, the Caspian region, Venezuela and the straits of Hormuz and Malacca.

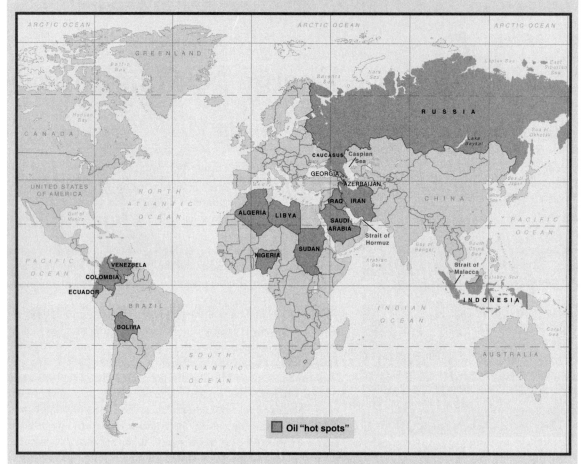

Source: U.S. Department of Energy

their oil resources. Moreover, the leaders of some petrostates are imposing new political agendas on their oil sectors, notably Putin and Venezuela's combative socialist president Hugo Chávez.

"Everywhere there is a return to oil nationalism," says Jean-Marie Chevalier, director of the energy geopolitics center at Paris-Dauphine University. [4]

In the three decades since the world's first great oil shock in 1973, oil prices have periodically climbed and crashed as shortages were followed by surpluses. But this time around, the high prices are likely to stay high, many experts warn. To be sure, the war in Iraq and a looming confrontation over Iran's nuclear program are feeding the high prices. And escalating global markets, led by booming China and India, also intensify demand.

But rising energy nationalism is also triggering anxiety in global oil markets. A dramatic shift has occurred in world oil supplies since 30 years ago, when roughly three-quarters of the world's oil production was managed by private multinational oil companies — the so-called Seven Sisters — and the rest belonged to a handful of state-owned oil companies. "Today, that is about reversed," Former CIA Director John M. Deutch succinctly told the House Foreign Affairs Committee. [5]

As of 2005, 12 of the world's top 20 petroleum companies were state-owned or state-controlled, according to *Petroleum Intelligence Weekly* (PIW). [6] (*See chart, p. 270.*) "There has been a very significant change in the balance of power between international oil companies, and it's clear today that it is the national companies that have the upper hand," said Olivier Appert, president of the French Oil Institute. [7]

"One of the favorites of headline writers is 'Big Oil,' " says Daniel Yergin, author of *The Prize: The Epic Quest for Oil, Money & Power.* "But it's the wrong Big Oil. 'Big Oil' today means the national oil companies."

The nationalization of foreign oil company interests in Venezuela and Bolivia in the past two years is the hard edge of this new chapter in oil politics, echoing the same raging denunciations of Western governments and oil companies that accompanied Iran and Libya's nationalizations of foreign oil interests in the 1950s and '60s. [8] "The nationalization of Venezuela's oil is now for real," said Chávez at a ceremony in May marking the takeover of the country's last foreign-run oil fields. "Down with the U.S. empire!" he shouted as newly purchased Russian jet fighters roared overhead. [9]

Oil-production arrangements vary widely among the dozen leading national oil companies. In Nigeria and Brazil,

Pipeline Politics Play Pivotal Role

New and proposed oil and gas pipelines from fields in Russia, the Caspian region and Africa will likely play crucial roles in meeting the world's future energy needs. But global politics will influence when, where and whether the pipelines will be built. For instance, China covets oil and gas from eastern Siberia, but Russia's leaders have delayed building a proposed pipeline into Daqing, China. They want the pipeline to go to Russia's Pacific coast, to serve competing customers in Asia and the United States.

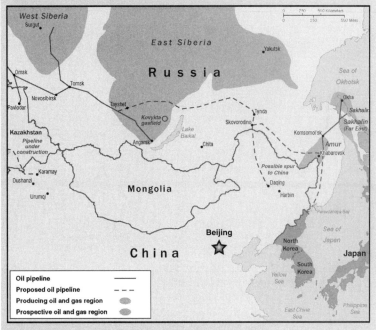

Source: U.S. Department of Energy

the government invites foreign companies to develop their oil regions, while Kuwait keeps them out. Ecuadorian President Rafael Correa, a Chávez ally who took office in January, has demanded a higher share of revenues from foreign oil companies but needs outside help to expand refining facilities. [10] Russia is forcing Shell and BP to give up majority positions in oil and gas joint ventures but hasn't thrown them out. And neither have Chávez and Correa.

Kazakhstan, after becoming independent in 1991, combined existing state firms into KazMunaiGaz — a new company that it intends to take public — while maintaining government influence through a parent company. The China National Offshore Oil Corp. is publicly traded but state-controlled.

World Oil Prices Respond to Events

Oil prices reached an all-time high of $78* a barrel in 1981, two years after the U.S.-Iran hostage crisis began. Prices dropped for the next 17 years as new non-OPEC (Organization of Petroleum Exporting Countries) supplies came online and demand declined. After bottoming out at $15.50 a barrel in 1998, prices have risen, largely due to increased demand from India and China, Middle East conflicts and the growing state control of oil operations around the world.

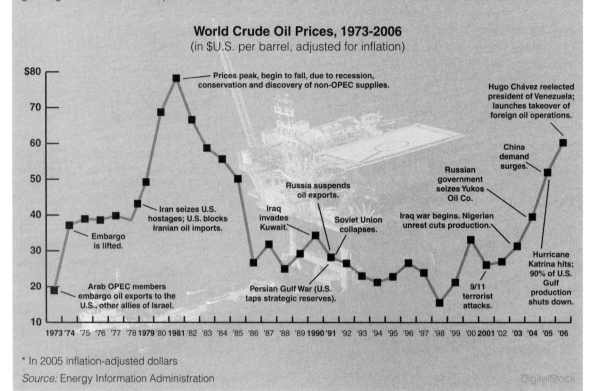

World Crude Oil Prices, 1973-2006
(in $U.S. per barrel, adjusted for inflation)

Prices peak, begin to fall, due to recession, conservation and discovery of non-OPEC supplies.

Hugo Chávez reelected president of Venezuela; launches takeover of foreign oil operations.

China demand surges.

Russian government seizes Yukos Oil Co.

Russia suspends oil exports.

Iran seizes U.S. hostages; U.S. blocks Iranian oil imports.

Iraq invades Kuwait.

Soviet Union collapses.

Iraq war begins. Nigerian unrest cuts production.

Embargo is lifted.

Arab OPEC members embargo oil exports to the U.S., other allies of Israel.

Persian Gulf War (U.S. taps strategic reserves).

9/11 terrorist attacks.

Hurricane Katrina hits; 90% of U.S. Gulf production shuts down.

* In 2005 inflation-adjusted dollars

Source: Energy Information Administration

But whatever model a petrostate adopts, *PIW* says the trend is largely the same: Major oil companies are finding their interests "increasingly subordinated to the nationalistic political agendas of key reserve-holding host countries." [11]

The new oil nationalism has been fed by energy prices at or near peak levels — when adjusted for inflation — reached after the 1970s oil shocks. (*See "Background," p. 271, and chart above.*) [12]

Rising energy prices also have produced a vast shift in wealth — over $970 billion in 2006 — from consuming nations to producing countries, a $670 billion jump in four years, and most has gone to a handful of countries, according to the Federal Reserve Bank of New York. [13]

Some industry experts say new sources of oil coming online — often from politically unstable hot spots in Africa and Central Asia — could mean lower consumer prices if Russia and the Central Asian petrostates remain independent of the Organization of Petroleum Exporting Countries (OPEC), which seeks to set international oil prices. On the other hand, the dramatic changes occurring in the industry could boost prices and — eventually — lead to declining supplies if state-run companies reduce exploration investments or botch operations, as some have done.

The International Energy Agency estimates that at least $2.2 trillion will need to be invested in the global oil sector over the next 30 years to meet rising demand for oil, but oil nationalism "is slowing or even discouraging this needed investment," according to the James A. Baker III Institute for Public Policy at Rice University. [14]

Consolidation of the world's oil supplies into government hands also raises questions about whether the new oil producers will break the historic "curse of oil" pattern, in which petrostate leaders used oil profits to line their pockets and buy arms rather than lift indigent populations out of poverty. Still others worry that intensified competition for energy between nations will sow new conflicts around the globe.

In addition to oil shortages and high prices, the International Energy Agency says Earth is facing "twin energy-related threats" — inadequate and insecure supplies of affordable oil and, paradoxically, environmental harm caused by excessive oil consumption. [15]

High prices and dangerous climate-changing energy emissions are fostering conservation-oriented responses similar to those prompted by skyrocketing oil prices in the 1970s, including the use of smaller cars and investments in energy-efficient manufacturing, construction and appliances. [16]

But short supplies also can trigger intense competition between consuming nations, and experts are closely watching the political fallout as major powers vie for control over oil and gas resources. The construction of new pipelines to carry oil and gas from Central Asia to Asia and Europe has already sparked disputes among Russia, China and the United States, and more could follow. [17]

China's worldwide search for oil is causing particular concern because its aggressive attempts to secure important new reserves in countries such as Sudan and Myanmar (formerly Burma) have ignored human rights abuses in those countries that the international community is trying to halt, critics say. [18]

Trends in oil discoveries and price moves have long defied accurate forecasting. An escalation of Persian Gulf conflicts, a terrorist attack on Saudi Arabian oil facilities or congested sea channels could shoot oil prices past $100 a barrel. [19]

For the moment, the world is consuming oil faster than it is finding new supplies, and the historic trend of gradual increases in the world's hydrocarbon reserves has shifted to one of "stagnation and modest decline." Global oil reserves were down by nearly 1 percent in 2006, according to the *PIW's* latest reserves survey. [20]

A banner at a natural gas plant in Tarija, Bolivia, proclaims: "Nationalized: Property of the Bolivians," after President Evo Morales nationalized foreign oil and gas operations in May 2006. "The looting by the foreign companies has ended," he declared.

As increased oil nationalism and global conditions trigger tight supplies, high prices, nervous markets and potential conflict, here are some questions being asked by the oil industry, its investors and critics:

Will emerging petrostates undermine OPEC's control over oil prices, benefiting consumers?

The first Arab oil embargo, in 1973, established oil as a pivotal political and economic lever. Since then, the OPEC cartel has sought to keep world oil prices high enough to maximize producers' returns without tipping global economies into recession.

It is widely assumed that OPEC's continued control over prices depends on whether emerging African, Caspian and Latin American producers reject OPEC membership and create excess global supply.

Of course, a widespread economic recession or financial crisis could slash oil demand, generating a surplus and a collapse in oil prices. In the past, OPEC has responded by cutting production to shore up prices, with mixed results.

So far, Russia has rejected OPEC requests to limit production. Neither Russia nor its Caspian neighbors are strong candidates to join OPEC, says Robert E. Ebel, senior adviser at the Center for Strategic and International Studies (CSIS). "Why would they want to join? Why

Have the World's Oil Supplies Peaked?

After 50 years, the debate continues.

It's called the "peak oil" theory, and ever since American geologist M. King Hubbert developed it in 1956, oil experts have been divided into two camps — those who believe Earth's oil supplies have peaked, and those who don't.

If proponents of the theory are correct — that the world has used up half of the planet's oil stocks and the remaining supplies will face rapid depletion — the future promises even higher prices and more energy shocks. But critics of the theory say the high point in oil production is still 20 or 30 years away, that oil production is not likely to decline precipitously thereafter and that political events and energy prices — not hydrocarbon shortages — will dictate the industry's course until near the mid-century mark.

According to industry estimates, world oil reserves increased by 24 billion barrels during 2006 to 1.3 trillion barrels — a gain of about 2 percent over 2005. [1] Reserve estimates are periodically recalculated based on new geological and engineering data and new discoveries. But the 2006 increase cannot be documented because two of the countries reporting the greatest increases were Iran and Saudi Arabia, and their governments don't let outsiders check their figures.

"No one knows the amount of oil really contained in reservoirs," says Leonardo Maugeri, an economist and oil industry analyst with the Italian oil and gas company ENI. Such knowledge evolves over time after new wells are drilled and more sophisticated technology is developed.

"In fact," he adds, "countries such as Saudi Arabia or Iraq (which together hold about 35 percent of the world's proven reserves of oil) produce petroleum only from a few old fields, although they have discovered, but not developed, more than 50 new fields each." [2]

The peak oil argument begins with the controversial 1956 prediction by Hubbert that oil production from the lower U.S. 48 states would top out in 1968. The actual peak occurred two to four years later, depending on which measure of oil production is used. As a result of Hubbert's controversial prediction, "He found himself being harassed and vilified," says one of Hubbert's champions, Chris Skrebowski, editor of the monthly magazine *Petroleum Review*, published by the Energy Institute in London. [3]

But Peter M. Jackson, a director of the international research firm Cambridge Energy Research Associates (CERA), argues Hubbert erred in not considering how new drilling technologies could increase output from older fields or how energy prices affect exploration and production. [4]

He is even more critical of Hubbert's present-day disciples who say an oil field peaks when half of its available oil has been extracted. Their model is illustrated with a simple, smoothly rising and falling bell-shape curve.

Jackson says Hubbert's curve ignores the typical expansion of oil field dimensions as more exploration and development occurs. Oil production from the lower 48 states since 1970 has been 66 percent higher and 15 billion barrels greater that Hubbert predicted, Jackson writes, citing U.S. Geological Survey findings and his company's oil field analysis.

When admittedly high-priced, "unconventional" sources such as shale and tar sands or Arctic fields are counted, the world's total supply of oil is 4.8 trillion barrels,

would they want other people telling them what they can produce and export? They can derive all the benefits [of OPEC's pricing strategies] without being a member."

But experts disagree over whether Russia might support creation of an OPEC-style cartel for natural gas — of which it has the world's largest supply. In November 2006, a confidential NATO economic study warned Russia may be seeking to assemble a gas cartel with Algeria, Qatar, Libya, the countries of Central Asia and perhaps Iran. [21]

But Dmitry Peskov, deputy Kremlin spokesman, has denied the suggestion. "Our main thesis is interdependence of producers and consumers. Only a madman could think that Russia would start to blackmail Europe using gas, because we depend to the same extent on European customers." [22]

Whatever Russia does, the supply-demand balance is running tight for oil and gas, even with new petrostate supplies coming online, and new conflicts in oil-rich "hot spots" would only worsen conditions. "Many of the world's major oil-producing regions are also locations of geopolitical tension," said Daniel S. Sullivan, assistant secretary of State for economic, energy and business affairs. "Instability

Jackson stated. That is enough, at current growth rates, to delay a peak until 2030 or later, and even then, the peak will not be followed by a sharp decline, he said.

BP chief economist Peter Davies complains that Hubbert's theory also ignores the impact of increased conservation and the switching to alterative fuels that occurs as oil prices rise, which tend to extend oil supplies. Since 1980, for instance, the world's economic output has doubled while oil consumption has only increased by a third, he noted in a June 14, 2006, speech in London. "Year by year, a combination of exploration, investment and the application of technology is ensuring that every unit of oil and gas that is produced is replaced by new proved reserves," he said. [5]

Jackson likened peak oil advocates to sidewalk doomsayers who predict the end of the world. "Peakists continue to criticize those who disagree, but their projections of the date of the peak continue to come and go," he said in his CERA report. "One of the most recent peak oil dates was supposed to have occurred just after the U.S. Thanksgiving Day 2005, and we still wait for the evidence."

Skrebowski replied furiously that Jackson and the anti-peak oil crowd were either Polyannas or paid shills for an oil industry that must persuade investors that untapped oil abounds. [6]

But, when one gets beyond the name calling, the two sides appear less far apart. Skrebowski says Jackson's 4.8 trillion barrels may be technically available "but is only of interest if it can be discovered, mobilised and marketed within a reasonable time period. "This," he says, "is the entire debate: Can all the unfound and unproven resources be exploited quickly enough to more than offset the peaking and decline of the known and proven reserves?"

A leading peak oil advocate, Dallas energy financier Matthew R. Simmons, argues that Saudi Arabia's reserves are being greatly overestimated. [7] But he also says more than half the world's conventional oil and a larger share of its unconventional oil remain to be extracted. "What the world is running out of is cheap oil — the $20 oil we built our civilization around," he writes. [8]

That sounds close to the views of CERA chairman Daniel Yergin. However, he asks, will economics and government decisions in a politicized oil world permit enough new exploration and production to keep pipelines full?

Although energy companies will be prospecting in more difficult environments, he says, "the major obstacle to the development of new supplies is not geology but what happens above ground: namely, international affairs, politics, decision-making by governments and energy investment and new technological development." [9]

[1] "World Proved Reserves of Oil and Natural Gas," Energy Information Administration, Jan. 9, 2007; www.eia.doe.gov/emeu/international/reserves.html.

[2] "The Cheap Oil Era is Far from Over," *Alexander's Oil and Gas Connections*, June 2, 2004; www.gasandoil.com/goc/features/fex42299.htm.

[3] Chris Skrebowski, "Open letter to Peter Jackson of CERA," *Energy Bulletin*, Dec. 21, 2006; www.energybulletin.net/23977.html.

[4] Peter M. Jackson, "Why the 'Peak Oil' Theory Falls Down," Cambridge Energy Research Associates, Inc., Nov. 10, 2006; http://cera.ecnext.com/ coms2/summary_0236-821_ITM.

[5] Peter Davies, "BP Statistical Review of World Energy 2005," presentation, London, June 14, 2006, p. 9.

[6] Skrebowski, *op. cit.*

[7] "Twilight in the Desert," *The Oil Drum*, June 13, 2005; www.theoildrum.com/classic/2005/06/twilight-in-desert.html.

[8] Randy Udall and Matthew R. Simmons, "CERA's Rosy Oil Forecast — Pabulum to the People," *ASPO-USA's Peak Oil Review/Energy Bulletin*, Aug. 21, 2006.

[9] Daniel Yergin, "Ensuring Energy Security," *Foreign Affairs*, March/April 2006, p. 75; www.foreignaffairs.org/20060301faessay85206/daniel-yergin/ ensuring-energy-security.html.

in producing countries is the biggest challenge we face, and it adds a significant premium to world oil prices." [23]

When supplies are tight, consumers lose. And tight supplies could persist since government-controlled energy operations may not develop new reserves or build pipelines as aggressively as the international oil companies. Instead, national oil companies tend to use more of their profits to fund social improvements and provide cheap, subsidized energy for citizens. [24]

To make matters worse, demand for more energy — led by booming China and India — is accelerating. Assuming their growth bubbles don't burst, experts predict China's energy use would have to grow by 150 percent by 2020 and India's to double to maintain current economic expansion. [25]

However, China's continued growth is not a certainty, according to a study from the Stanley Foundation, in Muscatine, Iowa. [26] "China faces immense problems, including pollution, disease, poverty, inequality, corruption, abuses of power, an aging population and a shrinking labor force," contend authors Michael Schiffer, a foundation program officer,

Saudi Arabia and Russia Have Biggest Reserves

Saudi Arabia and Canada lead the world in oil reserves, with nearly 450 billion barrels — more than half as much as the next 10 nations combined. Russia has the most natural gas reserves, with 1.68 quadrillion cubic feet — almost three-quarters more than Iran.

Oil Reserves*			Natural Gas Reserves*		
Rank	**Country**	**Barrels** (in billions)	**Rank**	**Country**	**Cubic ft.** (in trillions)
1.	Saudi Arabia	262.3	1.	Russia	1,680.0
2.	Canada	179.2	2.	Iran	974.0
3.	Iran	136.3	3.	Qatar	910.5
4.	Iraq	115.0	4.	Saudi Arabia	240.0
5.	Kuwait	101.5	5.	United Arab Emirates	214.4
6.	United Arab Emirates	97.8	6.	United States	204.4
7.	Venezuela	80.0	7.	Nigeria	181.9
8.	Russia	60.0	8.	Algeria	161.7
9.	Libya	41.5	9.	Venezuela	152.4
10.	Nigeria	36.2	10.	Iraq	112.0
11.	Kazakhstan	30.0	11.	Kazakhstan (tie)	100.0
12.	United States	21.8	11.	Turkmenistan (tie)	100.0

* As of Jan. 1, 2007

Source: "World Proved Reserves of Oil and Natural Gas, Most Recent Estimates," Energy Information Administration, Jan. 9, 2007

and Gary Schmitt, director of the American Enterprise Institute's advanced-strategic studies program. "China's leaders today are, thus, holding a tiger by the tail. They have built the legitimacy of their continued rule largely on meeting the rising expectations of a billion-plus people, but to meet those expectations they eventually have to release the reins of economic and political power they are clutching so tightly." [27]

Some experts hope China and India — which are eyeing Persian Gulf oil — could eventually add their considerable consumer weight to efforts by others to restrain OPEC's pricing strategies. "Much of the recent discussion in Washington about the growing oil demand of China — and to a lesser extent India — has focused on the threats posed to the U.S. economy and foreign policy, but that often obscures the fact that the oil interests of China, India and the United States are also broadly aligned," writes Xuecheng Liu, a senior fellow at China's Institute of International Studies. [28]

Will nationalizing oil wealth help the poor?

In May 2006, newly elected President Evo Morales ordered troops to occupy Bolivia's oil and gas fields and gave foreign companies 180 days to renegotiate their energy leases or leave the country. "The looting by the foreign companies has ended," he declared. [29]

Morales was elected partly on a populist platform to take over energy resources in Bolivia, which has Latin America's second-largest gas reserves after Venezuela. "We are the owners of this noble land," he said during the campaign, "and it is not possible that [natural resources] be in the hands of the transnationals." [30]

Echoing former Mexican President Lazaro Cardenas, who nationalized 17 foreign oil companies in 1938, leaders of Bolivia, Ecuador and Venezuela have called their energy reserves a critical tool for helping poor, indigenous populations.

Since the oil age began more than a century ago, governments in the developing world — on both the right and left — have promised their people a fair share of the wealth created by geological forces. But few leaders have followed through. Instead, "black gold" has spawned corruption, economic hardship, vast class differences and civil war.

"Look what oil is doing to us, to the oil-exporting countries," said OPEC founder Juan Pablo Pérez Alfonzo, a Venezuelan, nearly 30 years ago. [31] "It is the excrement of the devil."

Oil bonanzas often leave developing economies worse off — a phenomenon economists call the "resource curse." [32] PEMEX, Mexico's state-run oil company, pays an estimated 60 percent of oil earnings to fund government programs. But Mexico has overborrowed to keep production going and has more than $30 billion in pension liabilities, leaving it with a huge longstanding debt and too little money for maintaining old oil fields or finding new ones. [33] And Mexico's biggest field is in decline, raising fears that a chronic slippage in oil revenues could trigger a budget disaster. [34]

Similarly, OPEC members had an average gain of 1.3 percent in per capita gross domestic product (GDP) between 1965 and 1980, while the rest of the world saw GDP grow 2.2 percent annually. [35]

Sudden oil windfalls have also triggered what economists call the "Dutch disease" — skyrocketing currency values that depress local manufacturers' exports and trigger huge jumps in imports. The economic paradox got its nickname from a drastic decline in economic growth in the Netherlands after natural gas was discovered there in the 1960s. [36]

Oil's easy money also often ends up filling government officials' Swiss bank accounts rather than benefiting public health or education. Some of the most egregious excesses are in Africa. Since oil was discovered in Nigeria's Niger Delta in 1956, for example, the country's infamous kleptocracy has used oil billions to enrich elites, leaving delta residents trapped in pollution and poverty. "Everything looked possible — but everything went wrong," *National Geographic*'s Tom O'Neill reports. [37]

Now the situation "has gone from bad to worse to disastrous," said Senan Murray of BBC News. [38] The Movement for the Emancipation of the Niger Delta (MEND) has stepped up attacks on foreign oil facilities and the police who protect them, including an oil rig 40 miles offshore. In May, six Chevron employees were kidnapped and released after a month, but other kidnappings followed. [39] The oil companies — in conjunction with the Nigerian government — have pledged to support rural education, environmental cleanup and other social programs, but armed rebels in the delta say improvements aren't being implemented fast enough. [40]

In Venezuela, Chávez has kept his promises to channel petrodollars to health care, roads and housing. The percentage of Venezuelans living in poverty has shrunk from 42.8 percent to 30.4 percent under Chávez, according to government statistics. Researchers at Catholic University, near Caracas, estimate that about 45 percent of the population lives in poverty, less than in 1999. [41]

Chávez also uses oil money to promote his anti-capitalism ideology by investing in social programs in other Latin American countries. But he hasn't made a dent in Venezuela's chronic corruption, according to Transparency International. The Berlin-based nonprofit puts Venezuela in the bottom quarter of its 2002 and 2006 rankings. [42]

A forest of oil derricks lines the Caspian shore just outside of Azerbaijan's capital Baku. The oil-rich Caucasus republic is expected to be a significant source of the world's oil in the future, some of it delivered via new pipelines.

AFP/Getty Images/Mladen Antonov

At the same time, the Washington-based advocacy group Freedom House says Chávez has presided over the "deterioration of the country's democratic institutions," replacing the Supreme Court, filling civilian government posts with military personnel, blacklisting political opponents from government positions and shutting down a leading opposition television station. [43]

Russia, China, Mexico and Iran also provide cheap, subsidized energy to their populations, in a tradeoff that carries a stiff economic price. The policy has backfired in Iran, where the government imposed gasoline rationing in June 2007, triggering violent protests that led to more than a dozen gas stations being set on fire. [44] Iran's subsidized gasoline prices are among the lowest in the world, so Iranian motor fuel consumption has been climbing fast. But the government was forced to ration gasoline because it has not used its oil profits to build enough refinery capacity, and gasoline imports have not kept up with demand.

Oil wealth has generated violence and even civil war in many developing countries. For instance, factions from northern and southern Sudan, where oil was discovered in 1978, fought a civil war in the 1980s over the nation's oil revenue. Although a peace accord was signed in 2005, the largely Arab and Islamist ruling party in the north has dragged its feet on sharing the oil wealth with the largely black, Christian southerners.

Meanwhile, some analysts say oil has played a key role in the international community's failure to stop the rape,

C H R O N O L O G Y

1951-1979 *Oil surpluses keep crude prices low; U.S. restricts oil production to maintain prices.*

1951 Soviet Union builds first deep-sea oil platform.

1956 Geologist M. King Hubbert's "peak oil" theory contends half of U.S. oil stocks would be depleted by the 1960s, and the remaining supplies face rapid depletion.

1960 Iran, Iraq, Kuwait, Saudi Arabia and Venezuela form the Organization of Petroleum Exporting Countries (OPEC) to stabilize world oil prices.

1970s OPEC gains control of global oil pricing; Arab countries begin using oil as a political weapon.

1972 Oil production from Lower 48 states peaks; limits on U.S. production are lifted.

1973 Major Arab oil producers impose embargo on oil exports to United States and several allies in retaliation for their support of Israel in Yon Kippur War; oil prices quadruple.

1979 Shah flees Iran; Iranian students seize hostages at U.S. Embassy, triggering more price shocks.

1980s *Oil from non-OPEC sources breaks the cartel's market hold, helping to create an oil glut.*

1980 Iraq attacks Iran, triggering an eight-year war.

1981 Global oil prices drop after a severe recession.

1983 Production from the North Sea and Alaska's North Slope swells global oil supply.

1985 Saudis boost output; prices plummet.

1988 Iran-Iraq War ends.

1990s *Breakup of Soviet Union raises hope for development of Caspian Sea oil and gas; oil production increases in Africa; global warming emerges as environmental issue.*

1990 Iraq invades Kuwait.

1991 U.S.-led coalition drives Iraq from Kuwait; Soviet Union collapses.

1993 Crude prices drop to $15 a barrel.

1996 Giant Sakhalin oil project announced in Russian Far East.

1997 Violence, protests disrupt Nigerian and Colombian production; Caspian pipeline consortium formed to deliver Caspian Sea oil to Black Sea ports; Kyoto global warming protocol drafted.

1999 Oil production flattens; prices rise.

2000s *Terrorist attacks in U.S. lead to new Iraq war; China becomes fastest-growing oil importer; oil prices climb.*

Sept. 11, 2001 Arab terrorists attack World Trade Center, Pentagon; oil prices surge.

2002 Oil workers strike in Venezuela.

2003 Iraq War begins; attacks close some oil platforms in Nigeria. . . . Major Iraq pipeline is sabotaged; violence escalates.

2004 Oil production in Russia, former Soviet states continues to recover, surpassing 1991 Soviet Union totals.

2005 China's oil demand soars. . . . Hurricane Katrina strikes the U.S. Gulf Coast, shutting down nearly 90 percent of oil and gas production in federal waters.

2006 Venezuelan President Hugo Chávez reelected, launches takeover of foreign-run oil operations. . . . Bolivian President Evo Morales announces the nationalization of all remaining natural gas reserves in the country. . . . Baku-Tblisi-Ceyhan pipeline opens, bypassing the Bosporus Strait.

2007 In a tariff dispute with Belarus, Russia's state-owned Transneft oil company shuts down a pipeline supplying oil to several European countries. . . . Dissidents attack three major pipelines in Nigeria's Niger Delta. . . . On May 1, Chávez takes control of the last remaining privately run oil operations in Venezuela.

murder and wholesale destruction of villages in western Sudan's Darfur region, where the Coalition for Darfur says as of 2005 Sudanese militia reportedly had killed 140,000 villagers, 250,000 have perished from disease, famine or exposure and 2 million more are homeless. The Sudanese government disputes the figures. [45]

Until recently, U.N. Security Council efforts to sanction Sudan have been hampered by China, which buys two-thirds of Sudan's oil and has invested more than $8 billion in its oil sector. [46] "Business is business," said Deputy Foreign Minister Zhou Wenzhong in 2004. "We try to separate politics from business." [47]

But this year, after critics threatened to make Darfur an issue during China's preparations to host the 2008 Summer Olympic Games, China shifted course. It now supports a combined U.N.-African Union peacekeeping force in Sudan, which Sudan agreed to accept in June. However, skeptics doubt the agreement will be fully carried out. [48]

In an effort to buffer the negative impact of oil wealth on developing countries, industrialized nations have launched the Extractive Industries Transparency Initiative, announced by then British Prime Minister Tony Blair in October 2002. By requiring oil, gas and other "extractive" companies to report what they pay foreign governments for their natural resources, the initiative aims to expose corruption and foster accurate reporting of oil revenues and spending.

"Knowing what companies pay and what governments receive is a critical first step" to creating accountability in the handling of oil wealth, says the initiative's statement of purpose. [49] Members include industrialized countries as well as the World Bank, major oil companies and about 20 oil-producing developing nations.

However, transparency efforts are still hampered by national oil companies that keep their energy books closed and ignore international accountability guidelines.

Nevertheless, BP chief economist Peter Davies is optimistic about the initiative. "There is still a broad tendency toward transparency," he says. "There are forces that counteract this from time to time, [but] the forces for progress are there."

Will the growing competition for energy trigger new international conflicts?

The Cold War that dominated the last half of the 20th century was about ideology. As a new century begins, a widely shared concern is that energy will become a new arena for superpower or regional confrontations.

Conflicts over oil historically have centered in the Middle East. Now, because of the new petrostates, other hot spots claim attention in Central Asia, Africa and Latin America. The risks are magnified by the recent escalation of energy prices, which have made oil and natural gas resources an even bigger prize for rulers seeking to take or keep power.

New York Times columnist Thomas L. Friedman recently described a perverse relationship between oil prices and democracy: The higher oil prices go, the more democracy suffers and authoritarianism grows in the countries with oil. "Not only will some of the worst regimes in the world have extra cash for longer than ever to do the worst things," Friedman wrote, "but decent, democratic countries — India and Japan, for instance — will be forced to kowtow or turn a blind eye to the behavior of petro-authoritarians, such as Iran or Sudan, because of their heavy dependence on them for oil. That cannot be good for global stability." [50]

Japan and China see themselves competing for access to natural gas reserves in eastern Russia. Poland fears that Russia's construction of a new "North Stream" natural gas pipeline to Germany, now under way, will enable Russia to cut gas deliveries to Poland if tensions between those two countries erupt. [51] (A large portion of Russia's lucrative gas sales to Germany now transit through Poland, but that route could be bypassed by the North Stream project, Polish leaders fear.)

In Latin America, Bolivia's seizure of majority control over its natural gas industry in 2006 was a direct challenge to Brazil, which needs Bolivia's gas and whose state energy company Petrobras is a major gas producer in Bolivia. [52]

Some experts especially worry about the possibility of conflicts over energy between the United States and China, which is on a path to challenge U.S. economic and military leadership within two decades unless its hyper-growth spins out of control. Maureen S. Crandall, a professor of economics at the Industrial College of the Armed Forces, says that while China badly wants to import oil and natural gas from eastern Russia, it is not clear that pipelines will be built to deliver those resources. So China is looking hard at Caspian gas production and at the prospects for a pipeline through Iran to bring gas to seaports for export in liquefied form aboard tankers. [53]

World Crude Supplies Remain Vulnerable

Oil "hot spots" are most at risk.

On Feb. 24, 2006, a small band of al Qaeda gunmen attacked Saudi Arabia's giant oil processing facility at Abqaiq — the first such attack since terrorist leader Osama bin Laden publicly targeted Saudi oil installations in a 2004 audio message.

Although the Saudis repulsed the assault, the incident was a wake-up call as to what terrorists' intentions were concerning oil supplies, warned Simon Henderson, director of the Gulf and Energy Policy Program at the Washington Institute for Near East Policy. "Saudi oil production remains extremely vulnerable to sabotage," he wrote shortly after the attack, and the kingdom's estimated 12,000 miles of pipelines are also "at particular risk." A Saudi police raid on a terrorist hideout the previous year had reportedly uncovered copies of maps and plans of the new Shaybah oil field, he pointed out. [1]

Had the terrorists succeeded in destroying the sulfur-clearing towers at Abqaiq — through which about two-thirds of Saudi crude passes — it would have driven the price of crude to more than $100 a barrel for months, perhaps even up to bin Laden's goal of $200 a barrel, according to R. James Woolsey, a former CIA director. [2]

World leaders have been warning since the onset of the Industrial Age that the key to energy security lies in diversification of supplies. When Winston Churchill — then the First Lord of the Admiralty — shifted the Royal Navy from coal to oil on the eve of the First World War, he presciently warned, "Safety and certainty in oil lie in variety and variety alone." [3]

The conflicts and crises that have periodically disrupted Middle East oil supplies — from the oil shocks of the 1970s to Saddam Hussein's invasion of Kuwait in 1990 — have repeatedly reinforced the wisdom of Churchill's advice: find more sources of oil outside the Persian Gulf.

Today, the world is once again seeking to diversify its energy supplies, turning to sources in Central Asia, Africa and Russia. But while the emergence of these rising petrostates has increased the diversity of energy supplies, it has not increased energy security. Many of those new producers appear along with Saudi Arabia on the U.S. Energy Information Administration (EIA) list of various "hot spots" in world oil markets.

Saudi Arabia tops the list, but it is followed by other "emerging" oil producing states: Russia, Iran, Iraq, Nigeria, the Caspian region, Sudan, Venezuela and seven other countries where energy facilities are considered at risk from saboteurs or unstable domestic policies. [4] The EIA projects that by 2010 at least 50 million barrels of oil per day — 58 percent of worldwide daily production — will be in jeopardy because it originates or passes through oil hot spots.

"The security of the energy infrastructure is becoming progressively in doubt," says Massachusetts Institute of Technology Professor John Deutch, also a former CIA director. "Oil facilities, pipelines [and] control systems for the energy distribution systems are all very much more vulnerable to terrorist attack and national disaster." [5]

The choke points for seaborne oil — and, increasingly, natural gas — create some of the worst risks. According to Daniel Yergin, author of *The Prize: The Epic Quest for Oil, Money & Power*, those ocean chokepoints include the:

- Strait of Hormuz, at the entrance to the Persian Gulf;
- Suez Canal, which connects the Red Sea and the Mediterranean;
- Bab el Mandeb Strait at the Red Sea's entrance;
- Bosporus Strait, a major transit channel for Russian and Caspian oil; and
- Strait of Malacca between Malaysia and Indonesia, a conduit for 80 percent of the oil used by Japan and South Korea and about half of China's oil. [6]

That puts China in opposition to the Bush administration's top-priority campaign to isolate Iran to prevent it from developing nuclear weapons — a goal Iran denies it is seeking. The Iran issue headed America's agenda for the U.S.-China Senior Dialogue between top diplomats from both nations in June 2007, while China pushed for assurances the United States was not boosting its support for China's rival, Taiwan. [54]

The two nations are not consciously pointed toward conflict, says the National Intelligence Council's 2020

The Malacca strait is only 1.5 miles wide at its narrowest point, and if terrorists or pirates scuttled a ship at that choke point it could disrupt supplies for a long time, Yergin warns.

"It may take only one asymmetric or conventional attack on a Ghawar [Saudi oil field] or tankers in the Strait of Hormuz to throw the market into a spiral, warns Anthony H. Cordesman, a scholar at the Center for Strategic and International Studies in Washington. [7]

"Assuring the security of global energy markets will require coordination on both an international and a national basis among companies and governments, including energy, environmental, military, law enforcement and intelligence agencies," Yergin writes. "But in the United States, as in other countries, the lines of responsibility — and the sources of funding — for protecting critical infrastructures, such as energy, are far from clear."

Countries are trying a wide range of policies and practices to increase security of energy production and delivery, experts say. Colombia has military units — trained and partly supplied by the United States — tasked with combating rebel attacks on oil pipelines. The natural gas networks of Qatar and the United Arab Emirates are being connected to shipping terminals in Oman that lie outside the vulnerable Strait of Hormuz. [8] China is expanding its naval forces in order to protect oil shipments through Asian sea lanes where piracy is a threat.

But Gal Luft, executive director of the Institute for the Analysis of Global Security in Washington, says security efforts have been hampered by uncertainty over whether private companies or governments should pay for the additional security.

"NATO is looking into defining the roles of industry and government," Luft says. "Each wants the other to do more. In places where you can introduce technology or more manpower economically, you do it. But on the ground not a lot is happening."

Building in redundancy and the availability of alternative sources are also popular strategies for assuring energy deliveries, says Mariano Gurfinkel, associate head of the Center for Energy Economics at the University of Texas.

Separatist rebels show their firepower in Nigeria's oil-rich Niger Delta in February 2006. Insurgents have kidnapped foreign oil workers and sabotaged oil facilities to protest the slow pace of economic development in the delta.

"Since it is very hard to avoid all incidents on all elements of the energy infrastructure, efforts are made to minimize the consequences."

[1] Simon Henderson, "Al-Qaeda Attack on Abqaiq: The Vulnerability of Saudi Oil," Washington Institute for Near East Policy, www.washingtoninstitute. org/templateC05.php?CID=2446.

[2] R. James Woolsey, "Global implications of Rising Oil Dependence and Global Warming," testimony before the House Select Committee on Energy Independence and Global Warming, April 18, 2007, p. 2.

[3] Daniel Yergin, "Ensuring Energy Security," *Foreign Affairs*, March/April 2006, p. 69.

[4] "World Energy Hotspots," Energy Information Administration, Sept. 2005, www.eia.doe.gov/emeu/cabs/World_Energy_Hotspots/Full.html.

[5] John M. Deutch, testimony before the House Foreign Affairs Committee, March 22, 2007.

[6] Yergin, *op. cit.*, p. 79.

[7] Anthony H. Cordesman, "Global Oil Security," Center for Strategic and International Studies, Nov. 13, 2006, p. 14.

[8] Energy Information Administration, "Oman" country analysis, April 2007, www.eia.doe.gov/emeu/cabs/Oman/NaturalGas.html.

Project report — the most recent public forecast by the CIA's research arm. "[T]he growing dependence on global financial and trade networks increasingly will act as a deterrent to conflict among the great powers — the U.S., Europe, China, India, Japan and Russia," says the report. [55]

But, the report adds, inadvertent conflicts could erupt as a result of growing oil nationalism, the lack of effective international conflict-resolution processes or raw emotions exploding over key issues. For instance, a naval arms race could develop between China, intent on pro-

Majority of Oil Companies Are State-Owned

Thirteen of the world's 25-largest oil companies are entirely owned or controlled by national governments, including all the companies in the Middle East; three other oil firms are partially state-owned. In 1973, by comparison, roughly three-quarters of the world's oil production was managed by the privately owned "Seven Sisters" — the seven major Western oil companies.*

World's Largest Oil Companies

Rank (2005)	Company	Country of origin	Percentage of firm owned by state
1	Saudi Aramco	Saudi Arabia	100
2	Exxon Mobil	United States	0
3	NIOC	Iran	100
4	PDVSA	Venezuela	100
5	BP	United Kingdom	0
6	Royal Dutch Shell	United Kingdom/Netherlands	0
7	PetroChina	China	90
8	Chevron	United States	0
8	Total	France	0
10	Pemex	Mexico	100
11	ConocoPhillips	United States	0
12	Sonatrach	Algeria	100
13	KPC	Kuwait	100
14	Petrobras	Brazil	32
15	Gazprom	Russia	50.002
16	Lukoil	Russia	0
17	Adnoc	United Arab Emirates	100
18	Eni	Italy	0
19	Petronas	Malaysia	100
20	NNPC	Nigeria	100
21	Repsol YPF	Spain	0
22	Libya NOC	Libya	100
23	INOC	Iraq	100
24	EGPC	Egypt	100
24	QP	Qatar	100

* The Seven Sisters were: Exxon, Mobil, Chevron, Texaco, Gulf, Shell, British Petroleum

Source: Petroleum Intelligence Weekly

favors maintaining a credible U.S. military posture in Asia, they argue, but if U.S. actions are seen as a bid for supremacy or a check on China's rightful regional role, "it might fuel further resentments and incite precisely the reaction we don't seek, a redoubling of countervailing military, economic and diplomatic strategies."

"The United States and China are not seeking to make war on one another," agrees Michael Klare, a political science professor at Hampshire College. "But they are inadvertently contributing to the risk of conflict in Africa and Central Asia by using arms transfers as an instrument of influence."

China, for instance, has sent troops to Sudan to protect its energy investment there, he points out, and the U.S. military maintains a presence in Central Asia. In the same vein, former Chinese deputy chief of staff Gen. Xiong Guangkai told an international conference on energy security last December that "the strategic race for the world's energy may result in regional tension and even trigger a military clash." [57]

The recent deterioration of U.S.-Russian relations is a case study of what should not be allowed to happen between the United States and China, say some experts. The dialogue has grown raw, escalated by Russia's sharp swing toward an aggressive nationalism. But the division also has been fostered by arrogant and short-

tecting vital seaborne oil shipments, and the United States, determined to maintain strategic leverage in Asian waters. While China's interest "lies with a peaceful and stable regional and international order," write Schiffer and Schmitt, China's ambitions or internal political conflicts could take it in a different direction. [56] Prudence

sighted U.S. moves over the past 15 years that treated Russia as a defeated world power and dictated terms to them instead of seeking a working relationship, says Blair Ruble, director of the Kennan Institute in Washington.

"It has been a bipartisan failure," adds Ruble's colleague, program associate F. Joseph Dresen. After the

Soviet Union's collapse, the United States "had tons of leverage" but "we needed more influence. It starts with diplomacy."

A win-win relationship with China that minimizes potential for conflict "will take far more sophistication than U.S. policymakers from either political party have previously shown," Schiffer and Schmitt conclude. [58]

BACKGROUND

OPEC Is Born

In 1960, representatives of Iran, Iraq, Kuwait, Saudi Arabia and Venezuela met in Baghdad to form a cartel designed to stabilize world oil markets. Today the 12-member Organization of Petroleum Exporting Countries — now based in Vienna, Austria — also includes Qatar, Indonesia, Libya, the United Arab Emirates, Algeria, Nigeria and Angola. Ecuador and Gabon joined in the '70s but dropped out in the '90s. [59]

Despite the cartel's promise of stability, oil markets have been chaotic since the 1970s, characterized by four distinct periods.

Two oil shocks hit world energy markets in the 1970s. Resentful of U.S. efforts to suppress oil prices and angered by U.S. support for Israel in the 1973 Yom Kippur War, several Arab OPEC members on Oct. 17, 1973, imposed an oil embargo on the United States and other countries aiding Israel, followed by a production cut. [60] The world suddenly faced a crude-oil shortage of 4 million barrels a day, 7 percent below demand. Prices shot up from $3 a barrel to $12. [61] Long lines formed at gasoline pumps in the United States and some European countries.

To limit the impact on American consumers, President Richard M. Nixon imposed price controls on the U.S. economy, and President Gerald Ford created the U.S. Strategic Petroleum Reserve, which today holds more than 688 million barrels of crude oil in underground caverns. [62]

The embargo ended five months later — in March 1974 — after Arab-Israeli tensions eased. Egyptian President Anwar el-Sadat, intent on moving toward a peace agreement, argued successfully that the "oil weapon had served its purpose." [63]

But memories of the embargo continued to drive a search for new energy policies. On April 18, 1977, shortly

Motorists in London queue up for petrol in 1973. The world's first oil shock was caused by an Arab oil embargo, which established oil as a pivotal political and economic lever.

after being inaugurated, President Jimmy Carter warned about America's overdependence on foreign oil supplies, calling the energy crisis "the moral equivalent of war." With the exception of preventing war, Carter said, "this is the greatest challenge our country will face during our lifetimes." [64]

Then in early 1979, after a year of paralyzing strikes and demonstrations by supporters of militant Iranian Shia Muslim cleric Ayatollah Ruhollah Khomeini, Iran's Shah Mohammad Reza Pahlavi fled Tehran, opening the door to the founding of an Islamic republic.

As the impact of the Iranian Revolution on world oil prices began to be felt, Carter in July 1979 unveiled a comprehensive energy plan to help America combat its overdependence on unstable Middle Eastern oil, promoting conservation, alternative fuels and higher taxes on gasoline and gas-guzzling cars. [65]

Four months later, on Nov. 4, Islamist zealots and students took over the U.S. Embassy in Tehran, holding 52 hostages for 444 days — until Ronald Reagan replaced Carter. [66] During the crisis, oil prices nearly doubled. [67] World oil markets got even tighter in 1980, when Iran's oil production nearly dried up after Iraq invaded — beginning an eight-year-long conflict. Panic

Pollution and poverty abound in the swampy Niger Delta region of Nigeria, where international oil companies are drilling for the country's rich oil resources. Shanties reflect the slow rate of development, which has sparked violent protests in recent years.

purchases by governments, companies and consumers made the shortage worse, and, once again, motorists in industrialized countries queued up at gas stations.

The 1970s price shocks triggered a determined campaign to reduce energy dependence. Congress in 1975 directed U.S. auto manufacturers to double the efficiency of their cars within a decade, and businesses made serious efforts to shrink energy use. [68]

But the pendulum would soon be reversed. A sharp recession stunted energy demand, the search for oil outside the Persian Gulf intensified and the balance between supply and demand was set to shift again.

Oil Glut

Discoveries and exploitation of vast oil and gas reserves in the North Sea, Mexico and Alaska's North Slope in the early 1980s led to a tide of new production, tipping events in consumers' favor.

North Sea development, called "one of the greatest investment projects in the world," required intrepid drilling crews, path-breaking technology and platforms able to withstand crushing waves and 130-mile-per-hour winds. [69] By the early 1980s, daily North Sea production had reached 3.5 million barrels — more than Kuwait and Libya combined — and a new 800-mile pipeline to the port of Valdez from Alaska's landlocked North Slope was supplying up to 2 million barrels of oil a day to the Lower 48 states — a quarter of U.S. production. [70] In 1985, non-OPEC production had increased by 10 million barrels a day over 1974 levels, more than double the cartel's daily output. [71]

Moreover, by 1983 energy conservation was working. Americans were consuming less gasoline than in 1973, even with more cars on the road, and the U.S. economy had become 25 percent more energy efficient. Conservation efforts in Europe and Japan also were cutting consumption. [72] The two trends sent energy prices into a nosedive. By 1985 crude was below $10 a barrel ($20 in inflation-adjusted, 2006 prices), prompting Saudi Arabia to abandon efforts to control cartel production and boost its own output. Analysts have since interpreted the Saudis' decision as a strategic move to hamper the ability of Iran and Iraq to continue their war, raging just across the Saudi border. Others say the move hastened the demise of communism — by draining the Soviet Union's treasury at a time when it was facing rising internal pressures and fighting a war in Afghanistan.

But the lower oil prices also knocked the wind out of the conservation movement. The push to continue raising vehicle performance stalled in Congress, and gas-slurping minivans and SUVs became wildly popular. [73]

New Petrostates

Oil prices spiked briefly in 1991 after Saddam Hussein invaded Kuwait, and the U.S.-led coalition counterattacked, knocking out 3 percent of world oil output. After Iraq's defeat, the oil industry focused on the rising petrostates in Africa and Central Asia and on the collapse — and stunning recovery — of Russia's oil production. [74]

The Caspian Sea — about the size of California — holds one of the world's oldest-known concentrations of petroleum. The Caspian has long triggered fears that its oil, known since Alexander the Great's day, would become a conflict flashpoint. "It will be sad to see how the magnet of oil draws great armies to the Caucasus," wrote journalist Louis Fischer in 1926. [75]

The Caspian is bordered by Russia on the northwest, Kazakhstan on the north and east, Turkmenistan to the east, Iran to the south and Azerbaijan in the west. (*See map, p. 258.*) The rise of the independent former Soviet satellites triggered extravagant hopes that the Caspian could become "the Middle East of the next millennium." The State Department fanned the hyperbole, estimating Caspian oil reserves at 200 billion barrels, or 10 percent of the world's total potential reserves. [76]

Then developers began hitting dry holes, and war and separatist violence spread through the region. Caspian countries disagreed over how to divide the Caspian's energy reserves and whether the Caspian is, in fact, a "sea" or a "lake" — a definition that could affect the ultimate distribution. "The dreams have faded as the hard realities of energy development and politics have set in," says economist Crandall at the Industrial College of the Armed Forces, who predicts Caspian reserves will top out at 33-48 billion barrels, or 3 percent of the world's total. [77]

But even with the lower estimates, the Caspian reserves still are larger than Alaska's North Slope, big enough to attract not only Russia and Iran but also Europe and China. By 2010, the Energy Information Agency projects the Caspian region will be producing 2.9-3.8 million barrels a day — more than Venezuela. [78]

Dreams for a birth of democracy in the region also have faded. Most of the region's governments have become more authoritarian and corrupt since the demise of the Soviet Union, says Martha Brill Olcott, a senior associate at the Carnegie Endowment for International Peace. [79] Indeed, says Crandall, most Central Asian states are "one-bullet regimes" that would fall into chaos if current leaders were deposed. [80]

In Africa, the discovery of oil in Algeria in 1955 — and later in the Niger Delta and Libya — seemed like gifts from the gods for the planet's poorest continent. The riches lured flocks of petroleum companies.

As exploration expanded, Africa's proven reserves more than doubled from 1980 to 2005, to 114.3 billion barrels, far ahead of overall reserve gains worldwide. In 2004, Nigeria ranked eighth among the world's biggest oil exporters, followed by No. 10 Algeria and 12th-place Libya. [81] Angola soon joined Africa's oil club: In the past 10 years, Angola's estimated oil reserves have nearly tripled and its crude oil production doubled. [82]

Oil also was found in Sudan, where production has been climbing since completion in 1999 of an oil

In the shadow of Istanbul's historic Blue Mosque (left), the Hagia Sophia Museum (center) and Topkapi Palace (right), an oil tanker enters the Bosporus Strait. The 21-mile-long waterway is the sole route for Caspian oil shipped through pipelines to the Black Sea, where it is then loaded onto tankers for the trip through the strait to the Mediterranean. Turkey fears increased tanker traffic could bring an environmental catastrophe to the already busy Bosporus, so it has encouraged development of an overland pipeline that would bypass the strait.

pipeline for exports, despite years of civil war. In 2006, estimates of proven reserves topped 5 billion barrels, a 10-fold increase over the year before. [83]

Africa also has abundant natural gas. Nigeria has the continent's largest reserves and the world's seventh-biggest, while Algeria's reserves rank eighth. [84] Both are on a par with Saudi Arabia and the United States. Algeria in 1964 became the first nation to ship liquified natural gas (LNG) aboard tankers. But Nigeria, convulsed by tribal wars and coups, has been unable to capitalize on its gas deposits until recently. It still "flares," or burns away, 40 percent of the natural gas produced with its oil, although Nigeria is beginning to expand LNG production. [85]

The New Nationalism

China's staggering expansion and modernization have overtaken its energy resources. Twenty years ago, China was the largest oil exporter in East Asia. Now it is the world's second-largest oil purchaser, accounting for nearly one-third of the global increase in oil demand, note David Zweig and Bi Jianhai of the Hong Kong University of Science. [86] Similarly, India's oil consumption doubled

President Vladimir Putin addresses executives of Russia's Rosneft oil company in September 2005 after visiting the Tuapse oil terminal, pictured behind him. Putin is attempting to reclaim Russia's position as a superpower by harnessing its considerable energy resources.

between 1990 and 2004, and other industrializing Asian nations nearly matched that pace. [87]

Fortunately for the world's consumers, the explosive growth of China's oil demand was matched by a remarkable recovery in Russia's oil output. The fall of the Soviet Union and a financial credit crisis had devastated Russia's oil industry. Starved for capital and leadership, it was producing only 6 million barrels a day in 1995. But oil output had rebounded to average 9.4 million barrels a day this year, making Russia currently the world's largest oil producer, ahead of Saudi Arabia, which has trimmed its output. With the world's largest production and reserves of natural gas, it is poised to be Europe's prime supplier while developing its immense Far East gas reserves for eventual use by China, the rest of Asia and North America.

Russia's energy wealth also has transformed its self-image and ambitions, as it pulls away from the West. "In the late 19th century, Russia's success was said to rest on its army and its navy; today, its success rests on its oil and gas," writes Dmitri Trenin, deputy director of the Carnegie Moscow Center. [88]

Today, says Leonid Grigoriev, president of the Institute for Energy and Finance in Moscow, "We see ourselves as a great power." [89]

That power has frightened Russia's neighbors, especially after the Putin government took control of major petroleum reserves and energy pipelines, forcing Western energy companies to surrender equity positions in the country's largest new gas fields. Putin "has a very traditional Soviet view of the nature of power," says the Kennan Institute's Ruble. "He views oil and gas as strategic playing cards to reassert Russia in the world scene."

Now Europe anxiously faces growing dependence on Russia for its energy. "Russia is a natural, reliable and stable supplier" for Europe, insists Grigoriev.

"They see things strictly through the eyes of Russia: What is in their national interest?" responds CSIS's Ebel.

"The issue of security of supply is critical for European consumers," says BP economist Davies. "That debate is continuing."

Like Putin, Venezuela's Chávez is an architect of oil's rising nationalism. Following in the footsteps of Argentinean strongman Juan Perón and Cuba's Fidel Castro, Chávez is using Venezuela's oil and gas reserves — the Western Hemisphere's largest — to promote his socialist "Bolivarian Revolution." [90] While Chávez delights in confronting U.S. policy goals in Latin America, he also finds willing listeners in the Middle East and Asia. Having survived a coup attempt and an oil-workers' strike that stunted output in the winter of 2002-03, the former rebel paratrooper is firmly in control.

At home, Chávez has steered energy export earnings toward the three-quarters of the population that comprise Venezuela's poor. Their plight worsened in the 1980s and '90s despite market reforms recommended by globalization advocates at the International Monetary Fund (IMF) and World Bank. Chávez rejects free-market, capitalist economic approaches and vows to establish a socialist, classless society. [91] Social spending by Petróleos de Venezuela S.A. (PDVSA), the state-run oil and natural gas company, has increased 10-fold since 1997.

Abroad, Chávez seeks a coalition of allies who will help him parry opposition from the United States and pursue his agenda. He has offered low-priced oil to Latin America. (He also has donated heating oil to the poor in the United States.) PDVSA has forced major oil companies to give up majority holdings in Venezuela's oil fields and has signed oil deals with China, Iran, Vietnam, Brazil and Belarus. [92]

Has a new Cold War begun over oil that could lead to conflict?

YES Michael T. Klare
Five College Professor of Peace and World Security Studies (Amherst, Hampshire, Mount Holyoke and Smith colleges and the University of Massachusetts, Amherst)

Written for *CQ Researcher*, June 2007

Two simultaneous developments are likely to intensify future conflicts over oil. On one hand, increasing competition for a finite resource will become more intense in the years ahead. With China and India leading the growth in demand, competition is going to soar, and supply isn't likely to expand nearly as fast as demand. In addition, oil supplies increasingly will be located in areas of tension and inherent friction — the Middle East, Africa, Central Asia and other unstable places.

During the Cold War, the superpowers competed for influence by providing arms for various proxies in Africa, the Middle East and Asia. We are seeing the same thing happening in the oil cold war.

The United States, Russia and China, in their pursuit of oil allies, are again providing arms to proxies and suppliers, which is intensifying the risk of internal conflicts. It is an exceedingly dangerous development. The United States and China are not seeking to make war on one another. But they are inadvertently contributing to the risk of conflict in Africa and Central Asia by using arms transfers as an instrument of influence.

Ultimately, the only solution will be to reduce our craving for imported oil. That is easier said than done. It is a craving, and cravings lead to irrational behavior. For China, its close embrace of the Sudanese government — including supplying arms — is bringing the Chinese terrible criticism. The United States, for its part, engages in equally irrational behavior in creating close ties with — for example — the leaders of Kazakhstan and Azerbaijan — alienating the pro-democracy movements in those countries.

Ultimately, the most dangerous piece in all of this is the U.S.-China competition for energy. We have a cold war today, but it could become a hot war, although not through a deliberate act over oil. But we are engaged in competitive arms competition in Africa and Asia, and this could lead to inadvertent local conflicts and an accidental clash between the United States and China, much the way World War I began.

Neither side would choose such a conflict, but it would arise from a clash of proxies, eventually involving U.S. and Chinese advisers and troops.

Such an outcome may not be highly probable, but it is an exceedingly dangerous possibility.

NO Amy Myers Jaffe
Wallace S. Wilson Fellow in Energy Studies, James A. Baker III Institute for Public Policy; Associate Director, Rice University Energy Program

Written for *CQ Researcher*, June 2007

Competition over energy may contribute to fundamental global conflicts, but the conflicts would have happened with or without the energy situation. North Korea is not an oil issue. Kosovo was not about oil. The Iran confrontation is not an oil issue.

The Persian Gulf remains a special case. Saudi Arabia controls most of the world's excess oil production. In the case of the Iraq War in 1991 — which followed Iraq's invasion of oil-rich Kuwait — the United States was not going to let Saddam Hussein control 40-50 percent of the world's oil reserves. Saudi oil facilities have been targeted by terrorists, and Iran has threatened in the past to use military force to interfere with oil shipments through the Strait of Hormuz.

A future confrontation with Iran would greatly increase the risk to essential oil exports through the Persian Gulf. On the other hand, Iran is critically dependent upon revenues from its own oil sales and must import gasoline from foreign refiners to meet its population's requirements.

The overriding concern, however, is that the sudden loss of the Saudi oil network would paralyze the global economy. The United States — and the rest of the world — has a concrete interest in preventing that. But most conflicts facing the United States today, like North Korea or Afghanistan, are not going to change whether the price of oil is $50 a barrel or $70 a barrel.

Nor is Central Asia likely to become a flash point. We have been watching a revival of the so-called Great Game competition over Caspian oil for a decade. Why? Because the leaders in those countries have chosen to delay, trying to get the best economic and geopolitical deals they can. The Russians play the Japanese off the Chinese. The Chinese are trying to take care of their needs. Their motivations vary from country to country, but it is a dynamic that is very unlikely to lead to conflict. We are not likely to go to war with Russia over a pipeline in Kazakhstan.

The United States and China, as the world's largest oil importers, are economic partners by virtue of their trade and, consequently, potential political rivals. But both share a common interest in reasonable oil prices.

If the United States and China ever go to war over Taiwan, oil will not be the trigger.

Nigerians work on a French gas-drilling installation in Nigeria's Niger Delta, aided by Chinese contractors. The Chinese are competing with other international oil companies for the delta's rich oil reserves.

But Venezuela now spends more on social programs than on maintaining and expanding its oil production capacity, according to the Baker Institute. The current production rate of 2.4 million barrels a day is down from 3.1 million barrels when Chávez took office in 1999. [93]

"He is good at giving oil away, but he's not good at producing oil," says Chávez opponent Luis Giusti, who headed PDVSA in the 1990s.

While Chávez is a thorn in the side to the U.S. government and international oil companies, his overtures to China and Iran and his willingness to slow future development in favor of higher returns today represent a new reality in the world's energy story. [94]

CURRENT SITUATION

Majors Shut Out

Government-owned or controlled petroleum companies today control a majority of the world's hydrocarbon reserves and production. By 2005, nationalized oil companies had taken over 77 percent of the world's 1.1 trillion barrels of oil reserves. And, while Western oil companies have absorbed their share of the short-term windfall created by recent higher prices, their long-term future does not look particularly rosy. Major oil firms now control only 10 percent of global petroleum reserves. [95]

"International majors have been relegated to second-tier status," concluded the Baker Institute. In the 1970s and '80s, Western companies were invited to explore the new fields in the North Sea, Alaska and the Gulf of Mexico, but today key future resources in Russia and Central Asia are government-controlled.

"The bulk of the resources remain in a number of key countries, which are dominated by states, and we have to be dependent on governments and state companies to deliver the capacity," says BP's Davies.

"Access really is a consideration," adds Cambridge Energy Research Associates chairman Yergin. "Where can you go to invest money, apply technology and develop resources and bring them to market? Terms get very tough. The decision-making slows down, if you can get there at all."

China's strategy for feeding its oil appetite is a major source of concern, says former CIA Director Deutch. Its oil companies scour the world seeking access to oil and gas resources, effectively reducing supplies on the world market.

"China — and now India — are making extensive efforts in Africa and elsewhere in the world to lock up oil supplies," says Deutch. These state-to-state deals typically are not based solely on market terms but include sweeteners such as political incentives, military assistance, economic aid or trade concessions, he explains.

International oil companies, while banking record profits, are facing higher taxes or demands to surrender parts of their stakes in projects. For instance, say Western analysts, Putin's government has shown its knuckles to Royal Dutch Shell and Exxon Mobil in disputes over control of two huge projects on Sakhalin Island, off Russia's Pacific coast. Shell had to give up controlling interest in the Sakhalin-2 pipeline project to Russia's natural gas monopoly Gazprom after suffering cost overruns. Russia wants to determine where the gas goes, says its oil minister. [96]

Emboldened by rising oil prices, Russia and nations in South America and West Africa that once relied on Western oil companies are now "increasingly calling the shots," said *The Wall Street Journal.* [97]

Producer Windfalls

Oil prices have more than tripled since 2002, sparking an unprecedented transfer of wealth from consuming to producing nations. The amount energy-importing nations must spend for oil has leaped from $300 billion in 2002 to nearly $1 trillion in 2006 (roughly the gross domestic product of Spain or South Korea). [98] The higher prices, of course, affect not only oil production but also the current value of oil in the ground. The IMF reports the value of energy exporters' oil reserves increased by more than $40 trillion between 1999 and 2005. Thus if prices stay at current levels, it would translate into an enormous increase in future wealth for the exporting nations, concentrated in the Middle East, Russia, Central Asia and Africa. [99]

Higher oil prices leave all consumers with less to spend and save, but the impact is harshest in poor countries with no oil. Without oil or other high-value exports to offset increased energy costs, poor countries go deeper in debt.

"Debt is the central inhibitor of economic development," says former CIA Director R. James Woolsey Jr. "Importing expensive oil is helping bind hundreds of millions of the world's poor more firmly into poverty." [100]

The flow of petrodollars also is profoundly affecting the United States — the world's richest nation but also its largest oil consumer. When the U.S. buys oil from abroad, dollars pile up in the exporting nations' coffers. The oil-dollar outflow has added enormously to the U.S. "current account" deficit, or the dollar difference between U.S. imports and exports and international financial transactions. The United States is the only major nation that pays for its oil imports by borrowing heavily from the rest of the world. [101]

"The U.S. now borrows from its creditors — such as China and Saudi Arabia — over $300 billion per year, approaching a billion dollars a day of national IOU-writing, to import oil," according to Woolsey. [102]

A consequence of the increasing role of national oil companies is that most U.S. dollars paid for oil go into accounts controlled by foreign governments, according to the Federal Reserve Bank of New York. A crucial question is what those governments will do with their petrodollars, bank experts said. [103]

The outward tide of U.S. petrodollars has been matched by purchases of U.S. securities and properties by exporting countries, providing crucial support for U.S. stock and bond markets, the Federal Reserve report notes. In a dramatic example, China recently purchased $3 billion in stock of the Blackstone Group, a prominent U.S. equity firm that buys and turns around distressed companies.

Getty Images/Stanton R. Winter

Uncertainty over the construction of new oil and gas pipelines is heightening political tensions among the central players in the global competition for energy. New pipelines will be increasingly vital in moving energy resources from new fields in Russia, Central Asia and Africa.

"Officials in Beijing have $1.2 trillion of reserves they want to invest more profitably than in U.S. Treasuries. They lack the expertise to do it themselves and don't want to pay money managers millions in fees," said financial columnist William Pesek. [104]

For its part, Blackstone will get the increased access to China's surging economy that it covets. [105]

But such purchases are full of complexities, the Federal Reserve report notes. The Blackstone stock purchase was made by China's new state-owned investment fund, and other oil exporters have set up similar "sovereign wealth funds" to make direct investments in the United States and other oil-buying countries, writes

Gas stations in Tehran were torched and looted on June 26, 2007, after the Iranian government announced plans to begin fuel rationing. The state-controlled National Iranian Oil Co. has subsidized consumer fuel prices, sparking increased demand for oil.

columnist Sebastian Mallaby. "Chunks of corporate America could be bought by Beijing's government — or, for that matter, by the Kremlin." The economic and political fallout could be seismic, he adds. [106]

If events make oil exporters less willing to put dollars back into the United States, U.S. interest rates could increase to keep the foreign investment coming. Otherwise, U.S. consumers would have to cut their spending to reduce the outflow of dollars. A big shift of petrodollars away from the United States would pull a vital prop out from under stock markets. [107]

The flow of untraceable petrodollars also affects world security. Because so much oil revenue goes into the Middle East and from there into untraceable channels, some of it is being used to finance terrorist organizations opposed to the United States. "Thus . . . when we pay for Middle Eastern oil today, this long war in which we are engaged becomes the only war the U.S. has ever fought in which we pay for both sides," Woolsey says. [108]

Pipeline Politics

Over the next quarter-century, the world will rely on new oil and gas fields in Russia, Central Asia and Africa for a critical part of its energy needs. But uncertainty over when, where and if new pipelines will be built to access those new fields is heightening political tensions among the central players in the global competition for energy.

China covets oil and gas from eastern Siberia, but Russia's leaders have delayed building a pipeline into China, unwilling to hinge such a costly project on a single customer. Instead, Russia wants to channel those resources to its Pacific coast, where they can be shipped to competing customers not only in China but also in Japan, the rest of Asia and the United States.

Europe depends on Russian natural gas delivered over a Soviet-era pipeline network, which must be expanded to handle future growth. But Russia itself needs more gas and thus wants to build new pipelines into Central Asia to transport gas from Caspian fields — at market prices — to Europe.

Many Russian pipelines carrying Caspian oil terminate at the Black Sea. But Turkey opposes plans to expand that route because it fears a catastrophic oil spill from tanker traffic through the Bosporus Strait.

The most direct export route for Caspian oil is southward, by pipeline through Iran — a project China would welcome. But the United States opposes the route because it seeks to block Tehran's suspected nuclear-weapons development. [109]

Pipeline infighting is further reflected in BP's controversial $4 billion, 1,100-mile BTC pipeline from Baku, Azerbaijan, past Tbilisi, Georgia, and on to the Mediterranean port of Ceyhan, Turkey. The world's second-longest pipeline threads through mountains and volcanic regions and had to withstand unrest in Georgia, environmental opposition and sabotage threats. Its completion in 2005 fulfilled a hardball strategy by the United States to keep the pipeline out of Russian territory and block a shorter, cheaper route through Iran. [110] Leaders in Moscow and Tehran were infuriated.

"We really put all our cards on the table on that one," said Ebel, of CSIS.

But Russia has high cards to play, too, in the current pipeline tug-of-war over the undeveloped natural gas riches on the Caspian's eastern coast. The only gas pipeline through this region now leads north from Turkmenistan, through Kazakhstan into Russia, and Moscow controls it. [111]

The United States is pushing for a new pipeline across the Caspian seabed to carry Turkmenistan's gas westward to Baku.

From there it could travel into Turkey and connect with a new pipeline that the European Union wants to see built into Austria, (the "Nabucco" project), thus completing a pathway for Caspian gas to Europe without setting foot on Russian soil.

"We would love to see the Trans-Caspian Gas Pipeline put in place," Deputy Assistant Secretary of State for European and Eurasian Affairs Matthew Bryza said in January. [112]

Putin has other ideas. He is pressing Turkmenistan and Kazakhstan to support a Russian-built pipeline around the north end of the Caspian into Russia to move the gas into Europe over old and new Russian lines. Russia insists that no pipeline may cross the Caspian Sea unless all five adjoining nations agree — and Moscow is ready with its veto.

Speaking in Turkey recently, Bryza took a shot at Gazprom's natural gas pipeline monopoly, saying Russia uses its pipelines to intimidate governments in Europe that depend on them. "Europeans are finally waking up to the reality, I'm sorry to say, that Gazprom isn't always the most reliable partner for them. The more gas that moves from Central Asia and Azerbaijan to Europe via Turkey, the better." [113]

Russian officials contend the United States is still trying to throw its weight around, telling Moscow what to do.

In May, Moscow claimed the advantage after Putin and President Gurbanguly Berdymukhammedov of Turkmenistan agreed to the Russian plan for moving Caspian gas, but the United States says the door is still open for its favored route. [114] "These two pipelines are different," Bryza said in June, speaking of the Russian plan and trans-Caspian pipeline.

Meanwhile, Turkmenistan continues to talk with China about an eastward pipeline connection for its gas.

Currently, however, most of the pipeline-route disputes remain on paper. Soaring steel prices continue to inflate the costs of the billion-dollar pipeline networks. "The watchword today is delay," says Yergin of Cambridge Energy Research Associates, "not only because of political issues, but also because construction costs are going through the roof."

OUTLOOK

Curbing Demand

The race for Earth's remaining energy resources increasingly is splitting the world into two camps: countries that sell oil and natural gas and those that buy them.

The buyers — led by the United States, Europe, China and India and Japan — have a clear imperative, according to the International Energy Agency (IEA) and other energy experts: Start curbing demand. [115]

Energy security is the primary reason. Two-thirds of the growth in oil supplies over the next quarter-century will likely come from the Middle East, Russia, the Caspian region, Africa and Venezuela — areas beset by conflict or political instability. [116]

Climate change is also driving the need to curb demand. Total world economic output is projected to more than double by 2030, accelerating the discharge of greenhouse gases into the atmosphere. Eighty percent of the growth will come from China, India, Brazil and other developing countries. [117]

To avert potentially catastrophic climate disasters before the end of this century, both industrial and developing countries must agree on strategies for conserving energy and reducing greenhouse gases without halting economic growth, says the Intergovernmental Panel on Climate Change. [118]

Both energy insecurity and climate threats demand greater international cooperation than in the past decade, experts say. The United States has, until now, mainly sought to deal with its energy challenges by producing more oil and gas outside its borders, said a 2004 report for the Baker Institute for Public Policy.

After the Sept. 11, 2001, terrorist attacks, influential members of the Bush administration saw regime change in Iraq as a way to shake OPEC's hold on oil production, the Baker Institute authors wrote. Instead of taking responsibility for reducing energy consumption, however, the U.S. addressed the challenge "by attempting to control the Middle East." [119] But the strategy "has fallen flat on its face," the authors have asserted.

No matter how the Iraq War ends, the authors continue, the United States must move more decisively to reduce its energy demands if it wants credibility in seeking cooperation from China. China is quickly catching up to the United States in energy production and greenhouse-gas emissions, according to a recent report by U.S. climate experts Jeffrey Logan, Joanna Lewis and Michael B. Cummings. [120]

China has been building on average one new electric power plant a week for the past few years, and its automobile sales are booming (though they're small by U.S. standards). [121] But by the end of the decade, China will have 90 times more motor vehicles than it had in 1990, and by 2030 — or sooner — there may be more cars in China than in the United States. [122]

This year China announced new climate goals, including a 10 percent reduction in carbon-dioxide emissions over five years. "[W]e have to take responsibility for lowering greenhouse emissions," said Zhang Zhang Guobao, vice chairman of the energy-policy-setting National Development and Reform Commission. [123]

But China has adopted a "wait-and-see" attitude toward international climate-change agreements, unwilling to make binding commitments until it is clear what the United States and the developed world will do, according to Logan, Lewis and Cummings. The United States must lead by example, they said.

"Thinking about how to alter our energy-consumption patterns to bring down the price of oil is no longer simply a hobby for high-minded environmentalists or some personal virtue," says *Times* columnist Friedman. "It is a national-security imperative." [124]

"It must be recognized," says Yergin of Cambridge Energy Research Associates, "that energy security does not stand by itself but is lodged in the larger relations among nations and how they interact with one another." [125]

NOTES

1. The Associated Press, "Putin: Soviet Collapse a 'Genuine Tragedy,'" MSNBC, April 25, 2005, www.msnbc.msn.com/id/7632057.

2. "Russia Cuts Ukraine Gas Supplies," BBC News, Jan. 1, 2006; http://news.bbc.co.uk/1/hi/world/europe/4572712.stm.

3. "Russia and the West; No Divide, No Rule," *The Economist*, May 17, 2007, p. 12.

4. "Oil Nationalism Troubling Multinationals," *Iran Daily*, Oct. 23, 2006, p. 11, http://irandaily.ir/1385/2691/pdf/i11.pdf.

5. John M. Deutch, testimony before the House Foreign Affairs Committee, March 22, 2007.

6. "PIW Ranks the World's Top Oil Companies," *Energy Intelligence*, www.energyintel.com/DocumentDetail.asp?document_id=137158.

7. *Iran Daily, op. cit.*

8. Peter Katel, "Change in Latin America," *CQ Researcher*, July 21, 2006, pp. 601-624.

9. Natalie Obiko Pearson, "Chávez takes over Venezuela's last private oil fields," The Associated Press Worldstream, May 2, 2007.

10. Alexandra Valencia, "Ecuador says started review of oil contracts," Reuters, June 6, 2007; www.reuters.com/article/companyNewsAndPR/idUSN0645081020070607.

11. *Energy Intelligence, op. cit.*

12. U.S. motorists were paying over $1.42 a gallon for regular gasoline in March 1981. Adjusted at 2006 price levels to account for inflation, that cost would be $3.22 a gallon; www.eia.doe.gov/emeu/steo/pub/fsheets/petroleumprices.xls.

13. Matthew Higgins, Thomas Klitgaard and Robert Lerman, "Recycling Petrodollars: Current Issues in Economics and Finance," Federal Reserve Bank of New York, December 2006, p. 1; www.newyorkfed.org/research/current_issues/ci12-9.pdf.

14. "The Changing Role of National Oil Companies in International Energy Markets," James A. Baker III Institute for Public Policy, April 2007; http://bakerinstitute.org/Pubs/BI_ Pol%20Rep_35.pdf, page 2; see all reports www.rice.edu/energy/publications/nocs.html.

15. "World Energy Outlook 2006," International Energy Agency, p. 1; www.worldenergyoutlook.org/summaries2006/English.pdf.

16. For background, see Colin Woodard, "Curbing Climate Change," *CQ Global Researcher*, February 2007, pp. 27-50; and the following *CQ Researchers*: Barbara Mantel, "Energy Efficiency," May 19, 2006, pp. 433-456; Marcia Clemmitt, "Climate Change," Jan. 27, 2006, pp. 73-96; Mary H. Cooper, "Energy Policy," May 25, 2001, pp. 441-464; Mary H. Cooper, "Global Warming Treaty," Jan. 26, 2001, pp. 41-64; Mary H. Cooper, "Global Warming Update," Nov. 1, 1996, pp. 961-984.

17. Maureen S. Crandall, *Energy, Economics and Politics in the Caspian Region: Dreams and Realities* (2006), pp. 23, 46.

18. Amy Myers Jaffe and Matthew E. Chen, James A. Baker III Institute for Public Policy, testimony before the U.S.-China Economic and Security

Review Commission, hearing on China's Role in the World, Aug. 4, 2006; www.uscc.gov/hearings/2006hearings/written_testimonies/06_08_3_4wrts/06_08_3_4_jaffe_amy_statement.php.

19. R. James Woolsey, "Global Implications of Rising Oil Dependence and Global Warming," testimony before the House Select Committee on Energy Independence and Global Warming, April 18, 2007, p. 2.

20. "PIW Survey: Oil Reserves Are Not Rising," *Petroleum Intelligence Weekly*, April 16, 2007; www.energyintel.com/DocumentDetail.asp?document_id=199949. See also "Performance Profiles of Major Energy Producers 2005," Energy Information Agency, pp. 20-21; www.eia.doe.gov/emeu/perfpro/020605.pdf.

21. Michael Connolly, "Fragmented Market Would Hamper Russian-Iranian 'Gas OPEC,' " *Wall Street Journal* online, Feb. 2, 2007.

22. Daniel Dombey, Neil Buckley, Carola Hoyos, "NATO fears Russian plans for 'gas OPEC,' " *Financial Times*, Nov. 13, 2006.

23. Daniel S. Sullivan addressed the Energy Council's Federal Energy & Environmental Matters Conference, March 9, 2007.

24. James A. Baker III Institute for Public Policy Report, *op. cit.*; also Baker Institute Report, "Introductions and Summary Conclusions," pp. 7-19; www.rice.edu/energy/publications/docs/NOCs/Presentations/Hou-Jaffe-KeyFindings.pdf.

25. "Mapping the Global Future: Report of the National Intelligence Council's 2020 Project," National Intelligence Council, December 2004; www.dni.gov/nic/NIC_globaltrend2020.html.

26. Michael Schiffer and Gary Schmitt, "Keeping Tabs on China's Rise," The Stanley Foundation, May 2007, p. 1; www.stanleyfoundation.org/publications/other/SchifferSchimitt07.pdf.

27. *Ibid.*, p. 9.

28. Xuecheng Liu, "China's Energy Security and Its Grand Strategy," The Stanley Foundation, September 2006, p. 13; www.stanleyfoundation.org/publications/pab/pab06chinasenergy.pdf.

29. Quoted in Paulo Prada, "Bolivia Nationalizes the Oil and Gas Sector," *The New York Times*, May 2, 2006, p. A9.

30. Quoted in Juan Forero, "Presidential Vote Could Alter Bolivia, and Strain Ties With U.S.," *The New York Times*, Dec. 18, 2005, p. A13.

31. Alfonzo quoted by Stanford University's Terry Lynn Karl, Senior Fellow at the Institute for International Studies, Stanford University, in "The Oil Trap," Transparency International, September 2003; ww1.transparency.org/newsletters/2003.3/tiq-Sept2003.pdf.

32. Richard M. Auty, *Sustaining Development in Mineral Economies: The Resource Curse Thesis* (Routledge), 1993. Summarized in Richard M. Auty, "The 'Resource Curse' in Developing Countries Can Be Avoided," United Nations University, Helsinki; www.wider.unu.edu/research/pr9899d2/pr9899d2s.htm.

33. "Country Analysis Briefs: Mexico," Energy Information Administration, January 2007; www.eia.doe.gov/emeu/cabs/Mexico/Oil.html; and "Major Non-OPEC Countries' Oil Revenues," www.eia.doe.gov/cabs/opecnon.html.

34. Robert Collier, "Mexico's Oil Bonanza Starts to Dry Up," *San Francisco Chronicle*; www.sfgate.com/cgi-bin/article.cgi?file=/c/a/2006/06/30/MNGAAJN9JG1.DTL.

35. Karl, Transparency International, *op. cit.*, p. 1.

36. See "The 'Dutch Disease': Theory and Evidence," *Poverty and Growth Blog*, The World Bank, http://pgpblog.worldbank.org/the_dutch_disease_theory_and_evidence.

37. Tom O'Neill, "Hope and Betrayal in the Niger Delta," *National Geographic*, February 2007, p. 97.

38. Senan Murray, "Tackling Nigeria's Violent Oil Swamps," BBC News, May 30, 2007; http://news.bbc.co.uk/2/hi/africa/6698433.stm.

39. Karl Maier, "Nigeria Militants Release Six Chevron Oil Workers," Bloomberg, June 2, 2007; www.bloomberg.com/apps/news?pid=20601087&sid=aXT6yOlwMVGY&refer=home.

40. Daniel Dalint Kurti, "New Militia is a Potent Force," *The Christian Science Monitor*, March 7, 2007; www.csmonitor.com/2006/0307/p04s01-woaf.html.

41. Bernd Debusmann, "In Venezuela, obstacles to 21st Century socialism," Reuters, June 20, 2007.

42. Transparency International, Corruption Perceptions Index, 2006; www.transparency.org/policy_research/surveys_indices/cpi/2006.

43. Freedom House, "Countries at the Crossroads 2006; Country Report: Venezuela," www.freedomhouse.org/template.cfm?page=140&edition=7&ccrpage=31&ccrcountry=141.

44. "Iran fuel rations spark anger, pump stations burn," Reuters, June 27, 2007, www.reuters.com/article/worldNews/idUSDAH72595420070627.

45. "New Analysis Claims Darfur Deaths Near 400,000," Coalition for Darfur, April 25, 2005, http://coalitionfordarfur.blogspot.com/2005/04/new-analysis-claims-darfur-deaths-near.html.

46. Jaffe, *op. cit.*

47. David Zweig and Bi Jianhai, "China's Global Hunt for Energy," *Foreign Affairs*, Sept./Oct. 2005, p. 32.

48. Scott McDonald, "China Welcomes Darfur Agreement," The Associated Press, June 14, 2007; www.boston.com/news/world/asia/articles/2007/06/14/china_welcomes_darfur_agreement/.

49. "Fact Sheet," Extractive Industries Transparency Initiative, 2007; www.eitransparency.org/section/abouteiti.

50. Thomas L. Friedman, "The First Law of Petropolitics," *Foreign Policy*, May/June 2006, p. 4; www.foreignpolicy.com/story/cms.php?story_id=3426.

51. Ariel Cohen, the Heritage Foundation, "The North Eureopean Gas Pipeline Threatens Europe's Energy Security," Oct. 26, 2006; www.heritage.org/Research/Europe/bg1980.cfm.

52. Alexandre Rocha, "Burned by Bolivia, Brazil Goes to Africa and Middle East Looking for Gas," *Brazzil Magazine* (online), June 20, 2007; www.brazzilmag.com/content/view/8368/1/.

53. Crandall, *op. cit.*, p. 143.

54. Foster Klug, "U.S. Presses China on Iran in Latest Talks," The Associated Press, June 20, 2007.

55. "Mapping the Global Future," *op. cit.*

56. Schiffer and Schmitt, *op. cit.*, p 14.

57. Evan Osnos, "U.S., China vie for oil, allies on new Silk Road," *Chicago Tribune*, Dec. 19, 2006, p. 4.

58. Schiffer and Schmitt, *op. cit.*, p. 15.

59. "About Us," Organization of Petroleum Exporting Countries, www.opec.org/aboutus/history/history.htm.

60. Until 1972 production limits set by the Texas Railroad Commission effectively set a ceiling on oil prices in the United States and the rest of the world. But U.S. output peaked then, opening the way for OPEC's moves to control oil markets; http://tonto.eia.doe.gov/dnav/pet/hist/mcrfpus1m.htm.

61. For background, see Mary H. Cooper, "OPEC: Ten Years After the Arab Oil Boycott," *Editorial Research Reports*, Sept. 23, 1983; available in *CQ Researcher Plus Archive*, www.cqpress.com.

62. "U.S. Strategic Petroleum Reserve," Fact Sheet, U.S. Department of Energy, May 30, 2007; www.fossil.energy.gov/programs/reserves.

63. Daniel Yergin, *The Prize: The Epic Quest for Oil, Money & Power* (1991), p. 631.

64. "Carter Energy Program," *CQ Historic Documents Series Online Edition.* Originally published in *Historic Documents of 1977*, CQ Press (1978), CQ Electronic Library; http://library.cqpress.com/historicdocuments/hsdc77-0000106610.

65. *Ibid.*

66. "Iranian Hostage Crisis, 1980 Special Report," *Congress and the Nation, 1977-1980* (Vol. 5); CQ Press; available at CQ Congress Collection, CQ Electronic Library, http://library.cqpress.com/congress/catn77-0010173673.

67. "Real Gasoline Prices," Energy Information Administration; www.eia.doe.gov/emeu/steo/pub/fsheets/real_prices.html.

68. For background, see R. Thompson, "Quest for Energy Independence," *Editorial Research Reports*, Dec. 23, 1983, available in *CQ Researcher Plus Archive*, CQ Electronic Library, http://library.cqpress.com.

69. Yergin, *op. cit.*, p. 669.

70. *Ibid.*, p. 666.

71. "Annual Energy Review 2005, World Crude Oil Production, 1960-2005," Energy Information Administration; www.eia.doe.gov/emeu/aer/pdf/pages/sec11_11.pdf.

72. Yergin, *op. cit.*, p. 718.

73. Mary H. Cooper, "SUV Debate," *CQ Researcher*, May 16, 2003, pp. 449-472.

74. For background, see Kenneth Jost, "Russia and the Former Soviet Republics," *CQ Researcher*, June 17, 2005; pp. 541-564.

75. Louis Fischer, *Oil Imperialism* (1926), cited by Robert E. Ebel, Center for Strategic and International Studies, July 25, 2006.

76. Bruce W. Nelan, "The Rush for Caspian Oil," *Time*, May 4, 1998, p. 40.

77. Crandall, *op. cit.*, p. 1.

78. "Caspian Sea," Energy Information Administration, 2007; www.eia.doe.gov/emeu/cabs/Caspian/Full.html.

79. Martha Brill Olcott, "Will Central Asia Have Another 'Second Chance'?" speech, Carnegie Endowment for International Peace, Sept. 15, 2005.

80. Crandall, *op. cit.*, p. 3.

81. "Top World Oil Producers, Exporters, Consumers, and Importers 2004," Information Please Database, 2007; www.infoplease.com/ipa/A0922041.html.

82. "BP Statistical Review 2006," *British Petroleum*, p. 8; www.bp.com/sectiongenericarticle.do?categoryId=9017903&contentId=7033469.

83. "Sudan," Energy Information Administration, April 2007; www.eia.doe.gov/emeu/cabs/Sudan/Background.html.

84. "Libya — Natural Gas," Energy Information Administration, March 2006; www.eia.doe.gov/emeu/cabs/Libya/NaturalGas.html.

85. "Nigeria/Natural Gas," Energy Information Administration, April 2007, www.eia.doe.gov/emeu/cabs/Nigeria/NaturalGas.html.

86. Zweig and Jianhai, *op. cit.*, p. 25.

87. "International Energy Outlook, 2007," Energy Information Administration, p. 83; www.eia.doe.gov/oiaf/ieo/pdf/ieorefcase.pdf.

88. Dmitri Trenin, Deputy Director, Carnegie Moscow Center, "Russia Leaves the West," *Foreign Affairs*, July/August 2006.

89. Leonid Grigoriev, speaking at the Kennan Institute, Feb. 5, 2007; www.wilsoncenter.org/index.cfm?topic_id=1424&fuseaction=topics.event_summary&event_id=215229.

90. *Oil and Gas Journal*, quoted in www.eia.doe.gov/emeu/cabs/Venezuela/Oil.html. Conventional reserves do not include the extensive Canadian tar sands or Venezuela's extra-heavy oil and bitumen deposits.

91. Michael Shifter, "In search of Hugo Chávez," *Foreign Affairs*, May/June 2006, p. 47. For background, see Peter Katel, "Change in Latin America," *CQ Researcher*, July 21, 2006, pp. 601-624.

92. Baker Institute for Public Policy, *op. cit.*, p. 6.

93. "Venezuela," Energy Information Administration, September 2006; www.eia.doe.gov/emeu/cabs/Venezuela/Oil.html.

94. Baker Institute, *op. cit.*, p. 5.

95. *Ibid.*, p. 1.

96. Gregory L. White and Jeffrey Ball, "Huge Sakhalin Project Is Mostly on Track, As Shell Feels Pinch," *The Wall Street Journal*, May 7, 2007, p. 1.

97. *Ibid.*, p. 1. Also see Amy Myers Jaffe, James A. Baker III Institute for Public Policy, "Russia: Back to the Future?" testimony before the Senate Committee on Foreign Relations, June 29, 2006, p. 1.

98. Higgins, Klitgaard and Lerman, *op. cit.*, p. 1.

99. "World Economic Outlook, April 2006," Chapter 2, p. 24, International Monetary Fund; www.imf.org/external/pubs/ft/weo/2006/01/pdf/c2.pdf.

100. Woolsey, *op. cit.*, p. 3.

101. Higgins, Klitgaard and Lerman, *op. cit.*, p. 6.

102. Woolsey, *op. cit.*, p. 3.

103. Higgins, Klitgaard and Lerman, *op. cit.*, pp. 3-4.

104. William Pesek, "Blackstone + China = Bubble," Bloomberg, May 23, 2007; www.bloomberg.com/apps/news?pid=20601039&sid=aU7bs9CJazGI&refer=columnist_pesek.

105. Ransdell Pierson and Tamora Vidaillet, "China flexes FX muscle with $3 bln Blackstone deal," Reuters, May 21, 2007.

106. Sebastian Mallaby, "The Next Globalization Backlash," *The Washington Post*, June 25, 2007, p. A19.

107. Higgins, Klitgaard and Lerman, *op. cit.*, p. 6.

108. Woolsey, *op. cit.*, p. 4.

109. The United States has its own huge pipeline project on the table, a plan to transport natural gas from Alaska's North Slope into the U.S. Midwest, which would reduce some of the future need for natural gas imports by LNG tankers from Russia and the Middle East.

110. Robert E. Ebel, "Russian Energy Policy," Center for Strategic and International Studies, testimony before the U.S. Senate Committee on Foreign Relations, June 21, 2005; Crandall, *op. cit.*, p. 23.

111. "Central Asia," Energy Information Administration, September 2005; www.eia.doe.gov/emeu/cabs/Centasia/NaturalGas.html.

112. "Washington Pushes for Trans-Caspian Pipeline," *New Europe*, Jan. 15, 2007; www.neurope.eu/view_news.php?id=69019.

113. Press statement, State Department, Consulate General-Istanbul, Remarks by Matthew Bryza, deputy-assistant secretary of State for European and Eurasian affairs, May 11, 2007; http://istanbul.usconsulate.gov/bryza_speech_051107.html.

114. "Turkmenistan open oil, gas to Russia," UPI, June 13, 2007.

115. "World Energy Outlook 2006," International Energy Agency, p. 3; www.worldenergyoutlook.org/summaries2006/English.pdf.

116. "International Energy Outlook 2007," Energy Information Administration, p. 187; www.eia.doe.gov/oiaf/ieo/pdf/ieopol.pdf.

117. "Fighting Climate Change Through Energy Efficiency," United Nations Environment Program, May 30, 2006; www.unep.org/Documents.Multilingual/Default.asp?DocumentID=477&ArticleID=5276&l=en.

118. "Working Group III Report," Intergovernmental Panel on Climate Change, May 2007; www.mnp.nl/ipcc/pages_media/AR4-chapters.html.

119. Joe Barnes, Amy Myers Jaffe, Edward L. Morse, "The Energy Dimension in Russian Global Strategy," James A. Baker III Institute for Public Policy," 2004, p. 5; www.rice.edu/energy/publications/docs/PEC_BarnesJaffeMorse_10_2004.pdf.

120. Jeffrey Logan, Joanna Lewis and Michael B. Cummings, "For China, the Shift to Climate-Friendly Energy Depends on International Collaboration," *Boston Review*, January/February 2007; www.pewclimate.org/press_room/discussions/jlbostonreview.cfm.

121. Logan, Lewis and Cummings, *op. cit.*

122. Global Insight Forecast, "Outlook Still Buoyant for Chinese Auto Market," March 2007; www.globalinsight.com/SDA/SDADetail9307.htm.

123. Catherine Brahic, "China to promise cuts in greenhouse gases," NewScientist.com news services, Feb. 14, 2007, http://environment.newscientist.com/article/dn11184.

124. Friedman, *op. cit.*, p. 10.

125. Yergin, "Ensuring Energy Security," *op. cit.*, p. 69.

BIBLIOGRAPHY

Books

Crandall, Maureen S., *Energy, Economics, and Politics in the Caspian Region: Dreams and Realities,* **Praeger Security International, 2006.**
An economics professor at the National Defense University argues that the Caspian region's oil development will accelerate global and regional military, ethnic and religious conflict.

Klare, Michael, *Resource Wars: The New Landscape of Global Conflict,* **Henry Holt, 2001.**
A political science professor describes how the demand for scarce resources among growing populations has led to wars over the past century.

Yergin, Daniel, *The Prize: The Epic Quest for Oil, Money & Power,* **Simon & Schuster, 1991.**
In a Pulitzer Prize-winning work, the chairman of Cambridge Energy Research Associates chronicles the political and economic history of the oil industry.

Articles

"PIW Ranks the World's Top Oil Companies," *Energy Intelligence,* **www.energyintel.com.**
Petroleum Intelligence Weekly, a leading industry publication, ranks Saudi Aramco of Saudi Arabia and Exxon Mobil of the United States as the world's top two oil companies.

O'Neill, Tom, "Curse of the Black Gold," *National Geographic*, February 2007, p. 88.
The writer examines the politics and corruption of multinational petroleum companies that critics claim have created poverty and violence in the wake of Nigeria's oil boom.

Schiffer, Michael and Gary Schmitt, "Keeping Tabs on China's Rise," The Stanley Foundation, May 2007, www.stanleyfoundation.org.
Two foreign policy experts encourage the West to continue diplomatic relations with the Beijing government amid China's rise as a global superpower.

Shifter, Michael, "In Search of Hugo Chávez," *Foreign Affairs*, May-June 2006, p. 45.
According to a vice president of the Inter-American Dialogue, the profits from nationalization of Venezuela's oil have yielded only modest gains for the country's poor.

Trenin, Dmitri, "Russia Leaves the West," *Foreign Affairs*, July-Aug. 2006, p. 87.
Russia's vast energy resources make it a potential threat to the United States and other Western nations, according to the deputy director of the Carnegie Moscow Center.

Udall, Randy, and Matthew R. Simmons, "CERA's Rosy Oil Forecast — Pabulum to the People," *ASPO-USA's Peak Oil Review/Energy Bulletin*, Aug. 21, 2006, www.energy bulletin.net.
Two energy experts refute a recent optimistic oil study by Cambridge Energy Research Associates, contending that in actuality oil will be in shorter supply and more expensive by 2015.

Yergin, Daniel, "Ensuring Energy Security," *Foreign Affairs*, March-April 2006, p. 69.
The chairman of Cambridge Energy Research Associates explores new tactics for safeguarding the world's energy supplies and alleviating energy-related conflicts.

Zweig, David, and Bi Jianhai, "China's Global Hunt for Energy," *Foreign Affairs*, Sept.-Oct. 2005, p. 25.
Two foreign policy professors at Hong Kong University argue that China must find new energy sources if it wants to maintain rapid economic growth.

Reports

"Challenge and Opportunity, Charting a New Energy Future," Energy Future Coalition, 2002, www.ener gyfuturecoalition.org.
A bipartisan energy research group advocates alternative energy strategies to reduce dependence on foreign oil.

"The Changing Role of National Oil Companies in International Markets," James A. Baker III Institute for Public Policy, Rice University, May 1, 2007, www.rice.edu.
Energy researchers provide case studies analyzing the problems of private petroleum companies amid the rise of oil nationalism.

Ebel, Robert E., "Russian Energy Policy," testimony before Senate Foreign Relations Committee, June 21, 2005.
A senior energy adviser at the Center for Strategic and International Studies stresses the United States' need for a diplomatic energy-policy dialogue with Russia.

Jaffe, Amy Myers, "Russia: Back to the Future?" testimony before Senate Foreign Relations Committee, June 29, 2006.
A noted energy analyst reviews Russia's increasingly nationalistic energy policies.

Woolsey, R. James, "Geopolitical Implications of Rising Oil Dependence and Global Warming," testimony before Select Committee on Energy Independence and Global Warming, April 18, 2007.
A former CIA director offers solutions for curbing the United States' dependence on oil and natural gas.

For More Information

American Enterprise Institute, 1150 17th St., N.W., Washington, DC 20036; (202) 862-5800; www.aei.org. Public-policy research group studying economic and social issues.

American Petroleum Institute, 1220 L St., N.W., Washington, DC 20005-4070; (202) 682-8000; www.api.org. Industry group representing oil and gas producers.

Cambridge Energy Research Associates, 55 Cambridge Parkway, Cambridge, MA 02142; (617) 866-5000; www.cera.com. Renowned energy consultancy to international energy firms, financial institutions, foreign governments and technology providers.

Center for Strategic and International Studies, 800 K St., N.W., Washington, DC 20006; (202) 887-0200; www.csis.org. Public-policy research group specializing in defense, security and energy issues.

Council on Foreign Relations, 1779 Massachusetts Ave., N.W., Washington, DC 20036; (202) 518-3400; www.cfr.org. Think tank focusing on international issues; publishes Foreign Affairs.

Energy Future Coalition, 1800 Massachusetts Ave., N.W., Washington, DC 20036; (202) 463-1947; www.energyfuturecoalition.org. A bipartisan advocacy group for energy conservation and alternative fuels.

Energy Information Administration, 1000 Independence Ave., S.W., Washington, DC 20585; (202) 586-8800; www.eia.doe.gov. The primary source of federal data and analysis on energy.

Extractive Industries Transparency Initiative, Ruseløkkveien 26, 0251 Oslo, Norway; +47 2224 2110; www.eitransparency.org. Advocates responsible energy use and public disclosure of energy-based revenues and expenditures on behalf of more than 20 nations.

Human Rights Watch, 350 Fifth Ave., 34th floor, New York, NY 10118-3299; (212) 290-4700; www.hrw.org. Advocates for human rights.

International Energy Agency, 9 rue de la Fédération, 75739 Paris Cedex 15, France; 33 1 40 57 65 00/01; www.iea.org. The principal international forum for global energy data and analysis.

James A. Baker III Institute, 6100 Main St., Rice University, Baker Hall, Suite 120, Houston, TX 77005; (713) 348-4683; http://bakerinstitute.org. Academic research group specializing in energy.

Kennan Institute, Woodrow Wilson International Center for Scholars, Ronald Reagan Building and International Trade Center, One Woodrow Wilson Plaza, 1300 Pennsylvania Ave., N.W., Washington, DC 20004-3027; (202) 691-4000; www.wilsoncenter.org. Think tank specializing in social, political and economic developments in Russia and the former Soviet states.

Organization of the Petroleum Exporting Countries, Obere Donaustrasse 93, A-1020 Vienna, Austria; +43-1-21112-279; www.opec.org. Coordinates and unifies petroleum policies among its 12 oil-exporting member nations.

Transparency International, Alt-Moabit 96, 10559 Berlin, Germany; 49-30-3438 20-0; www.transparency.org. Advocacy group that campaigns against corruption worldwide.

World Bank, 1818 H St., N.W., Washington, DC 20433; (202) 473-1000; www.worldbank.org. Provides financial and technical assistance to developing countries.

VOICES FROM ABROAD

Abdalla Salem El-Badri

Secretary General, OPEC

Oil is important to all

"Any talk of energy security must take into account both supply and demand perspectives. The role of oil is equally important to the economic growth and prosperity of consuming-importing countries, as well as to the development and social progress of producing-exporting countries."

— *Speech, Second Asian Ministerial Energy Roundtable, May 2007*

Ngozi Okonjo-Iweala

Minister of Finance, Nigeria

Niger Delta problems present an opportunity

"The government is determined to address the genuine problems of the Niger Delta people but will not allow gangsterism to prevail. . . . There will be no going back on the present reforms no matter what political configuration is in place, because Nigeria can not afford to miss this opportunity."

— *This Day (Nigeria), April 2006*

Editorial

Gazeta (Russia)

Russia: 'Oil is its everything'

"In 2009 oil prices will fall. [Putin] understands perfectly well that it is the falling of oil prices and not at all the elections that could return the demand for liberal reforms. This is the kind of country Russia is — oil is its everything."

— *February 2006*

Rafael Ramírez

Minister of Energy and Petroleum, Venezuela

Oil stability requires social stability

"There cannot be stability in the international oil market if there is no stability within the oil producing countries, which in turn presupposes political and social stability, justice and a truly national and fair distribution of the oil rent."

— *Speech during Third OPEC International Seminar, September 2006*

Xu Weizhong

African Studies Director
China Institute of Contemporary International Relations

It's not just about oil

"[Western media] believed that China became interested in Africa only because of oil. But . . . Africa has always been a focus of China's foreign policy over the past half-century. . . . China has broad cooperation with African countries, including both energy-rich countries and resource-lacking ones. Western media's accusation against China [regarding Darfur] was not objective."

— *Xinhua news agency (China), October 2006*

Luiz Inacio Lula da Silva

President, Brazil

Brazil has rights too

"Bolivia's nationalization of its gas reserves was a necessary adjustment for a suffering people seeking a greater measure of control over their own resources. However, the fact that Bolivia has rights does not deny the fact that Brazil has rights in the matter as well."

— *AP Worldstream, May 2006*

Dmitry Peskov

Deputy Presidential Spokesman, Russia

Russia depends on Europe, too

"I think the authors of such an idea [gas OPEC] simply fail to understand our thesis about energy security. Our main thesis is interdependence of producers and consumers. Only a madman could think that Russia would start to blackmail Europe using gas, because we depend to the same extent on European customers."

— *Financial Times, November 2006*

Carlos Lopes

Political Analyst, Brazil

Lula is weak

"Presidential meetings don't resolve technical questions. They're symbolic, and the symbolism was bad from Brazil's viewpoint. Bolivia's sovereignty defends Bolivia, not Brazil. Brazil's role is to defend its interests. . . . Its attitude was very weak, but that's Lula."

— *AP Worldstream, May 2006*

Uzeir Jafarov

Military Expert, Azerbaijan

Iran threatens U.S. oil interests

"Even if Azerbaijan gives no consent to using its territory by U.S. troops, it should be not ruled out that Tehran, being in a desperate situation, would strike objects of U.S. economic interests in Azerbaijan: works in the Caspian Sea, the Baku-Tbilisi-Ceyhan pipeline."

— *United Press International, April 2006*

Arcadio Esquivel/La Prens., Panama

11

Oil Jitters

Peter Katel

Heavy traffic in Beijing last August reflects the rising demand for energy in China and other developing nations. China had just 22 million cars and "light-duty vehicles" in 2005, with 10 times as many projected by 2030. By comparison, the United States, with a quarter of China's 1.3 billion population, had 250 million motor vehicles.

AFP/Getty Images/Teh Eng Koon

O n a recent trip to Beijing, David Sandalow saw the world's energy future, and it wasn't pretty. "They tell me there are almost 1,000 new cars a day on the streets," says Sandalow, a senior fellow at the Brookings Institution think tank. "If those cars and trucks use oil in the same way the current fleet does, we're in trouble, for a lot of reasons."

Sandalow, author of the 2007 book *Freedom From Oil*, isn't alone. [1] The top economic researcher at the International Energy Agency (IEA) recently gave oil industry representatives in London a dire warning. "If we don't do something very quickly, and in a bold manner," said Fatih Birol, "our energy system's wheels may fall off." [2]

Demand for the key fuel of modern life is shooting up, especially in the developing world, but production isn't keeping pace, the IEA reports. Within the next seven years, Birol predicted, the gap will exceed 13 million barrels of oil a day — or 15 percent of the world's current output. [3]

"Rising global energy demand poses a real and growing threat to the world's energy security," said the IEA's 2007 annual report. "If governments around the world stick with current policies, the world's energy needs would be well over 50 percent higher in 2030 than today. China and India together account for 45 percent of the increase in demand in this scenario." [4]

The IEA delivered its message when intense oil jitters had pushed crude oil prices as high as they've ever been: close to $100 a barrel in December 2007 and more than $3 per gallon at U.S. gas pumps.*

From *CQ Researcher*,
January 4, 2008.

---

* The IEA was founded in Paris in 1974 during the first post-World War II oil crisis to help ensure a steady supply of reasonably priced fuel for the world's industrialized nations.

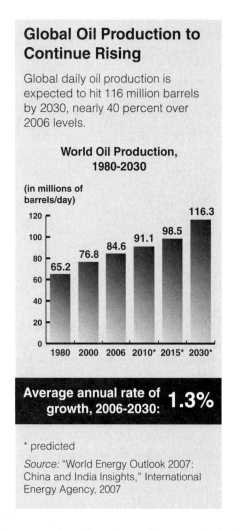

Global Oil Production to Continue Rising

Global daily oil production is expected to hit 116 million barrels by 2030, nearly 40 percent over 2006 levels.

World Oil Production, 1980-2030

(in millions of barrels/day)

Year	Production
1980	65.2
2000	76.8
2006	84.6
2010*	91.1
2015*	98.5
2030*	116.3

Average annual rate of growth, 2006-2030: 1.3%

* predicted

Source: "World Energy Outlook 2007: China and India Insights," International Energy Agency, 2007

The increases reflected a variety of concerns, including worries that supplies would be interrupted by possible U.S. or Israeli military strikes against Iran or a potential Turkish incursion into northern Iraq. "The latest run-up . . . has to do with fear," said Lawrence J. Goldstein, an economist at the Energy Policy Research Foundation. [5]

Fears of Middle East war choking off oil flow have hit several times since 1973, when Arab nations launched an oil embargo against the United States and other countries in retribution for their support for Israel in a war with its neighbors. Iraqi dictator Saddam Hussein prompted another scare when he invaded Kuwait in 1990.

This time, though, the headline-induced jitters have emerged along with deeper worries about a variety of developments: rising oil demand from rapidly industrializing China and India; depletion of oil reserves in the United States, Europe and possibly the Middle East and the fact that since the 1960s, most of the world's oil has switched from corporate to government ownership, as in Iran, Venezuela and Russia. [6]

"Nationally owned companies are less efficient, and the traditional international majors [big oil firms] don't control as much of the resource as they used to," says Kenneth B. Medlock III, an energy studies fellow at the James A. Baker III Institute for Public Policy at Rice University in Houston.

Meanwhile, the world's total production of about 84 million barrels a day is spoken for. There is virtually no spare oil — "excess capacity," in industry jargon. [7] The United States alone consumes nearly a quarter of today's world production — about 20 million barrels a day.

Concern about rising demand for oil by industrializing nations is compounded by the fact that oil is a nonrenewable resource and plays such a major role in other parts of the global economy.

"Oil (and natural gas) are the essential components in the fertilizer on which world agriculture depends; oil makes it possible to transport food to the totally non-self-sufficient megacities of the world," writes Daniel Yergin, an oil historian and chairman of Cambridge Energy Research Associates, a consulting firm. "Oil also provides the plastics and chemicals that are the bricks and mortar of contemporary civilization — a civilization that would collapse if the world's oil wells suddenly went dry." [8]

Oil's central role in the world marketplace means that an economic slow-down can push down demand for oil, while an economic boom raises demand. With the subprime mortgage crisis slowing down the U.S. economy, oil prices are likely to fall somewhat, says J. Robinson West, chairman of PFC Energy, a Houston-based consulting firm. "Then the economy rebounds, and oil demand picks up again. That's when you're going to see prices go through the roof. There's going to be a crunch, where demand outstrips supply."

* On Jan. 2, 2008, crude oil prices hit the milestone $100-a-barrel mark for the first time. Violence in Nigeria's oil-producing region and speculative trading were blamed for the jump. In April 1980, during the turmoil that followed the 1979 Iranian revolution, prices were actually higher when adjusted for inflation: $102.81 a barrel.

West, who directed U.S. offshore oil policy during the Reagan administration, doesn't think the world is about to run out of oil altogether. He is a member of the chorus of oil-watchers who generally fault state-owned oil companies (except Saudi Arabia's and Brazil's) for not reinvesting at least some of their oil income in exploration and equipment maintenance — so they can keep the oil cash pouring in. "Politicians don't care about the oil industry, they care about the money."

Some other experts question how much of the run-up in oil prices is driven by doubts over supply capacity, and how much by financial speculators who benefit financially if prices move in the direction they have forecast. "The biggest thing that traders are now playing is the fear card," says Fadel Gheit, head energy analyst at Oppenheimer & Co., a Wall Street investment firm. "Commodity traders are spinning every piece of information that can embellish their position."

A 2006 report by the Senate's Permanent Subcommittee on Investigations of the Committee on Homeland Security and Governmental Affairs traced an energy futures trading boom to congressional action in 2000 that freed energy commodity trading on electronic exchanges from regulatory oversight. [9]

But traders make a convenient target, one economics writer argues. "They are speculating against real risks — the risk that oil from the Persian Gulf could be cut off; that hurricanes in the Gulf of Mexico could damage U.S. oil rigs and refineries; that political events elsewhere (in Russia, Nigeria, Venezuela) could curtail supplies," columnist Robert Samuelson wrote in *The Washington Post.* "High prices reflect genuine uncertainties." [10]

Further complicating the oil-supply picture, Saudi Arabia and other big producers are devoting an increasing percentage of their petroleum to expanding their own economies — effectively withholding oil from the market (*See p. 306.*) Advocates of the "peak oil" thesis argue that major global oil reserves — including those in Saudi Arabia — have hit the point at which about half of the oil they can yield has already been produced.

"Over the years, we've just always assumed that over time we always find more oil — because over time we always found more oil," says Houston energy consultant Matthew R. Simmons, a leading proponent of the peak oil theory. But the world seems to have run out of mega-fields, he says.

In fact, Simmons says, major discoveries since the late 1960s can be counted on the fingers of one hand. In 1967 came Prudhoe Bay in Alaska; about 10 billion of its 13 billion barrels of recoverable oil already have been pumped, according to BP, which operates the field. [11]

Since then, exploration has yielded a 13-billion-barrel Caspian Sea reservoir owned by Kazakhstan, a 3-to-5-billion-barrel U.S. field 3,500 feet under the Gulf of Mexico and a 5-to-8-billion-barrel field off the Brazilian coast. [12]

Some experts say such recent discoveries suggest that new exploration and production technology will supply the world with oil into the indefinite future. "What's really happening is the opening up of a whole new horizon in the ultra-deep waters of the Gulf of Mexico, and it looks like the upside is very significant," said Yergin, a critic of peak oil theory. But, he added, "It will take time and billions of dollars to get there." [13]

U.S. Oil Consumption Exceeds Production

The U.S. has continually consumed more oil than it has produced. The disparity between consumption and production exceeded 12 million barrels per day in 2006, forcing America to import more oil.

U.S. oil consumption and production, 1965-2005

Source: U.S. Energy Information Administration

A gas station burns in Tehran on June, 27, 2007, during protests against efforts by the Iranian government to reduce consumption by imposing gas rationing.

Indeed, recent discoveries come nowhere near the spectacular discoveries that launched the oil age. The Middle East set the standard for mega-discoveries. Even after decades of production, its reserves were estimated at 266.8 billion barrels in 2006. Oil behemoth Saudi Arabia, for example, was producing 8.6 million barrels a day in August 2007. [14] U.S. production for 2006 was 5.1 million barrels a day.

But because Saudi Arabia doesn't release detailed figures on oilfield-by-oilfield production, Simmons questions the country's reserve estimates. "I don't think there's a shred of evidence" to back up Saudi reserve numbers, he says. More cautiously, the Government Accountability Office (GAO) notes the "potential unreliability" of reserve data from members of the Organization of Petroleum Exporting Countries (OPEC), among whom Saudi Arabia leads in reported reserves. That issue is "particularly problematic," the GAO reports, because OPEC countries together hold more than three-quarters of the world's known oil reserves. [15]

Cambridge Energy Research Associates estimates Middle Eastern reserves at 662 billion barrels as of November 2006 — or about 15 percent of the world's total reserves of 4.82 trillion barrels. "Key producing countries such as Saudi Arabia have a vast reserve and resource base," the firm reported. "There is no credible technical analysis that we are aware of that demon-

strates its productive capacity will suddenly fall in the near term." [16]

Other experts see production problems even if the peak oil theorists are wrong. Edward L. Morse, chief energy economist at Lehman Brothers, a New York investment bank, calculates that if Venezuela, Nigeria, Iraq and Iran were producing oil more efficiently, 6 million barrels a day more would be available to the world market. By contrast, the peak debate centers on technical issues, including the geology of oil reservoirs. Consequently, "Why should I believe in peak oil?" asks Morse, a deputy assistant secretary of State for energy policy during the Carter administration. The International Energy Agency guardedly shares Morse's skepticism about supply. "New capacity additions . . . are expected to increase over the next five years," the agency said. "But it is far from clear whether they will be sufficient to compensate for the decline in output at existing fields." [17]

To compensate, Birol said China, India and other big energy consumers need to step up energy efficiency efforts "right away and in a bold manner. We want more action, instead of more targets, more meetings and more talks." [18]

As oil-watchers monitor trends and conservation plans, here are some of the issues in debate:

Have global oil supplies peaked?

When a country's oil resources peak — or hit the point where half the oil is gone — it happens without warning, said a veteran energy company executive and researcher, Robert L. Hirsch, who conducted a peak-oil study in 2005 for the U.S. Department of Energy. That's what happened in North America, Britain, Norway, Argentina, Colombia and Egypt, Hirsch said. "In most cases, it was not obvious that production was about to peak a year ahead of the event. . . . In most cases the peaks were sharp, not gently varying or flat-topped, as some forecasters hope. In some cases, post-peak production declines were quite rapid." [19]

But Cambridge Energy Research Associates argues that a global peak — when it is reached many decades from now — will not mark the beginning of a precipitous drop-off. "Global production will eventually follow an "undulating plateau" for one or more decades before declining slowly," the firm said. [20]

A study by the nonpartisan GAO adds to the uncertainty over oil reserves. "The amount of oil remaining in the ground is highly uncertain," the agency concluded, "in part because the Organization of Petroleum Exporting Countries controls most of the estimated world oil reserves, but its estimates . . . are not verified by independent auditors." [21]

In part, debate turns on the extent to which oil producers can turn to so-called "unconventional" sources. Shale oil — a form of petroleum extracted by applying very high temperatures to certain types of rock formations abundant in parts of the American West — has been viewed for decades as an alternative to conventional crude oil. The GAO reported that one-half million to 1 million barrels a day could be extracted from U.S. shale within 10 years, though the process is expensive and energy-intensive. [22]

Oil can also be extracted from tar sands which have become one of Canada's major sources of petroleum. An oil-sands boom is under way in Canada, which is producing about 1.2 million barrels of oil from sands in Alberta Province, though the process requires burning so much natural gas that emissions have done considerable environmental damage. [23]

Cambridge Energy Research Associates said in its rebuttal of the "peak" thesis that oil sands and other unconventional sources may account for 6 percent of global production by 2030. [24]

Peak oil thesis advocates argue that unconventional sources won't suffice for the world's needs. They turn the argument back to the region still considered the globe's main petroleum reservoir, the Middle East. Houston investment banker Simmons says that a lack of verifiable information about Middle Eastern reserves lies at the heart of peak oil theory.

"These optimists — I'm happy they're so happy about things — but they have no data to base their case on," Simmons says. "We have passed peak oil, and demand is not going to slow down." Simmons' 2005 book, *Twilight in the Desert*, is a major text of the hypothesis. [25]

Simmons insists his projections and forecasts are more data-driven than those of peak oil critics. "That's one of the reasons I boldly predicted in 1995 that the North Sea was likely to peak by 1998-2000," Simmons says. "The major oil company people said I was nuts. All I did was look at the reports."

Experts agree the North Sea passed its high point and that the industry is doing its best to pump out the remaining crude. "Oil and gas production has peaked, [and] the industry is concentrating on managing the decline," said Trisha O'Reilly, communications director of Oil and Gas UK, the trade association of North Sea oil producers. "There's still a sizable prize out there." [26]

Some oil insiders accept parts of the peak oil argument, but others dismiss it as panic-mongering that only drives up prices for the benefit of price speculators. "Peak oil theory is a lot of baloney," says energy analyst Gheit, at Oppenheimer & Co. "We are consuming more, but we are finding more than we consume; reserves continue to bulge."

Vastly improved technology has facilitated the discovery of new reservoirs even in well-developed fields, Gheit and others argue. For example, he says, "In the old days, when they built the first platform in the North Sea, it was like a very big table made of concrete with hollow legs. Now there is something called sub-sea completion, where all the equipment is sitting on the ocean floor, and everything is robotically controlled."

West of PFC Energy agrees that while onshore U.S. fields and the North Sea have peaked and been squeezed "dry" thanks to technological advances, "there are parts of the Middle East and Russia that are virtually unexplored."

But peaking may be more widespread than some industry insiders say, another oil expert argues. "People are asking the right questions about peak oil, but they're asking about the wrong country," says David Pursell, managing director of Tudor Pickering, a Houston-based investment firm. "We know that Mexico has peaked. When does Russia peak?"

Will the rising energy needs of India, China and other developing countries keep oil prices high?

The newest twist in the volatile world of global oil economics is growing petroleum demand by Earth's two population giants — China (1.3 billion people) and India (1.1 billion people) — which together account for more than a third of the planet's 6.6 billion population. The two huge nations have been maintaining annual economic growth of about 10 percent a year, sparking intense demand among new members of their rising middle classes for cars and other energy-intensive consumer goods.

China had 22 million cars and "light-duty vehicles" on the road in 2005, with 10 times as many projected in 2030. In India, a tenfold increase is also expected — from 11 million to 115 million, according to the Paris-based International Energy Agency (IEA). [27] By comparison, there are about 250 million cars and other motor vehicles in the United States, or slightly more than one for each of the approximately 240 million adults in the population. [28]

Most Oil Belongs to OPEC Nations

Members of the Organization of Petroleum Exporting Countries (OPEC) held more than three-quarters of the world's 1.2 trillion barrels of crude oil reserves in 2006 (left). Most OPEC oil reserves are in the Middle East, with Saudi Arabia, Iran and Iraq holding 56 percent of the OPEC total (right).

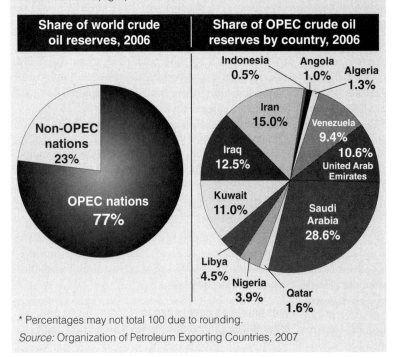

Share of world crude oil reserves, 2006

Non-OPEC nations 23%

OPEC nations 77%

Share of OPEC crude oil reserves by country, 2006

Indonesia 0.5%
Angola 1.0%
Algeria 1.3%
Iran 15.0%
Venezuela 9.4%
10.6% United Arab Emirates
Iraq 12.5%
Kuwait 11.0%
Saudi Arabia 28.6%
Libya 4.5%
Nigeria 3.9%
Qatar 1.6%

* Percentages may not total 100 due to rounding.

Source: Organization of Petroleum Exporting Countries, 2007

If all countries maintain their present energy policies, the IEA says developing countries will account for 74 percent of the increase in worldwide energy use from all sources between 2005 and 2030, with China and Indian accounting for 45 percent of that boost. Developing countries now make up 41 percent of the global energy market. By 2030, if no policies change, those countries would account for 54 percent of world consumption. [29]

All in all, the IEA concludes, "The consequences for China, India, the OECD [Organization for Economic Cooperation and Development] and the rest of the world of unfettered growth in global energy demand are alarming . . . the world's energy needs would be well over 50 percent higher in 2030 than today."

The report goes on to recommend international efforts to reduce demand — for environmental reasons as well as to conserve oil and keep prices from skyrocket-

ing. But some experts say the growing presence of China and India in the world energy market will keep prices high no matter what measures are taken.

"You're talking about economic development in two countries that comprise a little over one-third of the world population," says Medlock at the Baker Institute. "It's going to be difficult for the energy supply to expand production at a significant enough pace to drive down prices." Only an international economic slowdown could have that effect, he adds.

But Gheit of Oppenheimer & Co. argues that major price increases generated by continued growth in demand will force China and India to adapt, just as other nations do. "Energy conservation accelerates when prices go higher — even in China and India," he says. "That's the mitigating factor. Any developing economy becomes more energy-efficient with time."

Gheit adds that the Chinese and Indian governments have a highly efficient tool at their disposal if they want to curb demand: Both countries keep gasoline prices low through subsidies. "If gasoline subsidies were to cease, demand would crash," he says. "Roads will be half-empty."

But some oil experts say China's energy demands reflect far more than stepped-up car use. "The big thrust on Chinese demand is really on production of energy-intensive goods for their export industry," says Morse at Lehman Brothers. China's policy of keeping its currency undervalued to make exports cheaper is maintaining that effort — and causing the high energy demand that results.

Communist Party leaders in China oppose ending gasoline price subsidies, according to a Lehman Brothers analysis. And even if they were eliminated, "Chinese motorists might dip into their savings, and businesses might borrow more from banks to foot higher energy bills." In the long run, however, higher prices likely would force down demand, the analysis says. [30]

In the United States, meanwhile, high gasoline prices, perhaps combined with wider economic troubles, have reduced demand. Normally, lower demand would send prices down. But some experts say the high oil demand from China and India has changed the outlook. Long term, says Pursell of Tudor Pickering in Houston, prices are going to be higher in the next 10 years than in the past 10 years.

Nonetheless, the market system continues to function, some economists point out. "At these prices, an enormous incentive exists to develop new [oil] sources," says Robert Crandall, a senior fellow at the Brookings Institution and former director of the Council on Wage and Price Stability in the Ford and Carter administrations. "My guess is that after three-four-five years, new pools will be found."

But, Crandall cautions, new oil fields may sit in regions that are difficult to reach, for geographical or political reasons.

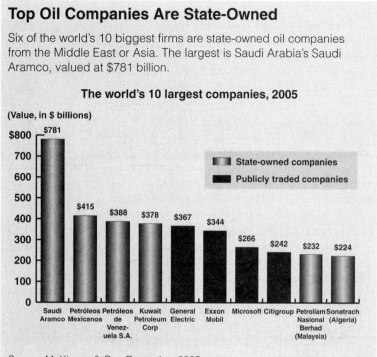

Top Oil Companies Are State-Owned

Six of the world's 10 biggest firms are state-owned oil companies from the Middle East or Asia. The largest is Saudi Arabia's Saudi Aramco, valued at $781 billion.

The world's 10 largest companies, 2005

Source: McKinsey & Co., December 2005

Can the federal government do anything to significantly reduce energy demand?

American worries about oil dependence and its effects on the global environment reached critical mass in December, when Congress passed, and President Bush signed, an energy bill designed to force major reductions in U.S. petroleum consumption. Bush, a former oilman, had previously acknowledged that the political climate now favors energy conservation. In his 2006 State of the Union address, he said, "America is addicted to oil." [31]

The new energy law includes tougher corporate average fuel efficiency (CAFE) requirement for cars and light trucks (including SUVs). They will have to meet a fleetwide average standard of 35 miles per gallon by 2020, compared with the present 27.5 miles per gallon for cars and 22.2 miles per gallon for light trucks. The bill also requires the production of 36 billion gallons of ethanol, the plant-based gasoline substitute, by 2022 — five times more than present production levels. [32]

Due to the combined effects of the fuel efficiency standard and the ethanol production boost, "We will save as much oil as we would import from the Persian Gulf — 2.59 million barrels a day," says Brendan Bell, Washington representative of the Union of Concerned Scientists, citing projected oil demand if the law hadn't been enacted.

Some disappointment could be heard amid the cheers, however, because lawmakers balked at dealing with renewable electricity. "It's really unfortunate that we didn't have the renewable electricity standard or the incentives for wind and solar," Sen. Barbara Boxer, D-Calif., chairwoman of the Senate Environment and Public Works Committee, said. "But we'll fight for those another day." [33]

Still, opposition hasn't entirely died away. Rep. F. James Sensenbrenner Jr., R-Wis., who voted against the bill, had argued at a Nov. 14 hearing of the House Select Committee on Energy Independence and Global Warming that the new energy-use standards were unlikely to have much global effect on auto efficiency or on tailpipe emissions. "These regulations may work if everybody all over the world agreed to them and then actually complied with them," Sensenbrenner said. [34]

In addition to skepticism about the likely impact of a U.S. law on world energy use, critics are also asking whether markets can be relied on, without government involvement, to resolve supply-demand imbalances. That is, will prices rise in response to scarcity? In the classic supply-demand scenario, higher prices encourage companies to find and produce more oil, because they'll make more money — though if prices rise too much, demand drops.

Some experts who hold that world oil supplies are diminishing argue that the resulting problems are too big for the market alone to handle. "Intervention by governments will be required because the economic and social implications of oil peaking would otherwise be chaotic," said the report to the Energy Department directed by former energy executive Hirsch in 2005. [35]

But two years later, Hirsch warns that government action to reduce demand won't produce immediate results. "We have to do it, but we can't be unrealistic in our expectations," Hirsch says. "If you pass a dramatic increase in CAFE now, a significant number of new cars will not show up for about three years. It takes that long to get prepared with parts suppliers, assembly lines and so forth. And people may not buy the cars unless they're feeling pained or are required to by the government."

Government intervention would do far more harm than good, argues Jerry Taylor, a senior fellow at the Cato Institute, a libertarian think tank. "One thing markets are good at doing is allocating scarce resources among competing users, based on ability to pay," he says. "A peak in global oil production would send a very strong signal to consumers that oil is going to become scarce. If government decides to help steer the economy through a peak scenario, its main mission will be to dull that price signal to make sure consumers don't get it in the teeth."

But even some Wall Street energy experts argue that tougher fuel efficiency standards are long overdue. "If we'd had [the 35-miles-per-gallon] standard in place in 1990," says Morse of Lehman Brothers, "we'd be consuming 2 million barrels a day less now, and we'd be consuming 3 million barrels a day less if we had imposed the fuel efficiency standards on trucks that we have on cars."

No new standards or sudden consumer preference for fuel-efficient gasoline-electricity hybrid cars in the near future will have a dramatic effect on oil demand, another industry expert says. "It's a feel-good measure in the near term," says Pursell of Tudor Pickering in Houston. "In the long term, it probably makes sense. But we have

roughly 150 million cars on the road." With so many cars, he says, requiring better fuel efficiency for new cars would take years to show results.

"So what can you do in the near term?" Pursell asks. "Drive less." He adds that his fellow Texans, who favor big vehicles on the long roads they travel, don't cotton to the idea of cutting back on time behind the wheel.

Another veteran oil analyst argues that market reaction to changing conditions is already well under way. "We have reached a saturation point on cars," says Gheit of Oppenheimer & Co., citing anecdotal but plentiful evidence of jam-packed streets and highways throughout the country. "Everywhere you go you're stuck in traffic. You go out and you can't find parking. These things are beginning to take a toll on the number of cars sold in North America."

And the cars that are sold are more fuel-efficient than earlier models, Gheit says. Hence the market is coming up with its own solutions. "You're seeing more and more advancement. Economic advancement comes with much more energy efficiency."

BACKGROUND

Energy Shock

In 1956, M. King Hubbert, a geologist for Shell Oil, told the American Petroleum Institute (API) that he had determined when U.S. oil production would hit its peak. After calculating the maximum reserves of U.S. oil fields (200 billion barrels) and the rates at which oil companies would keep pumping, he announced that the peak year would arrive in the 1970s. [36]

As it happened, U.S. production peaked in 1970, many experts say, when the United States was producing about 10 million barrels a day. Today, production has fallen by about half. [37] "We picked up again in the late '70s but still didn't go back to the previous high," says Ron Planting, an API economist.

But in 1956, Americans in general and the oil industry in particular believed American wells would be spouting oil and gas into the indefinite future. So when Hubbert announced his conclusion, "It was as if a physician had diagnosed virulent, metastasized cancer; denial was one of the responses," writes Kenneth S. Deffeyes, a retired professor of geology at Princeton University who was a protégé of Hubbert's at Shell. [38]

Some analysts take issue with the notion that Hubbert has been proved right. Technological advances have made it possible to probe oil and gas formations more accurately, leading to increased production in some cases, and recalculation — upwards — of reserves.

At the time of Hubbert's forecast, there was growing resentment among the oil-producing countries of the Middle East and Latin America of the power wielded by the "big eight" foreign oil companies, half of them American (the so-called "Seven Sisters," plus France's state-owned oil company). While the foreign companies controlled the price of a resource that the world depended on, the supplying countries had little say. [39] After a few years of quiet discussion, ministers from Saudi Arabia, Venezuela, Kuwait, Iraq and Iran convened in Baghdad in 1960 to form the Organization of Petroleum Exporting Countries. The objective was simple: to manage prices by controlling production.

In its early years, however, OPEC swung little weight, largely because the big oil companies were making major discoveries in countries that weren't — yet — members of the new organization. Over the years, the membership expanded to include Qatar, Indonesia, Libya, Nigeria and Angola. Two other countries — Ecuador and Gabon — joined in the 1970s but dropped out in the '90s.

As soon as the United States began depending on foreign oil, events showed that dependency had made the country vulnerable.

Following the 1973 Yom Kippur War, which pitted Israel against Egypt, Syria and Iraq, Arab OPEC nations retaliated against the United States and other Israeli allies by launching an oil embargo against them.

The embargo began on Oct. 17, 1973, and almost overnight 4 million barrels of oil a day were removed from world supplies. Demand rose 7 percent above supply, and international prices quadrupled from $3 a barrel to $12. Some saw the boycott as vindication of predictions that the energy foundation on which Western civilization depended would dry up. "The party is over," declared E. F. Schumacher, a British economist who had long prophesied an end to cheap oil. [40]

To prevent the high oil price from rippling through the economy, President Richard M. Nixon imposed price controls on oil. And his successor, Gerald R. Ford, established the Strategic Petroleum Reserve, an emergency stockpile that today has about 695 million barrels. [41]

But the boycott that gave rise to those measures ended in March 1974 — five months after it had begun. Egyptian President Anwar Sadat declared that the supply cutoff had served its purpose: to demonstrate to the West that it needed to push Israel to resolve its longstanding conflict with its Arab neighbors and with the Palestinians.

Even as the memories — and frustrations — of the Arab boycott faded, Ford's successor warned the country about potential future emergencies. "This is the greatest challenge our country will face during our lifetimes," President Jimmy Carter said in a nationally televised speech on April 18, 1977. [42] Some commentators said the speech paved the way for Ronald Reagan's 1980 election as president. Reagan portrayed himself as the optimistic alternative to gloomy Democrats.

Meanwhile, however, the 1979 Iranian revolution renewed America's sense of energy vulnerability after Shah Mohammed Reza Pahlavi — a close U.S. ally who ruled an oil superpower — was toppled by Muslim radicals who made anti-Americanism a tenet of their doctrine.

On Nov. 4, 1979, Iranian revolutionaries seized the U.S. Embassy and took 52 employees hostage — holding them for 444 days. Panic took hold of energy markets again, and prices shot up to the $45-per-barrel range, as high as they'd ever been. [43] During both the 1973 and 1979 crises American motorists sat in long lines at service stations, and some station owners who were short on supplies began rationing gasoline. During the second "oil shock," Congress funded research into alternative fuels and encouraged Americans to conserve fuel.

Then, even before the hostages were released in early 1981, Iraqi dictator Saddam Hussein attacked Iran. Oil exports by the two countries virtually ceased for a time, as production facilities were bombed during the first months of fighting in 1980. About 4 million barrels a day vanished from the market, setting off a new round of panic buying. The eight-year war eventually had little lasting effect on oil markets.

Conoumoro Co Wild

After the disruptions caused by war and revolution, market forces restored stability to oil trade. The law of supply and demand got a big assist from Saudi Arabia, the world's biggest oil producer. Worried that a prolonged period of high prices would cut oil demand by newly conservation-minded Western countries — and force

CHRONOLOGY

1950s-1970s *Oil imports ease concerns about decreasing U.S. oil supplies — until big oil-producing nations suspend their shipments.*

1956 Shell Oil geologist forecasts that the U.S. oil supply will plateau in the early 1970s.

1960 Saudi Arabia, Venezuela and other oil giants form Organization of Petroleum Exporting Countries (OPEC).

1970-1972 U.S. oil reserves peak, as predicted.

1973 Arab members of OPEC cut off oil exports to the United States and other allies of Israel, causing oil prices to skyrocket. The embargo ends in March 1974.

1975 President Gerald R. Ford signs the Energy Policy and Conservation Act, imposing fuel economy standards on carmakers.

1977 President Jimmy Carter calls energy conservation the country's biggest challenge.

1979 Revolution topples the U.S.-backed shah of Iran, prompting oil price spikes in the United States and other big oil-consuming nations.

1980s *New non-OPEC oil sources are discovered or come online, vastly expanding world oil supplies and causing prices to plummet.*

1980 Non-OPEC oil supply expands by about 6 million barrels a day after Mexico's daily production rises, new North Sea sources come online and drilling is stepped up in Alaska. . . . Iraq attacks Iran.

1983 OPEC cuts prices from $34 a barrel to $29.

1985 Oil falls to $10 a barrel; Saudi Arabia steps up output and abandons efforts to prop up prices.

1988 Iran-Iraq War ends, removing source of potential oil-market disruption.

1990s *Steady supply of cheap oil sparks popularity of gas-guzzling sport-utility vehicles (SUVs), but trouble looms by decade's end.*

1990 Automakers sell 750,000 SUVs; annual sales hit 3 million 10 years later. . . . Iraqi leader Saddam Hussein invades Kuwait, prompting fears about Saudi oil security.

1991 U.S.-led forces oust Iraq from Kuwait, maintain protective presence in Saudi Arabia.

1996 Russia begins developing oil production facilities in its Far East region. . . . Saudi Islamist Osama bin Laden releases manifesto attacking U.S. military presence in Saudi Arabia.

1998 Socialist Hugo Chávez is elected president of Venezuela.

2000s *Terrorism, war and fear of war disrupt oil prices in the Middle East.*

Sept. 11, 2001 Arab terrorists crash hijacked U.S. jetliners into the World Trade Center and Pentagon, killing nearly 3,000 people.

2002-2003 Venezuelan oil workers strike against the Chávez government's efforts to reduce production, pushing prices up.

2003 U.S.-led coalition invades Iraq, topples Saddam.

2004 Insurgents attack Iraqi oil facilities, prompting price fluctuations.

2005 Gas hits $3 a gallon in the U.S. . . . Author of a report on "peak oil" tells lawmakers government should prepare for possible oil shortage.

2006 Saudi Arabia's oil consumption rises by 2 million barrels a day in one year. . . . Chávez pledges to sell China 1 million barrels of oil a day by 2012.

2007 International Energy Agency warns of looming oil shortfall. . . . Crude oil price nears $100 per barrel. . . . President George W. Bush signs new energy bill including a fuel-efficiency standard of 35 miles per gallon for cars and light trucks by 2020. . . . Environmental Protection Agency denies California and 16 other states the right to set auto emission standards.

Jan. 2, 2008 Crude oil price hits $100.

prices lower — Saudi Arabia had been steadily increasing its production. Non-members of OPEC followed suit.

Other developments were at work as well. After the oil shocks of the 1970s, energy companies stepped up exploration outside the turbulent Middle East. By the early 1980s, the results began pouring in.

At least 6 million barrels a day were added to world oil supplies by Britain and Norway's production in the North Sea, a new pipeline from Alaska's rich North Slope to the port of Valdez and a major discovery in Mexican waters in the Gulf of Mexico. The new output, coming from outside the OPEC circle, was within striking distance of Saudi Arabia, which in 1981 reached a top daily production level of about 9.8 million barrels. [44]

Meanwhile, the effects of conservation measures adopted during the 1970s kicked in. The most significant was a 1975 law setting tough corporate average fuel efficiency (CAFE) standards for new cars of 27.5 miles per gallon by 1985. The measure would save about 2 million barrels of gasoline a day. [45]

Production from the new oil fields combined with new conservation efforts would have been enough by themselves to push oil prices down. But a third factor emerged as well: In a newly restabilized geopolitical environment, oil companies began selling off oil that they'd been holding in storage against the possibility of long-lasting shortages. Companies couldn't justify the considerable expense of warehousing the oil.

By March 1983, OPEC was feeling the pressure from an oil glut that it couldn't control by shutting down production, because much of the new supply came from outside the organization's control. So OPEC took the unprecedented step of cutting prices from about $34 per barrel to about $29. With the world oil supply still plentiful and with new CAFE standards reducing demand, prices kept falling even further. In 1985, with oil at $10 a barrel, Saudi Arabia gave up trying to limit OPEC output and stepped up its own shipments.

American automakers and consumers, meanwhile, reacted in their own ways. Unconcerned (for the moment) about oil prices and supplies, manufacturers began expanding their production of popular SUVs. Classified by the government as "light trucks," the gas-guzzling SUVs were subject to less rigorous fuel efficiency standards.

"Gasoline remained readily available, and its price stayed flat instead of soaring to the $20 a gallon level once predicted by energy forecasters," a journalist specializing in the auto industry wrote in 1996. [46]

In 1990, carmakers sold 750,000 SUVs nationwide. By 2000, annual sales were approaching 3 million.

By the mid-1990s, however, there were warning signs that the latest cheap-oil era might be ending. The signs included a little-noticed 1996 anti-American manifesto by a Saudi Arabian millionaire and veteran of Afghanistan's U.S.-aided war against Soviet occupation in 1979-1989. By then, Osama bin Laden had developed a deep hatred for the United States, and he decried the presence in Saudi Arabia of American troops, which had been providing security for the oil giant ever since Saddam Hussein invaded Kuwait during the Persian Gulf War of 1990-1991. [47]

Tide Turns Again

The terrorist attacks of Sept. 11, 2001, for which bin Laden later claimed responsibility, might have been expected to cause a major disruption in the oil market. Indeed, only hours after the terrorists struck, prices on the International Oil Exchange in London rose by 13 percent, to $31.05 a barrel. And as rumors of major shortages swept through parts of the United States, some drivers in Oklahoma City saw prices at the pump surge to $5 a gallon. [48]

But the wholesale and pump price spikes proved momentary. No terrorists hit any oil facilities, and OPEC immediately issued a market-calming declaration that it would not use the oil weapon against the United States for whatever military action it took to answer the attacks. Overall, the average wholesale price paid by U.S. refineries in September was lower than they'd paid the previous month — a drop from $24.44 a barrel to $23.73. "By October 2001, the economy was having more effect on the price of oil — in terms of weakening oil demand and reducing oil prices — than the price of oil was having on the economy," the Congressional Research Service concluded in a report a year after the attacks. Demand weakened in part because airplane travel dropped in the immediate aftermath of the attacks. [49]

As the decade wore on, however, a series of developments began to push prices higher. By late 2004, oil was commanding about $50 a barrel. Analysts cited the effects of the war in Iraq in reducing that country's production and export capacity, as well as the economic booms already under way in China and India.

How Times Have Changed

Now petrostates are bailing out U.S. firms

Only a few decades ago, American oil companies stood among the petroleum giants that controlled most of the world's oil, and their profits largely were recycled back into the United States.

But times have changed. "For some time now," writes former Treasury Secretary Lawrence H. Summers, "the large flow of capital from the developing to the industrialized world has been the principal irony of the international financial system." [1]

In today's world, a tiny Persian Gulf state can rescue a major American bank from financial catastrophe using money earned from selling millions of barrels of oil. And politicians in Europe and the United States are nervous about their nations' companies being bought up by cash-swollen petrostates.

"Their wealth is a reminder to our politicians that the West is no longer the force it once was in the world," wrote Michael Gordon, fixed-income director at Fidelity International, a giant investment-management firm. "And just maybe, business leaders are ahead of the politicians in welcoming this infusion of new money into the global financial system." [2]

Last year, U.S. lawmakers of both parties scuttled a deal that would have allowed a company owned by the government of Dubai* to run six major U.S. ports. "This proposal may require additional congressional action in order to ensure that we are fully protecting Americans at home," wrote House Speaker J. Dennis Hastert, R-Ill. [3]

---

* Dubai is one of seven Arabian Peninsula city-states that constitute the United Arab Emirates.

Political jitters over the wide range of foreign government funds invested don't all center on the oil-rich countries. China, which has grown rich selling cheap goods to the rest of the world, has set alarm bells ringing on Wall Street over attempted investments in American and other Western companies. In 2005, a political firestorm forced China's state-owned oil company to abandon a bid to buy Unocal, a U.S. oil company. [4]

China's sheer size and strategic importance guarantee continuing interest in its investment projects. But high oil prices in 2007 have focused attention on efforts by oil-exporting countries to invest their profits — totaling a mind-boggling $3.4-$3.8 trillion — much of it in the West, according to the McKinsey Global Institute.

And the developing world's cash situation is expected to get even more dramatic in the future. "The most conservative assumptions you could think of, absent some catastrophic event, would have [these assets] double by 2012," Diana Farrell, the institute's director, said in December. [5]

In fact, even if the price of oil falls from current levels (now above $90 a barrel) to $50 a barrel, petrodollar assets would expand to $5.9 trillion by 2012, the institute says, fueling investment at a rate of about $1 billion a day. [6]

Political resistance to Middle Eastern oil profits buying up American companies surfaced even before oil prices sky-rocketed in 2007. In 2006, Dubai PortsWorld bought a British firm that ran port operations in New York City, New Jersey, Philadelphia, Baltimore, Miami and New Orleans. Lawmakers of both parties lost no time in denouncing the deal with an Arab nation as a threat to

---

By 2005, gas prices nationwide had passed $3 a gallon. Oil and marketing experts had long contended that the $3 price was a critical threshold. Rebecca Lindland, an automotive industry analyst for Global Insight, a research firm in Waltham, Mass., had told *The New York Times* in 2004 that consumers would change their driving and car-buying behavior if prices at the pump exceeded $3 a gallon for at least six months. [50] The forecast proved accurate. As higher prices stayed steady, SUV lovers started shying away from sport-utility vehicles. "I

really want my Explorer back, but I'm thinking about not getting it because of gas prices," said Angie Motylinski, a bank teller in Sylvania, Ohio, whose lease was expiring. "If they gave me an awesome, awesome deal, I might consider it. But who's going to want it when gas is $3.19 a gallon?" [51]

Other Sylvanians were thinking similar thoughts. "If I had a dollar for every time that somebody said I'm looking for something with better gas mileage, I'd be a wealthy man," said Bill Roemer, the manager

national security, and the government of Dubai eventually sold its interest in the U.S. operations. [7]

But some international finance experts urge politicians and others to look at other implications, such as whether foreign-owned companies could end up unduly influencing domestic policy. "What about the day when a country joins some 'coalition of the willing' and asks the U.S. president to support a tax break for a company in which it has invested?" Summers asked, using Bush administration terminology for U.S. allies in the Iraq War. "Or when a decision has to be made about whether to bail out a company, much of whose debt is held by an ally's central bank?" [8]

In the 1950s, the oil-rich countries worried about foreign involvement in their economic and political affairs. For instance, the Iranians did not take kindly to the U.S.-organized 1953 coup in Iran that ousted Prime Minister Mohammed Mossadeq, who had nationalized a British-owned oil company. And oil-producing countries also resented foreign oil companies' control of petroleum pricing and marketing. Eventually, most countries nationalized their oil resources. [9]

Now the situation is almost reversed, with the industrialized countries coming to depend on the oil countries for oil as well as cash.

But that's not necessarily a bad thing, some experts note, because investments in the industrialized world give the oil

A firm owned by the government of Dubai backed out of a 2006 deal to run six U.S. ports after U.S. lawmakers protested.

countries a stake in maintaining stability and prosperity, not to mention a market for petroleum. "If the U.S. goes in the tank, the whole world goes in the tank," says Kenneth Medlock III, an energy research fellow at the James A. Baker III Institute for Public Policy at Rice University in Houston. "That would put a crimp in oil demand."

[1] See Lawrence Summers, "Sovereign funds shake the logic of capitalism," *Financial Times* (London), July 30, 2007, p. A11.

[2] See Michael Gordon, "Ignore the murk and myths on sovereign funds," *Financial Times* (London), Dec. 12, 2007, p. A13.

[3] Quoted in Jim VandeHei and Jonathan Weisman, "Bush Threatens Veto Against Bid to Stop Port Deal," *The Washington Post*, Feb. 22, 2006, p. A1.

[4] See Jad Mouwad, "Foiled Bid Stirs Worry for U.S. Oil," *The New York Times*, Aug. 11, 2005, www.nytimes.com/2005/08/11/business/worldbusiness/11unocal.html?_r=1&oref=slogin.

[5] See "Sovereign Wealth Fund Briefing," (transcript) Brookings Institution, Dec. 6, 2007, p. 16, www.brookings.edu/~/media/Files/events/2007/1206_sovereign_wealth_funds/1206_sovereign_wealth _funds.pdf.

[6] See "The New Power Brokers: How Oil, Asia, Hedge Funds, and Private Equity are Shaping Global Capital Markets," McKinsey Global Institute, October 2007, pp. 12-13, www.mckinsey.com/mgi/publications/The_New_Power_Brokers/index.asp.

[7] See Richard Simon and Peter Wallsten, "Bush to Fight for Port Deal," Los Angeles Times, Feb. 22, 2006, p. A1; "Dubai Firm Details Plans for U.S. Ports," *Los Angeles Times* (The Associated Press), March 16, 2006, p. C3.

[8] See Summers, *op. cit.*

[9] See Daniel Yergin, *The Prize: The Epic Quest for Oil, Money, and Power* (1992), pp. 511-512, 467-470.

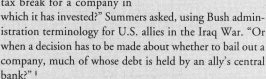

of a local Chevrolet dealership. "With gas prices the way they are, people just aren't looking at minivans, SUVs, trucks." [52]

Petro-Nationalism

As prices spiraled upwards, a trend that had begun decades earlier suddenly took on new importance for oil-watchers. In the 1970s, publicly owned firms — all in the West — owned roughly three-quarters of global petroleum; today, state-owned oil companies own three-quarters of the oil. [53] That poses a potential problem for the U.S because governments that control oil supplies may have economic and/or political reasons to limit their foreign sales. The 1973 OPEC oil embargo serves as a reminder of the potency of oil as a political weapon against the United States. And some producing countries may decide to increase the amount of oil they use at home. (*See p. 306.*) To be sure, the No. 1 international oil supplier, Saudi Arabia, still cooperates closely with the United States and other consuming countries. And

Plug-in Hybrids Offer Clean-Energy Future

New technology may enable motorists to burn less oil.

Its cities separated by hundreds of miles of windswept, open spaces, Texas may not be the place to start up a conversation about carpooling. "That's a very unpopular discussion to have here in Houston," says Kenneth B. Medlock III, speaking from his car.

"You look out on a freeway," says Medlock, an energy studies fellow at the James A. Baker III Institute for Public Policy at Houston's Rice University, "and all you see is car after car with a driver and no passengers."

Texans may be especially fond of their cars — but Lone Star State drivers aren't unique. Transportation (including airplanes and trucking) accounts for two-thirds of U.S. petroleum use, according to a July 2007 study by the National Petroleum Council. [1]

That's hardly a surprising statistic, given the size of the U.S. car and truck fleet: nearly 250 million vehicles in a nation of about 300 million. Relying on fuel efficiency standards alone to hold gasoline use in 2017 to what it was in 2005 would require improving average vehicle performance to 22 miles per gallon — a 25 percent improvement over today, researchers at the Baker Institute calculate. [2]

To reduce oil consumption to 2005 levels by conservation alone, every American would have to drive 45 miles a week less. "Basically, it's a lifestyle change," says Medlock, who worked on the study.

But some energy experts are arguing that new automotive technology will allow Americans to keep driving while burning less oil. They tout the plug-in hybrid electric vehicle (PHEV), a variant of the gasoline-electric hybrid car whose electric motor gets recharged from an ordinary wall socket. Limited-edition PHEVs — Toyota Priuses retrofitted by conversion companies or by enthusiasts — boast bigger batteries that allow drivers to cruise for about 20 miles on electric power alone, burning no gasoline. Unmodified Priuses can travel only about a half-mile on electricity alone, according to the Institute of Electrical and Electronics Engineers. PHEV advocates also say that recharging the cars at night uses surplus electricity that utilities hold in reserve for emergencies. [3]

The reliance on wall current, though, raises the question of whether the plug-ins wind up burning as much energy as the hybrid models now on sale. Alternative-energy advocates raise another objection. "If you start plugging in hundreds of cars all at once, you'll be finding out what the limits of the electricity grid are real quick," Paul Cass, a representative of Ballard Power Systems, a Canadian firm, told the *Los Angeles Times* at an alternative-vehicle convention. [4]

Nigeria and Brazil invite foreign companies to help develop national petroleum resources.

But Venezuela is headed by an anti-American president who has threatened more than once to cut off sales to the United States by its state-owned oil firm. President Hugo Chávez also plans to sell less oil to the United States and more to China. In fact, in 2006 the pugnacious Chávez vowed to sell 1 million barrels a day to China by 2012. [54]

And then there is Russia. A major buildup of production capacities in the country's Far East region has turned Russia into an oil behemoth. As such, it once again sees itself as a great power. And some of Russia's neighbors say it uses petroleum as a weapon. In winter 2006, vitally needed natural gas stopped flowing from Russia to the Republic of Georgia, headed by a president who tried to defy Russian supremacy in the region. Russia blamed a technical problem — an explanation Georgians rejected. [55]

But the major concern for private oil companies and oil-consuming countries such as the United States is not a cutoff in service by a state-owned oil firm. The big issues are access to oil fields and participation in production ventures. "Access really is a consideration," said oil historian and consultant Yergin. "Where can you go to invest money, apply technology and develop resources and bring them to market? Terms get very tough." [56]

In an ironic twist, some state-owned oil companies that have grown enormously wealthy recently have ridden to the rescue of some ailing U.S. companies. Notably, the Abu Dhabi Investment Authority spent $7.5 billion on a stake in Citigroup, bailing the big

Ballard makes hydrogen fuel cells for use in cars. Hydrogen technology, attractive to many because it uses no fossil fuels at all, is getting a big push from the government — $195.8 million in research and development money from the Department of Energy. Electric and hybrid-electric car research is getting $50.8 million. [5]

Technical arguments aside, the PHEV is far closer to dealer showrooms. "There are no truly viable hydrogen fuel cells on the market today," acknowledged Bud DeFlaviis, government-affairs director of the U.S. Fuel Cell Council, a trade group. [6]

The argument that plug-in hybrids don't reduce energy consumption overall has been persuasive, because non-nuclear power plants burn fossil fuels. That issue is especially important on the environmental-protection side of the alternative-energy debate.

But a July 2007 report gives ammunition to the PHEV advocates. After an 18-month study, the Electric Power Research Institute and the Natural Resources Defense Council (NRDC), an environmental group, concluded that widespread use of plug-in hybrids would, in 2050, reduce oil

Toyota and France's state-owned energy company plan to develop recharging stations for plug-in hybrid cars in major European cities.

consumption by 3-4 million barrels a day. It would also cut greenhouse gas emissions by 450 million metric tons a year — the equivalent of taking 82.5 million cars off the road. "Our results show that PHEVs recharged from low- and non-emitting electricity sources can decrease the carbon footprint in the nation's transportation sector," said David Hawkins, director of the NRDC Climate Center. [7]

Those numbers might be persuasive, even in Texas.

[1] "Hard Truths: Facing the Hard Truths About Energy," National Petroleum Council, July 2007, p. 46, www.npchardtruthsreport.org.

[2] See Kenneth B. Medlock III and Amy Myers Jaffe, "Gas FAQ: U.S. Gasoline Markets and U.S. Oil Import Dependence," James A. Baker III Institute for Public Policy, Rice University, July 27, 2007, pp. 3, 13, www.rice.edu/energy/publications/FAQs/WWT_FAQ_gas.pdf.

[3] See "Take This Car and Plug It," *IEEE Spectrum*, July 2005, http://iee explore.ieee.org/iel5/6/31432/01460339.pdf?arnumber=1460339.

[4] Quoted in Ken Bensinger, "The Garage: Focus on autos; 2 'green' technologies race for driver's seat," *Los Angeles Times*, Dec. 8, 2007, p. C1.

[5] *Ibid.*

[6] *Ibid.*

[7] See "EPRI-NRDC Report Finds Environmental Benefits of Deploying PHEVs," July 19, 2007, www.nrdc.org/media/2007/070719.asp. Report accessible at www.calcars.org/calcars-news/797.html.

bank out of trouble. (A Saudi prince is also a major stockholder.) [57]

Abu Dhabi already owned shares in Advanced Micro Devices, a computer chip manufacturer, and bought a major American private-equity firm, the Carlyle Group. A "sovereign wealth fund" owned by Dubai, another Persian Gulf city-state, was forced to back out of a deal to manage some major U.S. ports. (*See sidebar, p. 300.*) The fund bought fashion retailer Barney's of New York in 2006, as well as a $1.2 billion stake in a U.S. hedge fund, the Och-Ziff Capital Management Group. These purchases are only the tip of the iceberg, and have prompted public worrying by Treasury Secretary Henry M. Paulson Jr. and finance ministers from the industrial countries about a lack of transparency in high-stakes global investing by petrostates. [58]

In fact, geopolitics experts including former Central Intelligence Director R. James Woolsey say profits from these investments could find their way into the coffers of terrorists, putting the United States in the ironic position of financing both sides in the war against terrorism.

CURRENT SITUATION

New Conservation Law

At year's end, environmentalists and the auto industry finally developed a fuel-efficiency standard they could agree on. The agreement opened the way for enactment on Dec. 18 of the first major petroleum-conservation law in decades. In addition to the new gasoline mileage requirements for cars and light trucks (including SUVs), the law

President George W. Bush celebrates with House Speaker Nancy Pelosi, D-Calif., Secretary of Energy Samuel Bodman, left, and other lawmakers after signing the 2007 Energy Act on Dec. 19. The legislation raises vehicle fuel economy standards for the first time in 32 years.

demands a major increase in production of ethanol, the alcohol substitute made from corn or other plants.

Environmentalists and automakers alike say the new mileage standard is a breakthrough that ends a long standoff over different requirements for cars and light trucks. The latter category includes SUVs — a favorite target of environmentalists who call them gas-guzzlers.

Under the new system, the 35-miles-per-gallon standard applies to the entire fleet of new cars and light trucks, by all makers, sold in the United States. Then, each manufacturer would have to meet an individual standard — one for each company — based on each of its models' "footprint," a size measurement based on a vehicle's wheel base and track width.

The legislation does demand that separate sets of standards be devised for cars and light trucks. "That wasn't our favorite provision," Hobson of the Union of Concerned Scientists says, "but since the overall target — the 35-miles-per-gallon standard — has to apply across both of those fleets, it was a compromise we accepted."

Industry leaders expressed support as well. "This tough, national fuel economy bill will be good for both consumers and energy security," Dave McCurdy, president of the Alliance of Automobile Manufacturers, said in a statement. "We support its passage." [59] McCurdy is a Democratic ex-House member from Oklahoma. The alliance is made up of the Big 3 U.S. automakers and some of the biggest foreign-owned firms, including Toyota, Volkswagen and Mitsubishi.

Another endorsement came from the Association of International Automobile Manufacturers. "It's not perfect, but I think we're going to be pleased," said Mike Stanton, president and CEO of that trade group, which represents Honda, Nissan, Hyundai and others, including Toyota. [60]

EPA Blocks States

The era of good feelings between environmentalists and the Bush administration that opened with the Dec. 18 passage of the energy bill proved short-lived. The very next day, the Environmental Protection Agency (EPA) prohibited California and 16 other states from setting their own carbon dioxide emission standards for cars and trucks. Tougher state standards were designed to step up action against global warming.

But the new energy bill makes such moves by states unnecessary because cars will be polluting less because they'll burn less fuel, EPA Administrator Stephen L. Johnson told reporters. "The Bush administration is moving forward with a clear national solution, not a confusing patchwork of state rules," he said. "I believe this is a better approach than if individual states were to act alone." [61]

California Gov. Arnold Schwarzenegger, a Republican sometimes out of step with the Bush administration, immediately vowed to challenge the decision in court. "It is disappointing that the federal government is standing in our way and ignoring the will of tens of millions of people across the nation," Schwarzenegger said. "We will continue to fight this battle." [62]

Twelve other states — New York, New Jersey, Connecticut, Maine, Maryland, Massachusetts, New Mexico, Oregon, Pennsylvania, Rhode Island, Vermont and Washington — had proposed the same standards as California. And the governors of Arizona, Colorado, Florida and Utah had pledged to follow suit. Had the EPA decision gone their way, an estimated one-half of the new vehicles sold in the United States would have had to meet the higher-than-federal air-pollution standards.

McCurdy saluted the EPA decision, tacitly referring to the potential widespread effect of the state-proposed standards. "We commend EPA for protecting a national, 50-state program," he said. "A patchwork quilt of inconsistent and competing . . . programs at the state level would only have created confusion, inefficiency and uncertainty for automakers and consumers." [63]

Environmentalists say they are confident the states will win out in the end. The EPA decision is a "short-

Are higher vehicle fuel-economy standards good energy policy?

YES
Michelle Robinson
Director, Clean Vehicles Program, Union of Concerned Scientists

Written for *CQ Researcher*, December 2007

Requiring automakers to build more fuel-efficient cars and trucks is the patriotic, common-sense thing to do. Strengthened corporate average fuel economy (CAFE) standards will reduce our dependence on oil, save consumers billions of dollars, create hundreds of thousands of domestic jobs and dramatically cut global warming pollution. And it can be done using existing technology. How could anyone argue with that?

The fuel-economy standards instituted in 1975, albeit outdated, worked. If our cars and light trucks still had the same fuel economy they did in the early 1970s, we would have burned through an additional 80 billion gallons of gasoline on top of the 140 billion gallons we will consume this year. That would have amounted to an extra 5.2 million barrels of oil per day. At an average price for regular gasoline of about $2.50 per gallon, we would have forked over an extra $200 billion to the oil companies.

After decades of inaction, Congress has strengthened the standard. Cars, trucks and sport utility vehicles (SUVs) will be required to average at least 35 miles per gallon (mpg) by 2020, a 10-mpg increase over today's levels. A Union of Concerned Scientists (UCS) analysis found this would save 1.1 million barrels of oil per day in 2020, about half of what the United States currently imports from the Persian Gulf. Consumers would save $22 billion in 2020 — even after paying the cost of the improved fuel-economy technology. It would prevent more than 190 million metric tons of global warming emissions in 2020, the equivalent of taking 28 million of today's average cars and trucks off the road. And the new fuel-economy standard would create jobs. According to a UCS study, the standard would generate some 149,300 new domestic jobs in 2020.

Clearly, requiring cars and trucks to average at least 35 mpg by 2020 is smart energy policy. However, a better standard by itself would not ensure that we would avoid the worst consequences of global warming or conquer our national addiction to oil. To tackle these problems, the federal government also must require utilities to generate more of their electricity from clean, renewable energy sources; enact a low-carbon fuel standard to ensure that alternatives to oil are produced in an environmentally friendly way and adopt an economy-wide cap-and-trade program. That said, improving fuel-economy standards is a big step in the right direction.

NO
Robert W. Crandall
Senior Fellow, The Brookings Institution

Written for *CQ Researcher*, December 2007

Proponents of increases in mandated corporate average fuel economy (CAFE) standards often claim that they would be good for consumers, promote job formation and solve various environmental and energy-security problems. It is important, therefore, to disentangle these claims and to ask if there are not better options available.

First, any claim that raising fuel economy would be good for consumers and create additional jobs is surely incorrect. A highly competitive new-vehicles market delivers cars and trucks that are responsive to consumer demand. Any attempt to mandate greater fuel economy will lead to smaller, less powerful vehicles with more expensive fuel-saving technology than demanded by consumers. Inevitably, this will lead some consumers to hold their vehicles a little longer before trading them in. The result: lower consumer satisfaction, lower vehicle output and fewer auto industry jobs. Is it any wonder that auto producers oppose these proposals?

Second, any proposal to raise CAFE standards must be based on offsetting, non-market "externalities" associated with new-vehicle use. The current proposals are motivated in part by the desire to reduce carbon emissions, the precursors to potential global warming. But new U.S. vehicles generate a very small share of these greenhouse gases. To reduce carbon emissions efficiently, everyone on the globe should face a similar marginal cost of emitting a gram of carbon into the atmosphere.

Surely, it makes little sense to legislate mandatory reductions in carbon emissions (through CAFE) for new U.S. passenger cars while letting older cars, buses and trucks off the hook and — indeed — even encouraging the continued use of these older cars. More important, it is sheer folly to try to reduce global warming by setting high fuel-economy standards in California, Massachusetts or Hawaii while ignoring the much-lower-cost opportunities available in constraining emissions from coal-fired power plants or coke ovens in China, India, Europe or the U.S. Raising U.S. fuel-economy standards is a very high-cost approach, even by Washington standards, to reducing the threat of global warming.

Third, if the goal is to reduce oil imports for national-security purposes, increased fuel-economy standards are still an inefficient, blunt instrument. We burn oil in power plants, home furnaces, industrial boilers and about 250 million cars, trucks and buses already on the road. Any attempt to reduce oil consumption and, therefore, imports, should impose equal per-gallon costs on all of these alternatives. Higher CAFE standards will not do this and will even exacerbate the problem by encouraging Americans to use older gas-guzzlers more intensively.

term roadblock," says Eli Hobson, Washington representative of the Union of Concerned Scientists, which is active in energy-conservation issues. "The states will move forward."

Meanwhile, some lawmakers launched their own response to the EPA decision. Rep. Henry A. Waxman, D-Calif., chairman of the House Committee on Oversight and Government Reform, as well as Sen. Boxer, announced they had begun investigating the action. Waxman warned the EPA staff to "preserve all documents" relating to the decision. [64]

New Paradigm

China and India aren't the only countries that have some oil-watchers worrying about global oil supplies. Traditional oil-exporting countries are now using more of their petroleum for their own needs, shipping less to foreign buyers.

Saudi Arabia, for example, consumed 2 million barrels a day more in 2006 than in 2005, a one-year increase of 6.2 percent. Some projections have Saudi Arabia burning more than one-third of its oil by 2020. [65]

The Middle East isn't alone in putting its own oil to work in newly expanded fleets of cars, as well as homes and factories. Even countries such as Mexico, whose oil fields are said to be nearly played out, are consuming more and shipping less. "Production is declining in Mexico," says West of PFC Energy, in part because the national oil company has been lax in exploration and maintenance.

"One country that's making a huge investment is Saudi Arabia," West says. "They're going to raise production capacity to about 12.5 million barrels a day, with surge capacity to 15 million barrels a day. My people are skeptical they can do more."

Saudi Arabia also has an aggressive and ambitious industrial expansion program on the drawing boards or already under way, including aluminum smelters, petrochemical plants, copper refineries and new power plants. But Saudi industrialist Abdallah Dabbagh, director of the Saudi Arabian Mining Co., which is building a smelter, confessed some doubt to *The Wall Street Journal.* "I think the Saudi government will have to stop and think at some point if this is the best utilization of Saudi's crude." [66]

At street level, new cars are clogging the streets and highways of most of the world's oil giants, in large part because government subsidies keep gasoline prices low.

Saudi Arabians, whose home electricity costs are also subsidized, typically leave their air conditioners running when they go on vacation. Air conditioning accounts for nearly two-thirds of Saudi Arabia's electricity production. [67]

In Venezuela, motorists pay 7 cents a gallon. As a result, Hummers — perhaps the ultimate in gas-guzzling SUVs — are much in demand. The seeming disconnect between Venezuela's growing fleet of massive vehicles and President Chávez' plans for a socialist society prompted an outburst from the president. "What kind of a revolution is this — one of Hummers?" Chávez asked on his television show in October. [68]

And in Iran, where gasoline costs only slightly more, a government attempt in 2007 to cut back on consumption by rationing — instead of cutting or lessening the subsidy — caused violent street protests. Venezuelans predict the same thing would happen if their gasoline subsidy disappeared or shrank. [69]

Concern about consumption is an issue that also applies to China and India — can they be persuaded to moderate their taste for the same amenities that people in developed countries have been enjoying for decades? The International Energy Agency says the issue isn't one of fairness but of numbers. "A level of per-capita income in China and India comparable with that of the industrialized countries would, on today's model, require a level of energy use beyond the world's energy resource endowment." [70]

By comparison, the question of whether Saudi Arabia should be building more power plants to fuel more air conditioners seems like an easier question — at least for non-Saudis.

OUTLOOK

Production Crunch?

Dire predictions invariably swirl around the question of Earth's energy resources. Oil historian and consultant Yergin counts present-day forecasts of imminent decline as the fifth set of such predictions since the petroleum industry began. "Cycles of shortage and surplus characterize the entire history of the oil industry," he wrote in 2005, dismissing the idea that this phase is inherently different. [71]

Still, even some oil-watchers who agree with Yergin on the fundamentals argue that the global panorama has changed enough to cause serious problems in the near term.

If world economic growth stays on track, says West of PFC Energy, "We believe in the likelihood of a production crunch coming between 2012 and 2014. The economic impact will be severe and the geopolitical impact will be severe."

The end result could be heightened competition for resources and "massive" transfer of wealth to oil-producing countries, West says.

To avoid such an outcome, research needs to focus — quickly — on finding technology that provides an alternative to petroleum as an energy source, West says.

"What energy research should do is prioritize limited numbers of areas, whether it's battery efficiency, or light materials with which to build automobiles." Up to now, he says, research has been unfocused.

The Brookings Institution's Sandalow argues that research has already developed a solution that's ready to go — "plug-in hybrids" — hybrid cars that are converted to recharge their electric motors on household current. Sandalow drives one himself. "In 10 years, all Americans will be aware of the option of buying a car that plugs into the power grid," he says. "We have a vast infrastructure for generating electricity in this country that does us almost no good for getting off oil. This is the breakthrough."

As he envisions it, the president could order all government vehicles to use plug-in technology. Overloads of the electricity system would be avoided by drivers plugging in at night, using reserve capacity that utilities build into their systems.

But some energy experts sound a note of caution. Hirsch, who directed the peak-oil study for the Department of Energy, supports plug-ins but says they can create as many problems as they solve. "Imagine you have a lot of plug-in hybrids, enough to make a difference in U.S. oil consumption. Recharging them in off-peak hours — you can do that for a while. But if you're going to have a big impact, then you're going to have to build a lot of power plants."

In general, Hirsch sees an unhappy energy future not very far down the road. Oil supplies will shrink, he says. "I think there's not much question we will be in serious, long-term recession, deepening recession," he says. "With oil shortages, you'll have much higher prices — and shortages meaning you just simply won't be able to get it."

The world economy will adjust, Hirsch says, but until then, "It's not a pretty picture. Companies will be cutting back on employment; a lot of people will lose their homes because they can't afford to meet mortgages. International trade will go down."

Energy analyst Medlock at the Baker Institute is far less pessimistic. "I see conservation forces coming to bear over the next decade, which will tend to trim the growth of demand. I do see new supplies coming on line, and a major interest in developing unconventional oil."

Such developments would avoid the continued price spikes that some predict. "I think it's well within the range of possibility to see oil prices in the range of $60 to $70 a barrel," Medlock says.

Saudi Arabia, Canada Have Biggest Reserves

Saudi Arabia and Canada lead the world in oil reserves, with nearly 450 billion barrels — more than half as much as the next 10 nations combined.

Rank	Country	Barrels (in billions)
1.	Saudi Arabia	262.3
2.	Canada	179.2
3.	Iran	136.3
4.	Iraq	115.0
5.	Kuwait	101.5
6.	United Arab Emirates	97.8
7.	Venezuela	80.0
8.	Russia	60.0
9.	Libya	41.5
10.	Nigeria	36.2
11.	Kazakhstan	30.0
12.	United States	21.8

* As of Jan. 1, 2007

Source: "World Proved Reserves of Oil and Natural Gas, Most Recent Estimates," Energy Information Administration, Jan. 9, 2007

Simmons, widely seen as the leading voice of the peak oil thesis, sees no grounds for such optimism. Oil producers can indeed use natural gas liquids and other unconventional sources of energy to make up a shortfall in crude oil supplies, but that will only hasten the day when the real crunch begins, he says. "We are basically living on borrowed time," he says. The gap between demand and supply "creates social chaos and war" by 2020.

Or, in the best of all possible worlds, Simmons says, a government-directed effort will come up with alternatives to petroleum. "But if we spend three more years arguing if it's time to get into a program like that," he says, the future is grim.

Gheit, the veteran oilman now on Wall Street, dismisses all such talk.

Oil-exploration and production technology isn't standing still and will enable oil companies to keep producing petroleum, he says. "I can assure people we are not going to run out of oil any time soon."

NOTES

1. David Sandalow, *Freedom From Oil: How the next President can End the United States' Oil Addiction* (2007).

2. Quoted in "Transcript: Interview with IEA chief economist," FT.com, Nov. 7, 2007, www.ft.com/cms/s/0/3c8940ca-8d46-11dc-a398-0000779fd2ac.html?nclick_check=1.

3. *Ibid.*

4. "World Energy Outlook 2007 — China and India Insights," International Energy Association, p. 41, www.worldenergyoutlook.org (only executive summary available to public).

5. Quoted in Jad Mouawad, "Record Price of Oil Raises New Fears," *The New York Times*, Oct. 17, 2007, p. C1.

6. For background, see Peter Behr, "Energy Nationalism," *CQ Global Researcher*, July 2007, pp. 151-180.

7. For oil demand statistics, see "World Petroleum (Oil) Demand 2003-2007," Energy Information Administration, U.S. Department of Energy, updated Nov. 5, 2007, www.eia.doe.gov/ipm/demand.html.

8. Daniel Yergin, *The Prize: The Epic Quest for Oil, Money and Power* (1992), p. 15.

9. Gretchen Morgenson, "Dangers of a World Without Rules," *The New York Times*, Sept. 24, 2006, Sect. 3, p. 1.

10. Robert J. Samuelson, "Is There an Oil 'Bubble,' " *The Washington Post*, July 26, 2006, p. A17.

11. "Fact Sheet — Prudhoe Bay," BP, updated August 2006, www.bp.com/liveassets/bp_internet/us/bp_us_english/STAGING/local_assets/downloads/a/A03_prudhoe_bay_fact_sheet.pdf.

12. Heather Timmons, "Oil Majors Agree to Develop a Big Kazakh Field," *The New York Times*, Feb. 26, 2004, p. W1; "Chevron Reports Oil Find in Gulf of Mexico," *The New York Times* [Bloomberg News], Dec. 21, 2004, p. C5; Alexei Barrionuevo, "Brazil Discovers an Oil Field Can Be a Political Tool," *The New York Times*, Nov. 19, 2007, p. A3.

13. Quoted in Steven Mufson, "U.S. Oil Reserves Get a Big Boost," *The Washington Post*, Sept. 6, 2006, p. D1.

14. "Crude Oil Production by Selected Country," Energy Information Administration, U.S. Department of Energy, November 2007, www.eia.doe.gov/emeu/mer/pdf/pages/sec11_5.pdf. For historical reserves figure, see Yergin, *op. cit.*, pp. 499-500. For Saudi Arabia reserve estimate, see "Crude Oil — Uncertainty about Future Oil Supply Makes It Important to Develop a Strategy for Addressing a Peak and Decline in Oil Production," Government Accountability Office, February 2007, p. 62, www.gao.gov/new.items/d07283.pdf.

15. Government Accountability Office, *ibid.*, p. 20.

16. Peter Jackson, "Why the 'Peak Oil' Theory Falls Down," Cambridge Energy Resource Associates, November 2006, pp. 2, 10.

17. "World Energy Outlook 2007," *op. cit.*, p. 64.

18. Quoted in "Transcript: Interview with IEA chief economist," *op. cit.*

19. "Testimony on Peak Oil, Dr. Robert L. Hirsch, Senior Energy Program Advisor, SAIC," House Subcommittee on Energy and Air Quality, Dec. 7, 2005, http://energycommerce.house.gov/reparchives/108/Hearings/12072005hearing1733/Hirsch.pdf.

20. "Peak Oil Theory — 'World Running Out of Oil Soon' — Is Faulty; Could Distort Policy and Energy Debate," Cambridge Energy Research Associates, (press release), Nov. 14, 2006, www.cera.com/aspx/

cda/public1/news/pressReleases/pressReleaseDetails.aspx?CID=8444.

21. "Crude Oil — Uncertainty about Future Oil Supply . . .," *op. cit.*, p. 4.

22. *Ibid.*

23. See Tim Reiterman, "Canada's black gold glitters but tarnishes," *Los Angeles Times*, July 8, 2007, p. A1.

24. Jackson, *op. cit.*, p. 6.

25. Matthew R. Simmons, *Twilight in the Desert: The Coming Saudi Oil Shock and the World Economy* (2005).

26. Quoted in Thomas Catan, "UK prepares for the day the oil runs out," *Financial Times* (London), May 27, 2005, p. A20.

27. "World Energy Outlook," *op. cit.*, p. 122.

28. "USA Statistics in Brief — Population by Age, Sex, and Region," U.S. Census Bureau, updated Nov. 6, 2007, www.census.gov/compendia/statab/files/pop.html.

29. "World Energy Outlook," *op. cit.*, pp. 122, 77.

30. "Olympic Trials: China's bout with $90 oil," Lehman Brothers, Fixed Income Research, Nov. 16, 2007, p. 3 (not publicly available).

31. "President Bush Delivers State of the Union Address," The White House, Jan. 31, 2006, www.whitehouse.gov/news/releases/2006/01/20060131-10.html.

32. John M. Broder, "House, 314-100, Passes Broad Energy Bill," *The New York Times*, Sept. 19, 2007, p. A16; Steven Mufson, "House Sends President an Energy Bill to Sign," *The Washington Post*, Sept. 19, 2007, p. A1.

33. Quoted in Broder, *op. cit.*

34. "House Select Committee on Energy Independence and Global Warming Holds Hearing on State Efforts Towards Low-Carbon Energy," *Congressional Transcripts*, Nov. 14, 2007.

35. Robert L. Hirsch, *et al.*, "Peaking of World Oil Production: Impacts, Mitigation & Risk Management," Science Applications International Corp., February 2005, p. 5, www.projectcensored.org/newsflash/the_hirsch_report.pdf.

36. Kenneth S. Deffeyes, *Hubbert's Peak* (2001), pp. 1-5.

37. See "Crude Oil," *op. cit.*, Government Accountability Office.

38. Deffeyes, *op. cit.*, p. 134.

39. For background, see Behr, *op. cit.* Material in this sub-section is also drawn from Yergin, *op. cit.*

40. Quoted in *ibid.*, p. 615.

41. "Current SPR Inventory As Of Nov. 29, 2007," Strategic Petroleum Reserve, Department of Energy, www.spr.doe.gov/dir/dir.html.

42. "Speeches by President J. Carter Outlining the Critical Nature of the Energy Crisis and Recommendations for Legislation to Deal with Issue," April 18, 1977, *CQ Public Affairs Collection.*

43. Yergin, *op. cit.*, p. 702; "Imported Crude Oil Prices: Nominal and Real," Energy Information Administration, Department of Energy, undated, www.eia.doe.gov/emeu/steo/pub/fsheets/real_prices.html.

44. Yergin, *op. cit.*, pp. 699-703.

45. *Ibid.*, p. 718.

46. Doron P. Levin, "How Ford Finally Found the Road to Wellville," *Los Angeles Times Magazine*, March 10, 1996, p. 16.

47. See "The 9/11 Commission Report: Final Report of the National Commission on Terrorist Attacks Upon the United States," 2004, p. 48.

48. Neela Banerjee, "After the Attacks: The Energy Market," *The New York Times*, Sept. 13, 2001, p. A7; Brad Foss, "Gas Prices Shoot Up," *The Washington Post* (The Associated Press), Sept. 12, 2001, p. E4.

49. Gail Makinen, "The Economic Effects of 9/11: A Retrospective Assessment," Congressional Research Service, Sept. 27, 2002, p. 16, www.fas.org/irp/crs/RL31617.pdf.

50. Simon Romero, "Laissez-Faire My Gas-Guzzler, Already," *The New York Times*, Sept. 7, 2004, p. C1.

51. Quoted in Jeremy W. Peters, "On Auto-Dealer Lots, a Shift Away from Gas-Guzzling Vehicles," *The New York Times*, Sept. 1, 2006, p. C6.

52. *Ibid.*

53. Unless otherwise indicated, material in this sub-section is drawn from Behr, *op. cit.*

54. "China seals oil deal with China," BBC News, Aug. 25, 2006, http://news.bbc.co.uk/1/hi/business/5286766.stm.

55. "Millions in Georgia Without Heat," CNN, Jan. 24, 2006, www.cnn.com/2006/WORLD/europe/01/24/russia.gas/index.html. See also "Top World Oil Producers," Energy Information Administration, U.S. Department of Energy, www.eia.doe.gov/emeu/cabs/topworldtables1_2.htm.

56. Quoted in Behr, *op. cit.*

57. Steven R. Weisman, "Oil Producers See the World and Buy It Up," *The New York Times*, Nov. 28, 2007, www.nytimes.com/2007/11/28/business/worldbusiness/28petrodollars.html.

58. "Sovereign Wealth Funds: A Shopping List," DealBook, *The New York Times*, Nov. 27, 2007, http://dealbook.blogs.nytimes.com/2007/11/27/sovereign-wealth-funds-a-shopping-list/.

59. Quoted in John M. Broder and Felicity Barringer, "E.P.A. Says 17 States Can't Set Greenhouse Gas Rules for Cars," *The New York Times*, Dec. 20, 2007, p. A1.

60. *Ibid.*

61. *Ibid.*

62. Waxman letter to Johnson, Dec. 20, 2007, http://oversight.house.gov/documents/20071220111155.pdf; and Janet Wilson, "EPA chief is said to have ignored staff," *Los Angeles Times*, Dec. 21, 2007, p. A30.

63. See "Statement of President and CEO Dave McCurdy on National Fuel Economy Agreement," Alliance of American Automobile Manufacturers, Dec. 1, 2007, www.autoalliance.org/archives/archive.php?id=427&cat=Press%20Releases.

64. Quoted in Dave Shepardson, "Auto industry backs CAFE deal," *Detroit News*, www.detnews.com/apps/pbcs.dll/article?AID=2007712010414.

65. Neil King Jr., "Saudi Industrial Drive Strains Oil-Export Role," *The Wall Street Journal*, Dec. 12, 2007, p. A1.

66. Quoted in *ibid.*

67. *Ibid.*

68. Quoted in Simon Romero, "Venezuela's Gas Prices Remain Low, But the Political Costs May Be Rising," *The New York Times*, Oct. 30, 2007, www.nytimes.com/2007/10/30/world/americas/30venezuela.html?n=Top/Reference/Times%20Topics/People/C/Chavez,%20Hugo.

69. Ramin Mostaghim and Borzou Daragahi, "Gas rationing in Iran ignites anger, unrest," *Los Angeles Times*, June 28, 2007, p. A5; Najmeh Bozorgmehr, "Iran pushes on with fuel rationing in face of riots," *Financial Times* (London), June 28, 2007, p. A7. Also see Romero, *op. cit.*

70. "World Energy Outlook," *op. cit.*, p. 215.

71. Daniel Yergin, "It's Not the End of the Oil Age," *The Washington Post*, July 31, 2005, p. B7.

BIBLIOGRAPHY

Books

Huber, Peter W., and Mark P. Mills, *The Bottomless Well: The Twilight of Fuel, the Virtue of Waste, and Why We Will Never Run Out of Energy*, Basic Books, 2005.
A lawyer and a physicist argue that energy in all its forms is plentiful.

Sandalow, David, *Freedom From Oil: How the Next President Can End the United States' Oil Addiction*, McGraw-Hill, 2007.
A former Clinton administration official lays out a plan for reducing U.S. oil usage.

Simmons, Matthew R., *Twilight in the Desert: The Coming Saudi Oil Shock and the World Economy*, John Wiley & Sons, 2005.
A leading "peak oil" proponent cites evidence that Saudi Arabia has vastly exaggerated the amount of its oil reserves.

Yergin, Daniel, *The Prize: The Epic Quest for Oil, Money and Power*, Simon & Schuster, 1992.
An American oil expert provides a classic history of the global oil industry and its role in contemporary geopolitics.

Articles

Bradsher, Keith, "Trucks Propel China's Economy, and Foul Its Air," *The New York Times*, Dec. 8, 2007, p. A1.
China's reliance on trucking is growing by leaps and bounds, far ahead of the government's ability to regulate the industry.

Hagenbaugh, Barbara, "Gas pump gulps more of family pay," *USA Today*, May 17, 2007, p. A1.
Average American consumers suddenly are shelling out appreciably more to fill their tanks.

Hoyos, Carola, and Demetri Sevastopulo, "Saudi Aramco dismisses claims over problems meeting rising global demand for oil," *Financial Times* (London), Feb. 27, 2004.
The Saudi oil company responds to the first major stirrings of the "peak oil" movement.

King, Neil Jr., "Saudi Industrial Drive Strains Oil-Export Role," *The Wall Street Journal*, Dec. 12, 2007, p. A1.
Saudi Arabia's rapidly expanding consumption of its major product is making even some Saudi industrialists nervous.

Morse, Edward L., and James Richard, "The Battle for Energy Dominance," *Foreign Affairs*, March-April 2002, p. 16.
Two Wall Street energy specialists presciently examine the geopolitical effects of Russia's sudden emergence as a major player in world energy markets.

Murphy, Kim, *et al.*, "Oil's Winners and Losers," *Los Angeles Times*, Nov. 24, 2007, p. A1.
High oil prices spell progress for some and disaster for others as new petroleum-market dynamics play out globally.

Rosenberg, Tina, "The Perils of Petrocracy," *The New York Times Magazine*, Nov. 4 2007, p. 42.
Focusing on Venezuela, a veteran writer reports that state-owned oil companies tend not to be models of efficient performance, nor reliable explorers for new energy deposits.

Weisman, Steven R., "Oil Producers See the World and Buy It Up," *The New York Times*, Nov. 28, 2007, p. A1.
Wall Street and Washington try to grasp the implications of oil-producing countries buying big chunks of major U.S. and European companies.

Reports and Studies

"Crude Oil: Uncertainty about Future Oil Supply Makes It Important to Develop a Strategy for Addressing a Peak and Decline in Oil Production," Government Accountability Office, February 2007, www.gao.gov/new.items/d07283.pdf.
The government should begin planning now for world oil supplies to peak, even if that moment is several decades away.

"Hard Truths: Facing the Hard Truths About Energy," National Petroleum Council, July 2007, http://downloadcenter.connectlive.com/events/npc07 1807/pdf-downloads/NPC_Facing_Hard_Truths.pdf.
The United States needs to rapidly prepare for a world in which oil is more difficult and more expensive to obtain, according to top energy experts and executives.

Medlock, Kenneth B. III, and Amy Myers Jaffe, "Gas FAQ: U.S. Gasoline Markets and U.S. Oil Import Dependence," James A. Baker III Institute for Public Policy, Rice University, http://bakerinstitute.org/Pubs/WWT_FAQ_Gas2.pdf.
Two experts from a think tank in the U.S. oil capital explain the basics of energy use in the United States.

Rosen, Daniel H., and Trevor Houser, "China Energy: A Guide for the Perplexed," Center for International and Strategic Studies, Peterson Institute for International Economics, May 2007, www.iie.com/publications/papers/rosen0507.pdf.
China's manufacturing expansion, not automobile fleet growth, accounts for most of the country's rising oil demand.

For More Information

American Petroleum Institute, 1220 L St., N.W., Washington, DC 20005; (202) 682-8000; www.api.org. Lobbies for the U.S. oil industry; supports loosening restrictions on oil exploration on public lands.

Cambridge Energy Research Associates, 55 Cambridge Parkway, Cambridge, MA 02142; (617) 866 5000; http://cera.com. A widely cited consulting firm that provides public summaries of studies performed for clients.

Energy Information Administration, U.S. Department of Energy, 1000 Independence Ave., S.W., Washington, DC 20585; (202) 586-8800; http://eia.doe.gov. The government's energy statistics division provides access to a wide range of data on all aspects of oil and gas production and use.

International Energy Agency, 9, rue de la Fédération, 75739 Paris Cedex 15, France, (011-33 1) 40.57.65.00/01; www.iea.org. An organization of industrialized countries, almost all in Europe, that studies energy trends and recommends policies on conservation and related topics.

James A. Baker III Institute for Public Policy, Energy Forum, Rice University, 6100 Main St., Baker Hall, Suite 120, Houston, TX 77005; (713) 348-4683; www.rice.edu/energy/index.html. Nonpartisan think tank that sponsors research and forums on oil-related topics.

The Oil Drum; www.theoildrum.com. A collective blog (with separate editions for the United States, Canada, Europe and Australia/New Zealand). Part of the "peak oil" community; provides a discussion forum on issues of conservation and alternative energy sources.

Organization of Petroleum Exporting Countries, Obere Donaustrasse 93, A-1020, Vienna, Austria; (011-43-1) 21112-279; www.opec.org. The cartel publishes statistics, forecasts and policy documents on global oil supplies.

12

Dealing with the 'New' Russia

Roland Flamini

Russian President Vladimir Putin, left, and U.S. President George W. Bush held a lighthearted press conference in November 2001 at Crawford High School in Texas after a three-day summit at Bush's ranch. At the time, Bush said he looked Putin in the eye and saw a man who was "straightforward and trustworthy." But the good working relationship they seemed to be developing has since deteriorated.

From *CQ Researcher*, June 6, 2008.

When Russian voters went to the polls to elect a new president on March 2, the outcome was hardly in doubt. Deputy Prime Minister Dmitry Medvedev, 42, is both genuinely popular and had been picked by the even more popular incumbent, President Vladimir Vladimirovich Putin. Indeed, Medvedev garnered 72 percent of the votes. [1] "It was not really an election, it was an appointment," observed Fraser Cameron, director of the European Union's Russian Center, expressing a widespread Western view. [2] Medvedev was inaugurated on May 7 and immediately nominated Putin — barred by the constitution from serving a third term — as prime minister at the head of his United Russia party government.

Medvedev has defined Russia's new leadership structure as "a single team" that would "be able to solve the most difficult and large-scale tasks." [3] Political commentators in Moscow are calling the partnership a diarchy, or a government by two joint leaders. [4] But finding the right label is a lot easier than figuring out how the power-sharing arrangement will work in practice.

Since the fall of the Soviet Union in 1991, the position of prime minister has been largely administrative and no threat to the presidency, but Putin has already indicated that he will broaden its political scope.

Medvedev, on the other hand, has never held elected office and has spent most of his career in Putin's shadow as a trusted deputy, so the most likely scenario seems to be that Putin will continue to dominate the government. If public opinion polls are to be believed, this sits well with the majority of Russians. According to surveys, more than 80 percent expect Putin to continue as chief guide and

The World's Largest Country

At 6.6 million square miles, Russia is by far the world's largest country, covering about one-eighth of Earth's land area. Its 141 million people make it the ninth-largest in population. The breakup of the Soviet Union in December 1991 led to the independence of Russia and 14 other republics. Today the Commonwealth of Independent States (CIS) consists of Russia and 11 former Soviet Republics: Azerbaijan, Armenia, Belarus, Georgia, Kazakhstan, Kyrgyzstan, Moldova, Tajikistan, Turkmenistan, Uzbekistan and Ukraine. The three Baltic states — Lithuania, Latvia and Estonia — are in the European Union and NATO.

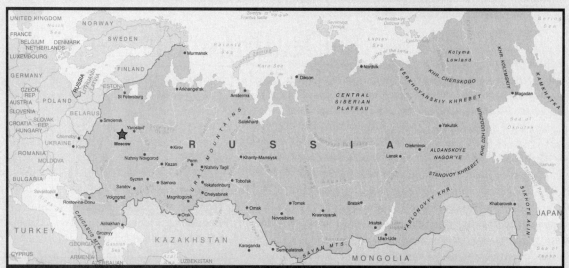

Russia at a Glance

Area: 6.6 million sq. miles. Russia is the world's largest country, nearly twice the size of the U.S.

Population: 140.7 million (July 2008 est.), less than half the U.S. population.

Population growth: Declining 0.47% (2008 est.)

Infant mortality: 10.81 deaths per 1,000 births

Labor force: 75.1 million (November 2007 est.)

Unemployment rate: 5.9% (November 2007 est.)

Religion: Russian Orthodox (Christian) 75%, Muslim 19%, other Christians 6% (2006 est.)

Languages: Russian, in addition to many minority languages recognized in the constituent republics and autonomous areas.

Government: The most powerful political leader is the president, who is elected by popular vote. The bicameral Federal Assembly, made up of the Federation Council, consists of two representatives from each of Russia's territorial units, and the State Duma, which fills half of its seats from single-member constituencies and half by proportional representation from party lists. The chair of the government or prime minister is the second-highest political official, appointed by the president. The Federation Council, the upper house, appoints the for-life members of the Judicial branch, including the Constitutional Court, Supreme Court and Supreme Arbitration Court.

Economy: The gross domestic product was $2.08 trillion in 2007, with about 15.8% of the population living below the poverty line. Russia's major oil and natural gas exports helped it end its ninth-straight year of growth, averaging 7% annually since the financial crisis of 1998. Over the last six years, personal incomes have increased 12% per year. The country's main sources of revenues are from oil, natural gas, metals and timber. Manufacturing is virtually nonexistent.

Communications hardware: There are 40.1 million telephone landlines, 150 million mobile phones and 2.8 million Internet hosts serving 25.6 million users.

Sources: Political Handbook of the World, 2008, CQ Press, 2008; *The World Factbook*, Central Intelligence Agency, 2008

arbiter of the nation's fate. More than 50 percent would be happy to make him president for life. [5]

Yet Fyodor Lukyanov, editor of the Moscow-based *Russia in Global Affairs* magazine, says things may not be that clear-cut. Two-headed power is without precedent in Russia — never mind that, ironically, the double-headed eagle was for centuries the Russian imperial symbol.

"The Russian political tradition is to have one single leader — one czar," Lukyanov observes. "Now we will get two centers of power, which is extremely unusual. If anyone tells you he knows how the system is going to work, don't believe it."

Meanwhile, with the U.S. presidential election looming, time is running out for any significant improvement in the U.S.-Russian tension that has developed during the Bush administration. Still, President George W. Bush telephoned Medvedev on March 4 to express the hope — in the words of a Medvedev spokesperson — that "the two [leaders] can establish a close working relationship that will help them deal with important world issues." [6]

A working relationship is what Bush no longer seems to have with Putin. In 2001, President Bush said he looked Putin in the eye and saw a man who was "straightforward and trustworthy." But it has been downhill from there. [7]

"In 2001 the Russians thought they were entering into a new strategic alliance [with the United States] against global terrorism, "says Michael McFaul, a senior associate at the Carnegie Endowment for International Peace in Washington, D.C. When the Bush administration sought to establish military bases in Uzbekistan and other former Soviet satellites in Central Asia to support a U.S. attack on al Qaeda in Afghanistan, Putin agreed. But when Bush turned on Iraq, Putin strongly opposed the invasion.

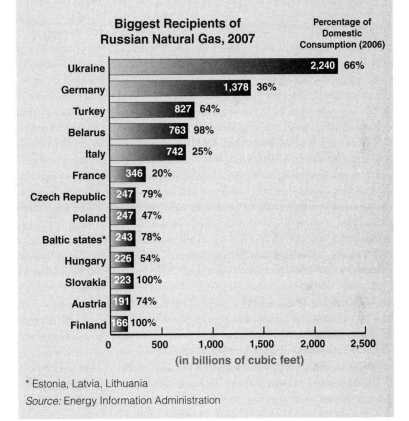

Europe Depends on Russian Natural Gas

Russian natural gas exports account for a high percentage of the natural gas used in many neighboring countries. Russia's biggest energy customer by far is Ukraine, which received more than 2.2 trillion cubic feet of natural gas in 2007, or 66 percent of its domestic consumption. Germany was the largest Western European recipient, importing nearly 1.4 trillion cubic feet, or more than a third of the nation's supply.

Biggest Recipients of Russian Natural Gas, 2007

Percentage of Domestic Consumption (2006)

Country	Billions of cubic feet	Percentage
Ukraine	2,240	66%
Germany	1,378	36%
Turkey	827	64%
Belarus	763	98%
Italy	742	25%
France	346	20%
Czech Republic	247	79%
Poland	247	47%
Baltic states*	243	78%
Hungary	226	54%
Slovakia	223	100%
Austria	191	74%
Finland	166	100%

(in billions of cubic feet)

* Estonia, Latvia, Lithuania

Source: Energy Information Administration

Relations between Washington and the Kremlin continued to worsen, with each side blaming the other for the deterioration and some experts warning that further worsening could lead to a new Cold War. "Now, relations are the worst in 20 years," says McFaul. "The central belief of Russian foreign policy is: If it's bad for the United States, it's good for Russia."

The contours of U.S.-Russian differences have emerged in disagreements over Iran's nuclear ambitions, U.S. support for Kosovo's independence, efforts by Ukraine and Georgia to join NATO and construction of gas and oil pipelines in the region. Moreover, Bush and top administration officials have lectured Putin on human rights violations by a presidency "based on the uncontested primacy of the top executive, with controlled politics and a growing intolerance towards public dissent, let alone political autonomy," as *Washington Post* columnist Masha Lipman wrote from Moscow early this spring. [8]

Some Russian analysts advance the argument that Putin's autocratic rule — also known as "Putinism" or "managed democracy" — was necessary to stabilize the country. Says Veronika Krasheninnikova, director of U.S. operations for the Council for Trade and Economic Cooperation and author of a recent book (in Russian) on U.S.-Russian relations. "Putin is putting order where there was chaos: The collapse of the Soviet Union had destroyed the state in every function."

Meanwhile, Putin charges that the Bush administration has aggressively moved to encircle Russia with military bases, install missiles on its borders, topple allied regimes in Central Asia and incite political upheaval in Moscow through U.S.-backed pro-democracy groups.

Arguably the most contentious single issue between Washington and the Kremlin is the Bush administration's plan to install an anti-missile defense system in Eastern Europe with the long-range missile interceptors deployed in Poland and a tracking radar system in the Czech Republic. Bush says the missiles are needed to protect the West against possible nuclear attack from Iran or North Korea.

To remove legal obstacles to the system, the Bush administration in 2002 withdrew from the 1972 Anti-Ballistic Missile Treaty (ABM), which prohibited missile defense systems in the region. Putin calls U.S. concerns over Iran overblown and complains that the proposed missile shield "will work automatically with the entire nuclear capability of the United States" functioning as one unit. The missile system also will trigger "a new arms race," Putin adds, since it will force Russia to update its own antiquated missile network. [9]

Some blame unrealistic expectations on both sides for the existing tensions. After the Soviet Union collapsed, Zbigniew Brzezinski, a former White House national security adviser, said, "There was too much euphoria; too much inclination to declare that Russia was a democracy; and too much pretension. . . . All of that has created ambiguity when clarity is needed." [10]

The United States has been disappointed that the hoped-for democracy has failed to take root in Russia after the fall of communism. For their part, the Russians had expected more from the United States in terms of support. Instead, a weakened Moscow was pressed into signing arms-control agreements. Furthermore, by welcoming former Soviet Eastern Europe and the Baltic states into NATO, the Atlantic alliance planted itself right on Mother Russia's front porch — a move that Putin, not surprisingly, saw as a serious threat.

But when that happened, Russia was weak and poor, and with its economy in free fall, the country was too eager to integrate itself into the West to object too strenuously. Russia's latest prosperity has brought a marked change in attitude. Thanks to rising world energy prices, revenues from Russia's vast natural gas and crude oil reserves have contributed significantly to putting Russia back on its feet — rich, resentful and nationalistic and seeking to regain its great-power status. [11] (After the collapse of the Soviet Union, Russian oil production fell about 50 percent, largely because of a lack of much-needed investments and poor management. The situation remained unchanged during Russia's financial crisis in the 1990s. The dramatic turnaround came in 1999, after two new pipelines were completed, the ruble was devalued, making Russian oil and gas cheap, and world energy prices spiked, triggering new foreign investments.) [12]

Grateful Russians, their pride restored, credit Putin with the country's resurgence and its consistent 7 percent annual growth rate, and the Russians gave him great latitude to exercise his "tsarist" style, which — unlike democracy — does have its roots in Russia.

Caught in the middle, as usual, is Europe, the historic battlefield of Russian expansionism. French President Nicolas Sarkozy expressed the general concern — increasingly reflected in the polls — that "Russia is imposing its return on the world scene by playing its assets, notably oil and gas, with a certain brutality." [13] He was referring to Putin's use of Europe's dependence on Russian energy supplies (some 36 percent in the case of Germany) to pressure Europe into supporting Moscow's positions. [14]

As policy experts gauge relations between Russia and the United States, here are some of the questions they are asking:

Can Medvedev be more than a surrogate for Putin?

Calling the Medvedev-Putin partnership a power-

Out of the Shadows Steps Russia's New President

Dmitry Medvedev is said to idolize Putin, his longtime mentor.

Vladimir Putin, a one-time officer in the Soviet intelligence service, the KGB, has a reputation for surrounding himself with other former agents. In that respect, Putin's choice to succeed him as president, Dmitry Medvedev, differs fundamentally from his mentor: He does not have an intelligence background. But the soft-spoken 42-year-old lawyer — Putin's loyal collaborator for 17 years — does share an important trait with other members of the Putin team. He belongs to what the *Financial Times* recently called "the new clan of power brokers" — officials who were members of Putin's foreign relations committee when Putin was deputy mayor of St. Petersburg. [1]

Medvedev had a respectable childhood in an intellectual family. His father was a professor at Leningrad Technical Institute, and his mother a teacher. He studied law in Leningrad, and by the late 1980s was head of the law faculty of Leningrad (now St. Petersburg) State University, at the same time he was moonlighting as a legal adviser to city hall, where he first met Putin. In 1991, when Putin became deputy mayor, Medvedev went to work full time as legal adviser to the foreign relations committee. [2]

When Putin went to the Kremlin as President Boris Yeltsin's prime minister, Medvedev followed, first as Putin's deputy chief of staff and three years later as chief of staff. [3] Putin also appointed him chairman of natural gas producer Gazprom, where he gradually replaced its independent-

Medvedev addresses students in Beijing on May 24, 2008. Some Russia-watchers saw his visit to China as significant, given tension between Moscow and the U.S.

AFP/Getty Images/Natalia Kolesnikova

minded executives with a management more loyal to the government. Throughout his rise, Medvedev quietly operated in the shadow of his mentor, whom many said he treated as a father figure. But *Der Spiegel* magazine reports that when German Chancellor Angela Merkel met him following his election, she sized him up as — in the magazine's words — "a seasoned, ambitious apparatchik who knows what he wants." [4]

Medvedev is energetic, good-natured and said to be unfailingly polite, with a taste for trendy clothes and American rock music. On the campaign trail, he made speeches about reducing taxes and slashing red tape while freeing the media and boosting the independence of the court system. But analysts point out that his background shows little promise of independent action. As the *Financial Times* put it, "His record as one of Mr. Putin's most senior officials, as the president rolled back many of those freedoms, throws these pledges into doubt." [5]

[1] Caroline Belton, "Anointed enigma: the quiet rise of a dedicated Dmitry Medvedev," FT.com, Feb. 28, 2008, www.ft.com/cms/s/0/72 ede4b6-e626-11dc-8398-0000779fd2ac,dwp_uuid=7ee6a12e-7d74-11 dc-9f47-0000779fd2ac.html?nclick_check=1.

[2] Matthias Schepp, "Don't Get Too Excited About Medvedev," *Der Spiegel*, March 3, 2008, www.spiegel.de/international/world/0,1518, 540313,00.html.

[3] Owen Matthews, "From a Mouse to a Tsar," *Newsweek*, March 3, 2008, www.newsweek.com/id/114679/page/3.

[4] Schepp, *op. cit.*

[5] Belton, *op. cit.*

sharing arrangement may be naive. In a typical comment, Russian political analyst Lilia Shevtsova wrote in the *London Daily Telegraph*: "In the Putin-Medvedev tango, Prime Minister Putin is going to be the lead dancer. President Medvedev is left with a somewhat humiliating role." [15]

Russia Holds Quarter of World's Gas Reserves

Russia holds the world's largest natural gas reserves — nearly 1.7 quadrillion cubic feet, or more than a quarter of the total. Its share of global crude oil reserves is the eighth-largest.

Global Natural Gas Reserves
(in cubic feet)

- **Russia 27.2%** (1.68 quadrillion cu. ft.)
- **Rest of world 26.2%** (1.62 quadrillion cu. ft.)
- **Iran 15.3%** (948.20 trillion cu. ft.)
- **Qatar 14.7%** (905.30 trillion cu. ft.)
- **Saudi Arabia 4.1%** (253.11 trillion cu. ft.)
- **United Arab Emirates 3.5%** (214.40 trillion cu. ft.)
- **United States 3.4%** (211.09 trillion cu. ft.)
- **Nigeria 3.0%** (183.99 trillion cu. ft)
- **Venezuela 2.7%** (166.26 trillion cu. ft.)

Crude Oil Reserves
(in billions of barrels)

- **Saudi Arabia 20%** (266.75)
- **Rest of world 21.3%** (371.16)
- **Canada 13.4%** (178.59 billion barrels)
- **Iran 10.4%** (138.40)
- **Iraq 8.6%** (115.00)
- **Kuwait 7.8%** (104.00)
- **United Arab Emirates 7.3%** (97.80)
- **Venezuela 6.5%** (87.04)
- **Russia 4.5%** (60.00)

* Percentages do not total 100 due to rounding.

Source: Energy Information Administration

staff when he was prime minister under President Boris Yeltsin. Later, Putin made Medvedev his presidential chief of staff. Medvedev was also chairman of Gazprom, the world's largest producer of natural gas, but it is widely believed that Putin called the shots.

Having spent almost a decade doing Putin's bidding, Medvedev "is chemically conditioned to obey Mr. Putin," argued Andrei A. Piontkovsky, a political commentator and Putin critic. "This artificial construction of two czars creates a real factor of instability. But Putin . . . chooses the person with minimal potential damage for him." [17]

Still, Medvedev may be helped by the fact that Russia's political elite "is beginning to understand that political stability based on personal popularity is fragile," comments *Global Affairs* editor Lukyanov. After all, Putin himself was against tampering with the constitution to secure a third presidential term even though such a move would have had popular support. And Medvedev talks of the importance of strengthening the institutions.

"They [the elite] understand that to preserve the spirit of Putinism they have to transform the system," says Lukyanov.

In other words, the somewhat cynically termed "managed democracy" established by Putin — based on firm control of all primary levers of power and influence, including the internal security forces, mass media and expanded state monopolies — can survive only by evolving from its current cult of personality.

But a month after Medvedev was sworn in there is still ambiguity about who is really in charge. In the division of labor, "foreign policy is the responsibility of the presidency and can't be moved to the prime minister's office

Medvedev himself knows that the new diarchy will draw fire from skeptics. "I am sure that there are some people who are going to interpret this arrangement in their own way, and look for holes in it. . . . We will manage," he said in an interview shortly after his election. [16]

Putin brought the young St. Petersburg law professor to Moscow in 1999 to serve as a Kremlin deputy chief of

because that would be in violation of the Russian constitution," Lukyanov says. Even so, in June Russia's ambassador to Washington, Yuri Ushakov, was recalled to Moscow to head Prime Minister Putin's foreign policy team, a move the *Moscow Times* said, "effectively snatched away an area of authority held by President Dmitry Medvedev and the Kremlin administration." The *Times*, however, also quoted a government official as saying Ushakov's appointment did not upset the balance of power. The news about Ushakov emerged as Putin concluded a high-profile visit to Paris that was described as "presidential," including dinner with President Sarkozy, a rare honor for a visiting foreign prime minister. [18]

Lukyanov points out that national security is a Kremlin issue, and for Putin to assume its direction "would be a contradiction of the way it has been handled in the past," although, as prime minister Putin remains a member of the presidential Security Council. Medvedev may have been sending his mentor a message last week when he chaired his first meeting of the Security Council while the prime minister was out of town. Russian media observed that it was the first meeting of the council Putin had missed in eight years. [19]

But will the complicated arrangement survive? Lukyanov concludes it will last "for a period of months, if not years, but then Russian tradition will prevail, and one man will emerge as the ruler. I cannot imagine a situation in which Medvedev fires Putin, but Putin could resign, saying my task is done — I can retire."

Aleksei Makarkin, an analyst at the Center for Political Technologies in Moscow, told *The New York Times* he does not foresee any serious contradictions between the two leaders, but he and others fully expect a power struggle "between the teams around them." [20]

Of course, Putin is running the greater risk — in at least two respects. For one thing, history is full of stories of intended surrogates who turned on their benefactors. For another, as political analyst Shevtsova pointed out, "As Putin undermines Medvedev's influence, he also undermines the presidency. Putin, it seems, is busy dismantling his major legacy — presidential hyperpower."

The low-key election campaign revealed little of Medvedev's laid-back personality and still less of his policies. But in his one main campaign speech, analysts found traces of a more liberal approach than his predecessor's. "Freedom is the soul of all things, and without it all is as if dead," he said, quoting Catherine the Great.

"Freedom does not mean chaos, but respect for the country's laws." [21]

If Medvedev decides to free himself from the embrace of his mentor, analysts say, liberal policies could help him to establish his own separate identity. But would he risk a breakup? "He may not yet know the answer," wrote Shevtsova.

Meanwhile, the Russian media have yet to decide on whom to lavish the most attention, and "a very pronounced balance" is being observed in TV coverage of the two leaders, according to a media analyst in Moscow. As for the general public, a survey on May 17 and 18 found that 1 in 10 Russians thinks that Putin is still the country's president. [22]

Are the West and Russia heading for a new Cold War?

The current, tense relations between the United States and Russia have stirred memories of the half-century face-off between the West and the Soviet Union after World War II. Some commentators warn the situation today has the makings of a second Cold War; a few believe we are already there.

Talk of a new Cold War increased after President Putin, speaking at a conference in Munich, Germany, accused the United States of abusing its power and trying to establish a "uni-polar" world, which he defined as "one, single center of power, one, single center of force. . . . This is the world of one master." The rhetoric "reminds [us of] Cold War times," commented Sergei Rogov, director of the U.S.A.-Canada Institute at the Russian Academy of Sciences, in the online daily *Kommersant.* [23]

President Bush, Rogov wrote recently, wants it both ways. He is turning NATO into the dominant military political force in Europe by expanding the alliance into post-Soviet territory, yet at the same time "would like to avoid a breach with Russia and a new Cold War." Democratic Sen. Joseph Biden of Delaware, chairman of the Senate Foreign Relations Committee, is among those who believe "relations between the United States and Russia are at their lowest ebb since the end of the Cold War." He calls for a "new [U.S.] approach" to managing relations with Moscow. But Biden is also critical of Kremlin leaders for reverting "to a Cold War, zero-sum mentality in their dealings abroad." [24]

The components of the Cold War were two opposed nuclear superpowers, a propaganda offensive that never let up and a series of proxy wars in different parts of the world, with the superpowers or their surrogates backing the warring sides. But the perception of an even balance of forces between East and West, and the fear of starting a nuclear war, prevented a third world war.

Today, "there can be no Cold War because Russia is in no position to wage either a hot or cold war," says former White House national security adviser Brzezinski. The Russian nuclear arsenal is antiquated and badly serviced — if at all; the Warsaw Pact (the Soviet Union's military response to NATO) has been dismantled, and Russian ground forces are widely judged to have performed poorly in Chechnya, Russia's most recent armed conflict. [25]

Perhaps because he is Russian, *Global Affairs* editor Lukyanov sees a diminution of power on both sides. "The Cold War stage in international relations was when everything was determined by confrontation between the two superpowers," he says. "They could do what they wanted. But the time when Russia and the United States could determine world events is over. The international environment is absolutely different. There are other important players — the European Union, China, India."

The Russians, he continues, "are not so insane to believe that they could challenge the United States militarily or economically, but there is a feeling that after the Cold War, when Russia fairly disappeared from the international scene, the United States had the opportunity to shape the world into what it wanted, and it failed. So the Russians see the limits of American power, and it makes Russians arrogant towards the United States."

For Mark Brzezinski, a former Russia specialist in the Clinton White House (and, incidentally, son of Zbigniew), "what exists today is a cold peace" between the United States and Russia. While Putin rails against the United States, the Bush administration, distracted by Iraq, has if anything been "rather passive" in not challenging some of Putin's actions, Brzezinski says. For example, he says, "Bush has been silent about Putin's rollback of democracy."

In fact, in a rare public comment about Russia last June, Bush said, "In Russia, reforms that once promised to empower citizens have been derailed, with troubling implications." [26] But most analysts agree the Bush administration has soft-pedaled its criticism of Putin, even as anti-government media have been intimidated or suppressed — and several journalists even assassinated, such as Anna Politkovskaya — and leading figures like industrialist Mikhail Khodorkovsky have been arrested.

Cold War or not, the slowdown in the democratic process is a major sticking point for the United States, according to Andrew C. Kuchins, director of the Russia and Eurasian Program at the Center for Strategic and International Studies in Washington. "For the United States, Russia will never be a very trusted partner until it more fully embraces Western values and becomes really democratic," he says. "Until that happens, Russia will remain in the category of countries that are partners and allies of convenience or necessity. Russia, for at least the near term, appears fated to trust nobody and have no genuine allies, but only partners of convenience and necessity."

Does Putin have legitimate grievances with the Bush administration?

"One of the historic blunders of this administration has been to antagonize and alienate Russia, the winning of whose friendship was a signal achievement of [Presidents] Ronald Reagan and George H. W. Bush," wrote Pat Buchanan, the conservative commentator and former presidential candidate. "And one of the foreign policy imperatives of this nation is for statesmanship to repair the damage." [27] Buchanan lists a number of by-now-familiar actions taken by the George W. Bush administration (and by the Clinton administration before that) that have angered, and even alarmed, the Russians, including:

- The Bush administration's criticism of Putin's brutal handling of the war in Chechnya, the would-be separatist, predominantly Muslim republic;
- its attacks on Putin's increasingly negative human-rights record; and
- criticism of apparent attempts by the government to manipulate recent elections, including the March presidential election.

A Russian monitoring group claimed there were irregularities in both the December government elections and the presidential election. [28] And the Organization for Security and Cooperation in Europe refused to oversee both elections because of what it called excessive restrictions placed on it by Moscow. The group acknowledged, however, that Medvedev would have won even in a clean election.

Another major U.S.-Russian controversy centers on admitting former Warsaw Pact members Poland, Hungary and Czechoslovakia into NATO. Putin says, with some justification, that support for their admission was a betrayal of clear but implicit promises made by the West in 1990-1991. [29]

In 2004, a second NATO enlargement added Romania, Bulgaria and — over Moscow's protests — Lithuania, Latvia and Estonia. The inclusion of the Baltic States aroused Putin's great resentment because the Kremlin considered them, with their significant Russian minorities, within Moscow's sphere of influence. The second NATO expansion, Buchanan wrote, "moved a U.S.-led military alliance into [Russia's] front yard, and onto [its] side porch." [30]

In the Caucasus, Ukraine and Georgia (the birthplace of former Russian leader Josef Stalin) also want to join NATO to protect themselves from a bellicose Russia. Zbigniew Brzezinski contends if Russia's former satellites are running for protective cover in NATO, it is Russia's fault. Russian "nostalgia for an imperial status creates sustained and extensive hostility with all of its neighbors. . . . Russia's influence probably would be greater if Putin had had the intelligence to use the Moscow events to promote a genuine reconciliation, instead of following . . . a kind of not-very-intelligent, nostalgic policy of rehabilitating partially Stalinism and certainly rehabilitating imperial nostalgia." [31]

When Bush announced that the United States was withdrawing unilaterally from the 29-year-old Anti-Ballistic Missile Treaty in 2001, Putin called the withdrawal "a mistake." [32] The pullout meant the Bush administration could launch its plan to put 10 interceptor rockets in Poland, with a radar tracking station in the Czech Republic. [33] Bush insists the missiles are not directed at Russia but once in place will form a line of defense against "rogue states" — in other words, Iran and North Korea. A skeptical Moscow responded by testing new tactical and strategic missiles in May 2007, in a situation Putin said was "certainly growing into a new arms race" in Europe. [34]

In making his own case, Putin recently pointed out to a group of Western journalists that, "For the first time in history — and I want to emphasize this — there are elements of the U.S. nuclear capability on the European continent. It simply changes the whole configuration of international security."

Putin said the United States justifies the deployment "by the need to defend themselves against Iranian missiles. But . . . Iran has no missiles with a range of 5,000 to 8,000 kilometers. In other words, we are being told that this missile defense system is there to defend against something that doesn't exist. Our military experts cer-

tainly believe that this system affects the territory of the Russian Federation in front of the Ural Mountains. And, of course, we have to respond to that." [35]

After failing for months to get the Russians to agree to the missile project, the Bush administration in April changed tactics, trying to interest Moscow in a sweeping American offer to participate in existing NATO and U.S. missile defenses, and in the development of future defense technology. The Russians are warily examining the proposal.

Bush and Putin want to finish their respective presidencies "in the soft glow of mutual legacy-burnishing rather than the glare of a clash over future NATO expansion and U.S. missile deployments," wrote *Washington Post* columnist Jim Hoagland. "They will leave relations between the White House and the Kremlin mired in a rare, soggy middle ground of extended ambivalence." [36]

But Robert Joseph and J. D. Crouch II, former Bush administration officials who had worked on the missile-deployment project, maintain Putin has rejected earlier offers of cooperation. "Over five years, the United States has made proposal after proposal to work with Russia's military and industry on missile defense, offering modest cooperative activities . . . and projects that would be more technically and politically challenging," they wrote, but "each time cooperation has been deflected or rejected."

Putin's refusal, they say, "reflects [Russia's] increasing assertiveness as a major player on the international scene, helped by the price of energy exports. Moscow is eager to regain great-power status and thinks the path to success requires painting the United States as the threat." [37]

BACKGROUND

Authoritarian Terror

It's one of the grim ironies of modern Russian history that of the 13 leaders who preceded Medvedev in the Kremlin since the Bolshevik Revolution in 1917, most had as much power as the autocratic czars.* The Union

---

* The 13 leaders before Medvedev were Vladimir Ilyich Lenin (1917-1924), Aleksei Rykov (1924-1930), Vyachezlov Molotov (1930-1941), Josef V. Stalin (1941-1953), Georgi M. Malenkov (1953-1955), Nikolai A. Bulganin (1955-1958), Nikita S. Khrushchev (1958-1964), Leonid I. Brezhnev (1964-1982), Yuri V. Andropov (1982-1984), Konstantin U. Chernenko (1984-1985), Mikhail S. Gorbachev (1985-1991), Boris Yeltsin (1991-1999) and Vladimir Putin (2000-2008).

Communist Era *Russian Revolution eradicates Romanov dynasty and establishes Union of Soviet Socialist Republics (USSR).*

October 1917 Communist regime takes over Russia; Vladimir Lenin is first Soviet leader.

1920s-1950s Josef Stalin eventually succeeds Lenin. Millions of peasants and potential dissidents are killed or imprisoned. . . . After World War II, Stalin negotiates with allies for control over Eastern Europe.

1950s-1980s U.S. and Soviet Union vie for nuclear dominance and reach a Cold War standoff.

1985 Mikhail Gorbachev takes power and initiates political reforms.

1990s *Soviet Union fragments into 15 republics.*

1990 U.S. helps ease food shortage.

1991 Hard-liners stage unsuccessful August coup against Gorbachev, triggering dissolution of USSR.

1992 Russian President Boris Yeltsin launches economic reforms. . . . United States commits $24 billion in aid. . . . Yeltsin and Bush sign Strategic Arms Reduction Treaty (START).

1993 Yeltsin orders attack on Russian legislature to end opposition to economic program. . . . Voters approve new constitution giving president broader powers.

1994 Yeltsin starts war against separatist Chechen republic. . . . First U.S.-Russian space mission is launched.

1995 U.S. and Russia agree to START II.

1997 Russia and NATO agree to cooperate on defense issues.

1999 Yeltsin resigns and designates Prime Minister Vladimir Putin as acting president. Putin re-starts suspended Chechen offensive. Over Russian objections, Poland, Hungary and Czech Republic become NATO members.

2000-Present *Improving relations between Russia and the U.S. soon sour.*

2000 Newly elected Putin moves against oligarchs and independent media. . . . President Bill Clinton addresses Russian parliament, discusses Iran's nuclear program and Chechnya with Putin.

2001 After Sept. 11 terrorist attacks on New York and the Pentagon, Putin allows U.S. to use bases in Central Asia to launch war in Afghanistan. . . . President George W. Bush and Putin meet for first time in Crawford, Texas.

2002 United States buys uranium from dismantled Russian warheads. . . . Government shuts down Russia's last independent TV station.

2003 U.S.-led coalition invades Iraq; Putin calls invasion "big mistake."

2004 Putin re-elected; Freedom House downgrades Russia's rating to "not free." . . . Ukraine's "Orange Revolution" ends with election of opposition leader Viktor Yushchenko over Russian-backed candidate. . . . Baltic States join NATO.

2005 Bush extols democracy during visits to Latvia and Georgia; raises issue privately with Putin in Moscow. . . . Yukos oil company founder Mikhail Khodorkovsky is convicted of financial crimes and sent to prison.

2006 Putin hosts G8 summit in St. Petersburg. . . . Poll shows 57 percent of Russians see U.S. as "threat to global security." . . . U.S. aid to Russia totals $949 million.

2007 Putin accuses U.S. of seeking a "uni-polar world," with itself as "one single master." . . . Bush administration asks Poland and Czech Republic to allow deployment of anti-missile system to prevent nuclear attack by "rogue states."

2008 NATO summit in Bucharest, Romania, supports Bush anti-missile plan but shelves NATO membership for Georgia and Ukraine due to Kremlin opposition. . . . Putin protégé Dmitry Medvedev is elected president in March. . . . Bush and Putin meet for the last time as presidents, easing tension, but leaving missile issue unresolved.

of Soviet Socialist Republics (USSR) was, as historian Robert Service has noted, a "highly centralized, one-party dictatorship" that directed a predominantly state-owned economy and imposed "severe restrictions on national, religious and cultural self-expression." [38] And, democracy in the emergent Russian Federation remains a work in progress.

Lenin started the country on a path of industrialization and agricultural collectivization. After his death in 1924, communist party official Josef Stalin promoted himself as Lenin's political heir and gradually outmaneuvered his rivals. Although others held positions equivalent to prime minister, by the late 1920s Stalin was the de facto dictator of the Soviet Union. Stalin speeded up industrialization and used brutal methods to enforce agricultural collectivization — causing widespread famine and an appalling death toll in some regions: at least 1 million Kazakhs and between 5-8 million Ukrainians. [39]

Having eliminated his chief rival, Leon Trotsky, Stalin consolidated his own position through purges, political show trials and executions that all but wiped out the generation of politicians who had led the revolution. Hundreds of thousands were exiled to Siberian slave labor camps, known as the "gulag." Stalin's ruthlessness affected even his closest associates.

However, some modern historians have produced a revisionist view of Stalin's role in the purges. Using Russian source material uncovered since the collapse of the Soviet Union, some historians maintain that although Stalin remains the central figure in the terror, which he certainly initiated, the brutality may have gained a momentum beyond the dictator's intentions. Local authorities interpreted Stalin's orders in their own way, the historians argue, and Stalin had to keep regaining the initiative. [40]

As an ally of the United States and Great Britain during World War II, the Soviet Union suffered an estimated 27 million civilian and military deaths and extensive devastation. In the postwar conferences, President Franklin D. Roosevelt and British Prime Minister Winston Churchill allowed Stalin to bring the Baltic States into the Soviet Union and to establish Eastern Europe as a zone of Soviet influence. [41]

By the time of his death in 1953, Stalin had dropped what Churchill called an "Iron Curtain" over Eastern Europe and made the Soviet Union a nuclear power and political and economic competitor with the United States. The resulting nuclear "balance of terror" — or

theory of nuclear deterrence — is credited by many with keeping the superpowers from going to war: Neither side would start a conflict for fear of nuclear retaliation leading to mutually assured destruction (M.A.D.). Instead, the United States and the Soviet Union competed in an ideologically driven Cold War.

Brinkmanship

Nonetheless, there were moments of dangerous brinkmanship, such as the 1948 Berlin airlift. On June 24, the Soviet Union blocked road and rail access in and out of the U.S.-British-French sectors of West Berlin across Moscow-controlled highways in East Germany. In response, the British and U.S. air forces launched a massive airlift lasting continuously from June 28, 1948, to May 11, 1949. Allied planes airlifted 2.3 million short tons of food and necessities — ranging from milk to coal — to the people of West Berlin and made 266,600 flights. The success of the operation humiliated Moscow, forcing the Soviets to lift the blockade. [42]

Then in 1962, the Cuban Missile Crisis, which brought the world close to nuclear war, resulted from Soviet leader Nikita S. Khrushchev's decision to deploy intermediate-range missiles in Fidel Castro's Cuba in response to an emerging U.S. lead in strategic missiles. American ICBMs (intercontinental ballistic missiles) could reach targets in the Soviet Union, but Russian warhead-carrying rockets still could not reach U.S. shores. To Khrushchev, positioning missiles in the Caribbean evened the score. [43]

The story of the crisis is making something of a comeback these days because Putin has incorporated the incident into his argument against the planned deployment of missiles in Poland. Putin points out that for President John F. Kennedy, the positioning of Soviet missiles on America's doorstep could not be tolerated. After the missiles were discovered, JFK warned Khrushchev on Oct. 22 that a nuclear missile attack from Cuba would be regarded as an attack from the Soviet Union, and answered accordingly.

Kennedy demanded the removal of the nuclear missiles already in position in Cuba and ordered a naval blockade of the island to prevent further shipments of weapons. After six days of intense diplomatic activity, coupled with a massive deployment of U.S. forces to combat-ready levels, Khrushchev agreed to remove the missiles in return for a U.S. commitment not to invade Cuba. [44]

Russia Swimming in Profits from Energy Exports

But need seen for diversification of economy.

On Jan. 7, 2007, Russian oil suddenly stopped flowing to Germany and other European customers, without any warning from Moscow. Though the details are unclear, either Russia or Belarus had shut off the so-called "Friendship" pipeline because of a pricing dispute. But the end result was the same: suspension of crude deliveries to points further down the line including Poland and Germany. [1]

The cutoff, though brief, underscored Europe's dependence on Russia for its oil and gas supplies. Europe imports a quarter of its natural gas and 30 percent of its crude oil from Russia. [2]

Indeed, Russia's energy trump card is natural gas. It controls over a quarter of the world's natural gas reserves — more than any other country. [3]

Some politicians in Europe's capitals worry that their energy dependence makes them vulnerable to Kremlin pressure, but others argue that energy exports account for a large part of Russia's newfound prosperity, so why would they want to jeopardize their market?

Still, the Kremlin has been accused of hiking gas prices to express its displeasure with former Soviet neighbors seeking closer ties with the West, such as Ukraine and Moldova. But while Moscow has been known to use oil as a political weapon, price increases are more likely to be dictated by the market — and the need of the energy sector, and particularly the state-owned Russian oil company, Rosneft, to finance expensive modernization programs. [4]

In addition, in late 2007, Russian oil production reached a peak of 9.9 million barrels a day accounting for 65 percent of its exports, and the energy bonanza has pushed Russian central bank reserves to the third-highest in the world after Japan and China. The Russian stock market, considered negligible a dozen years ago, is now worth $1 trillion. [5] In 2008, however, crude production has declined as old wells dried out and the oil industry faced the challenge of developing new Siberian fields. [6]

The ever-present danger of a price slump has brought warnings — even from former President Vladimir Putin himself — that the Russian economy needs to diversify. That won't be easy, according to Marshall Goldman, an economics professor at Wellesley College in Massachusetts and a specialist in the Russian economy.

"Russia was never strong as a manufacturer and lacks a sense of working with the market," he said. [7]

But diversification needs entrepreneurs, and Russia was going in the opposite direction, towards greater state control.

The 1979 Soviet invasion of Afghanistan ended the period of East-West detente established during President Richard M. Nixon's administration (1969-74). In response, President Jimmy Carter asked the Senate to postpone action on the SALT II nuclear weapons treaty that he and Soviet Premier Leonid Brezhnev had already signed and recalled the U.S. ambassador to Moscow. The United States also boycotted the 1980 Summer Olympics in Moscow. Carter feared that the Soviet presence in Afghanistan would threaten the stability of strategic neighboring countries, such as Iran and Pakistan, and could lead to Soviet control over much of the world's oil supplies.

Reagan Talks Tough

In 1980, Carter lost the presidency to Ronald Reagan, who revived Cold War policies and rhetoric. Reagan called the Soviet Union "the evil empire" and escalated the nuclear arms race. He also began covert support of anti-Soviet resistance in Afghanistan, secretly sending billions of dollars to arm and train the mujahedeen rebel forces battling the Soviets. The effort was successful, but with unintended consequences: It helped give rise to the oppressive Taliban regime and Osama bin Laden's al Qaeda terrorist organization.

In attempting to keep up with Reagan's arms escalation, the Soviets crippled their already ailing economy, and in 1989 the Soviet Union rapidly began to disintegrate. The Berlin Wall came down, and Germany was reunified. As communist governments collapsed all over Eastern Europe, the Soviet Union was deprived of its reason for existence and in 1991 fractured into 15 independent nations, with Russia as the first and largest. [45]

Nowhere was that more evident than in the energy sector. Under President Boris Yeltsin, Russia's so-called oligarchs had become fantastically rich by acquiring state-owned energy companies and other businesses at bargain prices. Putin leveraged tax and environmental laws to get the energy sector back under state control.

In 2004, Russia's largest private corporation, Yukos, was forced into bankruptcy by a flood of back-tax claims, and its assets were taken over by the state. [8] A year later, Yukos' owner, billionaire Mikhail Khodorkovsky, was sentenced to eight years at hard labor for fraud and tax evasion. [9] The $40 billion company's struggle with the Putin government over what Yukos said were trumped-up charges came to symbolize the bare-knuckled rules of Russian capitalism. Yukos' oil operations were taken over by Rosneft, and in 2006 Russia forced foreign corporations to reduce their stakes in energy production in Russia. [10]

Thus Russian oil — which was under tight state control in the Soviet era and then was grabbed by well-connected entrepreneurs in the euphoric rush towards capitalism — had all but in name come full circle.

AFP/Getty Images/Tatyana Makeyeva

Russian oil tycoon Mikhail Khodorkovsky is serving eight years in prison for fraud and tax evasion.

[1] Steven Lee Myers, "Russian Crude Stops Flowing to Europe," *The New York Times*, Jan. 8, 2007, www.nytimes.com/2007/01/08/world/europe/08cnd-belarus.html.

[2] Michael Richardson, "Russia Puts Energy Importers Over a Barrel," *YaleGlobal*, July 10, 2008, http://yaleglobal.yale.edu/display.article?id=9418.

[3] *Ibid.*

[4] Nadejda M. Victor, "Russia's Gas Crunch," *The Washington Post*, April 6, 2008, www.washingtonpost.com/wp-dyn/content/article/2006/04/05/AR2006040501954.html.

[5] Peter Clarke, "Oil revenues help fuel Russia tech revival," *EETimes*, June 16, 2008, www.eetimes.eu/199904409.

[6] "Trouble in the pipeline," *The Economist*, May 8, 2008.

[7] Quoted in "Russia: Energy based economy tries to diversify," Radio Free Europe, Feb. 9, 2007, www.rferl.org/featuresarticle/2007/02/5520e102-b5db-4805-8b68-73dc922bf344.html.

[8] Vidya Ram, "Former Yukos Billionaire on Hunger Strike," *Forbes*, Jan. 30, 2008, www.forbes.com/2008/01/30/mikhail-khodorkovsky-yukos-face-cx_vr_0130autofacescan02.html.

[9] Tom Bergin, "BP may have to give up control of Russian venture," Reuters India, April 4, 2008, http://in.reuters.com/article/oilRpt/idINL0438309620080404.

[10] Kari Liuhto, "A future role of foreign firms in Russia's strategic industries," Pan-European Institute, undated, www.tse.fi/FI/yksikot/erillislaitokset/pei/Documents/Julkaisut/Liuhto04_07.pdf. Also see Peter Behr, "Energy Nationalism," *CQ Global Researcher*, July 2007, pp. 157-180.

In September 1994, President Boris Yeltsin came to Washington to seek financial aid from President Bill Clinton. From 1992 to 1994, the United States provided $40.4 billion in aid to Russia and post-communist Eastern Europe. In 1998, the International Monetary Fund (IMF) earmarked an additional $11.2 billion in aid to the Russians. In 1991, a group of experts connected with Harvard University formed the Russian Project and worked closely with Moscow on a sweeping overhaul of the economy. The aim was swift privatization and the introduction of free-market policies to replace communist economic controls.

But the U.S.-encouraged "shock therapy" had disastrous consequences. The new free market opened the way for "tycoon capitalism," which benefited a corrupt political oligarchy. By December 1992, for example,

90,000 state companies had been privatized, but less than 14 percent had been sold at auction. Most enterprises had changed hands at shockingly low valuations through insider deals. Key figures in the Harvard Russian project were accused by the Justice Department of using federal funds for personal gain. The charge of "knowingly defrauding the government" was originally extended to the university itself, but Harvard was able to establish that it was not involved. [46]

"Since Clinton's presidency, everybody miscalculated the chances of establishing a sustainable democracy in Russia, and the time it would take to build a democracy," says Krasheninnikova, of the Council for Trade and Economic Cooperation. "The Americans thought it should all go faster and should follow the American way, and were not prepared to recognize the progress that had

Journalists' Murders Blamed on Putin's Government

Victims were critics of Chechnya war, corruption and crackdown on freedoms.

Twenty-one Russian journalists have been murdered since 2000, according to Reporters Without Borders, a Paris-based international organization that champions freedom of the press. Three were killed in 2006: The well-known investigative reporter Anna Politkovskaya was shot in the elevator of her Moscow apartment building on Oct. 7; Yevgeny Gerasimenko, a reporter at the regional weekly *Saratovski Rasklad*, was found by his mother with his head in a plastic bag and his body showing signs of torture; [1] and Ivan Safronov, the prominent military correspondent of the business daily *Kommersant*, fell to his death from his Moscow apartment building. The authorities labeled the death a suicide for "private reasons," after what some commentators regarded as only a perfunctory inquiry. [2]

Politkovskaya's was the most high-profile slaying since the 2004 shooting in Moscow of American journalist Paul Klebnikov, editor of the Russian edition of *Forbes* magazine.

Official investigations have avoided linking the deaths to the victims' reporting, but other sources have pointed out that each one was known as a critic of Putin's government. Politkovskaya, for example, was an outspoken opponent of the war in Chechnya and a critic of corruption and shrinking freedoms in Russia. Politkovskaya's final article was published by a Russian tabloid newspaper, along with tran-

scripts of videotaped torture sessions of Chechens that she obtained. [3] Klebnikov reportedly had been warned not to publish a scoop about Russian arms sales to Syria and Iran.

Yelena Tregubova, a former member of the Kremlin press corps, sought political asylum in the United Kingdom after writing an unflattering book on government corruption, *Tales of a Kremlin Digger.* She lost her job as a result, and a bomb was exploded outside the door of her apartment. [4]

The killings are seen as part of a government campaign to control the media. "Putin has shut all independent TV channels, introduced harsh censorship, blocked access to the press for the democratic opposition," wrote Tregubova. [5] In 2007, Putin acknowledged that journalists in Russia faced serious threats and promised to protect them, but Nina Ognianova from the New-York-based Committee to Protect Journalists, said research by the committee shows that "Putin's pledge to protect the press has been seriously undermined by his own actions and those of his government." [6]

For example, Putin has signed press laws making criticism of public officials a criminal offense in certain circumstances. The law is vaguely written, giving the authorities considerable leeway in interpreting it, and thereby making political reporting more hazardous. Some analysts suggest that Putin himself, a product of a repressive regime, is indif-

been made. There is actually a widespread feeling in the Russian establishment that Russia may not be quite ready for democracy."

Despite their country's current prosperity, a generation of older Russians still remembers the financial crisis of 1998, when falling oil prices brought the emerging Russian economy — and Yeltsin's administration — to the brink of disaster. Even as the value of the ruble plummeted, a major liquidity shortage paralyzed the banking system. When, early in 1998, the International Monetary Fund delayed payment of a much-needed $670 million loan payment because economic reforms were going too slowly, Yeltsin's government declared a moratorium on repayments of foreign debts. The central bank even halted ruble-dollar trading because it didn't want to give out more cash. At the same time, a panicked

public began withdrawing their savings en masse, causing many banks to simply close their doors. By the end of the year, the Russian government had negotiated a $22 billion loan, but foreign confidence had suffered a blow from which it took several years to recover. [47]

Meanwhile, a massive organized-crime wave took hold. The FBI was called in to advise on how to combat the "Russian mafia," which was said to include more than 5,700 different groups. The greatest danger of all was the possible theft and sale to terrorists of weapons-grade plutonium from the poorly guarded Russian nuclear arsenals. [48]

Putin's Rise

Putin was Yeltsin's last prime minister and his choice to succeed him. On his election as president in 2000, Putin

ferent toward a free press. A BBC report quotes him as saying in 2003, "Russia has never had a free media, so I don't know what I am supposed to be impeding." [7]

Based on his campaign remarks on the importance of a free press, some observers are hopeful that new President Dmitry Medvedev will allow the media greater latitude. In early June, he took what some saw as a step in the right direction by effectively stopping in its tracks a press law amendment giving authorities power to close down a media outlet suspected of libel.

Medvedev did this by writing on the draft amendment that had already passed the committee stage in the Russian parliament: "It would be logical to remove this draft from further discussion." Reports said the amendment — ironically introduced after a Russian magazine had

Investigative reporter Anna Politkovskaya, a fierce critic of then-President Putin, was shot dead in 2006.

reported that Vladimir Putin was planning to divorce his wife and marry a 24-year-old Olympic gymnast — would almost certainly be scrapped. [8]

[1] "Russia-Annual Report 2007," Reporters Without Borders, www.rsf.org/article.php3 ?id_article=20823.

[2] See Nina Ognianova, "Putin's Broken Promise," *The Huffington Post*, Feb. 14, 2008, www.huffingtonpost.com/nina-ognianova/putins-broken-promise_b_86 763.html.

[3] C.J. Chivers, "Slain Reporter's Final Article Points to Torture in Chechnya," *The New York Times*, Oct. 13, 2006, p. A3.

[4] Yelena Tregubova, "Why I fled Russia," *The Independent*, June 5, 2007, www.independent.co.uk/opinion/commentators/yelena-tregubova-why-i-fled-putins-russia-and-why-the-west-must-appease-him-no-longer-451724.html.

[5] *Ibid.*

[6] Ognianova, *op. cit.*

[7] Paul Jenkins, "Russian journalism comes under fire," BBC News, July 2, 2004, http://news.bbc.co.uk/2/hi/europe /3860299.stm.

[8] Guy Faulconbridge, "Medvedev sinks tougher media libel law," Reuters, June 2, 2008, www.reuters.com/article/GCA-Russia/idUSL023778902008 0602.

spoke of furthering the democratic process; but many wondered whether the former intelligence officer really had been converted to democracy. In 2004, Putin fired Prime Minister Mikhail Kasyanov, a Yeltsin appointee who — according to a BBC analysis — had "strong sympathies for the oligarchs who made their fortunes in the chaotic days of privatization." [49]

A year earlier, Putin had arrested billionaire businessman Mikhail Khodorkovsky, one of the world's richest men and head of the Yukos oil group, on charges of tax evasion — "a move widely interpreted as a declaration of war against the so-called oligarchs," wrote Marshall Goldman in *Foreign Affairs* magazine. The oligarchs were an easy target, and Khodorkovsky's arrest was a popular move. Putin's own popularity jumped from 70 percent to 80 percent. [50]

Putin's relationship with his American counterpart, George W. Bush, appeared to start warmly but has shifted to cold and distant. Early on, when Putin visited Bush at his ranch in Crawford, Texas, Bush waxed eloquent about their meeting. "The more I get to know President Putin," Bush said, "the more I get to see his heart and soul, and the more I know we can work together in a positive way." [51]

But developments have undermined that early promise. On more than one occasion Bush has publicly criticized Putin for the slow pace of democratic reforms in Russia. "Strong countries are built by developing strong democracies. I think Vladimir heard me loud and clear," Bush said at a summit press conference with Putin in Slovakia in February 2005. [52]

Bush's comments clearly irritated Putin. "We are constantly being taught about democracy, but . . . those who

A natural gas pipeline is installed near St. Petersburg. Profits from Russia's natural gas reserves — the world's largest — as well as the country's substantial oil reserves, have helped usher in a new era of prosperity in Russia.

teach don't want to learn themselves," he said on one occasion. [53] And in 2006, with the Iraq insurgency raging, Putin snapped, "We certainly don't want to have the same democracy as they have in Iraq." [54]

Starting in 1995, when Russia signed an $800 million deal to help Iran complete two nuclear reactors, the United States has objected to Moscow helping the Iranians' nuclear ambitions. As work progressed very slowly on the light-water reactor at Bushehr, the Bush administration charged that Tehran wanted to produce enriched uranium so it could develop nuclear weapons — which the Iranians denied. Moscow has offered to supply enriched uranium for the Iranians, so Tehran would not have to develop its own. The Russians said they would keep track of the nuclear fuel, taking back the spent fuel to prevent the Iranians from extracting weapons-grade plutonium from it. The Iranians, however, had turned down the offer, arguing that dependence on a foreign supplier would make them vulnerable to supply cut-offs. [55]

The United States and Russia also are on opposite sides on the issue of independence for Kosovo — a Serbian province whose ethnic Albanian majority unilaterally declared independence from Serbia in February, with the West's acquiescence. Washington backs Kosovo's separation from Belgrade, Russia opposes it. The Albanians are mostly Muslims. Moscow considers the Orthodox Christian Serbs natural allies. [56]

The Russian leaders are also upset about the Bush administration's decision to unilaterally scrap the 1972 Anti-Ballistic Missile treaty so the United States could resume nuclear testing — which the treaty expressly forbade. Bush contended the treaty was a Cold War relic, since one of its two signatories — the former Soviet Union — no longer exists. To the Russians, however, it's still the cornerstone of nuclear deterrence. But Bush's plan to deploy an anti-missile system in Eastern Europe meant the treaty had to go.

And the Russians are nervous that the United States still occupies military bases in Uzbekistan and Kyrgyzstan in Central Asia, which they used — with Putin's blessing — to invade Afghanistan after 9/11. Five years after the attack on bin-Laden and the Taliban in Afghanistan, the Russians have asked the Americans to leave or set an exit date. No date has been set.

CURRENT SITUATION

Russian Discontent

Every four years, global relations are virtually put on hold while Americans elect their next president. This election year, the periodic hiatus began earlier because of the longer-than-usual primary campaign. Thus, for example, a NATO summit in Bucharest, Romania, on April 2-4 left a solid unfinished agenda for the next White House, and the Bush-Putin meeting that followed — a swan song for both — did little more than put gloss on the personal relationship and try to project the mood of goodwill to the future.

Meanwhile, despite strong support from President Bush, Georgia and Ukraine — two former Soviet republics on Russia's southwestern border — remain outside the North Atlantic alliance, which they want to join. NATO postponed their entry until an unspecified date following strong Russian objections to their entry into the alliance. [57]

Is Western-style democracy possible in Russia?

YES
Fyodor Lukyanov
Editor, Russia in Global Affairs, a Moscow-based foreign-policy quarterly

Written for *CQ Researcher*, June 2008

Vladimir Putin has views of his own about how Russia should be governed. These views often do not fit in with the picture the West would like to see. But Putin has never said that Russia does not seek to build a modern democracy. He does insist, however, that Russia must come to democracy following its own path — but he does not question the destination.

This distinguishes his approach from the classical Russian conservatism, which maintained that Russia has its own unique path to follow, which leads to its own special goal. That is, we should not only abandon the particular way of the West, but we should go opposite ways to different goals. Therefore, Putin's view marks a serious historical change: He acknowledges that we share a common destination with the West.

But what exactly is "Western-style democracy"?

Democratic development in various countries went through different stages and took different periods of time — from several centuries (as in England and Holland) to several decades (for example, Japan and Spain) or even a few years (Poland, Hungary and South Korea). The results differed, as well. Democracy, Italian-style, is different from Swedish democracy, while Japanese-style democracy cannot be compared with U.S. democracy. The difference is even greater with Indian or Taiwanese democracy.

All democratic countries are united in one thing — they recognize a set of a few general principles on which state administration is built, among them the separation of powers, an independent judiciary and political pluralism.

How these principles are translated into life is another matter, and every country does it in its own way.

It would be naïve to believe that a country that for centuries existed as a centralized empire of states can turn into a modern democracy within a few years. Conditions for that do not emerge overnight; society must ripen first. However, there are no grounds to believe that Russia is less capable of such ripening than other countries. As Russia becomes more mature, its society and political class will demonstrate a demand for state administration mechanisms that have proved effective in other countries.

Outside interference is often counterproductive. The process of democratic maturing can hardly be speeded up artificially — especially in such a huge and inert country as Russia. Yet, there is no doubt that, strategically, Russia will move precisely in this direction.

NO
Veronika Krasheninnikova
Director of U.S. Operations, Council for Trade and Economic Cooperation

Written for *CQ Researcher*, June 2008

There is a widespread consensus in the Russian establishment that the Russian people are not ready for a Western-type of democracy. This belief is shared by a number of experts as well as by society at large. In other words, the people themselves do not believe they are ready.

This stark fact is substantiated by opinion polls: In the recent presidential election, 64 percent of Russians had no objection to changing the constitution so that President Putin could run for a third term; 68 percent were willing to vote for anyone Putin presented as his "successor."

Despite pro forma progressive declarations, those who achieve positions of power quickly slip into timeworn habits: They govern by issuing orders from above. Furthermore, the majority of the governed prefer to be ordered around rather than taking responsibility. The Russian tradition of "Please come and rule over us" — dating back to the 9th century, when Slavic tribes invited the Varangians (Norsemen) to come and rule their country — remains pervasive.

Exterior factors also slow down the progress of democracy in Russia. Western accusations of "rolling back democracy" imply there was democracy in Russia in the 1990s. Although there may have been incipient institutions moving in the direction of democracy, to ordinary Russians the 1990s are associated with anarchy and chaos — if that is democracy, they want no part of it.

Moreover, the U.S. administration's democratizing pressure always equates democracy with American interests. People want to be democratic, but they do not want to be dominated by the U.S.A. This goes for countries all around the world, not only Russia.

Democracy, by definition, has to grow from within the *demos* in question; it cannot be imposed from the outside or from above. People themselves have to take responsibility for their own human dignity and rights. This realization grows with wealth and with rising living standards. The middle class has been continuously expanding in recent years, and this may be the greatest hope for the future. When people have nothing to lose but their chains, they tend to believe in simple solutions that produce October revolutions. When they have much to lose, people tend to behave much more responsibly.

Today, the Russians sacrifice their democratic liberties in the name of order and a fast economic recovery — just as the Americans sacrifice theirs in the name of security.

Administration efforts to enroll Ukraine and Georgia as members of NATO had angered the Russian leader. Moscow may have sulked when the Balkan states joined NATO, but membership for the two republics along east-west oil and gas routes are a much more serious issue. Putin says the West would be crossing a red line into an area of Russian influence.

Germany and France, anxious not to alienate Russia even further, led a campaign to put the U.S. proposal on hold. [58]

Le Monde calls Georgia "the most faithful American ally after Britain in overseas operations." Georgia (population 4.6 million) has 180 soldiers stationed in Kosovo, 2,000 deployed in Iraq and has pledged to shortly send 500 to Afghanistan. The Georgian army is U.S.-trained and equipped under the Pentagon's Train and Equip, and Sustainment and Stability Operations programs; and the United States covers two-thirds of Georgian soldiers' pay. [59]

Both Georgia and Ukraine are deeply disappointed at their continued exclusion from NATO and are surprised that Bush's support was insufficient to open NATO's door. When NATO's Secretary General Jaap de Hoop Scheffer tried to console them, saying membership would happen some day, he got a sharp response from Moscow. Any attempt by the alliance to re-open the issue, declared Sergei Ryabkov, director of the Russian Foreign Ministry's Department of European Cooperation, would be "the biggest possible strategic error." [60]

Meanwhile, NATO approved Bush's anti-missile project despite Putin's objections. The alliance encouraged Russian participation along lines previously outlined to Moscow by Secretary of State Condoleezza Rice and Defense Secretary Robert Gates. The Russians thus have on the table the most comprehensive offer yet to cooperate in the anti-missile project by combining respective technologies.

To agree, however, would imply that Putin considers Iran — which Moscow regards as a friendly nation — a potential nuclear threat. In a closed-door NATO meeting, the Russian leader repeated his earlier argument that, "No one can seriously think that Iran would dare attack the United States." Instead, he said, NATO should explore ways "to help Iran become more predictable and transparent." [61]

In another NATO decision favoring Washington, French Mirage combat planes have been deployed in Iceland to close a gap left in the alliance's defenses when the United States closed its 60-year-old base in Keflavik in 2006. The base had been closed because the Pentagon regarded it as a relic of the Cold War, but when the Russians resumed Soviet-era strategic patrols near Iceland, the Bush administration appealed to NATO, which agreed to send interceptors to Iceland to monitor the Russians.

'Strategic Framework'

Just after the Bucharest summit, the two outgoing presidents met at Putin's home in the Black Sea resort of Sochi in what would be their last chance to shape their legacy of eight years of U.S.-Russian relations. They put on a show of camaraderie, stressing that there was "no change in our fundamental attitude" — as Putin put it — over U.S. anti-missile plans. The two leaders agreed to leave the issue to their successors but drew up a "strategic framework" on future U.S.-Russian cooperation.

"We reject the zero-sum thinking of the Cold War," the document says. "Rather, we are dedicated to working together and with other nations to address the global challenges of the 21st century." The document lists an agenda of future cooperation on counter-terrorism, trade and Russia's long-standing bid to join the World Trade Organization — long blocked by the U.S. Congress. On nuclear non-proliferation, the leaders agreed on a managed reduction of thousands of nuclear weapons in their arsenals almost two decades after the fall of the Berlin Wall. [62]

While the arguments over missile deployment and NATO enlargement continued to dominate the East-West debate, other issues got pushed into the background — including the slow progress of democracy. In that respect, said independent Russian military analyst Aleksandr Golts, Putin had dominated the summit agenda. "By keeping up the rhetoric on the missile shield and NATO membership for Georgia and Ukraine, there was no mention of issues which Putin didn't want raised — freedom of expression and other similar problems," Golts told the Italian newspaper *la Repubblica*. "Putin imposed on Europe, on the United States and NATO an agenda of the 1980s." [63]

OUTLOOK

Who Will Run Russia?

When President Bush met Medvedev at Sochi, Russia's president-elect trotted out standard remarks about the importance of the U.S.-Russian relationship, calling it "a key factor of international security," and expressed his intention "to keep up that relationship . . . so there will be constructive engagement between us." [64]

Yet within less than a year after his swearing in on May 6, Medvedev will have to engage a new U.S. president, with a new agenda. Even so, the same national interests will be at stake, and the same key issues will be awaiting resolution.

The presumptive GOP candidate, Sen. John McCain, R-Ariz., says he would "take a hard line on Russia" and has even vowed to try to evict Russia from the G8 summit of industrialized nations — something the other G8 members probably wouldn't allow. McCain also seems determined to push ahead with the missile shield. [65]

Sen. Barack Obama, D-Ill., the presumptive Democratic nominee, has promised to be tougher than Bush was on Russia and to continue efforts to get Georgia and Ukraine into NATO. [66]

Medvedev, however, remains an unknown quantity, with the overriding question being: To what extent will Putin be speaking through Medvedev? Developments in Moscow will be closely watched for indications of a working relationship. Medvedev's first appearance on the international scene is likely to be at the G8 summit on July 7 in Tokyo. An early indication of who's in control could be whether Putin goes along as well.

European Union countries can be expected to ensure that the Georgia-Ukraine NATO membership question remains in abeyance, but it can always be brought up to pressure Moscow if the situation warrants it. Meanwhile, the Kosovo situation seems resolved since the Albanian declaration of independence. The main thrust now is for the United Nations and the international community to ensure full safeguards for Kosovo's 10 percent Serb minority.

Some analysts believe that, left to his own devices, Medvedev might adopt a liberal agenda, easing the pressure on Russia's persecuted democrats, journalists and other embattled groups. Much of this perception is based on his major campaign speech. Stephen Sestanovich, the top Russia expert at the Washington-based Council on Foreign Relations, called it "a kind of manifesto for a more liberal and democratic formula for governing Russia," citing Medvedev's call for more rule of law, an independent judiciary, reduced state interference and a crackdown on corruption. [67]

But Sestanovich also hedges his bets. "Nobody can be sure what [the speech] means," he said. "Nobody knows how seriously to take it. . . . I think Medvedev will have very little power to do anything, at least at the outset, without clearing it . . . with Putin." [68]

Meanwhile, Putin has already embarked on the new phase of his political career. He was formally elected leader of the United Russia party at its annual congress and received parliamentary approval as prime minister on May 8. Thus, Putin's prime ministerial appointment at the head of a party that dominates the State Duma (315 seats out of 450) has changed the basis of political power in Russia, making Putin's new office more than the rubber stamp position it was before.

On the economic front, by year's end Russia could finally be celebrating its accession to the 152-member World Trade Organization after nearly 15 years of negotiations. In 2006, Moscow and Washington signed an agreement clearing the major hurdle of American opposition to Russian membership. [69] WTO membership is important to Russia because it builds foreign investor confidence and is seen in Moscow as confirmation that Russia has emerged as a free-market economy. [70]

The shadow over Russia's bright economic picture is the steady decline in oil production, the instrument of Putin's successful presidency. In recent months production has dropped 2 percent below last October's peak of 9.9 million barrels a day — mostly due to aging Siberian wells running dry, poor handling of the industry and huge taxes (up to 90 percent). There are still massive reserves in remote eastern Siberia and the Sakhalin region, but exploiting them will require sizable investments. Still, the fact that oil and gas account for 50 percent of Russia's budget revenues and 65 percent of its exports should be incentive enough. [71]

As for U.S. relations with Russia, the new occupant in the Kremlin needs to remember one thing about his counterpart in the White House, according to McFaul at the Carnegie Institute: "Russia sees itself as the No. 1 interlocutor with the United States, but Washington doesn't. That asymmetry is not understood by Moscow." Perhaps each side needs to re-examine its priorities.

NOTES

1. David Morgan, "Bush phones Medvedev after Russian election win," Reuters, March 3, 2008, http://uk.reuters.com/article/gc07/idUKL28835238 20080304.

2. "Cameron: EU-Russia relations should be more positive," *EurActiv*, April 9, 2008, www.euractiv.com/en/foreign-affairs/cameron-eu-russia-relations-positive/article-171457.

3. Clifford J. Levy, "Putin Agrees to Be Protégé's Prime Minister," *The New York Times*, Dec. 18, 2007, www.nytimes.com/2007/12/18/world/europe/18russia.html.

4. Felix Goryunov, "Beware of the WTO," *Moscow Times*, May 28, 2008, www.moscowtimes.ru/article/1016/42/367803.htm.

5. Simon Tisdall, "Putinism could be the next Russian export," *The Guardian*, Nov. 21, 2007, www.guardian.co.uk/world/2007/nov/21/tisdallbriefing.simontisdall.

6. "Bush congratulates Russian President-elect Medvedev," *Novosti*, March 4, 2008. http://en.rian.ru/russia/20080304/100642522.html. See also www.reuters.com/article/topNews/idUSL2883523820080304?feedType=RSS&feedName=topNews.

7. See White House press conference at www.whitehouse.gov/news/releases/2001/06/20010618.html.

8. Masha Lipman, "Medvedev's Chance to Lead?" *The Washington Post*, March 26, 2008, p. A19, www.washingtonpost.com/wp-dyn/content/article/2008/03/25/AR2008032502347.html.

9. Peter Finn, "Putin, in Speech, Accuses U.S. of Setting Off 'New Arms Race,' " *The Washington Post*, Feb. 9, 2008, p. 9.

10. "Zbigniew Brzezinski Assesses U.S.-Russia Relations," Radio Free Europe, May 11, 2005, www.rferl.org/featuresarticle/2005/05/b62307e1-832c-4fbc-ab91-ba8fa7a0eb24.html.

11. See Finn, *op. cit.*, p. 9.

12. Background information on Russia from Energy Information Administration, www.eia.doe.gov/cabs/Russia/Background.html.

13. Robert Kagan, "New Europe, Old Russia," *The Washington Post*, Feb. 6, 2008, p. A19, www.washingtonpost.com/wp-dyn/content/article/2008/02/05/AR2008020502879.html.

14. "Russian oil supply stop unsettles Germany," United Press International, Feb. 25, 2008, www.upi.com/International_Security/Energy/Briefing/2008/02/25/russian_oil_supply_stop_unsettles_germany/5189/.

15. Lilia Shevtsova, "Russians should prepare for the unexpected," *Daily Telegraph*, Feb. 18, 2008, www.telegraph.co.uk/opinion/main.jhtml?xml=/opinion/2008/02/20/do2003.xml.

16. "Russia's Medvedev hints at Kremlin power struggle," Reuters, March 27, 2008, www.reuters.com/article/worldNews/idUSL2735802820080327.

17. Levy, *op. cit.*

18. "Putin Seen Tapping Ambassador to U.S.," *Moscow Times*, June 2, 2008, www.themoscowtimes.com/article/1010/42/367910.htm.

19. Jonas Bernstein, "Putin Makes Foreign Policy Abroad, Medvedev Chairs Security Council at Home," *Eurasia Daily Monitor*, June 2, 2008, www.jamestown.org/edm/article.php?article_id=2373106.

20. Levy, *op. cit.*

21. See transcript at "Major Speeches: Speech at the Krasnoyarsk Economic Forum," Feb. 15, 2008, www.medvedev2008.ru/english_2008_02_15.htm.

22. Bernstein, *op. cit.*

23. Sergei Rogov, "U.S. to face choice: Partnership or Confrontation," *Kommersant*, March 28, 2008, www.kommersant.com/p872195/r_527/U.S.-Russia_relations_reached_turning_point/.

24. Joseph Biden, "U.S. must take a new look at Russia's soul," *Moscow Times*, March 25, 2008, p. 11.

25. For background, see Roland Flamini, "Nuclear Proliferation," *CQ Global Researcher*, January 2007, pp. 1-26.

26. Michael Fletcher, "Russia Has 'Derailed' Its Reforms, Bush Says," *The Washington Post*, June 6, 2007, www.washingtonpost.com/wp-dyn/content/article/2007/06/05/AR2007060500148.html.

27. Patrick J. Buchanan, "Doesn't Putin Have a Point?" *VDare.com*, Feb. 12, 2007, www.vdare.com/buchanan/070212_putin.htm.

28. Nabi Abdullaev, "Complaints of Fraud, Bribery and Pressure," *Moscow Times*, March 3, 2008, www.cdi.org/russia/johnson/2008-47-12.cfm.

29. Anatole Lieven, "A New Iron Curtain," *The Atlantic*, January 1996, www.theatlantic.com/issues/96jan/nato/nato.htm.

30. Buchanan, *op. cit.* For additional background, see

Mary H. Cooper, "Future of NATO," Feb. 28, 2003, *CQ Researcher*, pp. 177-200.

31. Zbigniew Brzezinski Assesses U.S.-Russia Relations," *op. cit.*

32. "America withdraws from ABM Treaty," Dec. 13, 2001, BBC News, http://news.bbc.co.uk/2/hi/amer icas/1707812.stm.

33. *Ibid.*

34. "Russian President Putin Interviewed by Journalists from G8 Countries," *Global Research.ca*, June 11, 2007. www.globalresearch.ca/index.php?context= va&aid=5938.

35. *Ibid.*

36. Jim Hoagland, "NATO's Middling Agenda," *The Washington Post*, March 28, p. A19, www.washing tonpost.com/wp-dyn/content/article/2008/03/27/A R2008032702618.html.

37. Robert Joseph and J. D. Crouch II, "Moscow's Missile Gambit," *The Washington Post*, March 13, 2008, p. A17, www.washingtonpost.com/wp-dyn /content/article/2008/03/12/AR2008031203394.html.

38. Kenneth Jost, "Russia and the Former Soviet Republics," *CQ Researcher*, June 17, 2005, pp. 541-564.

39. *Ibid.*

40. See "Stalinist Terror: New Perspectives," essays edited by John Arch-Getty and Roberta Thompson Manning, Cambridge University Press, 1993.

41. Jost, *op. cit.*

42. For chronology of the Berlin Airlift, see "Dates and Statistics," British Berlin Airlift Association, www .bbaa-airlift.org.uk/statistics.html.

43. "Cuban Missile Crisis," GlobalSecurity.org, www .globalsecurity.org/military/ops/cuba-62.htm.

44. *Ibid.*

45. For background, see Victoria Pope, "Soviet Republics Rebel," *CQ Researcher*, July 12, 1991, pp. 465-488.

46. George W. Krasnow, "Would Harvard Ever Help Russia?" *Johnson's Russia List*, March 10, 2006, www .cdi.org/russia/johnson/2006-62-24.cfm.

47. "Chronology of Russian Financial Crisis," *The Washington Post*, Aug. 27, 1998, www.washington post.com/wp-srv/inatl/longterm/russiagov/stories /russiachron.htm.

48. "Mr. Yeltsin Goes to Washington," BNET, Sept. 26, 1994, http://findarticles.com/p/articles/mi_m0 EPF/is_n4_v94/ai_16805514.

49. Sheila Barter, "Analysis: Putin moves against old guard," BBC News, Feb. 23, 2004. http://news .bbc.co.uk/2/hi/europe/3517867.stm.

50. Marshall Goldman, "Putin and the Oligarchs," *Foreign Affairs*, Nov/Dec 2004, www.foreignaf fairs.org/20041101faessay83604/marshall-i-goldman /putin-and-the-oligarchs.html.

51. "President Bush and President Putin Talk to Crawford Students," Office of the Press Secretary, White House, Nov. 15, 2001, www.whitehouse .gov/news/releases/2001/11/20011115-4.html. For additional background, see David Masci, "U.S.-Russia Relations," *CQ Researcher*, Jan. 18, 2002, pp. 25-48.

52. "Bush criticizes Putin on democracy's slide," *China Daily*, Feb. 2, 2005, www.chinadaily.com.cn/eng lish/doc/2005-02/25/content_419378.htm.

53. Text of speech to Munich Conference on Security Policy, Munich, Germany, Feb. 10, 2007, www.securityconference.de/konferenzen/rede.php? sprache=en&id=179.

54. David Jackson, "A Changing Relationship," *USA Today*, July 1, 2007, www.usatoday.com/news/wash ington/2007-07-01-bush-putin_N.htm.

55. Michael Gordon, "Against U.S. wishes, Russia will sell reactors to Iran," *The New York Times,* July 3, 1998, www.fas.org/news/iran/1998/980307-iran-nyt.htm; also see Jean-Christophe Peuch, "Were Moscow Talks just about Uranium Enrichment?" Radio Free Europe, Feb. 22, 2008, www.rferl.org /featuresarticle/2006/02/A5B0EBF6-2E6E-43AE-96B3-BBCAB7268B4A.html.

56. Dan Bilefsky, "Battle lines drawn over Kosovo," *Scotsman*, Feb. 24, 2008, http://news.scotsman.com /latestnews/Battle-lines-drawn-over-Kosovo.380992 7.jp. For additional background, see Brian Beary, "Separatist Movements," *CQ Global Researcher*, April 2008, pp. 85-114.

57. "NATO allies rebuff Bush on expansion," *Think Progress*, April 4, 2008, http://thinkprogress.org /2008/04/04/bush-nato/.

58. "Putin to NATO: Star guest or party pooper," ABC News, March 31, 2008, www.abc.net.au/news/stories/2008/03/31/2203620.htm.

59. Piotr Smolar, "Recalee, la Georgie, allie militaire des Etats-Unis, attend son heure," *Le Monde*, April 5, 2008, p. 6. Also see www.nytimes.com/2008/04/03/world/europe/03nato.html?_r=1&hp&oref=slogin.

60. "Nato denies Georgia and Ukraine," BBC News, April 3, 2008, http://news.bbc.co.uk/2/hi/europe/7328276.stm.

61. "No Cold War, but no deals at NATO-Russia summit," Agence France-Presse, April 4, 2008, http://afp.google.com/article/ALeqM5hqyJUgrTTt5hqddsGEOwL8dH6OpA.

62. "Bush, Putin and their successors," *International Herald Tribune*, April 8, 2008, www.iht.com/articles/2008/04/08/opinion/edrussia.php. The document is at www.whitehouse.gov/news/releases/2008/04/20080406-4.html.

63. "Il Cremlino cerca credibilita' per il neo leader Medvedev," *la Repubblica*, April 5, 2008, p. 13.

64. "President Bush Meets with President-Elect Dmitry Medvedev of Russia," White House press release, April 6, 2008, www.whitehouse.gov/news/releases/2008/04/20080406-1.html.

65. Erik Christiensen, and William Partlett, "The Candidates and Russia," *Foreign Policy in Focus*, www.fpif.org/fpiftxt/5043; also see Elisabeth Bumiller and Larry Rohter, "Foreign Policy: 2 Camps Seek McCain's Ear," *The New York Times*, April 10, 2008, p. 1.

66. Abdul Ruff, "Vote 2008: Candidates united in foreign policy," *Global Politician*, June 1, 2008, http://globalpolitician.com/24828-elections-foreign-policy.

67. Transcript, Medvedev's Krasnoyarsk speech, *op. cit.*

68. "Sestanovich: Behind the Scenes 'Warfare' As Russia Awaits Putin Successor," Council on Foreign Relations, Feb. 26, 2008, www.cfr.org/publication/15602/sestanovich.html?breadcrumb=%2Fissue%2F.

69. See Helen Cooper, "U.S. and Russia Sign Accord on W.T.O. Membership," *The New York Times*, Nov. 19, 2006, www.nytimes.com/2006/11/19/world/asia/20prexycnd.html?_r=2&fta=y&oref=slogin&oref=slogin.

70. "Russia inches closer to WTO accession," *EurActiv*, Feb. 18, 2008, www.euractiv.com/en/trade/russia-inches-closer-to-wto-accession/article-170367.

71. "Trouble in the pipeline," *The Economist*, May 8, 2008, www.economist.com/business/displaystory.cfm?story_id=11332313.

BIBLIOGRAPHY

Books

Baker, Peter, and Susan Glasser, *Kremlin Rising: Vladimir Putin's Russia and the End of Revolution*, updated edition, Potomac Books, 2007.
Two former Moscow hands (both news correspondents and married to each other) trace Putin's path to power and his major role in creating the new Russia.

Goldgeier, James M., and Michael McFaul, *Power and Purpose: U.S. Policy Towards Russia after the Cold War*, Brookings Institution Press, 2003.
The director of the Institute of European, Russian, and Eurasian Studies at George Washington University (Goldgeier) and a senior fellow at the Hoover Institute (McFaul) examine how American policy makers coped with the opportunities and challenges presented by the "new" Russia.

Politkovskaya, Anna, *Putin's Russia: Life in a Failing Democracy*, Metropolitan Books, 2005.
A prominent Russian journalist who was assassinated in 2006 paints a critical portrait of President Vladimir Putin's autocratic rule.

Satter, David, *Darkness at Dawn: the Rise of the Russian Criminal State*, Yale University Press, 2003.
A Russia specialist based in Washington traces the rise of the Russian mafia and the economic chaos that followed the collapse of the Soviet Union.

Talbott, Strobe, *The Russia Hand: A Memoir of Presidential Diplomacy*, Random House, 2002.
A former deputy secretary of State and the Clinton administration's top specialist on Russia provides a first-hand account of President Clinton's handling of Boris Yeltsin.

Articles

Arbatov, Alexei, "Are things really so bad?" *Russia in Global Affairs*, Aug. 8, 2007, www.foreignaffairs.org /20040301faessay83204/andrei-shleifer-daniel-treis man/a-normal-country.html.
A member of the Russian Academy of Science downplays fears the U.S. and Russia are heading for a new Cold War.

Belton, Catherine, "Anointed enigma: The quiet rise of Dmitry Medvedev," FT.com, Feb. 28, 2008, www.ft .com/cms/72ede4b6-e626-11dc-8389-0000779fd2ac,d wp_uuid=03d100e8.
A *Financial Times* correspondent details how Medvedev rose to the presidency.

Levy, Clifford, "Putin Protégé Secures Election Victory," *The New York Times*, March 3, 2008, p. A1.
Levy reports on Dmitry Medvedev's expected victory in the Russian presidential election.

Lyne, Sir Roderic, "Russia and the West: Is Confrontation Inevitable?" *Russia in Global Affairs*, January-March 2008, pp. 86-103.
A British expert says Russian-Western tensions made the idea of a partnership "unrealistic."

Myers, Stephen Lee, "U.S. Frustrated by Putin's Grip on Power," *The New York Times*, Oct. 15, 2007.
Myers describes problems the Bush administration is having in dealing with Putin.

Ramonet, Ignacio, "The World's New Look," *Le Monde Diplomatique* (English Edition), December 2001, www.mondediplofriends.org.uk/t_dec01art1.htm.
An international-affairs commentator looks at the world after the 9/11 attacks, with special reference to Russia.

Schleifer, Andre, and Daniel Treisman, "A Normal Country," *Foreign Affairs*, March/April 2004, www .foreignaffairs.org/20040301faessay83204/andrei- shleifer-daniel-treisman/a-normal-country.html.
A Harvard economics professor (Schleifer) and an associate professor of political science at the University of California, Los Angeles question the critical majority view of post-Soviet Russia.

Reports and Studies

"The Russian Federation," Brookings Institution, 2006, www.brookings.edu/reports/2006/10russia.aspx.
A team of Brookings fellows and researchers studies the policies and realities of energy powerhouse Russia.

Bovt, Georgy, "Too Alien for Europe," *Russia Profile*, May 7, 2008, www.russiaprofile.org/page.php?page id=Politics&articleid=a1210173951.
A Russian economist says the relationship between Brussels and Moscow has reached a stalemate.

Nikitin, Alexander, "The End of 'Post-Soviet' Space," Chatham House Briefing Papers, February 2007, www.chathamhouse.org.uk/files/3406_bpnis0207.pdf.
An environmental activist gives his view of the changing political orientation of the newly independent former Soviet states.

Robertson, Lord, "NATO'S Transformation," NATO News Articles, Nov. 28, 2003, www.nato.int/docu /articles/2003/a031027a.htm.
The North Atlantic Alliance's then-secretary general outlines NATO's policy on enlargement in the post-Soviet era.

For More Information

Brookings Institution, 1775 Massachusetts Ave., N.W., Washington, DC 20036; (202) 797-6000; www.brookings.edu. A nonprofit, public policy organization conducting research to "create a more open, safe, prosperous and cooperative international system."

Carnegie Moscow Center — Carnegie Institute for International Peace, 1G/2, Trevskaya, Moscow, 125009, Russia; (495) 935-8904; www.carnegie.ru/en. The Moscow branch of a Washington think tank, with foreign and Russian researchers working on a broad range of policy issues.

Center for National Security Studies, 2 Skovorody St., 04070 Kiev, Ukraine; (38-044) 416-6048; www.ukma.kiev.ua. Concentrates on studies and analyses of internal and external threats to Ukraine's national security.

Center for Russian and East European Studies, University Center of International Politics, 4400 Wesley W. Posvar Hall, University of Pittsburgh, Pittsburgh, PA 15260; (412) 648-7404; www.ucis.pitt.edu/crees. Conducts in-depth studies on Russian affairs.

Council on Foreign Relations, 58 East 68th St., New York, NY 10065; (212) 434-9400; www.cfr.org. An independent, non-partisan think tank dedicated to improving global understanding; publishes the authoritative *Foreign Affairs* magazine.

Gramsci Institute, Fondazione Istituto Gramsci, Via Portuense 95c, 00153 Rome, Italy; (396) 580-6646. A think tank devoted to the left-wing philosopher Antonio Gramsci; its archives hold the papers of leading Italian communists, including Palmiro Togliatti, who spent years living in Moscow, and Enrico Berlinguer, founder of Eurocommunism.

Institute for U.S. and Canadian Studies (ISKRAN), 2/3 Khlebny per., Moscow 123995, Russia; (7095) 290-5875; http://iskran.iip.net/engl/index-en.html. A Russian think tank focusing on U.S. and Canadian foreign and economic policy.

Institute of Economics — Russian Academy of Science (IERAS), 32 Nakhimovskiy prop., 117218 Moscow, Russia; (7499) 724-1541; www.inecon.ru. Studies the social transformation and modernization practices of countries in transition to a market economy and democracy.

Institute of European Affairs, Migration and Eastern Policy Program, Ul Szpitalna 5 lok 22, 00-031 Warsaw, Poland; (48-22) 556-4260; www.isp.org.pl. A think tank concerned with Poland's relations with neighboring states.

Institute of World Economy and International Affairs — IMEMO, Profsoyuznaya St. 23, Moscow GSP-7, Russia; (495) 120-5236; imemo.ru.en. A well-known center of fundamental and applied socioeconomic, political and strategic research, with close ties to the Russian establishment.

Kennan Institute for Advanced Russian Studies, Woodrow Wilson Center; One Woodrow Wilson Plaza, 1300 Pennsylvania Ave., N.W., Washington, DC 20004-3027; (202) 691-4100; www.wilsoncenter.org. Brings scholars and governmental experts together to discuss political, social, and economic issues affecting Russia and other successor states of the Soviet Union.

Russia and Eurasia Program, Royal Institute of International Affairs — Chatham House; 10 St James's Square, London SW1Y 4LE, England; (44207) 7957-5700. Studies the foreign and domestic policies of Russia and the members of the Commonwealth of Independent States.

13

The New Latin America

Roland Flamini

The changing face of Latin American leaders is reflected in, from left, Brazil's Luiz Inacio Lula da Silva, a former steel worker and an admirer of Cuba's Fidel Castro; Cristina Fernández de Kirchner, Argentina's first female president; and Bolivia's Evo Morales, an Aymara Indian and Latin America's only indigenous head of state.

W hen Cuban leader Fidel Castro announced on Feb. 19 that he was stepping down after nearly 50 years in power, the news — though widely reported — had limited impact in other Latin American countries. Once, revolutionary Cuba was an influential force in the region, but Latin America has since moved on.

Of course, the legendary Castro is still an icon of the left. But, while Latin America's current crop of leaders are socialist or left-leaning — like Brazil's President Luiz Inacio Lula da Silva, a lifelong admirer of Fidel — their governments are far removed from his dogmatic and ruinous communist system.

Developments in Cuba were quickly overshadowed by tension in the Andes, where Venezuela and Ecuador moved troops to their respective borders with Colombia after Colombian security forces on March 1 killed a top leader of a Colombian Marxist guerrilla group who was hiding in Ecuador's border area. However, an armed confrontation was considered unlikely, and the stand-off failed to dim the good news from the region.

This is Latin America's season of promise. In recent years the 22 countries that make up Latin America have quietly transformed a hemisphere once plagued by civil wars, brutal repression, mass murder, dictatorships and military juntas into functioning democracies focusing increasingly on their daunting social problems. *

Leftist administrations of one sort or another have been elected in Argentina, Brazil, Chile, Uruguay, Nicaragua, Venezuela, Bolivia,

From *CQ Researcher,*
March 2008.

---

* In this report, Latin America refers to South America, Central America, Mexico and Cuba.

Latin Countries Leaning to the Left

The 22 predominantly Spanish-, Portuguese- and French-speaking countries that make up Latin America stretch from Mexico in the north to Chile at the continent's southern tip and have a population of more than 500 million. Four countries, including Cuba, lean decidedly to the left, five are more centrist to right-wing and the rest follow moderate socialist policies.

Legend:
- ■ Communist
- ■ Leftist/Populist
- ■ Center-Right
- ☐ Moderate Socialist

* Having election in April and leftist candidate is expected to win.

Source: The World Bank

Ecuador and, in all likelihood after April elections, in Paraguay. All promised better conditions to the underclass: more employment, better social benefits and a larger share of the country's wealth. Only Colombia, Mexico and Honduras are run by more market-oriented, centrist or right-leaning leaders.

However, pigeon-holing the new generation of leaders is not easy, warns Antonio de Aguilar Patriota, Brazil's ambassador to Washington. "The categories of leftists and rightists don't apply so well to what's happening today in South America," he said recently. "They don't capture the political dynamics of the moment. These days democracy is taking root. All governments in South America are democratically elected." [1] In other words, pragmatism tends to win out over ideology among today's Latin American leaders.

Asked to review a book on the current situation in Latin America, Moisés Naím, a former government minister in Venezuela and now editor-in-chief of Washington-based *Foreign Policy* magazine, headlined his article "Ugly Betty Getting Prettier." His play on the title of the popular U.S. sitcom (itself inspired by a Colombian telenovela, or television soap opera) is, he says, "a good metaphor for what is happening throughout most of the region: Inflation is plummeting, financial debt gone, public financing under control — a fiscal system superior to the that of United States."

Governments have moved toward open societies and pragmatically embraced the global economy. By carefully managing their economies and benefiting from global trade tailor-made for Latin America's natural resources, the once debt-ridden region has enjoyed five continuous years of respectable growth almost across the board. (*See chart.*) Overall, Latin American economies grew an estimated 5.4 percent in 2007, and Mexico and Central America by 4.1 percent. [2]

On the political front, with two elected female presidents, Latinas are emerging as a new political force, as are the region's more than 650 indigenous groups. [3] (*See sidebar, p. 352.*) Mestizo, mixed-race and Indian groups are gaining influence, particularly in some Andean states, where Indians supported socialist Rafael Correa Delgado in Ecuador and Evo Morales — an Aymara Indian and Latin America's only indigenous head of state — in Bolivia. *

As the region tackles its chronic high poverty rates, it has even begun to export its poverty-alleviation systems. Bangladesh and Brazil are among the countries that have adopted Mexico's highly effective *Bolsa Familia* (Family Fund), an initiative that helped cut the number of Mexican families living in extreme poverty by 49 percent between 1998 and 2004. [4] A Venezuelan youth orchestra program that trains at-risk teenagers as musicians has been copied by 23 countries across the hemisphere. A 26-year-old Venezuelan conductor once linked to the program, Gustavo Dudamel, was recently appointed musical director of the Los Angeles Philharmonic. [5]

To be sure, corruption, injustice, high crime rates, drug smuggling and dismal social problems still cast a dark shadow over much of Latin America, where the gap between the rich and the poor is the largest in the world.

Latin Incomes on the Rise

Per capita income grew 12.3 percent in Latin America between 1995 and 2005, but incomes fell in Paraguay and oil-rich Venezuela. The biggest increases occurred in Belize and Chile.

Per Capita GDP
(in $US, adjusted for inflation)

Country	1995	2005	% Change
Argentina	$7,199.30	$8,130.80	12.9%
Belize	$2,905.70	$4,024.90	38.5%
Bolivia	$947.70	$1,033.40	9.0%
Brazil	$3,327.10	$3,573.70	7.4%
Chile	$4,261.70	$5,729.20	34.4%
Colombia	$2,076.40	$2,156.90	3.9%
Costa Rica	$3,607.60	$4,504.90	24.9%
Cuba	$2,055.60	n/a	n/a
Ecuador	$1,333.90	$1,550.20	16.2%
El Salvador	$1,993.10	$2,128.60	6.8%
Guatemala	$1,588.50	$1,720.40	8.3%
Guyana	$706.90	$798.60	13.0%
Honduras	$917.80	$977.30	6.5%
Mexico	$4,866.00	$5,993.20	23.2%
Nicaragua	$688.50	$835.10	21.3%
Panama	$3,470.60	$4,433.80	27.8%
Paraguay	$1,483.90	$1,296.20	-12.6%
Peru	$1,978.90	$2,340.40	18.3%
Suriname	$1,727.80	$2,247.40	30.1%
Uruguay	$5,622.20	$6,083.90	8.2%
Venezuela	$5,119.60	$4,939.20	-3.5%
Latin America	**$3,602.20**	**$4,044.10**	**12.3%**

Source: "Statistical Yearbook for Latin America and the Caribbean, 2006," U.N. Economic Commission for Latin America and the Caribbean, 2007

In his perceptive new book, *Forgotten Continent: The Battle for Latin America's Soul*, British journalist Michael Reid describes the region's struggle as being between durable mass democracies (Brazil, Chile) that follow pragmatic, moderate economic policies while addressing poverty and democratic reform and the autocratic, left-wing, populist model of Venezuela's flamboyant, radical President Hugo Chávez. [6]

Chávez is Fidel Castro with oil. Like Castro, he is virulently anti-American and embraces revolutionary social

---

* In addition to Bolivia and Ecuador, the Andean states — which border on or contain portions of the Andes Mountains — include Peru, Chile, Colombia, Argentina and Venezuela.

Three Economies Dominate the Region

Brazil, Mexico and Argentina generated nearly three-quarters of Latin America's $2.2 trillion gross domestic product (GDP) in 2005, largely thanks to their rich natural resources and extensive agricultural and ranching industries.

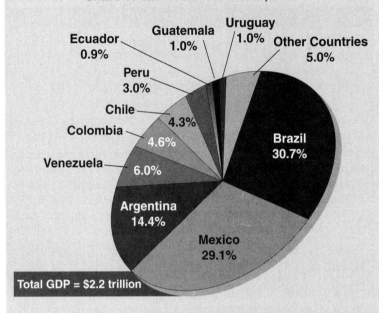

Share of Latin America's GDP, 2005

Ecuador 0.9%
Guatemala 1.0%
Uruguay 1.0%
Other Countries 5.0%
Peru 3.0%
Chile 4.3%
Colombia 4.6%
Venezuela 6.0%
Argentina 14.4%
Mexico 29.1%
Brazil 30.7%

Total GDP = $2.2 trillion

Source: "Statistical Yearbook for Latin America and the Caribbean, 2006," U.N. Economic Commission for Latin America and the Caribbean, 2007

policies that he wants to spread beyond his own borders. Using money from Venezuela's vast oil reserves — the largest in the hemisphere — Chávez extends his influence by selling oil at discounted rates to cash-strapped neighbors or lending them billions of dollars.

Domestically, the former paratrooper's tenure has been marked by turbulence largely because of his failure to deliver on promises to improve conditions for the poor. Growing public discontent led to several crippling national strikes — and in 2002 to a coup that removed him from office. Two days later, however, Venezuela's underclass took to the streets to demonstrate in his favor, and he was reinstated. Chávez accused the Bush administration of being behind the coup, and many analysts agreed.

Two years later the opposition engineered a referendum against him, but he emerged unscathed — actually

strengthened — by promising more social reforms. But by December 2007 the sense of neglect among his supporters had deepened so dramatically — heightened by massive food shortages in recent months — that his own referendum to amend the constitution and remove presidential term limits was narrowly defeated, his first electoral defeat in nine years. [7]

"I see Chávez traveling and traveling abroad, and the money ends up somewhere else," said Jesus Camacho, 29, a street vendor selling coffee in a Caracas slum who makes about $8 a day. Although he supported Chávez in the past, Camacho says he has lost faith in politics. [8]

Meanwhile, the U.S. government has often appeared indifferent to the problems of Latin America, especially since the terrorist attacks of Sept. 11, 2001. "Has Washington lost Latin America?" asked the December issue of the French foreign affairs monthly *Le Monde Diplomatique.* [9] And former U.S. ambassador to Belize Carolyn Curiel wrote in *The New York Times* recently: "Our mostly Spanish-speaking neighbors have reason to suspect that, except for occasional military and economic interventions, American leaders don't pay them much mind." [10]

Some analysts say that in the post-9/11 world, the United States is primarily concerned about Latin America as it relates to domestic security. The most recent security assessment given to the U.S. Senate by Director of National Intelligence J. Michael McConnell lays out perceived threats posed by Venezuela and Cuba and complains of "sharply anti-U.S. rhetoric" by leftist leaders in Bolivia, Nicaragua and Ecuador. The report alleges that Chávez allows illegal drug shipments by the Colombian guerrilla group known as the FARC (Revolutionary Armed Forces of Colombia) and others to pass through Venezuela en route to the streets of Europe and the United States. Cocaine exports are a main source of FARC's revenue. [11]

While the United States remains either the first or second largest trading partner of most Latin American countries — including Venezuela — the region has been broadening its ties to the European Union, China, Iran (in the case of Chávez) and others. For example, Brazil is actively lobbying to join the U.N. Security Council's five permanent members — the United States, Britain, France, Russia and China. And Brazil — home to 10 million people of Arab origin — just sent Foreign Minister Celso Amorim on an extended tour of the Middle East to strengthen bilateral relations. [12] A second Latin American-Arab summit — the first was in 2005 — is scheduled for later this year in the Persian Gulf state of Qatar.

A new regional cohesion and cooperation is also taking hold, particularly on the economic front. While the dynamics and mechanisms of change differ from country to country, "there is something that's really Latin American, and it's not only historical," says Peter Hakim, president of Inter-American Dialogue, a Washington-based think tank. "There is a huge circulation of ideas, people and common institutions."

Indeed, if Latin America could ever overcome its perennial internal rivalries and disharmony and act in concert, it could make a formidable bloc. "Our first priority is Latin America," Amorim said recently. Trading within the region itself accounts for about 27 percent of overall trade, he points out, followed by the European Union with 24 percent and the United States with 15 percent. "But like our trade, our foreign relations are also diverse. . . . We have excellent relations with [both] Cuba and with the United States." [13]

As Latin Americans consider how to deal with their economic and political issues, here are some of the questions they are asking:

Are Chávez's days numbered?

Chávez's Dec. 2 referendum defeat — 51 percent to 49 percent — "was a stunning setback . . . and may slow down his movement towards authoritarian rule and implementation of his vision of 21st-century socialism," Intelligence Director McConnell told the Senate Select Committee on Intelligence in February.

But does that mean Chávez's position is seriously threatened? No, says Carlos Malamud, a Latin America specialist at the Real Instituto Elcano, a think tank in Madrid, Spain. Chávez is "very far from being a lame duck" or as unsteady in the saddle as some people think.

Opponents flood Bolivar Avenue in Caracas, Venezuela, on Nov. 27, 2007, to protest the referendum proposed by President Hugo Chávez calling for constitutional changes that would give him more power and eliminate term limits. A week later it was defeated, delivering a stunning setback to Chávez.

"He still has significant popular backing and wide-ranging powers." All of the Venezuelan National Assembly seats are held by pro-Chávez parties, thanks to an opposition election boycott in 2005, although one group calling itself *Podemos* ("We can") did break ranks and vote against him in the referendum. The Chávez government also controls the judiciary, the state oil company and all but one provincial government.

"There are problems of inflation, weak investment in the oil sector and food shortages," says Malamud, who also could have added widespread crime to the list. "But internationally, Chávez still has oil as a powerful bargaining tool."

However, Francisco R. Rodríguez, a former economic adviser to the Venezuelan National Assembly and now a

Brazil Emerging as a Global Power

Pragmatic reliance on trade has helped boost economy.

In the not too distant past, jokesters perennially quipped: "Brazil is the land of the future — and always will be." [1] No longer. "Brazil's future is now," wrote *New York Times* columnist Roger Cohen recently, citing its raw materials, energy, vast and varied ecology and trade with China. [2]

Many would add another reason: Luiz Inacio Lula da Silva, the former metalworker and union leader who has been president since 2002. By electing Lula, voters gave Brazil's political elite its comeuppance. And while Lula's presidency has not been without problems — including charges of corruption in his government — his leadership has played a key role in putting to rest the myth that Brazil would remain unable to live up to its tremendous potential.

Lula's innovative social initiatives have begun making a dent in poverty, notably his *Fome Zero* (Zero Hunger) drive, which distributes money for food to the most needy. In addition, the *Bolsa Familia* (Family Fund) program — which provides aid to families earning less than $100 a month if they keep their children in school and their kids' vaccinations current — is considered highly successful. [3]

Although during the campaign Lula threatened to withdraw Brazil from the International Monetary Fund (IMF) if elected, he ended up complying with previously set IMF fiscal targets and followed his predecessor's macroeconomic policies. Lula has achieved "impressive results in economic stability," writes Jorge G. Castañeda, a former Mexican foreign minister and now Global Distinguished Professor of Politics and Latin American Studies at New York University. [4] Moreover, thanks to a fiscal surplus every year, Lula has paid off Brazil's $3 billion in foreign debt.

Much of Brazil's success is attributed to its aggressive export strategy. Brazil is the world's largest exporter of coffee, beef, sugar and orange juice. It also exports huge amounts of soy beans and $4.2 billion worth of chickens in 2007 — up from $2.9 billion in 2006. The discovery in 2007 of a huge, 5-8-billion-barrel deepwater oil field off Brazil's southeastern coast boosted the country's oil reserves by about 40 percent and narrowed its oil gap with Venezuela. China has invested heavily in Brazil and purchases many of its products, including iron ore.

"For the first time in a generation Brazilians are benefiting from stable economic growth, low inflation rates and improvements in social well-being," the World Bank stated in a recent report on Brazil. [5]

Latin America's largest country also has become a world leader in producing and exporting plant-based fuels, particularly ethanol from sugar cane. In 2007 Brazil signed an ethanol deal with the world's other large producer, the United States, to promote the development of new bio-fuel technologies — a rare example of U.S.-Brazilian cooperation.

"Brazil's independent approach to foreign policy has led to periodic disputes with the United States on trade and political issues, including Brazil's vocal opposition to the war in Iraq," says a U.S. Congressional Research Service report. [6]

"Brazilian foreign policy has recently aimed to strengthen ties with other South American countries, engage in multilateral diplomacy through the United Nations and the Organization of American States (OAS) and act at times as a countervailing force to U.S. political and economic influence in Latin America," the report continues." [7]

professor of political science and Latin American affairs at Wesleyan University in Middletown, Conn., thinks Chávez's days may indeed be numbered. The test, he says, will come in the October provincial elections. Chávez's political machine currently controls 22 of the 23 provinces, but the referendum defeat reflected "growing popular discontent with the regime," he continues, "and Chávez is going to lose badly in the elections, including control of Caracas. Things can deteriorate pretty quickly after that, whether due to a popular revolution, or even the army."

If the opposition gains control of two-thirds of the provincial seats, "a constitutional assembly could unseat Chávez," Rodríguez says. "But there has to be at least a pretext of constitutionality. What you are likely to see is movement in the Venezuelan supreme court." And then there's the worsening economic situation. "It will be difficult for him to hold on to power in the midst of an economic crisis."

Lula also has earned the Bush administration's disapproval with his neighborly dealings with Venezuela's anti-U.S. leader Hugo Chávez and Cuba's recently retired communist dictator Fidel Castro. Now a leftist social democrat, the former union leader has what Castañeda calls "a lingering emotional devotion to Cuba," but "it has not led to subservience to Castro." [8]

The Bush administration also has been less than supportive of Brazil's vigorous campaign to gain a permanent seat on the U.N. Security Council, joining the five original veto-wielding permanent members: China, Russia, the United Kingdom, France and the United States. And, although Brazil has reinforced its military and police presence on its long border with Colombia, Lula has refused Washington's entreaties to become more actively involved in Plan Colombia, the multimillion-dollar U.S. effort to curb Colombia's virulent drug trade.

The darker side of Brazil's emergence as a world player includes its gargantuan social problems and high levels of violent crime. More than 7,000 homicides occurred in Rio de Janeiro alone in 2007, according to Amnesty International, and some of the country's lawless *favelas* — teeming squatter settlements — are considered impenetrable to police. [9]

Workers at a meat-processing plant in Brazil's Sao Paulo state prepare beef for export to Europe, the Middle East and Asia. Brazil has made significant economic strides in recent years, in part because of its heavy reliance on exports.

AP Photo/Dario Lopez-Mills

As a Brazilian commentator put it recently, "The immediate problem that Brazil faces is less to solve these issues — that will take a generation — than to build a consensus on how to solve them. . . . For the country as a whole this is a moral as much as a political challenge." [10]

[1] Clare M. Ribando, "Brazil-U.S. Relations," Congressional Research Service, Feb. 28, 2007, www.wilsoncenter.org/news/docs/RL33456.pdf.

[2] Roger Cohen, "New Day in the Americas," *The New York Times*, Jan. 6, 2008, p. 13, www.nytimes.com/2008/01/06/opinion/06cohen.html; also see Amnesty International, "Brazil: Submission to the UN Universal Periodic Review," April 7-11, 2008, http://archive.amnesty.org/library/pdf/AMR190232007ENGLISH/$File/AM R1902307.pdf.

[3] Gina-Marie Cheeseman, "The Spread of Leftist Politics in Latin America," *American Chronicle*, March 20, 2007, www.americanchronicle.com/articles/22437.

[4] Jorge G. Castañeda, "Latin America's Left Turn," *Foreign Affairs*, May/June 2006, www.foreignaffairs.org/20060501faessay85302/jorge-g-castaneda/latin-america-s-left.html.

[5] "Brazil Country Brief," The World Bank, http://web.worldbank.org/WBSITE/EXTERNAL/COUNTRIES/LACEXT/BRAZILEXTN/0,,contentMDK:20189430~pagePK:141137~piPK:141127~theSitePK:322341,00.html.

[6] Ribando, *op. cit.*

[7] *Ibid.*

[8] Castañeda, *op. cit.*

[9] *Ibid.*

[10] Arthur Ituassu, "Brazil: the moral challenge," openDemocracy, April 18, 2007, www.opendemocracy.net/democracy-protest/brazil_challenge_4544.jsp.

Peter DeShazo, director of the Americas program at the Washington-based Center for Strategic and International Studies, said, "Clearly, Chávez's own political agenda in Venezuela is now off track, so that will definitely hurt his overall image." [14]

Chávez himself managed to sound defiant while acknowledging the setback, which he interpreted as a signal that he had moved too far ahead of rank-and-file Venezuelans. "I'm obliged to apply the brakes," the president said on his weekly television show "Aló Presidente" ("Hello President"). "The main motor seized up, so we'll have to go by donkey instead." He said he would try again to persuade voters to go along with him. "I haven't been weakened," he told the opposition, "nor have I been pushed back one millimeter. . . . Prepare yourself, because a new offensive will come with a proposed reform," he warned the opposition, either "that one, or transformed or simplified." [15]

AP Photo/Kent Gilbert

Costa Ricans protest the Central America-Dominican Republic Free Trade Agreement (CAFTA-DR) in San Jose, the capital, on Feb. 5, 2006. Although the controversial pact went into effect in 2005, Costa Rica didn't ratify it until voters, by a thin margin, approved a referendum on the treaty after a contentious campaign last fall.

"When I was minister of finance in Venezuela, imports ran at a fifth of what they are today, and the population is not five times what it was," observes *Foreign Policy* editor Naím. "Luxury goods are coming in for the new elite, but the country is without milk and very fundamental things like cooking gas." The imported Humvees and other signs of ostentatious wealth flaunted by rich Venezuelans and Chávez's cronies — nicknamed the "Bolivarian bourgeoisie" — contrast sharply with the shortages faced by ordinary citizens, further fueling the unrest. *

"I cannot find beans, rice, coffee or milk," said Mirna de Campos, 56, a nurse's assistant who lives just outside Caracas. "What there is to find is whiskey — lots of it." [16]

The recent food shortages have been caused in part by price controls imposed by Chávez. Food manufacturers and distributors find it more profitable to smuggle their goods into Colombia or Ecuador, where they can make as much as 300 percent profit, rather than sell them in Venezuela at low government-set prices. Milk shortages have been caused in part by dairies converting their price-controlled milk into butter and cheese, which are not subject to price caps. Chávez has recently threatened to nationalize food distribution to discourage hoarding and has beefed up border surveillance to discourage the smuggling — with some success, according to the government.

"Problems of scarcity are being caused by the private sector, which opposes Chávez," says Rodríguez. But the government's actions so far have been a confusing mixture of carrot and stick. "Chávez does not grasp the seriousness of the situation, and does not understand the consequences of what's happening."

Chávez's December defeat gave a boost to the loose alliance of political forces that opposes him because it showed that he was not unbeatable. Malamud believes Chávez's challengers would have even more success if they could find a leader to unite them. Venezuelan students emerged as strong opponents of the referendum, led by Yon Goicoechea, a 23-year-old Caracas law student who is revered as a fearless opponent of Chávez's policies despite the government's relentless harassment of him and his family.

But the anti-Chávez group spans all ages and ideologies, from the Roman Catholic Church to Gabriel Puerta, a former left-wing guerrilla and now leader of the Red Flag opposition organization. Media opponents include 75-year-old Teodoro Petkoff, respected editor of the Venezuelan paper *Tal Cual.* The more conventional resistance comes from middle-class business and professional groups and the Social Christian Party, which Chávez ousted in his first presidential election and is now returning to the political fray after a long boycott.

Whether an ousted Chávez would go quietly is anybody's guess. Malamud points out that while Chávez "talks a lot about revolution, there's been no revolution in Venezuela." Chávez gained his power through the ballot and has repeatedly resorted to the ballot to introduce changes in Venezuela's government.

A report by the Brussels-based International Crisis Group, an independent peace-advocacy organization, said Chávez "is not yet a dictator and for the most part

---

* Chávez calls his socialist program a "Bolivarian Revolution" in honor of the South American hero Simón Bolívar.

has not tried to act in a dictatorial manner, but the trend towards autocracy is strong." Chávez has been building personal power at the expense of other institutions and militarizing much of the government and political life, risking internal conflicts, the report continued. [17]

Are moderate governments proving more sustainable than Chávez-style radical populism?

When Chávez was first elected in 1998 with 56 percent of the vote, he was the first in a string of successful left-wing candidates across Latin America, each of whom has followed a different course in solving pressing social and economic problems.

Chávez's flashy Bolivarian Revolution programs for reducing poverty caught wide attention, but the populist leader hasn't delivered, according to his critics. His protégés — Morales in Bolivia and Correa in Ecuador — have also faced problems instituting their socialist agendas. Some say the region's more moderate left-wing governments, which have pushed modified macroeconomic programs, retained many liberalizing reforms of the 1990s and instituted gradual social improvements, will have more staying power.

Rather than trying to reform the government's inefficient services, Chávez quickly established social welfare "missions" in the barrios (poor neighborhoods), financed mainly with oil revenues, to address needs ranging from health and education to housing and employment. One mission, for instance, distributed money to enable the poor to buy new homes or repair old ones.

But Wesleyan University's Rodríguez contends the ambitious missions program never lived up to expectations because of understaffing, corruption and underfunding. Writing in *Foreign Affairs* magazine, Rodríguez — who as economic adviser to the National Assembly watched from a ringside seat as Chávez's economy began to crumble — recalls that the government was supposed to ensure that Chávez's social programs benefited from rising oil revenues. "But when oil revenues started to go up [the government] ignored the provision." The fact that the percentage of Venezuelans living in poverty declined from a peak of 54 percent in 2003 to 27.5 percent in 2007, says Rodríguez, was due to the impact on the economy of a tripling of oil prices rather than to Chávez's poverty programs. [18]

By 2006 Venezuela's economy had already begun to unravel, but Chávez was re-elected by an overwhelming margin. Oil revenues were high, and Venezuela had enjoyed three years of double-digit growth. But inflation was also double digit — equivalent to an annual rate of 67.7 percent in 2007, the highest in Latin America. [19]

According to Rodriguez, "Cháveznomics" — which economists Rudiger Dornbusch and Sebastian Edwards have called "the macroeconomics of populism" — is merely a reformulation of "the disastrous experiences of many Latin American countries during the 1970s and 1980s," such as the economic policies followed by Juan Perón in Argentina, Salvador Allende in Chile and Alan García in Peru. Populist macroeconomics usually involves expansionary fiscal and economic policies, coupled with an overvalued currency designed to accelerate growth and income redistribution. Fiscal and foreign exchange constraints are usually disregarded, and price controls are used to control inflation.

"The result is by now well known to Latin American economists: the emergence of production bottlenecks, the accumulation of severe fiscal and balance-of-payments problems, galloping inflation and plummeting real wages," wrote Rodríguez.

Which is what appears to be happening in Venezuela, he asserted. "Chávez's mismanagement of the economy and his failure to live up to his pro-poor rhetoric have finally begun to catch up with him," he wrote. As food shortages spread, Chávez's poll numbers declined. In September 2007 — three months before the referendum — 22 percent of Venezuelans thought the poverty situation had improved under Chávez; 50 percent thought it had gotten worse and the rest said there had been no change. [20]

Not surprisingly, both Morales and Correa were also planning constitutional changes to introduce their own variations of Chávez's as-yet-undefined "Socialism for the 21st Century." Among other controversial measures, Morales wants to restore Bolivia's indigenous tribal courts, making them available as an alternative to the normal judicial system. But Morales failed to get a majority in the constituent assembly drafting the new laws, so everything depends on a referendum to be scheduled later this year. Correa, whose government is drafting a similar document, is in a stronger position but also needs voter approval in a referendum. Correa is seeking sweeping changes, including increased presidential powers to strengthen his hand in dealing with foreign oil corporations operating in Ecuador — and analysts say he is likely to get them. [21]

Workers Abroad Sent $60 Billion Home

Workers from Mexico and South America sent nearly $49 billion home to their families in 2006 — 81 percent of the total remittances to the region.

Remittances to Latin America, 2006
(by region, in $US billions)

Total = $59.7 billion

Source: "Sending Money Home: Worldwide Remittance Flows to Developing Countries," International Fund for Agricultural Development, 2008

Some in Latin America question whether the outside world isn't giving the Andean neo-populists a disproportionate amount of attention. Norman Gall, executive director of the Fernand Braudel Institute of World Economics in Sao Paolo, Brazil, argues that the more significant trend in Latin America is not what's happening in places like Bolivia and Ecuador — which Gall calls two "marginal and chronically unstable countries" — but the shift "towards domestic stability" among the "more important republics" of Argentina, Brazil, Chile, Peru and Mexico. These more moderate governments have battled poverty and inequality, but not at the expense of their economic growth. In the past four years, for instance, South American economies as a whole have grown on average 4.4 percent. [22]

As for the populist leaders' social agendas, Venezuela and Ecuador spent 11.7 percent and 6.3 percent of GDP on education, respectively, in 2006 while Chile spent 28.7 percent and Brazil 22 percent — more than any other Latin American countries. [23] Raising education levels is a high priority because Latin America's traditional pool of cheap labor is no longer an asset in an increasingly high-tech world. Rodríguez writes that despite Chávez's claim to have eradicated illiteracy, a recent survey showed that illiteracy is still widespread in Venezuela. [24]

And Chávez hasn't really succeeded in narrowing the income gap between Venezuela's rich and poor — something he has blamed on free-market policies adopted by his predecessors and advocated by rich Western countries. "One would expect pro-poor growth [policies] to be accompanied by a marked decrease in income inequality," Rodríguez argued. "But according to the Venezuelan Central Bank, inequality has actually increased during the Chávez administration."

Other countries across the region, however, are making steady economic progress, including some progress in narrowing the income-inequality gap. The challenge now for the moderate left-wing governments, analysts say, is to convince the public that gradual but reliable improvement is better than unpredictable, flashy bursts of progress that are undermined by setbacks.

In addition, argues former Mexican foreign minister Jorge G. Castañeda, a political science professor at New York University, Latin Americans need to focus on the institutional underpinnings of their new democracies and eradicate "the region's secular plagues: corruption, weak or non-existent rule of law, ineffective governance" and the enduring temptation to concentrate power in the hands of a few. [25]

Can narco-terrorism be eradicated?

On March 1, 2008, Colombian troops crossed into neighboring Ecuador and attacked a FARC camp, killing the Marxist guerrilla group's second-ranking leader, known as Raúl Reyes, along with 22 other guerillas. Taking out Reyes was a major success for Colombia in its long struggle with FARC, which has waged a 40-plus-year insurgency against the Colombian state. But the incident plunged the region into a crisis, as Chávez mobilized 10 armored divisions on the Venezuelan-Colombian border, and Ecuador closed its embassy in

Bogotá in protest over the breach of its sovereignty and expelled Colombia's diplomats from Quito.

FARC guerrillas, categorized around the world as terrorists, have long used remote areas of Ecuador and Venezuela along the Colombian border as safe havens. [26] The incursion into Ecuador reflects the growing strength and confidence of the Colombian counter-insurgency forces, largely boosted by Washington's multibillion-dollar Plan Colombia.

The United States has spent $7 billion on the plan, launched in 2000 to halt cocaine production at the source. It was soon broadened to include combating the FARC, which funds its operations by selling drugs and kidnapping the wealthy. According to U.S military advisers, Colombian security forces have regained control over the country's major cities and large areas of the countryside, long overrun by the narco-terrorists, squeezing the over 10,000-strong group into jungle enclaves. [27]

The U.S. Congress has allotted $545 million to Plan Colombia for 2008, even though the program has yet to succeed in achieving either of its ultimate objectives — eradicating Colombia's cocaine crop and ending the FARC insurgency.

The last vestige of South and Central America's 1980s-era armed struggles, FARC still remains a serious threat to daily life in Colombia. But today it pays only lip service to its Marxist ideology, and its political objective to seize power has long been out of reach.

"Although the FARC has by no means been defeated, it is on the run and has been for the last few years," the *Los Angeles Times* reported from Florencia, Colombia, last month, quoting Colombian and U.S. military analysts. [28]

"The plan has been a success in boosting the Colombian military to contain FARC, but a failure in stopping cocaine production," says former Venezuelan minister Naím. "No assault on drugs will work unless an effort is made to reduce demand. The United States has spent $40 billion on the war on drugs, but very little of it went for demand abatement."

Analysts say eradicating the guerrillas would require an extensive military operation that even the improved and motivated Colombian military cannot launch. A major concern is the fate of the 70 foreigners and more than 700 Colombian citizens being held hostage by FARC. Their lives would be jeopardized by a full-scale military confrontation, and the Colombian government would not take that risk.

That's why many believe the inevitable answer is negotiation. "I don't know how it will work or when it will happen," says Wesleyan University's Rodríguez, "but I think direct talks will happen." [29]

As for cocaine production in Colombia, it is at roughly the same level as in 2000. Eradicating the $2.2-to-$5-billion-a-year cocaine trade — equivalent to 3 percent of the country's GDP — would require a massive operation and an unyielding political will. Both the anti-FARC and anti-cocaine initiatives would require full cooperation from Colombia's neighbors — Brazil, Venezuela and Ecuador — an unlikely prospect since Chávez openly backs FARC, with whom he says he shares some Marxist ideals. Furthermore, the Colombians claim that information gained from two laptop computers captured in the Reyes operation reveals that FARC has the support of top Ecuadorian officials — an allegation denied by the Ecuadorians.

Chávez has urged the European Union nations and others not to classify the Colombian guerrillas as terrorists, arguing that they are freedom fighters, and ordered a two-minute silence in Venezuela for Reyes.

"Drugs and kidnapping finance the FARC, and as long as they have the drug trade and Chávez's support and can count on Venezuela to help them export the drugs, FARC will survive," says Naím. Based on other evidence found in the computers, the Colombian government also alleged that Chávez had given FARC $300 million, but the Venezuelan government has denied the charge. [30]

Meanwhile, U.S.-supported aerial herbicide spraying has not succeeded in destroying Colombia's coca crops. The eradication program is controversial because the weed-killer damages nearby crops and causes breathing difficulties. [31] Spraying coca fields along the border also brought protests from neighboring Ecuador, where chemicals drifted across the boundary and ruined crops.

The Colombian government recently resorted to uprooting the coca bushes by hand, but the farmers simply switched from open fields to smaller, less detectable areas in the jungle. Recent CIA monitoring shows Colombia's cocaine crop is about as large as when aerial spraying began in 2001 — though that doesn't necessarily mean cocaine production hasn't taken a hit, argues the Bush administration. [32]

"The illegal drug trade in Colombia is as robust and as resilient as ever," says John Walsh, a senior associate at the Washington Office on Latin America, a human rights group generally opposed to U.S. policy in the region. "It's business as usual: the trade is regrouping, adapting and coming on in worse form."

Without regional cooperation, the drug trade could move across neighboring borders, or move to other countries like Panama. Brazil, for example, has reinforced its borders with troops and police in an attempt to prevent the FARC from spilling over.

Although Colombia is the Bush administration's most consistent ally in the region, American lawmakers have balked at approving a long-awaited bilateral trade agreement, in part because of Bogotá's failure to suppress the cocaine trade and Democrats' objections that President Álvaro Uribe has not done enough to halt the killing of Colombian labor union officials, apparently by right-wing paramilitary assassins.

"The total economic consequence of the delay is microscopic here in the United States, but very important there," says Naím. "For one thing, it raises the question: What is the point of being a U.S. ally if we can't even get a trade agreement?"

BACKGROUND

Empire to Independence

For three centuries, Latin America — the great colonial empires of Spain and Portugal — stretched from modern-day California to the southernmost tip of the Americas at Cape Horn. The empires collapsed in the early 19th century because of a combination of European power politics and local unrest and rebellion. The newly independent nations of Latin America established governments democratic in form but less so in substance. [33]

In the 1500s Spanish conquistadores destroyed thriving Aztec and Incan civilizations and laid the foundation for colonial rule and economic exploitation. Portugal explored and colonized Brazil under a 1494 papal decree that gave it the lands east of the mouth of the Amazon River. Colonial administration improved in the 1700s, but liberalized trade policies heightened social stratification by benefiting upper-class whites and mixed-race mestizos without helping the indigenous Indian populations or Negro slaves in Brazil. By 1800, professional and business classes were ripe for revolt, as were many of the Indians.

The wars of independence that threw off Spanish and Portuguese rule spanned a little more than a decade, from 1810 to the early 1820s. Spain, distracted by the Napoleonic wars, was unable to counter the revolutions that spread throughout its empire. South America's two great "liberators" — Bolívar and José de San Martín of Argentina — survived repeated reversals to eventually gain decisive military victories in 1821: Bolívar in his native Venezuela, San Martín in Peru. Meanwhile, Brazil won independence from Portugal under a monarchy established in 1822 by Dom Pedro — son of a former regent — with support from British and Brazilian liberals.

In Mexico, a liberal parish priest, Miguel Hidalgo y Costilla, ignited the war for independence in September 1810 but was executed a year later after government forces recovered from initial rebel victories. A guerrilla war succeeded in winning independence in 1821 only after defections by several royal officers and their troops. One of the colonels proclaimed himself emperor, but anti-monarchists succeeded in establishing Mexico's first republic three years later. Similar rebellions won independence in the kingdom of Guatemala, which then broke into separate states in the late 1820s.

Bolívar envisioned a United States of South America, but the nation he established, called Gran Colombia, broke into separate states — Colombia, Venezuela and Ecuador — before his death in 1830. Meanwhile, the colony of Upper Peru had broken away, declared its independence as Bolivia and given Bolívar dictatorial powers as president. Bolívar was no democrat: He favored a system headed by a strong president chosen for life. Shortly before his death, he wrote: "America is ungovernable."

However, South American independence was not accompanied by social or economic reform, according to historian Edwin Williamson. No new classes came to power, and the oligarchic structures of the colonial period remained unchanged. Politically, the era saw the rise of the *caudillos* — strongmen who came to power through patronage or force and exercised power with scant regard for legal technicalities. Political participation was limited to upper classes that themselves had no tradition of political culture.

Despite such handicaps, a few countries — Chile and Costa Rica, for example — established viable democracies. Historians David Bushnell and Neill Macaulay note that liberalism was advancing in the latter decades of the 19th century. Still, many countries had long periods of authoritarian rule — notably, Mexico under the 34-year dictatorship of Porfirio Diaz that began with his election as president in 1876.

The United States had wielded influence over Latin American affairs since President James Monroe proclaimed his doctrine barring European intervention in hemispheric affairs in 1823. The United States reached the Pacific Coast by wresting half of Mexico's territory in a two-year war, 1846-48. At century's end, the U.S. victory in the Spanish-American War helped Cuba win independence. The United States also sent gunboats to support Panama's secession from Colombia in 1903 in order to secure agreement for construction of the Panama Canal. A year later, President Theodore Roosevelt added his corollary to the Monroe Doctrine, asserting a right to intervene as an "international police power" in any cases of "chronic wrong-doing."

'Men on Horseback'

In the 20th century, democracy continued to compete with the tradition of turning to strongmen — figuratively, if not literally, men on horseback — at times of national crisis. Some of the 20th-century *caudillos* were military leaders bent on preserving the status quo. Others — notably, Juan Perón in Argentina and Castro in Cuba — challenged the status quo in the name of the dispossessed and disenfranchised masses. The 20th century also saw the formation of mass political parties and revolutionary movements with mixed results for democratic government.

Mexico experienced the hemisphere's first social revolution of the 20th century. A revolution that spanned two decades (1910 to 1929) — and had to overcome two invasions from the United States — led later to the nationalization of foreign-owned companies and wide-scale land reform for peasants. But democratic procedures — presidential elections every six years, with no right of succession — proved no obstacle to one-party rule by the PRI, Mexico's preeminent political party from 1929 until the early 1990s.

Widely supported leftist parties also formed in Argentina in the 1890s and in Peru in the 1930s. In Argentina, the Radical Civic Union gained the presidency in 1916 and led the country on the road to liberal democracy until a military coup in 1930. Thirteen years later, Perón was among a new generation of nationalist military officers who staged coups. Perón then was elected president in 1946 and gained a devoted following among the urban and rural poor until he was ousted by a conservative military coup in 1955.

In 1959, Cuban revolutionary Castro overthrew the regime of dictator Fulgencio Batista. A powerful speaker and charismatic leader, Castro exercised an almost mystical hold over the Cuban masses. By 1965 he had established the first communist state in the Western hemisphere and become a symbol of socialist revolution for Latin America. The mission of "converting" the region through revolution was entrusted to Ernesto "Che" Guevara, a revolutionary legend in his own time, who was killed in Bolivia in 1967.

In Peru, the American Popular Revolutionary Alliance (APRA) — led by Victor Raúl Haya de la Torre, a charismatic intellectual — drew support from workers and the urban middle class to vie for the presidency in 1931. Haya de la Torre's refusal to accept his apparent defeat touched off violence from both sides. Military governments banned APRA for most of the next three decades. And when Haya came close to winning the presidency in 1962, military rulers nullified the election.

With the exception of Mexico and Costa Rica, every Latin American country has experienced at least one military coup in the 20th century. Colombia's military stepped in to end an undeclared civil war in 1953. In Paraguay, Gen. Alfredo Stroessner seized power in 1954 after years of civil war and political squabbling — and held power until his ouster in 1989. Guatemala's military stood by in 1954 while a U.S. invasion ousted the pro-communist leader Jacobo Arbenz Guzmán. In Brazil, a military coup ousted the left-leaning President Joao Goulart in 1964, instituting two decades of semi-authoritarian rule.

Shock Therapy

Although the region has been called Latin America since the late 19th century — referring both to its predominant Catholicism and its Spanish and Portuguese colonial origins — it has never seemed less Latin or colonial than it does now, during the profound political, social and economic changes that are occurring.

"The region has been transformed in the past 30 years," observes Malamud, the Latin America specialist in Madrid. During the 1970s, he points out, all Latin American nations except Mexico, Costa Rica, Colombia and Venezuela were run by military regimes.

In the aftermath of the 1959 Cuban Revolution, militant left-wing movements proliferated in Latin America, often against a background of faltering economies and

CHRONOLOGY

1930s-1950s *Dictators control most of Latin America. In Cuba, Fidel Castro overthrows Batista regime.*

1932 Brazil and Uruguay become the first Latin American countries to grant women the right to vote.

1936 Dictatorial Somoza dynasty comes to power in Nicaragua.

1939 Fulgencio Batista era begins in Cuba; his regime is a byword for corruption and, wrote historian Hugh Thomas, "formalized gangsterism."

1946 Populist Army Col. Juan Perón is elected president of Argentina.

1948 Organization of American States is formed.

1954 Strongman Gen. Alfredo Stroessner takes over in Paraguay.

1959 Cuban revolutionaries, led by Castro, overthrow Batista.

1960s-1970s *Castro establishes communist regime in Cuba, forms alliance with Soviet Union, triggering long period of tension with the United States. Cuban missile crisis brings world to brink of nuclear war.*

1961 U.S.-backed Cuban exiles unsuccessfully try to overthrow Castro.

1961 Paraguay is last Latin American country to give women the vote.

1962 President John F. Kennedy blockades Cuba after spy photographs reveal bases being built in Cuba for Soviet-controlled nuclear missiles. Soviets agree to withdraw the missiles, and the U.S. agrees to withdraw its missiles from Turkey.

1970 Chile's Salvador Allende is first democratically elected socialist leader in Latin America.

1973 Allende is killed in CIA-supported coup; right-wing Gen. Augusto Pinochet takes over.

1976 Rabidly right-wing military junta takes over Argentina, launches deadly wave of "disappearances."

1980s-1990s *Neo-liberal reforms are short-lived. Former Lt. Col. Hugo Chávez, leader of a failed 1992 coup, wins his first presidential election. Rise of Chávez and Luiz Inacio Lula da Silva in Brazil signals shift to the left in region.*

1983 U.S. invades Grenada to stop alleged Cuban military buildup on the island and, the administration says, to protect Americans there.

1994 North American Free Trade Agreement (NAFTA) takes effect, lowering trade barriers between the United States, Mexico and Canada.

1998 Chávez is elected president of Venezuela.

2000s *Socialists are elected in several key Latin American countries.*

2001 Argentina defaults on its debt.

2002 Left-wing labor leader da Silva wins Brazilian presidential election.

2005 Evo Morales, an indigenous coca grower and labor leader, is elected president in Bolivia, vowing to nationalize the country's gas industry.

2006 Socialist Michelle Bachelet is elected first woman president in Chile. In Venezuela, Chávez is re-elected.

2007 Christina Fernández de Kirchner is elected president in Argentina, succeeding her husband. Chávez suffers setback when his proposed constitutional reforms are defeated. . . . Chávez proposes Bank of the South; seven countries join. . . . U.S. Congress approves U.S.-Peru free trade agreement.

2008 Ailing Castro, 81, retires as president of Cuba and is succeeded by his brother Raúl, 76. . . . On March 1 Colombian troops enter neighboring Ecuador and kill the second-ranking FARC guerrilla leader. In response, FARC supporter Chávez mobilizes 10 armored divisions on the Venezuelan-Colombian border, and Ecuador closes its embassy in Bogotá.

weak, inept governments. In response, right-wing military regimes — often secretly aided by the United States — took power in many South American and Central American countries. [34]

The epidemic of coups d'etat — a periodic affliction in Latin American history since independence — lasted until the 1980s, when it ran out of steam, eventually leaving democratically elected governments to deal with the shattered economies and civil institutions.

The Argentine junta, for example, gave up the ghost in 1983, humiliated by its defeat in the war with Britain over the Falkland Islands and burdened by failed fiscal policies. But it left behind a legacy of brutal murders of political opponents and mass arrests — the so-called dirty war. The Chilean military regime lasted until 1990 and eventually laid the foundation for economic recovery. More benign, the Brazilian military junta eased the country into democracy in 1985.

Saddled with skyrocketing foreign debt and hyperinflation, many of the governments turned to a neoliberal economic regime — the so-called Washington Consensus — promulgated by the World Bank and the International Monetary Fund (IMF). It advocated free-market reforms such as privatization of state-owned businesses, free trade, balancing budgets and attracting foreign investment.

It was shock therapy, and it worked — but only for a while, and at a cost. Inflation plummeted, and economies began to recover. But governments were forced to make draconian cuts in public spending — including on social programs — and slash price controls, leaving the majority of the population worse off than before — and angry. Meanwhile, widespread corruption and mismanagement undermined the system, and the wealthy, European-descended class — which has always controlled a disproportionate share of the region's wealth — was able to further enrich itself, in part by buying up former state enterprises. [35]

Rise of the Left

It was time for a backlash. By the end of the 20th century, it appeared that "a veritable left-wing tsunami" was about to hit the region, observed former Mexican Foreign Minister Castañeda. Beginning with Chávez's election victory in Venezuela in 1998, "a wave of leaders, parties and movements generically labeled 'leftist' swept into power in one Latin American country after

another." And, surprisingly, in a region with a history of abusive military dictatorships, support for democracy dropped from 61 percent in 1996 to 57 percent by 2002, according to a U.N. Development Programme poll. [36]

"As a result of neoliberal policies, the continent was severely impoverished," says Francisco Domínguez, head of the Latin American department at Great Britain's Middlesex University. "The level of poverty in the region went from around 25 percent to 44 percent in 2005, or roughly 227 million people." The wealth, he says, "was in the hands of a small elite."

In Venezuela, former Lt. Col. Chávez made his first bid for power in 1992 when he led an unsuccessful coup against President Carlos Andrés Pérez. He spent the next two years in jail but was eventually pardoned. In 1998, he campaigned for president and was elected for his first term.

After Chávez came da Silva and his Workers' Party in Brazil. The small, bearded former metal worker from northeast Brazil, who has a well-earned reputation for lengthy speeches, rose through Brazil's union ranks before making three unsuccessful bids for the presidency. On his fourth attempt, in 2002, he won, and then won re-election in 2006.

In Argentina, President Nestor Kirchner had been the successful governor of Patagonia's oil-rich Santa Cruz province for 12 years when he was elected in 2003 — by default because his rival, former President Carlos Menem, pulled out of the race. Kirchner managed to turn Argentina's deep economic crisis into four years of economic success, but then he declined to stand for a second term so that his wife Cristina, an influential senator, could successfully campaign for the job. [37]

In 2004 Tabaré Vázquez, a 68-year-old cancer specialist and former mayor of Montevideo, was elected president of Uruguay on his third attempt, becoming its first left-wing head of state. The economy was already on the upturn after years in the doldrums, but public resentment had ousted his conservative predecessors because one Uruguayan in three still lived below the poverty line. [38]

In Chile, Michelle Bachelet, a 56-year-old pediatrician and single parent, was elected president in 2006 after serving first as minister of health and then defense. A longtime socialist, she had been active in the underground during the military regime of Gen. Augusto Pinochet and had been arrested along with her mother but allowed to leave the country.

Latin Women Finding Their Political Voices

Gender quotas have helped women get elected.

Women politicians are making dramatic strides in the continent long known for its machismo and ubiquitous military dictators in dark glasses.

Since 2006, two women — Michelle Bachelet and Cristina Fernández de Kirchner — have been elected heads of state of Chile and Argentina, respectively. This spring former education minister Blanca Olevar is running for president of Paraguay, and in Brazil presidential chief of staff and former energy min-

making Cuba the third-highest in the world in the proportion of women parliamentarians. [3] Overall, women hold 19.7 percent of Latin America's lower-house legislative seats and 15.8 percent of upper-house seats — compared to 16 percent in the U.S. Congress, which is also the worldwide average. [4]

The sudden prominence of female leaders in influential Latin American countries reflects deep socioeconomic and demographic changes as well as gender quotas adopted by many countries that earmark a certain percentage of legislative seats to women.

The Inter-American Development Bank (IADB) attributes women's progress primarily to strides in education. According to a 2000 IADB study, girls in Latin America today outperform boys in enrollment rates at all levels of schooling — a dramatic reversal from the 1970s. [5] By 2000, close to 60 percent of females were enrolled in secondary schools and 17 percent in higher education — about the same rate as boys.

The rise of women in Latino politics is also linked to the establishment in the 1990s of gender quotas for the parliaments in more than a dozen Latin American countries, effectively turning their legislatures into training grounds for female political leaders.

International organizations have advocated gender quotas for parliaments since the 1975 U.N. First World Conference on Women, and some political parties — particularly in the Nordic countries — have had quotas since the 1970s. In Latin America the quotas vary, but most designate a minimum of 30 percent of seats for female delegates; Costa Rica has the highest, at 40 percent. [6]

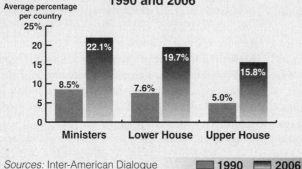

Number of Female Lawmakers and Ministers Has Surged

Female representation in Latin American senates, or upper houses, more than tripled between 1990 and 2006 — from 5 percent on average to nearly 17 percent. The percentage of female legislators in lower houses and ministers has more than doubled.

Political Posts Held by Women in Latin America, 1990 and 2006

Average percentage per country

Ministers: 8.5%, 22.1%
Lower House: 7.6%, 19.7%
Upper House: 5.0%, 15.8%

Sources: Inter-American Dialogue — 1990, 2006

ister Dilma Rousseff is widely expected to run for president when President Luiz Inacio Lula da Silva's term ends in 2010. [1]

While Hillary Rodham Clinton's campaign for the White House is considered groundbreaking in the United States, more than two dozen Latin American women have run for president since 1990. In fact, women have held the chief executive's position in 13 Latin American countries since 1974, although it was usually for brief stints in small countries. [2]

And women's political advancement in Latin America has not been limited to the president's office. Between 2000 and 2006 the percentage of women legislators in the region jumped 39.2 percent. After Cuba's national elections in January, women now make up 43 percent of the National Assembly,

Argentina's quota law was the first to apply to all political parties, so it offered the greatest opportunity to increase women's representation in the entire legislature. In the 1993 election — the first held after the quota law went into effect — the percentage of women elected to the Chamber of Deputies went from 5 percent to 14.4 percent. Today, Argentina's lower house is 48 percent female, and 31 percent of the senators are women. In Ecuador, women make up 25 percent of the legislature — up from 15 percent before the 2006 election. But in Venezuela, despite President Hugo Chávez's rhetoric about gender equality, only 31 out of 167 deputies — 18.6 percent — in the parliament are women. [7]

As with Clinton's bid for the presidency, there was a "husband factor" in Fernández's campaign: Her husband, President Nestor Kirchner, campaigned strongly for her. But Latina women haven't all risen to power on their husbands' coattails. In Chile, for instance, pediatrician and single mother Bachelet rose from political obscurity to the presidency in six years without male help.

Moreover, some experts see Latin women's political achievements as a rejection of male politics rather than an extension of it. "We gave men a chance and now it's our turn," says former presidential candidate Ivonne A-Baki of Ecuador. "Traditional political parties failed to give people what they need — stability, education, incorruptible government. Women still enjoyed respect in society; it's automatic that they should go into politics."

Chilean diplomat and writer Jorge Heine maintains that it's much more than a backlash against males. "As old-fashioned political parties with strong credibility problems struggle to come to terms with this rapidly changing environment, women leaders — often perceived as less corrupt, more task-oriented and with a warmer, more people-friendly leadership style — have moved in and occupied newly emerging political spaces," he wrote in the Indian newspaper *The Hindu* recently, when he was Chile's ambassador in New Delhi. [8]

The IADB report also predicts that the "the trend towards feminization of Latin America's democracy is here to stay." For instance, by the end of the 1990s women made up 53.9 percent of the continent's over-60 population. In this century Latin America will age faster, the report said, and the majority of the elderly will be women, who tend to outlive men. And polls have shown that Latin American women prefer women candidates. [9]

Has the feminization of Latin American politics advanced public policy issues embraced by women leaders? Apparently not yet, the London-based *Economist* pointed out recently. In Argentina, the magazine concluded, "the prominence of women in politics has not led to feminist policies. Proposals for equal pay and [legalizing] abortion have got nowhere." [10] Abortion is still illegal in Venezuela and throughout Latin America, except for Cuba.

But A-Baki says that rather than shifting focus to women's issues, the biggest change has been a change in style. "Women's approach to problems is different from men's," she says. "For example, women are better negotiators than men and tend to get better results."

President Michelle Bachelet of Chile, left, and Argentinean President Cristina Fernández de Kirchner are part of Latin America's new wave of female leaders.

AP Photo/Claudio Santana

Still, analysts say the impact across the region is mixed. Brazil, for example, has eliminated adultery from the penal code, but the legal concept of "legitimate defense of honor" — excusing the killing of an adulterous spouse or the spouse's lover — remains on the books. [11] Meanwhile, family issues generally are getting more attention in Brazil, as is income inequality (the gap between the rich and the poor), which is the highest in the world.

Moreover, say critics, a gender quota can be a two-edged sword because it can be manipulated to limit the number of female candidates or the number of women holding parliamentary seats. But few will deny that it has served a useful purpose in raising awareness. Ultimately, however, says Mala Htun, political science professor at New York's New School for Social Research, "advancing women's rights in the region depends on the consolidation of democracy, sustainable development and the promotion of equitable economic growth." [12]

[1] See "Women in the Americas: Paths to Political Power, A Report Card on Women in Political Leadership," Inter-American Development Bank, Inter-American Dialogue and League of Women Voters, January 2008; and Monte Reel, "South America Ushers In The Era of La Presidenta; Women Could Soon Lead a Majority of Continent's Population," *The Washington Post*, Oct. 31, 2007, p. A12.

[2] "Women in the Americas: Paths to Political Power," *op. cit..*, p. 7.

[3] According to Leslie Schwindt-Bayer, political science professor at the University of Missouri.

[4] Alexei Barrionuevo, "Political Tango, Women in the Lead," *The New York Times*, Nov. 4, 2007, p. 4; also see Diana Cariboni, "Women — Latin America: Politics, A Territory Still to be Conquered," Inter Press Service, http://ipsnews.net/interna.asp?idnews=27812, and Justin Vogler, "Latin America: woman's hour," Open Democracy Web site, March 17, 2006, www.opendemocracy.net/democracy-protest/womens_hour_3364.jsp.

[5] Mayra Buvinic and Vivian Roza, "Women, Politics, and Democratic Prospects in Latin America," Inter-American Development Bank, www.iadb.org/sds/doc/women.pdf.

[6] Mala N. Htun, "Women in Political Positions in Latin America," Institute for Democracy and Election Assistance, 2002, www.idea.int/publications/wip/upload/Chapter1-Htun-feb03.pdf.

[7] "Women in the Americas: Paths to Political Power," *op. cit.*

[8] Jorge Heine, "Women to the Fore: Feminising Latin Politics," *The Hindu*, Dec. 12, 2007, www.thehindu.com/2007/12/13/stories/2007121356641200.htm.

[9] Buvinic and Roza, *op. cit.*

[10] "Gaucho feminism," *The Economist*, Dec. 13, 2007, www.economist.com/world/la/displaystory.cfm?story_id=10286252.

[11] Cariboni, *op. cit.*

[12] Htun, *op. cit.*

Combating Coca, by Land and Sea

Colombian police officers beat a hasty retreat after blowing up a cocaine lab in rural Tumaco, along the southern Pacific coast, on June 9, 2005 (top). Colombian sailors unload 13.5 tons of cocaine seized in Tumaco (bottom).

greater power and increase state control over Bolivia's natural gas industry. [39]

Socialist Daniel Ortega served as Nicaragua's president from 1985 to 1990 after his Soviet-backed Sandinista National Liberation Front overthrew the Somoza dynasty by defeating the U.S.-supported counter-revolutionaries, called the *contras*. He returned to office in January 2007 after winning the 2006 presidential elections.

At the opposite end of the political spectrum, Colombia's Uribe — a conservative lawyer educated at Oxford and Harvard — is an implacable enemy of his country's Marxist guerrillas, whom he has vowed to defeat. Re-elected in 2006 for his second term, he is Washington's staunchest ally in the region and because of his distrust for Chávez tends to be wary of the region's trend towards closer cooperation. [40]

Today's Latin American politicians, Middlesex's Domínguez says, are promising social benefits, employment and a larger share of the country's wealth to the region's hitherto forgotten masses, the 38.5 million indigenous people and other poor, non-whites. Chávez and Morales were elected by mobilizing mestizos and other mixed-race or indigenous voters, many of whom were voting for the first time.

Castañeda identifies two main strains in the Latin American left wing. One, represented by Brazil and Chile, is "modern, open-minded, reformist and internationalist," he says. The other — represented by Venezuela, Bolivia and Ecuador — is "born of the great tradition of Latin American populism" and is "nationalist, strident and close-minded."

U.S. Director of Intelligence McConnell warned a Senate panel in February that "a small group of radical,

Morales, the Indian coca grower elected president of Bolivia in 2006, played a role in the conflicts between coca farmers and the U.S.-backed drug-eradication program and was involved in clashes with police during political demonstrations. Like his ally Chávez, he is seeking constitutional changes that would give the presidency

populist governments continue to project a competing vision that appeals to many of the region's poor." [41] So far, however, that vision is still more a promise than a reality.

The Chávez Factor

Chávez used Venezuela's oil money to become "the only Latin American politician in the past half-century to acquire the type of worldwide name recognition and star power" enjoyed by Guevara, wrote *Foreign Policy* editor Naím. The Bush administration became Chávez's No. 1 rhetorical target, since he "understood very quickly that the emperor had no clothes and that challenging the American empire and its internationally unpopular leader was a sure bet." [42]

Chávez has been the driving force behind the launching of the seven-nation Bank of the South — a potential regional competitor to the World Bank and the Inter-American Development Bank — with a projected $7 billion in start-up capital. He also pledged billions of dollars to help build oil refineries in Brazil, Nicaragua and Ecuador and has established a strategic alliance with Cuba, at one point importing 20,000 Cuban teachers, doctors and party activists.

"Most of all, he has been attempting, with some success, to split the hemisphere into two camps: one pro-Chávez, and one pro-American," wrote Castañeda. [43] But even as Chávez calls President Bush "the devil," the United States remains Venezuela's main oil customer, buying 1.5 million barrels per day of petroleum products, making Venezuela America's fourth-largest oil supplier. [44] Trade between the two countries totaled $7 billion in 2007.

Meanwhile, as if to poke the U.S. president in the eye, Chávez also has reached out to Iran's President Mahmoud Ahmadinejad, who is persona non grata in the United States for his refusal to halt Iran's uranium enrichment program. McConnell told the Senate committee that while Chávez and Ahmadinejad have "visited each other seven times since 2005" and have discussed nuclear energy, apparently no "significant developments" have followed these discussions. What causes anxiety among Venezuela's neighbors, McConnell said, is the fact that "military cooperation between Tehran and Caracas is growing." Venezuela has also purchased well over $3 billion in arms from Russia. As regional tensions heightened following the Colombian incursion into Ecuador on March 1, Chávez threatened to deploy his new Russian combat planes against Colombia.

Latin America's most stridently anti-U.S. leftist leaders include communist Fidel Castro (center), former president of Cuba, and his socialist protégés, Venezuela's President Hugo Chávez (left) and Bolivia's President Evo Morales (right).

Chávez's saber-rattling, together with Ecuador's decision to follow Venezuela's lead and move troops to the Colombian border, have drawn the Bush administration's attention to a region it has left largely unattended since 9/11.

"We're not using our power very well in general, and certainly not vis-a-vis Latin America," said Col. Lawrence Wilkerson, former chief of staff for Secretary of State Colin Powell and now a professor of government at the College of William and Mary in Williamsburg, Va. "There is very little attention paid to Latin America, and that's a mistake." [45]

Latin Americans, too, have felt the neglect. Ivonne A-Baki, speaker of the Ecuadorian national congress, calls Washington's lack of interest in Latin America since the attacks "patronizing." Terrorism is a global phenomenon, she says, noting, "9/11 could have originated in our region as well as any other part of the world. We need to be strengthening our ties, not weakening them." But, she acknowledges, "We Latin Americans haven't given the problem much attention either."

Inter-American Dialogue's Hakim isn't worried about what some have called Washington's benign neglect of Latin America. "There's nothing urgent we need to do in Latin America," he says. "There's the migration issue with Mexico, but that's really a U.S. border-control issue." [46] And unlike in the 1980s, when "nasty, vicious wars" were compounded by serious economic

Major Trade Agreements Affecting the Western Hemisphere

NAFTA — Implemented on Jan. 1, 1994, the North America Free Trade Agreement eliminates tariff barriers among the United States, Canada and Mexico until 2009. Increases in agricultural trade and investment fostered by NAFTA have made Mexico and Canada the largest and second-largest U.S. markets. From 1993 to 2006, overall trade in goods among the three countries jumped 198 percent — to an estimated $883 billion. During that same period, U.S. exports to Canada and Mexico jumped 157 percent, while imports from those countries increased by 231 percent, according to the International Trade Administration of the U.S. Commerce Department.

CAFTA-DR — The Central America-Dominican Republic-United States Free Trade Agreement went into effect on Aug. 2, 2005. Along with prior agreements, it will eliminate 80 percent of the trade barriers among Costa Rica, the Dominican Republic, El Salvador, Guatemala, Honduras, Nicaragua and the United States. The remaining tariffs are scheduled to be eliminated by 2020. CAFTA-DR also sets guidelines for workers' rights, provides access to sugar markets in the Dominican Republic and Central America and protects patents and trademarks for digital products like U.S. software.

FTAA — The Free Trade Agreement of the Americas, proposed at the First Summit of the Americas in 1994, calls for the gradual abolition of trade and investment barriers among the 34 democracies in the Western Hemisphere. The agreement was to have been signed by Jan. 1, 2005, but numerous countries, including Venezuela and Bolivia, refused to accept the proposed model. At the fourth Summit of the Americas in 2005 in Buenos Aires, 29 countries shelved the agreement until an unspecified future date.

MERCOSUR — Created in March 1991 by Brazil, Argentina, Paraguay and Uruguay, the *Mercado Común del Sur* (the Southern Common Market) is the largest trading bloc in South America, responsible for regulating imports and exports and overseeing trade disagreements among its members. Venezuela is awaiting ratification as the group's fifth member. Associate members include Bolivia, Chile, Colombia, Ecuador and Peru. Although several trade disagreements have arisen between members, MERCOSUR's overall goal is to establish a free-trade area across South America.

---

woes, he says, Latin America is now largely at peace, except for Colombia. And, for all Chávez's bombast, Hakim dismisses him as a "rather peripheral figure" from a second-tier country.

Trade Issues

Virulent anti-Americanism is one thing; commercial interests are another. Chávez may rail against President Bush, but not many other countries besides the United States are equipped to refine Venezuela's low-grade crude. Hence the United States remains the main customer for Venezuela's oil. Similarily, other Latin American leaders may distance themselves from Washington, but in the end they still want access to the U.S. market.

On the U.S. side, successive presidents have hoped to establish a hemisphere-wide free-trade area stretching from Alaska to Tierra del Fuego, but the U.S. Congress has been notoriously skeptical about trade accords.

U.S. lawmakers first and foremost scrutinize trade agreements for their impact on American jobs and exports. Then they often become the political instrument for forcing change abroad — such as improving human rights, intensifying the fight against drug trafficking and cooling relations with Cuba. In 1994, the United States, Canada and Mexico signed the North American Free Trade Agreement (NAFTA). (*See box.*) The accord significantly boosted Mexican trade with the United States but has always had its skeptics at home — including, most recently, both the Democratic presidential candidates, Sen. Hillary Rodham Clinton of New York and Sen. Barack Obama of Illinois.

Once NAFTA was approved, the United States switched its focus to regional agreements in Central and South America. But the Central America-Dominican Republic-United States Free Trade Agreement (CAFTA-DR) — approved by Congress in 2005 — is the only one approved so far. It has since been adopted by all the signatories except Costa Rica, where strong public opposition led the government to hold a referendum on the agreement last October. It was approved — but only by a hair — and the national assembly now has until October 1 to ratify the treaty.

Opponents of free-trade agreements include Latin American farmers who fear cheaper, subsidized U.S. agricultural goods flooding their markets, trade unionists afraid of losing jobs to southern lands with cheap, non-unionized labor and others who see such deals as a Trojan horse for "Yanqui" hegemony.

The alternative approach of bilateral trade pacts has had mixed success as a result of conflicting political interests. Congress passed a free-trade agreement with Peru after nearly three years of delays caused by American unions' concerns about jobs and farmers' fears of cheaper Peruvian agricultural imports. Ironically, it was a Democratic majority in Congress that unblocked the deal, on which the Republicans had been stonewalling since 2005. Democrats, who have heavy support from unions and environmental groups, voted for the $9 billion agreement after provisions to protect human rights and Peru's environment were added. [47]

In January, faced with strong Democratic resistance to the proposed U.S.-Colombia free-trade accord, Secretary of State Rice took the unusual step of inviting several Democratic lawmakers to accompany her to Colombia in order to assuage their complaints about Colombia's human rights record and failure to protect union leaders from right-wing violence.

In February Ecuadorian legislator A-Baki visited Washington with a group of Andean parliamentarians to lobby for renewal of the special trade preferences enjoyed by Colombia, Peru, Ecuador and Bolivia under the Andean Trade Promotion Agreement, which in February was extended for 10 months for the third time, but not renewed. Congress is balking at renewing the deal because Ecuador and Bolivia have close ties to Chávez. Supporters of extending the agreement argue that denial will drive the two countries even further into Venezuela's orbit, and other Latin American countries will view the cut-off as unjust and high-handed.

But today's Latin Americans have also developed their own approach to trade accords. In 1991, in a push towards greater regional integration, Brazil, Argentina, Uruguay and Paraguay launched Mercosur (*Mercado*

Comun del Sur or Common Market of the South). The United States was not invited to join, but Venezuela is awaiting ratification as a full member; Bolivia, Chile, Colombia, Ecuador and Peru are associate members.

Modeled after the European Union and designed to ensure free movement of goods, capital, services and people among its member states, the union has survived internal squabbles to reflect what observers see as a growing interest among Latin American states in cooperating with one another. [48]

CURRENT SITUATION

Tense Times

Two recent events have forced the world — including the United States — to focus its attention on Latin America. The first was Castro's announcement that he would step down from the presidency. The ailing Cuban leader's decision led to intense speculation whether the hand-picked new leadership in Cuba would change the repressively dogmatic communist course that Castro had steered for five decades.

But on March 4, the spotlight shifted to the Andes, where tension mounted as both Venezuela and Ecuador sent troops to their Colombian borders after Colombian forces killed FARC leader Reyes inside Ecuadorian territory. In Bogotá, President Uribe's government did not respond to the implied threat but said computer documents captured in the FARC camp revealed ties to both Venezuelan and Ecuadorian government officials. Both governments denied the allegations.

The Colombians also claimed seized documents showed Chávez had contributed $300 million to FARC — which, if true, raises the question of why the group needs to continue smuggling drugs and kidnapping in order to raise money. But Chávez's alleged contribution can also be seen in the context of another Colombian allegation: that FARC was seeking to buy uranium. [49]

The incident came on the heels of Chávez's high-profile role in getting FARC to release six hostages since Christmas, an intervention that the Colombian government first encouraged then opposed.

Amidst a flurry of negotiations to resolve the border standoff, President Uribe said he is considering action against Chávez in the International Criminal Court for aiding terrorists. [50] But official public reaction in Latin

America has tended to criticize Colombia for trespassing across the border. Not so President Bush, who condemned Chávez's "provocative maneuver" in sending troops to the border and called on Congress to pass the stalled U.S.-Colombia Free Trade agreement as a sign of support.

"If we fail to approve this agreement, we will let down our close ally, we will damage our credibility in the region and we will embolden the demagogues in our hemisphere," Bush said. "President [Uribe] told me that the people across the region are watching to see what the United States will do." [51]

The bombastic Venezuelan leaders' saber rattling is widely seen as an attempt to distract attention from growing domestic discontent over food shortages and his failure to improve the quality of life for the population. According to the Venezuelan Finance Ministry, food supplies are falling short of demand by "up to 60 percent" despite three consecutive years of production growth. In addition to tightening controls on food distribution and tightening border surveillance, Chávez has lifted restrictions on food imports and says the government is considering reviewing mandated price limits on foodstuffs.

The latest crisis overshadows the good news in Latin America, which is experiencing "a period of economic prosperity that may well continue," says Nora Lustig, a George Washington University professor of international relations specializing in Latin America. In fact, the recent global economic boom plays to the strength of the resource-rich region, where economic growth in the larger commodity-exporting countries, such as Brazil, is spilling over into neighboring countries.

Among the more centrist governments, Mexico is hoping the United States will not follow through with its plan to block illegal border crossings with a wall or electronic "fence." Officials in Mexico City are trying to calculate the impact America's current economic problems will have on bilateral trade, which involves 80 percent of Mexico's business.

The successful Colombian incursion into Ecuador was indicative of the improved effectiveness of the country's U.S.-trained and financed security forces. President Uribe has made progress in "improving security while energetically implementing a comprehensive counternarcotics strategy," Intelligence Director McConnell told the Senate committee. "Bogotá now holds the strategic advantage because of the Colombian military's sustained combat operations in the FARC's rural heartland," McConnell said.

Indeed, ordinary Colombians say the security situation has improved considerably. Military roadblocks have made highway travel between cities safer. According to U.S. statistics (accepted by Colombians as accurate), kidnappings are down 76 percent, homicides by 40 percent. Wealthier Colombians in cities like Cali, for example, can again visit country retreats that had been out of reach for years. [52]

Meanwhile, the Colombian government is negotiating the dismantlement of the right-wing paramilitaries that formed as an antidote to FARC. This is causing congestion in the judicial system and has led to political scandal for Uribe. More than 50 paramilitary commanders have confessed to their involvement, in hopes of obtaining lenient sentences, but some have alleged that several Uribe allies had colluded with the paramilitary. [53] So far, however, investigators have only looked into paramilitary confessions from three of Colombia's 32 provinces. [54]

Skepticism, however, surrounds McConnell's claim that "Bogotá's counterdrug program continues to show impressive results" and that "U.S.-supported aerial eradication has diminished coca cultivation in some areas." [55] But Chávez is undermining counternarcotics operations in the region, McConnell charged, "by giving traffickers access to alternative routes and transit points." The U.S. government recently confirmed earlier press reports that Chávez was allowing Colombian cocaine to be shipped to international markets through Venezuela. McConnell told the Senate panel that Venezuela was "a major departure point for South American — predominantly Colombian — cocaine destined for the U.S. market, and its importance as a transshipment center continues to grow." [56]

But a Feb. 3 *London Observer* report said the cocaine trail from Venezuela leads mainly to Europe, not the United States: "Thirty percent of the 600 tons of cocaine smuggled from Colombia each year goes through Venezuela. Most of that 30 percent ends up in Europe, with Spain and Portugal being the principal ports of entry."

The paper said there was no indication that Chávez himself had a direct role in the trafficking. Nevertheless, the reporter's sources doubted that "Chávez was not aware of the collusion between his armed forces and the leadership of FARC." [57]

Has the United States lost its influence in Latin America?

YES
Janette Habel
Professor, Institute of Latin American Studies, Paris

Written for *CQ Researcher*, February 2008

Over the past decade, the United States has suffered a number of setbacks in Latin America. Washington's ambitious plan for a Free Trade Area of the Americas (FTAA) stretching from Alaska to Tierra del Fuego is a dead duck. The demise of neo-liberalism has opened the way for a series of left-wing coalition governments, each anxious to demonstrate in different ways its independence from the United States. Then in 2002, there was the failure of a U.S.-supported coup against Venezuelan President Hugo Chávez.

Finally, the setbacks in Iraq made it unlikely that the United States could contemplate another military action to enforce its will. This state of affairs prompted some observers to ask whether the United States was "losing" Latin America, or had indeed already lost it. To put this loss in perspective, French diplomat Alain Rouquie argued that the collapse of the Soviet Union meant that "Latin America ceased to be of strategic interest to the United States."

The U.S. has regained some lost ground by ratifying a number of new free-trade agreements with Latin America. The failure of the FTAA should not detract from U.S. successes in signing bilateral free-trade accords. Washington also has been trying to beef up military cooperation within the framework of its war on terror and the fight against narco-trafficking.

Furthermore, despite the growing rejection faced by the United States, trade trumps politics. U.S. investments in Latin America and the Caribbean totaled $353 billion in 2005, and U.S. exports to Latin America increased by 12.7 percent in 2006.

As Latin America expands its horizons, the discipline imposed by globalization and world markets tends to reduce the risk of political upheavals. Thus, the old style of Washington arm-twisting would in any case seem less necessary.

Washington also has learned more subtle methods of exerting its influence. By waving the banner of democracy while using more acceptable persuasive measures, the Americans can target different groups and communities and work on their differences to achieve their objectives. North American hegemony over the continent may not be what it was, but its foundations remain solid.

NO
Francisco Rodríguez
Assistant Professor of Economics and Latin American Studies, Wesleyan University
Former chief economist, Venezuelan National Assembly (2000-2004)

Written for *CQ Researcher*, February 2008

I don't think the United States has neglected Latin America. The United States does have other priorities, and I think those are also important. If you have to neglect anywhere, it had better not be the Middle East. Policymakers have limited capacities to give priority to different regions.

At the same time, Latin America has been doing relatively well in the last few years, both in terms of economic growth and the consolidation of democracies.

Yes, there has been a surge to the left, but in most of Latin America it's a benign left, with a few exceptions. In Brazil, for instance, voters elected Luiz Inacio Lula da Silva as president, but he has been making good efforts at ensuring Brazil's institutions are compatible with democratic ideals. In Peru, there was the emergence of a radical left, but voters rejected it. Hugo Chávez in Venezuela and Evo Morales in Bolivia — and possibly Manuel Ortega in Nicaragua — are the exceptions, but they are isolated.

There's a broader phenomenon that has occurred in Latin America. In the 1990s the United States and the international financial institutions decided to back very aggressive market reforms. These reforms did not have the results that had been expected, causing a political backlash. The lesson was that it may not be a good idea to try to define Latin American policy with a very active involvement by Washington.

Rather, Latin America is developing home-grown market economies in which moderate, left-wing governments such as Brazil's are respecting the market, but they are also addressing their respective country's social problems, and they are doing it in their own way.

The United States could still help more. It would be a great step for Washington in its relations with Latin America if it lowered agricultural subsidies that hurt the agricultural exports of many countries in the region.

An active initiative to financially support anti-poverty programs could also be very productive in improving the relationship of the United States with Latin America.

Bolivian Discontent

In Bolivia, the government is trying to avert secessionist threats over Morales' efforts to codify his "democratic revolution."

Last year, a constituent assembly approved Morales' draft constitution, which would give Bolivia's 30-plus indigenous groups full citizenship and redistribute natural gas revenues to favor the central government. The proposal drew violent opposition from the eastern provinces, where Bolivians of European descent are concentrated — as are the country's rich natural gas deposits. Some indigenous communities in the area are also part of the opposition movement.

With emotions running high, some provinces threatened outright secession while others declared their autonomy from La Paz. In January, the government and provincial governors began a series of reconciliation talks aimed at reaching a compromise and paving the way for the national referendum on the constitution later in the year.

Although the talks began promisingly with a joint statement stressing the need for unity, in late January they were suspended after Morales suddenly cut gas revenues to the provinces by 30 percent.

OUTLOOK

Uncharted Waters

While analysts don't believe that the Venezuelan-Colombian border face-off will escalate, the residual bad feeling will make the Andes an area of tense relations for some time to come.

Of wider regional concern is the faltering U.S. economy. "Latin Americans don't really know to what extent they are insulated from the economic problems of the United States," says George Washington University's Lustig. "We're sailing in uncharted waters. How will they impact the Latin American macro-economy?" A loss of jobs stateside would reduce the amount of remittances Latin American workers in the United States send home — an amount that totaled $45 billion in 2006. [58]

Meanwhile, says Middlesex University's Domínguez, "the amount of investment from the United States has been almost non-existent, but Europe and China are investing very heavily in raw materials." He also sees the level of collaboration within the region improving. The Mercosur trade agreement and the recently launched Bank of the South (once it is funded) could become useful instruments for creating a closer economic — and, eventually, even political — union of Latin American countries. But other observers feel that such progress requires a greater degree of cooperation and political will than exists at present.

Two Latin American ballots this year could affect the region by potentially leaving the Venezuelan and Bolivian governments in an even more unpredictable state. What will Chávez do if — as seems likely — the growing opposition deals another blow to his prestige by winning a significant number of provincial seats? With his second term ending in 2012, "He'll be focused on concentrating power this year," predicts Daniel Varnagy, a political science professor at Simón Bolívar University in Caracas." [59]

Chávez's ally Morales faces a similar test later this year, when Bolivia holds a national referendum on his proposed constitution. Without some compromises with the opposition, Bolivia could be heading into a dangerous confrontation.

But for all Latin America's considerable — some might say "miraculous" — progress, Inter-American Dialogue's Hakim says its "most daunting challenges" remain "high and persistent rates of poverty; an egregious scale of income and wealth inequality; the dismal performance of public services available to low-income groups; and rampant crime and violence that mainly affect poor people."

Failure to make rapid and significant inroads into these problems, he warns, will deepen the mass discontent already afflicting the region and undermine its gains in other areas.

NOTES

1. Quoted in Larry Luxner, "Despite Some Leftist Leanings, Democracy Takes Root in Latin World," *The Washington Diplomat*, February 2008, p. 14.

2. Eric Green, "Economic Growth Continues in Latin America, Caribbean, U.N. says," america.gov Web site, July 26, 2006, www.america.gov/st/washfile-english/2006/July/200607261646411xeneerg2.906436e-02.html.

3. See "Indigenous peoples of Latin America: old inequities, mixed realities and new obligations for democracies in the twenty-first century," U.N. Economic Mission for Latin America and the Caribbean, ww.eclac.org/publicaciones/xml/4/27 484/PSI2006_Cap3_IndigenousPeople.pdf.

4. Jorge G. Castañeda, "Latin America's Left Turn," *Foreign Affairs*, May/June 2006, www.foreignaf fairs.org/20060501faessay85302/jorge-g-castaneda /latin-america-s-left-turn.html.

5. Jens Erik Gould, "Venezuela youths transformed by music," BBC News, Nov. 28, 2005, http://news.bbc .co.uk/2/hi/americas/4457278.stm.

6. Michael Reid, *Forgotten Continent: The Battle for South America's Soul* (2007).

7. "BBC News Profile: Hugo Chávez," Dec. 3, 2007, http://news.bbc.co.uk/2/hi/americas/3517106.stm.

8. Quoted in Simon Romero and Sandra La Fuente, "In Venezuela, Faith in Chávez Starts to Wane," *The New York Times*, Feb. 9, 2008, p. A1.

9. Janette Habel, "Washington a-t-il perdu l'Amerique Latine?" *Le Monde Diplomatique*, December 2007, p. 1.

10. Carolyn Curiel, "Hello Neighbor," *The New York Times*, Feb. 5, 2008, www.nytimes.com/2008/02 /03/books/Curiel-t.html?r=1&ref=review&page.htm.

11. J. Michael McConnell, "Annual Threat Assessment by the Director of National Intelligence for the Senate Select Committee on Intelligence 2008," testimony before Senate Select Committee on Intelligence, Feb. 5, 2008, www.dni.gov/testimonies /20080205_testimony.pdf.

12. Francisco Peregil, "Nuestra prioridad es jugar un gran papel en Suramerica," *El País*, Feb. 9, 2008, www.elpais.com/solotexto/articulo.html?xref=20080 209elpepiint_8&type=Tes&anchor=elpepiint.

13. *Ibid.*

14. Quoted in Pablo Bachelet, "Sunday's defeat likely to hurt Chávez's international standing," *Free Republic*, Dec. 3, 2007, www.freerepublic.com/focus/f-news /1934295/posts.

15. Quoted in Juan Forero, "Chávez Turns Bitter Over His Defeat in Referendum; Foes of Amending Charter Have 'Nothing to Celebrate,'" *The Washington Post*, Dec. 6, 2007, p. A20.

16. Romero and La Fuente, *op. cit.*

17. "Venezuela: Hugo Chávez's Revolution," Executive Summary, International Crisis Group, Feb. 27, 2007, www.crisisgroup.org/home/index.cfm?l=1&id =4674.

18. Francisco R. Rodriguez, "An Empty Revolution: The Unfulfilled Promises of Hugo Chávez," *Foreign Affairs*, March/April 2008, www.foreignaffairs.org /20080301faessay87205/francisco-rodriguez/an-empty-revolution.html.

19. *Ibid.*

20. *Ibid.* Rodríguez is citing pollster Alfredo Kellner Associados.

21. Monte Reel, "Bolivia's Burning question: Who May Dispense Justice?" *The Washington Post*, Feb. 2, 2008, p. 4, www.washingtonpost.com/wp-dyn/con tent/article/2008/02/01/AR2008020103426.html. For Ecuador: Brian Wagner, "Ecuador referendum may bring sweeping government changes," Voice of America, April 13, 2007, www.voanews.com/eng lish/archive/2007-04/2007-04-13-voa38.cfm?text mode=0.

22. "Statistical Yearbook for Latin America and the Caribbean, 2006," U.N. Economic Commission for Latin American and the Caribbean, 2007, p. 3 (their p. 85), www.eclac.cl/publicaciones/xml/4/28074 /LCG2332B_2.pdf.

23. "Social Panorama of Latin America — 2007," U.N. Economic Mission for Latin America and the Caribbean, www.eclac.org/publicaciones/xme/9 /30309/PSI2007_Sintesis_Lanziamento.pdf.

24. Rodríguez, *op. cit.*

25. Castañeda, *op. cit.*

26. Tyler Bridges and Sibylla Bridzinsky, "Latin America On the Brink," *The Miami Herald*, March 3, 2008, p. A1.

27. "FARC frees hostages in deal brokered by Chávez," NPR, Jan. 11, 2008, www.npr.org/templates/story /story.php?storyId=18021246.

28. Chris Kraul, "Colombia's military toughens up," *Los Angeles Times*, Jan. 18, 2008, www.latimes.com /news/nationworld/world/la-fg-colombia18jan18,0, 4255537.story. For background, see Peter Katel, "War on Drugs," *CQ Researcher*, June 2, 2006, pp. 481-504.

29. "FARC frees Colombian hostages," Al Jazeera, Feb. 27, 2008, http://english.aljazeera.net/NR/exeres/88961720-F807-47B8-B93B-0AB5E5C4ED77.htm.

30. "Files in Colombian rebel laptop show Chávez's ties to rebels," Fox News, March 5, 2008, www.foxnews.com/story/0,2933,335128,00.html.

31. PBS OnlineNewsHour, "Colombia's Civil War," www.pbs.org/newshour/bb/latin_america/colombia/trade.html.

32. Juan Forero, "Colombia's low-tech assault," *The Washington Post*, July 7, 2007, p. A1.

33. Early history of Latin America adapted from Kenneth Jost, "Democracy in Latin America," *CQ Researcher*, Nov. 3, 2000, pp. 881-904.

34. For background, see Peter Katel, "Change in Latin America," *CQ Researcher*, July 21, 2006, pp. 601-624.

35. James Surowiecki, "Morales's Mistake," *The New Yorker*, Jan. 23, 2006, www.newyorker.com/archive/2006/01/23/060123ta_talk_surowiecki.

36. "History of Latin America," www.britanica.com.

37. "BBC profile: Kirchner: President by default," May 15, 2003, http://news.bbc.co.uk/2/hi/americas/2981797.stm.

38. "Uruguay elects left wing leader," BBC News, Nov. 1, 2004, http://news.bbc.co.uk/2/hi/americas/3968755.stm.

39. "BBC profile: Evo Morales," Dec. 11, 2005, http://news.bbc.co.uk/2/hi/americas/3203752.stm.

40. "Uribe sworn in amid high security," BBC News, Aug. 7, 2006, http://news.bbc.co.uk/2/hi/americas/3214685.stm.

41. McConnell, *op. cit.*

42. Cristina Marcano and Alberto Barrera Tyszka, *Hugo Chávez: The Definitive Biography of Venezuela's Controversial President* (2004), pp. xiii-xiv.

43. Castañeda, *op. cit.*

44. Cesar J. Alvarez, "Council on Foreign Relations Backgrounder — Venezuela's Oil-Based Economy," Council on Foreign Relations, Nov. 27, 2006, p. 2, www.cfr.org/publication/12089/venezuelas_oil based_economy.html.

45. Luxner, *op. cit.*

46. For background, see Alan Greenblatt, "Immigration Debate," *CQ Researcher*, Feb. 1, 2008, pp. 97-120.

47. David T. Rowlands, "Peru: Free Trade Deal an Andean Tragedy," *Green Left Weekly*, Feb. 6, 2008, http//:upsidedownworld.org/main/content/view/1118/68/.

48. "Profile: Mercosur — Common Market of the South," BBC News, Jan. 29, 2008, news.bbc.co.uk/2/hi/americas/5195834.stm.

49. Carin Zissis, "Colombia's Border Crisis," America's Society Web site, March 4, 2008, www.as-coa.org/article.php?id=926.

50. For background, see Kenneth Jost, "International Law," *CQ Researcher*, Dec. 17, 2004, pp. 1049-1072.

51. Quoted in Michael Abramowitz, "Bush Attends to Foreign Policy Issues; President Talks to Medvedev, Pushes Colombian Free-Trade Pact, Discusses Mideast," *The Washington Post*, March 5, 2008, p. A3.

52. "The Case for the U.S.-Colombia Trade Promotion Agreement," U.S. Department of State, December 2007, www.state.gov/e/eeb/tpp/colombia/.

53. Marcela Sanchez, "Rethinking Plan Colombia," *The Washington Post*, March 16, 2007.

54. *Ibid.*

55. McConnell, *op. cit.*

56. *Ibid.*

57. John Carlin, "Revealed: Chávez role in cocaine trail to Europe," *The Observer*, Feb. 3, 2008, www.guardian.co.uk/print/0,,332351756-111259,00.html.

58. "Migrant remittances from the United States to Latin America to reach $45 billion in 2006, says IDB," Inter-American Development Bank, Oct. 18, 2006, www.iadb.org/NEWS/articledetail.cfm?artid=3348&language=En.

59. James Ingham, "Crucial Year for Chávez Revolution," BBC News, Jan. 11, 2008, http://news.bbc.co.uk/2/hi/americas/7179055.stm.

BIBLIOGRAPHY

Books

Chasteen, John Charles, *Americanos: Latin America's Struggle for Independence*, Oxford University Press, 2008.

A professor of history at the University of North

Carolina offers a compact history of Latin America's revolutions.

Marcano, Cristina, and Alberto Barrera Tyszka, (translated by Kristina Cordero), *Hugo Chávez: The Definitive Biography of Venezuela's Controversial President,* **Random House, 2004.**
Chávez's rise to power is traced by two Venezuelan journalists, who neither extol not attack the Venezuelan president. Based on numerous interviews with enemies as well as those close to him and on documents, the authors emphasize Chávez the man and his quest for power rather than his policies.

Marquez, Gabriel Garcia, *One Hundred Years of Solitude,* **Harper and Row, 1967.**
This is *the* Latin American novel and required reading for students of the region. Set in the fictional village of Macondo, Garcia Marquez's family saga is widely seen as an impeccably researched metaphor for the history of Colombia, in particular, and Latin America generally.

Oppenheimer, Andres, *Saving the Americas: The Dangerous Decline of Latin America and What the U.S. Must Do,* **Random House Mondadori, 2007.**
An acclaimed reporter and columnist at *The Miami Herald* sees Latin America as a commodity-rich but stagnant continent desperately in need of a strategy for survival in the 21st century.

Reid, Michael, *Forgotten Continent: The Battle for Latin America's Soul,* **Yale University Press, 2007.**
The Economist's Latin America editor says the continent's recent transformation to democracy deserves more attention.

Winn, Peter, *Americas: The Changing Face of Latin America and the Caribbean,* **Berkeley Books, 2006 edition.**
Companion book to the PBS 1992 series of the same name, updated in 2006. Winn, professor of Latin American studies at Tufts University, was the academic director on the series, responsible for its acclaimed historical accuracy.

Articles

Barrionuevo, Alexei, "Political Tango, Women in the Lead," *The New York Times,* **Nov. 4, 2007, p. 4WK.**

Women in Latin America are rising to top positions in politics as voters seek change.

Phillips, Tom, "Blood on the streets as drug gang and police fight for control of the favelas," *The Guardian,* **June 29, 2007, www.guardian.co.uk/world/2007/jun /29/brazil.international.**
A British correspondent describes life in Rio de Janeiro's combat zone.

Rodriguez, Francisco, "An Empty Revolution: The Unfulfilled Promises of Hugo Chávez," *Foreign Affairs,* **March/April 2008, www.foreignaffairs.org /20080301faessay87205-p0/francisco-rodriguez/an-empty-revolution.html.**
A Wesleyan University professor of economics and Latin American studies and former chief economist of the Venezuelan National Assembly says President Hugo Chávez's social reforms have failed because they were underfunded and mismanaged.

Reports and Studies

"Social Panorama of Latin America, 2007," Economic Council for Latin America and the Caribbean, www.eclac.org/publicaciones/xml/9/303 09/PSI2007Sintesis_Lanziamento.pdf.
The council provides an up-to-date picture of the social and ethnic structure in Latin America and the Caribbean.

Behrman, Jere R., Alejandro Gaviria and Miguel Székely, "Social Exclusion in Latin America: Introduction and Overview," Inter-American Development Bank, March, 2002, http://idbdocs .iadb.org/wsdocs/getdocument.aspx?docnum=773155.
The authors blame Latin America's income inequality — the highest in the world — on the absence of opportunities for large segments of the population due to outright or implicit exclusion of people on the basis of gender, ethnicity, place of residence or social status.

McConnell, J. Michael, "Annual Threat Assessment by the Director of National Intelligence for the Senate Select Committee on Intelligence 2008," Feb. 5, 2008, www.dni.gov/testimonies/20080205_testimony.pdf.
This unclassified country-by-country assessment lays out threats to the United States posed by leftist agendas and "sharply anti-U.S. rhetoric" in Venezuela, Cuba and, to

some extent, Bolivia, Nicaragua and Ecuador. Especially worrisome are these countries' efforts to undercut checks and balances on presidential power, seek lengthy presidential terms, weaken media and civil liberties and emphasize economic nationalism at the expense of market-based approaches.

The WWW Virtual Library: International Affairs Resources, www2.etown.edu/vl/latamer.html.
The Inter-American Development Bank and other sources provide a huge list of accessible statistics and information about Latin America.

For More Information

Argentine Council for International Relations, Uruguay 1037, Piso Primero, C1016ACA Buenos Aires, República Argentina; 54-11-4811-0071; www.cari.org.ar. Pluralist academic institution that encourages analysis of international affairs from an Argentinian perspective.

Center for Latin American Studies, Edmund Walsh School of Foreign Service, Georgetown University, ICC484, Washington, DC 20057; (202) 687-0140; http://clas.georgetown.edu/index.html. Offers undergraduate and graduate degrees emphasizing democratic governance, economic integration, inter-American affairs and culture and society.

Center for Latin American Studies, University of California, Berkeley, 2334 Bowditch St., Berkeley, CA 94720; (510) 642-2088; http://socrates.berkeley.edu:7001/index.html. Promotes research and community awareness of issues affecting Latin America.

Council on Foreign Relations, 58 E. 68th St., New York, NY 10065; (212) 434-9400; www.cfr.org. An independent, nonpartisan organization dedicated to improving global understanding and the foreign policy choices facing the United States and other countries.

Council on Hemispheric Affairs, 1250 Connecticut Ave., N.W., Suite 1C, Washington, DC 20036; (202) 223-4975; www.coha.org. Provides research and information promoting the common interests of the hemisphere.

Fernand Braudel School of World Economics, Rua Ceará 2, Sao Paulo, Brazil 01243-010; (5511) 3824-9633; www.braudel.org.br/en. Conducts research and public debate seeking solutions for the international problems of Brazil and its neighbors.

Institute for International Relations, Rua Marquês de São Vincente, 225, Vila dos Diretórios, Casa 20, Gávea, Rio de Janeiro, RJ, Brazil, 22453-900; (5521) 3527-1557; www.puc-rio.br/sobrepuc/depto/iri. Research and graduate-teaching institution dedicated to international affairs.

Inter-American Development Bank, 1300 New York Ave., N.W., Washington, DC 20577; (202) 623-1000; www.iadb.org. Dedicated to accelerating economic and social development in Latin America and the Caribbean.

Inter-American Dialogue, 1211 Connecticut Ave., N.W., Suite 510, Washington, DC 20036; (202) 822-9002; www.thedialogue.org. A center for policy analysis, exchange and communication on issues in the Western Hemisphere.

Latin American and Caribbean Institute for Economic and Social Planning, Avenida Dag Hammarskjöld 3477, Vitacura, Casilla 179-D, Santiago, Chile; (56-2) 206-6104; www.eclac.cl/ilpes. Primary training center for the U.N.'s Economic Commission for Latin America and the Caribbean.

Organization of American States, 17th Street and Constitution Ave., N.W., Washington, DC 20006; (202) 458-3000; www.oas.org. Promotes social and economic development in the Western Hemisphere.

U.N. Economic Commission for Latin America and the Caribbean, Avenida Dag Hammarkjold 3477, Vitacura, Casilla 179-D, Santiago, Chile; (56-2) 210-2380; www.eclac.cl/default.asp?idioma=IN. One of the five regional commissions of the United Nations, founded to contribute to the economic development of Latin America.

Elsa Cardozo

Foreign policy expert Central University of Venezuela

Chávez's defeat
"Up until now this appeared to be an indestructible government, but now people realize it is possible to find its weaknesses. This can also be a lesson for the opposition in Bolivia and Ecuador. Here [the opposition] found the government's Achilles' heel and attacked it democratically at the polls."

The Christian Science Monitor, December 2007

José Miguel Vivanco

Americas director Human Rights Watch

Demobilization of Colombia's paramilitary
"The original demobilization law said individuals could receive reduced sentences only for crimes related to their membership in an armed group. The government is now letting drug traffickers get around that rule just by claiming they had a loose connection to the paramilitaries."

The Irish Times, September 2006

Marcos Tarre

Security analyst, Secure Venezuela

Venezuelans resent attention to Colombian hostages
"There is still kidnapping by the guerrillas, though it's easy to say it's criminal gangs. What is clear is that there's a great resentment [among] Venezuelan families who believe there's not even minimal interest in helping them, while there's this media show to help Colombian hostages."

The Washington Post, February 2008

Alfredo Keller

Independent pollster Caracas, Venezuela

Chávez is new symbol for the left
"Chávez has already achieved a certain level of influence, but with Fidel out of the scenario he becomes the only reference point for the symbol of the leftist revolution. But he is trying to build something new, a kind of third world front against the first world, and has a lot of money to do it."

The Christian Science Monitor, February 2008

Francisco Rodríguez

Chief Economist for Venezuela's national assembly until 2004

Economic diversification unlikely in Venezuela
"Under Chávez the economy has become more dependent on oil, and non-oil exports have been falling. There is nothing in the constitutional reform that promises to alter this trend. There is no indication that the government even thinks that de-industrialization is a problem."

Financial Times (London), November 2007

Carlos Alarcón

Columnist, La Razón

Bolivian government cannot unify fractured nation
"Instead of looking for real and effective solutions for the crisis of unity and integration of Bolivia, [politicians] offer artificial measures that result in greater polarization, racism, violence and confrontation."

Los Angeles Times, December 2007

Carlos Toranzo

Political analyst, La Paz

Bolivian election creates uncertainty
"It's complete madness, chaos. We're in the midst of a grand political and territorial impasse, and the country is being turned into an electoral gymnasium."

Los Angeles Times, December 2007

Álvaro Uribe

President of Columbia

Chávez's use of oil wealth challenged
"You cannot mistreat the continent, set it on fire as you do, speaking about imperialism when you, on the basis of your budget, want to set up an empire."

The Christian Science Monitor, November 2007

Teodoro Petkoff

Editor, TalCual

Chávez criticized for hand-picking leaders
"His tireless finger won't stop singling out those who are going to be the bosses."

The International Herald Tribune, January 2007

Jorge Quiroga

Former President of Bolivia

Chávez's "totalitarian project" for Latin America
"Chávez is not just a clown or a buffoon: he is a very intelligent person, obsessive, vengeful and he has a photographic memory and a great capacity for communication."

BBC Monitoring Latin America, July 2007

Christo Komarnitski, Bulgaria

14

Afghanistan on the Brink

Roland Flamini

A Pakistani army helicopter patrols the troubled tribal area of North Waziristan, along the Pakistan-Afghanistan border in February 2007. The region has been a refuge for Taliban and al Qaeda militants since a U.S.-led alliance toppled the fundamentalist Taliban regime in Afghanistan in 2001. Some experts question whether the U.S-NATO alliance is swimming against the historical tide in trying to reshape the destiny of Afghans, often called unconquerable and ungovernable.

AP Photo/B. K. Bangash

From *CQ Researcher,* June 1, 2007.

The fabled Khyber Pass — linking Pakistan and Afghanistan — has long been synonymous with warfare in Central Asia. Since before Alexander the Great, invaders have used the rugged route through the Kush Mountains as the gateway to the Indian subcontinent. The British marched through it as well, coming from India, in three unsuccessful attempts to conquer Afghanistan.

Today, the Khyber is a paved road jammed with trucks, cars and brightly colored "jingle buses," and thousands of Taliban fighters and al Qaeda terrorists freely use it to cross from safe havens in Pakistan to try to take back Afghanistan from its fragile, new government.

It's been five years since a U.S.-led alliance toppled the fundamentalist Taliban regime after it refused to give up al Qaeda leader Osama bin Laden following the Sept. 11, 2001, terrorist attacks in the United States. The defiance cost the Taliban dearly. Its ranks decimated, it fled with its al Qaeda allies into the mountainous border areas between Afghanistan and Pakistan. But bin Laden is still at large and the regime is attempting a comeback, leaving Afghanistan's future far from certain.

The West has been only partially successful in establishing secular statehood and political and economic stability. President Hamid Karzai maintains a tenuous hold on just part of the country. But the Taliban — flush with money from a revived and booming opium trade — has garnered new recruits and weapons and is pushing to restore its draconian version of Islamic law in Kabul, the capital. As summer approaches and melting mountain snows clear the routes into Afghanistan, the Taliban has vowed to renew its efforts.

Afghans Live in a Dangerous Neighborhood

As the gateway to Central Asia, Afghanistan serves as a link between China, the Middle East and the Indian subcontinent. But it's a dangerous neighborhood. To the east is nuclear-armed Pakistan, where the Taliban and al Qaeda find refuge in lawless tribal areas along the border. (*See map, p. 369.*) India and China — two other nuclear powers — are also in the neighborhood, which includes Iran, Tajikistan, Uzbekistan and Turkmenistan.

Afghanistan at a Glance

Area: 647,500 sq. km.

Population: 31.9 million; growing at 2.63%/year (July 2007 est.)

Infant mortality: 157 deaths per 1,000 (2007 est.)

Labor force: 15 million (2004)

Unemployment rate: 40% (2005)

Religion: Sunni Muslim, 80%; Shiite Muslim, 19%; other, 1%

Languages: Dari (Afghan Persian) and Pashtu spoken by 50% and 35% of the population, respectively. Turkic languages — primarily Turkmen and Uzbek — are spoken by 11%. Balochi and Pashai are among Afghanistan's 30 minor languages.

Government: The president and two vice presidents are elected by direct vote for five-year terms. A president can be elected for two terms. The bicameral National Assembly consists of the Wolesi Jirga (House of People), which is allotted no more than 249 seats via direct election, and the Meshrano Jirga (House of Elders), which has 102 seats.

Economy: Recovering from decades of conflict, the economy has improved significantly since the fall of the Taliban in 2001, largely due to an infusion of international aid, recovery of the agricultural sector and growth of the service sector. The gross domestic product was $8.8 billion in 2006, and the per-capita GDP was around $275. In 2003, 53% of the population was living below the poverty line.

Communications hardware: 280,000 telephones, 1.4 million mobile phones and 22 Internet hosts serving around 30,000 users (2005).

Source: The World Factbook 2007, Central Intelligence Agency, 2007

Meanwhile, the Afghanistan conflict has put NATO's credibility and role in the post-Cold War era at stake. The venerable alliance has 36,750 troops serving in Afghanistan — the first time its forces have been deployed outside Europe. Also on the line is the Bush post-9/11 doctrine to bring democracy to Islamist regimes that could breed global jihadists.

Some question whether the NATO alliance is swimming against the historical tide in trying to reshape the destiny of Afghans, often called unconquerable and ungovernable. Others say America's quick-fix mentality is the wrong approach. The international community "needs to operate on a 10-to-20-year horizon," says Ashraf Ghani, former Afghan minister of finance and now chancellor of Kabul University.

To improve strained relations between Kabul and Pakistan, considered crucial for Afghanistan's recovery, a telephone hotline was installed early this year linking Karzai's office and that of his Pakistani counterpart, Gen. Pervez Musharraf. But since neither leader wants to talk to the other, it remains silent.

Karzai complains Musharraf is not doing enough to halt attacks in Afghanistan by the Pakistan-based Taliban. [1] Musharraf, who faces growing political unrest at home, counters that Karzai merely wants a scapegoat for his own inability to provide security. Their open hostility blocks Afghanistan's recovery and undermines the bilateral relationship between the two countries, felt most strongly along their 1,400-mile border of rugged, mountain terrain. [2]

Taliban militants, who controlled most of Afghanistan from 1996 until 2001, openly cross the porous border

Tribal Areas Harbor Guns, Drugs and Terrorists

Pakistan's Federally Administered Tribal Areas, stretching along the Pakistan-Afghanistan border, consist of seven Pashtun-dominated "agencies": Khyber, Kurram, Orakzai, Mohmand, Bajaur, North Waziristan and South Waziristan. The British created the enclave to give maximum autonomy to the fiercely independent Pashtuns and to serve as a buffer between then-undivided India and Afghanistan. Smuggling, drug trafficking and gun-running flourish in the region, often described as "lawless." During the 1980s, the tribal areas served as a base for the mujaheddin fighting the Soviet occupiers in Afghanistan. Today they are a safe haven for Taliban and al Qaeda insurgents.

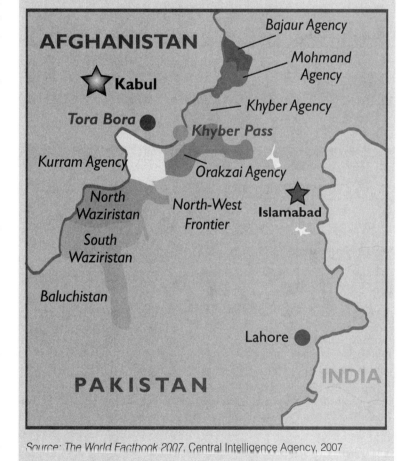

Source: The World Factbook 2007, Central Intelligence Agency, 2007

into Afghanistan and attack Afghan and Western troops or anyone thought to be cooperating with them. They then return to safety in Pakistan's North-West Frontier Province, Baluchistan and the lawless Federally

Foreign Troop Level Hits 50,000

Of the nearly 50,000 allied troops in Afghanistan, 27,000 are Americans: 12,000 serving in the U.S.-led coalition and 15,000 with NATO. The coalition has increased troop levels participating in Operation Enduring Freedom by only 2,800 since invading Afghanistan in 2001. NATO has more than quadrupled its troop levels since first deploying to Afghanistan in 2003.

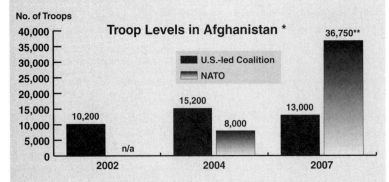

No. of Troops

Troop Levels in Afghanistan *

- ■ U.S.-led Coalition
- ▨ NATO

2002: 10,200 / n/a
2004: 15,200 / 8,000
2007: 13,000 / 36,750**

* U.S.-led coalition figures do not include U.S. troops serving under NATO.

** As of April 20, 2007

Sources: NATO, U.S. Department of Defense

Administered Tribal Areas (FATA) — all said to be sympathetic to or actually controlled by the Taliban.

"Waziristan [in the Federally Administered Tribal Areas] is virtually a criminal state, and Baluchistan is equally lawless," says Italian parliamentarian and foreign-policy specialist Margherita Boniver. "One has to wonder how much control Musharraf actually has over this situation."

Without question, his continued lack of determination in suppressing or denying refuge to the Taliban has been indispensable to its rapid recovery and resurgence. "Long-term prospects for eliminating the Taliban threat appear dim, so long as sanctuary remains in Pakistan," U.S. National Intelligence Director John Michael McConnell recently told the Senate Armed Services Committee. "And there are no encouraging signs that Pakistan is eliminating it." [3]

The cross-border antipathy doesn't help, and Karzai shares the blame for that. "Unless Afghanistan is good neighbors with Pakistan, it cannot survive," says Ishak Shahryar, Afghanistan's first ambassador to the United States after the defeat of the Taliban. "It doesn't make sense to antagonize Musharraf. For one thing, 90 percent

of Afghanistan's imports come through Pakistan."

But Pakistan is a tricky country with which to share a border, even without the Taliban threat. "We live in a very dangerous neighborhood," says former Afghan Foreign Minister Abdullah Abdullah. Indeed. Besides Pakistan, which has nuclear weapons, Afghanistan also shares the neighborhood with two other nuclear powers — India and China — plus Iran, Tajikistan, Uzbekistan and Turkmenistan.

The Taliban's re-emergence from its Pakistan sanctuary hampers the international community's efforts to establish a democracy in Afghanistan, as does Karzai's inability to control corruption or extend his authority over the entire country. With much of the country a patchwork of warlord-controlled fiefdoms, and the Taliban edging its way back into the south, critics derisively call Karzai "the mayor of Kabul."

There has been "an irrefutable loss of legitimacy [by] the government of Afghanistan among its people," said American Lt. Gen. Karl Eikenberry, deputy chairman of NATO's military committee. "People are asking, what is the government delivering? They have moved from a phase of pride in achieving democracy to disappointment in the government's delivery of services." [4]

In a 2002 speech to the Virginia Military Institute (VMI), President George W. Bush proclaimed his goal was "a stable government" in Afghanistan and launched a recovery plan he said would rival Gen. George C. Marshall's post-World War II reconstruction of Europe.

But has the international community lived up to its early promises to help? Close to $25 billion has been pledged in economic aid for reconstruction, but it's anyone's guess how much actually has been delivered or how it has been spent. Afghanistan became something of a black hole for foreign aid, analysts say, due to a dizzying combination of factors — security problems, questionable contracting practices, corruption, inefficiency, an initial preference for foreign contractors over cheaper

Afghan contractors, haste to show results at the expense of quality control and poor bookkeeping.

"Beltway bandits" — Washington-based contractors — saw to it that 80 cents of every U.S. aid dollar "went back to the United States," Ghani alleges.

So far, only about $13 billion of that $25 billion has been committed by the United States and Europe since 2001 — $10 billion of it from the United States — but those who keep track of the donations are unsure how much Japan and the Gulf States have contributed. [5] But even at $25 billion, the international community's pledge was less than the $30 billion over five years — plus another $15 billion in private investment — that Ghani and others have estimated would be needed to rebuild the war-torn country.

In February — five years after his VMI speech — Bush was less upbeat about progress in Afghanistan. The strengthened Taliban, operating out of "remote regions of Pakistan," was a renewed threat, he told the American Enterprise Institute (AEI), a conservative think tank in Washington. "We face a thinking [and] a tough enemy. They watch our actions. They adjust their tactics." [6]

With its military strength stretched due to the war in Iraq, the United States has turned to the North Atlantic military alliance for help, and Taliban fighters have been feeling the effect of battling modern, well-trained allied forces. The NATO deployment consists of troops from most of its 26 member countries, including 15,000 U.S. troops. Another 13,000 coalition forces (including 12,000 Americans) are still engaged in Operation Enduring Freedom, whose main task includes the continuing search for bin Laden.

Dutch Maj. Gen. Ton van Loon, until recently the NATO commander in Afghanistan's volatile south, told *The Washington Post* that insurgents have been pushed out of the southern regions where they had sought to gain a foothold, including Kandahar city and parts of Helmand province. The Taliban "will still be a force, but they don't have the initiative we have," van Loon said, and the anticipated major spring offensive had failed to materialize. [7] Military officials say they could hit the Taliban even harder if they were not barred from pursuing the enemy into their Pakistani hideouts.

But minor, daily clashes across the country are causing collateral damage among civilians — at least 380 deaths in the first four months of this year — and an angry, war-weary Afghan public is blaming U.S. and NATO firepower — especially airstrikes. [8]

AP Photo/Xinhua, Yu Zhixiao

Italian NATO soldiers guard a helicopter during a February 2007 operation in Herat province, where alliance forces are fighting Taliban insurgents. With most of its military resources tied up in Iraq, the Bush administration persuaded NATO to help fill the gap in Afghanistan. NATO now has nearly 38,000 troops in Afghanistan — 15,000 of them Americans.

A concerned President Bush dispatched Vice President Dick Cheney to the region in March to warn Musharraf that a new Democrat-dominated Congress intended to link further U.S. aid to Pakistan to greater efforts to restrain al Qaeda and the Taliban. On the same trip, Cheney also urged Karzai to beef up security and suppress Afghanistan's newly burgeoning $3 billion narcotics trade — a principal income source for Islamic militants and a major embarrassment to the Bush administration. (*See sidebar, p. 378.*) [9]

"Drug traffickers have a symbiotic relationship with insurgent and terrorist groups," wrote Antonio Maria Costa, executive director of the U.N. Office on Drugs and Crime. "Opium buys protection and pays for weapons and foot soldiers." [10] U.S. military forces in

Casting Off the Burqa: Still a Dream for Many

Taliban has executed those who teach, advocate for women.

Television broadcasts of Afghan parliamentary sessions routinely show male and female members sitting side by side, and even show women rising to debate with their male colleagues. To the Afghan public — and to Afghan women in particular — such scenes are surreal.

In the real world, proximity between men and women is generally forbidden, and a woman who has the temerity to argue with a male, especially in public, could be putting herself in harm's way.

This disconnect captures the schizophrenic state in which Afghan women find themselves. The new constitution mandates that women, who make up 50 percent of the population, hold 27 percent of the parliamentary seats (68 out of 249 members) — a higher share than in the U.S. Congress. But in almost every other respect, the promise of a bright future for women in the "new" Afghanistan has faded.

In the "old" Afghanistan ruled by the repressive Taliban regime from 1996 to 2001, girls were barred from going to school, and women were forced to cover their bodies and faces in public. Even when they were encased in the famous, blue, face-hiding burqas, however, women could not leave their homes — to work or even to shop for food — unless accompanied by a male relative. Those who violated these or other rigid rules of behavior were subject to public punishment — and even execution. Thousands of women widowed by Afghanistan's decades of war — or who had no other male relative to accompany them — became prisoners in their own homes with no way of supporting their families — vividly portrayed in the critically acclaimed 2003 movie "Osama."

While the Taliban is no longer in charge and burqas are optional today, new laws passed to protect women are not being enforced. With the Taliban resurgent in some areas, Afghan women still live in fear. The burqa has returned to the streets, even in Kabul, and the continued savagery of a deep-rooted male-dominated culture coupled with disastrous economic conditions have combined to stifle hope and break the spirit.

Small wonder that 65 percent of Kabul's 50,000 widows, each responsible for an average of six dependents and left with no means of support, have told pollsters that they feel suicide is their only way out, reflecting their sense of helplessness even in today's society. [1] And it's not just the widows.

Despite new laws banning forced or child marriages or the exchange of girls to settle a debt or tribal score, up to 80 percent of Afghan women face forced marriages, and 57 percent of girls are married before the legal age of 16, according to the U.N. Development Fund for Women (UNIFEM). "Men in my country think that women are not . . . completely human," Afghan women's rights advocate Homa Sultani recently told CNN. [2] Some who see no escape from chronic abuse commit suicide by setting themselves on fire: 106 cases of self-immolation by women were reported in 2006, according to UNIFEM. [3]

"Young girls are killing themselves from frustration and because they feel there is no way out for them," Medica Mondiale spokeswoman Ancil Adrian-Paul told the BBC. [4] Why do they choose self-immolation? Kerosene and matches are easy to come by.

Small wonder, too, that the life expectancy of Afghan women is around 44 — some 20 years less than in Europe. [5] Afghanistan ranks second worldwide in deaths at childbirth, according to Hangama Anwari, commissioner of the Afghanistan Independent Human Rights Commission, who called the human rights situation of Afghan women "disastrous."

Speaking at a conference in Rome on Afghan womens'

Afghanistan originally resisted calls to help eradicate the country's poppy opium trade, arguing that it was not part of their assignment. But eventually the military agreed to provide logistical support once it became clear the illicit drug income was being used to arm the Taliban.

As the war in Afghanistan enters its sixth year, here are some of the questions being asked:

Did the United States desert Afghanistan for Iraq?

In February 2003, when the United States was mobilizing to invade Iraq, President Karzai flew to Washington to plead

rights in the post-Taliban era, she said, "Women do not have a place in the justice system and they are not guaranteed de facto equality of rights. The laws of divorce and the family need to be reviewed. Discrimination and abuse form part of a firmly rooted mentality, and rates of domestic violence and suicide are still high." [6]

President Karzai recently rebutted criticism of the lack of progress on women's rights by observing that women participate in government. But he has only one female cabinet minister, and she is responsible for women's affairs. Karzai also pointed out that 35 percent of Afghanistan's 6 million schoolchildren are girls — a major improvement from the days of the Taliban. [7]

But scholastic attendance has been dropping because the Taliban has been burning schools — 198 in 2006 — and murdering teachers, especially women who teach girls. [8] As of December, Taliban insurgents reportedly had killed at least 20 educators for teaching girls — dragging one male teacher from his school and beheading him. [9] According to a July 2006 Human Rights Watch report, most of the destroyed schools are in the southern provinces, where the Taliban has been most active. [10]

Karzai — who has told Western reporters that it will take a long time for attitudes about women to change in Afghanistan — shrugs off the burnings. "Schools get burned, but not every day," he told the Council on Foreign Relations in September 2006.

Last September the country was shocked when Taliban gunmen assassinated Safia Ama Jan, the local women's affairs director in the southern city of Kandahar and a well known, longtime champion of women's education. She was killed in broad daylight as she left for work.

So as they wait for long-held misogynist attitudes to change, many Afghan women are choosing to don the shapeless head-to-toe burqa again — just to be on the safe side in a land of hidden dangers.

AFP/Getty Images/Shah Marai

The face-hiding burqa is now optional in Afghanistan, but with the Taliban resurgent in some areas, many Afghan women, fearing violence, have donned them again.

---

[2] Anderson Cooper, Peter Bergen and Nic Robertson, "Afghanistan: The Unfinished War," transcript of "Anderson Cooper, 360 Degrees," CNN, May 10, 2007.

[3] UNIFEM, "Fact Sheet," *op. cit.*

[4] "Afghan women seek death by fire," BBC World News, Nov. 15, 2006.

[5] UNIFEM, "Fact Sheet," *op. cit.*

[6] Agenzia Italia, Feb. 16, 2007.

[7] "Afghanistan Five Years On," Council on Foreign Relations backgrounder, Oct. 5, 2006.

[8] Ann Jones, "Not the Same as Being Equal: Women in Afghanistan," www.truthout.org/docs_2006/020507H.shtml, Feb. 5, 2007.

[9] "Taliban Kills 2 Sisters for Crime of Teaching," The Associated Press, *The New York Times*, Dec. 10, 2006.

[10] See "Lessons in Terror Attacks on Education in Afghanistan," Human Rights Watch, July 2006; www.hrw.org/reports/2006/afghanistan0706/.

---

[1] "Afghanistan: Democracy and Development: The Future Belongs to the Women," U.N. Development Fund for Women (UNIFEM), conference in Rome, Feb 15, 2007; and "Fact Sheet 2007," UNIFEM, May 2007.

---

with the Bush administration not to abandon Afghanistan's recovery. [11] At the same time, seeing troops being rerouted from Afghanistan to Iraq, Foreign Minister Abdullah, complained, "The United States is leaving us in the lurch."

No reinforcements were arriving, Abdullah said, just when extra effort was needed to consolidate his coun-

try's recovery and finish mopping up remnants of the Taliban and al Qaeda. "Afghanistan is the real front line against terrorism, and yet the Bush administration is giving up," he said.

Two years later, Abdullah was more diplomatic, but the message was the same. He conceded, however, that

Afghan officials count ballots after the Oct. 9, 2004, election in which Hamid Karzai was elected president. Karzai maintains a tenuous hold on only part of the country while the Taliban — flush with money from a revived and booming opium trade — has garnered new recruits and weapons.

after the fall of the Taliban the Afghans, in some cases, had unrealistic expectations.

Abdullah warned there was no quick fix for Afghanistan. "A country which was destroyed for 25 years couldn't be rebuilt in three-and-a-half years," he said, especially one that must rely on foreign support for its security and stability while it rebuilds. [12]

The U.S. Senate Foreign Relations Committee also cautioned the Bush administration not to detour from its efforts to rebuild Afghanistan and establish a secure democracy. "Our commitment to Afghanistan is also a demonstration of how we will approach post-conflict Iraq," said Chairman Richard G. Lugar, a Republican from Indiana. "Our credibility is on the line in these situations, and we must understand that failure to follow through could have extremely negative consequences." [13]

The belief that Afghanistan's recovery suffered when it slipped a few notches on the Bush administration's priorities list is widespread in the United States, Europe and Central Asia. Pakistani commentator Karamatullah Ghori calls it a blunder of "Himalayan" proportions. Neo-conservatives who were "calling the shots" misled Bush, Ghori continues, making him believe "Iraq would be a cakewalk."

Michael Scheuer, a former Central Intelligence Agency (CIA) officer in Afghanistan, agreed. "With the finite number of people who have any kind of pertinent

experience," he said, "there was unquestionably a sucking away of resources from Afghanistan and al Qaeda to Iraq, just because it was a much bigger effort." [14]

Not surprisingly, conservative analysts reject this claim. "That's political posturing," snaps Danielle Pletka, vice president for foreign and defense policy at AEI. "We can certainly manage Afghanistan and Iraq. To suggest that the United States is only capable of handling one situation at a time is ridiculous. We certainly made some mistakes in Afghanistan, but we didn't neglect it." In fact, she contends, the United States was more effective at correcting mistakes in Afghanistan than in Iraq. "We woke up and smelled the coffee."

Defense specialist John Pike, who runs the globalsecurity.org Web site, says, "To say [Afghanistan] turned into a mess because of U.S. neglect, because Washington was too focused on Iraq, that's just a talking point. [It doesn't] explain what the U.S. mistakes are." [15]

Talking point or not, critics cite a variety of American mistakes in Afghanistan. At one period in 2004-2005, U.S. forces in Afghanistan had dropped to less than 10,000 personnel, compared to 130,000 in Iraq, and NATO was persuaded to step in to fill the gap. This was done by beefing up the International Security and Assistance Force (ISAF) originally established through U.N. mandate in 2002 to provide security and to train the Afghan army and police forces.

"The administration has picked the wrong fights at the wrong time, failing to finish the job in Afghanistan, which the world agreed was the central front in the war on radical fundamentalism, and instead rushing to war in Iraq," declared Sen. Joseph R. Biden, Jr., D-Del., now chairman of the Senate Foreign Relations Committee and an aspiring Democratic presidential candidate. [16]

Even former Republican House Speaker Newt Gingrich of Georgia is critical. "We are neither where we wanted to be, nor where we need to be: We have not defeated the Taliban in its sanctuaries in northwest Pakistan, and neither Afghanistan nor Pakistan is stable and secure," he told the AEI in 2006. [17]

U.S. economic-development aid also has been cut, even as reconstruction projects began to show signs of hasty and inferior workmanship. The aid budget request for Afghanistan fell from $2.2 billion in 2004 to $1.2 billion in 2005. In 2003 Congress earmarked $11 billion for Iraq and Afghan military operations, but less than $1 billion for reconstruction in Afghanistan. [18]

The United States wasn't the only country cutting back on aid. "The European Union . . . has not put into Afghanistan a tenth of the aid it has put into Iraq," despite the convening of four meetings of international donors, says Italian foreign policy specialist Boniver.

The Bush administration is defensive about charges of neglecting Afghanistan. "It was not possible to 'finish the job' in Afghanistan," Secretary of State Condoleezza Rice told Fox News last September. Bringing stability to Afghanistan "is going to be a long process." Nevertheless, she continued, "We have made enormous progress over the last four years. You actually have a national government that's elected. You now have for the people in Afghanistan the possibility of a better life." [19]

Still, the Taliban had returned "somewhat more organized and somewhat more capable than people would have expected," Rice admitted. But they were being beaten, she added. NATO "was destroying them in large numbers." [20]

Can Pakistan do more to clamp down on the Taliban?

In March 2007, Pakistani authorities arrested Mullah Obaidullah Akhund, a top Taliban strategist and the regime's former defense minister. Captured while visiting family in Quetta, the Baluchistan capital, Akhund is the most senior Taliban figure arrested in Pakistan since the U.S.-led Afghan offensive began in 2001. [21]

The timing of the arrest was seen as significant: Vice President Cheney was in Islamabad at the time, urging President Musharraf to do more to shut down the Taliban inside his country. "Akhund was arrested solely to keep Western governments at bay," former Pakistani Prime Minister Benazir Bhutto wrote a week later in *The Washington Post.* [22]

Since the 9/11 attacks the United States has paid Islamabad roughly $1 billion to apprehend terrorists. But according to *The New York Times*, Pakistan's patrols have diminished in the past eight months, in part because Musharraf signed a controversial agreement with border villages in September 2006 allowing local militias to secure the frontier. Musharraf agreed that tribal leaders in dangerous Waziristan province — an area bristling with AK-47s and rocket-propelled grenades — would prevent any Islamic militants from crossing into Afghanistan. In exchange, the Pakistani army would pull out of the region.

But Western military officials and diplomats say there is little sign the deal has lessened the flow of jihadists. Time

and again, NATO forces in Afghanistan have pursued fighters to the border, where the ban on hot pursuit into the latter's safe havens forces them to halt. But when NATO forces try to alert Pakistani authorities by radio of the location of the fighters, they get mixed results at best. [23]

"Calls to apprehend or detain or restrict these ongoing movements, as agreed, were sometimes not answered," said former NATO supreme commander from 2003 to 2006, Gen. James L. Jones. The Pakistani ambassador in Washington, however, denied any slackening of Pakistani border vigilance. [24]

Equally troubling are the insurgents' reported links with Pakistan's all-powerful Inter-Services Intelligence (ISI) agency. Its ties to the Taliban go back a long way. In 1992, it supported the Taliban's drive to seize control in Afghanistan in hopes of establishing stability in a neighboring country that had been engulfed in violent unrest since the Soviet withdrawal in 1989.

U.S. journalist Arnaud de Borchgrave, a specialist on Pakistani affairs, says the ISI had 1,500 officers and operatives in Taliban-ruled Afghanistan in the late 1990s. "The country represented Pakistan's defense indepth in the event of an Indian invasion," de Borchgrave wrote, referring to Pakistan's neighboring nuclear arch rival. "Many of the ISI agents were veterans of the anti-Soviet guerrilla campaign that was fought by the mujaheddin under ISI direction, with funding and weapons from Saudi Arabia and the United States." [25]

Others question how much control Musharraf has over the lawless Pashtun area in the Federally Administered Tribal Areas. The Pakistani government has always conceded that its laws exist there only on the paved roads and cease where the pavement ends. The area is considered so perilous an outsider who enters a village without welcome is asking for death.

Musharraf frequently argues that hot pursuit by NATO forces inside Pakistan would make his government appear weak and undermine his position, potentially destabilizing Pakistan and opening the way for Islamic fundamentalists to take over Pakistan and its nuclear arsenal.

But his theory is disputed as self-serving. "The notion of Musharraf's regime as the only non-Islamist option is disingenuous and the worst type of fear mongering," writes former Prime Minister Bhutto. [26]

Islamic parties have never gained a majority in any free parliamentary elections in Pakistan, according to

CHRONOLOGY

1900s-1930s *Afghanistan becomes independent; tribal chiefs oppose reforms. Moscow's influence grows.*

1919 Afghanistan gains independence from Britain.

1926 Amanullah Khan begins push for a reformist monarchy.

1929 Nadir Shah becomes king.

1933 Shah is assassinated; his teenage son, Zahir Shah, succeeds him.

1940s-1960s *Afghanistan remains neutral in World War II. U.S. competes with Moscow for influence.*

1953 Gen. Madmoud Daoud, the king's cousin, becomes prime minister and begins to modernize, underwritten by the Soviets.

1964 Daoud resigns under pressure from U.S. . . . Zahir Shah establishes a constitutional monarchy, with free elections and female suffrage, triggering resistance.

1965 Women vote for the first time.

1970s *Monarchist Afghanistan is declared a republic. Power struggle leads to Soviet invasion.*

1973 King Shah is deposed; Afghanistan becomes republic under Daoud.

1978 Daoud is killed in leftist coup.

1979 Leftist Hafizullah Amin becomes president. Conservative Islamic and ethnic leaders revolt. . . . Moscow invades in December. Amin is executed.

1980s *Soviets occupy Afghanistan; U.S. backs anti-Soviet jihadists.*

1980 Soviet-backed Babrak Karmal becomes president.

1985 Islamic fighters resist Soviets.

1989 Last Soviet troops leave.

1990s *Taliban regime takes control of Afghanistan.*

1992 Mohammad Najibullah is overthrown as anti-Soviet resistance morphs into a civil war.

1996 Taliban seizes control in Kabul, hangs Najibullah, introduces hard-line Islamic policies.

1999 U.N. imposes air embargo and financial sanctions on Afghanistan, seeking handover of Osama bin Laden for the 1998 bombings of U.S. embassies in Africa.

2000-Present *U.S.-led coalition overthrows Taliban regime, but bin Laden escapes. Taliban makes a comeback, financed by opium trade.*

2001 Weeks after Sept. 11 terrorist attacks, Operation Enduring Freedom begins. Kabul falls; Taliban retreats. . . . Hamid Karzai is appointed to head interim government.

2002 International Security and Assistance Force is deployed in Kabul; international donors pledge $4.5 billion for Afghanistan's reconstruction.

2003 Special tribal council (*Loya Jirga*) drafts new Afghan constitution.

2004 Draft constitution is approved. . . . Karzai is elected president on Oct. 9 for five years.

2005 Voters elect lower house of parliament and provincial councils. Upper house is later appointed.

2006 NATO takes over security. . . . International donors pledge another $10.5 billion.

2007 Pakistan President Gen. Pervez Musharraf and Karzai agree to coordinate efforts to combat Taliban, al Qaeda. Allied troops kill top Taliban leader, Mullah Dadullah. Opium trade reaps $3 billion. . . . Taliban's threatened spring initiative fails to materialize. . . . U.S. Defense Secretary Robert M. Gates expresses guarded optimism that the military campaign against the resurgent Taliban is succeeding.

Bhutto. In Pakistan's last election, in 2002, religious political parties received only 11 percent of the vote, while Bhutto's secular party gained more than 28 percent. [27]

Besides, the military has been Pakistan's most dominant institution for decades. "I am not particularly worried about an extremist government coming to power and getting hold of nuclear weapons," said Robert Richer, who was associate director of operations in 2004 and 2005 for the Central Intelligence Agency. "If something happened to Musharraf tomorrow, another general would step in." [28]

Still, the Taliban has never been very concerned with votes and elections. If its growing strength is bottled up in Pakistani border areas with the Afghan escape valve shut off, Musharraf fears it could become his problem instead of Karzai's.

Is a Western-style democracy the best solution for Afghanistan?

At the 2001 U.N.-sponsored conference in Bonn, Germany, to determine Afghanistan's future, it was assumed the country would become a Western-style parliamentary democracy. Six months later, an interim administration in Kabul appointed by the tribal council, or *loya jirga*, representing all the main ethnic groups set out to draft a constitution and prepare for unfettered nationwide elections.

But work on the new constitution was immediately stalled by a debate among the drafters, clerics and jurists over the role of sharia, or Islamic law. The finished document was a compromise that allows individual judges wide latitude to give an Islamic interpretation to the country's new laws.

In retrospect, some critics contend that if Afghanistan is going to have a Western-style democratic parliamentary system, the first step should have been to form political parties. Because this was not done, says Italian parliamentarian Boniver, the elected parliament "includes warlords, drug lords and criminals of various kinds who got themselves elected and who have everything on their minds except democracy."

Shahir Zahine, a former mujaheddin fighter who now runs an Afghan non-governmental organization and publishes two newspapers, agrees. "The imposition on our society of a system called Western democracy has produced a mask of democracy, but not democracy

itself," he complained. Afghanistan needs to forget about further elections and create political parties effective enough to eliminate the warlords from the system, he insisted. [29]

A recent report by the Brussels-based International Crisis Group, a respected independent organization working to study and resolve crisis situations, agrees the lack of formalized political blocs "has seen powerbrokers of past eras try to dominate proceedings." To fix the problem, "New moderate forces need to move quickly now to establish formal [political] groups within the [parliamentary] houses to ensure their voices are heard." [30]

Another major problem is leadership — or the lack thereof — says former Ambassador Shahryar. "Karzai is very busy keeping everybody satisfied and forgets to be a leader," he says. And his lack of experience "comes out as indecisiveness." Once, when Karzai needed to appoint a new minister of industry, Shahryar recalls, the president offered the job to seven people and each time withdrew the offer before they could respond. Because of Karzai's unpopularity, Shahryar contends, many talented Afghans in the worldwide Afghan diaspora have not been interested in returning to their homeland to help with its recovery.

The nation's recovery has been hampered by poor security, corruption and lack of funds, and that too is blocking development of democracy, according to Shahryar. "After 9/11 we had the greatest opportunity to develop because the whole world was behind us," he declares. "We could have been a model for the Islamic world," he says. Instead, continued poverty and lack of reconstruction progress have created fertile ground for the return of the Taliban, he contends.

Afghanistan is "still lagging behind in . . . constructing an effective state," Afghanistan expert Barnett R. Rubin of New York University told the Carnegie Council, a New York think tank, in March 2006. "Basically, that territory does not produce enough wealth to pay for the costs of governing it." In fact, Afghanistan "is so poor we can't even tell how poor it is." In other words, Afghanistan doesn't produce enough reliable data to be included in international reports. [31]

Still, former Afghan finance minister Ghani believes, "There is actually more international attention focused on Afghanistan than in 2002." But that has not led to an increase in either aid or investment because of uncertainty over security and over the effectiveness of the cur-

Fighting Afghanistan's Narco Trade

Taliban uses drug profits to finance insurgency.

When the fundamentalist Taliban regime ruled Afghanistan, it used a simple tactic to eradicate the country's opium poppy crop, according to New York University's Afghanistan expert Barnett R. Rubin. "Don't grow poppy," they would warn villagers. "We're going to come back in two months. If we see it, we'll hang you." [1]

Not surprisingly, the amount of opium poppy cultivated across Afghanistan plummeted. Between 1999 and 2001, the amount of land dedicated to growing poppies dropped from a high of 90,583 hectares to 7,606. (*See graph, p. 319.*) By 2005, four years after a U.S.-backed coalition ousted the Taliban, Afghanistan's poppy crop had reached record levels — 104,000 hectares, or about 257,000 acres — and is expected to hit a record high in 2007 for the third year in a row. Taliban insurgents — no longer opposed to poppy production — will reap about a third of the proceeds to buy recruits, weapons and bombs, according to the United Nations Office on Drugs and Crime. [2]

Afghanistan today is a virtual narco state, producing more than 90 percent of the world's opium, which is turned into heroin. Last year's harvest of 6,100 tons poured more than $2.8 billion in illicit revenue — 36 percent of the country's gross domestic product — into the pockets of warlords, traffickers and some government officials. [3]

"Drug-related crime and corruption are rife and permeate all levels of society," according to a recent British government memorandum to the House of Commons. The opium trade represents "one of the gravest threats to the long-term security, development and effective governance of Afghanistan," posing as much of a threat to the country's reconstruction as the resurgent Taliban, the report continued. [4]

Yet in Afghanistan's depressed economy, a hectare of poppies produces 27 times more income than a hectare of wheat, according to a 2005 Asian Development Bank report, so the poppy crop has become the primary source of income for millions of rural Afghans. [5] Thus, if the Afghan government wants to achieve its stated goal of reducing poppy cultivation by 70 percent by 2011 and altogether by 2016, it must provide alternative livelihoods for farmers.

That could prove a major challenge, given the slow progress of economic development and reconstruction.

Another complication: The Taliban now has "extensive financial and logistical links" to drug traffickers at all levels, according to the British memorandum. [6] Poppy farmers and drug traffickers in Taliban-controlled areas pay a "tax" to the insurgents for protection, who then hire "day fighters" from among the ranks of Afghanistan's unemployed. And smugglers who sneak the drugs out of Afghanistan return with weapons and bombs for the Taliban, say officials. [7]

Until recently, the U.S. military in Afghanistan refused to get involved in poppy eradication, despite signs the Taliban was using drug profits to finance its insurgency. The U.S. Army insisted that fighting the traffickers was the work of drug enforcement officers, in collaboration with the Afghan police. This brought complaints that the military was ignoring evidence that warlords and politicians friendly to the United States were involved in the illicit trade. The strategy was "the Afghan equivalent of failing to deal with looting in Baghdad," Andre D. Hollis, a former deputy assistant secretary of Defense for counternarcotics, told *The New York Times*. "If you are not dealing with those who are threatened by security and who undermine security, namely drug traffickers, all your other grandiose plans will come to naught." [8]

But after Donald H. Rumsfeld stepped down as secretary of Defense that policy changed. "Now people recognize that it's all related," said Thomas Schweich, the State Department's coordinator for counternarcotics in Afghanistan. "It's no longer just a drug problem. It is an economic problem, a political problem and a security problem." The U.S. military now provides logistical support for drug eradication — but still does not carry out operations. [9]

NATO officials also argue that expanding the alliance's mission to include drug eradication would alienate Afghans instead of winning their cooperation in fighting the Taliban. But under U.S. and U.N. pressure the multinational force is also cooperating — up to a point. The British memorandum specifies that NATO forces "can provide support to counternarcotics operations, such as training of

rent Afghan government, he says. Corruption and bureaucratic ineptitude are seen as barriers to the country's ability to handle aid.

Emma Bonino, Italy's minister of international trade and former head of humanitarian affairs at the European Union, says while problems remain, "Afghanistan has

Afghan counternarcotics forces and *in extremis* support (e.g. medical) to their operations within means and capabilities. . . . But they do not play a direct role on counternarcotics or take part in eradication." [10]

NATO's role is "to establish security throughout the country . . . not to dilute its focus in eradication and interdiction missions," writes Vanda Felbab-Brown, a research fellow at the Brookings Institution in Washington. Getting involved in the drug war, she adds, could jeopardize reconstruction efforts and weaken efforts at long-term development, potentially losing "the hearts and minds of the population." [11]

So what is the solution? Some commentators have suggested that if Western governments were to buy up the entire poppy crop, it would employ Afghan farmers while keeping the drugs off the world market. But that answer risks the international community being held for ransom by farmers threatening to sell to higher-paying drug traffickers, says Neil McKeganey, professor of drug misuse research at the University of Glasgow, Scotland. [12]

The Senlis Council, an international security and development policy group, advocates legalizing the poppy crop and using it to produce medicines like morphine. By locating the entire production process — from seed to tablet — in rural areas, Afghan villagers would have jobs and "an economic opportunity they would want to protect — particularly against drug traffickers," the group says. [13]

However, it will take at least 20 years to clean up the drug trade in Afghanistan, according to a U.N. report issued last November. And cutting demand in Iran, Pakistan, the United Kingdom, Italy, Spain and Germany — where the major consumers of Afghanistan's opium live — is a good way to start. But the current international approach to stemming the drug trade is wrong, according to Rubin.

"It should focus its efforts to removing big drug money from the political process," Rubin said. "But instead what we have done is put big drug traffickers in positions of power, failed to take or support strong actions against them while we attack the livelihoods of small farmers and laborers through eradication, and they then turn to the Taliban or warlords for protection." [14]

Afghan police destroy opium poppies in Tarin Kowt in April. For the third year in a row, a record poppy crop is expected, despite eradication operations by Afghan and Western drug enforcement teams. In a policy reversal, the Taliban now uses profits from the illicit drug trade to buy arms and recruits.

Also see Anderson Cooper, Peter Bergen and Nic Robertson, "CNN's Anderson Cooper 360 Degrees," transcript of "Afghanistan: The Unfinished War," May 10, 2007.

[3] Grant Curtis, "Afghanistan's Opium Economy," *ADB Review*, Asian Development Bank, December 2005, p. 8. Also see James Risen, "Poppy Fields Are Now a Front Line in Afghanistan War," *The New York Times*, May 16, 2007, p. A1.

[4] "Afghanistan Counter Narcotics Strategy," Memorandum from the Afghan Drugs Inter-Departmental Unit (ADIDU), May 2, 2007; www.publications.parliament.uk/pa/cm200607/cmselect/cmdfence/memo/408/ucm11.htm.

[5] Grant Curtis, *op. cit.*

[6] "Afghanistan Counter Narcotics Strategy," *op. cit.*

[7] Risen, *op. cit.*

[8] Quoted in *ibid.*

[9] *Ibid.*

[10] *Ibid.*

[11] Vanda Felbab-Brown, Brookings Research Fellow, "Afghanistan's Opium Wars," *The Wall Street Journal*, Feb. 20, 2007, p. 12.

[12] Tanya Thompson, "Call to declare war on Afghan poppy fields," *The Scotsman*, May 22, 2007, p. 1.

[13] *Ibid.*

[14] Quoted in Jason Straziuso, "Afghan police aiding drug traffickers, fight will take 20 years to win, U.N. report says," The Associated Press, Nov. 28, 2006.

[1] Barnett Rubin, "The Forgotten War: Afghanistan," transcript of lecture at the Carnegie Council, New York, March 14, 2006.

[2] "World Drug Report 2006," U.N. Office on Drugs and Crime, 2006.

embarked on the road but it still needs to reach its destination." It was unrealistic, she says, to expect Afghanistan "to transform itself into a model of democracy in the past

couple of years. Some say it has all gone bad and will get worse. I think the Afghans have reached the half-way mark, and to abandon them now would be irresponsible."

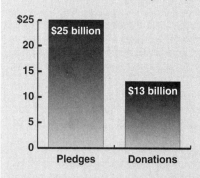

Donations Fall Short of Pledges So Far

Since the fall of the Taliban, the international community has pledged $25 billion to rebuild Afghanistan during donor conferences in Tokyo, Dubai, Berlin and London. However, only about half of that amount has actually been delivered so far.

International Aid to Afghan Reconstruction
(in $ billion U.S., as of May 2007)

Source: U.N. Office for the Coordination of Humanitarian Affairs

BACKGROUND

Prey to Invaders

Afghanistan has been perpetually beset by foreign invaders due to its geographic position as the Gateway to Central Asia — the link between China, the Middle East and the Indian subcontinent. The list of invaders goes back to before Alexander the Great conquered Afghanistan in 328 B.C. White Huns, Kushans, Persians and Arabs came and went, and Ghenghis Khan's hordes swept over it in 1219 A.D. [32]

Resistance against foreign domination became a way of life for Afghans, and internal turmoil was almost continuous. Throughout most of the 17th century the Safavids of Persia were in control. But in 1747 Persian strongman Nadir Shah was assassinated, and the Afghans seized the ensuing uncertainty over succession to stage a

revolt and gain their independence. The uprising was led by Ahmad Shah Abdali, a member of the Pashtun clan, which ruled the emergent Afghanistan nation in one form or another for the next 200 years. [33]

But Pashtun rule did not necessarily bring peace. The country was involved in at least 18 civil wars, foreign invasions or coups between 1816 and the U.S.-led invasion in 2001, including three wars with Persia and three with Britain.

While Pashtuns make up 42 percent of the population, the innumerable invasions and migrations have produced a demographically rich 31-million-plus Afghan population. Today, Afghanistan has at least a dozen other major ethnic groups, including Tajiks — the second-largest minority with 27 percent — Turkmen, Hazara, Uzbek, Nuristani, Arabs, Kirghiz and Persians. The Hazara and Uzbek are both at 9 percent, and the rest have much smaller percentages. [34]

The 'Great Game'

In the 19th century, Britain and tsarist Russia competed for control of Central Asia in a rivalry dubbed by historians as the "Great Game." The main "battleground" was Afghanistan, where the two powers waged a long and secret war of espionage, diplomacy and exploration.

Britain moved preemptively and invaded Afghanistan for the first time in 1839. The British later went to war with Afghanistan in 1878, and again in 1919. The first occupation ended in disaster when an uprising by Muslim Afghan tribesmen forced the British to withdraw, and every member of the retreating force and their families were either massacred or died — except for one doctor. More than three decades later, a second British occupation force also withdrew, but not before London retained the right to control Kabul's foreign policy.

Afghanistan remained a British protectorate until 1919, when Afghan Emir Amanullah — backed by Moscow's new Bolshevik government — declared his country independent. With its hands full elsewhere in World War I, Britain conceded Afghanistan's independence after a brief war, started by Amanullah in May, 1919. [35]

An Afghan monarchy was reestablished in the same year when Amanullah Khan changed his title from emir to padshah (king). In the ensuing period of political turmoil, warlords wrestled one another for power until a new king emerged, Muhammad Nadir Shah. He was assassinated by a student dissident in 1931 and was succeeded by his 19-year-old son, Muhammad Zahir Shah — the last king of Afghanistan — who would rule for the next 40 years.

Until the 1960s the real power was vested in the king's uncles and other relatives, but in 1964 the king fired his prime minister and cousin, Mahmoud Daoud, and established a constitutional monarchy with a two-chamber parliament and free elections and gave women the right to vote.

In 1973, Zahir Shah went to London for an eye operation. While he was convalescing in Italy, Daoud seized control in a bloodless coup, establishing a republic with himself as its president. Zahir Shah remained in exile in Rome until summer 2001.

The Russians finally made it to Kabul after a pro-Moscow coup in April 1978 by the People's Democratic Party of Afghanistan. Daoud was killed and a pro-Moscow government formed with Nur Mohammad Taraki as president and prime minister. In September 1979 Taraki was assassinated, and Deputy Prime Minister Hafizullah Amin seized control. But on Dec. 25 and 26, 1979, the Soviet Union stunned the world by invading Afghanistan, airlifting some 4,000-5,000 troops into Kabul. Amin was, in turn, killed on Dec. 27 and replaced by Babrak Karmal. By 1982, Karmal's regime would be supported by a build-up of more than 100,000 Soviet troops, and by 1986 Moscow would replace Karmal with President Mohammad Najibullah. [36]

In the meantime, on Jan. 4, 1980, American President Jimmy Carter condemned the invasion, saying it "threatened both Iran and Pakistan and is a stepping-stone to possible control over much of the world's oil supplies." [37] In protest, no U.S. athletes competed in the Summer Olympics in Moscow that year. A more purposeful action was the CIA's support for Afghan resistance — the so-called mujaheddin — to the communist regime. According to *The New York Times*, the CIA shipped about $3 billion worth of weapons to Afghan commanders fighting the Soviets in the 1980s — in "a struggle that left perhaps 1 million Afghans dead and up to 3 million in exile in Pakistan." [38]

The Russians called it quits in 1988 after nearly a decade of severe losses (up to 15,000 soldiers) in nearly continuous fighting against the U.S.- and Pakistan-supported mujaheddin. The last Soviet forces withdrew in February 1989. After that, a chaotic sequence of warlords — many of them corrupt and brutally oppressive — seized power until challenged and overthrown by the next one.

AP Photo/Pablo Martinez Monsivais

President Bush meets last September with Afghan President Hamid Karzai, right, and Pakistani President Gen. Pervez Musharraf to urge more cooperation between the two countries. Karzai and Bush want Musharraf to do more to rein in Taliban and al Qaeda insurgents using Pakistan's border tribal areas as a refuge. A telephone hotline was installed early this year linking the two leaders, but so far neither wants to talk to the other.

Taliban Emerges

If the Taliban movement was not actually created by the Pakistani intelligence services concerned about the instability of its neighbor, as some suggest, the ISI was certainly present at its birth, and the link has never been broken.

The Taliban's first recruits came from Pakistani madrassas, or Muslim religious schools. A few dozen of the more conservative institutions served as de facto training grounds for the jihadists fighting the Soviet occupation of Afghanistan, according to British Foreign Office official Alexander Evans.

"Many of these jihadists went on to become foot soldiers in later campaigns," Evans writes. "They also helped form the Taliban and gave succor and support to Osama bin Laden." [39]

The Taliban began seizing power in Afghanistan in 1994. By 1996 the fundamentalists had expelled the government from Kabul and established a repressive Islamic theocracy. Among other restrictive measures, television

An Afghan Army soldier packs rocket-propelled grenades into Helmand province, where Afghans are fighting alongside 5,500 British forces trying to clear out Taliban insurgents. NATO forces hope to restore peace in Helmand so they can help upgrade a hydroelectric dam that powers much of Afghanistan.

and music were outlawed. Men had to wear beards and women had to be fully veiled and could no longer work or go out alone. Those who infringed on these rules were publicly punished and even executed. An armed Northern Alliance resistance movement made up of Uzbeks, Tajiks and other ethnic Afghan minorities — aided by Iran, India and Russia — held out in the north.

The Taliban welcomed bin Laden and his al Qaeda followers when they were asked to leave Sudan. Bin Laden had already been a conduit of Saudi Arabian contributions during the struggle against the Soviet occupation and had been active in the resistance. The Taliban not only allowed al Qaeda to set up training camps but also gave them legitimacy of a kind by making the terror organization a part of the ministry of defense.

The Taliban might still have Afghanistan in its fanatical grip were it not for the terrorist attacks on New York and the Pentagon. Once 9/11 was attributed to al Qaeda, the wrath of a vengeful United States came down on its protectors' heads. When Taliban leaders refused U.S. demands to surrender bin Laden, the United States began bombing Afghanistan on Oct. 7, 2001, and providing air cover for a Northern Alliance offensive. By early December the offensive had cleared the Taliban out of the main cities, with the remnants fleeing to Pakistan along with bin Laden and his followers. [40]

Unlike Iraq, the war in Afghanistan had bipartisan support in Washington and broad support among America's European allies. It was also welcomed in Afghanistan itself. "An overwhelming number of Afghanis recognized the need for international help," points out Marvin G. Weinbaum, a scholar in residence at the Middle East Institute, and the Afghans never viewed the coalition's presence as an "occupation." [41]

New Government

The United Nations convened an international conference in Bonn on Nov. 27, 2001, to lay out a road map for Afghanistan's route towards democracy.

But while the Northern Alliance may have helped win the war, it lost the fight for political dominance. With Washington's support, the majority Pashtun emerged as the dominant force in the new Afghan political structure, with a Pashtun — Karzai — leading the interim government, and the exiled king, also a Pashtun, returning as the "father of the nation."

By December 2003, a new Afghan constitution had been drafted establishing the Islamic Republic of Afghanistan with a strong presidency and a national assembly. Islam was to be the country's religion, but freedom of worship was guaranteed. The constitution also gave — at least on paper — equal rights to men and women. [42] Ten months later, the presidential election of Oct. 9, 2004, confirmed Karzai for five years. Due to security fears, national assembly elections were postponed until 2005, when they were held under U.N. supervision with a large voter turnout.

As the Bonn conference was getting underway, 1,000 U.S. Marines were landing in Afghanistan and taking over the Kandahar airport — establishing the first U.S. beachhead in the country. The primary aims of the U.S. military were to find bin Laden and provide security while the Afghan army and police were formed and trained to take over.

The closest the United States came to capturing the terrorist leader was in December 2001, when a large number of retreating Taliban were surrounded at Tora Bora near the Pakistan border. Bin Laden was widely believed to have been present at the four-day battle, but the Americans let anti-Taliban militia take the lead in the fighting, and bin Laden was among those who slipped through the cordon. It's widely believed that some of the attacking militia looked the other way while he made his escape. U.S. troops did not intervene directly until the last day of the battle, and by then there was no bin Laden. Today the bin Laden trail has reportedly gone ice cold.

Its hands full with Iraq, Washington has increasingly called upon the North Atlantic alliance to help ensure security in Afghanistan to enable democracy to establish roots. Initially, NATO's ISAF forces were to be centered in Kabul. By late 2005, however, NATO had agreed to take over security throughout all of Afghanistan and battle the re-emerging Taliban — the alliance's first deployment outside Europe.

CURRENT SITUATION

Resurgent Taliban

Five years after its Islamic emirate in Afghanistan was defeated, the Taliban remains "a formidable enemy," writes Francoise Chipaux, an Afghanistan specialist and correspondent for the French newspaper *Le Monde.* "Despite its superior strength and weaponry, NATO has not been able to guarantee the peace and security that the Afghan population has been hoping for since 2001." [43] She blamed what she called the "carelessness" of the Afghan government, mistakes made by the international community and the support given the Taliban by Pakistan and al Qaeda.

However, Dutch Maj. Gen. van Loon, lately commander of NATO's forces in Afghanistan's volatile south, was optimistic, telling *The Washington Post* that Taliban fighters had been driven out of the regions they had gained in 2006, when North Atlantic alliance forces were thinner on the ground. Van Loon said the Taliban "no longer had the initiative," and there was no longer any basis for thinking that the country was slipping back under its control. [44]

Military sources are encouraged by the fact that the Taliban's threatened major spring offensive failed to materialize and by the news that allied forces in May had killed Mullah Dadullah, the Taliban's foremost opera-

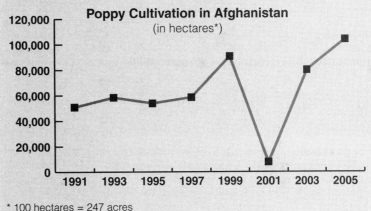

Opium Cultivation Increases Dramatically

Afghanistan's opium poppy crop has burgeoned to record levels since 2001, when the Taliban regime — which officially forbade poppy cultivation — was ousted. The booming drug trade now helps finance the growing Taliban insurgency.

Poppy Cultivation in Afghanistan
(in hectares*)

* 100 hectares = 247 acres

Source: "World Drug Report 2006," U.N. Office on Drugs and Crime, 2006

tional commander. [45] The Taliban, it seems, has learned from its defeat in open combat in September 2006 in southern Afghanistan against Canadian and British forces. [46] At the time, then-British commander Brig. Ed Butler said the insurgents had been "tactically defeated" for the time being. [47]

Even before the winter, the Taliban had switched from military-style coordinated attacks to guerrilla tactics, based on the "Iraq model." Small, highly mobile groups harass NATO forces, roadside bombs have become a standard hazard and suicide bomb attacks are on the increase. [48] But suicide bombs so far in 2007 are not up significantly over last year, even though they jumped fivefold between 2005 and 2006. [49]

The Pashtun Taliban has reportedly concentrated its efforts on southern Helmand province — which is also predominantly Pashtun — viewing it as a key area to test its ability to take and hold Afghan territory from NATO and Afghan troops. [50] But the Taliban also is following the money: Helmand produces 42 percent of Afghanistan's opium, a key source of the insurgents' income.

In April, Karzai and Musharraf, both under strong pressure from Washington to cooperate with one another, agreed to step up their efforts to halt terrorism

AP Photo/Rahmat Gul

Afghans shout anti-American slogans during a March 6, 2007, protest in Nangarhar province after U.S. Marines reportedly fired on civilian cars and pedestrians following a suicide bombing. NATO and U.S. military officials fear a spike in civilian casualties could spark anti-Western sentiment among war-weary Afghans. At least 380 civilians were killed in the first four months of 2007.

and drug smuggling. Meeting in Ankara, Turkey, they vowed "to deny sanctuary, training and financing to terrorists and to elements involving subversive and anti-state activities in each other's countries." [51]

Many observers wonder how much Musharraf can deliver on his commitment to police the tribal areas where the Taliban receive shelter, even if he wants to. In May 2007, Musharraf's position at home appeared weakened following violent public protests over the president's suspension of Pakistan's chief justice, who had accused government officials of corruption. But the Bush administration is keenly aware that it cannot allow the three-sided U.S.-Pakistan-Afghanistan partnership to break up, or the key issue of stabilizing the border to slip from view.

Visiting Rawalpindi, Pakistan, in February, U.S. Defense Secretary Robert M. Gates said after meeting Musharraf, "If we weren't concerned about what was happening along the border, I wouldn't be here."

Hearts and Minds

An insurgency cannot succeed without the support of the population, but neither can a counterinsurgency. Thus, winning the hearts and minds of the Afghan population is NATO's biggest challenge, concedes Gen. Eikenberry. [52]

To further that goal, NATO has established provincial reconstruction teams (PRTs), which combine reconstruction and security efforts into one group.

Last July, for example, the British launched a $55 million economic program in Helmand designed to bring employment and other benefits to 600,000 people. The Helmand PRTs, which typically consist of both British combat troops and soldiers from the Royal Engineers, will spearhead reconstruction of roads and public buildings.

One of the goals of the PRTs is to maintain a cooperative relationship with the local population, a task made more difficult by NATO's increased reliance on the heavy airstrikes that have been a part of its offensive against Taliban strongholds. The civilian death tolls, such as the loss of 57 villagers — nearly half of them women and children — in a Herat village during U.S. airstrikes on April 27 and 29 — are turning Afghans against the NATO forces and undermining an Afghan government that is already considered shaky. In a similar incident on May 9 in Helmand, 21 civilians were killed by gunfire from planes supporting a ground operation. [53]

President Karzai has condemned the rise in peripheral casualties, including those shot at roadblocks and caught in crossfire during clashes. According to press reports, the most serious episodes of civilian deaths have involved U.S. counterterrorism and Special Operations forces, which has created tension inside the alliance and focused a lot of the protest against the U.S. military presence. [54]

Still, NATO officials point out there are often no clear battle lines between civilians and Taliban insurgents. Taliban fighters often endanger — and implicate — villagers by firing on NATO troops from their homes. NATO officials say the alliance has done a poor job of reminding the public — both inside and outside Afghanistan — that it is the Taliban that endangers civilians by hiding among the local population.

In another more sinister twist, alliance forces are sometimes deliberately given erroneous information about the whereabouts of the Taliban in order to incite attacks against a rival village. In at least one incident that resulted in civilian deaths, NATO troops were misled into thinking Taliban fighters were hiding in a nearby village and mounted an attack based on what turned out to be false information.

Commanders point out, however, that airstrikes are needed to make up for a shortage of ground forces. "Without air, we'd need hundreds of thousands of

Has U.S. policy in Afghanistan succeeded?

YES James Phillips
Research Fellow, Allison Center for Foreign Policy Studies, The Heritage Foundation

Written for *CQ Researcher*, June 2007

The United States scored a major military victory in Afghanistan but has not yet been able to transform this military success into a stable peace. Less than three months after the Sept. 11, 2001, terrorist attacks, the United States overthrew the radical Taliban regime and uprooted the al Qaeda infrastructure in one of the most remote and inhospitable regions on Earth. Although Osama bin Laden escaped, he was forced to go to ground in the tribal badlands along the Afghanistan-Pakistan border, where he could not operate with impunity, as before. While Afghanistan remains a violent place, Taliban militants no longer have a free hand to massacre their opponents, violently repress freedom or provide secure bases for al Qaeda and other allies to export terrorism and Islamic radicalism.

The United States has made substantial progress in helping to create a democratic government, resettle over 3 million refugees, repair Afghanistan's war-torn infrastructure and build schools, hospitals and health clinics to raise living standards. Afghans enjoy much greater political, religious and social freedoms. Sunni zealots no longer systematically massacre Afghan Shiites. In contrast to life under the Taliban, women are free to attend school and work outside the home. There is a free press and lively political debate in the parliament.

Afghanistan still confronts major challenges. The Taliban movement has made a violent resurgence, in part because it enjoys sanctuary and support from Pushtun tribes inside Pakistan. The booming opium trade, which finances the Taliban and corrupts government officials, remains a long-term threat to stability. Warlords continue to thrive in the absence of law and order. But it is unrealistic to expect rapid change overnight. It will take at least a generation to consolidate a stable democracy in Afghanistan.

High-level U.S. attention is needed on a sustained basis to address Afghanistan's daunting problems. But all in all, most Afghans are far better off today than they were under the Taliban's harsh rule. Afghans have voted with their feet to return home from refugee camps in neighboring countries and from jobs farther away. Most important, Afghanistan is an ally, not an adversary, in the struggle against radical Islamic terrorism.

Washington must lead a coordinated international effort to bolster Afghanistan's embryonic democratic government and boost its capacity to provide services, security and higher living standards for its own people. In the long run, only Afghans — not Americans — can consolidate success in Afghanistan.

NO Barnett R. Rubin
Director of Studies, Center on International Cooperation, New York University; Author, The Fragmentation of Afghanistan

Written for *CQ Researcher*, June 2007

U.S. policy has not achieved its principal objectives in Afghanistan but, in contrast to Iraq, it still could.

From the beginning the Bush administration defined Afghanistan primarily as a counterterrorism mission. In President Bush's words, we were to show that those who harbored terrorists would "share in their fate." In Secretary of Defense Donald H. Rumsfeld's words, the mission was to "kill and capture terrorists faster than the madrassas are turning them out."

According to President Bush, the United States has failed in that mission. Last February, Bush told the American Enterprise Institute, the principal neoconservative think tank:

"Across Afghanistan last year, the number of roadside bomb attacks almost doubled, direct fire attacks on international forces almost tripled and suicide bombings grew nearly five-fold. These escalating attacks were part of a Taliban offensive that made 2006 the most violent year in Afghanistan since the liberation of the country."

Afghanistan's production of opiates has reached a record high, accounting for more than 90 percent of the world's heroin supply. Money from this illicit trade funds insurgents who fight us and corrupts the Afghan government we are trying to support.

Blinded by its opposition to nation building, the Bush administration actively opposed the measures Afghanistan most needed after the initial victory. It opposed expansion of the International Security Assistance Force to the provinces. It refused to authorize the U.S. military to help demobilize and disarm militias. It allied with any anti-Taliban leader, turning a blind eye to both human rights violations and drug trafficking. It refused to lead the reconstruction effort. It treated Pakistan as its major ally in the war on terror, ignoring the conflict between Islamabad and Kabul and ignoring the establishment of Taliban bases there. Most of all, the United States diverted resources from Afghanistan to a disastrous war in Iraq.

In Afghanistan, however, unlike in Iraq, most of the people and most of the international community want the effort to succeed. Both military and financial aid have increased. The United States cooperates with the U.N., NATO and all major aid donors. Despite civilian casualties, Afghans have not yet decided they want us to leave. The internationally approved Afghanistan Compact and the Afghan government's National Development Strategy provide solid bases for success. If the United States disengages from Iraq, it can devote to Afghanistan the resources needed to succeed.

AFP/Getty Images/Shah Marai

Getty Images/Paula Bronstein

Plight of the Children

Decades of warfare have left poverty deeply entrenched in Afghanistan, especially among Kabul's 50,000 street children. Many are war orphans who help support themselves or their families by polishing shoes or collecting scraps from war-torn ruins and garbage dumps to recycle or use as fuel (top). Non-governmental organizations like Aschiana ("the nest") help provide education, vocational training and outreach services to street children and their families (bottom).

troops," a senior NATO official said. [55]

The deaths are occurring even as many Afghans are questioning the price of liberation from the Taliban. "There is no confidence in any justice system, security is still a huge problem and corruption is the biggest failing of all," said BBC correspondent Alistair Leithead, reporting from Helmand province. "People don't trust the police or the government departments, and that makes persuading them that all is well so much more difficult." [56]

In the south, the Taliban is considered less corrupt and more efficient than government bureaucrats appointed since the 2004 elections. [57] A disaffected generation of unemployed young Afghans — the result of setbacks in the economic recovery — has turned to crime or joined the Taliban, often more out of anger than religious fervor.

"Sixty-five percent of the population is under 20 years of age, and that's the source of new Taliban recruits," says Kabul University Chancellor Ghani. "I know of men who for $20 will put bombs under bridges. The number of people who will commit violence for pay is very high."

Some join the jihadists to avenge family members killed in the fighting. Taking blood for blood is a strong cultural belief among the Pashtun. "Today, it's not just the Taliban who are willing to blow themselves up," said Mullah Naceem-ur-Rahman Hashimi, who reportedly has been responsible for training suicide bombers. "Ordinary people do it because they have a father or brothers in prison, or because they themselves were released but their lives are finished, their dignity gone, and they know that if they die in a suicide operation, they'll go to heaven." [58]

The lack of security has seriously hindered the work of the 1,200 non-governmental organizations (NGOs) — 383 of them from overseas — operating in Afghanistan. To avoid kidnapping, many NGO workers now travel in old, unmarked cars, maintain secret addresses and work in offices with no identifying signs. In the villages, "getting around is very dangerous, and we always try to take along members of the local choura (council)," says Esmatullah Haidary, director of the Afghan Development Association, a leading local NGO.

"Members of smaller NGOs are sincere, but often naive," says Anja De Beer, coordinator of the Agency Coordinating Body for Afghan Relief. "They believe that because they are doing good work for people they will protect them, but that idea is no longer true." [59]

U.S. officials say the slow progress of reconstruction that had been a major disappointment to Afghans initially has been corrected. By 2004, the U.S. Agency for International Development (USAID) had spent $73 million and completed only 100 of 1,000 promised projects, according to *The Washington Post*. [60] But by 2005, the reconstruction pace had improved, said USAID's mission director in Kabul, Alonzo Fulgham, and the United States had built or refurbished 312 schools and 338 clinics, laid 500 miles of new asphalt roads and resurfaced another 500 miles. [61]

Quality of Life

Although the new Afghan constitution guarantees religious freedom, that freedom "remains restricted," according to a Council on Foreign Relations (CFR) backgrounder. In addition, the new constitution guarantees women's participation in the Afghan parliament, but the bright promise of women's rights of three years ago has somewhat dimmed. (*See sidebar, p. 372.*)

"Domestic abuse is rampant," according to the CFR report, noting an alarming jump in suicides — often by self-immolation — among young girls. New laws to raise the marriageable age and outlaw forced marriages are often ignored, especially in the villages. [62]

On the positive side, eight or nine private banks have opened in Afghanistan. Foreign companies have invested $800 million in the telecommunications sector; more than 1.5 million Afghans now have their own mostly mobile phones — a figure Ghani says is expected to double in three

Al Qaeda leader Osama bin Laden is thought to be hiding in Taliban-infested tribal areas on the border between Afghanistan and Pakistan, but his trail has grown cold.

years. And bids worth more than $60 million are coming in from U.S. firms to develop copper mining, he adds.

But progress has been uneven between the various regions, and the widespread mood among Afghans is one of increasing anger and frustration at what they perceive as unfulfilled promises and expectations.

Zarguna Saleh, an Afghan living in Virginia who used part of a family inheritance to build and start a vocational school for orphans in Jalalabad, says many Afghans believe the United States is pushing the wrong priorities. "They're thinking too much in American terms," says Saleh whose family moved to America after the Russian invasion but who now visits her homeland regularly.

"People are angry," she says. "There's no work, no infrastructure and all they hear about is women's rights. Right now, what Afghanistan needs is a strong government; the situation for women will take time to change."

On the other hand, there's no shortage of mass media, Saleh says. The people may "have nothing," she says, but "they have 300 newspapers." And while there are a dozen television channels, "they have no electricity" with which to watch them.

OUTLOOK

Political Solution

NATO's provincial reconstruction teams slowly are coming into their own — albeit modestly — after a shaky start. In April 2007, British troops wrested control of the strategic town of Sangin, a center of poppy cultivation and drug smuggling in Helmand province, that had been in Taliban hands for months. The town lies on the road to the Kajaki dam — the main source of power in southern Afghanistan — earmarked for a $10 million renovation by the U.S. government. But work had been delayed for more than a year because of the Taliban presence. [63]

"Afghanistan has emerged from hell to purgatory but is still a long way from heaven," says Italian parliamentarian Boniver, expressing a view widely held in the international community. "And the danger is that it could slide back into hell once more."

To prevent that slide back, NATO urgently needs to improve the security situation. "The mission hangs in the balance," says Lt. Gen. Eikenberry succinctly. [64] Certainly, routing the Taliban in the field without inadvertently triggering a backlash among villagers would significantly boost morale. But the Afghan problem is as much a weak government as it is a strong enemy. The government must reform its judiciary and clean up its corruption if it hopes to survive.

"Where we are losing in Afghanistan is in the battle to create a fair legal and judicial system; overcome rampant corruption; build a police force; control the drug-proliferation epidemic and bring job opportunities to the Afghan people," wrote Gen. Jones, the retired NATO supreme commander. [65]

Karzai will bear the brunt of the country's failures and might not survive the year as president, say knowledgeable Afghan expatriates. But if early elections are held, many well-qualified Afghans are ready to step into Karzai's shoes, they add.

Many Afghans also doubt America's long-term intentions, and that makes them hold back in their commitment to the international presence in Afghanistan. Most, however, generally agree their country cannot yet go it alone.

Political fragmentation, security problems and failure to meet public expectations after the defeat of the Taliban threaten the region's stability and offer opportunities for those same insurgents. Most Afghans and international observers agree the solution in Afghanistan is a political one, not a military one.

"To prevail in Afghanistan, more than military force is needed," wrote Jones. "Until Washington, Brussels and Kabul address that concept . . . the outcome will be too close to call." [66]

In the long run, says Pakistani analyst Ahmed Rashid, a coalition government — made up of the Taliban and the present Afghan administration, presumably without al Qaeda — might bring peace and stability to Afghanistan. [67]

Karzai himself revealed for the first time in April that he had held "reconciliation talks" with Taliban members, but most observers think he would be excluded from such an alliance. [68]

President Musharraf's own destiny is also linked to Afghanistan. Karzai's growing closeness to India, with workers from the subcontinent arriving in Kabul by the planeload, is a cause of rising concern in Islamabad. His other worry must surely be that the U.S. Congress might begin to ask why the administration has so far stopped short of declaring the Taliban a terrorist organization. Presumably, Washington has avoided that step because countries that harbor terrorists are declared state sponsors of terrorism.

The one certainty is that Afghanistan's recovery will be a long haul. "Many pieces seem to be going well, some are going badly, some change as you watch them," says Ronald E. Neumann, who until recently was U.S. ambassador to Kabul. "It's true that NATO is doing well. But you need a political process."

But can Afghanistan recover? "My sense is that it can be done," he says. "But it can't be done quickly."

NOTES

1. Roland Flamini, "Corridors of Power," www.world-politicswatch.com, March 3, 2007.

2. David Sanger, "Danger Signal in a Bombing," *The New York Times*, Feb. 28, 2007, p. A1.

3. Transcript of testimony by John Michael McConnell before the Senate Armed Services Committee, March 3, 2007.

4. Eikenberry was addressing the Brookings Institution on the situation in Afghanistan, April 30, 2007.

5. U.N. Office for the Coordination of Humanitarian Affairs.

6. Quoted from Bush speech to AEI on Feb. 12, 2007, White House text.

7. Jason Ukman, "NATO General Tells of Taliban Setbacks," *The Washington Post*, May 30, 2007, p. A10.

8. *Ibid.*

9. Afghan drug production statistics from www.unodc.org/pdf/afghanistan_2005/annex_opium-afghanistan-2005-09-09.pdf.

10. Antonio Maria Costa, "An Open Market Mystery," *The Washington Post*, April 25, 2007, p. A16.

11. "Karzai's Challenge: Remain a Priority; Afghanistan implores: 'Do more for us,' " *The Washington Post*, Feb. 28, 2003, p. A6.

12. "A Conversation with H. E. Abdullah Abdullah on U.S.-Afghanistan Relations," Council on Foreign Relations transcript, May 25, 2005.

13. Text of Lugar statement before Senate Committee on Foreign Relations, Feb. 12, 2003.

14. James Fallows, "Bush's Lost Year," *Atlantic Monthly*, October 2004, p. 18. Scheuer headed the special CIA unit formed to hunt for Osama bin Laden.

15. Quoted by Tim Harper, "Afghanistan: U.S. 'Handed off a Mess' to NATO Forces," *Toronto Star*, Sept. 16, 2006, www.commondreams.org/headlines06/0916 02.htm.

16. *Ibid.*

17. "Where Do We Go from Here? Lessons from the First Five Years of the War," American Enterprise Institute, transcript, Sept. 11, 2006.

18. U.S. Budget, fiscal 2004 and 2005.

19. Fox News, "Sunday with Chris Wallace," transcript, Sept. 10, 2006.

20. *Ibid.*

21. "Report: Pakistan arrests one of Taliban's top three," Reuters; March 2, 2007; www.intelligence-summit.blogspot.com/2007/03/report-pakistan-arrests-one-of-talibans.html.

22. Benazir Bhutto, "A False Choice for Pakistan," *The Washington Post*, March 12, 2007.

23. David E. Sanger and David Rohde, "U.S. Pays Pakistan to Fight Terror, but Patrols Ebb," *The New York Times*, May 20, 2007, p. A1.

24. *Ibid.*

25. Arnaud de Borchgrave, "Commentary: Shock and Awe About-face," *The Washington Times*, Dec. 12, 2006, p. A16.

26. Bhutto, *op. cit.*

27. Mark Mazzetti, "One Bullet Away from What?" *The New York Times*, March 11, 2007, Sec. 4, p. 1.

28. Quoted in *ibid.*

29. "Afghanistan: Una Strada Senza Uscita," Interpress Service News Agency, Italy, July 28, 2006.

30. "Afghanistan's New Legislature: Making Democracy Work," International Crisis Group, Asia Report No. 116, May 15, 2006.

31. Barnett R. Rubin, "Afghanistan: The Forgotten War," lecture at the Carnegie Council, March 10, 2006.

32. See "Chronological History of Afghanistan"; www.afghan-web.com/history/chron/index2.html.

33. *Ibid.*, and Adam Ritscher, "Brief History of Afghanistan," on the Afghanistan government's Web site, www.AfghanGovernment.com.

34. CIA *World Fact Book*, https://www.cia.gov/library/publications/the-world-factbook/index.html.

35. See "Chronological History of Afghanistan," *op. cit.*; also Ronan Thomas, "Once More Up the Khyber," *Asia Times*, www.atimes.com/atimes/South_Asia/HF20Df02.html.

36. For background, see *Political Handbook of the World*, CQ Press, http://library.cqpress.com.

37. See The American Presidency Project; www.presidency.ucsb.edu/ws/index.php?pid=32911.

38. Tim Weiner, "At Large in a Rugged Land," *Week in Review, The New York Times*, March 11, 2007, pp. 4, 14.

39. Alexander Evans, "Understanding Madrasahs: How Threatening Are They?" *Foreign Affairs*, January/February 2006, pp. 9-16.

40. For background, see Kenneth Jost, "Rebuilding Afghanistan," *CQ Researcher*, Dec. 21, 2001, pp. 1041-1064.

41. *Ibid.*

42. "Karzai signs Afghan constitution," BBC, Jan. 26, 2004; http://news.bbc.co.uk/2/hi/south_asia/3428935.stm. For English text of Afghan constitution, go to www.servat.unibe.ch/law/icl/af00000_.html.

43. Francoise Chipaux, "Afghanistan: Le Taliban sont de retour," *Le Monde*, April 29, 2007, p. 1.

44. Ukman, *op. cit.*

45. *Ibid.*

46. "Plus de 200 taliban tues dans le sud de l'Afghanistan," *L'Express*, quoted in www.casafree.com/modules/news/article.php?storyid=7187.

47. "British armed forces in Afghanistan," p. 3; Answers.com; www.answers.com/topic/operation-herrick.

48. Chipaux, *op. cit.*

49. See Jason Straziuso, "New U.S. commander in Afghanistan expects rise in suicide attacks in 2007," The Associated Press, Jan. 30, 2007.

50. http://news.bbc.co.uk/2/hi/south_asia/5189316.stm.

51. "Musharraf, Karzai meet in Turkey," United Press International, April 30, 2007.

52. Eikenberry, *op. cit.*

53. "Afghanistan: 21 civili uccisi in raid Nato," *Il Sole 24 Ore*, May 9, 2007, p. 2.

54. Gall and Sanger, *op. cit.*

55. *Ibid.*

56. http://news.bbc.co.uk/1/hi/world/south_asia/6607211.stm.

57. Chipaux, *op. cit.*

58. Francoise Chipaux, "Dans le provinces afghans, des conditions de travail difficiles pour les ONG," *Le Monde*, May 2, 2007, p. 1.

59. *Ibid.*

60. Joe Stephens and David B. Ottaway, "A Rebuilding Plan Full of Cracks," *The Washington Post*, Nov. 20, 2005, p. A1.

61. Carlotta Gall and David Rohde, "Problems with U.S. Aid Alienate Afghans," *International Herald Tribune*, Nov. 7, 2005; http://iht.com/articles/2005/11/07/news/rebuild.php/php.

62. *Ibid.*

63. *Ibid.*

64. Eikenberry, *op. cit.*

65. "What Is at Stake in Afghanistan," letter to the editor, *The Washington Post*, April 10, 2007, p. A16. The letter was also signed by Harlan Ullman, Gen. Jones' former senior adviser and now a senior associate at the Center for Strategic and International Studies in Washington.

66. *Ibid.*

67. Giandomenico Picco, "Afghanistan il prezzo della pace," *La Stampa*, Jan. 22, 2007.

68. Carlotta Gall, "Karzai Says He Has Met With Some Taliban Members in an Effort at Reconciliation," *The New York Times*, April 7, 2007, p. A1.

BIBLIOGRAPHY

Books

Bergen, Peter, *The Osama bin Laden I Know: An Oral History of Al-Qaida's Leader*, Free Press, 2006.
A journalist and terrorism analyst chronicles bin Laden's life, based largely on the author's 1997 interview with the al Qaeda leader.

Coll, Steve, *Ghost Wars: The Secret History of the CIA, Afghanistan, and bin Laden, from the Soviet Invasion to September 10, 2001*, Penguin, 2007.
A staff writer for *The New Yorker* — who covered Afghanistan from 1989 to 1992 for *The Washington Post* — recounts the CIA's involvement with the Taliban and al Qaeda in the years leading up to the Sept. 11, 2001, terrorist attacks.

De Long, Michael, Noah Lukeman and Anthony Zinni, *A General Speaks Out: The Truth about the Wars in Afghanistan and Iraq*, Zenith Press, 2007.

This critique of the U.S. war in Afghanistan is written by a retired Marine lieutenant general who was deputy to Gen. Tommy Franks, commander-in-chief at U.S. Central Command, (De Long); the former commander of Central Command (Zinni) and writer Lukeman.

Dupree, Louis, *Afghanistan*, Princeton University Press, 1980.

While dated, this book by a former senior research associate for Duke University's Program in Islamic and Arabian Development Studies and a founder of the Afghan Relief Committee is still widely regarded as the definitive work on Afghanistan.

Jones, Ann, *Kabul in Winter: Life Without Peace in Afghanistan*, Metropolitan, 2006.

A New York-based authority on women and violence, who worked in Kabul for a non-governmental organization that helped Afghan war widows, assesses women's conditions in Afghanistan.

Rashid, Ahmed, *Taliban, Islam, Oil, and the New Great Game in Central Asia*, IB Taurus, 2006.

A Pakistani journalist based in Lahore who has covered Central Asia for 25 years examines in meticulous detail the reasons why the Taliban came to power, and the circumstances of its alliance with Osama bin Laden.

Rodriguez, Deborah, and Kristin Ohlson, *Kabul Beauty School: An American Woman Goes Behind the Veil*, Random House, 2007.

Michigan-born Rodriguez originally volunteered to go to Afghanistan as a nurse's aide as the Taliban regime was ending. She stayed on first as a women's hairdresser and eventually opened a hairdressing school. The book has rare insights into current conditions among Afghan women in the post-Taliban era. Ohlson is a freelance writer.

Articles

Baker, Aryn, "The Truth About Talibanistan," *Time*, March 22, 2007.

Pakistan's tribal region has become a sanctuary for the Taliban and other extremists.

Moreau, Ron, *et al.*, "The Rise of Jihadistan," *Newsweek*, Oct. 2, 2006, pp. 24-28.

Five years after the U.S.-led invasion of Afghanistan, the Taliban is fighting back hard.

Rubin, Elizabeth, "In the Land of the Taliban," *The New York Times Sunday Magazine*, Oct. 22, 2006, pp. 86-97, 172-175.

Pakistan's mountainous border with Afghanistan has become "a Taliban spa for rehabilitation and inspiration," says a contributing editor of the magazine, with Quetta as an assembly point for Taliban incursions into Afghan territory.

Reports and Studies

Patel, Seema, and Steven Ross, "Breaking Point: Measuring Progress in Afghanistan," Washington Center for Strategic and International Studies, March 2007.

Two members of the Post Conflict Reconstruction Project say Afghans are losing trust in their government because of an escalation of violence, and conditions in the country have deteriorated in all key areas except the economy and women's rights.

Rubin, Barnett, "Afghanistan's Uncertain Transition from Turmoil to Normalcy," Council on Foreign Relations, 2006.

One of the world's foremost experts on Afghanistan and a former U.N. adviser on Afghanistan assesses the situation in Afghanistan.

Summers, Christina Hoff, "The Subjection of Islamic Women," American Enterprise Institute, 2007.

A resident AEI scholar researches culture, adolescents and morality in Afghan society.

United Nations Office on Drugs and Crime, "UNODC Afghanistan Opium Winter Rapid Assessment Survey," February 2007.

Opium production in Afghanistan continues to increase at a record rate. For an assessment of the previous year's crop see, "UNODC Afghanistan Opium Survey," October 2006.

For More Information

Afghanistan Research and Evaluation Unit, Flower St./Street No. 2, Shahr-i-Naw, Kabul, Afghanistan; +93-(0)-799-608-548; www.areu.org.af. Promotes a culture of research and learning in Afghanistan by strengthening analytical capacity and facilitating debate.

Carnegie Council, 170 E. 64th St., New York, NY 10065; (212) 838-4120; www.cceia.org. Think tank advocating ethical decision-making in international policy.

Council on Foreign Relations, 58 E. 68th St., New York, NY 10065; (212) 434-9400; www.cfr.org. Promotes a better understanding of the foreign-policy choices facing the United States and other governments.

International Crisis Group, 149 Avenue Louise, Level 24, B-1050 Brussels, Belgium; +32-(0)-2-502-90-38; www.crisisgroup.org. Nongovernmental organization using field-based analysis and high-level advocacy to prevent violent conflict worldwide.

International Institute for Strategic Studies, 13-15 Arundel St., Temple Place, London WC2R 3DX, United Kingdom; +44-(0)-20-7379-7676; www.iiss.org. Think tank focusing on international security with emphasis on political-military conflict.

Islamabad Policy Research Institute, House No. 2, Street No. 15, Margella Rd., Sector F-7/2, Islamabad, Pakistan; +92-51-921-3680-2; www.ipripak.org. Evaluates national and international political-strategic issues and developments affecting Pakistan and surrounding countries.

Middle East Institute, 1761 N St., N.W., Washington, DC 20036; (202) 785-1141; www.mideasti.org. Seeks better relations between Middle East nations and American policymakers.

North Atlantic Treaty Organisation, Boulevard Leopold III, 1110 Brussels, Belgium; +32-(0)-2-707-50-41; www.nato.int. Oversees International Security Assistance Force in Afghanistan, a U.N.-mandated mission established in 2001.

United Nations Development Fund for Women, 304 E. 45th St., 15th Floor, New York, NY 10017; (212) 906-6400; www.unifem.org. Promotes women's empowerment and gender equality.

United Nations Office on Drugs and Crime, Wagramer Strasse 5, A-1400 Vienna, Austria; +43-1-26060-0; www.unodc.org. Monitors the global trade in illicit drugs.

United States Agency for International Development, 1300 Pennsylvania Ave., N.W., Washington, DC 20523; (202) 712-0000; www.usaid.gov. Principal U.S. agency dispensing foreign aid.

VOICES FROM ABROAD

Pervez Musharraf

President, Pakistan

Repatriation requires cooperation

"Problems along the bordering regions of Pakistan and Afghanistan are compounded by the continuing presence of over 3 million Afghan refugees, some of them sympathetic to the Taliban. The incentives offered to the refugees for their voluntary return by the international community are minimal. A serious international commitment is required to facilitate their repatriation."

— *Statement before U.N. General Assembly, September 2006*

Mohammad Nader Nadery

Commissioner, Afghan Independent Human Rights Commission

Afghanistan is a narco state

"If the governors in many parts of the country are involved in the drug trade, if a minister is directly or indirectly getting benefits from drug trade, and if a chief of police gets money from drug traffickers, then how else do you define a narco-state?"

— *The Christian Science Monitor, May 2005*

Hamid Karzai

President, Afghanistan

The world was warned

"I did expect a rise in militant activity. And for two years I have systematically, consistently and on a daily basis warned the international community of what was developing in Afghanistan and of the need for a change of approach in this regard. . . . The international community [must] reassess the manner in which this war against terror is conducted."

— *BBC News, June 2006*

Des Browne

Defence Secretary Great Britain

Taliban stronger than expected

"We do have to accept that it's been even harder than we expected. The Taliban's tenacity in the face of massive losses has been a surprise, absorbing more of our effort than we predicted it would, and consequently slowing progress on reconstruction."

— *The Guardian (United Kingdom), September 2006*

Shukria Barakzai

Editor, Aina-E-Zan (Afghanistan)

A long way to go for women

"But we cannot allow 10 years of demagogy and oppression to be the sole scale by which we judge progress or the character of Afghan women today. . . . It is also illogical to say that every problem has been solved and that Afghan women are relieved from all the miseries they have suffered. There remains a long and difficult path of showing each Afghan how to recognize and protect the values of the liberty he or she possesses."

— *Worldpress.org, March 2005*

Jaap de Hoop Scheffer

Secretary General, NATO

Afghanistan is everybody's problem

"If we don't go to Afghanistan and if we are not here, Afghanistan will come to us. . . . Consequences will be felt not only in Afghanistan but in other nations as well . . . we will not give the terrorists an opportunity to win."

— *BBC Monitoring Europe, September 2006*

Karim Rahimi

Presidential Spokesman Afghanistan

Taliban help not welcome

"It is true that we still have some problems . . . but these problems do not mean that the people will give their support to the Taliban. The people of Afghanistan have proved in the past years that they have strongly rejected those who impose terrorism, oppression, war, manslaughter, cruelty and killing of innocents, and will never go to them."

— *Sapa — Agence France-Presse, October 2006*

Hamidullah

Farmer, Musa Qala Helmand Province

Our poppy is safe

"No [one] has destroyed my poppy and no one will be able to destroy it. We are not paying the Taliban, but they tell us, 'As long as we are here, no one can destroy your poppy.' This year we have grown more than ever."

— *Institute for War & Peace Reporting, March 2007*

Editorial

Anis (Afghanistan)

Stop Pakistan's support of the Taliban

"If NATO wants to bring permanent peace and stability to Afghanistan, prevent casualties among its forces and avoid facing huge economic burdens as well as avoiding pressure from the public in their own countries, they should try 100 per cent to ensure that Pakistan renounces its support for the Taliban and shuts down religious, terrorist training centres and the channels that breed fanaticism and suicide attacks."

— *September 2006*

Patrick Chappatte, Le Temps, Switzerland

15

The Troubled Dollar

Peter Behr

Shanghai businessman Chen Haiwen holds a stack of Chinese yuan he exchanged for U.S. greenbacks. Although the yuan has strengthened against the U.S. dollar in the past two years, critics say it still is undervalued, which keeps China's exports unrealistically cheap. The U.S. trade deficit with China and other exporters is partly to blame for the 21 percent decline in the value of the dollar since 2002. The dollar's shakiness is prompting China to consider gradually reducing its reserves of more than $1 trillion in U.S. currency.

From *CQ Researcher,*
October 1, 2008.

On Sept. 15, 2008 — a Black Monday for financial markets — investors around the world dove for cover following the weekend collapse of legendary Wall Street firms Lehman Brothers and Merrill Lynch.

After dumping their tanking stocks, the stampeding investors — like others before them — began plowing billions of dollars into U.S. Treasury securities. [1]

Once again the dollar had proved to be a safe harbor in a financial storm.

It was a notable, if perhaps momentary comeback for the beleaguered greenback. Since 2002, the dollar has lost 21 percent of its value compared to other leading currencies, marking a profound loss of American economic clout. [2]

With the banking crisis spreading in Europe and Asia, confidence in U.S. economic leadership — and in the dollar — may have suffered an historic blow, some financial experts and government leaders say. Nonetheless, the financial firestorm now raging through Europe and Asia could send foreign investors running back to the dollar as their best option, other experts say.

The risk for the dollar largely stems from the $700 billion rescue package that the U.S. Treasury has been given to buy subprime mortgages and other "toxic" debt that is choking off day-to-day lending in the U.S. economy. Because the United States faces a deep budget deficit already, the federal government will have to borrow those funds, much of it from foreign banks and investors who already hold more than half of the $3.5 trillion in U.S. Treasury debt. But the increasing obligations are likely to further undermine the dollar, making foreigners less willing to increase their dollar investments, some experts say.

Dollar Has Declined Against Euro and Yen

Since 2002 the dollar's value has fallen about 40 percent against Europe's euro — and about 20 percent versus the Japanese yen — in part because U.S. interest rates have been kept low in order to stimulate the domestic economy. A cheaper dollar makes U.S. exports cheaper but boosts the price of imports. It also triggers increases in worldwide prices for oil, food and other commodities.

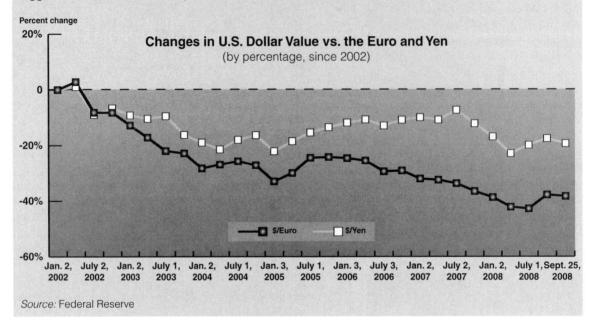

Source: Federal Reserve

"If international investors lose confidence in the ability of the American taxpayer to honor their debts, then the taps will be turned off, the dollar will plunge and interest rates will rocket, destroying demand," wrote Jeremy Warner, business columnist for *The Independent* in London, in early October. "The present crisis in banking would find itself mirrored on a national scale." [3]

"Financing of the losses by the American taxpayer may lead to an American disaster if the cost is simply added to the budget deficit," according to Jacques Attali, former president of the European Bank for Reconstruction and Development. [4]

German Finance Minister Peer Steinbrück is predicting that the crisis will shrink the dollar's role in global trade and finance. The United States will "lose its status as the superpower of the global financial system," he bluntly predicts. The Persian Gulf states, China and Russia will gain influence, in his view. The international financial community "has begun seeking a new world

order," says Kazuo Mizuno, the chief economist of Mitsubishi UFJ Securities Co. in Japan. [5]

But other nations and their currencies may fare worse than the dollar. Germany's economy — Europe's strongest — is facing a "pronounced slowdown" that could drag on to 2010, said Deutsche Bank's chief economist Norbert Walter. [6]

"Europe is sitting on a huge financial problem," says David Smick, publisher of *The International Economy* quarterly. "They don't have a European-wide way for handling the collapse of a major financial institution."

The average American may not know the dollar's exchange rate against, the yen, yuan, euro or rupee, but its place in the world economy matters immensely to Americans. Most world trade is conducted in dollars, and the greenback's value on world currency markets affects not only the price U.S. farmers and manufacturers get for their exports but also how much American consumers pay for their favorite Japanese car or high-definition TV set.

Dollar fluctuations also have global implications. Because most commodities are priced in dollars, the currency's slide helped to fuel the 2008 spike in oil prices to nearly $150 a barrel, for instance, triggering strikes, protests and hardships on every continent. A parallel increase in food prices — also sparked in part by the dollar's decline — spread hunger in the world's poorest regions and strained family budgets elsewhere, adding to fears of inflation in many countries. [7]

When the dollar drops in value, it produces both winners and losers. While U.S. buyers of imported products suffer from having to pay higher prices, American manufacturers who sell goods abroad get a break because their products become cheaper for foreign buyers. Conversely, a weaker dollar is handicapping manufacturers in Europe and Asia, making their products less competitive in the United States. Meanwhile, the dollar's slump has triggered a virtual fire sale for foreigners seeking to buy U.S. companies, real estate and other assets. For example, 15 percent of all Florida home sales in early 2008 involved foreign purchasers. [8]

The dollar has been the world's leading currency since 1944, when Allied leaders met in Bretton Woods, N.H., to plan the post-World War II economic order. With much of Europe, Russia, China and Japan prostrate and the British Empire collapsing, the dollar was established as the dominant global currency, and the United States became "the banker to the world." It remained so despite periodic ups and downs during economic booms, oil shocks and recessions. Thus, the dollar became the favored currency held by foreign banks in reserve accounts that back up their lending operations. [9]

Dollar's Decline Helps U.S. Trade Deficit

The dollar has declined 21 percent since 2002 when measured against the currencies of 26 major U.S. trading partners (top graph). The decline has made U.S. exports more affordable. As cheaper U.S. goods find more markets abroad, the U.S. trade deficit has begun to shrink, after peaking at $788 billion in 2006 (bottom).

Value of U.S. Dollar Compared to Average Value of Major Foreign Currencies

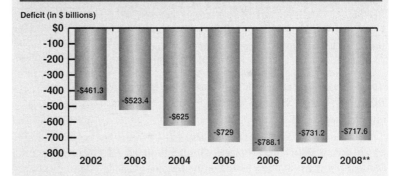

Deficit in U.S. Global Trade and Financial Transactions

* The base value was 100 in January 1980.

** Through second quarter.

Sources: Federal Reserve, Bureau of Economic Analysis

The dollar's value compared to other major currencies is tied to fundamental economic conditions. Falling U.S. interest rates make dollar-based investments less appealing to foreigners, while low inflation and strong growth in the United States make them more attractive. Ultimately, the dollar's value is based on investors' confidence in the U.S. economy.

But America's twin deficits — the $700 billion short-

外 国 為 替
■ドル   115.94-96 円 -0.24
■ユーロ 139.63-71 円 +0.08
区ポンド 202.66-75 円
●スイスフラン 90.03-08 円
四豪ドル 85.95-00 円
回カナダル 100.16-23 円

選、国民支持と党内信頼の両方大事

AFP/Getty Images/Toshifumi Kitamura

A currency trader in Tokyo monitors the dollar's value on world currency markets. Because most global trade is conducted in dollars, the greenback's value affects the price of commodities around the world. The dollar's two-year slide helped to fuel the recent spike in oil prices to nearly $150 a barrel, triggering strikes, protests and hardships on every continent.

fall in trade in 2007 and a projected $438 billion federal budget deficit in 2009 — have significantly weakened the dollar. [10] As the trade deficit increased in this decade, vast amounts of U.S. currency left the country: Americans spent $5 trillion more buying foreign goods than they earned exporting their own goods. Most of the dollar outflow has ended up in government-controlled banks in the Middle East, Russia, China and other Asian nations. To raise money to cover the budget deficit the U.S. government buys dollars back from foreign banks and investment funds by selling them Treasury securities, making the United States critically dependent on those foreign buyers.

Overall, the volume of worldwide government and private investment has soared in this decade to an estimated $167 trillion, accompanying a burst in global trade in manufactured goods led by the emerging economies of China and India. [11] The dollar figures in more cross-border transactions than any other currency.

But the current U.S. financial crisis — widely viewed as the worst since the Great Depression — has exposed the risks to American financial firms caused by those massive amounts of dollars circulating around the globe. The U.S. government's stunning takeover of the giant mortgage firms Fannie Mae and Freddie Mac three weeks ago exemplifies the risk. Early this year foreign investors, led by China, held $1.3 trillion in housing bonds issued by the two congressionally chartered institutions — up dramatically from the $107 billion they held in 1994. [12] As the U.S. housing market collapse morphed into a global credit crisis last summer, banks in China and elsewhere began an unprecedented sell-off of Fannie and Freddie's bonds, threatening to cripple the two firms whose purchases of mortgages support more than half of the U.S. housing industry. [13] The federal takeover followed.

Ironically, it is precisely the dollar's appeal as a safe currency over the past half-century that has enabled the United States to borrow dollars from international investors at reasonable costs to finance America's budget and trade deficits. Foreigners owned nearly one-fifth of the $49 trillion in overall U.S. government and private debt outstanding in mid-2007, according to official estimates. Foreigners — mainly government-controlled banks in Asia — also held more than half of the $3.5 trillion in marketable Treasury securities. [14] If foreign governments and investors grow doubtful of U.S. economic leadership or anxious about the amount of American debt they hold, they could slow their purchases of Treasury securities and other U.S. assets.

"At some point . . . foreign investors will balk at the growing concentration [of dollars] in their investment portfolios," former Federal Reserve Chairman Alan Greenspan has pointed out. "The well-established principle of not putting all your eggs in one basket holds for global finance as well as for the private household." [15]

A pullback by foreign investors would leave a gap in the budget and trade deficits that would force the government to dramatically cut spending and increase taxes or raise interest rates enough to attract more foreign investment — all of which would slow down the economy.

Until now, foreigners have been willing to accept relatively low returns on Treasury bills and bonds because of their stability, says Kenneth Rogoff, former chief economist of the IMF. He doubts that will continue. [16]

"After so many years of miserable returns on dollar assets, will global investors really be willing to absorb another trillion dollars in U.S. debt at anything near current interest rates and exchange rates?" he asks.

Others aren't so pessimistic, however. "Doomsday predictions about the dollar and interest rates, made year after year, have failed to materialize and are unconvincing," said Miranda Xafa, a member of the International Monetary Fund's (IMF) executive board and a former chief economic adviser to the Greek government. [17]

As economists, policymakers and investors nervously watch the weakened value of the U.S. dollar, here are some of the questions being debated:

Does the United States need a stronger dollar?

Among the first questions a new U.S. Treasury secretary is asked is whether the dollar's value will remain strong. It is a critical matter for nations in a closely linked global economy, where the dollar's value compared with other currencies can be a decisive competitive factor in each country's ability to sell its products abroad.

For more than half a century, the rote answer by Treasury secretaries was, the dollar will be strong.

Today the world has its doubts. The dollar lost 26 percent of its value between January 2002 and July 2008 compared to a large selection of currencies tracked by the Federal Reserve. (*See graph, p. 396.*) Even with a strong rally since late summer, the dollar was still 21 percent below the 2002 starting point. It has also recovered some ground against the euro, the common currency adopted by 15 members of the 27-nation European Union — a major U.S. competitor. [18] A euro was worth 90 U.S. cents when it went into circulation in January 2002. In early October,

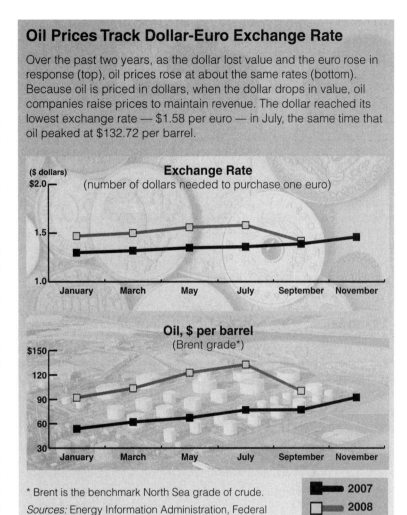

Oil Prices Track Dollar-Euro Exchange Rate

Over the past two years, as the dollar lost value and the euro rose in response (top), oil prices rose at about the same rates (bottom). Because oil is priced in dollars, when the dollar drops in value, oil companies raise prices to maintain revenue. The dollar reached its lowest exchange rate — $1.58 per euro — in July, the same time that oil peaked at $132.72 per barrel.

Exchange Rate
(number of dollars needed to purchase one euro)

($ dollars)

Oil, $ per barrel
(Brent grade*)

* Brent is the benchmark North Sea grade of crude.
Sources: Energy Information Administration, Federal Reserve

2007
2008

the price of a single euro was $1.38, down from $1.59 in July 2008. Under pressure from the Bush administration, China has let its currency, the renminbi, strengthen against the dollar (thus leaving the dollar weaker). *

By the summer of 2008, the dollar's slide and the corresponding rise for European and Asian currencies had begun to alarm financial officials. "European manufacturers are already screeching that the euro is too high," says Richard Koo, chief economist of Tokyo-based

---

* The renminbi, which means "the people's currency," is denominated in yuan units.

Where's the Best Place for a Big Mac Attack?

Undervalued currency makes the burger cheap in Beijing.

If you're going to have a Big Mac attack, have it in China. Last July a Big Mac that would have cost $3.57 in the United States cost only $1.83 in China — largely because the Chinese currency is undervalued by 49 percent, according to a currency benchmark developed by *The Economist* magazine.

The index was designed to answer questions such as: Is the euro overvalued? Is the dollar priced too low? What about Brazil's real or Norway's krona?

An undervalued currency can make a country's exports unrealistically cheap, giving that country an unfair advantage in international trade. With profits, jobs and global political standings at stake, questions about currency values cry for clear answers. But instead, the academic research on currency values is debated by experts, in part because of the difficulties in comparing the costs of living in wealthy and poor nations. Ideological differences about the advantages of strong and weak dollars also color the debate.

The currency exchange rate between two countries reflects many factors, such as interest rates and inflation pressures, investor and speculator hunches about where an economy and its currency rates are headed and sometimes government actions to try to change the rate by buying or selling their own currencies.

In trying to determine what currencies are really worth, *The Economist* created the "Big Mac Index" — a whimsical but seriously regarded benchmark for determining the purchasing power of various countries' national currencies. It compares the price — in each country's currency and in the dollar — for a hamburger in McDonald's franchises around the globe.

"The Big Mac Index is based on the theory of purchasing-power parity (PPP), which says exchange rates should move to make the price of a basket of goods the same in each country. Our basket contains just a single item, a Big Mac hamburger, but one that is sold around the world. The exchange rate that leaves a Big Mac costing the same in dollars everywhere is our fair-value yardstick," *The Economist* said in its latest index update in July 2008. [1]

In July a Big Mac cost $3.57 at a U.S. franchise participating in the survey. At the same time, an American tourist in Reykjavik, Iceland, paid 469 kronur for a Big

Nomura Research Institute. [19] French Finance Minister Christine Lagarde said in May that the euro's surge against the dollar was "a major misalignment." [20]

Mizuno of Mitsubishi Securities predicted at that time "the end of the strong dollar-based currency regime." [21]

The dollar's relative strength versus other major currencies is a critical matter for nations in a closely linked global economy where trade is a vital source of job and wealth creation.

From a U.S. perspective, the "right" value for the dollar can't be determined by looking at past history, says C. Fred Bergsten, director of the Peter G. Peterson Institute for International Economics in Washington. What's important, he said, is that the dollar needs to work as a lever, helping to boost U.S. exports and restrain imports enough to bring the American trade deficit down to an acceptable

level. So the right price for the dollar is whatever exchange value with the euro, the yen and other currencies will make that happen, Bergsten and other experts say.

The dollar has settled at a reasonable value versus the euro, he said. [22] But it needs to drop further against leading Asian currencies, including China's yuan and the South Korean won, he adds.

From 2002 into 2008, America's trade deficit widened as imports from China and other nations outstripped U.S. exports, creating a record $788 billion "current account" deficit in 2006 — nearly 7 percent of U.S. gross domestic product (GDP). [23] * A deficit that

---

* The current account deficit combines the deficit in traded goods with net U.S. financial transactions with the rest of the world.

Mac. Under the actual exchange rate for the two countries at the time, $1 was worth only 78.57 kronur, so the tourist had to pay $5.97 to buy enough kronur to buy the burger (469 kronur divided by 78.57 kronur per dollar equals the $5.97).

Thus, according to the index, the kronur is "overvalued," because the burger cost $2.40 more in Iceland than it does in the United States — or 67 percent more. So the "fair value" exchange rate for the kronur should be 67 percent higher, or 131 per dollar.

Conversely, China's currency appears "undervalued" in the Big Mac Index. The $3.57 burger in the United States costs 12.5 yuan in China. At the current exchange rate of 6.83 yuan per dollar, that comes to $1.83. Thus, the yuan is undervalued by the difference between $3.57 and $1.83, or 49 percent, according to the Big Mac Index.

The Economist found that, compared to the dollar, currencies from Britain, Europe, Norway, Brazil and Turkey are overvalued. Undervalued currencies included Saudi Arabia's riyal, the Japanese yen, Thailand's baht and Pakistan's rupee. (*See graph.*)

The results buttress the argument that China and other Asian exporters need to raise their currencies' values to create a fairer trading arena with the rest of the world.

----

[1] "The Big Mac Index: Sandwiched," *The Economist*, July 24, 2008, www.economist.com/finance/displaystory.cfm?story_id=11793125.

The 'Big Mac Index'

The whimsical but seriously regarded benchmark determines various currencies' purchasing power by comparing the price of a McDonald's hamburger around the world.

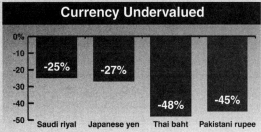

Source: The Economist; values are as of July 24, 2008

----

size is untenable economically and politically, according to the Peterson Institute, because it forces the United States to finance too much of its economy with loans from foreigners. [24]

Bergsten and other economists say the current account deficit must come down to about 3 percent of U.S. GDP to prevent a loss of confidence in the dollar. Such a decline, however, will require a cheaper dollar in order to raise the price of imports and lower the price of U.S. exports.

While a cheaper dollar would help the United States, it burdens other nations, especially Asia's big exporting countries. The dollar has fallen since 2002 against the currencies of Thailand, South Korea, Singapore, India and China (while gaining against Mexico). If the Asian nations agreed to increase their currencies' values against the dollar, their exports would become more expensive in the United States and presumably decline.

The dollar has been on a roller-coaster ride over the past quarter-century, dropping in value in the late 1970s, climbing in the early 1980s, falling again in the early 1990s and then recovering at decade's end. But as long as the United States was the main locomotive for world growth, U.S. policy called for a strong dollar, building wealth in the American economy, which could then afford to purchase more of the world's imports.

Clinton administration Treasury Secretary Robert Rubin made a strong dollar a priority and between 1995 and 2002, when the value of U.S. currency climbed by 40 percent compared with several other leading currencies. [25]

Paul O'Neill, President George W. Bush's first Treasury secretary, caused an international uproar early

AFP/Getty/Jed Aznar

A vast stockpile of rice sits in a warehouse in Manila last March as the Philippine government prepared for potential rice shortages. A decline in the value of the U.S. dollar helped to trigger a spike in global food prices earlier this year, leading to hoarding and shortages of grain and other commodities in scores of countries.

in 2001 by saying he wanted a "strong economy," not a "strong dollar." O'Neill promptly backpedaled, explaining, "I believe in a strong dollar, and if I decide to shift that stance, I will hire out Yankee Stadium and some rousing brass bands and announce that change in policy to the whole world." [26]

O'Neill did not last long enough in office to keep that promise, but with less fanfare the dollar did turn downward. After the Sept. 11, 2001, terrorist attacks, the Federal Reserve lowered short-term interest rates, which made dollar-denominated bonds less profitable to investors. Currency traders fix on differences in nations' interest rates, and after the Fed's actions the dollar began falling.

The Bush administration has maintained the strong-dollar mantra, but in fact kept hands off. "In reality, of course, the United States does not have a dollar policy — other than letting the market determine its value," said Martin Feldstein, former Council of Economic Advisers chairman under President Ronald Reagan. [27]

The United States has intervened in currency markets in the past to boost the dollar's value and calm volatile or speculative trading in the dollar or other currencies. But it has not done so since Secretary Rubin concluded that the amount of currency trading on foreign exchange markets was growing too large for effective intervention by the U.S. Treasury. [28]

Some experts say the United States must strengthen the dollar to keep its leadership among the world's economies, even if that requires painful decisions on shrinking trade and budget deficits. "The lower the dollar, the poorer we are as a country," says Jeffrey Garten, a professor at the Yale University School of Management and former undersecretary of Commerce for international trade in the Clinton administration.

A stronger dollar increases the value of American-made goods and services, which makes U.S. exports more expensive. But Garten says American firms can compete effectively using new technology, skilled workers and capital to increase the sophistication of products and processes.

"If we want to have influence in the world, we can't have that with a soft currency," Garten says.

Will the euro surpass the dollar as the world's anchor currency?

With President Nicolas Sarkozy on hand to lead the cheering, the French energy company Areva in November 2007 sold two advanced nuclear power reactors to China for a record $12 billion. [29] "In the history of the civilian nuclear industry, there's never been a deal of this magnitude," boasted Areva Chief Executive Anne Lauvergeon.

It was a milestone in another way. The China Guangdong Nuclear Power Corp. (CGNPC), which purchased the reactors, agreed to pay half the price in euros, the official currency of the European Monetary Union. China's policy until then had been to transact international business almost entirely in dollars. [30] Dividing the pie between the dollar and the euro was another visible mark of the European currency's growing prominence.

Much more than national pride in the greenback is a stake in the competition between the dollar and the euro. The United States has long enjoyed an "exorbitant privilege," as former French President Charles de Gaulle tersely put it, because of the dollar's status as the leading global currency. Foreign governments have been eager to hold dollars in their own vaults to support their financial systems — in a crisis a country wants dollars, not Russian rubles. [31] Governments then return those dollars to the United States when they invest them in U.S. Treasury securities. That has helped the United States fund its deficits and live beyond its means, *The Economist* notes.

A Currency Primer

Why a strong dollar is important.

What happens when the dollar's value shifts against other currencies? Consider the dollar and the Japanese yen. In January 2002, $1 would buy about 132 yen. At that exchange rate, a U.S.-made medical device priced at $1,000 would sell for 132,000 yen in Japan.

Fast-forward to March 2008, when the dollar's value against the yen had fallen so that $1 would buy only 100 yen. At that exchange rate, a Japanese hospital could buy the same $1,000 medical device for only 100,000 yen.

From a U.S. business perspective, the dollar's decline made the U.S.-made product a lot more affordable and thus more competitive in international trade.

But the lower dollar puts Japanese manufacturers at a disadvantage. When the dollar was trading for 132 yen in 2002, a Japanese-made television that sold for 150,000 yen in Japan would have cost $1,136 in the United States. But at the lower 2008 exchange rate of 100 yen per dollar, the same television would cost $1,500, potentially putting it out of range for many American consumers.

A weakened dollar has less purchasing power. For example, because of the dollar's slump American tourists in Tokyo would have to pay nearly 25 percent more for the same meal and lodgings in 2008 than their dollars would have bought in 2002.

However, when the dollar's value falls, the United States ends up repaying its debts to foreigners with cheaper — or less valuable — dollars. That's a break for the United States but not for foreigners, who will reconsider investing in U.S. securities.

If the dollar ends up sharing that privilege with the euro, the United States could find it significantly more costly to attract the foreign-held dollars it needs to square its trade accounts. [32]

Indeed, Europe's financial markets have nearly caught up with the United States, says the San Francisco-based McKinsey Global Institute. Total financial assets for the 15 euro nations (the "Eurozone"), plus Britain, Switzerland and four Scandinavian countries outside the euro network amounted to $53.2 trillion in 2006 — less than the U.S. total of $56.1 trillion but growing faster — McKinsey said. [33]

"The euro is emerging as a rival to the dollar as the world's global reserve currency, reflecting in part the growing vibrancy and depth of Europe's financial markets," the McKinsey analysts reported. In mid-2007, the value of euro currencies in circulation worldwide passed U.S. dollar currencies for the first time. The euro is also favored for international bond issues.

Whether the euro can overtake the dollar as the favored currency for international transactions is now discussed seriously by currency experts worldwide. (But most say it is less likely that the euro could replace the dollar as the preferred reserve currency held by central banks.)

Tokyo-based author and business consultant Kenichi Ohmae said, "The current weakness of the American economy that has resulted from borrowing abroad to sustain high growth, and of which the subprime crisis is a symptom, is also driving the dollar to historical lows. This is causing China, Japan, the Gulf states and Russia, among others, discreetly, but inexorably, to begin fleeing the declining dollar in favor of the sounder currency of the euro. When all is said and done, the European Union will have the world's largest consumer base and integrated infrastructure." [34]

In a 2008 survey of currency experts, a decided majority predicted either that the dollar would remain the leading currency or would gradually share the distinction with the euro or a basket of international currencies including the euro, and Chinese yuan. *The International Economy*, a Washington-based journal, asked 53 of the world's leading economists, bankers and currency experts to predict what the world's great global currency would be in 10 years. Thirty-one said the dollar would remain on top, although many saw it diminishing. [35]

Tadao Chino, former president of the Asian Development Bank, picked the dollar to hold its premier

CHRONOLOGY

1700s-Early 1800s *United States adopts a "sound" money policy; struggles over the dollar's role span the century.*

1791 The First Bank of the United States is established, advancing Treasury Secretary Alexander Hamilton's strategy for a sound, centrally managed currency.

1890s-1930s *Several financial crises lead to centralized control by Washington over the nation's money supply.*

1895 Foreign investors exchange U.S. securities for gold, nearly depleting the U.S. government's gold supply. Financier J. P. Morgan heads off a crisis by leading a private syndicate in selling gold bonds in Europe.

1900 United States ties the dollar's value to gold.

1913 Congress creates the Federal Reserve System as the U.S. "lender of last resort" in emergencies.

1933 The 1929 stock market crash is followed by a banking crisis on the eve of Franklin D. Roosevelt's presidential inauguration. He temporarily closes the banks and bans gold hoarding. The New Deal insures bank deposits, but global currency devaluations prolong the Great Depression.

1940s-1995 *United States establishes a stable post-World War II global currency regime based on the dollar.*

1944 World leaders at a meeting in Bretton Woods, N.H., establish the dollar as the world's primary or "anchor" currency, displacing the British pound.

1971 President Richard M. Nixon ends the Bretton Woods policy allowing nations to exchange dollars for U.S. gold, introducing floating currency rates.

1983-85 Dollar soars against the yen, making Japanese imports cheaper. U.S. manufacturers and unions demand a cheaper dollar so they can compete.

1985 Leaders from United States, Japan, West Germany, France and Britain sign the Plaza Accord lowering the dollar's value.

1985-1995 Yen rebounds against the dollar, leading to major Japanese investments in the United States. A massive real estate boom ends in a crash in 1990, triggering an enduring banking crisis in Japan.

1997-Present *Global trade and financial transactions expand rapidly, setting the stage for financial crises that eventually spread to the United States.*

1997-1999 Financial crises erupt in Thailand, Russia, Indonesia, South Korea and Brazil. The Clinton administration and the International Monetary Fund commit billions of dollars in emergency loans to stem the contagion.

1999 European Monetary Union creates a common currency, the euro, which enters circulation in 2002.

2002 The dollar begins a long decline compared to the euro, as higher European interest rates attract investors away from the greenback.

2005 China ends its policy of tying the yuan to the dollar, agreeing to U.S. requests to let the currency float within a controlled range to reduce a huge U.S. trade deficit with China.

2007 A decade-long U.S. housing market bubble bursts following the failure of high-risk, subprime mortgage investments. A chain reaction of financial losses spreads from Wall Street to the banking industry.

2008 Despite domestic inflationary pressures caused by the dollar's decline, Saudia Arabia keeps its currency tied to the dollar. . . . To prevent economic collapse, the Bush administration pledges more than $1 trillion in emergency support, including $700 billion to Wall Street plus loans to banks, mortgage lenders and the nation's leading insurer, American International Group. The rescue lifts the sagging dollar, but may undermine it in the future.

place. So did Il Sakong, former South Korean finance minister; Boris Fedorov, former Russian finance minister, and Pedto-Pablo Kuczynski, Peru's former top finance official.

Daniel Griswold, director of the conservative Cato Institute's trade policy studies, says the dollar was "still the best bet." Nearly two-thirds of central bank reserves worldwide are held in dollars, and almost 90 percent of all daily currency transactions involve dollars, he noted.

Eight survey responders picked the euro either to match or surpass the dollar within 10 years.

"The euro, for sure," said Maya Bhandari, senior economist at Lombard Street Research in London. About twice as many respondents said the dollar and euro would share leadership, and several said the yuan could eventually rival the dollar and euro, but not within a decade. "The euro is vying with the U.S. dollar for the status of leading global currency," said Chi Lo, a Hong Kong-based investment research director, but the race won't be won in 10 years.

A dozen respondents said a group of currencies including the dollar, euro and yuan would replace the dollar.

"During the next one or two decades, we will move toward a multilateral currency system with three or four major currencies," predicted Klaus Regling, director general for Economic and Financial Affairs at the European Commission. The dollar will probably be the most important currency, particularly in the Americas, but will no longer be the dominant world currency. The euro will be the currency for at least 25 countries, he added. And the Chinese yuan will gain importance, too. [36]

The euro's position would be significantly boosted if Britain gave up the pound and joined the Eurozone, providing the continent with a financial center in London to rival New York and Shanghai. But Richard H. Clarida, a former assistant Treasury secretary for economic policy, and other experts say that isn't likely in the foreseeable future. [37]

The dollar has remained on top for so long in part because it had no serious rivals. In the 1980s the Japanese yen and the German mark briefly threatened, but those economies stumbled, wrote Menzie D. Chinn, a University of Wisconsin economist, and Jeffrey A. Frankel, a professor of capital formation at Harvard. [38] However, the euro provides a credible option now, they contend.

Could the dollar's value plunge?

As leaders from Saudi Arabia and other oil producers in the Gulf Cooperation Council (GCC) prepared to meet in Qatar last Dec. 3, the dollar began rising and falling against the leading Gulf currencies.

The changes were small but significant all the same, because the dollar and most Persian Gulf currencies are not supposed to vary. Saudi Arabia, Qatar, Bahrain and the United Arab Emirates "peg" their currencies to the dollar in order to piggyback on its stability (and, say some observers, to acknowledge their reliance on U.S. military protection). [39] Thus, while the dollar's price rises and falls on world markets, the Saudi riyal and the other Gulf currencies generally move in sync with the greenback.

These small fluctuations signaled a much deeper uneasiness in world markets about the dollar at the end of last year, as the dimensions of the U.S. mortgage lending crisis became clearer. Worried experts and analysts began to speculate on the possibility the dollar's deep slump would force U.S. trading partners to cut their currencies' values in order to keep prices on their exported goods in line with U.S. competitors' prices. Others warned that the dollar's slide could spin out of control, leading to a free fall in its value and catastrophic losses in dollar-based investments worldwide.

"If we're not careful, monetary disarray could morph into economic war. We would all be its victims," French President Sarkozy said in an address to the U.S. Congress in November 2007. [40]

Those fears were present at the Gulf council meeting. The dollar's fall has reduced the value of Gulf state currencies, raising the prices of imported goods on which the desert kingdoms' breakneck expansion depends and pushing inflation toward economically and politically treacherous levels.

The previous May Kuwait had broken the official link between its dinar currency and the dollar in favor of a linkage to a group of currencies including the dollar. With the U.S. economy reeling from the subprime mortgage and credit crises, a decision by any of the five other states to follow Kuwait's lead could have rocked the dollar.

"This would be seen as a further loss of confidence in the greenback, accelerating its rout," said Gabriel Stein, chief international economist at London's Lombard Street Research. [41]

U.S. Treasury Secretary Henry M. Paulson Jr. said in Saudi Arabia last May that a decision by the Saudis to end

Gold bars are displayed at a bank in Seoul, South Korea. Nations keep gold reserves because their value goes up when inflation increases. After World War II, the gold-backed U.S. dollar was established as the world's "anchor" currency. But in 1971, President Richard M. Nixon stunned the world by cutting the historic linkage between gold and the dollar, blocking foreigners from exchanging dollars for gold from the U.S. government's reserves.

the dollar peg is "a sovereign decision," and not for the United States to decide. But he added, "The dollar peg, I think, has served this country and this region well." Saudi Arabia's Finance Minister Ibrahim al-Assaf settled the issue: "We have no intention of de-pegging or revaluation." [42]

Noriel Roubini, an economics professor at New York University, is among the experts who believe confidence in the American currency is seriously undermined by the growing U.S. debt to foreigners. Dubbed "Dr. Doom" in a recent *New York Times* profile, Roubini sounded an early warning that the United States was headed for a cataclysmic housing market bust and credit shock. [43]

Roubini's concern centered on U.S. dependence on foreign investors to channel dollars back into the United States to cover the federal budget deficit and balance the trade gap. An alarming portion of that return investment is coming from about a dozen government central banks, most of them in Asia, he said. "If foreign central banks stopped buying dollar-denominated bonds, the dollar would fall dramatically against their currencies," and U.S. interest rates would be forced sharply higher, pummeling the economy, Roubini wrote. [44]

As the housing and credit crises deepened this year, Roubini said the losses from mortgage foreclosures, bank

failures and bad debt would increase America's budget deficit by hundreds of billions of dollars. Will foreigners willingly take on massive, new U.S. debt? he asks. "Our biggest financiers are China, Russia and the Gulf states," he said. "These are rivals, not allies." [45]

But others contend the size, openness and resilience of the U.S. economy — even in hard times — will attract foreigners. And foreign central banks holding large numbers of dollars in their reserves have too much to lose from a free fall in the dollar.

If China tried to sell dollar assets precipitously, the worldwide prices of those assets — especially U.S. Treasury securities and the dollar itself — would likely fall, wrote Donald J. Boudreaux, chairman of the economics department at George Mason University, in Fairfax, Va. "And while Americans would suffer, the Chinese government would suffer even more," he added. [46]

The appeal of the United States to foreign investors goes beyond currency prices, says Adam S. Posen, deputy director of the Peterson Institute. "U.S. political leadership in security, commercial and even cultural affairs globally has a critical impact on the usage of the dollar in the monetary realm," he said. Foreigners invest in the United States in part to gain "insider access" to U.S. government and business decision-making. This desire for membership adds to a kind of unquantifiable "dark matter" that energizes support for the dollar, he adds. [47]

The risk of large, volatile swings in the dollar's value is somewhat lessened by the tremendous volume of dollar trading on world currency exchanges, says Derek Sammann, head of foreign exchange products at CME Group in Chicago, which runs the world's largest currency exchange. More than $3 trillion in currencies are traded on foreign-exchange markets on an average day. So even if China or one of the Gulf states were to sell as much as $1 trillion in dollars over a month, there is sufficient underlying trading activity or liquidity so that it would not overwhelm the dollar market, he says.

"You would see some selling pressure, but the impact on daily dollar trading on foreign exchange markets would be minimal," he says. As long as the U.S. economy holds its underlying strength, a run on the dollar isn't likely, he says.

Nevertheless, the dollar's new volatility worries many experts. The World Bank Commission on Growth and Development warned this year that the United States had been relying too much on foreign capital, which has "financed America's trade deficit, allowing the country to live beyond its means. This American spending has helped keep the world economy growing, but it is unlikely to be sustainable." [48]

BACKGROUND

Untying the Dollar

In 1944 an agreement on postwar international finance and trade forged by world leaders in Bretton Woods, N.H., established the right to convert a U.S. dollar for one-35th of an ounce of gold, a guarantee that anchored a system of stable currency exchange rates for all countries. [49] Gold has been struck into coins since at least the 7th century B.C. [50]

As a result of Bretton Woods, other nations' currencies were linked flexibly to the dollar, permitting countries to devalue or lower their exchange rates with the dollar in extreme economic crises in order to preserve their bank reserves. The goal was a stable, permanent formula for aligning currency values.

But on Aug. 15, 1971, President Richard M. Nixon stunned the world by cutting the historic linkage between gold and the dollar, blocking foreigners from exchanging dollars for gold from the government's vaults at Fort Knox, Ky. [51] Nixon's decision led to an array of different currency exchange policies that has continued to evolve.

The trend in exchange rate policies is for countries to let their currencies "float," with their value determined by the world's currency exchanges.

Foreign exchange trading is so huge that most governments would be unable to successfully control their currency's value by "intervention" — buying and selling their own currency on the exchanges. (In 2004, for example, the paper value of currencies traded on exchanges in a typical week matched the $9 trillion figure for the total output of the U.S. economy for the entire year.) [52]

Instead, countries with floating rates try to set short-term interest rates at levels that strengthen or weaken their currency values, and in that way hit their goals for exports and imports. Floating currency exchange rates are a cornerstone of economic globalization and a key reason for the huge increase in currency trading.

According to the International Monetary Fund, 23 countries — most of them small, including Bulgaria, Ecuador and Estonia — have adopted a "hard" peg,

tying their currencies to various other countries' currencies at fixed rates. Another 63 nations — including Argentina, Nigeria, Pakistan, Saudi Arabia and other oil-producing states — peg their money to a single currency. About half favor the dollar, and a third choose the euro. China's "crawling" peg arrangement allows its foreign exchange rate to be periodically adjusted against the dollar in small steps to meet China's economic goals. [53]

The United States, Britain, Mexico, Brazil, Australia, Israel and Eurozone countries were among 35 nations that let their currencies float freely, the IMF said. Japan allows the yen to float but has intervened at times to keep the yen's exchange value from falling so low that Japanese exports are depressed. Russia, most former Soviet satellite states and smaller Asian, South American and African nations were among the 48 countries that maintained a "managed" float, with their governments intervening to keep their currencies at desired exchange rates.

In general, advanced countries with large exports and imports were most likely to let currencies float. Smaller countries that had suffered from hyper-inflation were likely to peg their currencies to the dollar or euro, seeking protection against inflation. [54] Other countries with disproportionately large trade and financial flows — such as Saudi Arabia — peg to the dollar for the same reason. [55]

The dollar's long decline beginning in 2002 caused other floating currencies to move in the opposite direction. Moreover, as in the euro's case, the cheap dollar has given U.S. exporters a competitive trade advantage, causing tension between the United States and rival exporting nations. On the other hand, countries whose currencies are pegged to the dollar, such as Saudi Arabia, have suffered with rising prices for oil, food and other commodities. Higher commodity prices have triggered higher inflation and led to calls for a shift from a dollar peg to a linkage with a group, or "basket," of currencies, or ties to a mix of currencies combined with the price of oil itself. [56]

Before Nixon's 1971 move, a government or a foreign investor could switch to gold whenever inflation threatened to undermine a local currency's value (as inflation causes prices to rise, the dollar's purchasing power shrinks). Massive American spending on the Vietnam War, combined with Washington's refusal to cut other spending or raise taxes, meant the United States had to pay for the war by printing more money, causing inflation and lowering the dollar's value.

"When inflation eroded the greenback's purchasing power, gold was the more attractive option. Foreigners traded in their dollars until U.S. gold stocks were close to exhaustion. Higher U.S. interest rates could have lured foreigners back into dollars. But Nixon wouldn't tolerate high rates the year before an election," noted *Washington Post* columnist Sebastian Mallaby. [57]

Rescue Efforts

Concern about the dollar's strength dates from the first years of the republic, when U.S. Treasury Secretary Alexander Hamilton persuaded President George Washington to create a national bank and have the federal government take over the states' heavy Revolutionary War debts. Hamilton's policy enriched speculators who had bought the war debt from investors at cheap prices, infuriating Secretary of State Thomas Jefferson and others who feared concentrated national monetary power. [58]

But Hamilton solidly established the principle of a strong dollar that would be linked to gold for most of the U.S. peacetime history before Nixon's action.

Now the dollar — no longer tethered to gold — depends on the world's confidence in the U.S. economy in relation to other economies. "Money is a belief," writes Jason Goodwin, author of *Greenback, The Almighty Dollar and the Invention of America*. "We accept money because we believe others in turn will accept it, too." [59] It follows, then, that the dollar's position in the world depends on confidence.

In the worst-case scenario, if that confidence eroded and foreign governments abandoned the dollar or reduced the dollars they hold in their central banks, "the dollar could rapidly lose in popularity and value," wrote economists Christopher M. Meissner and Nienke Oomes in an IMF Working Paper. "A similar situation occurred in the early 1970s, when the British pound sterling quite suddenly disappeared as an anchor currency, despite . . . its international status during the preceding 150 years." [60]

Some experts — citing the potential for a sharp plunge in the dollar — call for a coordinated response by the world's leading economies, similar to the action taken by the five largest industrial democracies — in 1985. The finance ministers from France, Germany, Japan, Britain and the United States came together to resolve the problems caused by the large U.S. trade deficit and the dollar's strength against other currencies.

High interest rates engineered by the U.S. Federal Reserve to control inflation in the early 1980s had invited heavy foreign investment in the dollar, driving up its price, particularly against the yen. [61] American manufacturers were being beaten bloody by the high dollar, which penalized U.S. exporters and gave a critical advantage to Japanese exporters of cars, electronics and other products. Democratic Party leaders in Congress were threatening trade sanctions, and U.S. business leaders demanded a change.

The "Plaza" agreement, named for the New York City hotel where the ministers met, pledged to gradually lower the dollar's value and shrink global trade imbalances. (By the time the Plaza conference was held, U.S. interest rates and oil prices were falling, and the dollar had already begun to shift downward from its peak values. Thus, the ministers were able to "lean with the wind," as Japanese journalist Yoichi Funabashi put it.) [62]

The dollar did eventually stabilize, contributing to the economic growth and budget surpluses of the Clinton presidency. Political ferment over trade also eased, helping Clinton win bipartisan approval of the North American Free Trade Agreement (NAFTA) and formation of the World Trade Organization. [63]

The Peterson Institute's Bergsten argues that the current weakness of the dollar and persistent trade deficits require a new round of top-level cooperation among the United States and other economic powers. The major financial powers need an "Asian Plaza Agreement" with China, so that it will allow its currency to gain value against the dollar and the euro, Bergsten and other experts say. That, they say, will shrink the U.S. trade deficit to a sustainable level and head off a new round of congressional demands for trade penalties against China. [64]

Moreover, Bergsten says, any currency move by China must be accompanied by a unified, coordinated increase in foreign currency rates by other leading Asian nations, led by Japan and South Korea. Otherwise, some Asian countries could act independently, he says, suppressing their currency values to gain a competitive advantage and killing the initiative before it could work. Whether China would join such an effort is one of the unknowns in the dollar's future.

CURRENT SITUATION

Oil and the Dollar

The world's investors are viewing the dollar and oil as a linked gauge of anxiety over the ongoing global financial crisis. In a pattern that appeared early in this decade and has been especially pronounced since the credit crisis exploded last year, when the dollar weakens, oil prices rise. The price of Brent crude, the benchmark North Sea crude oil grade, jumped from $50 a barrel in mid-January 2007 to $142 a barrel by early July 2008, while the exchange rate for the euro rose from $1.29 per euro to $1.58. [65] Then the trend reversed. By the third week of August 2008 Brent was $110 a barrel and the dollar had retreated to $1.46 per euro. The linkage was unmistakable, said American oil analyst Philip K. Verleger Jr. [66]

Oil and the dollar had often behaved differently in the past, the Peterson Institute's Bergsten said in congressional testimony in July. In 1985-86, the price of oil sank from nearly $30 a barrel to $10 a barrel while the dollar's value compared to the currencies of the 10 largest industrial nations dropped by 40 percent. [67] Both oil and the dollar rose together again in the late 1990s, Bergsten added. [68]

Normally, oil and the dollar react independently to economic conditions, experts say. Interest rates differ among nations, affecting currency values as investors seek higher returns on bonds. And oil prices respond to shortages or surpluses, wars and political tensions in oil-producing regions or hurricanes that smash into oil fields and refineries.

So what has caused the unusual recent oil-dollar linkage?

Worldwide oil supplies have become increasingly strained since 2000, notes Daniel Yergin, chairman of Cambridge Energy Research Associates in Massachussetts. China's hyper-growth — and accompanying increased demand for oil — plus the Iraq War and violence in Nigeria's oil-producing region all contributed to the scarcity. [69]

The tight balance between oil supply and demand encouraged traders and speculators to sell the dollar on currency exchanges because the oil scarcity stoked higher prices for oil. And because most oil shipments are priced in dollars, a drop in the dollar's value meant lower revenues for producers, who then sought higher oil prices. Meanwhile, European, Chinese and Russian currencies were gaining value against the dollar, so they could afford to pay more for dollar-priced oil.

In addition, major investment and retirement funds rushed into the commodity markets to buy oil and grains instead of increasingly risky stocks, bonds and real estate. At a congressional hearing in June, Yergin called oil "the new gold" — an investment that offers protection against rising inflation, a declining dollar and collapsing real estate values. [70]

As a result, Yergin theorized, instead of the traditional "flight to the dollar" during a time of financial stress, there has been a "flight to commodities." "Although the correlation does not hold week-in and week-out, we believe that this trend — a falling dollar contributing to higher oil prices — is very strong," Yergin said. A Federal Reserve Bank of Dallas study, he said, estimated that about one-third of the $60 increase in oil prices between 2003 through 2007 was caused by the dollar's decline. [71]

"The crisis that started in the subprime mortgage market in the United States has traveled around the world. And through the medium of a weaker dollar it has come back home to Americans [as] higher prices at the pump," he said.

Although members of Congress have trained fire on oil traders and speculators, commodities analyst Peter Beutel, president of a Connecticut-based energy risk-management company, says the entry in 2006 of huge pension and investment funds into speculative commodity trading was a bigger factor in rising oil prices. The trend accelerated after the Federal Reserve cut interest rates repeatedly in 2007, which telegraphed to fund managers that the dollar would decline.

As an example, Beutel cites the California Public Employees' Retirement System (CalPERS) — the nation's largest public retirement fund — which disclosed in September 2006 that it planned to invest in commodities. "There may be serious money to be made by taking advantage of accelerating world demand for commodities and compelling investment opportunities in alternatives to diminishing resources, including cheap oil," said Charles P. Valdes, a CalPERS board member. [72]

Although energy is a relatively minor part of the fund's total capital, profit from energy and other commodity investments ballooned. "CalPERS has racked up a 68 percent return playing the commodities market in the past 12 months," reported the *Sacramento Bee*. [73] Critics in Washington and California say the fund is cashing in on consumers' pain at the gasoline pump.

But CalPERS spokeswoman Pat Macht responded, "Commodities are one small part of a diversification strategy that we . . . and all institutional investors use. We don't think we're causing a problem. There are many, many other factors at play here. Our intentions are honorable."

However, Michael Greenberger, a former U.S. Commodity Futures Trading Commission official, said investments by CalPERS and other pension and endowment funds "are completely distorting the market" and helping to push oil and other commodity prices higher. [74]

The Dollar and Food

A "silent tsunami" of hunger is afflicting the poorest communities in South Africa, where rice prices doubled between May 2007 and May 2008, a government survey reported this month. [75] South Africa's plight is matched throughout the world's poorest regions, all hit by an escalation of food prices connected to the dollar's downward trend in value.

Food has become another important option for investors seeking relief from a falling dollar.

In 2008, developing countries may spend four times what they paid for food imports in 2000, according to a "Food Price Index" study issued by two international agencies. [76] (The increase for developed countries is far less.) The fast-rising track for cereal prices on the index matches the path of crude oil and euros in 2007. And, imitating oil and euro prices on commodity exchanges, the index, covering five food commodities, has flattened out this spring, and sugar and dairy prices have tipped slightly downward, say the Organization for Economic Cooperation and Development (OECD) and the U.N. Food and Agriculture Organization (FAO).

The rising food prices ignited sometimes violent protests in a score of countries, from Haiti to Niger to Uzbekistan. Peruvian farmers blocked rail lines to protest higher fertilizer prices caused by higher oil prices. More than 75,000 protesters filled the streets of Mexico City in January 2007 demanding price controls after a 400-percent jump in the price of tortillas due to rising costs of maize imports. [77] Rice, an essential part of the developing world's diet, shot up from $300 a ton in May 2005 to $900 a ton three years later. A Haitian factory worker earns about $5 a day, so when rice triples to 67 cents a bowl, the worker ends up spending a day's pay for just seven bowls of rice, according to a report by the Progressive Policy Institute, a Washington, D.C., think tank. [78]

As in the case of oil, the escalation in food prices in 2007 followed increased trading in grains and other farm commodities by financial firms, banks, investment funds and other newcomers to these markets. Trading volumes in commodities like maize doubled between February 2005 and February 2008, in large part due to these "new agents." [79]

According to commodities analyst Beutel, the financial industry's move into commodity markets, like its investments in oil contracts, has a decidedly different impact than traditional commodity market activity. Traders and speculators purchase their oil or grain contracts seeking short-term profits and will sell out of their positions when they sense the time is right. The noncommercial newcomers are buying and holding positions in oil and farm commodities as if they were long-term investments in corporate stocks and bonds, says Beutel. "They buy and hold," and that puts upward pressure on oil prices, he adds.

All of that creates upward momentum toward higher prices until events cause a decisive change in investors' outlook. The activities of major funds in commodity markets have become a "key concern," according to a long-term outlook by the OECD and FAO. [80]

The two institutions predict that over the long term food price hikes will level off but remain historically high. The U.S. dollar is expected to regain some strength, they predicted, which will reduce food imports and encourage more local food production, allowing food prices to fall some. But farm commodity markets are expected to remain volatile, and the risk of more food price shocks continues, the agencies concluded. [81]

China's Challenge

The 2008 Olympics delivered to a global television audience the dazzling evidence of China's economic growth. [82] Hundreds of millions of rural Chinese have been lifted out of extreme poverty. China has taken a commanding position in world trade as the world's second-largest exporter — behind Germany and ahead of the United States — and the third-largest importer, trailing the United States and Germany. [83]

But China's remarkable rise has come at a high price. Environmental degradation, income inequality and inflation have accompanied the growth. [84] And China's success has stirred intense criticism over the "people's" currency, the renminbi (RMB).

Could the euro replace the dollar as the globe's anchor currency?

YES
Jeffrey A. Frankel
Professor of Capital Formation and Growth, Harvard Kennedy School

Written for *CQ Researcher*, September, 2008

The euro is a credible, long-term challenger to the dollar. The Eurozone — the 15 European countries that have adopted the euro currency — is roughly as big as the United States, and the euro has shown itself a better store of value than the dollar. It's true that in the current credit crisis, the dollar has retained its reputation as a safe haven for fearful investors around the world. I might have predicted the crisis would have begun to undermine the dollar's position by now. But U.S. Treasury bills have still been considered the safest thing around.

Taking a longer view, however, the causes of the crisis and the cost to the United States to prevent an economic collapse are negatives for the dollar. Whether measured in terms of a burgeoning federal budget deficit or in damage to New York's reputation as a financial center, the situation certainly appears to significantly undermine confidence in the dollar and in U.S. financial markets.

As the crisis eases, there will be more rethinking of the dollar. We will go back to the more mundane macroeconomic issues, which have been overshadowed by the recent crisis. The rising federal budget deficit could renew downward pressure on the dollar. The current account deficit may grow. Monetary authorities in China and the Persian Gulf have been reluctant to shift out of dollars because they are afraid of setting off a run on the dollar, and they would be the biggest losers. But once the crisis is past, they may see an incentive to quietly reduce dollar holdings.

To be sure, rankings of international currencies change very slowly. The United States surpassed the United Kingdom in economic size in 1872, in exports in 1915 and as a net creditor in 1917, yet the dollar did not surpass the pound as the No. 1 international currency until 1945. In 2005, when University of Wisconsin Professor Menzie Chinn and I created a model to determine the factors that create a dominant global currency, even our pessimistic scenarios had the euro not overtaking the dollar until 2022.

But the dollar has continued to lose ground. We updated our calculations earlier this year, particularly to recognize that London is usurping Frankfurt's role as the financial capital of the euro, even though the U.K. remains outside of the European monetary union. Now we find that the tipping point could come sooner; the euro could overtake the dollar as early as 2015.

For more information: http://papers.ssrn.com/sol3/papers .cfm?abstract_id=1083712

NO
Adam S. Posen
Deputy Director, Peterson Institute for International Economics

Written for *CQ Researcher*, September, 2008

Financial panics are rarely of lasting significance to the fate of nations or their currencies. Though calm is difficult to maintain while the United States experiences
a panic in its many interlocking markets, it would be a mistake to read too much into recent developments. The dollar will continue to benefit from the geopolitical sources of its global role, which the euro cannot yet — or soon, if ever — match.

The euro's ascent to at least comparable status with the dollar has a surface plausibility. Some analysts have argued that the euro's attaining co-dominance simply awaited a significant series of policy mistakes by the United States, similar to how the pound sterling began losing its role in the 1930s. The dollar was spared such a fate during the 1970s only because neither the deutschemark nor the yen were a viable alternative at the time.

It is time for observers to shed excessive doubts about the euro. Yet, the dollar will retain a dominant role in official reserve portfolios, partly because longer-term choices of international currency commitments are driven by both financial and political factors. Moreover, the Eurozone's monetary strengths cannot offset the European Union's economic and political weaknesses in global leadership.

These sources of dollar strength are ignored in a narrow, deterministic focus on why countries choose to hold dollars in official reserves. Other governments' exchange-rate management is influenced by security ties. From Taiwan to Saudi Arabia to Panama, decisions about pegging one's currency to the dollar (and thus to accumulate dollar reserves for intervention) depend as much on foreign policy as on economics. Foreigners' decisions to invest in the United States are influenced by their desire to gain insider access to key U.S. decision-making processes and to membership in transnational elites.

The European Union, let alone the Eurozone, is unable or unwilling to offer these systemic or security benefits beyond a very local area, and thus the euro's global attractiveness is fundamentally limited.

This dependence of the dollar on both political and economic factors, however, suggests that were the dollar no long dominant, the global monetary system would fragment into a multicurrency system, not result in parity between the dollar and the euro.

For more information: The International Economy, spring 2008, pp. 10-11.

The complaints are perhaps loudest in the United States, where critics contend China has kept the RMB's value too low against the dollar and other currencies in order to keep China's exports cheap. Although the RMB has risen this year against the dollar, lessening China's currency advantage, the huge U.S. trade deficit with China may yet trigger a political backlash in Congress.

Trade or currency restrictions could ignite a damaging trade conflict between the two countries. [85] Edwin M. Truman, former assistant Treasury secretary for international affairs, notes that China's government-controlled banking and currency policies and actions are deliberately hidden from public view.

"China is subject to multiple suspicions about its political and strategic objectives," he said. Unless China "can demonstrate that it is a good international financial citizen, it risks protectionist reactions." [86]

China contends critics overstate its currency-rate advantage. Low U.S. interest rates engineered by the Federal Reserve are largely responsible for the dollar's weakness, said Jin Zhongxia, chief representative in the United States of the People's Bank of China. [87] "There is no way for Chinese authorities to create a competitive advantage by choosing a specific currency regime," he said, "and they have no intention of doing so." [88]

Despite their differences, China and the United States are lashed together — climbers on a path with many risks. Foreigners owned $9.7 trillion worth of U.S. securities in June 2007, including bonds and stocks issued by government agencies and corporations. China's share — at $922 billion — was second only to Japan's. In fact, China nearly tripled its holdings from 2004 to 2007 as it poured dollars from exports sales back into the United States, primarily by buying Treasury bonds. [89]

"Why are the Chinese monetary authorities so willing to underwrite American profligacy? Not out of altruism," wrote British historian Niall Ferguson. [90] If China doesn't buy U.S. Treasury securities as fast as they are printed, the dollar's value could sink. "The Chinese authorities dread such a dollar slide," he adds. The prices of Chinese goods would climb, exports to the United States would decline and unemployment in China could spike upward when millions of workers from the countryside begin looking for factory jobs in China's cities.

Brad W. Setser, a fellow at the New York-based Council on Foreign Relations, calculates that a one-third decline in the value of the dollar and euro against the

renminbi would hit China with a $1 trillion financial loss. "That is a large sum even for a nation of over a billion people," he writes. [91]

The dollar's shakiness is clearly prompting China to consider gradually reducing its dollar holdings, which will tend to depress the dollar against the renminbi, Setser says. [92]

"With China, we have little concept of what is around the bend, yet there is no turning back," writes *International Economy* publisher Smick, in his 2008 book, *The World Is Curved*. [93]

OUTLOOK

Catch-22 Dilemmas

The 2008 global credit crisis has overturned the outlook for the world's leading currencies and sharpened the financial dilemmas facing their governments.

The euro's advantage is the diversity of the economies that make up the 15-nation European Monetary Union, from France and Germany to Slovenia and Greece. That is also its weakness, as Europe's leaders demonstrated in early October as they struggled to find a common response to the threat of bank failures and recession. [94]

"The European financial sector is on trial: We have to support our banks," said French President Sarkozy on Oct. 4 at the start of a European economic summit that brought British Prime Minister Gordon Brown, German Chancellor Angela Merkel and Italian Prime Minister Silvio Berlusconi to Paris. In the previous week, governments in Belgium, Britain, France, Germany, Luxembourg, the Netherlands and Iceland had been forced to shore up the finances of several banks. "We are all staring into the abyss," said German Finance Minister Steinbrück. [95]

But while the leaders expressed solidarity after the Paris meeting, they did not move to create a European emergency fund for banks so normal lending could resume. Prior to the summit, France had suggested Europe create a $415 billion emergency fund to mirror the U.S. financial rescue plan. But Germany and Britain quickly said no, unwilling to pledge their wealth to support other nations' banking systems. A lingering question is whether the fissures within Europe created by the banking crisis will weaken the euro.

Like China, Japan must decide how to handle its huge holdings of dollar-based assets. Japan has more than $1 trillion in foreign currency holdings, most of it in relatively low-yielding U.S. Treasury bills, according to reports from Tokyo. [96] Some financial experts suggest Japan could follow a path taken by China, Norway, Russia, Singapore and the United Arab Emirates in creating a "sovereign wealth fund" empowered to invest government-held dollars in higher-paying foreign securities or real estate. Japan needs improved investment earnings to help fund its rising social security costs.

Financial Services Minister Yuji Yamamoto told *The Japan Times* that with sovereign funds taking a significant role in global finance, "does Japan just sit back as an onlooker and flatly say, 'We don't have to do anything'? That's stubbornly conservative." [97]

But Finance Minister Fukushiro Nukaga rejects the idea, saying Japan's public prefers a safer strategy for investing government-held dollars. "Active management of public wealth involves high risks," he said in February. [98] Analysts note that any significant moves by Japan to reduce its dollar holdings through government investments in non-U.S. assets would undermine the dollar's value — eroding Japan's remaining dollar assets.

China has a similar Catch-22 dilemma, driven home during the current crisis by heavy losses on Wall Street and in U.S. government securities. China's sovereign wealth fund, China Investment Corp. (CIC), "has been bitten several times and is shy" about investing in U.S. financial securities, says Shanghai financial analyst Andy Xie.

"It would be too politically sensitive to buy [more] assets that do not perform well," adds Paul Cavey, chief China economist at Australia's Macquarie Bank in Beijing. [99]

An alternative option for China is to increase purchases in U.S. companies, particularly if the dollar remains weak. The cost of the Bush administration's financial rescue plan and the prospects of higher federal deficits compel the United States to continue borrowing hundreds of billions of dollars a year from foreign governments and banks.

Xie, formerly Morgan Stanley's chief Asia economist, said U.S. political leaders must accept increased foreign investment by China in U.S. companies — a controversial issue for Congress in the past. "If the U.S. is not willing to accept that," he said, "they will have to print money [to fund the deficits], and the dollar will fall. And we will be headed toward a global financial meltdown." [100]

Indeed, German Finance Minister Steinbrück predicted in early October: "One thing is clear: after this crisis, the world will no longer be the same." [101]

NOTES

1. "Five Days That Transformed Wall Street," *The Washington Post*, Sept. 20, 2008, p. A9.

2. Michael M. Grynbaum, "The Fed Holds Rates Steady, and Wall Street Turns a Bad Start Around," *The New York Times*, Sept. 17, 2008, Section C, p. 8.

3. Jeremy Warner, "UK Government may need to guarantee deposits," *The Independent* (London), Oct. 1, 2008, p. 36.

4. Jacques Attali, "Wall Street Meltdown: The First Authentic Global Crisis," *New Perspectives Quarterly*, Sept. 22, 2008.

5. "Subprime woes 'could end dollar regime,' " *The Daily Yomiuri* (Tokyo), March 20, 2008, p. 1.

6. Agence France-Presse, "Germany hit by a 'pronounced slowdown': economist," Aug. 30, 2008.

7. For background, see Marcia Clemmitt, "Global Food Crisis," *CQ Researcher*, June 27, 2008, pp. 553-576.

8. Paul Owers, "Foreign Home Buyers Are Flocking to Florida," *South Florida Sun-Sentinel*, April 12, 2008, p. 1D.

9. Menzi Chinn and Jeffrey Frankel, "Will the Euro Eventually Surpass the Dollar as Leading International Reserve Currency?" http://papers.ssrn.com/sol3/papers.cfm?abstract_id=884261.

10. "U.S. International Trade, Second Quarter 2008," U.S. Bureau of Economic Analysis (BEA), Sept. 11, 2008, Table 2, www.bea.gov/newsreleases/international/trade/2008/trad0708.htm; BEA, "International Transactions Account Data," www.bea.gov/international/bp_web/simple.cfm?anon=78423&table_id=1&area_id=3, and "The Budget and Economic Outlook: An Update," Congressional Budget Office, Sept. 8, 2008, www.cbo.gov/ftpdocs/97xx/doc9706/09-08-Update.pdf.

11. "Mapping Global Capital Markets, Fourth Annual Report," McKinsey Global Institute, January 2008, p. 10.

12. Jill Treanor and Larry Elliott, "Analysis: Failure of financial heavyweights could have caused markets to implode," *The Guardian* (London), Sept. 9, 2008, p. 9.

13. *Ibid.*

14. "Report on Foreign Portfolio Holdings of U.S. Securities as of June 2007," U.S. Treasury

Department, April 2008, pp. 6-8, www.treas.gov/tic/shl2007r.pdf ; also "Report to Congress on International Economic and Exchange Rate Policies," U.S. Treasury Department, November 2008, www.treas.gov/offices/international-affairs/economic-exchange-rates/112005_report.pdf.

15. Alan Greenspan, *The Age of Turbulence: Adventures in a New World* (2007), p. 352.

16. Miranda Xafa, "Global Imbalances: Do They Matter?" *Cato Journal*, winter 2007, p. 59.

17. Kenneth Rogoff, "Goodbye to the Dollar," *The International Economy*, spring 2008, p. 51.

18. "Fact Sheet," European Central Bank, www.ecb.int/home/html/index.en.html.

19. "Will dollar lose position as key currency," *The Daily Yomiuri* (Tokyo), April 19, 2008, p. 16.

20. Katrin Bennhold and Steven Erlanger, "French finance minister calls for realignment of currencies," *International Herald Tribune*, May 22, 2008, p. 13.

21. *The Daily Yomiuri*, March 20, 2008, *op. cit.*

22. C. Fred Bergsten, testimony before the House Committee on Financial Services, July 24, 2008, p. 1.

23. "International Economic Accounts," U.S. Bureau of Economic Analysis, June 17, 2008, www.bea.gov/newsreleases/international/transactions/transnewsrelease.htm.

24. "The Current Account Deficit," Peterson Institute of International Economics, www.iie.com/research/topics/hottopic.cfm?HotTopicID=9.

25. Bergsten, *op. cit.*

26. Jonathan Weisman, "Straight-talking Treasury chief stares down critics; O'Neill's remarks don't just ruffle feathers, they rattle markets," *USA Today*, Feb. 21, 2001, p. 1B.

27. Martin Feldstein, "The Dollar Will Fall Further," *The International Economy*, *op. cit.*, p. 16.

28. "Role of Central Banks," Federal Reserve Bank of New York, www.ny.frb.org/education/fx/role.html.

29. Jane Macartney and Robin Pagnamenta, "French seal $12bn Chinese nuclear deal," *The Times* (London), Nov. 27, 2007, p. 55.

30. Joelle Garrus, "Areva announces 8 bln euro nuclear deal with China," Agence France-Presse, Nov. 26, 2006.

31. Brad W. Setser, "Sovereign Wealth and Sovereign Power," Council on Foreign Relations, September 2008, p. 22.

32. "The Falling Dollar," *The Economist*, Nov. 11, 2004, www.economist.com/agenda/displayStory.cfm?Story_id=3372405.

33. McKinsey Global Institute, *op. cit.*, pp. 11-12.

34. Kenichi Ohmae, "The Coming Battle of the Atlantic: Euro vs. the Dollar;" *New Perspectives Quarterly*, April 14, 2008.

35. "The Next Great Global Currency," *The International Economy*, *op. cit.*, pp. 22-37.

36. The International Economy, *op. cit.*, p. 35.

37. Richard H. Clarida, "Reflections on Currency Regimes," *The International Economy*, *op. cit.*, p. 18.

38. Menzie Chinn and Jeffrey A. Frankel, "Will the Euro Eventually Surpass the Dollar as Leading International Reserve Currency?" *G7 Current Account Imbalances* (2007), p. 287.

39. Setser, *op. cit.*

40. "The Dollar in Free Fall," *The New York Times*, Nov. 11, 2007, p. 2.

41. Gary Duncan, "Dollar faces new sell-off if Gulf states end greenback pegs," *The Times* (London), Dec. 3, 2007, p. 45.

42. "Paulson says strong dollar in US interest, Saudi peg 'sovereign decision,' " Thomson Financial News, May 31, 2008, www.forbes.com/afxnewslimited/feeds/afx/2008/05/31/afx5066473.html.

43. Stephen Mihm, "Dr. Doom," *The New York Times Magazine*, Aug. 17, 2008, p. 26.

44. Brad Setser and Nouriel Roubini, "How Scary is the Deficit?" *Foreign Affairs*, July/August 2005.

45. Mihm, *op. cit.*

46. Donald J. Boudreaux, "A Dollar Dump? Not likely," *Pittsburgh Tribune-Review*, Nov. 30, 2007, www.pittsburghlive.com/x/pittsburghtrib/opinion/columnists/boudreaux/s_540383.html.

47. Adam S. Posen, "It's Not Just About The Money," *The International Economy*, *op. cit.*, p. 10.

48. "The Growth Report — Strategies for Sustained Growth and Inclusive Development," The World Bank Commission on Growth and Development, May 21, 2008, p. 96.

49. "The Role of the U.S. Dollar," Iowa State University, www.econ.iastate.edu/classes/econ355/choi/bre.htm. For background, see F. P. Huddle, "Bretton Woods Agreements," in *Editorial Research Reports*, April 27, 1945, available in *CQ Researcher Plus Archive*, http://library.cqpress.com.

50. Michael D. Bordo, "Gold Standard," *The Concise Encyclopedia of Economics*, www.econlib.org/library /Enc/GoldStandard.html.

51. The right of American citizens to own gold coins and currency ended in 1933 as part of President Franklin D. Roosevelt's emergency measures to end widespread gold hoarding during the nation's banking crisis in the Great Depression. For background, see Lawrence Sullivan, *Prelude to Panic: The Story of the Bank Holiday* (1936), pp. 87-103. For background, see R. C. Deans, "World Money Crisis," in *Editorial Research Reports*, Sept. 8, 1971, available in *CQ Researcher Plus Archive*, http://library.cqpress.com.

52. "Economic Report of the President 2007," p. 150, www.whitehouse.gov/cea/pubs.html.

53. "Review of Exchange Agreements, Restrictions and Controls," International Monetary Fund, Nov. 27, 2007, www.imf.org/External/NP/pp/2007/eng/112 707.pdf.

54. Christopher M. Meissner and Nienke Oomes, "Why do Countries Peg the Way They Peg? The Determinants of Anchor Currency Choice," *IMF Working Paper*, May 2008.

55. Brad W. Setser, "The Case for Exchange Rate Flexibility of Oil-Exporting Economies," Peterson Institute for International Economics, November 2007, pp. 1-13.

56. *Ibid.*, p. 4.

57. Sebastian Mallaby, "The Dollar in Danger," *The Washington Post*, Nov. 12, 2007, p. A21.

58. Richard Hofstadter, *The American Political Tradition* (1989), p. 42.

59. Jason Goodwin, *Greenback, The Almighty Dollar and the Invention of America* (2003), p. 5.

60. Meissner and Oomes, *op. cit.*

61. Kent H. Hughes, *Building the Next American Century, The Past and Future of American Economic Competitiveness* (2005), p. 383.

62. *Ibid.*, p. 393.

63. *Ibid.*, p. 340.

64. David M. Smick, *The World Is Curved* (2008), pp. 267-268.

65. "Weekly Europe (UK) Brent Blend Spot Price FOB," *Petroleum Navigator*, Energy Information Administration, http://tonto.eia.doe.gov/dnav/pet /hist/wepcbrentw.htm; and "Foreign Exchange Rates (Daily)," Federal Reserve Statistical Release, www.federalreserve.gov/releases/h10/Hist/.

66. Philip K. Verleger, Jr., "The Oil-Dollar Link," *The International Economy, op. cit.*, p. 48.

67. "Annual Oil Market Chronology," Energy Information Administration, www.eia.doe.gov/cabs /AOMC/Overview.html.

68. Bergsten testimony, *op. cit.*, p. 5.

69. Daniel Yergin, "Oil and the Break Point," testimony to the Joint Economic Committee of Congress, June 25, 2008, pp. 1-5, www2.cera.com/news/DYergin _June2008_Testimony.pdf.

70. *Ibid.*, p. 7.

71. Stephen P.A. Brown, Raghav Virmani and Richard Alm, "Economic Letter — Insights from the Federal Reserve Bank of Dallas," May 2008, p. 6.

72. CalPERS, press release, "CalPERS Explores Natural Resource/Commodities Investing, Sept. 12, 2006, www.calpers.ca.gov/index.jsp?bc=/about/press/pr-2006 /sept/natural-resources-commodities.xml, and www .calpers.ca.gov/index.jsp?bc=/investments/hom.xml.

73. Dale Kasler, "CalPERS profits as costs surge; While consumers fume over commodity prices, pension fund makes killing in market," *Sacramento Bee*, June 20, 2008, p. A1.

74. *Ibid.*

75. Lyse Comins and David Canning, "Surveys show silent hunger 'tsunami,'" *Pretoria News*, Sept. 1, 2008, p. E2.

76. "The FAO Price Index," Organization for Economic Cooperation and Development and the U.N. Food and Agriculture Organization, www.fao.org/docrep /010/ai466e/ai466e16.htm.

77. Jerome Taylor, "How the rising price of corn made Mexicans take to the street," *The Independent*, June 23, 2007, www.independent.co.uk/news/world/americas /how-the-rising-price-of-corn-made-mexicans-take-to-streets-454260.html.

78. "Trade and Global Markets," Progressive Policy Institute, June 4, 2008, www.ppionline.org/ppi_ci .cfm?contentid=254657&knlgAreaID=108&subsecid =900003.

79. "OECD-FAO Agricultural Outlook 2008-2017," Organization for Economic Cooperation and Development, Food and Agriculture Organization, 2008, pp. 37-38, www.oecd.org/dataoecd/54/15 /40715381.pdf.

80. *Ibid.*, pp. 37-38.

81. *Ibid.*, p. 53.

82. Bert Hoffman and Louis Kuijs, "Rebalancing China's Growth," in Debating China's Exchange Rate Policy (2008), Peterson Institute for International Economics, p. 110.

83. "Rank Order-Exports," *CIA World Factbook*, August 2008; https://www.cia.gov/library/publications/the-world-factbook/rankorder/2078rank.html.

84. Rowan Callick, "Communist Party hoping to kick off its 15 millenniums of fame," *The Australian*, Aug. 8, 2008, p. 8; Jim Yardley, "China sees inflation as its top fiscal priority," *The International Herald Tribune*, March 6, 2008, p. 5.

85. Morris Goldstein and Nicholas R. Lardy, "China's Exchange Rate policy: An Overview of Some Key Issues," in *Debating China's Exchange Rate Policy, op. cit.*, pp. 17-35, p. 44; Smick, *op. cit.*, p. 119.

86. Edwin M. Truman, "The Management of China's International Reserves: China and a Sovereign Wealth Fund Scoreboard," in *Debating China's Exchange Rate Policy, op. cit.*, pp. 182-183.

87. Jin Zhongxia, "The Open Economy Trilemma: An Alternative View from China's Perspective," in *Debating China's Exchange Rate Policy, op. cit.*, p. 102.

88. *Ibid.*, p. 105.

89. "Report on Foreign Portfolio Holdings of U.S. Securities, June 2007," *op. cit.*, p. 12.

90. Niall Ferguson, "Our Currency, Your Problem," *The New York Times*, March 13, 2005.

91. Setser, "Sovereign Wealth and Sovereign Power," *op. cit.*, p. 30.

92. "The Case for Exchange Rate Flexibility in Oil-Exporting Economies," Peterson Institute, November 2007, pp. 10-12.

93. Smick, *op. cit.*, p. 127.

94. Philippe Alfroy, "Divided Europe holds financial crisis summit," Agence France-Presse, Oct. 4, 2008.

95. Ambrose Evans-Pritchard, "Now Europe is staring into the abyss; Banks falling like dominoes have led to credit being almost impossible to find," *The Daily Telegraph*, London, Sept. 30, 2008.

96. Shinichi Terada, "LDP studying creation of sovereign wealth fund," *The Japan Times*, April 4, 2008.

97. *Ibid.*

98. "Japan needs to study risks before setting up government investment fund," The Associated Press, Feb. 22, 2008.

99. Ron Scherer, "Wall Street woes: why world's investors sit on sidelines," *The Christian Science Monitor*, Sept. 18, 2008.

100. Blaine Harden and Ariana Eunjung Cha, "Japan, China Locked In by Investments," *The Washington Post*, Sept. 20, 2008, p. D1.

101. Peter Wilson, "Europe wants US power shift," *The Australian*, Oct. 1, 2008, p. 36.

BIBLIOGRAPHY

Books

Goldstein, Morris, and Nicholas R. Lardy, eds., *Debating China's Exchange Rate Policy*, Peterson Institute for International Economics, 2005.
Two China experts present papers from a symposium on China's exchange rate policies and economic outlook.

Greenspan, Alan, *The Age of Turbulence: Adventures in a New World*, Penguin Press, 2008.
The former Federal Reserve chairman recounts a life at the center of economic policy.

Hughes, Kent H., *Building the Next American Century, The Past and Future of American Economic Competitiveness*, Woodrow Wilson Center Press, 2005.
A former Clinton administration official examines the global competitiveness challenges facing the United States.

Smick, M. David, *The World Is Curved*, Portfolio, 2008.
The publisher of *The International Economy* quarterly reviews the pluses and pitfalls of globalization with a warning about the future.

Soros, George, *The New Paradigm for Financial Markets: The Credit Crisis of 2008 and What it Means*, Public Affairs, 2008.
The billionaire investor, speculator and philanthropist describes where he thinks the global credit crisis may lead.

Zandi, Mark, *Financial Shock*, FT Press, 2008.
The founder and chief economist of Moody's economy.com dissects how the subprime mortgage scandal morphed into a global financial crisis.

Articles

Wilson, Peter, "Europe wants US Power shift," *The Australian*, Oct. 1, 2008, p. 36.
The global credit crisis demands a new world order for international finance, says European Union Trade Commissioner Peter Mandelson, with Europe and developing economies — such as China, Brazil and India — having greater regulatory power.

Reports and Studies

"The Dollar Issue," *The International Economy*, Spring 2008, www.international-economy.com/Spring 2008archive.htm.
Some 50 experts are surveyed on whether the dollar may be overtaken by the euro and the Chinese yuan as the leading global currency.

"Economic Report of the President 2008," Council of Economic Advisers, Feb. 11, 2008, www.whitehouse .gov/cea/pubs.html.
President Bush's economic advisers survey the economy.

"Mapping Global Capital Markets, Fourth Annual Report," McKinsey Global Institute, January 2008, www.mckinsey.com/mgi/publications/Mapping_Global /index.asp.
The McKinsey research organization charts worldwide capital flows.

"World Economic Outlook, Housing and the Business Cycle," The International Monetary Fund, April 2008, www.imf.org/external/pubs/ft/weo/2008 /01/index.htm.
The international lending agency assesses causes of the dollar's decline.

Chinn, Menzie, and Jeffrey Frankel, "The Euro May Over the Next 15 Years Surpass the Dollar as Leading International Currency," *International Finance*, February 2008, http://ksghome.harvard.edu/~jfrank el/EuroVs$-IFdebateFeb2008.pdf.
A professor of economics at the University of Wisconsin (Menzie) and a Harvard professor of capital formation and growth (Frankel) argue that the dollar may be eclipsed as the world's anchor currency.

Meissner, Christopher M., and Nienke Oomes, "Why do Countries Peg the Way They Peg? The Determinants of Anchor Currency Choice," *IMF Working Paper*, May 2008, Stanford Law School, http://papers.ssrn.com/sol3/papers.cfm?abstract_id= 1154294.
Two international economists examine various foreign exchange policies used by the world's nations. Meissner is at the University of California, Davis, and Oomes is resident representative in Armenia for the International Monetary Fund.

Posen, Adam S., "It's Not Just About the Money," Peterson Institute for International Economics, 2008, http://petersoninstitute.org/publications/papers/posen 0408.pdf.
The Peterson Institute's deputy director argues that the dollar can draw on the political strength and broad economic leadership of the United States.

Setser, Brad W., "Sovereign Wealth and Sovereign Power," Council on Foreign Relations, September 2008, www.cfr.org/publication/17074.
A former Treasury official now at the Council on Foreign Relations examines the political risks of U.S. foreign indebtedness.

For More Information

American Enterprise Institute, 1150 17th St., N.W., Washington, DC 20036; (202) 862-5800; www.aei.org. A research center devoted to the education and study of government, politics, economics and social welfare issues.

Bank for International Settlements, Centralbahnplatz 2, CH-4002 Basel, Switzerland; (41) 61 280 8080; www.bis.org. Serves as a bank for other banks and works to create global financial cooperation.

Brookings Institution, 1775 Massachusetts Ave., N.W., Washington, DC 20036; (202) 797-6000; www.brookings.edu. A nonpartisan organization dedicated to public policy research.

Competitiveness Institute, Imagina Building, Diagonal Av.177 1st floor, 08018 Barcelona, Spain; (34) 93 309 4834; www.competitiveness.org. An international network of policy makers and leaders working to increase competition in various sectors around the globe.

Economic Report of the President, www.gpoaccess.gov /eop/. Written by the chairman of the president's Council of Economic Advisors, describes the current economic status and progress of the United States.

Federal Reserve Bank of New York, 33 Liberty St., New York, NY 10045; (212) 720-5000; www.ny.frb.org. Helps create financial stability and carry out monetary policy. The New York Fed's president is the only regional Federal Reserve Bank president with a permanent vote on the Federal Open Market Committee, which sets monetary policy.

Federal Reserve Board of Governors, 20th St. and Constitution Ave., N.W., Washington, DC 20551; (202) 452-3000; www.federalreserve.gov. Seven-member panel nominated by the president that sets U.S. monetary policy.

International Monetary Fund, 700 19th St., N.W., Washington, DC 20431; (202) 623-7000; www.imf.org. Monitors economic stability and provides financial and technical assistance to ailing economies.

Peter G. Peterson Institute, 1750 Massachusetts Ave., N.W., Washington, DC 20036-1903; (202) 328-9000; www.iie.com. A nonprofit, nonpartisan think tank that studies international economic policy.

Progressive Policy Institute, 600 Pennsylvania Ave., S.E., Suite 400, Washington, DC 20003; (202) 547-0001; www.ppionline.org. A liberal research and education center.

Tax Policy Center, www.taxpolicycenter.org. A joint project of the Urban Institute and Brookings Institution that provides information and analysis on tax policies.

Woodrow Wilson International Center for Scholars, 1300 Pennsylvania Ave., N.W., Washington, DC 20004-3027; (202) 691-4000; www.wilsoncenter.org. Provides research and a forum for discussions on international affairs.

Tientip Subhanij

Professor, Chulalongkorn University, Thailand

America's leadership role at risk

"It would be too naive to say that the falling dollar can never hurt the U.S. In the long run, a currency reflects economic fundamentals, and the fall of the dollar may weaken America's status as the global leader."

Bangkok Post, May 2008

Valerie Hermann

CEO, Yves Saint Laurent

Dollar hurting foreign exporters

"I have never been as careful as I am now to look at the entry-level price of a product. Because I know that currently in the U.S. the market is driven by that, and, to a greater extent, by this currency problem."

Los Angeles Times, November 2007

Julian Jessop

Chief International Economist, Capital Economics, London

More problems may come

"The . . . U.S.'s huge current account deficit leaves the dollar vulnerable to all sorts of scare stories."

Guardian Unlimited (England), November 2006

Peer Steinbrück

Finance Minister, Germany

Sharing the spotlight

"It does not mean that the dollar will lose its function as a reserve currency, but it will be supplemented by the yen, the euro — which is already the second-biggest reserve currency — and also by the yuan. Over the next 10 years, we will be dealing with four big, important currencies."

Reuters, September 2008

Alan Waddell

COO, Visit USA, London

Cheap for Europeans

"You already got high-quality holidays and friendliness, and now you even got the good prices. It means we can come."

The New York Times, December 2007

Christine Lagarde

Economy Minister, France

Oil prices linked to dollar exchange

"The strengthening of the dollar I find satisfying. However, there is a cause/effect link between the stability of financial markets, the euro-dollar exchange and increasing prices of oil products."

Reuters, June 2008

Nicolas Sarkozy

President, France

Not our problem

"The (Chinese) yuan is already everyone's problem. The dollar cannot remain solely the problem of others. If we're not careful, monetary disarray could morph into economic war. We would all be its victims."

USA Today, November 2007

Shiekh Ahmed bin Mohammed Al Kalifa

Finance Minister, Bahrain

Continuing to peg

"We are fully committed to keeping the dollar peg. It has served us. Our exchange rate hasn't changed since 1980. We are very happy with it. And we maintain the dollar peg, and our monetary policy is going to continue, no change."

CNN.com, February 2008

José Manuel Barroso

President, European Commission

Falling dollar leads to inflation

"I believe it is important we show at the European level that we are committed to fighting inflation. We would like to see a more balanced relationship between the dollar and other major currencies, including the euro."

Reuters, July 2008

ONE DOLLAR

caglecartoons.com/espanol

Ares/Caglecartoons.com

16

China in Africa

Karen Foerstel

A Chinese supervisor (right) oversees Africans working on a Chinese-funded road project in Addis Ababa, Ethiopia, in April 2007. Sino-African trade has increased more than sixfold in recent years, bringing Chinese investment and cheap consumer goods to the continent but generating fears China could become Africa's newest colonizer.

Billboards displaying elephants, lions and giraffes roaming African savannas hung from every street corner. Woodcarvings of antelopes and other safari animals lined the streets of the main shopping district. And everywhere posters proclaimed, "Africa, the Land of Myth and Miracles." [1]

The three-day Forum on China-Africa Cooperation in Beijing in November 2006 ranked among China's biggest extravaganzas in years, with 43 of Africa's 53 heads of state attending the meeting to discuss how the two regions could expand economic, political and social ties. [2]

No expense — or detail — was spared. African drummers and Chinese acrobats greeted delegates as they entered the Great Hall of the People for the opening ceremonies. A 30-foot image of the Egyptian Sphinx looked down on passersby in downtown Beijing. Even the grass around the airport and conference venues was touched up with green paint. [3]

But China was offering its visitors more than just a good time. President Hu Jintao pledged to double China's assistance to Africa by 2009, an economic package that also included:

- Preferential loans and credits to Africa totaling $5 billion;
- A promise to increase two-way trade to more than $100 billion by 2010;
- A $5 billion development fund to encourage Chinese companies to invest in Africa;
- Cancellation of debts owed to China from the least-developed African countries;
- Doubling exports to China from Africa's least developed countries, which receive zero-tariff treatment, and

From *CQ Researcher,*
January 1, 2008.

China Is Making Oil Deals Throughout Africa

China is negotiating oil deals with 13 of the 19 African countries with proven oil reserves. Africa's total reserves are estimated at 103 billion barrels, or about the same as Kuwait.

African Countries with Oil Reserves

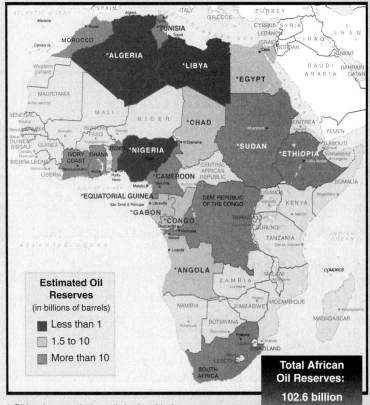

Estimated Oil Reserves
(in billions of barrels)

- Less than 1
- 1.5 to 10
- More than 10

Total African Oil Reserves: 102.6 billion

* China is negotiating oil deals with the government.

Source: Cindy Hurst, "China's Oil Rush in Africa," Energy Security, http://leav-www.army.mil/fmso/ documents/chinainafrica.pdf

- Construction of 30 hospitals, 30 malaria treatment centers and 100 schools in rural Africa. [4]

Apart from the promised government aid, Chinese companies and African governments and firms signed $1.9 billion in business agreements. [5]

"China is opening itself up to Africa, coming with assistance," said Zimbabwe's President Robert Mugabe. "We have nothing to lose but our imperialist chains." [6]

Many African leaders feel the same. After a history of often brutal and rapacious colonization and failed economic policies imposed upon them by the West, African nations are increasingly turning East. China presents itself as a partner that has never colonized Africa nor enslaved any African. And it emphasizes the fact that it is a developing country, so it understands the many issues Africa's developing nations face.

Since the Beijing forum, China-Africa trade has increased almost 30 percent, and Chinese diplomats have held nearly nonstop meetings with African leaders. [7] In early 2007, Foreign Minister Li Zhaoxing took a seven-nation tour across Africa to discuss public health, education, agribusiness and other areas of economic cooperation. [8] A month later, President Hu opened a Chinese-built hospital in Cameroon, a Chinese-funded malaria treatment center in Liberia and a Chinese-language after-school program in Namibia. [9] In September, representatives from 48 African countries met with their Chinese counterparts at U.N. headquarters in New York — the first such meeting of its kind between Africans and the Chinese. [10]

"African nations never had this level of attention before," says Chris Alden, head of the China in Africa program at the South African Institute of International Affairs and author of a new book, *China in Africa.* "African leaders have often been treated by the West as tin-pot dictators. Now they are being treated by China with a level of respect that all leaders crave."

And the attention is paying off — for both sides. Chinese firms have won contracts worth more than $30 billion for infrastructure projects in Africa, and nearly 800 Chinese companies now operate in Africa. [11] In 2005, Africa's economy grew a record 5.2 percent, which many credit at least in part to China's growing engagement. [12]

"If these trends continue, China will be the dominant economic trader across the continent," says Alden.

But many wonder whether China — while certainly helping Africa develop — is also becoming the continent's newest colonizer, extracting its vast natural resources, supporting corrupt governments for financial gain and making the African economy dependent on Chinese aid. Chinese exports — often surplus products that can be sold well below cost — are flooding African markets and putting many local manufacturers and companies out of business. Likewise, thousands of Chinese workers are streaming into Africa to build roads, hospitals and other infrastructure, displacing the African labor force. By some estimates, from 750,000 to 1 million Chinese now live and work in Africa. [13]

"The relationship between China and Africa does resemble the standard European relationship — you pay as little as you can for the resources you need," says Patrick Smith, editor and publisher of *Africa Confidential*, a London-based publication focusing on African issues and events. "There is a real risk of them becoming like Western colonizers."

While African leaders are embracing Chinese products and aid, average Africans increasingly are opposing the growing presence of China in their back yard. During the 2006 presidential election in Zambia, opposition candidate Michael Sata made China — and its growing control over the country's copper mines — a major platform of his campaign.

"Zambia is becoming a province — no, a district — of China," Sata said during his campaign. [14]

He threatened to cut diplomatic ties with China and instead support the Chinese breakaway state of Taiwan and its claim to regain its seat in the United Nations. Ultimately, Sata lost the election, garnering 28 percent of the vote. But his opposition Patriotic Front party won key seats in Zambia's mining regions. [15]

Anti-Chinese sentiment in Zambia grew in 2005 after 46 workers died in an explosion at a Chinese-owned copper mine. The blast was blamed on poor safety conditions. [16]

In addition to copper, timber, minerals and oil are all in high demand by China's rapidly growing economy. And as the Middle East becomes increasingly unstable, China and the West both are looking to Africa for oil supplies. Now the world's second-largest oil consumer behind the United States, China has negotiated oil deals in more than a dozen African nations and buys nearly a third of its oil from Africa — an amount likely to grow quickly. [17]

China's Trade with Africa Skyrockets

Sino-African trade jumped nearly sixfold since the establishment of the Forum on China-Africa Cooperation in 2000. The trade includes cheap manufactured goods from China and oil, commodities and raw materials from Africa.

Value of China-Africa Trade, 1991-2005*
(in $ billions)

\$5.6 billion — 1999
\$32.2 billion — 2005

* Through October 2005

Sources: International Monetary Fund, *Direction of Trade Statistics, Yearbook 2004*; and People's Republic of China, Ministry of Commerce

"The single, biggest future worry [for the West] is access to petroleum resources," says Stephen Chan, a professor of international relations at the University of London's School of Oriental and African Studies. "China is buying [oil-producing] acreage and putting a lot of sweeteners in the deals. . . . The real danger is about 20 years up the line. You will have intense competition."

China's growing thirst for oil has led it to deal with resource-rich nations that have been ostracized by the West for human-rights abuses. Sudan, for instance, where more than 200,000 people have died in fighting in the Darfur region since 2003, is one of China's biggest oil suppliers. [18] China repeatedly has blocked efforts by the West to impose sanctions against Sudan and until recently was reluctant even to pressure the Sudanese government to curb the fighting.

Oil-Rich Countries Get China's Transport Help

Energy-hungry China is giving low-interest loans to oil-rich sub-Saharan countries to help overhaul aging roads and rail lines. Major projects funded in 2006 included:

- **$1 billion to repair Nigerian rail lines and supply new equipment;**

- **Rebuilding nearly half of Angola's 754 roads;**

- **$500 million to overhaul Angola's railways and**

- **An offer of $1.5 billion to upgrade other parts of Angola's transportation network.**

Source: Raphael Kaplinsky, *et al.,* "The Impact of China on Sub Saharan Africa," Institute of Development Studies, April 2006

EU wants to remain a privileged partner and make the most of its relations with Africa, it must be willing to reinforce, and in some areas reinvent, the current relationship — institutionally, politically and culturally. . . . [I]t is now time to move on from a strategy for Africa towards **a political partnership *with* Africa**." [20] As China's influence continues to grow across the African continent, here are some of the questions analysts are beginning to ask:

Is China benefiting Africa's economy?

While the $70-billion U.S. trade with Africa overshadows China's $55.5 billion total, business between China and Africa is growing at a much faster pace. [21] Sino-African trade more than quintupled between 1999 and 2004 — rising from roughly $5.6 billion to $29.5 billion — while U.S.-African trade doubled to $58.9 billion during that same period. [22]

Beijing, meanwhile, has overtaken the World Bank in lending to Africa. In 2005, for instance, China committed $8 billion in loans to Nigeria, Angola and Mozambique while the World Bank distributed just $2.3 billion throughout the continent. [23]

China's increasing investments in Africa's oil fields, roads and telephone networks appear to have helped the currency of many African nations to rise in value. According to the Standard Bank Group, the Kenyan shilling, Nigerian naira, Zambian kwacha, Angolan kwanza and Ghanaian cedi have all gained strength this year. [24]

At the same time, China's growing exports to Africa have inundated the continent with low-cost consumer goods. Televisions, washing machines and cell phones are now available to many Africans who previously couldn't afford such items. But critics say the influx of cheap goods is forcing many African retailers and manufacturers out of business.

"A large proportion of our population is very poor, so they have to buy the cheapest products available. So, yes, there is a positive impact," says Brian Brink, executive director of the South African Textile Federation. "But if that continues, there won't be anyone with jobs and

The West has condemned China's failure to demand that African nations comply with democratic, environmental or human-rights standards before receiving financial aid. Without such demands, the West says, loans and investments will benefit despotic regimes but do little for average Africans.

"There can be no sustainable development without good governance. Development is much more than just financial aid," says Amadeu Altafaj, a spokesman for the European Commission. "There must be links between security and development, social issues and development, the environment and development. China is not doing that" in its dealings in Africa.

But even as the West criticizes China's policy of non-interference, it is taking notice of China's rapid success in Africa and beginning to play catch-up. In an obvious effort to counterbalance Beijing's spectacular Forum on China-Africa Cooperation, the European Union (EU) this past December hosted the EU-Africa Summit, which brought leaders from 53 African nations to Lisbon, Portugal, to discuss how to strengthen and expand political and strategic ties with Europe. [19] Although the EU says the summit was not a reaction to China's influence in Africa, the EU's own summary paper about the summit opens by describing China's growing trade and economic power in Africa:

"China . . . has rapidly emerged as Africa's third most important trade partner [behind the United States and the European Union] with total trade amounting to about 43 billion [about $32 billion] in 2006. . . . If the

money in their pockets. [Chinese goods are] destroying a lot more jobs" than they are creating.

As a result, tensions between African and Chinese merchants are on the rise. Fist fights and even riots have been reported in street markets across the continent, according to Brink and Chan. And migrant Chinese workers create additional tensions among average Africans by forming isolated communities across the continent.

"The Chinese tend to live in enclaves and don't contribute to the local economies where they're living," says Elizabeth Economy, director of Asian studies at the influential Council on Foreign Relations, a New York-based think tank. "If you export labor, people expect [them] to buy things [on the local market]. But the Chinese are very self-sufficient. It doesn't breed a sense that it's benefiting the local people."

And although Sino-African trade is growing rapidly, most African nations have a mounting trade deficit with China. [25] Many also worry that China's massive loans to African nations will plunge the continent deeper into debt. In 2006, the EU's European Investment Bank and the International Monetary Fund (IMF) warned that China's emergence as a major creditor was creating a wave of new debt for African countries, and the U.S. Treasury Department labeled China a "rogue creditor" practicing "opportunistic lending." [26]

"Africa sells raw materials to China, and China sells manufactured products to Africa. This is a dangerous equation that reproduces Africa's old relationship with colonial powers," said Moeletsi Mbeki, deputy chairman of the South African Institute of International Affairs. "The equation is not sustainable for a number of reasons. First, Africa needs to preserve its natural resources to use in the future for its own industrialisation. Secondly, China's export strategy is contributing to the de-industrialisation of some middle-income countries." [27]

Chinese officials tried to allay those concerns in May 2007, when Shanghai hosted the annual meeting of the African Development Bank. "We are truly sincere in helping Africa speed up economic and social development for the benefit of the African people and its nations," said Chinese Premier Wen Jiabao. [28] China then pledged an additional $20 billion for African infrastructure development over the next three years. [29]

China had already invested billions in Africa's infrastructure. In Angola — desperate to rebuild after a 27-year civil war — China International Fund Ltd., a Hong Kong

Chinese soldiers and engineers train in China before shipping out to Darfur in western Sudan. China recently agreed to send engineers, medics and transportation specialists to join U.N. peacekeepers in the war-torn region, partly to rebut Western criticism that China enables genocidal atrocities in Darfur by trading arms to the Sudanese government for oil. China has more than 1,200 peacekeepers building infrastructure and monitoring troubled villages in Africa.

construction company, funded a $300 million project to repair the heavily damaged Benguela Railroad. In Sierra Leone, also recovering after years of conflict, China has paid for the construction and repair of government buildings, bridges, hydroelectrical facilities, Sierra Leone University and the national football stadium. [30]

Western nations either have been reluctant to invest in these war-torn countries or demand preconditions many African nations are unwilling or unable to meet. "The Chinese are doing more than the G-8 to make poverty history," said Sahr Johnny, Sierra Leone's ambassador to Beijing, referring to the world's eight largest economies. "If a G-8 country had wanted to rebuild the stadium, we would still be holding meetings. The Chinese just come and do it. They don't hold meetings about environmental impact assessment, human rights, bad governance and good governance." [31]

Nicole Lee, director of TransAfrica, a Washington D.C., organization that promotes human-rights policies that benefit Africans and those of African descent, says China gives African leaders more power to decide what is best for their countries. "They can make their own choices and don't have to take loans from the U.S. with all these conditions and attachments," Lee says. "There

Voracious China Threatens the Environment

African forests are most at risk.

While China is focusing largely on Africa's oil, it is also reaching deeply into Africa's forests. China imports half of all the tropical trees being logged around the world, making it the world's largest importer of tropical timber. In the past 10 years, China's wood imports have jumped more than 400 percent — much of it harvested under conditions outlawed by local and regional laws from forests around the globe. [1]

Nearly half — 46 per cent — of Gabon's forest exports go to China, making it Gabon's largest timber trading partner. [2] Although Gabonese law requires timber to be processed before exportation — increasing its export value — China, with its abundance of cheap home-grown labor, wants only unprocessed logs. As a result, China encourages "flagrant disregard for the law," according to the Web site of GlobalTimber.org.uk, which compiles data and studies on the international trade of wood products. According to the group, 80 percent of Gabon's timber exports to China are illegal.

China's timber imports from other African nations are just as shady, according to the group. Eighty percent of wood exports from Cameroon to China are illegal, as are 90 percent of the wood exports from Equatorial Guinea and Congo, the group says. [3]

Ironically, China's growing demand for wood stems from recent policies it has enacted to protect its own forests. After deadly floods along the Yangtze River in 1998, the Chinese government instituted environmental protections aimed at preventing future disasters, including new restrictions on timber harvesting and reforestation projects to combat erosion. [4] While those strategies may be helping to protect China's forests, they are prompting China to look elsewhere for timber.

China's demand for oil also has caused environmental degradation in Africa's forests. Gabon recently forced China's Sinopec oil company to stop exploring for oil in a national forest after the company was found to be polluting, dynamiting and carving roads through the forest. [5]

African governments often are reluctant to prosecute China for its environmental activities because they "want the investments," says Elizabeth Economy, director of Asia studies at the New York-based Council on Foreign Relations.

But with pressure mounting from environmentalists, Beijing last August issued new guidelines to encourage Chinese logging companies working overseas to carry out their operations in a sustainable manner. [6] In November, China and Brazil announced they would give Africa free

may be some bad impacts from China, but African countries are being treated as partners, not subjects."

Indeed, she notes, Western preconditions on aid do not guarantee benefits to Africans. Often, those conditions — such as requiring aid recipients to slash public-sector work or privatize businesses — are designed only to "ensure that multinational corporations are getting rich off the privatization of Africa," says Lee. "But they are not always good for the lower or middle classes."

The Council on Foreign Relations' Economy says Africans have "a lot of mixed feelings" about China. "Certain people benefit, some don't. But the more China engages, the more the picture is mixed."

Do China's policies threaten human rights in Africa?

China's drive for oil and natural resources has prompted

it to forge close relationships with many governments that have been condemned by the West for corruption and human-rights abuses.

In 2003, China gave Angola a $2 billion loan in exchange for 10,000 barrels of oil a day, with no strings attached. [32] That allowed Angola to avoid good-governance conditions demanded by the IMF before it would provide aid. Shortly after the loan was granted, Transparency International ranked Angola as one of the world's most corrupt nations. [33]

In Sudan — where the government is accused of condoning years of wholesale rape, murder and pillaging by Arab *mujahadeen* in the Darfur region — China has invested billions in the oil sector, imports 60 percent of Sudan's oil and is Sudan's largest source of weapons. [34]

In May 2007, the United States imposed economic

satellite imaging of the continent to help it respond to threats from deforestation, desertification and drought. [7]

And in June, B&Q — one of China's largest home-improvement retail chains — announced it would guarantee that timber products in all its 60 stores come from legal sources. Moreover, the company pledged that within three years all its product lines will come from certified, ecologically responsible forestry operations. The move won high praise from the environmental group Greenpeace. [8]

But there is still concern that China will continue to put its need for resources above its concern for habitat protection, and that African leaders — desperate for Chinese investments — will ignore environmental regulations.

In October, environmental activists in Gabon expressed outrage over a deal they say could destroy one of the most beautiful natural waterfalls in central Africa. The watchdog organization Environment Gabon said the deal between Gabon and a Chinese iron mining consortium would exempt from taxes for 25 years the Belinga iron ore mining project — run by a predominantly Chinese company — and free it from responsibility for any "environmental consequences." [9]

The project is set to be powered by a hydroelectric dam built at the spectacular Kongou Falls. No environmental-impact studies have been conducted — as required by Gabonese law — but construction has already begun, authorized by Gabon's Ministry of Mines. [10]

The Chinese firm reportedly is ready to conduct environmental assessments if authorities request it. But Gabonese officials say the socio-economic benefits of the project outweigh environmental concerns.

"Belinga just reveals the tensions born of overlapping interests between the necessary development of the country and protecting the environment, as well as Chinese penetration into Africa," said a government official. [11]

---

[1] Tamara Stark and Sze Pang Cheung, "Sharing the Blame: Global Consumption and China's Role in Ancient Forest Destruction," Greenpeace, March 28, 2006, p. 1.

[2] Michelle Chan-Fishel, "Environmental Impact: More of the Same?," *African Perspectives of China in Africa*, p. 146.

[3] GlobalTimber.org.uk.

[4] Alex Kirby, "Plan to tame Yangtze floods," BBC News Online, Oct. 12, 2001.

[5] Ian Taylor, "China's environmental footprint in Africa," chinadialogue, Feb. 2, 2007.

[6] "China issues rules on overseas logging by its companies," Associated Press Worldstream, Aug. 29, 2007.

[7] "China, Brazil give Africa free satellite land images," Agence France-Presse, Nov. 28, 2007.

[8] "Greenpeace applauds B&Q's initiative to clean up timber trade in China," Greenpeace press release, June 12, 2007.

[9] Francesco Fontemaggi, "Chinese iron mine project in Gabon pits greens against developers," Agence France-Presse, Oct. 16, 2007.

[10] *Ibid.*

[11] *Ibid.*

sanctions against Sudan, barring 30 companies controlled by the Sudanese government from using the U.S. banking system. The sanctions also specifically prohibited three individuals — including Sudan's minister for humanitarian affairs — from doing business with U.S. companies or individuals. [35]

Until recently, China had been reluctant to leverage its billions in investments to demand that the Sudanese government halt the murder and destruction in Darfur. Instead, China had followed a policy of "non interference" in countries where it does business, refusing to become involved in internal conflicts and often ignoring human-rights abuses, corruption or other social problems.

China respects the sovereignty of African nations to "independently resolve African problems," according to the declaration adopted by China and 48 African nations during the 2006 Beijing forum. [36]

"Business is business. We try to separate politics from business," Chinese Deputy Foreign Minister Zhou Wenzhong said in 2004, when asked about his government's cooperation with Sudan. "Secondly, I think the internal situation in the Sudan is an internal affair, and we are not in a position to impose upon them." [37]

That attitude rankles human-rights groups. Amnesty International says the principle of non-interference in internal affairs of another country "must not become an excuse to remain silent when such states violate the human rights of their people. . . . Economic profits for China should not be built on the killings and displacement of Africans." [38]

Besides buying Africa's natural resources without demanding reforms, China provided one-tenth of the

Senegalese shop assistants in Dakar wait for clients under the watchful eye of the Chinese owner's sister — a visible sign of China's deep penetration into Africa's economies. Up to 800 Chinese companies operate in Africa — buying oil and raw materials, building infrastructure and helping China become a player in the continent's telecommunications and textile industries.

arms bought in Africa between 1996 and 2003. [39] In 2004, China sold arms to Zimbabwe, ignoring a U.S. and EU arms embargo imposed because of human-rights abuses. In Zimbabwe, where acute food and commodities shortages threaten social collapse and unemployment has reached 80 percent, China sold $200 million worth of military aircraft and vehicles. [40] Chinese businesses also reportedly designed Mugabe's 25-room mansion and provided radio-jamming equipment to block anti-government broadcasts. [41]

In the past year, however, China has begun to distance itself from Mugabe and other governments condemned by the West. Li Guijin, China's special envoy for Africa, announced last September that Beijing had halted development aid to Zimbabwe and would only provide humanitarian assistance. "China in the past provided substantial development assistance, but owing to the dramatic currency revaluations and rapid deterioration of economic conditions, the economic outcomes of these projects have not been so good." [42]

Meanwhile, after years of blocking U.N. efforts to impose sanctions on Sudan, China now is joining Western forces in peacekeeping missions. In 2007, China sent hundreds of engineers, medics and transport specialists to join U.N. forces sent in to keep peace in Sudan until 2011. It is China's longest peacekeeping

mission to date. Across Africa, China now has more than 1,200 peacekeepers building infrastructure and monitoring troubled villages. [43]

"China's policy of non-interference is coming apart at the seams," says Smith of *Africa Confidential*, because it is finding that doing business with corrupt, unstable governments is often less than profitable. Continued fighting in Sudan threatens oil production, and China is losing money on its investments in Zimbabwe, he says.

And, as China strives to become a global superpower, it apparently is beginning to pay more attention to Western criticism. "China wants to be seen as a serious, international player," Smith says.

China contends that — as a developing nation that has overcome imperialism — it has a sincere interest in helping Africans also succeed and thrive. In fact, China considers "economic rights" and "rights of subsistence" as the most important human rights for citizens in developing nations, more important than the personal, individual rights promoted by the West. [44]

China sent its first medical team to Algeria in 1963 and has since dispatched more than 15,000 medical professionals to 47 African countries. In addition, China has sent more than 500 teachers to Africa and trained more than 1,000 Africans in various professional skills. Each year, China provides more than 1,500 scholarships for African students. [45]

Chinese officials and others cite the hypocrisy they see in Western nations that criticize China for supporting tyrants in Africa while they themselves do business with despots elsewhere. "The United States is in Saudi Arabia," says Economy of the Council on Foreign Relations. "Chevron is in Burma. I'm certainly not an apologist for China, but before we call the kettle black we have to be very, very careful."

Are China and the West headed for a showdown over Africa's natural resources?

Western countries buy much more of Africa's oil than China does. China bought only 9 percent of Africa's petroleum exports in 2006, while the United States took 33 percent and Europe 36 percent. [46]

But both China and the West are growing increasingly dependent on African oil as oil-rich Middle Eastern nations become less stable. China already imports more oil from Angola than it does from Saudi Arabia, and the United States has nearly doubled its oil imports from

Africa since 2002. [47] In 2006, Africa provided more than 15 per cent of U.S. oil imports. Experts say recent explorations in the Gulf of Guinea region show potential reserves that could supply 25-35 per cent of U.S. imports within the next decade. [48]

As China's economy expands, its future oil needs are expected to have consequences for the West on several levels. "Chinese demand is driving up commodity prices," says Alden at the South African Institute of International Affairs. "It's making the cost of energy more expensive for the West."

Ian Taylor, a professor of international relations at Scotland's University of St. Andrews, said there might be another concern for the West. "Chinese oil diplomacy in Africa has two main goals: in the short-term, secure oil supplies to help feed growing domestic demand back in China; and in the long-term position China as a global player in the international oil market," Taylor wrote. "The recent upsurge in Chinese oil diplomacy may be linked to Chinese strategists at the national level who may well first and foremost be paying attention to the long-term goal of being in charge of oil resources at their source in a strategy to manipulate future prices." [49]

Some say China's strategy to bypass international market pricing by controlling products at the source does not stop at oil but includes nearly every natural resource Africa has to offer. "Thus the price that China pays for specific commodities will be negotiated at source with recipient governments rather than the price determined by the 'market,' " charges a report conducted by the Centre for Chinese Studies at Stellenbosch University in South Africa. "This is the underlying factor of China's strategic engagement of African commodity- and energy-endowed economies." [50]

West Is Still Africa's Biggest Trade Partner

Sub-Saharan Africa's trade with China — the value of both exports and imports — has grown dramatically since 2000, but its trade with industrialized countries is still far bigger. Africa's trade with China reached nearly $50 billion in 2006, or about one-seventh of its trade with the West.

Sub-Saharan Africa's Trade with China and the Industrialized Countries, 1980-2006

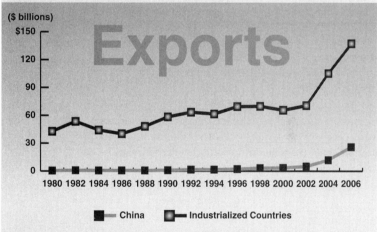

Source: Raphael Kaplinsky, *et al.*, "The Impact of China on Sub Saharan Africa," Institute of Development Studies, www.uk.cn/uploadfiles/2006428172021581 .doc

Others, however, say China is not deliberately trying to push Western companies out of Africa's oil market but has simply made the most of the opportunities available to it to meet its energy needs.

"There is a race for these resources," says Helmut Reisen, coordinator of the Finance for Development Unit at the Organization for Economic Cooperation and Development in Paris. But he says China has monopolized

CHRONOLOGY

1400s–1900s *Chinese explorers make first contact with Africa. Europeans expand across Africa, enslaving, colonizing and exploiting natural resources.*

1405-1423 Chinese Admiral Zheng He reaches the east coast of Africa.

1515 Portugal ships the first slaves from Africa to colonies in the Americas.

1884-1885 German Chancellor Otto von Bismarck convenes major Western powers to negotiate colonial control of Africa.

1914 Europeans finalize plan to divide Africa among themselves into 50 countries. Great Britain colonizes much of eastern and southern Africa, while France takes much of West Africa, and Portugal takes Mozambique and Angola.

1950s–1960s *African nations begin fighting for — and gaining — independence. China establishes diplomatic relations with more than a dozen African nations by 1969.*

1955 Africa-Asia summit in Bandung, Indonesia, promotes economic and cultural cooperation and opposes "colonialism in all of its manifestations."

1956 China establishes diplomatic relations with Egypt, the first official Sino-African ties.

1959 China establishes diplomatic relations with Sudan; then with eight more African countries, including Uganda, Congo, Kenya and Somalia.

1963-1964 Chinese Prime Minister Zhou Enlai makes a 10-country tour across Africa offering China's support for the continent's growing independence.

1980s–1990s *After turning inward following Mao Zedong's death in 1976, China reemerges and rapidly expands its outreach to Africa.*

1980 After years of support from China during its struggle for independence, Zimbabwe and China establish diplomatic relations on the same day Zimbabwe gains its independence.

1983 China establishes diplomatic ties with Angola.

1996 Chinese President Jiang Zemin tours six African nations, promising financial aid "without political strings."

1998 China begins a 957-mile-long pipeline in Sudan, the largest foreign oil project in China's history.

2000s *China invests billions in Africa, securing its hold across the continent.*

2000 Forum on China-Africa Cooperation (FOCAC) is founded, sparking increased trade between the two regions.

2003 FOCAC holds its second ministerial meeting in Ethiopia, during which China cancels $1.27 billion in African debt and vows to increase overall Sino-African trade to $28 billion by 2006. . . . China gives Angola $2 billion in exchange for 10,000 barrels of oil a day, allowing Angola to avoid IMF good-governance requirements.

2004 Trade between China and Africa reaches $29.5 billion. . . . China becomes second-largest consumer of oil, behind United States. . . . China sells Zimbabwe $200 million in arms, despite U.S., EU embargos.

2005 Nigeria signs $800-million deal to supply 30,000 barrels of crude oil per day to China.

2006 Forty-eight African nations attend FOCAC's Third Ministerial Meeting in Beijing, where Chinese President Hu Jintao announces $5 billion in preferential loans and credits to Africa and pledges to increase Sino-Chinese trade to $100 billion by 2010.

2007 China hosts African Development Bank's annual meeting in Shanghai, promising $20 billion for infrastructure development in Africa over the next three years. . . . European Union holds an EU-Africa Summit in Lisbon, Portugal, amid controversy over the attendance of Zimbabwean President Robert Mugabe, condemned by the West as a dictator and suppressor of human rights.

African oil markets "only where the West deliberately leaves an empty space. Zimbabwe, Sudan, Angola — that's exactly where the Chinese have jumped in."

The vast economic resources of China's state-controlled oil companies have enabled China to attach billions in development aid to oil contracts and out-bid international companies for rights to Africa's petroleum reserves. For example, in 2004, as India was preparing to close a $620 million deal to buy shares in an oil field in Angola, China at the last minute offered an additional $2 billion in aid for various projects in Angola. Not surprisingly, China got the contract. [51]

"The Chinese don't just go after the extractive resources," says Alden. "They produce a whole package. They build roads, hospitals and other things."

BP and ExxonMobil refused to comment for this report on China's growing hold on African oil. But during a September 2007 speech before the German Council for Foreign Policy, BP's regional president for Asia, Gary Dirks, said the West should not be concerned.

"Some rather simplistically see China as the root cause of rising oil prices. Others doubt the adequacy of the world's energy resources to meet the growing Chinese demand," Dirks said. "My own more narrow perspective is that the world has enough energy resources to meet growing energy demand for the foreseeable future, including from China, provided adequate investment is made in a timely manner." [52]

EU spokesman Altafaj agrees. "Most African countries are smart enough to diversify portfolios. We don't fear a monopoly."

But others say there is evidence the West is more than just concerned about China's oil investments in Africa. The United States, they charge, is in fact beginning to use its military to maintain control over Africa's oil. In October 2007, the United States announced creation of AFRICOM, a new military headquarters devoted solely to Africa. It will be located near the Gulf of Guinea — home to one of the largest untapped oil reserves in the world. [53]

By some estimates, by 2010 the gulf will contribute at least one out of every five new barrels of oil used on the global market. [54] The oil fields are scattered off the coast of southwest Africa in territorial waters claimed by Nigeria, Angola, Gabon, Equatorial Guinea and others.

AFRICOM's Web site denies that the new military force has anything to do with oil or China. Its homepage includes the question: "Is this an effort by the

A Chadian soldier mans a Chinese-made armored vehicle in April 2006 that reportedly was seized from rebel forces. Chad has accused neighboring Sudan — which gets most of its arms from China — of forming a new rebel army to attack Chad. China provided one-tenth of all arms bought in Africa between 1996 and 2003.

United States to gain access to natural resources (for example, petroleum)? Is this in response to Chinese activities in Africa?" AFRICOM's reply: "No. Africa is growing in military, strategic and economic importance in global affairs. We are seeking more effective ways to bolster security on the continent, to prevent and respond to humanitarian crises, to improve cooperative efforts with African nations to stem transnational terrorism, and to sustain enduring efforts that contribute to African unity." [55]

But many are skeptical. "I think it has everything to do with China and oil," says TransAfrica's Lee. "China has between 10 to 20 oil platforms off the coast. That is an absolute threat to our own energy interests in the Gulf of Guinea. The United States does not want to give up its hold there."

U.S. Rep. Marcy Kaptur, a Democrat from Ohio, agrees. "The hot, new area, of course, for exploration is Africa, and I imagine that may be a reason President Bush this week announced a new U.S-Africa Command," Kaptur told House colleagues last February. "China is interested in Africa's natural resources, including oil. And now the Bush administration is trying to play catch-up. [56]

China Floods Africa with Cheap Textiles

Hundreds of thousands of Africans have lost their jobs.

Since China began exporting large quantities of cheap clothing and fabric to Africa about seven years ago, more than 80 percent of Nigeria's textile factories have been forced to shut down, and an estimated 250,000 workers have been laid off. [1]

"It's very serious," says Brian Brink, executive director of the South African Textile Federation. The Chinese can supply materials at prices that are "very much below" local prices, and sometimes even "below the cost of raw materials. That's usually bloody impossible."

Africa's textile and clothing industry — perhaps more than any other sector — has been hit hardest by China's economic expansion across the continent. And South Africa and Nigeria have suffered the most.

In South Africa, textile business membership in Brink's federation has declined by nearly half — dropping from 75 to just 40 in the past seven years. If the trend continues, Brink says, the 150,000 textile and apparel workers across Southern Africa face a troubled future.

"Those who are less resilient will pack up and close their doors," he says. "There will be others that survive in areas that China is not yet operating in, such as in the technical areas, products supplied to technical specifications. China is not there — yet."

About 90 percent South Africa's clothing imports come from China, according to the federation, most of it surplus items from orders destined for the U.S. market. That's what allows China to sell them in Africa for below cost — despite South African regulations that prohibit such "dumping" trade practices.

Brink said relations between Chinese businessmen in South Africa and local textile workers have grown so tense that fist fights regularly break out in local markets. In the face of growing resentment that Africans feel toward Chinese businesses, Beijing officials have voluntarily agreed to cut back on textile exports to South Africa and to provide technical training and assistance to African textile manufacturers.

"The Chinese government does not encourage Chinese enterprises to take other countries' markets by purely increasing the quantity of their exports," President Hu Jintao said during an eight-nation tour of Africa in early 2007. [2]

Meanwhile, Chinese Commerce Minister Bo Xilai met last fall with his counterparts from Benin, Cote d'Ivoire,

Cheap Clothing Means Lost Jobs

Since China began exporting low-cost clothing to Africa, many textile workers in Southern Africa have lost their jobs. More than half the textile workers in Swaziland, for instance, lost their jobs between 2004 and 2005.

Decline in Textile Jobs in Southern Africa, 2004-2005

	2004	2005	% decline
Kenya	34,614	31,745	9.3
Lesotho	50,217	35,678	28.9
S. Africa	98,000	86,000	12.2
Swaziland	32,000	14,000	56.2

Source: Raphael Kaplinsky and Mike Morris, "Dangling by a Thread: How Sharp Are the Chinese Scissors?" Institute of Development Studies, University of Sussex, Brighton, England, 2006

Mali, Senegal and Togo to discuss how China can help the cotton industry in West Africa. In addition to sharing technology and sending experts to help increase production, China pledged to build clothing and textile factories and import more cotton from West Africa to boost textile jobs in Africa. [3]

Brink says those moves will help Africa's textile industry but won't solve all the problems. He admits that many African retailers are contributing to the flood of cheap Chinese goods by undervaluing or not declaring imports in order to avoid paying duties.

"It's not just China being efficient. It's not just the little beavers working hard," Brink says. "There is illegal activity, and that takes two to tango. We have to get our own house in order."

---

[1] Chris Alden, *China in Africa*, p. 81.

[2] "China, Africa build new partnership on old ties," Xinhua General News Service, Oct. 2, 2007.

[3] "Chinese minister meets officials on boosting cotton industry in west Africa," Xinhua News Agency, Oct. 2, 2007.

BACKGROUND

Breaking Colonial Ties

China's first encounter with Africa dates back to the early 15th century, when Admiral Zheng He led some 300 ships on seven journeys across the globe. Although his celebrated expeditions between 1405 and 1423 took him as far as the eastern coast of Africa, China had little to do with Africa for the next 500 years. Western nations, on the other hand, spent those centuries enslaving Africans and later colonizing the continent and extracting its raw materials to supply the needs of an industrializing Europe.

For more than 300 years, Europeans ran a lucrative and brutal trans-Atlantic slave trade, bringing an estimated 10 million Africans to the Americas — mainly Brazil. [57] After Britain abolished slavery in 1807, the Europeans began exploring Africa's interior, and by the late 1800s Europe's "Scramble for Africa" was in full swing. The colonial powers — primarily Britain, France, Belgium, Portugal and Germany — competed for vast tracts of Africa. And while they did build roads, railroads and other infrastructure — primarily to facilitate their exploitation of Africa's vast resources — millions of Africans died in the process.

As European nations expanded their control over Africa, they began to fear competition from one another for the continent's resources. In 1884, the European powers gathered at the so-called Berlin Conference to divvy up control of the continent. By 1902, all but 10 percent of Africa was under European control. [58]

But by mid-century the colonial powers had been weakened by the First and Second World Wars and could no longer afford to maintain vast colonies abroad. [59] Before World War II, Africa had only three independent countries: Liberia — which was founded by freed American slaves and declared itself independent in 1847; Ethiopia, which was never colonized by a European power; and Egypt, which had achieved independence in 1922. [60]

As Europe's colonies around the world gained independence after World War II, Mahatma Gandhi's struggle for Indian independence — achieved in 1947 — inspired similar efforts across Africa in the 1950s. [61]

During that time, China began reaching out to Africa. In 1955, emerging independent African and Asian countries gathered in Indonesia for the Bandung Conference — the first meeting of Third World nations

Kidnapped Chinese oil workers land in Addis Ababa, Ethiopia, last April after being released. Anti-government rebels held the six men for nearly a week after attacking a Chinese oil refinery in Ethiopia. Attacks on Chinese businesses have been on the rise in Africa.

— to promote Afro-Asian economic and cultural cooperation and spur political autonomy from the West. Attendees also launched the Non-Aligned Movement, pledging to support neither the United States nor the Soviet Union in their Cold War struggles. [62] Chinese Prime Minister Zhou Enlai played a particularly strong role in the conference and launched China's first foray into international politics. The first Sino-African diplomatic ties were established with Egypt in 1956, and within 10 years China had solidified relations with more than a dozen African countries. [63]

In the early 1960s, as African countries were gaining their independence, Zhou made a 10-country tour across the continent offering China's support. His trip was seen in part as a way to ensure Africa's opposition to Taiwan and to counter growing influence from the United States and Soviet Union, which supported "proxy" wars in Africa as offshoots of the global Cold War. China began sending doctors to Africa and provided aid to more than 800 projects across the continent, ranging from sports stadiums and the Tanzam railway — between Tanzania and Zambia — to providing scholarships to African students to study in Beijing. [64]

"People forget how much goodwill China gained in Africa during this liberation era," says Chan of London's School of Oriental and African Studies. "Africans were struck by the message Zhou Enlai put to them. It sustained

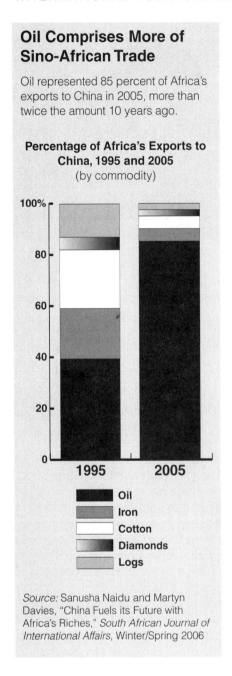

Oil Comprises More of Sino-African Trade

Oil represented 85 percent of Africa's exports to China in 2005, more than twice the amount 10 years ago.

Percentage of Africa's Exports to China, 1995 and 2005
(by commodity)

Legend:
- Oil
- Iron
- Cotton
- Diamonds
- Logs

Source: Sanusha Naidu and Martyn Davies, "China Fuels its Future with Africa's Riches," *South African Journal of International Affairs*, Winter/Spring 2006

Soviet influence. For instance, in Rhodesia (now Zimbabwe) — which did not gain its independence from Britain until 1980 — China backed the liberation movement of Robert Mugabe's Zanu party, while the Soviet Union backed that of Joshua Nkomo's Zapu party. In response, Mugabe's party turned profoundly anti-Soviet.

When Mugabe was elected prime minister in March 1980, Zimbabwe's close relationship with China was cemented. The two countries announced diplomatic ties on April 18, the day Zimbabwe won its independence from Britain. Shortly after that, Foreign Minister Simon Muzenda visited Beijing to thank the government for its support, and Mugabe himself went to Beijing the following year. [65]

Colonialism's Legacy

By the early 1980s, China had established diplomatic ties with nearly 40 African nations. However, during the political turmoil that followed the death of Chairman Mao Zedong in September 1976, China turned inward, and its influence and involvement in Africa waned. [66] But China's ideological goal of revolution and independence in Africa had been largely achieved. And having forged strong relationships with African leaders, China was not as fearful of Taiwan's influence in the region.

Despite their independence, African nations still faced many problems. Many lacked the technical and administrative skills needed to create healthy economies, and support structures — such as higher education, communications and armed forces — were poorly developed. [67]

During the post-independence era, the United States thought Africa did not have sufficient natural resources to warrant large U.S. investments, which could have helped to stabilize and strengthen the new African nations. "It is highly unlikely that most African countries will obtain external assistance or investment on anything approaching the scale required for sustained economic development," said a 1965 CIA assessment. "No African raw materials or other resources are essential to U.S. security." [68]

After the colonial rulers left, ethnic violence erupted across Africa in nations where colonizers had drawn artificial boundaries without regard to traditional tribal territories. Many of the new African countries also embraced socialism, prompting the United States — fearful that the continent might tilt toward the Soviet Union — to provide economic and military support to anti-communist despots or rebel groups. The beneficia-

the relationship between Africa and China. There was a genuine solidarity and empathy involved. Africans never forgot that."

Along with its ideological goal of spreading the "people's revolution" against Western imperialism, Communist China's outreach to Africa was also an attempt to counter

ries of U.S. funding during this period included notoriously corrupt strongmen such as Mobuto Sese Seko of Zaire (now the Democratic Republic of Congo), Jonas Savimbi of Angola and Hiseene Habre of Chad. [69]

In the 1980s, African nations borrowed heavily from the West. By 1986 Africa's foreign debt had reached $162 billion, and interest payments alone were eating up two-thirds of all the money the continent received in foreign aid. By 1989, the World Bank and International Monetary Fund (IMF) were forcing 30 heavily indebted sub-Saharan African nations to submit to "structural adjustment" programs designed to institute more market-oriented policies. [70]

The countries were forced to lower the value of their currencies to make their exports more attractive, shrink bloated budgets and bureaucracies and privatize state-run enterprises. But the spending limits kept many economies in deep recession and hurt Africa's poor. And although the requirements were initially said to be temporary, they soon become permanent World Bank and IMF policy. [71]

As the 1980s came to a close, African nations grew disillusioned with Western financial aid and the economic and political strings it carried. Many African leaders felt China could offer an alternative model in which "bread comes before the freedom to vote," in the words of Ndubisi Obiorah, director of the Center for Law and Social Action in Lagos, Nigeria. [72]

China's Return

As the 1990s dawned, Africa's economy continued to falter, Taiwan reached out to African leaders for support in regaining its seat in the United Nations and China re-emerged across the continent.

Earlier, African nations grateful for China's support during their struggles for independence had voted in 1971 to strip Taiwan of its U.N. seat and re-assign it to China. But in the 1990s, several African leaders began playing politics with their allegiances, switching back and forth between China and Taiwan. As a result, both Asian governments sent economic aid to Africa in hopes of winning African support at the U.N. [73] In 1996, Senegal moved its embassy from Beijing to Taipei, Taiwan's capital — for the third time — after receiving a large development aid package. Gambia got $48 million from Taiwan the previous year when it moved its embassy from China to Taipei. [74]

Youngsters — some only 8 years old — work at a copper mine in the Democratic Republic of Congo. The mineral-rich country's huge copper deposits are helping to fuel China's economic boom. To help move the minerals, China is investing $5 billion in Congo to build nearly 2,000 miles of roads and rail lines plus 31 hospitals, 145 health clinics, two new universities and 5,000 housing units.

Shortly after the Senegal move, Chinese President Jiang Zemin made a six-nation tour of Africa, promising financial assistance "without political strings" and pledging that "hand in hand the two sides will march towards the 21st century." [75] During the trip he offered Zaire $10 million for a cobalt and copper mining project, plus a "gift" of $3.6 million. [76] Also in 1996, China announced a $24 million investment in a gold mine in Sudan, despite U.N. Security Council sanctions against the country for "terrorist" activities. [77]

Besides countering Taiwan's influence, China was interested in Africa's consumer markets for its burgeoning exports and commercial enterprises. China's economy has grown an average of 9 percent each year over the last two decades. [78]

In 2000, the Forum on China-Africa Cooperation (FOCAC) was founded to promote stronger trade and investment relations between both the public and private sectors in China and Africa. It was wildly successful: Sino-African trade more than quintupled between 1999 and 2004 — from $5.6 billion to $29.5 billion — and continued to grow to $32.2 billion by the end of October 2005. [79] At the second FOCAC meeting in 2003, China promised to help train 10,000 African professionals, [80] cancel $1.27 billion in debt to 31 African nations and increase overall Sino-African trade to

AFP/Getty Images/Kambou Sia

Tons of fish were seized from two Chinese ships caught in Ivory Coast waters in December 2007. Fishing groups claim Chinese fleets are exploiting Africa's resources by illegally "bottom trawling" — which some equate with clear-cutting the ocean bottom of all flora and fauna.

$28 billion by 2006 — a target that was far exceeded. [81] During the third FOCAC meeting in Beijing in 2006, China dramatically pledged to increase Sino-African trade to $100 billion by 2010 and to pour billions more into financial aid, infrastructure development and social services.

China also has expanded its cultural ties to Africa, offering more than 18,000 government-sponsored scholarships to Africans through 2005, signing 65 cultural agreements with African countries, implementing 151 cultural exchanges and organizing visits by performing-arts troupes from each African region. [82]

"China is the largest developing country, and Africa is home to the largest number of developing countries," President Hu told the 2006 FOCAC summit. "Building strong ties between China and Africa will not only promote development of each side but also help cement unity and cooperation among developing countries and contribute to establishing a just and equitable, new international political and economic order."

He added: "We in China will not forget Africa's full support for restoring the lawful rights of the People's Republic of China in the United Nations. Nor will we forget the sincere and ardent wish of African countries and people for China to realise complete and peaceful reunification and achieve the goal of building a modern nation." [83]

Resource Envy

Many analysts believe China's biggest motivation for expanding its influence in Africa is its growing need for natural resources. Until the 1990s, China could meet its own energy needs by tapping its massive oil reserves in Daqing in northern China. [84] It also relied heavily on coal. But because of coal's low efficiency and negative environmental impacts, China has increasingly switched to gas and oil.

Once Asia's largest oil exporter, China became a net importer of oil in 1993. Between 1995 and 2005 oil consumption in China doubled to 6.8 million barrels per day. [85] In 2003, China became the world's second-largest oil consumer, behind the United States, and its oil demand is expected to continue growing steadily.

China has spent the last 10 years negotiating deals with African nations to secure oil supplies. In 1998, China sent 7,000 Chinese engineers and construction workers to Sudan to build a 957-mile pipeline, the largest contracted foreign oil project in China's history. [86] The project — Sudan's first step into oil exploration — was seen as a possible panacea to the war-torn country's problems. [87] Since then, China has become the leading developer of Sudan's oil reserves, importing 60 percent of the country's output. [88]

Using a combination of political prowess and technological contributions, China also has made oil deals with Angola, Equatorial Guinea, Gabon, Nigeria and others. [89] To gain a foothold in Nigeria, for instance — where Western companies had dominated the oil reserves for decades — China has promised to build and launch a communication satellite. In 2005, China and Nigeria signed an $800 million deal to supply 30,000 barrels of crude oil per day to China. More recently, China and Nigeria agreed China would provide a $4 billion infrastructure investment package in exchange for first-refusal rights on four oil blocks. Many believe China could easily replace some Western firms when their drilling licenses come up for renewal. [90]

Besides oil, China has an unquenchable thirst for minerals needed to produce everyday items, such as door knobs, faucets and cell phones for its 1.3 billion population. [91] "Anywhere there are extractive resources, if China hasn't moved in yet, they will," says Alden, of the South African Institute of International Affairs.

In 2004, China bought 14 percent of Africa's timber exports and 85 percent of its cobalt. [92] South Africa is

Is China becoming Africa's newest colonizer?

YES Adama Gaye

Visiting Fellow, Johns Hopkins University, School of Advanced and International Studies, and author, China-Africa: The Dragon and the Ostrich

Written for *CQ Researcher*, December 2007

Every time the colonial question is raised in relation to China's ties with Africa, the Chinese refute it. But the question cannot be easily whisked away.

Now casting itself as the world's largest developing country, China associates its destiny with that of Africa, insisting that both were once humiliated by foreign imperialists and colonial rulers.

But despite its claim that it wants to contribute to Africa's development, a closer look shows another face of China. No longer promoting "international proletarianism," China now strives to gain access to Africa's natural resources and isolate Taiwan. In the process, a colonial power with an Asian face may have entered the continent. And like previous colonizers, China, too, is in Africa to achieve a colonial strategy.

China's goal in Africa is geared toward fulfilling narrow national interests, and the goodwill surrounding it can be perceived as the softer side of a hard-core project. For all its debt cancellation and financial support of Africa, China gets even more in return. While grabbing Africa's natural resources, China dumps its cheap exports in Africa. So far, China's business investments have not reversed the unequal terms of trade that attracted criticism for Western colonizers of the past. The ports, refineries and railways being built by the Chinese serve China's eagerness to "exfiltrate" Africa's resources. And its equity investments in energy and mining industries are all part of its long-term interests.

Meanwhile, cynicism is China's watchword. Under the guise of non-interference and respect for sovereignty, China closes its eyes to lapses in good leadership, corruption, arms sales and violations of human rights and democratic norms.

Giving legitimacy to "rogue states" and providing loans under dubious conditions, China has indirectly rehabilitated political authoritarianism in Africa. Many African leaders now brag about China's achievements in poverty alleviation and economic recovery. Hailing this "model" from the East, they say that it "works" and does not "dictate." Contrasting it to the "failed" Western solutions, these leaders are too happy to have found in China their new tutor. They are no longer orphans of the demise of the Cold War nor do they need to go, bowl in hands, begging the now-discredited World Bank and International Monetary Fund.

Yet the ruthless, capitalistic behavior of China's businessmen in Africa is bound to produce a backlash. Soft-power alone will not prevent it.

NO Ronald D. Palmer

Former U.S. Ambassador to Togo and Mauritius

Written for *CQ Researcher*, December 2007

Colonialism consists of intricate politico-economic-juridical and socio-cultural structures. Traditional colonizing powers maintained authority and control by ruthless use, as necessary, of police power. By this definition, China is clearly not seeking to colonize Africa.

But China is seeking to increase its influence in Africa. For more than 50 years, China has had a strategy of developing soft power in Africa. They have been quietly making a place for themselves across the continent. The Chinese have established hundreds of businesses across the continent and have poured billions into roads, bridges and other infrastructure. Chinese officials meet regularly with African leaders.

We are seeing the product of years of careful planning. The Chinese worked closely with many African nations during their struggles for independence in the 1950s and '60s. Understanding Africa's resentment toward Western colonialists and the possibilities of exploiting that resentment, China moved into an influence vacuum when colonialism ended.

In desperate need of oil and working hard to become a global superpower, China is doing whatever it needs to do to achieve those goals. In the process, China has made mistakes, rousing the anger of some Africans and prompting many to accuse it of colonialism. Through grants and loans, the Chinese government has helped many small Chinese businesses open up shop in Africa, competing with Africans and forcing many workers to lose their jobs. And Chinese businesses in Africa are known for their poor labor rights and low wages.

But China doesn't have any intention of colonizing Africa. The Chinese are firmly planted in their own environment. Their concerns are with their homeland.

And Africans will not allow themselves to be re-colonized. Already, we have seen Africans protesting Chinese policies that hurt their livelihoods. Africans will simply not put up with another colonial power. By 2020, Africa will still be Africa. It will not be China. Africans don't plan to be dominated again. Africans will retain their concept of who they are and who they want to be.

Does China want to have influence? Yes. Does China need to use its military to colonize Africa? No. They've demonstrated that their investments in Africa's infrastructure can win and influence people. The Chinese are doing things the West did in the past to profit from Africa's resources. But the Chinese are doing it better and without the need to colonize.

To protest the genocide in Darfur, actress Mia Farrow holds an Olympic-style torch at a rally last Dec. 10 outside the Chinese Embassy in Washington. Activists are pressuring Beijing — which hosts the Olympics this summer — to use its influence in oil-rich Sudan to stop the killing.

China's fourth-largest supplier of iron ore. Gabon, South Africa and Ghana are among China's top five manganese suppliers and together account for more than a third of its total manganese imports. Minerals accounted for 97 percent of Sierra Leone's exports to China in 2005 and 87 percent of Zambia's. Minerals accounted for 92 percent of Tanzania's exports to China in 2004. [93]

"China's primary goal is to import from Africa those key raw materials that will sustain its booming economy," says David Shinn, former U.S. ambassador to Ethiopia and Burkina Faso and currently an adjunct professor at The George Washington University. "The Communist Party is more or less predicating its future on maintaining booming economic growth, and if it should stumble, then I think the party is in danger of losing power." [94]

CURRENT SITUATION

Communism to Capitalism

Today, China's outreach to Africa is no longer driven by ideological goals but by the economic and energy resources it needs to become a global superpower. "The West is worried about the impact of Chinese capitalism, not communism," says Alden.

China is Africa's third-largest trading partner, behind the European Union and the United States. [95] And it's doing everything it can to gain on the competition.

In the first quarter of 2007 senior Chinese officials — including President Hu and then-Foreign Minister Li — visited 15 African countries. [96] Besides hosting the African Development Bank's annual meeting in May and promising $20 billion for infrastructure development, Beijing pledged $8 million to the World Health Organization to beef up African countries' capacity to respond to public health emergencies. [97] In September China agreed to lend the Republic of Congo $5 billion in exchange for access to the country's extensive timber, cobalt and copper. Congo said the loan will help build roads, hospitals, housing and universities. [98]

Meanwhile, China is strengthening its political ties with Africa. In September, the first annual political consultation meeting between Chinese and African foreign ministers was held at U.N. headquarters in New York. Foreign ministers and representatives from 48 African countries attended the event chaired by Chinese Foreign Minister Yang Jiechi and Egyptian Foreign Minister Ahmed Aboul Gheit. [99]

"China has a long history of relationships with African countries," says Economy, of the Council on Foreign Relations. "The development aspect — providing doctors and engineers — has remained fairly constant. But now there's an extraordinary jump in the level of Chinese business deals. They're not pushing communism anymore."

Africa Reacts

African governments are welcoming China's financial aid and business investments. The African Union accepted China's offer to build — free of charge — a new conference center for the organization next to its headquarters in Addis Ababa, Ethiopia. [100]

For many Africans, China has become the new symbol of prosperity, replacing the United States as the land of opportunity. "The United States is a nice place to visit," said Ahmet Mohamet Ali, a trader in Chad who returned from his first trip to China in October. "China is a place to do business." [101]

Direct flights to more than 20 African cities leave weekly from Beijing, Shanghai, Guangzhou and Hong Kong. Regular flights from the United States, on the other hand, serve only eight African cities. [102]

In fall 2007, Chinese officials held a university exposition in the Kenyan capital of Nairobi to recruit even more African students for study in China. African students made up about 2.3 percent of the 162,000 foreign students in China last year. The Chinese government, which already allocates one-fifth of its international scholarships to Africans, plans to double the number of scholarships for Africa to 4,000 by 2009.

According to the official Xinhua news agency, more than 8,000 African students studied Mandarin last year. [103]

Violence against China and its businesses in Africa, however, is increasing. President Hu was forced to cancel a February 2007 trip to Zambia because of threats of massive protests against China's growing hold over the country's copper mines and poor labor policies toward mine workers. [104] In the past year, numerous Chinese businesses in Africa have been attacked. Rebels attacked a Chinese-run oil refinery in Ethiopia, killing 74 and kidnapping six Chinese employees. In Nigeria — where militants are seeking greater local share of oil revenues — 16 Chinese oil workers were kidnapped in three separate incidents. And gunmen in Kenya killed a Chinese engineer working on a highway project and injured another. Chinese officials, however, have pledged not to let the attacks hinder their business investments in Africa. [105]

Competition Heats Up

Western nations continue to criticize China's business practices in Africa while stepping up their own efforts to reach out to the continent.

"The increasing presence of China in Africa has worked as kind of a wake-up call among some European nations," says the European Commission's Altafaj. "We had a feeling that many Europeans didn't put Africa as high as it should be on its list."

In December, the European Union hosted an EU-Africa Summit in Lisbon, Portugal, in order to develop joint strategies on such issues as trade, human rights, climate change and security. The meeting had originally been scheduled for 2003 but was cancelled because of controversy over whether Zimbabwe's President Mugabe should be allowed to attend. Western countries condemn Mugabe as a dictator who uses violence against his opponents and has expropriated land from white farmers and plunged the country into economic collapse. The same controversy threatened to derail the December summit when Prime Minister Gordan Brown vowed that neither he nor any senior British cabinet member would attend if Mugabe participated. [106]

African leaders angrily threatened to boycott the summit if Mugabe was excluded and accused the West of resorting to its colonial ways. "This is again another way of manipulating Africa," Gertrude Mongella, the Tanzanian president of the Pan-African Parliament, said in response to Brown's boycott. "Zimbabwe is a nation which got independence. In the developed countries there are so many countries doing things which not all of us subscribe to. We have seen the Iraq War — not everyone accepts what is being done in Iraq." [107]

Despite Brown's opposition, other European leaders were quick to insist that Mugabe be allowed to attend. "There has been enough moralization from Europe," says Altafaj. "We should not underestimate the negative impact of former colonizers lecturing Africans. This summit will be a good opportunity to have conversations about good governance. We do not intend to give lectures." Earlier, German Chancellor Angela Merkel said it was up to African leaders to decide who should represent them at the summit — a sign of the growing pressure European countries feel to strengthen ties with Africa in the wake of China's influence. [108]

And U.S. Treasury Secretary Henry Paulson made a six-day tour to Ghana, South Africa and Tanzania in November to "shine a light" on a part of the world that investors have overlooked. At the end of the tour, President Bush pledged $250 million to start three government funds that will invest in African debt, stocks and companies. [109]

Robert Mosbacher, Jr., president of the Overseas Private Investment Corp., which will administer the government funds, said U.S. companies had to do "a bit of catch-up" in Africa after having focused in recent years on Eastern Europe, Russia and parts of Latin America. "There's no doubt the U.S. can do more to take advantage of growth opportunities in Africa," he said. [110]

As the West is taking notice of China's activities in Africa, China is beginning to listen to Western criticism of its dealings with African nations. After years of blocking U.N. sanctions against Sudan, China last year agreed to send more than 300 peacekeepers as part of the U.N. mission to end years of bloodshed in Darfur. [111]

In fact, President Bush's special envoy to Sudan, Andrew Natsios, last fall credited China for its work to help end the fighting in Darfur. It was Chinese influence, Natsios said, that finally convinced the Sudanese government to accept a July Security Council resolution to authorize a 26,000-member U.N. military and civilian peacekeeping operation in Darfur. "The Chinese are like a locomotive that is speeding up," he said. "They are even doing things we didn't ask them to do." [112]

Many observers say China is working hard to improve its global image with the approach of the 2008 Olympics in Beijing. "It's about reputational risks, especially with the build-up to the Olympics," says Alden, of the South African Institute of International Affairs. "They don't want to be seen as an evil face."

OUTLOOK

Belle of the Ball

China is expected to honor the promises it made at the Beijing summit to rapidly expand its business, cultural and infrastructure investments across Africa. In part, that commitment is dictated by China's need for resources. By 2020, analysts say, China will have 120 million private cars on the road and be forced to import at least 60 percent of its oil. [113]

But Western countries also are expected to invest more financial and diplomatic energy in Africa. "The West is already beginning to get off their duffs. This could mean greater trade and aid from the West," Alden says. "I sense the West is going to increasingly feel China as a source of pressure and provide more assistance and government investment to Africa in the coming years."

Increased attention from both the East and the West will undoubtedly inject much-needed infrastructure and economic support into developing Africa, which could benefit both sides. For decades the West has ignored the continent's potential as a business and political partner, generally seeing African governments as too corrupt or too weak to provide healthy investment environments. Or they saw Africa as a disaster zone — plagued by famine and disease — worthy of humanitarian assistance rather than financial investment. But China has proven that Africa can be a powerful ally.

"It's not too late [for the West], but it's getting late," says the European Commission's Altafaj. "We better upgrade our relationship now — for the benefit of both sides."

But along with China and the West, India, Russia, Brazil and others also are expected to look increasingly toward Africa as their energy needs grow and business opportunities expand. Russian trade with Africa has tripled since 2000, up to $3 billion a year. Russia also has invested $3.5 billion in oil exploration across the continent in recent years, and new energy deals in Algeria have been accompanied by $4 billion in arms sales. [114]

Meanwhile, Africa is relishing its newfound international popularity — opening its doors to a multitude of investors. "Angola and others have discovered it's in their best interest to stay diversified," says Reisen at the Organization for Economic Cooperation and Development. "You don't want to replace one monopolizer with another."

But some fear the new flood of investments — especially from countries such as China that put no restrictions on the funding — will actually feed the continent's already serious corruption problem.

"The Chinese are much more prone to do business in a way that today Europeans and Americans do not accept — paying bribes and all kinds of bonuses under the table," said Gal Luft, codirector of the Institute for the Analysis of Global Security, a Washington educational organization focusing on energy security. "These are things that have been rampant throughout Africa. . . . It will be much easier for those countries to work with Chinese companies rather than American and European companies that are becoming more and more restricted by this 'publish what you pay' initiative and others calling for better transparency." [115]

International pressure is also forcing China to play a bigger role in confronting human-rights abuses in Africa.

China has already softened its policy of "non-interference" and sent peacekeepers to Darfur. "The pressure on China is immense, especially with the Olympics coming up" in China, says the Council on Foreign Relations' Economy. "China is getting the message that it's not enough just to be a global superpower."

It is unclear, however, whether China's recent actions to protect human rights in Africa is simply a short-term public relations campaign or a long-term change in policy. "If you're a glass half-full person, then you'll say there won't be that much difference between Western policy and Chinese policy in the future," says Alden. "If you're a glass half-empty person, you'd say it's just window dressing."

But Africans say the onus is not just on China. Africans themselves must act to ensure they do not fall prey to yet another colonial power.

"China's stance on Africa is likely to harden in the long term, with more manipulation and exploitation and less benefit for the continent," said Moreblessings Chidaushe, a lobby and advocacy program officer with the African Forum and Network on Debt and Development, based in Harare, Zimbabwe. "One way out would be the development of a comprehensive African policy on China."

Chidaushe called on the African Union to "increase African countries' security" and make it easier for them to deal with China — which she called a "superpower wannabe" — rather than making individual approaches "that are easily susceptible to manipulation." [116]

Some say China's growing involvement in Africa is giving leaders across the continent the power they need to improve social conditions and human rights. "Human rights cannot be imposed upon a nation. It's indigenous," says TransAfrica's Lee. "China is opening more options for these governments and for their people. Africans now have more room, more flexibility to determine how they can improve their countries."

But even those who question China's motives, business practices and human-rights policies say the renewed interest could benefit the continent economically, politically and socially. "Africans will rise up significantly in the coming years," says Chan at the University of London's School of Oriental and African Studies. "They will rise up with the assistance of everyone — not just China."

NOTES

1. Jonathan Watts, "The savannah comes to Beijing as China hosts its new empire," *The Guardian* (London), Nov. 4, 2006, p. 24; "China-Africa Forum Opens in Beijing Today," *Ghanaian Chronicle*, Nov. 3, 2006.

2. Bates Gill, Chin-hao Huang and J. Stephenson Morrison, "Assessing China's Growing Influence in Africa," *China Security*, Summer 2007, World Security Institute, p. 3, http://yaleglobal.yale.edu/about/pdfs/china-africa.pdf.

3. "China-Africa Forum Opens in Beijing Today," *op. cit.*

4. "China announces package of aid measures for Africa at historic summit," Xinhua News Agency, Nov. 4, 2006.

5. "Chinese, African entrepreneurs sign billion-dollar worth agreements," Xinhua News Agency, Nov. 5, 2006.

6. Watts, *op. cit.*; also see http://news.xinhuanet.com/english/2006-12/08/content_5452301.htm.

7. Sarah DiLorenzo, "China thanks Africans for help stopping Taiwan vote, heralds 30 percent trade increase," The Associated Press, Sept. 27, 2007.

8. Bates Gill, Chin-hao Huang and J. Stephenson Morrison, "China's Expanding Role in Africa and Implications for the United States," Center for Strategic and International Studies, January, 2007.

9. Danna Harman, "China Takes Up Civic Work in Africa," *The Christian Science Monitor*, June 27, 2007, p. 1.

10. "Full text of joint communiqué of Sino-African ministerial political consultations," Xinhua Economic News Service, Sept. 27, 2007.

11. "Promoting Growth in Africa: Working with China," British Department for International Development Fact Sheet, October 2006; also see Sanusha Naidu and Martyn Davies, "China Fuels its Future with Africa's Riches," *South African Journal of International Affairs*, Winter/Spring 2006, pp. 69-83.

12. Esther Pan, "Backgrounder: China, Africa and Oil," Council on Foreign Relations, Jan. 26, 2007.

13. Statistics come from Chris Alden and Helmut Reisen.

14. Chris Alden, *China in Africa* (2007), p. 75.

15. *Ibid.*

16. "Blast Kills 46 at a Copper Mine in Zambia," Reuters, April 21, 2005.

17. Cindy Hurst, "China's Oil Rush in Africa," Institute for the Analysis of Global Security, July 2006, p. 3.

18. Barbara Slavin, "Olympics seen as leverage for Darfur; China moving to solve crisis," *USA Today*, Sept. 21, 2007, p. 6A.

19. "An Awkward Meeting: Europe and Africa," the Economist.com, Dec. 9, 2007. www.economist.com/world/africa/displaystory.cfm?story_id=10273503.

20. "Communication from the Commission to the European Parliament and the Council: From Cairo to Lisbon — The EU-Africa Strategic Partnership," Commission of the European Communities, June 26, 2007, p. 3.

21. Heidi Vogt, "Chinese Mark on Africa Means Commerce," The Associated Press, Sept. 2, 2007.

22. Peter Brookes and Ji Hye Shin, "China's Influence in Africa: Implications for the United States," Heritage Foundation, Feb. 22, 2006, p. 6.

23. Harman, *op. cit.*

24. Jake Lee, "China inflows give African currencies a boost," *International Tribune Herald*, June 5, 2007, p. 18.

25. "China's Interest and Activity in Africa's Construction and Infrastructure Sectors," Centre for Chinese Studies, Stellenbosch University, South Africa, Nov. 2006, p. 7.

26. Brookes and Shin, *op. cit.*, p. 6.

27. Quoted in Firoze Manji and Stephen Marks, *African Perspectives on China in Africa* (2007), p. 5, available at www.fahamu.org/downloads/cia_download.pdf.

28. "China defends its role in Africa," *East African Business Week*, May 28, 2007.

29. Gill, Huang and Morrison, "Assessing China's Growing Influence in Africa," *op. cit.*, p. 5.

30. Stellenbosch University, *op. cit.*, pp. 21, 33.

31. Richard Beeston, "West could learn from straight-forward approach," *The Times* (London), Nov. 2, 2006, p. 42.

32. Don Lee, "China Barrels Ahead in Oil Market," *Los Angeles Times*, Nov. 14, 2004, p. C1.

33. Peter Ford, "China woos African trade," *The Christian Science Monitor*, Nov. 3, 2006, p. 1.

34. Hurst, *op. cit.*, p. 7; and Slavin, *op. cit.*

35. Deb Riechmann, "Bush announces new sanctions against Sudan for its role in Darfur," The Associated Press, May 29, 2007.

36. "Beijing Summit adopts declaration, highlighting China-Africa strategic partnership," Forum on China-Africa Cooperation press release, Nov. 6, 2006.

37. Howard W. French, "China in Africa: All Trade, With No Political Baggage," *The New York Times*, Aug. 8, 2004, p. 4.

38. "Appeal by Amnesty International to the Chinese government on the occasion of the China-Africa Summit for Development and Cooperation," AI Index: AFR 54/072/2006, Nov. 1, 2006.

39. Pan, *op. cit.*

40. Jane Macartney, "Beijing turns its back on embattled Robert Mugabe," *The Times* (London), Sept. 19, 2007, p. 34; also see Brookes and Shin, *op. cit.*, p. 4.

41. Abraham McLaughlin, "A rising China counters US clout in Africa," *The Christian Science Monitor*, March 30, 2005, p. 1.

42. Macartney, *op. cit.*, p. 4.

43. Harman, *op. cit.*

44. Margaret C. Lee, Henning Melber, Sanusha Naidu and Ian Taylor, "China in Africa," *Current African Issues*, No. 33, Nordiska Afrikainstitutet, Uppsala, Sweden, p. 11.

45. For statistics on China's assistance to Africa, see the Forum on China-Africa Cooperation, http://english.focacsummit.org/.

46. David Shinn, "Africa, China, the United States, and Oil," Center for Strategic and International Studies Africa Policy Forum, May 8, 2007.

47. Guy Raz, "New U.S. Command in Africa Faces Skeptics, National Public Radio, Oct. 18, 2007; and Shinn, *op. cit.*

48. Christopher Thompson, "The Scramble for Africa's Oil," *The New Statesman*, June 14, 2007. www.newstatesman.com/200706180024.

49. Lee, Melber, Naidu and Taylor, *op. cit.*

50. Naidu and Davies, *op. cit.*

51. Hurst, *op. cit.*, p. 10.

52. See www.bp.com/genericarticle.do?categoryId=98&contentId=7036566.

53. Raz, *op. cit.*

54. Manji and Marks, *op. cit.*, p. 18.

55. See www.africom.mil/africomFAQs.asp.

56. "Big Oil and Energy Independence," *Congressional Record*, Feb. 8, 2007, p. H1404, www.govtrack.us/congress/record.xpd?id=110-h20070208-53.

57. See "The Trans-Atlantic Slave Trade," from About.com: African History, http://africanhistory.about.com/library/weekly/aa080601a.htm.

58. For background on European colonization of Africa and the Berlin Conference, see U.K.'s Channel 4 feature, "Empire's Children: The Scramble for Africa," at www.channel4.empireschildren.co.uk.

59. For background, see David Masci, "Aiding Africa," *CQ Researcher*, Aug. 29, 2003, pp. 697-720.

60. For background on Africa's fight for independence, see the BBC, "The Story of Africa: Independence," at www.bbc.co.uk/worldservice/africa/features/storyofafrica.

61. *Ibid.*

62. Slobodan Lekic, "Historic Asia-Africa conference was marked by superpower hostility, tragedy," The Associated Press, April 24, 2005.

63. For background on diplomatic relations between China and Africa, visit http://english.focacsummit.org.

64. Manji and Marks, *op. cit.*, p. 35.

65. Joshua Eisenman, "Zimbabwe: China's African ally," China Brief 5 (15), the Jamestown Foundation, July 5, 2007.

66. Stellenbosch University, *op. cit.*, p. 13.

67. Masci, *op. cit.*, p. 710.

68. For background, see Peter Katel, "Ending Poverty," *CQ Researcher*, Sept. 9, 2005, pp. 733-760.

69. *Ibid.*

70. Masci, *op. cit.*, p. 749; also see Kathy Koch, "Economic Turnabout in Africa," *Editorial Research Reports*, Nov. 7, 1986, available in *CQ Researcher Plus Archive*, www.cqpress.com.

71. Katel, *op. cit.*, p. 749.

72. Manji and Marks, *op. cit.*, p. 44.

73. "Africa and Asia. Hallo, China — or is it Taiwan?" *The Economist*, Sept. 14, 1996, p. 44.

74. Jonathan Manthorpe, "Asia courts Africa in Chinese rivalry," *The Vancouver Sun* (British Columbia), June 5, 1996, p. A1.

75. "Visiting Chinese president pledges support with no strings attached," BBC, May 27, 1996.

76. *The Economist, op. cit.*

77. David Hecht, "Taiwan Loses 1 Big African Nation But Still Has 8 Little Ones," *Africa News*, Dec. 5, 1996.

78. Pan, *op. cit.*

79. Brookes and Shin, *op. cit.*, pp. 5-6.

80. For background, visit FOCAC's Web site at http://english.focacsummit.org/.

81. Alden, *op. cit.*, p. 31.

82. For background on China's aid to Africa, see http://english.focacsummit.org/.

83. "Full text: Address by Hu Jintao at the Opening Ceremony of the Beijing Summit of The Forum on China-Africa Cooperation," http://english.focacsummit.org/2006-11/04/content_4978.htm.

84. Hurst, *op. cit.*, p. 3.

85. Lee, Melber, Naidu and Taylor, *op. cit.*, p. 14.

86. "Set to Build Pipeline for Sudan," Xinhua News Agency, July 31, 1998.

87. Michela Wrong, "Sudan looks to oil for new lifeblood," *Financial Times*, June 11, 1998, p. 4.

88. Hurst, *op. cit.*, p. 7.

89. *Ibid.*, p. 6.

90. *Ibid.*, p. 11.

91. Manji and Marks, *op. cit.*, p. 143.

92. Naidu and Davies, *op. cit.*

93. Stellenbosch University, *op. cit.*, p. 74.

94. Sebastian Junger, "Enter China the Giant," *Vanity Fair*, July 2007, p. 126.

95. Lee, Melber, Naidu and Taylor, *op. cit.*, p. 41.

96. Gill, Huang and Morrison, *op. cit.*, p. 3.

97. *Ibid.*, p. 6.

98. China opens coffers for minerals," BBC, Sept. 18, 2007, http://news.bbc.co.uk/2/hi/africa/7000925.stm.

99. "Chinese, African foreign ministers launch consultation mechanism at UN," BBC Worldwide Monitoring, Sept. 27, 2007.

100. David White, "The China Factor: A spectacular resurgence," *Financial Times*, Nov. 20, 2006, www.ft.com/cms/s/0/e6afc19a-6e5d-11db-b5c4-0 000779e2340,dwp_uuid=1f2588a0-765d-11db-8 284-0000779e2340.html.

101. Stephanie McCrummen, "Struggling Chadians Dream Of a Better Life — in China," *The Washington Post*, Oct. 6, 2007, p. A17, www .washingtonpost.com/wp-dyn/content/article/2007 /10/05/AR2007100502484.html.

102. Heidi Vogt, "Chinese Mark on Africa Means Commerce," The Associated Press, Sept. 2, 2007, www.mcclatchydc.com/staff/shashank_bengali/story /20987.html.

103. Shashank Bengali, "To soften its image, China courts African students," McClatchy News Service, Nov. 4, 2007.

104. Danna Harman, "In Sudan, China Focuses on Oil Wells, Not Local Needs," *The Christian Science Monitor*, June 25, 2007, p. 11, www.csmonitor.com /2007/0625/p11s01-woaf.htm.

105. Anita Powell, "Ethiopia Blames Eritrea for Attack," The Associated Press, April 25, 2007.

106. "Zimbabwe poses dilemma for EU-Africa summit host," Agence France-Presse, Nov. 25, 2007.

107. Philip Webster and David Charter, "Brown offers summit a lifeline: I'll go — but only if Mugabe stays away," *The Times* (London), Sept. 21, 2007, p. 21, www.timesonline.co.uk/tol/news/world /africa/article2496374.ece.

108. Tracy McVeigh, "Mugabe can attend summit," *The Guardian* (London), Oct. 12, 2007, p. 6.

109. "U.S. funds to purchase Africa debt and stocks," *The International Herald Tribune*, Nov. 20, 2007.

110. Alec Russell, "US business worried over China's expansion in Africa," *Financial Times*, Nov. 20, 2007, p. 5, www.ft.com/cms/s/0/93944ea8-96f3-11 dc-b2da-0000779fd2ac,dwp_uuid=5cdb1d20-feea-11db-aff2-000b5df10621.html.

111. Mohamed Hasni, "Darfur rebels tell China peacekeepers to go home," Agence France-Presse, Nov. 25, 2007.

112. William C. Mann, "China Credited with Progress on Darfur," The Associated Press, Sept. 19, 2007.

113. Hurst, *op. cit.*, p. 3.

114. Owen Matthews, "Racing for New Riches," *Newsweek*, Nov. 19, 2007, www.newsweek.com/id /68910.

115. Hurst, *op. cit.*, p. 15.

116. Manji and Marks, *op. cit.*, pp. 110-111.

BIBLIOGRAPHY

Books

Alden, Chris, *China in Africa*, Zed Books, 2007.
The head of the China in Africa program at the South African Institute of International Affairs offers a comprehensive overview of China's new engagement in Africa, examining China's motives, Africa's reaction and the ultimate outcome of the new relationship.

Lee, Margaret C., Henning Melber, Sanusha Naidu and Ian Taylor, *China in Africa: Current African Issues No. 3*, Nordic Africa Institute, 2007.
The authors, all researchers with extensive experience in African and Asian studies, examine China's scramble for Africa's resources, its economic investments in the continent and case studies on Uganda and South Africa.

Manji, Firoze, and Stephen Marks (eds.), *African Perspectives on China in Africa*, Fahamu, 2007.
Essays by some of Africa's leading academics and activists look at a variety of issues arising from China's growing influence across the continent — from environmental impacts to colonialism to economic growth.

Articles

Gill, Bates, Chin-hao Huang and J. Stephenson Morrison, "Assessing China's Growing Influence in Africa," *China Security*, Vol. 3, No. 3, summer 2007, World Security Institute, pp. 3-21, www.wsichina .org/cs7_all.pdf.
The authors explore China's rapidly growing engagement in Africa over the past decade and highlight milestones that have led to their strong relationship.

Harman, Danna, "China Takes up Civic Work in Africa," *The Christian Science Monitor*, June 27, 2007, p. 1, www.csmonitor.com/2007/0627/p01s05-

woaf.html.

Is China helping or hurting Africa? Both sides of the debate are presented.

Junger, Sebastian, "Enter China, the Giant," *Vanity Fair*, July 2007, p. 126.

A best-selling author examines China's activities in Sudan and Darfur.

Naidu, Sanusha, and Martyn Davies, "China Fuels its Future with Africa's Riches," *South African Journal of International Affairs*, Vol. 13 (2), winter/spring 2006, www.ccs.org.za/downloads/Naidu%20and%20Davies%20-%20SAIIA%20-%20Vol%2013.2.pdf.

Scholars at the Center for Chinese Studies in South Africa examine China's growing reliance on African resources and the opportunities and threats China's search for energy is creating for Africans.

Shinn, David H., "Africa, China, the United States and Oil," Center for Strategic and International Studies Online Africa Policy Forum, May 8, 2007, http://forums.csis.org/africa/index.php?s=Shinn&searchbutton=Go%21.

A former U.S. ambassador to Ethiopia and Burkina Faso discusses the role oil plays in the relationships among China, Africa and the United States.

Vogt, Heidi, "Chinese Mark on Africa Means Commerce," The Associated Press, Sept. 2, 2007, www.usatoday.com/news/world/2007-09-02-2865007898_x.htm.

A reporter provides an overview of the pros and cons of the proliferation of Chinese businesses and citizens working in Africa.

Reports and Studies

Brooks, Peter, and Ji Hye Shin, "China's Influence in Africa: Implications for the United States," The Heritage Foundation Backgrounder, No. 1916, Feb. 22, 2006, www.heritage.org/Research/Asiaandthe Pacific/bg1916.cfm.

Scholars at a conservative Washington think tank outline China's rapidly expanding political, social and economic influence across Africa and warn of threats to U.S. goals in the region.

Hurst, Cindy, "China's Oil Rush in Africa," The Institute for the Analysis of Global Security, July 2006, http://leav-www.army.mil/fmso/documents/chinainafrica.pdf.

A U.S. Navy officer and political-military research analyst offers an excellent overview of China's growing reliance on African oil.

Kaplinsky, Raphael, Dorothy McCormick and Mike Morris, "The Impact of China on Sub Saharan Africa," U.K. Department for International Development, April 2006, www.uneca.org/eca_programmes/acgd/Overview_Report.pdf.

The report examines why China and Africa are strengthening their ties and details China's impact on Africa's trade, textile and energy sectors.

Pan, Esther, "China, Africa and Oil," Backgrounder for the Council on Foreign Relations, Jan. 26, 2007, www.cfr.org/publication/9557/china_africa_and_oil.html?breadcrumb=%2Fpublication%2Fpublication_list%3Ftype%3Dbackgrounder%26page%3D5.

A researcher at the Council on Foreign Relations addresses some of the most frequently asked questions about China in Africa.

For More Information

African Union, P.O. Box 3243, Roosevelt St., WK1K19, Addis Ababa, Ethiopia; +251 11 551 77 00; www.africa-union.org. A diplomatic organization that fosters economic and social cooperation among 53 African nations and other governments.

Center for Strategic and International Studies, 1800 K St., N.W., Washington, DC 20006; (202) 887-0200; www.csis.org. A nonprofit public policy research institution that provides analysis on defense, security and international issues.

Council on Foreign Relations, 1779 Massachusetts Ave., N.W., Washington, DC 20036; (202) 509-8400; www.cfr.org. A nonpartisan think tank that offers extensive resources, data and experts on foreign policy issues.

Department for International Development, 1 Palace St., London SW1E 5HE, UK; +44 020 7023 0000; www.dfid.gov.uk. The United Kingdom agency working on international development issues.

Directorate General for External Trade, European Union, 200 rue de la Loi-Wetstraat, B-1049 Brussels, Belgium, 00 800 67891011; http://ec.europa.eu/trade. Oversees the European Commission's global trade policy.

Forum on China-Africa Cooperation, No. 2, Chaoyangmen Nandajie, Chaoyang District, Beijing, 100701; +86-10-65961114; www.focac.org/eng. A Ministry of Foreign Affairs organization that works to strengthen economic, social and political ties between China and Africa.

Institute for the Analysis of Global Security, P.O. Box 2837, Washington, DC 20013; (866) 713-7527; www.iags.org. A nonprofit educational organization focusing on energy security.

South African Institute of International Affairs, P.O. Box 31596, Braamfontein, 2017, South Africa; +27 (011) 339-2021; www.saiia.org.za. Its China in Africa Project studies the emerging relationship between China and Africa.

Textile Federation of South Africa, P.O. Box 53, Bruma, 2026, South Africa; +27 (011) 454-2342; www.texfed.co.za. The trade association for South Africa's textile businesses; offers information about the economic stability of the industry, particularly China's impact.

Jacques Chirac

Former President, France

Cooperation is positive, even for Europe

"With China's heft in the international arena growing, China's role in Africa is also increasing. I think it is a positive thing. It is good for China, Africa and Europe because [in this process] China has gained new room to develop itself, Africa has got new investment and Europe has been stimulated to be competitive."

Xinhua news agency (China), December 2007

Liu Jianchao

Foreign Ministry Spokesman, China

Our projects do no harm

"When China is building roads and schools and providing health infrastructure and agricultural technology to African countries, are we damaging human rights in Africa? Are we hurting good governance in those countries? African people are benefiting from China's projects."

The Associated Press, November 2006

Amare Kifle

Small-business Contractor, Ethiopia

Doing it our way

"We are tired of the condescending American style. True, the American government and American companies have done and do a lot here, but I always feel like they think they are doing us a favor ... telling us how to do things and punishing us when we do it our own way. These Chinese are different. They are about the bottom line and allow us to sort out our side of the business as we see fit."

The Christian Science Monitor, June 2007

Spokesman for Nigerian militants

(Anonymous)

Colonialism abounds

"The Chinese used to be more populist. But now they are turning into colonialists themselves."

The Boston Globe, June 2007

Edmundo Vaz

Former Adviser, Guinea-Bissau Finance Ministry

We need money, no strings attached

"China is not like the World Bank. They don't attach all these conditions on the money. The West makes us wait, but we're a poor country, we don't have time to wait."

Chicago Tribune, January 2007

Editorial

New Vision, Uganda

Understanding China

"Before declaring China as a close and dependable friend, African policymakers need to ask themselves one important and valid question: That is, does Africa understand communist China well? If the answer is no, then, Africans need to find a way of understanding this ... emerging Asian economic giant."

July 2007

Neva Seidman Makgetla

Economist, Congress of South African Trade Unions

No benefits for the poor

"There's no question that for upper classes, [China's trade with South Africa] is a boon. The problem is any lower-class South Africans would rather have a job."

The Washington Post, June 2006

Wang Hongyi

African-relations Specialist, China Institute of International Studies

We don't impose our values

"The Western approach of imposing its values and political system on other countries is not acceptable to China. We focus on mutual development, not promoting one country at the expense of another."

The New York Times, November 2006

Festus Mogae

President, Botswana

We are equal in Chinese eyes

"China treats us as equals, while the West treats us as former subjects. That is the reality. I prefer the attitude of China to that of the West."

China-Africa Co-operation Summit, Beijing, November 2006

Gavin Coates/Hong Kong